중·고등 영어도 역시 **1위** 해커스다.

해커스북 중·고등

HackersBook.com

해커스 수능영어듣기 모의고사 20+4회가

특별한 이유!

최신 경향과 출제 패턴을 반영한 문제로 실전 대비!

1

최신 수능 출제경향을
그대로 반영한
**양질의
영어듣기 모의고사**

2

난이도 높은 문제로
만점 굳히기!
고난도 모의고사

3

대표 기출문제로
수능 기본기를 탄탄히!
**14개 유형별
핵심 전략**

해커스 수능영어듣기 모의고사 20+4회

기본   실전

다양한 버전의 음성으로 편리한 학습!

4

여러 가지 버전으로
실전에 대비할 수 있는
**기본 속도/고속 버전/
고사장 버전 MP3**

5

복습이 간편해지는
**딕테이션 MP3/
문항별 MP3**

6

모든 음성 버전을
한 손에 쏙!
**문제 음성 듣기
QR코드**

해커스 수능영어듣기 모의고사 시리즈를 검토해주신 선생님들

경기
김보경　성일고등학교
김성철　코코스영어학원
연원기　신갈고등학교
이지혜　리케이온 어학원
전상호　평촌 이지어학원

대전
신주희　파써블영어학원

부산
이승의　에이치큐(HQ)영수학원

서울
김종오　입시형인간학원
양세희　양세희 수능영어학원

해커스 어학연구소 자문위원단 2기

강원
안서아　숲어학원 남산캠퍼스
최현주　최샘영어

경기
강민정　김진성의 열정어학원
강상훈　평촌RTS학원
강유빈　일링영어수학학원
권계미　A&T+ 영어
김남균　SDH어학원 세교캠퍼스
김보경　성일고등학교
김세희　이화킴스영어전문학원
김은영　신갈고등학교
나한샘　해법영어교실 프라임수학학원
두형호　잉글리쉬피티 어학원
박은성　GSE 어학원
박지승　신갈고등학교
배동영　이바인어학원탄현캠퍼스
서현주　웰어학원
연원기　신갈고등학교
윤혜영　이루다학원
이미연　김상희수학영어학원
이선미　정현영어학원
이슬기　연세센크레영어
이승주　EL영어학원
이주의　뉴욕학원
이충기　영어나무
이한이　엘케이영어학원
장명희　이루다영어수학전문학원
장소연　우리학원
장한상　티엔디플러스학원
전상호　평촌 이지어학원
전성훈　훈선생영어학원
정선영　코어플러스영어학원
정세창　팍스어학원
정재식　마스터제이학원
정필두　정상어학원
조원웅　클라비스영어전문학원
조은혜　이든영수학원
천은지　프링크어학원
최지영　다른영어학원
최한나　석사영수전문

경남
김선우　이해성 김해 의대관
라승희　아이작잉글리쉬
박정주　타임영어 전문학원
이지선　PMS영재센터학원

경북
김대원　포항영신중학교
김주훈　아너스영어
문재원　포항영신고등학교
성룡　미르어학원
엄경식　포항영신고등학교
정창용　엑소더스어학원

광주
강창일　MAX(맥스) 에듀학원
김태호　금호고등학교
임희숙　설월여자고등학교
정영철　정영철 영어전문학원
조유승　링즈영어학원

대구
구수진　석샘수학&제임스영어 학원
권익재　제이슨영어교습소
김광영　e끌리네영어학원
김보곤　베스트영어
김연정　달서고등학교
김원회　글로벌리더스어학원
위영선　위영선영어학원
이가영　어썸코칭영어학원
이승현　학문당입시학원
이정아　능인고등학교
조승희　켈리외국어학원
주현아　강고영어학원
최윤정　최강영어
황은진　상인황샘영어학원

대전
김미경　이보영의토킹클럽유성분원
성태미　한울영수학원
신주희　파써블영어학원
이재근　이재근영어수학학원
이혜숙　대동천재학원
최애림　ECC송촌제우스학원

부산
고영하　해리포터영어도서관
김미혜　더멘토영어
김서진　케이트예일학원
김소희　윤선생IGSE 센텀어학원
박경일　제니스영어
성현석　닉쌤영어교습소
신연주　도담학원
이경희　더에듀기장학원

이아린　명진학원
이종혁　대동학원
이지현　7번방의 기적 영어학원
전재석　영어를담다
채지영　리드앤톡영어도서관학원

서울
갈성은　씨앤씨(목동) 특목관
공현미　이은재학원
김시아　시아영어교습소
김은주　열정과신념영어학원
박병배　강북세일학원
신이준　정영어학원
신진희　신진희영어
양세희　양세희수능영어학원
윤승완　윤승완영어학원
이계윤　씨앤씨(목동) 학원
이상영　와이즈(WHY's) 학원
이정욱　이은재학원
이지연　중계케이트영어학원
정미라　미라정영어학원
정용문　맥코칭학원
정윤정　대치명인학원 마포캠퍼스
조용현　바른스터디학원
채가희　대성세그루영수학원

세종
김주년　드림하이영어학원
하원태　백년대계입시학원
홍수정　수정영어입시전문학원

울산
김한중　스마트영어전문학원
오충섭　인트로영어전문학원
윤창호　로제타스톤어학원
임예린　와엘영어학원
최주하　더 셀럽학원
최호선　마시멜로영어전문학원

인천
권효진　Genie's English
송숙진　예스영어학원
임민선　SNU에듀
정진수　원리영어
함선임　리본에듀학원
황혜림　SNU에듀

전남
류성준　타임영어학원

전북
강동현　커넥트영수전문학원
김길자　군산맨투맨학원
김두환　해남맨체스터영수학원
김유경　이엘 어학원
노빈나　노빈나영어학원
라성남　하포드어학원
박지연　박지연영어학원
변진호　쉐마영어학원
송윤경　줄리안나영어국어전문학원
이수정　씨에이엔영어학원
장윤정　혁신뉴욕어학원

제주
김랑　KLS어학원
박자은　KLS어학원

충남
문정효　좋은습관 에토스학원
박서현　EiE고려대학교 어학원 논산
박정은　탑씨크리트학원
성승민　SDH어학원 불당캠퍼스
손세윤　최상위학원 (탕정)
이지선　힐베르트학원

충북
강은구　강쌤영어학원
남장길　에이탑정철어학원
이혜인　위즈영어학원

해커스

수능영어듣기 모의고사 20+4회

실전

해커스 어학연구소

CONTENTS

해커스 수능영어듣기 모의고사 20+4회 **실전**

교재 구성과 특징 ·························· 4

읽으면 정답이 들린다! 유형별 핵심 전략 ····· 6

영어듣기 모의고사

01회　영어듣기 모의고사 ············· 16

02회　영어듣기 모의고사 ············· 22

03회　영어듣기 모의고사 ············· 28

04회　영어듣기 모의고사 ············· 34

05회　영어듣기 모의고사 ············· 40

06회　영어듣기 모의고사 ············· 46

07회　영어듣기 모의고사 ············· 52

08회　영어듣기 모의고사 ············· 58

09회　영어듣기 모의고사 ············· 64

10회　영어듣기 모의고사 ············· 70

11회　영어듣기 모의고사 ············· 76

12회　영어듣기 모의고사 ············· 82

13회　영어듣기 모의고사 ············· 88

14회　영어듣기 모의고사 ············· 94

15회　영어듣기 모의고사 ············· 100

16회　영어듣기 모의고사 ············· 106

17회　영어듣기 모의고사 ············· 112

18회　영어듣기 모의고사 ············· 118

19회　영어듣기 모의고사 ············· 124

20회　영어듣기 모의고사 ············· 130

21회　**고난도** 영어듣기 모의고사 ······ 136

22회　**고난도** 영어듣기 모의고사 ······ 142

23회　**고난도** 영어듣기 모의고사 ······ 148

24회　**고난도** 영어듣기 모의고사 ······ 154

정답 및 해설 [책 속의 책]

교재 구성과 특징

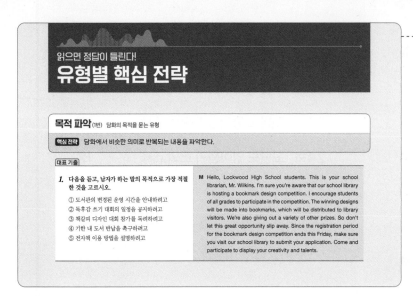

유형별 핵심 전략

수능에 반드시 출제되는 14개 대표 문제 유형의 핵심 전략과 기출 문제를 통해 보다 쉽고 빠르게 출제 경향을 확인할 수 있습니다.

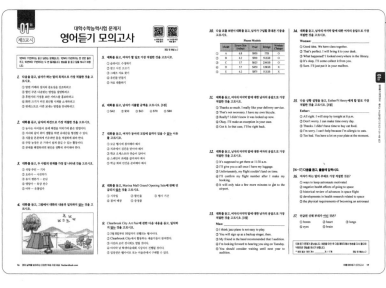

영어듣기 모의고사 20회

실제 수능 및 평가원 모의고사와 문제 유형, 출제 순서, 소재, 난이도가 동일한 모의고사를 풀면서 실전 감각을 키울 수 있습니다.

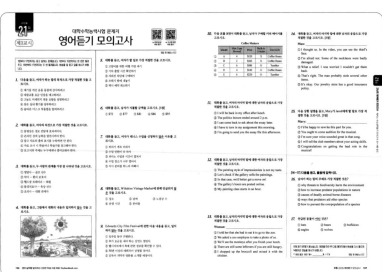

고난도 영어듣기 모의고사 4회

실제 수능보다 더 어려운 난이도의 문제로 구성된 고난도 모의고사를 통해 듣기 실력을 다지면 어렵게 출제될 때도 흔들리지 않고 만점을 받을 수 있도록 완벽히 대비할 수 있습니다.

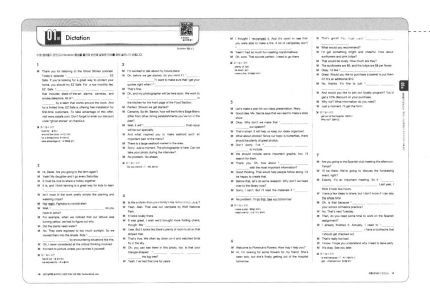

Dictation

매회 문제 풀이 후 Dictation을 하며 문제 풀이 시 놓쳤던 정답 단서를 확인하고 내용을 정확하게 듣는 연습을 할 수 있습니다.

듣기 필수 표현에 따로 정리되어 있는 시험에 자주 출제되는 표현들을 편리하게 복습할 수 있습니다

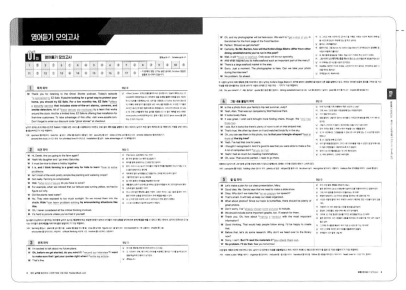

정답 및 해설

스크립트와 해석을 나란히 확인하며 지문 내용을 한눈에 빠르게 파악할 수 있습니다.

스스로 정답의 근거를 확인하고 상세한 해설을 읽어보면서 다시 틀리는 일이 없도록 오답을 점검할 수 있습니다.

다양한 버전의 MP3

- 수능과 동일한 속도의 **기본 속도 MP3**
- 실전보다 빠른 **고속 버전 MP3**
- 실제 수능 시험장에서 듣는 것 같은 **고사장 버전 MP3**
- 틀린 문제만 골라 다시 들으며 복습하는 **문항별 MP3**
- 영어 지문만 들으며 Dictation하는 **딕테이션 MP3**

MP3 스트리밍 QR코드

매회 모의고사와 Dictation에 있는 QR코드로 간편하게 음성을 이용할 수 있습니다.
HackersBook.com에서 MP3 파일 다운로드도 가능합니다.

유형별 핵심 전략

목적 파악 (1번) 담화의 목적을 묻는 유형

핵심 전략 담화에서 비슷한 의미로 반복되는 내용을 파악한다.

대표 기출

1. 다음을 듣고, 남자가 하는 말의 목적으로 가장 적절한 것을 고르시오.

① 도서관의 변경된 운영 시간을 안내하려고
② 독후감 쓰기 대회의 일정을 공지하려고
③ 책갈피 디자인 대회 참가를 독려하려고
④ 기한 내 도서 반납을 촉구하려고
⑤ 전자책 이용 방법을 설명하려고

M Hello, Lockwood High School students. This is your school librarian, Mr. Wilkins. I'm sure you're aware that our school library is hosting a bookmark design competition. I encourage students of all grades to participate in the competition. The winning designs will be made into bookmarks, which will be distributed to library visitors. We're also giving out a variety of other prizes. So don't let this great opportunity slip away. Since the registration period for the bookmark design competition ends this Friday, make sure you visit our school library to submit your application. Come and participate to display your creativity and talents.

의견 파악 (2번) 대화 속에 드러난 화자의 의견을 묻는 유형

핵심 전략 대화 중반에 직접적으로 언급되는 화자의 의견을 파악하여 정답을 고른다.

대표 기출

2. 대화를 듣고, 여자의 의견으로 가장 적절한 것을 고르시오.

① 사과를 먹으면 장운동이 원활해진다.
② 사과 껍질은 피부 상태 개선에 도움이 된다.
③ 충분한 수면은 건강한 피부 유지에 필수적이다.
④ 사과를 먹기 전에 껍질을 깨끗이 씻어야 한다.
⑤ 주기적인 수분 섭취는 피부 노화를 늦춘다.

M Honey, do you want some apples with breakfast?
W Sounds great. Can you save the apple peels for me?
M Why? What do you want them for?
W I'm going to use them to make a face pack. Apple peels are effective for improving skin condition.
M Where did you hear about that?
W I recently read an article about their benefits for our skin.
M Interesting. What's in them?
W It said apple peels are rich in vitamins and minerals, so they moisturize our skin and enhance skin glow.
M That's good to know.
W Also, they remove oil from our skin and have a cooling effect.
M Wow! Then I shouldn't throw them away.
W Right. Apple peels can help improve our skin condition.
M I see. I'll save them for you.

관계 파악 (3번) 대화 속 두 사람의 관계를 묻는 유형

핵심 전략 대화 초반을 듣고 두 사람의 직업을 파악한다.

대표 기출

3. 대화를 듣고, 두 사람의 관계를 가장 잘 나타낸 것을 고르시오.

① 평론가 — 영화감독
② 심판 — 수영 선수
③ 작가 — 수영 코치
④ 서점 주인 — 유치원 교사
⑤ 잡지사 편집장 — 광고주

W Hello, Mr. Roberts. I appreciate you taking the time to share your experience and knowledge.

M My pleasure, Ms. Lee. I've enjoyed all your bestselling books. So, I'm excited to help you.

W Thanks. Since I'm writing about world-class athletes, I wanted to hear how you've trained children who became Olympic swimming champions.

M Then we should start with what I observe on the first day of my swimming classes.

W Do some children stand out right away?

M Yes. Some kids are able to pick up my instructions quickly and easily.

W I see. So did many of those kids go on to become Olympic champions?

M Well, practicing is much more important. Those who consistently practiced made great improvements and ultimately became champions.

W This is good insight I can use in my book.

M I hope it helps.

그림 내용 불일치 파악 (4번) 주어진 그림에서 대화 내용과 일치하지 않는 요소를 묻는 유형

핵심 전략 선택지 순서대로 그림과 설명이 일치하는지 확인한 후, 일치하는 선택지를 하나씩 소거한다.

대표 기출

4. 대화를 듣고, 그림에서 대화의 내용과 일치하지 <u>않는</u> 것을 고르시오.

M Hi, Jane. What are you looking at on your phone?

W Hi, Brian. It's a picture I took at Grand Boulder National Park. I went hiking there last weekend.

M Let me see. I like the bear statue wearing the check pattern jacket.

W It's cute, right?

M Yeah. There's a park map between the lights. It seems to include useful information.

W It helps me pick a different trail each time I go hiking. Do you see the two flowerpots in front of the cabin?

M Yes. They look beautiful. Oh, there's a round table by the path.

W I had lunch there.

M What a nice place to enjoy lunch! Look at the bird on the tree branch.

W Isn't it lovely? I love going there and being close to nature.

할 일/부탁한 일 파악 (5번) 대화 속 화자가 앞으로 할 일 또는 상대방에게 부탁한 일을 묻는 유형

대화 후반에 화자가 할 일이 언급되므로, 대화 후반의 내용을 잘 확인한다.

대표 기출

5. 대화를 듣고, 남자가 할 일로 가장 적절한 것을 고르시오.

① 음식 재료 주문하기
② 와인 잔 포장하기
③ 추가 메뉴 선정하기
④ 초대 문자 메시지 보내기
⑤ 노래 목록 확인하기

W Honey, I'm so excited for our restaurant's reopening event tomorrow.
M So am I. Let's see. We've ordered enough ingredients, right?
W I think so. We need to remind our loyal customers of the event.
M I already sent text messages.
W Good. I hope people like the new menu items that we added.
M Don't worry. We have a great chef. So I'm sure the new dishes will be a hit.
W What about the live music? Did you confirm the song list with the band?
M Not yet. And we also need to wrap wine glasses to give as gifts for the customers.
W Okay. Could you wrap them?
M Sure. I'll do it now.
W Great! Then I'll contact the band.

금액 정보 파악 (6번) [고난도] 대화 속 화자가 지불할 금액을 묻는 유형

대화에서 언급되는 가격 정보와 구매하려는 품목의 개수를 간단하게 메모하며 듣는다.

대표 기출

6. 대화를 듣고, 여자가 지불할 금액을 고르시오. [3점]

① $36   ② $45   ③ $50
④ $54   ⑤ $60

M Welcome to Daisy Valley Restaurant.
W Hi. I'd like to order some food to go. How much is the shrimp pasta and the chicken salad?
M The shrimp pasta is $20, and the chicken salad is $10.
W I'll take two shrimp pastas and one chicken salad, please.
M Sure. Would you like some dessert, too?
W Yes. What do you recommend?
M The mini cheese cake is one of the best sellers in our restaurant. It's $5 each.
W Great! I'll order two of them.
M Okay. Let me confirm your order. Two shrimp pastas, one chicken salad, and two mini cheese cakes. Is that correct?
W Yes. And I have a birthday coupon here. Can I use it?
M Let me see. [Pause] Yes. You can get a 10% discount off the total.
W Terrific. I'll use this coupon. Here's my credit card.

이유 파악 (7번) 대화 속 화자의 행동에 대한 이유를 묻는 유형

핵심 전략 대화 후반에 진짜 이유가 언급되므로, 대화 후반의 내용을 잘 확인한다.

대표 기출

7. 대화를 듣고, 남자가 K-Trend Festival에 갈 수 <u>없는</u> 이유를 고르시오.

① 영화관에서 일해야 해서
② 유학 설명회에 참석해야 해서
③ 경제학 시험공부를 해야 해서
④ 태권도 시합에 출전해야 해서
⑤ 동생을 공항에 데려다줘야 해서

W Sam, do you want to go to the K-Trend Festival with me this Saturday?
M Hi, Olivia. Is that the festival held at Central Square?
W Yeah, that's it. There'll be many attractions including Taekwondo performances that incorporate K-pop dance moves.
M Really? Sounds cool! What time does it start?
W It starts at 5 p.m. Will you be working at the movie theater at that time?
M No, I'm not working this Saturday. But I can't come to the festival.
W Too bad. Do you have to study for your economics exam?
M Actually, I already took the exam yesterday.
W Then, what's the matter?
M I have to take my younger sister to the airport on Saturday evening.
W Where's she going?
M She's going to Canada to study abroad.
W That's awesome. I hope she has a good experience there.

언급 유무 파악 (8번) 대화에서 언급되지 않은 것을 묻는 유형

핵심 전략 선택지 순서대로 내용이 언급되는지 확인한 후, 언급된 선택지를 하나씩 소거한다.

대표 기출

8. 대화를 듣고, 졸업 사진 촬영에 관해 언급되지 <u>않은</u> 것을 고르시오.

① 날짜　　② 장소　　③ 복장
④ 참여 학생 수　⑤ 소요 시간

[Telephone rings.]
W Hello, Jennifer Porter speaking.
M Hi, Ms. Porter. This is Steve Jackson from Lifetime Photo Studio.
W Oh, how are you?
M Good. I'm scheduled to shoot your school's graduation photos on Wednesday, November 23rd. So, I'm calling to confirm the details.
W Sure. As we previously discussed, the place will be Lily Pond Park.
M Okay. Could you tell me the exact number of students taking part in the photo session?
W Let me check. *[Pause]* Well, it'll be 180 students.
M I see. The same as you said before.
W That's right. How long will it take to shoot the photos?
M It'll take almost three hours. We should finish by noon.
W Great. Is there any other information you need?
M No, I'm all set. Bye.

핵심 전략 선택지 순서대로 내용이 일치하는지 확인한 후, 일치하는 선택지를 하나씩 소거한다.

대표 기출

9. Greenville Houseplant Expo에 관한 다음 내용을 듣고, 일치하지 않는 것을 고르시오.

① 3일 동안 진행될 것이다.
② 식물 관리 방법에 관한 강의가 매일 있을 것이다.
③ 희귀종을 포함한 다양한 식물을 구입할 수 있다.
④ 티켓 구입은 온라인으로만 가능하다.
⑤ 에메랄드 컨벤션 센터에서 열릴 것이다.

W Hello, listeners. I'm Melinda Jones from the organizing committee of the Greenville Houseplant Expo. I'm here to announce that the expo will run for three days starting on March 17th, 2023. Just on the opening day, there'll be a lecture on plant care methods. This lecture will be given by Dr. Evans, host of the TV show *Plants Love You*. Most importantly, you can buy a variety of plants, including rare species, exhibited in the expo. Due to its popularity, you'd better get your tickets early. Tickets are available through online purchase only. If you're a plant lover, come to the expo, which will take place at the Emerald Convention Center, and refresh your houseplant collection.

도표 정보 파악 (10번) 주어진 도표에서 대화 속 화자가 선택할 것을 묻는 유형

핵심 전략 도표에 제시된 조건에 맞지 않는 선택지를 하나씩 소거하며 듣는다.

대표 기출

10. 다음 표를 보면서 대화를 듣고, 여자가 구매할 첼로 케이스를 고르시오.

Hard Cello Cases

	Model	Price	Interior Material	Length (inches)	Wheels
①	A	$140	Nylon	51	X
②	B	$160	Cotton	49	O
③	C	$175	Velvet	53	X
④	D	$190	Cotton	52	O
⑤	E	$215	Cotton	55	X

M Welcome to Uptown Music Shop. How can I help you?
W Hi, I'm looking for a hard cello case.
M All right. Here's our catalog. These are the ones we have in stock. How much are you willing to spend?
W I can spend up to $200.
M Okay. How about the interior material? Do you have a preference?
W Well, I don't want the velvet one. It seems difficult to take care of.
M Right. Then how about the length?
W I have a full-size cello, so I want a case that's at least 50 inches long.
M Now you have two options left. Do you need wheels on your case?
W No, I don't need them. I won't carry it around a lot.
M Then this is the one for you.
W Thank you. I'll take it.

핵심 전략 대화 속 마지막 말의 의도를 파악하여 적절한 응답을 추론한다.

대표 기출

11. 대화를 듣고, 남자의 마지막 말에 대한 여자의 응답으로 가장 적절한 것을 고르시오.

① Never mind. I'm selling my old helmet.

② All right. I'll buy a bigger one that fits you.

③ No way. You should not ride a bicycle at night.

④ Great. I think it matches your bicycle perfectly.

⑤ No. We don't have to worry about the tight schedule.

M　Mom, I'd like to get a new bicycle helmet. Can you buy me one?

W　I'll buy you a new helmet if you need it. But what's the problem with the one you have now?

M　My helmet feels too tight. It hurts my head.

긴 대화의 응답 파악 (13~14번) [고난도] 긴 대화의 마지막 말에 대한 가장 적절한 응답을 묻는 유형 (매회 2문항으로 출제)

핵심 전략 대화의 전체적인 흐름을 통해 마지막 말의 의도를 파악하여 적절한 응답을 추론한다.

대표 기출

13. 대화를 듣고, 남자의 마지막 말에 대한 여자의 응답으로 가장 적절한 것을 고르시오. [3점]

Woman: ＿＿＿＿＿＿＿＿＿＿＿＿＿＿

① Not really. It's better to speak in simple sentences.

② Yes. Try to memorize words by learning the root words.

③ That's right. I'm glad you've studied the proper examples.

④ Exactly. That way you can use the proper words in context.

⑤ I don't think so. Always use an Italian-to-Italian dictionary.

M　Can I come in, Professor Rossini?

W　Of course. Come on in, Ben. What brings you here?

M　I came to ask for advice on studying Italian.

W　Is there anything specific you're having trouble with?

M　Yes. I'm experiencing difficulty using words properly. Could I get some tips?

W　Sure. First, let me ask how you use your dictionary.

M　Well, I use it to look up words that I don't know the meanings of.

W　Dictionaries provide example sentences for most words. Do you read them, too?

M　No, I don't pay attention to the example sentences.

W　Knowing the meaning of words is important, but you should also understand the context in which the words are properly used.

M　I see. So you're suggesting that I study the example sentences as well, right?

상황에 적절한 말 파악 (15번) 고난도 담화 속 인물이 주어진 상황에서 하기에 가장 적절한 말을 묻는 유형

핵심 전략 담화 후반 wants to tell/suggest가 나오면 그 뒤에 이어지는 말을 확인한다.

대표 기출

15. 다음 상황 설명을 듣고, Katie가 Jacob에게 할 말로 가장 적절한 것을 고르시오. [3점]

Katie: _____

① You should check how many nursing homes there are.
② Why don't you reuse the activity you prepared last time?
③ How about preparing multiple activities for your next visit?
④ You need to gain more practical knowledge about nursing.
⑤ You'd better speak to the residents of the neighborhood.

M Jacob just started volunteering at a nursing home and is planning his next visit. He recalls that not every resident in the nursing home enjoyed the activity he had prepared last time. To avoid this situation, he tries to find an activity that all residents in the nursing home can enjoy. But he can't come up with one that everyone would like. He asks his friend Katie for advice because she has lots of experience volunteering at a nursing home. Katie thinks there's no single activity that can interest all the residents. So Katie wants to suggest to Jacob that next time he should plan more than one activity. In this situation, what would Katie most likely say to Jacob?

세트 문항 (주제/세부 내용 파악) (16~17번) 긴 담화 하나에 대해 두 개의 문제를 묻는 유형 (유일하게 두 번 반복해서 들려줌)

핵심 전략 16번 : 담화 초반 Today 뒤에 이어지는 말을 듣고 주제를 파악한다.
17번 : 선택지 순서대로 언급되므로, 언급된 선택지를 하나씩 소거하며 듣는다.

대표 기출

[16~17] 다음을 듣고, 물음에 답하시오.

16. 여자가 하는 말의 주제로 가장 적절한 것은?

① how metals advanced human civilization
② how techniques applied to metals improved
③ where most precious metals originated from
④ why metals were used in the fashion industry
⑤ why ancient civilizations competed for metals

17. 언급된 금속이 <u>아닌</u> 것은?

① gold ② silver ③ iron
④ aluminum ⑤ nickel

W Hello, students. Perhaps no material on earth has been more important in human history than metal. Today, we're going to discuss the contribution of metals to the development of civilization. First, gold was considered the most valuable metal due to its beauty and scarcity. Because of its visual appeal and ability to be easily shaped, it's been used to decorate religious places and objects. Second, silver was mainly prized for being the shiniest of all metals. It's been one of the main forms of currency since it was the chief metal used for making coins. Next, iron became widely used once humans discovered techniques to strengthen it. This metal was fashioned into tools that revolutionized farming, and later, machines that industrialized the world. Finally, aluminum is the most abundant metal in the world and is also lightweight. That's why it's been essential to countless industries in modern society from automotive to aerospace to household products. Now, let's watch a short related video.

수능 영어 듣기 Tip

수능 영어 듣기는 짧은 시간 동안 정확하고 효율적으로 문제를 푸는 것이 중요합니다. 어떤 문제 유형에도 적용할 수 있는 아래 세 가지 Tip을 기억하며 문제를 풀어보세요.

---

1. 문제 음성이 나오기 전 문제와 선택지 빠르게 읽기

음성이 나오기 전에 문제와 선택지를 꼼꼼히 읽어두면 어떤 내용이 나올지 미리 파악할 수 있고, 대화에서 여자와 남자 중 누구의 말을 더 주의 깊게 들어야 할지 확인할 수 있습니다. 문제 음성이 끝나면 문제를 푸는 시간이 주어지므로, 음성이 끝나면 바로 정답을 체크하고, 남은 시간 동안 다음 문제와 선택지를 확인해두면 좋습니다.

특히 '목적 파악', '의견 파악', '이유 파악' 유형과 선택지가 영어로 되어있는 11번~17번 문제는 음성이 시작되기 전에 빠르게 읽어 놓으면 더욱 수월하게 정답을 유추할 수 있습니다.

> **대화를 듣고, 여자의 의견으로 가장 적절한 것을 고르시오.**
> ① 사과를 먹으면 장운동이 원활해진다.
> ② 사과 껍질은 피부 상태 개선에 도움이 된다.
> ③ 충분한 수면은 건강한 피부 유지에 필수적이다.
> ④ 사과를 먹기 전에 껍질을 깨끗이 씻어야 한다.
> ⑤ 주기적인 수분 섭취는 피부 노화를 늦춘다.

 이 대화에서는 여자의 말에서 결정적인 정답 단서가 나오겠다고 예상할 수 있고, 선택지에 나온 단어를 여자가 언급하는지 유의하여 들으면 정답을 더 쉽게 찾을 수 있습니다.

2. 키워드 간단하게 메모하기

음성을 들으며 중요한 키워드는 빠르고 간단하게 시험지에 메모합니다. 시험지에 간단하게 메모를 해두면 음성 초반에 들은 정보를 잊어버릴 걱정이 없고, 음성이 끝난 후 문제를 스스로 검토할 때에도 확신을 가지고 정답을 검토해볼 수 있습니다.

특히 '금액 정보 파악' 유형은 다양한 품목의 가격이 나오고, 계산을 해야 하기 때문에 메모를 해두면 정보를 잊어버릴 걱정 없이 정확한 숫자 계산을 할 수 있습니다.

3. 음성 끝까지 주의하며 듣기

음성의 마지막에 결정적인 정답 단서가 나오는 경우가 있기 때문에 음성의 중간까지만 듣고 문제를 풀면 오답을 고르게 될 수도 있습니다. 음성이 끝나는 신호음 '딩동' 소리가 들릴 때까지 집중하여 음성을 끝까지 들으세요.

특히 '할 일 파악', '이유 파악', '짧은 대화의 응답 파악', '긴 대화의 응답 파악', '상황에 적절한 말 파악' 유형은 음성의 마지막에 결정적인 정답 단서가 나오므로, 음성을 끝까지 들어야 정답을 고를 수 있습니다.

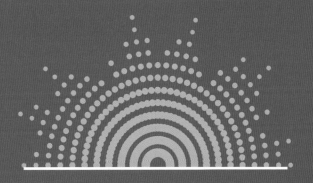

영어듣기
모의고사

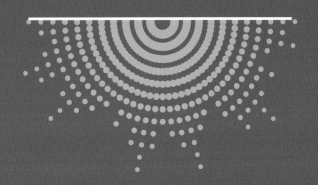

01회~20회	영어듣기 모의고사
21회~24회	**고난도** 영어듣기 모의고사

01 회

제3교시

대학수학능력시험 문제지
영어듣기 모의고사

▲ 문제 음성
바로 듣기
▲ 고사장 버전
바로 듣기

정답 및 해설 p.2

1번부터 17번까지는 듣고 답하는 문제입니다. 1번부터 15번까지는 한 번만 들려주고, 16번부터 17번까지는 두 번 들려줍니다. 방송을 잘 듣고 답을 하시기 바랍니다.

1. 다음을 듣고, 남자가 하는 말의 목적으로 가장 적절한 것을 고르시오.

① 방범 카메라 설치의 중요성을 강조하려고
② 할인 쿠폰 다운받는 방법을 설명하려고
③ 후원사의 가정용 보안 서비스를 홍보하려고
④ 화면 크기가 커진 최신형 시계를 소개하려고
⑤ 팟캐스트로 사연 보내는 방법을 안내하려고

2. 대화를 듣고, 남자의 의견으로 가장 적절한 것을 고르시오.

① 농사는 아이들이 문제 해결을 익히기에 좋은 방법이다.
② 자녀와 같이 취미 생활을 하면 유대감을 형성할 수 있다.
③ 식물을 튼튼하게 키우려면 물을 적절하게 줘야 한다.
④ 주말 농장은 온 가족이 쉽게 즐길 수 있는 활동이다.
⑤ 문제를 해결하려면 원인을 정확히 파악해야 한다.

3. 대화를 듣고, 두 사람의 관계를 가장 잘 나타낸 것을 고르시오.

① 식당 주인 — 기자
② 요리사 — 사진작가
③ 음식 평론가 — 손님
④ 영양사 — 육상 선수
⑤ 어부 — 유통업자

4. 대화를 듣고, 그림에서 대화의 내용과 일치하지 않는 것을 고르시오.

5. 대화를 듣고, 여자가 할 일로 가장 적절한 것을 고르시오.

① 슬라이드 수정하기
② 참고 사진 고르기
③ 그래프 자료 찾기
④ 유인물 만들기
⑤ 자료 대출하기

6. 대화를 듣고, 남자가 지불할 금액을 고르시오. [3점]

① $42　　② $50　　③ $63　　④ $70　　⑤ $80

7. 대화를 듣고, 여자가 동아리 모임에 끝까지 있을 수 없는 이유를 고르시오.

① 모금 행사에 참석해야 해서
② 치과에서 검진을 받아야 해서
③ 학교 오케스트라 연습이 있어서
④ 스페인어 과제를 끝마쳐야 해서
⑤ 학급 회의 안건을 준비해야 해서

8. 대화를 듣고, Marina Mall Grand Opening Sale에 관해 언급되지 않은 것을 고르시오.

① 시작일　　② 할인율　　③ 행사 기간
④ 참여 매장　　⑤ 증정품

9. Clearbrook City Art Fair에 관한 다음 내용을 듣고, 일치하지 않는 것을 고르시오.

① 5월 8일부터 10일까지 진행되는 행사이다.
② Clearbrook City에서 활동하는 예술가들이 참여한다.
③ 사진과 조각 전시회도 열릴 것이다.
④ 마지막 날 학생미술대회 시상식이 진행될 것이다.
⑤ 입장권은 웹사이트 또는 미술관에서 구매할 수 있다.

10. 다음 표를 보면서 대화를 듣고, 남자가 구입할 휴대폰 기종을 고르시오.

Phone Models

	Model	Screen Size (inches)	Price	Storage	Wireless Charger
①	A	6.8	$950	1TB	O
②	B	6.2	$910	512GB	O
③	C	5.7	$625	256GB	O
④	D	5.7	$450	128GB	X
⑤	E	6.2	$875	512GB	X

11. 대화를 듣고, 여자의 마지막 말에 대한 남자의 응답으로 가장 적절한 것을 고르시오.

① Thanks so much. I really like your delivery service.
② That's not necessary. I have my own bicycle.
③ Really? I didn't know it was locked up now.
④ Okay. I'll make an exception in your case.
⑤ Got it. In that case, I'll be right back.

12. 대화를 듣고, 남자의 마지막 말에 대한 여자의 응답으로 가장 적절한 것을 고르시오.

① It's supposed to get there at 11:30 a.m.
② I'll give you a call once I have my luggage.
③ Unfortunately, my flight couldn't land on time.
④ I'll confirm my flight number after I make my booking.
⑤ It will only take a few more minutes to get to the airport.

13. 대화를 듣고, 여자의 마지막 말에 대한 남자의 응답으로 가장 적절한 것을 고르시오. [3점]

Man: _____

① I think jazz piano is not easy to play.
② You will sign up as a backup singer, then.
③ My friend in the band recommended that I audition.
④ I'm looking forward to hearing you sing on Tuesday.
⑤ You should consider waiting until next year to audition.

14. 대화를 듣고, 남자의 마지막 말에 대한 여자의 응답으로 가장 적절한 것을 고르시오.

Woman: _____

① Good idea. We have class together.
② That's perfect. I will bring it to your desk.
③ What happened? I looked everywhere in the library.
④ It's okay. I'll come collect it from you.
⑤ Sure. I'll just put it in your mailbox.

15. 다음 상황 설명을 듣고, Esther가 Henry에게 할 말로 가장 적절한 것을 고르시오. [3점]

Esther: _____

① All right. I will stop by tonight at 8 p.m.
② Don't worry. I can make time every day.
③ Thanks. I didn't have time to buy cat food.
④ I'm sorry. I can't help because I'm allergic to cats.
⑤ Too bad. You have a lot on your plate at the moment.

[16~17] 다음을 듣고, 물음에 답하시오.

16. 여자가 하는 말의 주제로 가장 적절한 것은?

① ways to keep astronauts motivated
② negative health effects of going to space
③ historical review of advances in space flight
④ developments in health research related to space
⑤ the physical requirements of becoming an astronaut

17. 언급된 신체 부위가 <u>아닌</u> 것은?

① bones   ② heart   ③ lungs
④ eyes   ⑤ brain

> 이제 듣기 문제가 끝났습니다. 채점을 마친 후 다음 페이지에서 방송을 다시 들으며 딕테이션 연습을 하시기 바랍니다.
>
> * 채점 결과: 맞은 개수 _____개 / 17개   정답 및 해설 p.2

Dictation 정답 p.2

01회 영어듣기 모의고사 Dictation 음성을 들으며 빈칸에 알맞은 단어를 채워 넣으시기 바랍니다.

1

M Thank you for listening to the *Ghost Stories* podcast. Today's episode 1)_____ _____ _____ EZ Safe. If you're looking for a great way to protect your home, you should try EZ Safe. For a low monthly fee, EZ Safe 2)_____ _____ _____ _____ that includes state-of-the-art alarms, cameras, and smoke detectors. All of 3)_____ _____ _____ _____ by a team that works around the clock. And for a limited time, EZ Safe is offering free installation for first-time customers. To take advantage of this offer, visit www.ezsafe.com. Don't forget to enter our discount code "ghost stories" at checkout.

↘ **듣기 필수 표현**
· look for ~을 찾다
· around the clock 24시간 내내
· for a limited time 한시적으로
· take advantage of ~의 혜택을 받다

2

W Hi, Derek. Are you going to the farm again?
M Yeah! My daughter and I go every Saturday.
W It must be nice to share a hobby together.
M It is, and I think farming is a great way for kids to learn 1)_____ _____ _____ _____ .
W Isn't most of the work pretty simple like planting and watering crops?
M Not really. Farming is complicated.
W Well, 2)_____ _____ _____ _____ do you have to solve?
M For example, when we noticed that our lettuce was turning yellow, we had to figure out why.
W Did the plants need water?
M No. They were exposed to too much sunlight. So we moved them into the shade. Kids 3)_____ _____ _____ by encountering situations like this.
W Oh, I never considered all the critical thinking involved.
M It's hard to picture unless you've tried it yourself.

↘ **듣기 필수 표현**
· figure out ~을 알아내다
· be exposed to ~에 노출되다

3

M I'm excited to talk about my future plans.
W Oh, before we get started, do you mind if I 1)_____ _____ _____ ? I want to make sure that I get your quotes right when I 2)_____ _____ _____ _____ .
M That's fine.
W Oh, and my photographer will be here soon. We want to 3)_____ _____ _____ _____ _____ in the kitchen for the front page of the Food Section.
M Perfect. Should we get started?
W Certainly. So Mr. Barton, how will the Knife's Edge Bistro differ from other dining establishments you've run in the past?
M Well, it will 4)_____ _____ _____ . Crab soup will be our specialty.
W And what inspired you to make seafood such an important part of the menu?
M There is a large seafood market in the area.
W Sorry. Just a moment. The photographer is here. Can we take your photo during the interview?
M No problem. Go ahead.

↘ **듣기 필수 표현**
· Do you mind if ~? ~해도 될까요?

4

M Is this a photo from your family's trip last summer, Judy?
W Yeah, Alan. That was our campsite by Wolf National Park.
M It looks lovely there.
W It was great. I wish we'd brought more folding chairs, though. We 1)_____ _____ _____ _____ .
M I see. But it looks like there's plenty of room to sit on that striped mat.
W That's true. We often lay down on it and watched birds fly in the sky.
M Oh, you can see them in this photo, too. Is that your triangle-shaped 2)_____ _____ _____ the big tree?
W Yeah. I've had that one for years.

M I thought I recognized it. And it's good to see that you were able to make a fire. A lot of campsites don't 3)_____ _____ _____ _____.

W Yeah! I had so much fun roasting marshmallows.

M Oh, wow. That sounds perfect. I need to go there.

↘ 듣기 필수 표현
· plenty of 많은
· lie down 눕다
· make a fire 모닥불을 피우다

5

M Let's make a plan for our class presentation, Mary.

W Good idea. Ms. Garcia says that we need to make a slide show.

M Okay. Why don't we make that 1)_____ _____ _____ our speech?

W That's smart. It will help us keep our ideas organized.

M What about photos? Since our topic is butterflies, there should be plenty of great photos.

W Don't worry. I've 2)_____ _____ _____ _____ to include.

M We should include some important graphs, too. I'll search for them.

W Thank you. Oh, how about 3)_____ _____ _____ with the most important information?

M Good thinking. That would help people follow along. I'd be happy to create that.

W Before that, let's do some research. Why don't we head over to the library now?

M Sorry, I can't. But I'll read the materials if 4)_____ _____ _____ _____.

W No problem. I'll do that. See you tomorrow!

↘ 듣기 필수 표현
· make a plan 계획을 세우다
· head over to ~으로 가다, 향하다

6

W Welcome to Florence's Flowers. How may I help you?

M Hi, I'm looking for some flowers for my friend. She's been sick, but she's finally getting out of the hospital tomorrow.

W That's great! You must want 1)_____ _____ _____.

M What would you recommend?

W I'd get something bright and cheerful. How about sunflowers and pink tulips?

M That would be lovely. How much are they?

W The sunflowers are $6, and the tulips are $8 per flower.

M Okay. I'd like 2)_____ _____ _____.

W Great. Would you like to purchase a basket to put them in? It's an additional $10.

M No, thanks. It's fine to just 3)_____ _____ _____ _____.

W And would you like to join our loyalty program? You'd get a 10% discount on your purchase.

M Why not? What information do you need?

W Just a moment. I'll get the form.

↘ 듣기 필수 표현
· get out of the hospital 퇴원하다
· Why not? 물론이죠.

7

M Are you going to the Spanish club meeting this afternoon, Tanya?

W I'll be there. We're going to discuss the fundraising event, right?

M Exactly. It's an important meeting. So it 1)_____ _____ _____ _____ _____. Last year, I think it took two hours.

W I have a few ideas to share, but I don't know if I can stay the whole time.

M Oh, is that because 2)_____ _____ _____ your school orchestra practice?

W No. That's next Tuesday.

M Then, do you need some time to work on the Spanish assignment?

W I already finished it. Actually, I need to 3)_____ _____ _____ _____. I have a toothache that I should get checked out.

M That's really too bad.

W I know. I hope you understand why I need to leave early.

M It's okay. See you later.

↘ 듣기 필수 표현
· Is that because ~? ~하기 때문이니?
· get ~ checked out 검진을 받다

8

M Hey, Gina. Did you see that a new mall is opening up near us?

W I did. I keep seeing ads about the Marina Mall Grand Opening Sale.

M Yeah, do you want to go on Saturday? It ¹⁾_____ _____ _____ _____.

W I guess. But won't it be too busy?

M Probably so, but there are discounts of up to 50% at a bunch of stores.

W Wow, that's great. Do you know ²⁾_____ _____ _____ _____?

M Hmm... I only remember that Lana's Boutique will. You love their clothes, right?

W Yes, I do. I used to drive 30 minutes to shop at one of their locations.

M And I heard that ³⁾_____ _____ _____ _____ _____ as a special gift to the first 500 customers.

W Well, we better get there early, then.

M I'll pick you up at 8?

W Okay, sure!

↘ 듣기 필수 표현
· up to ~까지
· a bunch of 많은
· pick up ~를 (차로) 데리러 가다

9

W Welcome back to *Jazz Night* on K-BRMC Radio. Before we get back to the music, I'd like to let you know about the upcoming Clearbrook City Art Fair. It will be held at Somerset Auditorium from May 8th to May 10th. This annual event features artwork made right here in Clearbrook City by some of our ¹⁾_____ _____ _____ _____. This year, in addition to paintings, the festival will include photography and sculpture exhibits. Starting things off on the 8th, there will be a ceremony ²⁾_____ _____ _____ of this year's student art contest. The winning piece will be displayed throughout the festival. Tickets for the event ³⁾_____ _____ _____ _____ the city government's website or in person at Clearbrook Gallery. They will cost $25.

↘ 듣기 필수 표현
· in addition to ~뿐만 아니라
· start ~ off ~을 시작하다

10

M Melissa, did you get a new phone?

W Hi, Fred. I did. This is the latest model.

M I've been thinking of getting a new phone, but I can't make up my mind about which one.

W Maybe one of the first things to consider is the size of the device.

M The one you have looks ¹⁾_____ _____ _____ _____ _____.

W Fair enough. Mine has a 6.8-inch screen, so you should ²⁾_____ _____ _____ _____. And what's your price range?

M I can spend up to $900.

W That narrows it down a little. Is memory a big factor?

M It's ³⁾_____ _____ _____. I'm fine with anything over 200 gigabytes.

W I see. And do you care if it comes with a wireless charger?

M Yes. That's very important to me.

W In that case, I think there's only one good option for you.

↘ 듣기 필수 표현
· make up one's mind 결정하다
· narrow down 좁히다
· come with ~이 딸려 있다

11

W Excuse me, sir. You ¹⁾_____ _____ _____ _____ inside.

M I'll just be here for a minute. I'm delivering something to Mr. Jensen.

W I'm afraid ²⁾_____ _____ _____ _____. You can lock up your bike at the rack next to the building.

↘ 듣기 필수 표현
· lock up (자물쇠, 문 등을) 잠그다

12

[Cell phone rings.]

M Hey, Chloe? This is Alex. I'll be able to ¹⁾_____ _____ _____ _____ at the airport tomorrow.

W Thanks! I have a lot of luggage, so that'll be very helpful. I'll be on Flight ZE 281.

M ²⁾_____ _____ _____ I can do. When is it scheduled to land?

↘ 듣기 필수 표현
· be scheduled to ~할 예정이다

13

W　Hi, Mr. Miller. I'm Emily. I wanted to ask about joining the high school jazz band.

M　To join, you'll have to [1)]_____ _____ _____ . The auditions are being held next week.

W　Sure, that's fine.

M　Great. So what instrument do you play?

W　I'm a singer, actually.

M　The audition for singers is on Tuesday, but I should warn you. There are a lot of [2)]_____ _____ trying out, and only one will be selected.

W　I understand. I'd still like to sign up.

M　Also, most of the students auditioning have been performing for years. And almost all of them are seniors.

W　I realize that. But I have a lot of experience, and I think [3)]_____ _____ _____ .

M　I love your confidence! Here's the sign-up sheet.

W　Thanks. I hope [4)]_____ _____ _____ _____ with my audition.

↘ 듣기 필수 표현
· try out (오디션에) 도전하다
· sign up 신청하다

14

[Cell phone rings.]

W　Hello?

M　Hi, Jessica. This is Adam Kim from biology class.

W　Hey, Adam. What's up?

M　I'm just calling to say that I [1)]_____ _____ _____ .

W　Oh, wow! I had almost given up looking. Where did you find it?

M　I saw it in the library's lost and found when I was collecting an umbrella I left there.

W　Hmm... That's weird. I [2)]_____ _____ _____ _____ recently. Are you sure it's mine?

M　It has your name in it!

W　I wonder if someone moved it. In any case, thanks for letting me know.

M　Of course. I bet you were pretty worried.

W　I was! Well, would you mind [3)]_____ _____ _____ _____ ?

M　Don't you need it for your homework tonight? I can take it to your house now if you want.

↘ 듣기 필수 표현
· give up 포기하다

15

M　Henry and Esther are friends who live in the same apartment building. Henry is leaving for a summer vacation next week, and he needs someone [1)]_____ _____ _____ _____ his cat. Esther knows about his plans and offers to come feed it. However, Henry wants someone who can visit his house and look after his cat every day. He thinks that Esther is [2)]_____ _____ , _____ _____ _____ , so he plans to hire a cat sitter. Esther believes that she has [3)]_____ _____ _____ _____ . Therefore, she wants to tell Henry that she can come by to cat-sit daily, so he can leave it to her. In this situation, what would Esther most likely say to Henry?

↘ 듣기 필수 표현
· look after 돌보다
· come by 들르다
· leave A to B A를 B에게 맡기다

16~17

W　Good morning, everyone. In our class on Friday we discussed the history of space flight. Today, I want to talk about how journeys to space [1)]_____ _____ _____ . First, let's consider the effect on their bones. Studies show that in low gravity conditions, the body mostly stops building up bones. So they will often [2)]_____ _____ _____ _____ when astronauts get back to Earth. Second, the heart can be hurt by space travel. This is due to radiation, which can damage and harden the heart's tissues. The eyes are also [3)]_____ _____ _____ _____ in space. In fact, 80% of astronauts experience some difficulty seeing. For some, this damage becomes permanent. Lastly, the brain can change shape in zero-gravity conditions. As a consequence, astronauts' mental abilities get worse the longer [4)]_____ _____ _____ _____ . This can affect astronauts' judgment and problem-solving skills. Now, let's take a look at an interview with an astronaut about her space travels.

↘ 듣기 필수 표현
· build up 강하게 만들다
· due to ~ 때문인
· as a consequence 그 결과
· take a look 살펴보다

대학수학능력시험 문제지
영어듣기 모의고사

▲ 문제 음성 바로 듣기　▲ 고사장 버전 바로 듣기

정답 및 해설 p.8

1번부터 17번까지는 듣고 답하는 문제입니다. 1번부터 15번까지는 한 번만 들려주고, 16번부터 17번까지는 두 번 들려줍니다. 방송을 잘 듣고 답을 하시기 바랍니다.

1. 다음을 듣고, 여자가 하는 말의 목적으로 가장 적절한 것을 고르시오.

① 테니스 수업 장소 변경을 공지하려고
② 테니스 대회 개최 소식을 홍보하려고
③ 다가오는 보수 공사 일정을 안내하려고
④ 테니스 수업 수강생을 모집하려고
⑤ 센터의 경기장 예약 시스템을 설명하려고

2. 대화를 듣고, 남자의 의견으로 가장 적절한 것을 고르시오.

① 조별 과제에서는 활발할 토론이 필수적이다.
② 숙제는 마감 기한 전에 미리 끝내놓아야 한다.
③ 시간을 낭비하지 않으려는 태도가 집중력을 높인다.
④ 관점을 바꾸면 창의적인 해결책을 찾을 수 있다.
⑤ 짧게 휴식을 취하면 생산성이 높아진다.

3. 대화를 듣고, 두 사람의 관계를 가장 잘 나타낸 것을 고르시오.

① 미술품 경매사 — 수집가
② 박물관 큐레이터 — 고고학자
③ 시상식 사회자 — 초청 강사
④ 라디오 진행자 — 역사학 교수
⑤ 도예가 — 도예공방 수강생

4. 대화를 듣고, 그림에서 대화의 내용과 일치하지 않는 것을 고르시오.

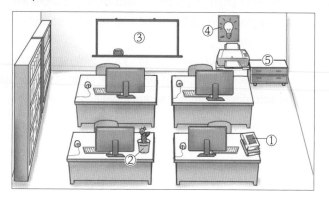

5. 대화를 듣고, 남자가 할 일로 가장 적절한 것을 고르시오.

① 설거지하기
② 식탁 닦기
③ 쓰레기 버리기
④ 청소기 돌리기
⑤ 책장 먼지 털기

6. 대화를 듣고, 여자가 지불할 금액을 고르시오. [3점]

① $36　② $54　③ $60　④ $81　⑤ $90

7. 대화를 듣고, 두 사람이 승용차로 이동할 수 없는 이유를 고르시오.

① 교통이 차단되어 있어서
② 정비소에 수리를 맡겨서
③ 동생에게 차를 빌려주어서
④ 고객을 태워주기로 해서
⑤ 퍼레이드로 인해 차가 막혀서

8. 대화를 듣고, Mayfield Woodcraft Program에 관해 언급되지 않은 것을 고르시오.

① 행사 시기　② 행사 기간　③ 참가자 수
④ 연령 제한　⑤ 신청 마감일

9. Chef Conference에 관한 다음 내용을 듣고, 일치하지 않는 것을 고르시오.

① 3월 3일에 시작해서 6일에 끝난다.
② 200명 이상의 요리사들이 참석할 예정이다.
③ 유명 요리사들이 대표 요리를 대접할 것이다.
④ 티켓 가격은 30달러이다.
⑤ 티켓은 현장에서 구입할 수 있다.

10. 다음 표를 보면서 대화를 듣고, 두 사람이 구입할 텐트를 고르시오.

Camping Tents

	Model	Number of People	Intended Season	Weight	Price
①	A	2-3	Summer	1.5 kg	$180
②	B	2-4	Winter	2 kg	$350
③	C	2-4	Summer	3 kg	$250
④	D	4-6	Winter	6.5 kg	$425
⑤	E	4-6	Winter	5 kg	$400

11. 대화를 듣고, 여자의 마지막 말에 대한 남자의 응답으로 가장 적절한 것을 고르시오.

① That's right. The bus fare is only $2.

② Sure. Let's pull over and ask for directions.

③ We should hurry. My train leaves in a few minutes.

④ Wait. I'll let you know when we get to the station.

⑤ Cross the street. Then, you'll see a bus stop.

12. 대화를 듣고, 남자의 마지막 말에 대한 여자의 응답으로 가장 적절한 것을 고르시오.

① Excuse me. Could you sit down?

② I understand. I'll move to your desk.

③ Sure. I'll go write it on the whiteboard.

④ Good. Just stay in the back and switch the lights on.

⑤ That's not true. I usually wear contacts instead of glasses.

13. 대화를 듣고, 여자의 마지막 말에 대한 남자의 응답으로 가장 적절한 것을 고르시오. [3점]

Man: _____

① If I do that, when will I be able to get the book?

② Unfortunately, I can't find another book on the topic.

③ Please click on "other options" in the online catalog.

④ You can check if it is available on the library's website.

⑤ I've been looking everywhere for information about diabetes.

14. 대화를 듣고, 남자의 마지막 말에 대한 여자의 응답으로 가장 적절한 것을 고르시오.

Woman: _____

① No. This is the kind of bracelet that I like to wear.

② I don't know. I don't think she needs two bracelets.

③ That's a great idea. Why don't we go and exchange it together?

④ Never mind. She's planning to get me a blouse or sweater.

⑤ That's not possible. The bracelet cost me a lot of money.

15. 다음 상황 설명을 듣고, Jennifer가 Steve에게 할 말로 가장 적절한 것을 고르시오. [3점]

Jennifer: _____

① Can I order the salad to go?

② I'm so sorry, but I can't eat shrimp.

③ I forgot you had that shrimp allergy.

④ You still remember my favorite foods.

⑤ I'm afraid I can't come over to your house tonight.

[16~17] 다음을 듣고, 물음에 답하시오.

16. 여자가 하는 말의 주제로 가장 적절한 것은?

① the benefits of traditional exercise

② improvements in diet and fitness methods

③ different forms of fitness training in history

④ how certain athletic activities became popular

⑤ methods used for training for various sports

17. 언급된 운동이 아닌 것은?

① weightlifting   ② running   ③ dancing

④ boxing   ⑤ Pilates

이제 듣기 문제가 끝났습니다. 채점을 마친 후 다음 페이지에서 방송을 다시 들으며 딕테이션 연습을 하시기 바랍니다.

* 채점 결과: 맞은 개수 _____ 개 / 17개   정답 및 해설 p.8

02회 Dictation

Dictation 정답 p.8

02회 영어듣기 모의고사 Dictation 음성을 들으며 빈칸에 알맞은 단어를 채워 넣으시기 바랍니다.

1

W Attention, please. This is an announcement for all visitors to the Parkview Tennis Center. Due to ongoing renovations to our outdoor courts, all beginner and intermediate tennis lessons 1)_____ _____ _____ _____ today. Beginners will meet with their coaches on Courts 3 and 4, while intermediate students will play on Courts 5 and 6. As a result, our indoor courts will not be open 2)_____ _____ _____ until classes have ended for the day. Any reservations made during class times or for our outdoor courts 3)_____ _____ _____. We expect to reopen our outdoor facility by next week. Our apologies for any inconvenience this may cause.

2

M Do you want to take a quick break, Jessica?

W I'd prefer to keep going. We still have a lot of work to do on the group project, and it's getting late.

M True, but I think 1)_____ _____ _____ _____.

W How do you figure? I don't want to waste any time.

M It would give us more energy, which would 2)_____ _____ _____ _____.

W Oh, that makes sense.

M Also, a break tends to make you more creative. If we come back to our work with a fresh perspective, it might be easier 3)_____ _____ _____ _____.

W Yeah. I do feel like we're stuck.

M Exactly. Don't you think we should take a few minutes to reset?

W I suppose so.

M See you back here at 4:30?

W Sounds good.

↘ 듣기 필수 표현
· take a break 휴식 시간을 가지다
· waste time 시간 낭비하다
· make sense 일리가 있다
· be stuck 막혀 있다

3

M Dr. Brown, thank you for meeting with me.

W I always enjoy a chance to visit the Museum of Archeology. What did you want to speak about?

M Well, I wanted to 1)_____ _____ _____ that I'm planning here.

W What did you have in mind?

M I'd like you to write an audio guide 2)_____ _____ _____ on some of the artifacts in the exhibit.

W I see. I presume these are famous pieces of Greek pottery?

M Right. You 3)_____ _____ _____ _____ several of them, so you have unique insights.

W Great. It would be my pleasure.

M We'd also like to invite you to come speak at an event when the exhibit opens.

W When would that be?

M Sometime next May.

W Let me check my schedule. If I'm not out of the country 4)_____ _____ _____, I'll be there.

↘ 듣기 필수 표현
· have ~ in mind ~을 생각하다, 계획하다
· out of the country 해외에, 국외에

4

W Welcome to Greenwich High School, Mr. Walker. I'll show you around.

M I appreciate that.

W Let's drop by the teacher's office first. You'll prepare 1)_____ _____ _____ here.

M Which one is my desk?

W It's in the front of the room, 2)_____ _____ next to the keyboard.

M I see it.

W My desk is to the left of yours. It's the one with the cactus plant on it.

M What's that whiteboard in the back of the room for?

W We use it for reminders. If we have a teachers' meeting, I'll 3)_____ _____ _____ there.

M It's blank right now, so there's no meeting today, right?

W Correct.

M Oh, is there a printer I could use?

W It's 4)_____ _____ _____ _____ of a light bulb. If you need more paper, there's some in the drawers on its right.

M Thanks!

↘ 듣기 필수 표현
· show ~ around ~를 안내하다
· drop by 들르다

5

W Okay, let's get to it, Daniel. We have a lot of cleaning to do before Mom and Dad get back home.

M Right. We 1)_____ _____ _____ earlier. We don't have much time.

W Let's get organized. How does the kitchen look?

M Well, I already washed and put away the dishes.

W What about wiping down the dining table? Did you do that?

M They look pretty clean, actually. We can probably 2)_____ _____ _____ _____.

W Great. That makes things easier. I'll 3)_____ _____.

M Should I dust the bookshelves?

W I think we need to take out the trash first.

M Okay, 4)_____ _____ _____.

W Mom and Dad will be happy to see that the house is in good shape.

↘ 듣기 필수 표현
· get organized 정리하다
· put away 넣어두다, 치우다
· wipe down (걸레, 행주로) 닦다
· take out the trash 쓰레기를 버리다
· in good shape 상태가 좋은

6

M Welcome to Sam's Home Décors. Can I help you?

W Hi, I'm wondering about these two picture frames. Do they have the same price?

M Actually, no. The gold one is $10 while the brown one is $15.

W Hmm... I prefer 1)_____ _____ _____. I'll take four of those, please.

M Do you need anything else?

W I'd like to buy a table lamp, too.

M This is our most popular model, and it's on sale right now.

W That's perfect. I'll 2)_____ _____.

M I can ring you up now if you like.

W Sure. And I have this coupon for 10% off. Can I use it?

M Certainly. I'll apply it 3)_____ _____ _____. So... you have four brown picture frames and the lamp. Is that right?

W Wait! The lamp is $30? That's more expensive than I thought. I 4)_____ _____ I'll buy it.

M No problem.

↘ 듣기 필수 표현
· on sale 할인 중인
· ring up 계산해주다

7

W Honey, are you almost ready to leave?

M Give me 10 minutes. I have to return a phone call. One of my clients has a quick question.

W Okay. But are you sure we're not going to be late to Marcia's science fair?

M We should be fine. The building where it's 1)_____ _____ is only a 15-minute drive away.

W But remember, we can't use the car.

M Really? Is it 2)_____ _____ at the shop?

W You really don't remember?

M Is traffic blocked off downtown? I thought the parade on Main Street was tomorrow.

W Honey, my brother 3)_____ _____ _____ _____ this weekend.

M Oh! Of course... Well, we better call a cab soon.

W I'll get the taxi. Can you be ready to leave in five minutes?

M Yes, I'll be ready!

↘ 듣기 필수 표현
· be ready to ~할 준비를 하다
· block off 차단하다

8

M Hey, Carla. Have you attended the Mayfield Woodcraft Program?

W I have. And I'm going back this year, actually. It's a great summer program.

M My art teacher recommended it to me, so I was thinking of [1]_____ _____ _____ _____.

W You should definitely come! You'd love it.

M It's a two-week-long program, right?

W That's right.

M And all of the participants are [2]_____ _____ _____?

W Yes. You have to be between 15 and 17 years old to attend.

M Okay, great. I might sign up for the furniture-making course in that case.

W Just make sure that you apply soon. The application deadline is coming up [3]_____ _____.

M Okay. I'll make up my mind soon.

W Hope to see you there!

↘ 듣기 필수 표현
· sign up for ~에 등록하다
· come up (날짜가) 다가오다
· make up one's mind 결정하다

9

M Hello, everyone. Thanks for tuning into *All Things Boston*. Today, we have some exciting news for you. Our city will hold the annual Chef Conference from March 3rd to 6th. [1]_____ _____ _____ from all over the country will participate in this event. The conference aims to introduce the trendiest dishes and provide information about new ingredients. This year, the conference will be open to the public. Celebrity chefs [2]_____ _____ _____ _____ to their signature dishes in addition to leading cooking workshops. If you want to visit, purchase a ticket for $30 on the conference website. Please note that tickets [3]_____ _____ _____ _____ on-site. Do you like to try delicious foods? Then, make sure to come!

↘ 듣기 필수 표현
· tune into (라디오를) 듣다
· aim to ~하는 것을 목표로 하다
· in addition to ~뿐만 아니라

10

W Honey, we need a tent for our vacation.

M I know. I've been looking online. I found a site that lists some good ones. Here, take a look.

W Oh, interesting. *[Pause]* Well, [1]_____ _____ _____ _____ would need to sleep in it, so this one isn't going to be a good option.

M That's true.

W The weather is expected to be chilly for this season. So how about [2]_____ _____ _____ _____?

M I think it's the safer choice.

W All right. That makes picking one a little bit easier. Is weight going to be a big factor?

M Um... anything under six kilograms would be fine for backpacking.

W That leaves us with two choices.

M I don't mind [3]_____ _____ _____ _____ for a better tent. We should get the more expensive one.

W That's fine with me.

M Great. I'll go ahead and buy it.

↘ 듣기 필수 표현
· Take a look. 한번 봐봐.
· be expected to ~일 것으로 예상되다
· I don't mind ~해도 상관없다

11

W Excuse me. Are you headed to Wentworth Train Station?

M No, ma'am. This bus is [1]_____ _____ _____ _____, toward downtown. Wentworth Station is on this side of the river.

W If you don't mind me asking, [2]_____ _____ _____ catch a bus going in the right direction?

↘ 듣기 필수 표현
· be headed to ~으로 가다, 향하다
· catch a bus 버스를 타다

12

M Gina, I need a favor. Can you [1]_____ _____ _____ _____?

W Why? I always sit here during class.

M I know, but I [2]_____ _____ _____ today. I won't be able to see the whiteboard from the back.

↘ 듣기 필수 표현
· I need a favor. 부탁이 있어.

13

[Phone rings.]

W You've reached the Sampson County Library help desk.

M Hi, I want to request that the library [1)]_____ _____.

W I may be able to help. What's the title of the book?

M It's called *The Understanding of Diabetes*. It was not in the library's online catalog.

W Let's see... Yes, I can confirm that we [2)]_____ _____ _____ _____.

M I need it for a class research project.

W Let me see what I can do. *[Typing sound]* Hmm, ordering the book may not be the best option for you.

M Oh, really? Is it not available?

W It's available for purchase, but this process [3)]_____ _____. The book would arrive in six to eight weeks.

M That won't help! My project is due at the end of the month.

W Then, we could borrow it [4)]_____ _____ _____. You just need to fill out an application.

↘ **듣기 필수 표현**
· fill out (양식을) 작성하다, 기입하다

14

M What's in the bag? Did someone give you a gift?

W No. I bought this bracelet [1)]_____ _____ _____ _____.

M Do you mean Grace?

W Yes. She is moving to Phoenix tomorrow.

M It's a nice present. I'm sure she'll love it.

W I'm not so sure. In the store, [2)]_____ _____ _____ _____ a light yellow-gold. But in this light, it looks silver.

M Is there anything wrong with that?

W She doesn't like silver. I should have known better than to buy this on impulse.

M Why don't you exchange it for another piece of jewelry?

W The shop won't let me. The receipt says "No returns, no exchanges."

M Oh, dear. What if you keep the bracelet for yourself, and [3)]_____ _____ _____ _____ _____?

↘ **듣기 필수 표현**
· move to ~로 이사 가다
· should have known better than to ~하지 말았어야 했다
· on impulse 충동적으로

15

M Steve invited Jennifer over for a meal at his apartment. He just learned [1)]_____ _____ _____ and wanted to try them out. He grilled some shrimp, put together a salad, and even made his own fish soup. All of the food was already prepared when Jennifer arrived. She was excited to try the food that Steve had cooked, but when he handed her a plate, she noticed that it had [2)]_____ _____ _____. Since Jennifer has a shrimp allergy, she knows that she would get ill if she ate it. Even though she doesn't want to make Steve feel bad, she has to tell him that she must [3)]_____ _____. In this situation, what would Jennifer most likely say to Steve?

↘ **듣기 필수 표현**
· put together 만들다; 조립하다
· get ill 탈이 나다, 병들다

16~17

W Good morning, everyone. Last time we talked about the importance of diet to maintain a high level of fitness. In today's class, I'd like to discuss [1)]_____ _____ throughout history. First off, weightlifting has been an essential workout for thousands of years. Stone weights have been found that were used in the ancient Olympics. Running is another exercise that is present [2)]_____ _____ _____. For instance, the gymnasiums all over the Roman empire usually included tracks where joggers could run. Next, let's talk about dancing. Dancing has been used to improve physical fitness since at least the medieval period. Some records show that knights [3)]_____ _____ _____ to get used to wearing their armor. Finally, we can take a recent example, Pilates. This is indeed a modern invention, which was created by a German physical trainer. People who practice it [4)]_____ _____ _____ and learn breathing techniques. Now, let's take a look at a brief video.

↘ **듣기 필수 표현**
· get used to ~에 익숙해지다

03회

제3교시

대학수학능력시험 문제지
영어듣기 모의고사

▲ 문제 음성
바로 듣기

▲ 고사장 버전
바로 듣기

정답 및 해설 p.14

1번부터 17번까지는 듣고 답하는 문제입니다. 1번부터 15번까지는 한 번만 들려주고, 16번부터 17번까지는 두 번 들려줍니다. 방송을 잘 듣고 답을 하시기 바랍니다.

1. 다음을 듣고, 여자가 하는 말의 목적으로 가장 적절한 것을 고르시오.

① 손 씻기 캠페인을 홍보하려고
② 기침에 좋은 음식을 소개하려고
③ 무료 건강 검진 일정을 안내하려고
④ 독감 예방 수칙 준수를 권고하려고
⑤ 백신 접종 신청 방법을 설명하려고

2. 대화를 듣고, 여자의 의견으로 가장 적절한 것을 고르시오.

① 관광지에서 기차를 이용하면 비용이 절약된다.
② 때로는 중심지보다 교외에 볼거리가 더 많다.
③ 여행 시 숙소는 도심에 위치한 곳이 좋다.
④ 탐방할 관광지들을 여행 전에 미리 찾아봐야 한다.
⑤ 여행에서 얻은 특별한 경험은 인생에 활기를 준다.

3. 대화를 듣고, 두 사람의 관계를 가장 잘 나타낸 것을 고르시오.

① 사진작가 – 배우
② 촬영 감독 – 드라마 작가
③ 플로리스트 – 패션모델
④ 잡지 기자 – 영화 제작자
⑤ 조명 기사 – 스타일리스트

4. 대화를 듣고, 그림에서 대화의 내용과 일치하지 않는 것을 고르시오.

5. 대화를 듣고, 남자가 할 일로 가장 적절한 것을 고르시오.

① 연설문 수정하기
② 농구팀 지도하기
③ 연설 듣고 의견 주기
④ 연설 대본 출력하기
⑤ 필기도구 가져다주기

6. 대화를 듣고, 여자가 지불할 금액을 고르시오. [3점]

① $210   ② $230   ③ $240   ④ $250   ⑤ $ 270

7. 대화를 듣고, 남자가 발표 때 노트북을 가져올 수 없는 이유를 고르시오.

① 수리를 맡겨야 해서
② 여동생이 빌려 가서
③ 학교에 가져오기 불편해서
④ 프로그래밍 수업에 필요해서
⑤ 휴대폰으로 발표할 예정이어서

8. 대화를 듣고, 발레 *Swan Lake*에 관해 언급되지 않은 것을 고르시오.

① 무용단 국적   ② 마지막 공연일   ③ 티켓 가격
④ 공연 장소   ⑤ 공연 길이

9. 10th Annual Charity Concert에 관한 다음 내용을 듣고, 일치하지 않는 것을 고르시오.

① 매년 2월에 열린다.
② 모금액의 일부만 동물 보호소에 기부될 것이다.
③ 시내의 Logan Ballroom에서 개최된다.
④ 라디오 DJ가 사회를 맡을 예정이다.
⑤ 티켓은 1인당 50달러로 웹사이트에서 구매할 수 있다.

10. 다음 표를 보면서 대화를 듣고, 두 사람이 구매할 서랍장을 고르시오.

Dressers

	Dresser	Price	Number of Drawers	Color	Material
①	A	$450	6	White	Oak
②	B	$550	4	Black	Maple
③	C	$600	8	Brown	Maple
④	D	$775	6	Black	Walnut
⑤	E	$850	8	Brown	Walnut

11. 대화를 듣고, 여자의 마지막 말에 대한 남자의 응답으로 가장 적절한 것을 고르시오.

① Good point. But let's visit somewhere quieter.

② No way. I was looking forward to traveling over the weekend.

③ Okay. I'll do my best so that I won't regret it afterwards.

④ Don't worry. The traffic will be better if we leave early.

⑤ I agree. We will have more fun relaxing at home.

12. 대화를 듣고, 남자의 마지막 말에 대한 여자의 응답으로 가장 적절한 것을 고르시오.

① I agree with you. The exhibit was really brilliant.

② Yes. I often come here with my friends during my free time.

③ Really? I can't believe it's been that long since we last saw each other.

④ Sure. How about getting some coffee at a nearby café?

⑤ Sorry. I couldn't chat because I had to leave early.

13. 대화를 듣고, 여자의 마지막 말에 대한 남자의 응답으로 가장 적절한 것을 고르시오. [3점]

Man: _____

① I'll do my best. But I can't promise a perfect result.

② I see. Well, no wonder that it got torn again so quickly.

③ Thanks so much. When should I come back to pick up my clothes?

④ I'm afraid not. We can't clean items like this one.

⑤ No. The material is a lot stronger than it looks.

14. 대화를 듣고, 남자의 마지막 말에 대한 여자의 응답으로 가장 적절한 것을 고르시오.

Woman: _____

① You're right. The manager was very kind.

② Why not? I've never tried the soup here before.

③ No, it's fine. You can use my napkin if you want.

④ Yeah. I can't eat this, so I'll ask for a salad instead.

⑤ This is unacceptable. The waiter brought me the wrong dish!

15. 다음 상황 설명을 듣고, Hank가 Kendra에게 할 말로 가장 적절한 것을 고르시오. [3점]

Hank: _____

① Would you mind me asking what score you got?

② Actually, I'm thinking of joining a study group.

③ I think you just need to spend more time studying formulas.

④ This class is way too difficult, so I'm starting to regret taking it.

⑤ Could you give me some tips on how I can get a better score next time?

[16~17] 다음을 듣고, 물음에 답하시오.

16. 남자가 하는 말의 주제로 가장 적절한 것은?

① unusual parenting methods of various animals

② the evolution of birds living on the ocean

③ unique ways animals hatch from eggs

④ why cooperative parenting is essential for mammals

⑤ the importance of high survival rates to wild animals

17. 언급된 동물이 <u>아닌</u> 것은?

① sea turtles　　② alligators

③ emperor penguins　　④ elephants

⑤ kangaroos

이제 듣기 문제가 끝났습니다. 채점을 마친 후 다음 페이지에서 방송을 다시 들으며 딕테이션 연습을 하시기 바랍니다.

* 채점 결과: 맞은 개수 _____개 / 17개　　　정답 및 해설 p.14

03회 Dictation

Dictation 정답 p.14

03회 영어듣기 모의고사 Dictation 음성을 들으며 빈칸에 알맞은 단어를 채워 넣으시기 바랍니다.

1

W Attention, Brook High School students. As you may know, the flu is going around right now. This viral disease is spread through human contact 1)_____ _____ _____. Consequently, schools are often a place where the flu spreads quickly. Therefore, we would like to advise students to take preventive measures to 2)_____ _____ _____ _____ and spreading it. Wash your hands often and use your sleeve if you need to sneeze or cough. It is also a good idea to wear a mask. Free vaccinations against this disease are offered by local hospitals and community health centers. Vaccinations are 3)_____ _____, but students are strongly advised to get vaccinated. Thank you.

↘ 듣기 필수 표현
· go around (질병이) 유행하다
· advise A to B A에게 B하기를 권고하다
· take a measure 조치를 취하다
· get vaccinated 예방 접종을 받다

2

W Hi, Carl. Did you book a hotel for your trip to Paris?

M Hey, Sheila. Not yet.

W Where do you want to stay?

M I was thinking of getting a hotel 1)_____ _____ _____. Then, I could take a train in to Paris to go sightseeing.

W Hmm... I think it's better to find accommodations in 2)_____ _____ _____ when you're traveling.

M Really? I could save 50 euros per night.

W Maybe so, but then you'll have to spend a lot of time going back and forth.

M It's 45 minutes each way. I guess that will get tiring.

W Exactly. That's why you need a place to stay in the middle of the city. You'll have 3)_____ _____ _____ _____ the attractions.

M Yeah... I want to have a special experience there.

W Then, keep looking!

M I will.

↘ 듣기 필수 표현
· go sightseeing 관광하러 가다
· go back and forth 왔다 갔다 하다
· That's why ~. 그게 바로 ~한 이유이다.

3

W Hi. Welcome to the studio!

M It's nice to meet you, Lauren.

W It's my pleasure. I'm a big fan of yours. I've watched all the movies 1)_____ _____ _____.

M Thanks. I've wanted to work with you since I saw your last collection of photos.

W Then, you're going to like today's shoot. It'll be based on the same theme.

M You mean we'll 2)_____ _____ using flowers?

W Yeah. I'm sure you're eager to begin. I know you have a meeting with the director of your new movie later.

M No rush. Is there anything in particular you want me to wear in the pictures?

W The stylist has a few choices for you.

M Great. And we'll take the pictures in this room?

W That's right. I have the 3)_____ _____ _____ _____. I think this magazine cover is going to look great!

M I hope so! I'll go ahead and get ready.

↘ 듣기 필수 표현
· be based on ~을 기반으로 하다
· be eager to 몹시 ~하고 싶다
· No rush. 서두르지 마세요.
· in particular 특별히

4

W Honey, do you mind taking a look at the room setup? I want to check if we're forgetting anything for Jake's graduation party.

M No problem. I love the balloon arch 1)_____ _____ _____.

W Thanks.

M Is there enough seating? I only see three tables.

W We're expecting 20 people, so I think everyone will have 2)_____ _____ _____ _____ _____.

M You've already put a stack of square plates on the table in the front.

W Right. We'll serve the snacks and cake on those plates.

M What about that photo of Jake ³)_____ _____? Is that the one you want to display?

W Yes. He wanted a sports-themed one.

M That makes sense. I see you have ⁴)_____ _____ _____ _____ in the back of the room.

W Right, we'll have music playing.

M I think everything is good to go.

↘ 듣기 필수 표현
· take a look at ~을 보다
· good to go 준비가 된, 순조로운

5

M Hey, Alison. What are you working on?

W I just finished revising the end of my speech, Uncle Steve.

M Oh, right. You're in a speech competition. When is it?

W It's next Friday afternoon.

M That's perfect. I'll be able to watch it.

W Do you want to come? I know you're ¹)_____ _____ your basketball team.

M No worries. Our team is taking a break. So I'll be free for a while.

W Really? Then, please help me with my speech. I'm nervous about it.

M Sure. Why don't you read it out loud for me? I'd be happy to listen to your speech and ²)_____ _____ _____ _____.

W That would be really helpful. Give me just a second to ³)_____ _____ _____ for you.

M Sure! Take your time. Oh, and please bring me a pen, too.

W Alright. One moment.

↘ 듣기 필수 표현
· take a break 휴식을 취하다
· for a while 당분간, 잠시
· read out loud 큰 소리로 읽다
· I'd be happy to ~. 기꺼이 ~할게.
· Take your time. 천천히 해.

6

M Welcome to the Hotel Marigold, ma'am. May I help you?

W Yes, thanks. I need a room for the next couple of nights. Do you ¹)_____ _____ _____?

M We do have a few rooms available. *[Typing sound]* It looks like you have two options. There's one room with a queen-sized bed for $100 per night, and one with a king-sized bed for $120 per night.

W I'll take the one with the queen-sized bed.

M And that's ²)_____ _____ _____?

W Right. Also, I have this discount voucher.

M Ah, sure. This would give you $20 off of the total on your bill.

W Great. And is breakfast included?

M There's an ³)_____ _____ _____ $15 per person for our breakfast buffet.

W Well, it's just me, but I would like it both mornings.

M All right, then. I just need an ID and credit card.

W I've got those right here.

7

W Hi, David. I heard you started a computer programming course. How is that going?

M It's really fun, Lisa. I practiced coding a website today.

W That's really interesting. Oh, I needed to ask you something. Can you bring your laptop for our class presentation tomorrow?

M I ¹)_____ _____ that's going to be possible.

W Did you lend it to your sister?

M Yes, but she gave it back to me already.

W Then, I guess you're not comfortable bringing it to school, right? That's understandable.

M I normally take mine to school. Actually, I have to take it to the shop ²)_____ _____.

W Oh... I see. Well, what are we going to do?

M We can use our smartphones to project the slideshow. Let me look up ³)_____ _____ _____ _____.

W Great! That should work.

↘ 듣기 필수 표현
· look up 찾아보다

8

W Hey, Patrick. How was the performance of *Swan Lake*?

M It was wonderful, Carrie! What a great ballet performance!

W Aren't the dancers ¹)_____ _____?

M That's right. The lead ballerina is one of the best dancers in the world.

W Wow. Is there still time to get tickets?

M Yeah, I think so. There are performances ²)_____ _____ _____.

W How much are they?

M Well, it's different depending on where you sit. The one I bought was $25, though.

W That's not so bad. Where are the performances being held?

M The shows are at the Sheldon Auditorium.

W That's perfect. That's close to my house. I'll ³)_____ _____.

M Well, let me know your plan. I'd be happy to go see it again.

W I will!

↘ 듣기 필수 표현
· depending on ~에 따라
· close to ~에서 가까운

9

W Hello, WBBZ Radio listeners. Before we get to the next program, I want to remind listeners about our radio station's 10th Annual Charity Concert. During this event, which is ¹)_____ _____, our station raises money for charity with the help of our loyal listeners. This year, ²)_____ _____ _____ raised will be donated to several local pet shelters. The event, which will take place on the sixth, will be held downtown at the Logan Ballroom on 1st Avenue. Jennifer Haley, the city's most popular radio DJ, will ³)_____ _____ _____. Food and beverages will be provided by Winston Catering Services. Tickets are $50 each and available on our website. Okay, now let's get back to your regularly scheduled program.

↘ 듣기 필수 표현
· raise money for charity 자선기금을 모금하다
· take place (행사가) 열리다, 개최되다

10

W Honey, shouldn't we get something for the bedroom? I think these dressers look good.

M Yeah, definitely. It would be nice to have a new dresser next to the bed.

W The problem is that there are so many choices in this showroom.

M Maybe we should ¹)_____ _____ _____ _____ first.

W We can't spend more than $800.

M That's fair. Well, what about this one? It looks pretty nice.

W Yeah, I like the style, but it only has four drawers. That ²)_____ _____ _____.

M Right, we need it to store a lot of clothes.

W Does the color make a big difference to you?

M I think any of these colors could work except for white.

W Okay. How about the material?

M I ³)_____ _____. It lasts a long time.

W That's exactly what I was thinking.

M Well, I think the decision is made for us, then.

↘ 듣기 필수 표현
· except for ~을 제외하고는

11

W Peter, I'm really ¹)_____ _____ _____ somewhere this weekend. How about heading to the beach?

M I'd like to, but I'm worried it will be crowded and the traffic will be awful.

W But if we stay at home, we'll ²)_____ _____ _____.

↘ 듣기 필수 표현
· head to ~으로 가다

12

M Jane! What a coincidence running into you here! I ¹)_____ _____ _____ in years.

W It's great to see you, Mark! Are you leaving the modern art exhibit?

M Yeah, I was about to go home. But why don't we go somewhere and ²)_____ _____ _____ _____?

↘ 듣기 필수 표현
· What a coincidence ~! ~하다니 이런 우연이!
· run into ~를 우연히 만나다
· be about to 막 ~하려던 참이다

13

M Hi! What can I do for you?

W I'd like to have these clothes dry-cleaned.

M Please set your items down here.

W Here they are.

M So I've got a woman's jacket, a short-sleeved dress, and a coat.

W Oh, I also have this shirt. Can you 1)_____ _____?

M What's wrong with it?

W There's a small tear down the back. You can hardly see it.

M Ma'am... I don't think I'll be 2)_____ _____ _____ this.

W Why not? It doesn't look too badly damaged. This is one of my favorite shirts.

M The material is too fine and fragile. I'm certain it will 3)_____ _____ even if I mend it.

W I 4)_____ _____ _____ if that happens. Can you please try mending it for me?

↘ 듣기 필수 표현
· have ~ dry-cleaned ~을 드라이클리닝 받다

14

M Hey, Samantha. What's wrong?

W Well, I think there's a 1)_____ _____ _____ _____.

M Are you sure? Can I take a look?

W It's right there on the side of the bowl.

M That doesn't look like a fly to me. I think it's probably a small piece of onion that's turned a little black from frying.

W Then, do you mind 2)_____ _____ _____ of the soup to check? I can't do it myself.

M Not at all. I'm going to 3)_____ _____ _____ this napkin.

W Go ahead. [Pause] Ah, maybe I was wrong.

M Yeah, that's not a fly. But it's not an onion either. I'm not sure if it's a part of your dish or not.

W Me neither. I should call over a manager to check it.

M You'd better 4)_____ _____ _____ _____ of soup or something else.

↘ 듣기 필수 표현
· take a look 한번 보다
· Go ahead. 그렇게 해.

15

W Kendra and Hank are friends who recently enrolled in an advanced physics class at an after-school program. Both of them are quite 1)_____ _____ _____. However, Hank is finding the class more difficult than he thought it would be, so he has to spend extra time studying the course materials every night. Today, everyone in the class 2)_____ _____ _____ of the first quiz of the semester. Despite his hard work, Hank was very disappointed with his score. However, he noticed that Kendra 3)_____ _____ when she saw her grade. So he wants to ask her if she can 4)_____ _____ _____ to help him improve his grade on the next test. In this situation, what would Hank most likely say to Kendra?

↘ 듣기 필수 표현
· be disappointed with ~에 실망하다

16~17

M Good afternoon, everyone. We previously learned about what kinds of animals lay eggs. Today, I want to talk about some of the unique ways that animals 1)_____ _____ _____. To begin, let's think about sea turtles that skip parenting entirely. When young turtles hatch, they have to get to the ocean 2)_____ _____ _____. Predictably, this means that very few of them survive to adulthood. In contrast, we have emperor penguins, who make a great effort to 3)_____ _____ _____. After laying an egg, the female penguin returns to the sea to look for food while its father holds on to it. Next up, elephants raise their young together. For them, parenting is a community-wide activity. Along with help from their mothers, baby elephants are fed, protected, and taught by elder females in the herd. Finally, we can consider kangaroos. Their babies are born tiny and underdeveloped. So kangaroos 4)_____ _____ _____ _____ in a pouch under their mothers' skin for warmth and protection. Now, let's take a look at a quick video.

↘ 듣기 필수 표현
· in contrast 대조적으로
· hold on to ~을 계속 품다, 잡다
· along with ~과 함께

대학수학능력시험 문제지
영어듣기 모의고사

▲ 문제 음성
바로 듣기

▲ 고사장 버전
바로 듣기

제3교시

정답 및 해설 p.20

1번부터 17번까지는 듣고 답하는 문제입니다. 1번부터 15번까지는 한 번만 들려주고, 16번부터 17번까지는 두 번 들려줍니다. 방송을 잘 듣고 답을 하시기 바랍니다.

1. 다음을 듣고, 여자가 하는 말의 목적으로 가장 적절한 것을 고르시오.

① 꾸준한 연주 연습을 독려하려고
② 변경된 수업 일정을 안내하려고
③ 음악 학원을 홍보하려고
④ 학원 위치 이전을 공지하려고
⑤ 음악 장르별 특징을 설명하려고

2. 대화를 듣고, 남자의 의견으로 가장 적절한 것을 고르시오.

① 집중을 방해할 요소들을 최소화해야 한다.
② 한 번에 여러 과제를 해결하는 능력을 키워야 한다.
③ 흥미 있는 과목을 공부할 때 집중이 더 잘 된다.
④ 과제를 미리 끝내 두는 습관은 스트레스를 줄여준다.
⑤ 시작한 과제를 끝마친 후에 다른 과제를 하는 것이 좋다.

3. 대화를 듣고, 두 사람의 관계를 가장 잘 나타낸 것을 고르시오.

① 광고주 — 카피라이터
② 건축가 — 가구 판매원
③ 호텔 매니저 — 투숙객
④ 인테리어 디자이너 — 고객
⑤ 페인트공 — 건물주

4. 대화를 듣고, 그림에서 대화의 내용과 일치하지 않는 것을 고르시오.

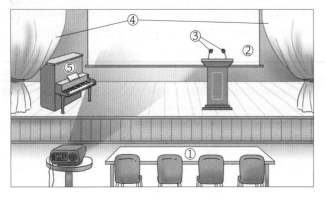

5. 대화를 듣고, 남자가 할 일로 가장 적절한 것을 고르시오.

① 춤 연습하기
② 피아노 치기
③ 노래 재생하기
④ 성당 위치 확인하기
⑤ 축하 선물 구입하기

6. 대화를 듣고, 남자가 지불할 금액을 고르시오. [3점]

① $24   ② $29   ③ $35   ④ $53   ⑤ $65

7. 대화를 듣고, 남자가 독서 동아리 모임에 참석할 수 없는 이유를 고르시오.

① 책이 마음에 들지 않아서
② 모임 장소가 너무 멀어서
③ 시험공부를 해야 해서
④ 고모 댁을 방문해야 해서
⑤ 1월까지 여행을 가서

8. 대화를 듣고, Maple Campsite에 관해 언급되지 않은 것을 고르시오.

① 개장 기간   ② 위치   ③ 운영 규칙
④ 제공 용품   ⑤ 이용 요금

9. Jacobs Department Store에 관한 다음 내용을 듣고, 일치하지 않는 것을 고르시오.

① 10월 24일에 재개장 세일이 열린다.
② 여름 원피스는 25% 할인된다.
③ 남성용 겨울 코트는 할인 대상에서 제외된다.
④ 최상층에는 아이들을 위한 놀이 공간이 있다.
⑤ 푸드 코트에는 12개가 넘는 다양한 식당이 있다.

10. 다음 표를 보면서 대화를 듣고, 두 사람이 주문할 케이크를 고르시오.

Red Panther Cakes

	Cake	Flavor	Custom Writing	Price	Number of Slices
①	A	Chocolate	O	$49.99	8-10
②	B	Carrot	X	$37.99	6-8
③	C	Vanilla	O	$67.99	8-10
④	D	Raspberry	X	$99.99	10-12
⑤	E	Lemon	O	$55.99	12-14

11. 대화를 듣고, 남자의 마지막 말에 대한 여자의 응답으로 가장 적절한 것을 고르시오.

① It's a nice day for a walk.
② There aren't any shops at the corner.
③ My favorite team plays in that arena.
④ It's about a 30-minute walk from here.
⑤ I don't have tickets to the basketball game.

12. 대화를 듣고, 여자의 마지막 말에 대한 남자의 응답으로 가장 적절한 것을 고르시오.

① Oh, could you pick me up a snack?
② We can cover that part in the morning.
③ I don't think it's going to be on the exam.
④ I'm tired, so I'm going to head to bed early.
⑤ I find myself having trouble managing time.

13. 대화를 듣고, 여자의 마지막 말에 대한 남자의 응답으로 가장 적절한 것을 고르시오. [3점]

Man: _____

① Probably. Could you call me back later?
② No. I don't recommend the fried octopus.
③ Yes. I'll have the check for you in a moment.
④ That depends. Are you dining alone or with someone?
⑤ No problem. I'll be back with your order in about 15 minutes.

14. 대화를 듣고, 남자의 마지막 말에 대한 여자의 응답으로 가장 적절한 것을 고르시오.

Woman: _____

① I'm excited to see who the winner will be.
② How about the water fountain next to Exit 2?
③ Of course you can come watch the dance battle with me.
④ Let's cheer for the dancers as loudly as we can.
⑤ I'll get there an hour before the show starts.

15. 다음 상황 설명을 듣고, Harry의 어머니가 Harry에게 할 말로 가장 적절한 것을 고르시오. [3점]

Harry's mother: _____

① To be honest, I would prefer if you didn't film me.
② Why don't you post the videos on a different website?
③ You should be more cautious when shooting private scenes.
④ That's not going to make for a good scene in your movie.
⑤ I'll always support your dream of being a film director.

[16~17] 다음을 듣고, 물음에 답하시오.

16. 남자가 하는 말의 주제로 가장 적절한 것은?

① how yoga influences people's health
② drawbacks to jogging every day
③ causes of health disorders
④ strategies for reducing stress levels
⑤ ways that people get injured exercising

17. 언급된 신체 부위가 아닌 것은?

① heart   ② spine   ③ shoulder
④ wrist   ⑤ legs

이제 듣기 문제가 끝났습니다. 채점을 마친 후 다음 페이지에서 방송을 다시 들으며 딕테이션 연습을 하시기 바랍니다.

* 채점 결과: 맞은 개수 _____ 개 / 17개   정답 및 해설 p.20

04회 영어듣기 모의고사 Dictation 음성을 들으며 빈칸에 알맞은 단어를 채워 넣으시기 바랍니다.

1

W Attention, Channel 15 viewers. Is there a musician inside you wanting to come out? Then, call Harmony Music Academy at 555-9283, and let us help you [1]_____ _____ _____! We offer a great variety of music classes for both beginners and more advanced students. Our classes will not only provide you with theoretical and historical knowledge of [2]_____ _____ _____, from classical music to rock music, but will also give you the practice you need to develop and [3]_____ _____ _____ _____. Our academy is located next to city hall, in front of the bus terminal. Call or stop by.

↘ 듣기 필수 표현
· come out 나오다
· a variety of 다양한
· stop by 들르다

2

M Kaylie, what are you working on? Are you finished with your chemistry homework?

W Oh, I was getting bored with chemistry, so I started an essay for my English class.

M I'm not sure that's a good idea.

W Why not? I have to [1]_____ _____ _____ _____.

M I think it's better to finish one task [2]_____ _____ _____ _____.

W I was having trouble focusing.

M I understand. But switching back and forth between different assignments wastes time.

W Maybe you're right.

M And finishing one thing always feels better. Doing another assignment only adds something else [3]_____ _____ _____.

W Yeah, now I'm worrying about both assignments.

M That's why you should stick to one thing at a time!

W Okay, I'll get back to my chemistry homework so I don't have to think about it anymore.

↘ 듣기 필수 표현
· get bored with ~에 신물이 나다
· back and forth 왔다 갔다
· stick to ~을 고수하다

3

M Hi, Ms. Williams. Did you see my draft of [1]_____ _____ _____?

W It looks good, but it's a big change from the old lobby, don't you think?

M That's true. But considering your company is an advertising agency, the change should [2]_____ _____.

W I guess. Maybe I'm not used to the bold colors.

M This is just a prospective design. If there are some things that you want to tone down, we can do that.

W It needs a carpet that stands out less.

M Sure, Ms. Williams. You can choose [3]_____ _____ _____ _____.

W I also think we should go with different furniture. Those chairs don't look comfortable.

M Got it. I'll show you some different samples.

W Good. Can I also see your design of the area near the elevators?

M Of course. You'll see I included a mirror across from each elevator, [4]_____ _____ _____.

↘ 듣기 필수 표현
· be used to ~에 익숙하다
· tone ~ down ~의 색상을 은은하게 하다
· stand out 눈에 띄다
· across from 바로 맞은편에

4

W Nathan, is the auditorium ready for the speech contest?

M I think so, Principal Hill. I just finished setting up the judges' table in front of the stage.

W Did you lower the projector screen at the [1]_____ _____ _____ _____ yet?

M I did. And I placed two microphones on the podium on the right side of the stage.

W By the way, did you replace the old curtains?

M Yes. I installed the [2]_____ _____ _____ a few days ago. Do you want me to do anything with the piano?

W Is it in the way?

M No. I pushed it to 3)_____ _____ _____.

W Let's leave it there, then. It's not worth the trouble of moving it off the stage.

M Sounds good.

W I think we're all set. Thanks, Nathan.

5

M Did you hear? Jennifer is getting married!

W Really? I can't believe that! I didn't even know she was in a relationship.

M She told me that the wedding will be in September. The ceremony 1)_____ _____ _____ at St. Mary's Church downtown.

W That's so great. It'll be fun to visit the city then. The weather in September is beautiful.

M Anyway, I think we should 2)_____ _____ _____ for her at the wedding.

W Sure. What should we do?

M How about performing a dance at the reception?

W Oh, you know I'm a bad dancer!

M Then, what about a song? You can play the piano, and I will sing.

W That sounds better. Do you have a song in mind?

M I do, actually! Let me 3)_____ _____ _____ for you on my phone.

W You've already worked everything out!

6

W Good afternoon, sir.

M Hi. I'd like to buy some tickets for the art museum.

W It's $10 per person for 1)_____ _____ _____ and $20 per person for the guided tour.

M Okay. When does the next guided tour start?

W Let's see. *[Pause]* The next one leaves at 2 p.m.

M Hmm... That's 2)_____ _____ _____. I'll stick with the audio tour. Three tickets, please.

W Got it. And are you a student?

M Yes. Is there a discount?

W It's 20% off the ticket price if you have a 3)_____ _____ _____.

M Thanks for mentioning it. Here you go.

W Okay, that's three audio tour tickets at the student rate. And would you like a copy of our exhibition catalog? It's a great souvenir, and it's only $5.

M Sure, I'll 4)_____ _____.

W Great. Here you are. I hope you enjoy the exhibit today.

7

W Tom, are you coming to the book club meeting?

M Hi, Marta. I can't make it.

W Oh, no. Again? You don't like the novel we're reading, do you?

M It's 1)_____ _____ _____. I'm enjoying the book.

W It must be the meeting place, then. I could have scheduled it at a café closer to the school.

M No. I've just been busy with the end of the semester. I need to focus on studying 2)_____ _____ _____ at the moment.

W Got it. It's too bad that you can't come this time. I haven't seen you there since you went to 3)_____ _____ _____ in December.

M Yeah, I wish I could go. But I'll be back soon.

W When do you think you can come to a club meeting again?

M I'll return in January. See you soon!

8

W Hey, Alex. Do you have special plans for next week?

M Yeah. I'm going to Maple Campsite! I've been looking forward to this for a long time.

W Oh, was it closed for a while?

M Yes. Visitors are only allowed there ¹⁾_____ _____ _____.

W And the campsite is in Maple Forest, right? Doesn't it get cold there in the autumn?

M You're right. But don't worry. I think I'm well prepared.

W Really? You'll have to ²⁾_____ _____ _____ to stay warm.

M No, actually. That's against campsite rules. The rangers won't let us build one.

W Oh, that must be to prevent forest fires.

M Right. But they ³⁾_____ _____ _____ a tent, so I just have to bring a thick sleeping bag.

W I see. Well, it sounds like you've got everything covered. Have a nice trip!

↘ 듣기 필수 표현
· look forward to ~을 기대하다
· for a while 한동안
· It sounds like ~. ~인 것 같다.

9

M Hi. I'm Michael Jacobs, owner of Jacobs Department Store. I want to invite everyone in the Peterville area to our Reopening Sale on October 24th. To celebrate our ¹⁾_____ _____ _____ on Madison Street, we're cutting prices throughout the store. On the second floor, where women's casual wear has been relocated, summer dresses are marked 25% off. In the men's fashion section, which is now on the third floor, ²⁾_____ _____ _____ _____ are discounted. Kids' clothing can now be found ³⁾_____ _____ _____ _____, along with a supervised playground area for your children. Also, make sure to stop by our food court in the basement. We have over a dozen different restaurants that will be offering free samples from their new menus. I hope you'll join us.

↘ 듣기 필수 표현
· cut prices 가격을 인하하다
· make sure to 꼭 ~하다
· over a dozen 12개가 넘는

10

W Patrick's birthday party is coming up. We need to order a cake soon.

M Why don't we get one from that new bakery on the corner?

W Right! Red Panther Bakery. I'll open their website.

M Let's make sure ¹⁾_____ _____ _____ a carrot cake. Patrick wasn't happy with the one we got last year.

W Fair enough. Well, there are still plenty of good options here.

M Should we get one with a custom message?

W Yeah. I think that would be cute.

M But I don't want to ²⁾_____ _____ _____. Some of these are expensive.

W No problem. We can go up to $60.

M Perfect.

W What about size? We're expecting five people, and some will want an extra serving.

M Let's not get something too small. But at the same time, we don't need to overdo it. ³⁾_____ _____ _____ _____ is probably excessive.

W I agree.

↘ 듣기 필수 표현
· plenty of 많은
· up to ~까지
· at the same time 동시에

11

M Excuse me. Do you know ¹⁾_____ _____ _____ _____ the Foster Center Basketball Arena from here?

W Just turn right at the corner, and then go straight. But are you sure you want to walk there? I ²⁾_____ _____ _____ _____.

M No? Why not?

12

W Toby, I'm ¹⁾_____ _____ from all this studying. Should we call it a night?

M We've covered almost everything that will be on the exam. Is ²⁾_____ _____ _____ _____ _____?

W I can manage that. I need to run over to the convenience store, though.

↘ 듣기 필수 표현
· call it a night (이날 밤의 일을) 여기서 끝내다, 중지하다
· run over to ~에 잠시 들르다

13

M Welcome to Antonio's Restaurant. What will you be having this afternoon?

W I'd like to [1)]_____ _____ the shrimp salad.

M Fantastic. Would you like cocktail sauce or the chef's special dressing?

W The special dressing is fine. I'd also like a bowl of soup.

M Okay. We have tomato, potato, and clam chowder.

W I'm in the mood for seafood. Clam chowder, please.

M Excellent choice. Now, [2)]_____ _____ _____ _____ the main course?

W I'm thinking about the fried octopus. How is that served?

M It's served with a fresh herb sauce. It's also our special of the day, which means it's half off.

W Oh, that sounds lovely.

M So that's a clam chowder, a shrimp salad, and the fried octopus?

W Correct. Can you bring everything [3)]_____ _____ _____ _____ ?

↘ 듣기 필수 표현
· be in the mood for ~하고 싶다
· half off 반값의

14

M Sally, do you have plans tonight?

W I'm going to the Street Dance Battle.

M Oh, I heard about that event. Don't the performers dance to hip-hop music?

W Yeah. There's a famous DJ doing the music, and the dancers are supposed to be spectacular.

M Why do they [1)]_____ _____ _____ _____ _____ ?

W It is a competition, with a winner and loser after each performance.

M I see. But who judges the dancers?

W The fans pick the winners. It's based on [2)]_____ _____ _____ _____ _____ .

M Wow. That sounds like a lot of fun.

W Do you want to come? It starts at 8:30 in Central Park.

M Sure! Where should we meet?

W I was going to take the subway to Murray Station. See you there at 7:30?

M Okay, but let's pick a [3)]_____ _____ _____ .

↘ 듣기 필수 표현
· be based on ~을 근거로 하다

15

W Harry is a high school student who wants to become a film director. Recently, his mother [1)]_____ _____ _____ _____ _____ to support his dream. Since then, he has been filming almost everywhere he goes. This includes in his school, where Harry often makes videos of [2)]_____ _____ . Then, he posts nearly all of these on his website without asking for permission. Now, Harry's mother has begun to worry. She thinks that he is filming and sharing [3)]_____ _____ _____ _____ . She is concerned that this will upset or embarrass someone. So she wants to tell Harry that he should be careful [4)]_____ _____ _____ other people's privacy. In this situation, what would Harry's mother most likely say to Harry?

↘ 듣기 필수 표현
· ask for ~을 구하다, 요청하다

16~17

M Good afternoon, everyone. We've been discussing the effects of jogging on the body lately. But today I want to look at some of the effects yoga has [1)]_____ _____ _____ _____ . First of all, the heart does benefit from such exercise. High levels of stress-related chemicals are a major cause of heart disease. Since the practice of yoga [2)]_____ _____ , it lowers the chances of a heart attack. Next, we see a notable improvement in spine health. This is because deep stretching helps to maintain good posture and strengthens core muscle groups. However, there are some downsides. For example, a sprained wrist is a [3)]_____ _____ _____ _____ who practice yoga. This occurs when people put too much weight on the wrist, and it can be painful. Also, the legs can be put under [4)]_____ _____ _____ _____ when people do yoga poses inappropriately. Stretching too deeply can lead to pulled and torn muscles. But these risks are minimal with proper technique. Now, we'll see some examples of yoga poses for beginners.

↘ 듣기 필수 표현
· This is because ~. ~하기 때문이다.
· lead to ~으로 이어지다

05회

제3교시

대학수학능력시험 문제지
영어듣기 모의고사

▲ 문제 음성
바로 듣기

▲ 고사장 버전
바로 듣기

정답 및 해설 p.26

1번부터 17번까지는 듣고 답하는 문제입니다. 1번부터 15번까지는 한 번만 들려주고, 16번부터 17번까지는 두 번 들려줍니다. 방송을 잘 듣고 답을 하시기 바랍니다.

1. 다음을 듣고, 여자가 하는 말의 목적으로 가장 적절한 것을 고르시오.

① 지역의 관광명소를 소개하려고
② 생존 수영 교육 이수를 권유하려고
③ 물놀이 사고의 인명 피해 현황을 발표하려고
④ 호숫가에서의 다이빙 금지 조치를 안내하려고
⑤ 잠수 시간이 길어질 때 겪을 수 있는 위험을 경고하려고

2. 대화를 듣고, 남자의 의견으로 가장 적절한 것을 고르시오.

① 빨리 적는 것보다 깔끔하게 필기하는 것이 중요하다.
② 노트북으로 필기하는 것은 학습에 도움이 되는 방법이다.
③ 학생 편의를 위해 다양한 학습용 앱이 개발되어야 한다.
④ 수업 시간에 필기한 부분을 다시 찾아 복습하는 편이 좋다.
⑤ 전자기기를 활용한 수업은 학생들의 주의력을 산만하게 할 수 있다.

3. 대화를 듣고, 두 사람의 관계를 가장 잘 나타낸 것을 고르시오.

① TV쇼 진행자 — 댄서
② 보컬 코치 — 가수 지망생
③ 방송 작가 — 배우
④ 신문 기자 — 발레리나
⑤ 아나운서 — 운동선수

4. 대화를 듣고, 그림에서 대화의 내용과 일치하지 <u>않는</u> 것을 고르시오.

5. 대화를 듣고, 여자가 할 일로 가장 적절한 것을 고르시오.

① 가방 확인하기
② 윤리 교과서 빌리기
③ 친구에게 전화하기
④ 영어 선생님과 면담하기
⑤ 생물 수업 들으러 가기

6. 대화를 듣고, 여자가 지불할 금액을 고르시오.

① $18   ② $20   ③ $25   ④ $27   ⑤ $29

7. 대화를 듣고, 남자가 운전면허증이 <u>없는</u> 이유를 고르시오.

① 면허 시험에 떨어져서
② 운전할 필요가 없다고 생각해서
③ 면허 취득 연령에 미달해서
④ 사고가 날까 봐 염려되어서
⑤ 환경 오염을 유발할까 봐 걱정해서

8. 대화를 듣고, Greenhills Apple Picking Festival에 관해 언급되지 <u>않은</u> 것을 고르시오.

① 개최 장소   ② 시작 시간   ③ 입장료
④ 참가 활동   ⑤ 기념품

9. Falcon Crest National Park에 관한 다음 내용을 듣고, 일치하지 <u>않는</u> 것을 고르시오.

① 혼자 등산하는 것은 권고되지 않는다.
② 표지판으로 표시된 등산로만 이용해야 한다.
③ 등산객은 마실 물을 지참하는 것이 좋다.
④ 휴대용 버너를 사용하는 것은 금지되어 있다.
⑤ 반입 금지 물품은 적발되는 즉시 압수 조치된다.

10. 다음 표를 보면서 대화를 듣고, 두 사람이 예약할 가이드 투어를 고르시오.

Guided Tours of Rome

	Tour	Mode of Transportation	Length (in hours)	Price	Meal
①	A	Walking	2-3	$50	X
②	B	Walking	4-5	$40	O
③	C	Bus	1-2	$20	O
④	D	Cycling	1-2	$35	O
⑤	E	Cycling	2-3	$25	X

11. 대화를 듣고, 여자의 마지막 말에 대한 남자의 응답으로 가장 적절한 것을 고르시오.

① Roast beef would be good.

② I'm not picky, so any store is fine.

③ Sure, I'll grab a sandwich for you.

④ I'd prefer to pay for it by credit card.

⑤ I bought milk at the convenience store.

12. 대화를 듣고, 남자의 마지막 말에 대한 여자의 응답으로 가장 적절한 것을 고르시오.

① I'll ride my bike there tomorrow.

② Thanks, and I'll let you know if I do.

③ I can call the doctor's office right now.

④ It's a long drive to the soccer stadium.

⑤ My doctor told me not to play soccer for a while.

13. 대화를 듣고, 여자의 마지막 말에 대한 남자의 응답으로 가장 적절한 것을 고르시오. [3점]

Man: _____

① Good thinking. The socks are very practical.

② Sure. Do you know what size your dad wears?

③ Look here. What do you think of this jacket?

④ I don't know. It still seems a little expensive.

⑤ Of course. I'll get you a pair of socks from the back room.

14. 대화를 듣고, 남자의 마지막 말에 대한 여자의 응답으로 가장 적절한 것을 고르시오. [3점]

Woman: _____

① That's a good idea. Then, I'll join you.

② Okay. Let's study for the exam together.

③ Great! In that case, I'll pick you up at 8 p.m.

④ You're right. The festival runs until after midnight.

⑤ I'll pass. Actually, I don't really like horror movies.

15. 다음 상황 설명을 듣고, Billy가 Erica에게 할 말로 가장 적절한 것을 고르시오. [3점]

Billy: _____

① I'll invite someone else to go with me on Saturday.

② If you want to get your money back, check the refund policy.

③ We should go to the first show because the band is better.

④ I got tickets to the other show, but do you want to go to both?

⑤ Can you exchange yours so we can go on the next day instead?

[16~17] 다음을 듣고, 물음에 답하시오.

16. 남자가 하는 말의 주제로 가장 적절한 것은?

① the impact of eating various fruits

② vitamins in different kinds of food

③ benefits of getting proper nutrition

④ a method for choosing a healthier diet

⑤ problems caused by overeating healthy foods

17. 언급된 식재료가 아닌 것은?

① tuna ② pineapples ③ spinach

④ avocados ⑤ broccoli

이제 듣기 문제가 끝났습니다. 채점을 마친 후 다음 페이지에서 방송을 다시 들으며 딕테이션 연습을 하시기 바랍니다.

* 채점 결과: 맞은 개수 _____ 개 / 17개 　　　　정답 및 해설 p.26

05회 Dictation

Dictation 정답 p.26

05회 영어듣기 모의고사 Dictation 음성을 들으며 빈칸에 알맞은 단어를 채워 넣으시기 바랍니다.

1

W Hello, Radio 602 listeners. It's time for the 5 o'clock news. Local officials have announced new restrictions at Herald Lake. The lake has long been 1) _____ _____ _____ among both locals and visitors. However, recent diving accidents have created worries about its safety. The problem is, people who jump in from nearby rocks are not 2) _____ _____ _____ the lake is less than two meters deep in spots. As a consequence, they risk injuries to their heads or necks on the bottom of the lake, which can be fatal. Thus, to 3) _____ _____ _____, the city government has decided to ban all diving at the lake. For more information, visit the city government's website.

↘ 듣기 필수 표현
· in spots 군데군데
· as a consequence 결과적으로

2

M Claire, can I borrow your laptop charger?

W I don't have it. Do you need it during class?

M Yeah. I usually use my laptop for note-taking. I think typing my notes makes it 1) _____ _____ _____ lessons.

W Why don't you just use pen and paper?

M I can type a lot faster than I can write by hand, so using a laptop 2) _____ _____ _____ more detailed information.

W But don't you get distracted?

M Not really. I only use apps relevant to the class.

W Oh, good thinking.

M The best part is that I have 3) _____ _____ _____, so I can quickly search through my notes when I study later.

W Yeah, typing on a laptop is helpful for studying. See if one of our classmates has a charger.

M Okay. I better go do that now.

↘ 듣기 필수 표현
· get distracted 정신이 산만해지다
· relevant to ~에 관련된

3

M Hello, Ms. Simmons. Welcome to *Music and People*.

W Thank you for having me on your show.

M I wanted to discuss your recent win in *The National Talent Competition* that 1) _____ _____ _____ _____ last week. How did you prepare for it?

W It took a lot of preparation. I began rehearsing my dance months ago.

M Wow, really?

W Yes. I wanted my performance to be perfect.

M It was really incredible. Can you tell our viewers how you created your 2) _____ _____ _____ ?

W I've been taking ballet and tap-dancing lessons for a long time. So I tried to combine those two styles.

M Were you nervous when you finally 3) _____ _____ _____ ?

W Absolutely. I was so scared I'd mess up one of my moves.

M Well, it ended up going well for you after all. Thank you so much for talking about it with us today.

W You're welcome.

↘ 듣기 필수 표현
· for a long time 오랫동안
· mess up 망치다
· end up ~으로 끝나게 되다
· after all 결국

4

M Julia, come and see! This is my bedroom.

W It's beautiful. Did you 1) _____ _____ _____ _____ I introduced you to?

M Yes, I did. He picked out the floral print on the rug.

W I love it. What about the striped chair by the window?

M Yeah, he recommended that, too.

W I thought so. The 2) _____ _____ _____ is a nice touch, too.

M Thanks.

W Do you normally keep all 3) _____ _____ _____ on the bed like that?

M Honestly, no. They're just for decoration. I usually put them in that box by the foot of the bed right before I go to sleep.

W Good idea. They would get in the way while you are sleeping.

M You're telling me. Now, why don't we go downstairs and take a look at the kitchen?

W Sounds good.

↘ 듣기 필수 표현
· pick out ~을 고르다
· get in the way 방해가 되다
· You're telling me. 내 말이 바로 그 말이야.
· take a look at ~을 보다

5

M Jess, is everything okay?

W Oh, I'm a little stressed out, Dad.

M Are you looking for something?

W Yeah. I can't ¹⁾_____ _____ _____ _____. I thought it was in my bag, but it's not there.

M Which one is it?

W It's my ethics textbook. I need it for my exam on Tuesday.

M Let's retrace your steps. Where did you go ²⁾_____ _____ _____ _____?

W Well, I had biology class in the last period. After school, I met with my English teacher. Then, I went to a German club meeting with my friend Jill.

M Does that help you remember?

W Actually, yes! I showed Jill something in the book while we were waiting for the meeting to begin. Maybe she took it by accident!

M ³⁾_____ _____ _____ her to see if she has it.

W I'll do that.

↘ 듣기 필수 표현
· be stressed out 스트레스를 받다
· retrace one's steps 왔던 길을 되짚다
· by accident 실수로

6

M Welcome to Barry's Burgers. What can we make for you today?

W Hi. I was wondering ¹⁾_____ _____ _____ in the combo meal.

M The combo meal includes a burger, fries, and a soda for $9. If you just want the burger, it's $6.

W Oh, so I can't get a milkshake with a combo?

M Actually, you can ²⁾_____ _____ _____ for an additional $2.

W I see. Well, I'll take three combo meals. I'd like two with sodas, and one with a vanilla milkshake.

M So you want three combos, one with a shake upgrade. Does that complete your order?

W Yes. That's all. But I do have a discount coupon for $2 off.

M [Pause] I'm afraid this coupon is ³⁾_____ _____ _____.

W Why not?

M This is ⁴⁾_____ _____ at our downtown location.

W Ah, well. I understand. Here's my credit card.

↘ 듣기 필수 표현
· complete one's order 주문을 완료하다

7

W Terry, did you get your driver's license yet?

M No, Grandma, I haven't gotten it.

W Oh, that's right. You're ¹⁾_____ _____ _____ _____.

M No, I am eligible to get one. I turned 18 in January.

W Oh, did you fail the test? I know it is a little tricky. But you can ²⁾_____ _____ _____!

M I haven't taken the test. And to be honest, I don't think I'm ever going to.

W You're concerned about the environment, right?

M That's not it. I think it's eco-friendly to ³⁾_____ _____ _____ _____. I'm just worried that I would get in an accident.

W Hmm... You may change your mind about that when you're older.

M We'll see.

↘ 듣기 필수 표현
· be eligible to ~할 자격이 되다
· fail the test 시험에 떨어지다
· to be honest 솔직히 말해서
· get in an accident 사고를 당하다

8

M Hailey, didn't you mention something about a class trip on Monday?

W Yeah. We're going to the Greenhills Apple Picking Festival, Dad.

M Oh, where ¹⁾_____ _____ _____ _____?

W The event is in Parkerville. I think it's about 25 kilometers from my high school.

M Ah, okay. When are you supposed to leave?

W The festival begins at 10 a.m., so we'll leave at 9:30.

M Good. Are there ²⁾_____ _____ other than picking apples?

W Yes. We'll have a chance to bake some apple cinnamon cookies. They also have a gift shop I want to visit. Could I borrow some money?

M Why not? Here's $50. Buy ³⁾_____ _____ _____. And can you get one for our family?

W Sure. I heard that the apple-shaped magnets are popular. I'll buy one.

M Thanks. Your mom will love it.

↘ 듣기 필수 표현
· be supposed to ~해야 한다
· other than ~ 외에

9

W Welcome to Falcon Crest National Park. For your safety, the following guidelines are in place. First of all, we recommend that you ¹⁾_____ _____ _____ _____. In the event of an accident, you would not have someone with you to call for help. We also ask that you only ²⁾_____ _____ _____ that have signs posted. Going off the trails may damage precious wildlife. There are water fountains, but there is no guarantee the water is clean. Therefore, we strongly recommend bringing drinking water with you. Lastly, because of recent dry weather, lighters and portable burners are prohibited. Those caught with ³⁾_____ _____ _____ will be removed from the park. Thank you for your cooperation, and I hope you all have a great visit.

↘ 듣기 필수 표현
· be in place 준비되다
· in the event of 만약 ~할 경우

10

W Okay, we've got the hotel and plane tickets for Rome. What else do we need to plan, Mike?

M What about a guided tour? It would be a good way to learn more about ¹⁾_____ _____ _____.

W Sure. Let's look up some tour options.

M Okay... well, this website lists a few. What do you think?

W I don't want to go on a bus tour. Let's do ²⁾_____ _____ _____!

M Fair enough. We can rule this one out.

W Let's keep it short, too. We need plenty of time to explore on our own.

M Alright. Anything ³⁾_____ _____ _____ would be too much.

W That leaves us with a couple of options. Is price a factor?

M I'm okay as long as we ⁴⁾_____ _____ _____ than $40 on it.

W I agree. And let's go with the one that includes a meal.

M I'll book it!

↘ 듣기 필수 표현
· look up 검색하다, 찾다
· Fair enough. 좋아.
· rule out 제외하다
· as long as ~하기만 한다면

11

W Carl, I'm headed down to the convenience store. Should I pick anything up for you?

M Yes, please. Do you mind ¹⁾_____ _____ _____ for me? Here's my card.

W Sure. Is there ²⁾_____ _____ _____ that you wanted?

↘ 듣기 필수 표현
· pick up ~을 사다

12

M Kate, do you need a ride to your doctor's appointment tomorrow afternoon?

W No. I'm okay, Dad. The hospital is ¹⁾_____ _____ _____, so I was thinking of walking there after soccer practice.

M Sounds good. Call me if you change your mind, though. I'll be ²⁾_____ _____ _____.

↘ 듣기 필수 표현
· change one's mind 생각을 바꾸다

13

W Hi. I'm looking for a gift for my father.

M We have some great leather jackets. I think you could find one that your dad would love.

W Yeah, I think this 1)_____ _____ _____. How much are they?

M They're priced at $160 to $200 each.

W Whoa! That's way 2)_____ _____ _____. Could you suggest something else?

M Well, what about something practical?

W You mean like some underwear or socks? That doesn't seem very exciting.

M Maybe not, but he might appreciate something like that. Wool socks really come in handy this time of year.

W Hmm... I don't think he needs socks, but something warm could be good. Can I see 3)_____ _____ _____?

M They're right over here. Most of them are $30 to $40.

W Perfect. Do you have a red and black one?

↘ 듣기 필수 표현
· come in handy 유용하다

14

M Hey, Sally. I'm going to a film festival tonight with some friends. Do you care to join us?

W What are they showing?

M Some 1)_____ _____ _____ from the 1980s.

W Oh, I read about that. That's at the Jacobson Theater, right?

M That's the one. I can give you a ride to it if you want.

W Thanks, but I don't think I can make it.

M I thought you loved scary movies.

W I do, but I stayed up too late studying for my history exam last night.

M Oh, you 2)_____ _____ _____ _____.

W Yeah, so I'm not sure I'd be able to stay awake the whole time.

M How about coming for only the first movie?

W When does it start?

M 8 p.m. There are three movies, 3)_____ _____ in between. You can just get a ticket for the first one.

↘ 듣기 필수 표현
· Do you care to ~? ~할래?
· make it (모임 등에) 가다
· stay up late 늦게까지 깨어있다

15

W Billy and Erica are best friends who love jazz music. They always go to jazz concerts together. So when either Billy or Erica buys tickets 1)_____ _____ _____, he or she takes it for granted that the other will go, too. This is why they always buy two tickets. Unfortunately, they 2)_____ _____ _____ for two different shows scheduled on Saturday at the same time. When Billy realizes the problem, it is already too late to get a refund for his tickets. However, he knows that the band Erica wants to see is playing again on Sunday. Therefore, Billy wants to suggest that Erica 3)_____ _____ _____ for ones on Sunday so that they can go together. In this situation, what would Billy most likely say to Erica?

↘ 듣기 필수 표현
· either A or B A나 B 중 하나
· take ~ for granted ~을 당연하게 여기다
· at the same time 동시에
· get a refund 환불받다

16~17

M Hi, class. We've been talking about the importance of a healthy diet lately. Today, I'll point out some of 1)_____ _____ _____ associated with having too much of any healthy food. First, what about tuna? It's wonderful in many ways, with lots of protein and fatty acids. But it also 2)_____ _____ _____ _____ mercury. So if you eat it every day, it can eventually damage your brain. Next, we have pineapples. Pineapples have a large amount of vitamin C, but they are slightly toxic when uncooked. If you eat too many, they'll make your mouth sore or give you a rash. Thirdly, avocados can 3)_____ _____ in large amounts. Their high fiber content is great for you, but it can cause diarrhea when avocados are overeaten. Last, we need to talk about broccoli. It helps keep your heart healthy. But when you eat too much, it can lower your energy level and even cause you 4)_____ _____ _____. I hope you'll take more care from now on when eating these foods.

↘ 듣기 필수 표현
· point out 지목하다
· associated with ~과 관련된
· from now on 앞으로

06회
제3교시

대학수학능력시험 문제지
영어듣기 모의고사

▲ 문제 음성
바로 듣기

▲ 고사장 버전
바로 듣기

정답 및 해설 p.32

1번부터 17번까지는 듣고 답하는 문제입니다. 1번부터 15번까지는 한 번만 들려주고, 16번부터 17번까지는 두 번 들려줍니다. 방송을 잘 듣고 답을 하시기 바랍니다.

1. 다음을 듣고, 남자가 하는 말의 목적으로 가장 적절한 것을 고르시오.

① 계주 경기의 참가자를 모집하려고
② 가정통신문 발송 지연을 사과하려고
③ 학교 체육대회 취소를 공지하려고
④ 천둥이 칠 때 조심해야 할 사항을 설명하려고
⑤ 가을철 학교 운동장 야간 개방을 홍보하려고

2. 대화를 듣고, 남자의 의견으로 가장 적절한 것을 고르시오.

① 숙면은 부상 회복을 돕는 가장 좋은 방법이다.
② 다친 부위는 재활 운동을 통해 꾸준히 움직여줘야 한다.
③ 건강에 좋은 음식을 먹으면 상처 회복 속도가 빨라진다.
④ 간단한 준비 운동으로 부상을 방지할 수 있다.
⑤ 함부로 약물을 오남용하면 안 된다.

3. 대화를 듣고, 두 사람의 관계를 가장 잘 나타낸 것을 고르시오.

① 카페 주인 — 아르바이트생
② 라디오 쇼 진행자 — 창업주
③ 쇼호스트 — 바리스타
④ 광고 감독 — 영화배우
⑤ 방송 작가 — 원두 판매자

4. 대화를 듣고, 그림에서 대화의 내용과 일치하지 않는 것을 고르시오.

5. 대화를 듣고, 여자가 할 일로 가장 적절한 것을 고르시오.

① 안경 수리 맡기기
② 반창고 갖다주기
③ 자리 바꿔주기
④ 병원 예약하기
⑤ 전동 킥보드 반납하기

6. 대화를 듣고, 여자가 지불할 금액을 고르시오. [3점]

① $17 ② $20 ③ $24 ④ $25 ⑤ $29

7. 대화를 듣고, 남자가 야구 경기를 보러 갈 수 없는 이유를 고르시오.

① 주말 아르바이트를 하러 가야 해서
② 추운 날씨를 견딜 자신이 없어서
③ 이사 준비를 해야 해서
④ 과제 발표 연습을 해야 해서
⑤ 동생을 대회장에 데려다줘야 해서

8. 대화를 듣고, *Elite Singer* 리얼리티 쇼에 관해 언급되지 않은 것을 고르시오.

① 첫 방영일 ② 담당 프로듀서 ③ 정규 방송 시간
④ 촬영 장소 ⑤ 특별 출연자

9. Natural History Museum의 특별 체험 프로그램에 관한 다음 내용을 듣고, 일치하지 않는 것을 고르시오.

① 11세에서 13세 사이의 어린이들을 대상으로 한다.
② 기초 발굴 기술에 대한 설명으로 시작할 것이다.
③ 하루에 30명의 어린이만 참가할 수 있다.
④ 신청 마감일은 4월 15일이다.
⑤ 자녀와 동행하는 성인에게는 참가비를 받지 않는다.

10. 다음 표를 보면서 대화를 듣고, 여자가 구입할 책가방을 고르시오.

School Backpacks

	Model	Capacity (liter)	Laptop Pocket	Price	Color
①	A	18	O	$55	red
②	B	18	O	$70	green
③	C	24	X	$95	black
④	D	24	O	$115	green
⑤	E	28	X	$130	blue

11. 대화를 듣고, 여자의 마지막 말에 대한 남자의 응답으로 가장 적절한 것을 고르시오.

① Sorry. I can't lend it to you right now.
② No problem. I'll put it back in the box.
③ It's a little heavy. Be careful carrying it.
④ Okay. I'll go down there now and get it.
⑤ Yes. It's right next to the Christmas tree.

12. 대화를 듣고, 남자의 마지막 말에 대한 여자의 응답으로 가장 적절한 것을 고르시오.

① Of course. But they are still out of stock at the moment.
② I'm nervous. I was supposed to get a refund by now.
③ I have. And it shows that they haven't shipped yet.
④ No. I ordered it from the online store.
⑤ My apology. I'll send them right now.

13. 대화를 듣고, 여자의 마지막 말에 대한 남자의 응답으로 가장 적절한 것을 고르시오. [3점]

Man: _____

① You have my word. I'll surely give it my all.
② Sure. I included information about wind power, too.
③ Right. We printed your interview in the politics section.
④ Okay. I'll make those corrections with your feedback.
⑤ No. The construction will be completed early.

14. 대화를 듣고, 남자의 마지막 말에 대한 여자의 응답으로 가장 적절한 것을 고르시오.

Woman: _____

① No worries. I've practiced speaking a lot.
② Okay. We will have a deep discussion on the topic.
③ Sure. I think that will help you evaluate your ideas.
④ You're right. I need to participate in discussions more.
⑤ Thank you. You helped me finish the assignment on time.

15. 다음 상황 설명을 듣고, Christine이 Rick에게 할 말로 가장 적절한 것을 고르시오. [3점]

Christine: _____

① Could you help me get my car fixed?
② I'm going to ask for a second opinion.
③ The engine is damaged, so please treat it gently.
④ I appreciate you suggesting this car to me.
⑤ Can I take you out to dinner to thank you?

[16~17] 다음을 듣고, 물음에 답하시오.

16. 여자가 하는 말의 주제로 가장 적절한 것은?

① the evolutionary history of animals
② adaptations that help animals breed
③ survival strategies of various parasites
④ how different animals aid other species
⑤ ways plants protect themselves against animals

17. 언급된 동물이 <u>아닌</u> 것은?

① rhino bird　　　　② crocodile bird
③ white-eye bird　　④ woolly bat
⑤ clownfish

> 이제 듣기 문제가 끝났습니다. 채점을 마친 후 다음 페이지에서 방송을 다시 들으며 딕테이션 연습을 하시기 바랍니다.
>
> * 채점 결과: 맞은 개수 _____개 / 17개　　　　정답 및 해설 p.32

06회 Dictation

Dictation 정답 p.32

06회 영어듣기 모의고사 Dictation 음성을 들으며 빈칸에 알맞은 단어를 채워 넣으시기 바랍니다.

1

M Good afternoon, students. This is Principal Simmons. I have an announcement regarding the school sports day. Unfortunately, tomorrow's forecast calls for a severe thunderstorm and hail. In these conditions, it would be dangerous to be outside on the school field. So in the interest of safety, tomorrow's 1)_____ _____ _____. I know this is disappointing. However, we do have another sports day scheduled this fall. You'll still get a 2)_____ _____ _____ _____ the relay race and jump rope competition this year. The school will send out messages informing your parents about this cancellation, but please 3)_____ _____ _____ _____ come. Enjoy your evening, and we'll see you back in school tomorrow.

↘ 듣기 필수 표현
· call for (날씨를) 예상하다
· in the interest of ~을 위하여
· send out ~을 보내다

2

W How are you feeling today, Mark?

M Much better, Abbey. I got some good rest for the first time since I broke my arm.

W That's good to hear!

M I'm really happy about it. I think the best way to 1)_____ _____ _____ is to get enough sleep.

W Is it better than taking medicine?

M That's important, too. But your body 2)_____ _____ _____ when you sleep.

W Is that right? Please tell me more.

M Your body produces a lot of extra hormones when you sleep. They are called human growth hormones, and they help 3)_____ _____ _____ faster.

W Wow. I didn't know that. Well, let me know if I can do anything to help. And make sure to eat healthy as well.

M Thanks. I will!

↘ 듣기 필수 표현
· for the first time 처음으로
· That's good to hear! 다행이다!

3

M Hello, Julia Michaels. Welcome to *The Morning Break*.

W Thanks for inviting me. I 1)_____ _____ _____ every morning.

M We're always happy to have a fan on the show! So Julia, I hear you're opening a new coffee shop.

W That's right. Fresh Beans Coffee is 2)_____ _____ _____ _____ right here in Murton.

M This will be on Main Street?

W That's correct. To celebrate, I've organized a grand-opening event there on the 23rd.

M I'm sure many of our listeners will be interested in attending. Isn't this 3)_____ _____ _____?

W Actually, this will be the 11th.

M Wow. When you founded Fresh Beans Coffee, did you imagine it would become a successful chain?

W I just wanted to make sure 4)_____ _____ _____ _____.

M Well, I think you've achieved that. Now, for a brief word from our sponsors. We'll be right back.

↘ 듣기 필수 표현
· be interested in ~할 의향이 있다
· make sure (that) 꼭 ~하다

4

W Honey, what's this framed photograph? Are you planning to hang it up?

M Yeah. That's my grandfather's farm about 20 years ago.

W So is that your grandfather wearing 1)_____ _____ _____?

M Exactly. And those are his two old dogs walking alongside him.

W Is that the farmhouse down at the 2)_____ _____ _____ with the triangle-shaped roof?

M Yeah. It looks totally different now.

W Oh, I didn't realize he used to 3)_____ _____. It looks like there's a group of them in that field next to the farmhouse.

M Yeah, he sold them 10 years ago.

W What about the tree on the right? Is that still there?

M It is. It's just 4)_____ _____ _____ these days.

W We should go visit your grandfather soon.

M We should. I miss him.

↘ 듣기 필수 표현
· hang up (그림 등을) 걸다
· used to (과거에) ~했다

5

W What happened, Eric? Your face is scratched.

M I fell off my electric scooter 1)_____ _____ _____ _____ _____.

W Maybe you should go to the doctor.

M No need. I feel more embarrassed than anything else. A bunch of people saw me fall.

W I think you'd better put a bandage on your face, though.

M I'm okay. It's just a few scratches.

W Then, how about applying some medicine so that you don't get an infection?

M It'll be fine. *[Pause]* But... do you think 2)_____ _____ _____ _____? I dropped them in the crash.

W Yeah. I think you'll need to bring them to the shop to get them fixed.

M Hmm... I better not wear them. Do you mind 3)_____ _____ _____ me so I can see the board better?

W Of course. Let me know if you need anything else.

M I will.

↘ 듣기 필수 표현
· more than anything else 무엇보다도
· a bunch of 많은

6

M Good evening. Welcome to Celebration Cinema.

W Hi. We'd like three tickets to the animated film, *Space Cadets*. Two for my husband and I, and one for our son.

M Sure. Adult tickets are $8. By the way, how old is your son?

W Oh, he's only six.

M Well, you're in luck. Tickets for children under age seven are 1)_____ _____.

W I wasn't expecting that. It saves us a few dollars.

M Yes, it certainly does. And did you park your car in the mall parking garage? We can give you 2)_____ _____ _____.

W We did.

M It's only $5 if you pay here.

W Okay, let's do that.

M Great. I'll ring you up now.

W Thanks. My son has been looking forward to seeing this movie for weeks.

M That's 3)_____ _____ _____. Here are your tickets. You'll be in Theater 6.

↘ 듣기 필수 표현
· by the way 그런데
· You're in luck. 운이 좋으시네요.
· ring up 계산하다
· look forward to ~을 기대하다

7

W Hey, Justin. Are you still interested in going to the baseball game on Saturday?

M Oh! It's the first 1)_____ _____ _____ _____ on Saturday. I forgot about that!

W So... you can't make it?

M I'm afraid not.

W That's too bad. You have your part-time job on the weekends, right?

M Actually, that was 2)_____ _____ _____ _____. The job ended in February.

W Then, are you worried about the weather? I haven't checked the forecast yet.

M No. It's supposed to be warm and sunny on Saturday.

W Then, what's the problem?

M I'll be out of town. I 3)_____ _____ _____ my brother to St. Louis. He's in a speech contest.

W That makes sense. Well, let's go to a game soon, then.

M For sure.

↘ 듣기 필수 표현
· I'm afraid not. 안 될 것 같아.
· That's too bad. 유감이야.

8

W Hey, Billy. What are you watching?

M It's a reality show about young musicians. It's called *Elite Singer*.

W Oh, I wanted to see that. I didn't realize it had started.

M Yeah. The ¹⁾_____ _____ _____ last week, on the 19th. They're going to come out every Tuesday at 7 p.m.

W I see. Doesn't the whole show take place in Los Angeles?

M Yeah. All of the participants ²⁾_____ _____ _____ _____ in a house together.

W I didn't know that. *[Pause]* Oh, is that Tina Sanders?

M Yeah! She is a special guest star. She's ³⁾_____ _____ _____.

W Cool! I love her singing.

M Me too. Why don't you sit down and watch it with me?

W Okay. I think I will.

↘ 듣기 필수 표현
· come out 나오다

9

M Hello, visitors. I'd like to remind you that the Natural History Museum is holding a special hands-on program. It's for children aged 11 to 13 who are interested in ¹⁾_____ _____ _____ for a day. The four-hour program will be held for three days only. It ²⁾_____ _____ _____ a presentation on basic digging techniques. The group will then participate in a simulation of an archeological dig. If you're interested, please apply soon. Each day, the group of participants will be ³⁾_____ _____ _____ _____ _____, so there will only be 30 in all. The last day for signing up is April 15th, and the fee is $10 per student. Adults who ⁴⁾_____ _____ _____ their children will not be charged. Thank you.

↘ 듣기 필수 표현
· participate in ~에 참여하다

10

M Carrie, you need a backpack for the new school year, right?

W I do, Dad.

M Well, I found a website with a few good options. What do you think of this one?

W Hmm... I like the style, but it's ¹⁾_____ _____ _____!

M Right, a capacity of 25 liters should be plenty.

W Okay, so there are four to look at.

M Do you usually bring your laptop to school? If so, you should get one ²⁾_____ _____ _____ _____ for it.

W Good point. I'll definitely need one of those.

M Okay, but let's keep the price down. Some of these are too expensive.

W How much can we spend?

M Let's ³⁾_____ _____ _____ $100. *[Pause]* What about the color?

W I really like this green one.

M Why don't I order it?

W Okay! Thanks, Dad.

↘ 듣기 필수 표현
· Good point. 좋은 지적이에요.
· keep ~ down ~을 낮추다

11

W Jason, there you are! Can you lend me a hand ¹⁾_____ _____ _____?

M Sure, Mom. What do you need me to help you with?

W There's a box down in the basement with Christmas decorations in it. Please ²⁾_____ _____ _____ _____ to the living room.

↘ 듣기 필수 표현
· lend ~ a hand ~를 도와주다

12

[Phone rings.]

M BBM Electronics customer service, this is Liam speaking. How may I help you?

W Hi. ¹⁾_____ _____ _____ the headphones I ordered recently. I think they were supposed to arrive yesterday.

M Okay. Have you checked ²⁾_____ _____ _____ on our website?

↘ 듣기 필수 표현
· be supposed to ~하기로 되어 있다

13

W Mr. Robinson, can you step into my office?

M Sure, Ms. Porter. I hope you have positive feedback
1) _____ _____ _____ _____ .

W I think you did a fine job.

M Thanks. I worked hard on that story about the construction of wind farms.

W I can tell. That's why I'd like to give you another
2) _____ _____ .

M What's that?

W I'd like you to write an article on the government's upcoming clean energy program.

M They're 3)_____ _____ _____ a lot of money in solar energy, right?

W That's what I hear, but I want you to do some hard reporting and get all the details.

M Okay, I'll call my contacts in the energy department and do some interviews.

W I think this will be a front-page story, so make it your
4) _____ _____ .

↘ 듣기 필수 표현
· I can tell. 그래 보여요.

14

W I felt embarrassed when Mr. Wallace called on me last class. I hope he doesn't do that again today.

M He probably will. 1)_____ _____ _____ is required.

W I know, but the discussions seem unnecessary and stressful.

M I don't agree. Having a discussion is a great way to learn.

W Really? I'm not an expert. Why are my thoughts so important?

M By putting our thoughts into words, we can 2)_____
_____ _____ _____ .

W And what if those ideas are totally wrong?

M That can be good! Another student has to explain why they're wrong.

W That sounds time consuming.

M It can be. But if you can make a good argument, you'll
3) _____ _____ _____ on a deeper level.

W I see what you mean, but I'm not very good at that.

M Then you should practice by speaking more often during class!

↘ 듣기 필수 표현
· put ~ into words ~을 말로 나타내다
· be good at ~을 잘 하다

15

M Christine is planning to buy a used car. She recently found one she was interested in online. But she
1)_____ _____ _____ whether it was a good buy. So she called her friend Rick who knows a lot about cars. He advised her not to buy the car. Even though the 2)_____ _____ _____ for a low price, he thought Christine would have to spend a lot of money to repair it. He recommended that she look for
3)_____ _____ _____ . Thanks to his advice, Christine found a good car. Therefore, she wants to tell Rick that she will 4)_____ _____ to a great dinner to return the favor. In this situation, what would Christine most likely say to Rick?

↘ 듣기 필수 표현
· thanks to ~ 덕분에
· return favor 호의에 보답하다

16~17

W Good afternoon, everyone. Last week, we discussed parasites that harm the animals they are attached to. This week, we'll discuss ways in which 1)_____
_____ _____ with one another. First off, let's take the rhino bird. It sits on the back of large mammals and eats the 2)_____ _____ that collect in their fur. This helps to keep the large animal clean. Another example is the white-eye bird. It lives on the nectar of flowers. It helps the plants to reproduce 3)_____
_____ _____ . Third, we have the woolly bat. These winged animals use an insect-eating plant as their nest. At the same time, their droppings provide the nitrogen that the plant needs. Finally, let's consider the clownfish. It is provided shelter by sea anemones that are poisonous to other fish. While there, the clownfish's bright colors 4)_____ _____ to the anemone. So the clownfish gets a place to stay while the anemone gets some food. Now, let's take a moment to watch a brief video describing how this process works.

↘ 듣기 필수 표현
· with one another 서로서로
· live on ~을 먹고 살다

대학수학능력시험 문제지
영어듣기 모의고사

▲ 문제 음성
바로 듣기
▲ 고사장 버전
바로 듣기

정답 및 해설 p.38

1번부터 17번까지는 듣고 답하는 문제입니다. 1번부터 15번까지는 한 번만 들려주고, 16번부터 17번까지는 두 번 들려줍니다. 방송을 잘 듣고 답을 하시기 바랍니다.

1. 다음을 듣고, 남자가 하는 말의 목적으로 가장 적절한 것을 고르시오.

① 촬영장 내 보안 규칙을 안내하려고
② 방송 촬영 일정 지연을 공지하려고
③ 새로운 예능 프로그램을 홍보하려고
④ 공개 방송 참여 신청 방법을 설명하려고
⑤ 프로그램 방청 소감 작성을 부탁하려고

2. 대화를 듣고, 남자의 의견으로 가장 적절한 것을 고르시오.

① 긍정적인 마음가짐이 승패를 좌우한다.
② 공동의 목표를 세우면 팀워크를 강화하는 데 도움이 된다.
③ 지나간 과거를 곱씹다 보면 능력을 발전시키기 어렵다.
④ 접전 끝에 지는 것이 큰 점수 차로 지는 것보다 더 괴롭다.
⑤ 경기에서 이기는 것보다 기량 향상에 목표를 두어야 한다.

3. 대화를 듣고, 두 사람의 관계를 가장 잘 나타낸 것을 고르시오.

① 오토바이 수리공 — 배달 기사
② 부품업체 공장장 — 안전감독관
③ 자동차 판매원 — 택시 운전기사
④ 피자 가게 직원 — 유통업자
⑤ 기계 엔지니어 — 카레이서

4. 대화를 듣고, 그림에서 대화의 내용과 일치하지 않는 것을 고르시오.

5. 대화를 듣고, 여자가 할 일로 가장 적절한 것을 고르시오.

① 창작시 쓰기
② 러시아 시 번역하기
③ 과제 주제 바꾸기
④ 세 편의 시 분석하기
⑤ 작품 심층 조사하기

6. 대화를 듣고, 남자가 지불할 금액을 고르시오. [3점]

① $44   ② $46   ③ $51   ④ $53   ⑤ $56

7. 대화를 듣고, 여자가 학교 뮤지컬을 관람하러 갈 수 없는 이유를 고르시오.

① 아직 몸 상태가 좋지 않아서
② 뮤지컬을 좋아하는 편이 아니라서
③ 배우들의 실력이 마음에 들지 않아서
④ 아버지와 여행을 가기로 해서
⑤ 입양할 새를 데려올 준비를 해야 해서

8. 대화를 듣고, National Science Fair에 관해 언급되지 않은 것을 고르시오.

① 프로젝트 주제   ② 개최 장소   ③ 우승 상금
④ 참가자 수   ⑤ 평가 방식

9. Merkel Park Tree-Planting Event에 관한 다음 내용을 듣고, 일치하지 않는 것을 고르시오.

① Greenwood 주민 센터에서 주최한다.
② 350여 그루의 나무를 심을 예정이다.
③ 많은 지역 주민들이 행사에 자원해주었다.
④ 행사에 쓸 묘목은 대량 구매했다.
⑤ 간식과 물이 참석자들에게 제공될 것이다.

10. 다음 표를 보면서 대화를 듣고, 두 사람이 예약할 호텔 객실을 고르시오.

Hotel Room Options

	Room	Price	Maximum Occupancy	Pet-Friendly Room	View
①	A	$220	3	O	Mountain
②	B	$175	4	X	Ocean
③	C	$145	3	X	City
④	D	$135	2	O	Mountain
⑤	E	$125	2	O	City

11. 대화를 듣고, 여자의 마지막 말에 대한 남자의 응답으로 가장 적절한 것을 고르시오.

① Mom wants you to clean your bedroom right now.
② Sorry for interrupting, and I'll turn off my phone.
③ Oh, I didn't realize that it was out of power.
④ Can I ask what book you're reading?
⑤ I guess I must have slept too late.

12. 대화를 듣고, 남자의 마지막 말에 대한 여자의 응답으로 가장 적절한 것을 고르시오.

① My flight leaves at 2:15 p.m.
② Can you point me to the elevator?
③ Well, I can't seem to find my ticket.
④ I'm looking for information about the airport.
⑤ Be careful, the floor is slippery at the moment.

13. 대화를 듣고, 여자의 마지막 말에 대한 남자의 응답으로 가장 적절한 것을 고르시오.

Man: _____

① Thanks a lot. I don't like taking out the trash.
② I've been busy, too. That's not a good excuse.
③ Don't worry. I'll take care of it in the morning.
④ I can't. I'm expecting to get a phone call at that time.
⑤ Don't mention it. Mom will be happy that you remembered.

14. 대화를 듣고, 남자의 마지막 말에 대한 여자의 응답으로 가장 적절한 것을 고르시오. [3점]

Woman: _____

① I see. It looks like we put the shirts in the wrong box.
② Oh, really? I thought you said they were sold out.
③ That's fine. I just want them wrapped properly.
④ No, thanks. I'd like to ask for a refund.
⑤ Good. I'll take the large size, please.

15. 다음 상황 설명을 듣고, Jackie가 Scott에게 할 말로 가장 적절한 것을 고르시오. [3점]

Jackie: _____

① Wait! I need to get off right now!
② Wake up! You need to get off the bus.
③ Don't worry. Why don't we just walk home from here?
④ Okay. I guess you didn't sleep well last night.
⑤ Pardon me. Don't we go to the same school?

[16~17] 다음을 듣고, 물음에 답하시오.

16. 여자가 하는 말의 주제로 가장 적절한 것은?

① what different colors stand for
② effects of colors on people's emotions
③ how colored clothing was developed
④ importance of colors to cultural ceremonies
⑤ why some colors are more popular than others

17. 언급된 색깔이 <u>아닌</u> 것은?

① purple　　② white　　③ black
④ brown　　⑤ red

> 이제 듣기 문제가 끝났습니다. 채점을 마친 후 다음 페이지에서 방송을 다시 들으며 딕테이션 연습을 하시기 바랍니다.
>
> * 채점 결과: 맞은 개수 _____ 개 / 17개　　　　정답 및 해설 p.38

07회 영어듣기 모의고사 Dictation 음성을 들으며 빈칸에 알맞은 단어를 채워 넣으시기 바랍니다.

1

M Attention, visitors. Thanks for coming to today's recording of *The Angela Ross Comedy Hour*. I'm Jeff Bennett, chief security manager at this studio. Before it begins, I want to remind you that certain items 1)_____ _____ _____ in the television studio. These include any 2)_____ _____ _____ and outside beverages. Also, we will ask that you keep your smartphones turned off during your time in the studio. And don't forget that children under the age of 16 must be accompanied by a parent or guardian at all times. Any visitors caught breaking these rules will be asked to 3)_____ _____ _____. Does anyone have any questions?

↘ 듣기 필수 표현
· turn off (전원을) 끄다
· be accompanied by ~을 동반하다
· break a rule 규칙을 어기다

2

M Amy, are you doing okay?

W I'm fine, Dad. But I am still disappointed about my team losing the championship soccer match on Saturday.

M You don't need to be. You played well.

W Thanks. But it was 1)_____ _____ _____ _____. I thought we were going to win.

M I understand. But I don't think feeling bad about the past will help you win.

W What do you mean?

M You 2)_____ _____ _____ _____. So when you think that way, you feel powerless. It's a very negative mindset.

W But I care about my team. Should I feel nothing?

M No! I just mean that it's hard to 3)_____ _____ _____ _____ if you keep thinking about the past.

W I see.

M Maybe it would help to set some new goals for yourself.

W I'll think about it.

↘ 듣기 필수 표현
· feel bad about ~을 후회하다
· set a goal 목표를 세우다

3

[Phone rings.]

M You've reached Bruno's Auto. This is Bruno speaking.

W Hi. It's Rachel Miller. I brought in a motorbike for repairs this morning.

M Oh, you 1)_____ _____ _____ with your brakes, correct?

W That's right. I was wondering how much the repairs would cost.

M I'd estimate they 2)_____ _____ about $100.

W That's more than I expected.

M That includes 3)_____ _____ _____. I found your tire was flat while inspecting your brakes.

W I see. And how long will that take? I use the bike to deliver pizzas, so I'd like to have it back as soon as possible.

M Not to worry. I ordered a new part, and it should be here by tomorrow.

W So will it 4)_____ _____ _____ Thursday?

M It should be. I will call you if there's any delay.

W Okay. I really appreciate that.

↘ 듣기 필수 표현
· as soon as possible 가능한 한 빨리

4

M Thanks for letting me sleep here in your home office, Aunt Roberts.

W Certainly! The weather is terrible. It's not safe to go out in this storm.

M It must be nice to do remote work here. It's lovely. I really like that poster 1)_____ _____ _____ on it.

W Thanks.

M Should I sleep on the couch 2)_____ _____ _____?

W It's a bit short for you. I'll bring in an air mattress.

M Is it okay if I place it here on the striped rug?

W Of course. And if you need 3)_____ _____ _____, you can move that computer chair by my desk out into the hall.

M Okay.

W Just be careful that you don't bump into the round table by the door.

M Got it. The vase on top of it [4)]_____ _____.

W I'll be right back with that air mattress.

M Thanks again!

↘ 듣기 필수 표현
· remote work 원격근무
· bump into ~에 부딪치다

5

W Hello, Mr. Brown. Can I ask a question about the essay assignment?

M Sure. You mean the poetry analysis essay?

W Right. You mentioned that we should [1)]_____ _____ _____ by a single poet.

M Yes, that's correct.

W Well, the poet is Russian, and only one of her poems has been [2)]_____ _____ _____. So I couldn't find three poems to use.

M I see. Why did you pick this poet?

W Her poem inspired me to write my own poetry.

M Then, you could do [3)]_____ _____ _____ of that single poem using the critical approach I taught in class.

W I didn't think you'd accept an essay on only one poem.

M Under the circumstances, it would be fine.

W Great!

M But remember your essay will be the same length. I expect you to [4)]_____ _____ _____ more thoroughly so you have a deep enough analysis.

W Okay, I will.

↘ 듣기 필수 표현
· under the circumstances 사정이 그러니

6

W Welcome to Keith's Stationery. May I help you?

M Hi. I'm looking for a small-sized photo album.

W Sure. Those are right over here.

M How much is this photo album [1)]_____ _____ _____ _____?

W That's $20. We also have that in a blue leather version for $30.

M I'll take the blue one. Oh... and I should mention that I have a 10% discount coupon for this item.

W Great. [2)]_____ _____ _____ _____ when you check out. Do you need some paper?

M Yes. I'd like two packs of thick white paper.

W Those are $12 each.

M Sure, that's fine.

W Anything else, sir?

M I'll also take a pack of those silver stickers. It's $2, right?

W It is. Okay, so all I need is the coupon for that album, and I'll [3)]_____ _____ _____ _____.

M Here you go.

↘ 듣기 필수 표현
· check out 계산하다

7

[Cell phone rings.]

W Hey, Jonathan.

M Hi, Mary. How are you feeling?

W I'm [1)]_____ _____. I'll be back at school tomorrow.

M That's great. Well, I was calling to see if you could still go to the school musical on Saturday.

W I don't think I can make it.

M You must still be feeling a little under the weather, right?

W No. I'm fine.

M Ah, well, is it because you don't like musicals? Some people don't like that [2)]_____ _____ _____.

W No. I was excited to see it, and the actors in it are really talented. Actually, I promised my dad I would [3)]_____ _____ _____ _____ with him.

M Oh, I see.

W We're going birdwatching together. Sorry I forgot to [4)]_____ _____ _____.

M It's okay.

W Well, let's do something fun together soon.

↘ 듣기 필수 표현
· make it (모임 등에) 가다
· under the weather 몸이 좀 안 좋은

8

W Nick, are you still working on that 1)_____ _____? I thought you were finished.

M Well, I'm going to be participating in the National Science Fair.

W Whoa, really?

M Yeah. My project won first prize, so I 2)_____ _____ _____ the nationwide competition in Pinesburg City.

W That's so cool. Do you think you can win 3)_____ _____ _____, too?

M I hope so. The winner gets a cash prize. It's $5,000 this year.

W Wow. But I bet it's not easy. There must be a lot of people competing.

M Right. A 4)_____ _____ _____ _____ are going to be presenting their projects.

W How is it evaluated?

M It's decided by the science fair judges. They walk around the fair filling out score sheets and asking questions.

W That sounds a little stressful. But I bet you'll do really well!

M Thanks so much.

↘ 듣기 필수 표현
· win first prize 1등을 하다
· fill out 작성하다

9

W Welcome to the Merkel Park Tree-Planting Event. I'm Michelle Bach from the Greenwood Community Center. My organization put together today's event. Over the course of the afternoon, we're planning to plant around 350 trees 1)_____ _____ _____ _____ into a more beautiful and eco-friendly space. This is only possible because so many members of our local community have volunteered to do this hard work. Give yourself 2)_____ _____ _____ _____.
[Pause] I also want to thank Wilson Garden Store for 3)_____ _____ _____ _____ we'll be using today. And I should remind you of one more thing. As you're working today, remember to 4)_____ _____ _____. Water and snacks will be provided when you need them. Okay? Let's get started!

↘ 듣기 필수 표현
· put together 종합하여 만들다
· over the course of ~ 동안
· Let's get started! 시작합시다!

10

W Honey, we need to 1)_____ _____ _____ _____ in San Diego. The prices are already going up.

M I found one, but I wanted to check with you about which room to reserve. I'll send you a link.

W Hmm... all of these look good.

M I thought so! How much can we spend?

W Let's 2)_____ _____ _____ $200.

M Sounds good. And I don't think our room needs to be too big.

W True. It's just the two of us, so we don't need a room that can accommodate four.

M Also, don't forget we are traveling with our dog, which 3)_____ _____ _____ a little.

W Right, we need a room where pets are allowed. And we can choose what kind of view the room has.

M Oh, I'd 4)_____ _____ _____ _____.

W Sure. That's probably nicer.

M Okay, we're all set.

↘ 듣기 필수 표현
· go up (가격 등이) 오르다
· be all set 준비가 다 되어 있다

11

[Door knocks.]

W Hello, Jeremy? Are you in the bedroom?

M Yes, Liz. I was just reading. Is 1)_____ _____ _____?

W Mom was just trying to call you, but she 2)_____ _____ _____. Is your phone turned off?

12

M How may I help you?

W Is this where I can 1)_____ _____ _____ the express train to the airport?

M No, ma'am. This is just 2)_____ _____ _____. You need to go up to the top floor for that.

13

M Mom said we haven't been keeping up with our chores lately, Elena.

W I've been really busy lately, but I try my best!

M You forgot 1)_____ _____ _____ last night. I had to do them this morning.

W Are you sure about that? Wasn't it your turn last night?

M Go check the schedule on the fridge.

W Oh, you're right. I thought yesterday was Tuesday.

M How did that happen?

W I don't know... I was all mixed up.

M Okay. My point is that you're 2)_____ _____ _____ for someone else when you don't do your chores.

W You're right. But I have trouble keeping track of things. Do you have any ideas?

M I suggest that you 3)_____ _____ _____ _____ on your phone before each task.

W That's a good idea. Thank you for the tip!

↘ 듣기 필수 표현
· keep up with ~을 제때 하다
· try one's best 최선을 다하다
· be mixed up 헷갈리다, 혼란해지다
· keep track of ~을 기억하다

14

W Excuse me. I bought these shirts yesterday.

M Is there 1)_____ _____ with them?

W They were supposed to be a gift for my nephew, and I asked the clerk to wrap them. But when he opened the box, we discovered they were the wrong size.

M Are you sure you didn't buy 2)_____ _____ _____ by mistake?

W Yes, I double-checked before giving them to the clerk.

M Do you have the receipt?

W Here. It says "S" for small, but these are large.

M You're right. Well, it looks like we gift-wrapped the wrong package.

W Can I just exchange these for shirts in the correct size?

M One moment. I need to 3)_____ _____ _____.
[Typing sound] I'm afraid we're all sold out of small shirts in this style.

W That's very disappointing.

M I'm sorry, ma'am. But we do have other similar styles available.

↘ 듣기 필수 표현
· by mistake 실수로
· sold out 다 팔린

15

M Jackie and Scott live in the same area. They are in different grades at school, so they don't know each other very well. However, Jackie recognizes Scott because they 1)_____ _____ _____ _____ every day. She even knows that Scott gets off the bus at the stop right before hers. One afternoon 2)_____ _____ _____ _____ from school, Jackie notices that Scott has fallen asleep in his seat. Because she is about to get off the bus, she realizes that Scott has probably 3)_____ _____ _____. So Jackie wants to wake him up and tell him that he should exit the bus right away. In this situation, what would Jackie most likely say to Scott?

↘ 듣기 필수 표현
· get off 내리다
· fall asleep 잠이 들다
· be about to 막 ~하려는 참이다
· wake ~ up ~를 깨우다

16~17

W Hello, students. Although we usually think of colors as merely decorative, many have meanings tied to them. So today, we're going to discuss the symbolic meanings of 1)_____ _____ _____ _____ around the world. First, purple has been connected with wealth and power for centuries. This is because purple dye was 2)_____ _____ _____ in the past. Therefore, the dye was very expensive and was used for the clothes worn by royalty in places like ancient Rome. Next, white has different meanings depending on what part of the world you're in. In Western cultures, white is associated with 3)_____ _____ _____ _____ since it is seen as pure. However, it is tied to funerals and death in many Eastern cultures. Thirdly, brown is often connected with the earth. It symbolizes safety and reliability as the earth supports living things. Lastly, there is red. This color stands for 4)_____ _____ _____ in many cultures. But it's also used as a warning color since it catches attention easily. Now, let's watch a short related video.

↘ 듣기 필수 표현
· tied to ~과 관련된
· be connected with ~에 연관되다
· depending on ~에 따라
· be associated with ~과 관련지어지다
· stand for ~을 나타내다
· catch attention 주의를 끌다

08회

제3교시

대학수학능력시험 문제지
영어듣기 모의고사

▲ 문제 음성
바로 듣기

▲ 고사장 버전
바로 듣기

정답 및 해설 p.44

1번부터 17번까지는 듣고 답하는 문제입니다. 1번부터 15번까지는 한 번만 들려주고, 16번부터 17번까지는 두 번 들려줍니다. 방송을 잘 듣고 답을 하시기 바랍니다.

1. 다음을 듣고, 남자가 하는 말의 목적으로 가장 적절한 것을 고르시오.

① 수압이 약했던 이유를 설명하려고
② 배수관 교체 비용을 안내하려고
③ 누수 문제 해결에 대해 감사를 표하려고
④ 긴급 단수 조치를 공지하려고
⑤ 물을 아껴서 사용할 것을 당부하려고

2. 대화를 듣고, 여자의 의견으로 가장 적절한 것을 고르시오.

① 매일 스트레칭을 하면 건강에 좋다.
② 유연성이 부족하면 부상을 입기 쉽다.
③ 운동을 배울 때는 강사의 지도가 필요하다.
④ 운동 후에는 근육 회복 시간을 가져야 한다.
⑤ 고혈압 예방에는 아침 조깅이 가장 효과적이다.

3. 대화를 듣고, 두 사람의 관계를 가장 잘 나타낸 것을 고르시오.

① 도서관장 — 시인
② 서점 주인 — 인터넷 신문 기자
③ 홍보 전문가 — 경제지 편집장
④ 중고 매장 대표 — 시상식 진행자
⑤ 출판사 직원 — 국어 교사

4. 대화를 듣고, 그림에서 대화의 내용과 일치하지 <u>않는</u> 것을 고르시오.

5. 대화를 듣고, 남자가 할 일로 가장 적절한 것을 고르시오.

① 보고서 작성 돕기
② 먹을거리 사 오기
③ 도서관 방문하기
④ 잔돈 갖다주기
⑤ 사회학 과제 제출하기

6. 대화를 듣고, 남자가 지불할 금액을 고르시오. [3점]

① $110 ② $160 ③ $190 ④ $240 ⑤ $270

7. 대화를 듣고, 남자가 동아리를 탈퇴하려는 이유를 고르시오.

① 동물 보호소에서 봉사활동을 하기로 해서
② 로봇에 대한 흥미를 잃어서
③ 학교 밴드부 가입을 하고 싶어서
④ 입시 공부를 위한 시간이 더 필요해서
⑤ 동아리에서 너무 많은 활동을 요구해서

8. 대화를 듣고, International Food Festival에 관해 언급되지 <u>않은</u> 것을 고르시오.

① 행사 기간   ② 행사 장소   ③ 판매 음식
④ 입장료   ⑤ 공연 종류

9. Relay for Life에 관한 다음 내용을 듣고, 일치하지 <u>않는</u> 것을 고르시오.

① 이재민들을 돕기 위해 열릴 것이다.
② 9월 7일 오전 9시에 시작될 예정이다.
③ 10km 달리기와 5km 걷기 경주로 진행된다.
④ 5km 걷기 경주에는 연령 제한이 없다.
⑤ 기업에서 참가자 1명당 100달러씩 기부할 것이다.

10. 다음 표를 보면서 대화를 듣고, 여자가 구입할 게임용 마우스를 고르시오.

Gaming Mouse Options

	Model	Color	Wireless	Number of Side Buttons	Price
①	A	Red	O	4	$75
②	B	Black	X	2	$90
③	C	White	O	2	$55
④	D	Red	X	4	$60
⑤	E	White	O	2	$85

11. 대화를 듣고, 여자의 마지막 말에 대한 남자의 응답으로 가장 적절한 것을 고르시오.

① Okay. Then, we should probably leave early.
② Not really. We usually practice in the afternoon.
③ Thanks. You're a pretty good swimmer yourself.
④ No. You can actually get up around the same time.
⑤ Seriously. I won't be able to stay up late like I usually do.

12. 대화를 듣고, 남자의 마지막 말에 대한 여자의 응답으로 가장 적절한 것을 고르시오.

① Right. My goal is to pass the exam this year.
② Sure. But it's hard to find a parking space there.
③ That's right. It'll take us two hours to drive there.
④ I don't know. Traffic is very heavy this afternoon.
⑤ I'd love to. Why don't I pick you up in 10 minutes?

13. 대화를 듣고, 남자의 마지막 말에 대한 여자의 응답으로 가장 적절한 것을 고르시오. [3점]

Woman: _____

① Really? You could use your phone to take pictures.
② Are you sure? I thought you wanted to stay home.
③ No worries. I will wait here in the meantime.
④ It's okay. We don't have to get there early.
⑤ Good idea. I'll bring my camera as well.

14. 대화를 듣고, 여자의 마지막 말에 대한 남자의 응답으로 가장 적절한 것을 고르시오.

Man: _____

① That sounds good. How much does the package cost?
② Of course. Your booking confirmation number is 2827.
③ Are you sure? I still haven't received the itinerary.
④ Thanks again. Your directions were very helpful.
⑤ That's fine. Or you can contact me by e-mail.

15. 다음 상황 설명을 듣고, Jean이 Martin에게 할 말로 가장 적절한 것을 고르시오. [3점]

Jean: _____

① How about asking our teacher to let us work together today?
② Normally, chemistry problems are not as hard as they look.
③ Do you mind repeating the teacher's instructions for me?
④ If you're not feeling well, you can always go to the nurse's office.
⑤ Do you think we should ask him to do the experiment with us?

[16~17] 다음을 듣고, 물음에 답하시오.

16. 남자가 하는 말의 주제로 가장 적절한 것은?

① unique ways that people serve food
② how various food-related customs began
③ reasons that dining etiquette is changing
④ differences in table manners across cultures
⑤ reasons to behave politely when traveling abroad

17. 언급된 나라가 아닌 것은?

① China   ② India   ③ Chile
④ Mexico   ⑤ Spain

이제 듣기 문제가 끝났습니다. 채점을 마친 후 다음 페이지에서 방송을 다시 들으며 딕테이션 연습을 하시기 바랍니다.

* 채점 결과: 맞은 개수 _____ 개 / 17개   정답 및 해설 p.44

Dictation 정답 p.44

08회 영어듣기 모의고사 Dictation 음성을 들으며 빈칸에 알맞은 단어를 채워 넣으시기 바랍니다.

1

M Hello, residents! This is an announcement from the Riverside Hill Apartment Committee. We have discovered a damaged pipe in the basement, which needs to 1)_____ _____ _____. So please be aware that the water will be turned off from 10 a.m. to 1 p.m. today. We are sorry that we didn't announce this earlier. However, the leak will 2)_____ _____ _____ throughout the complex if we don't replace the pipe right away. Anyone who will need water during those hours should fill up their sink or bathtub beforehand. If the work takes 3)_____ _____ _____ _____ to finish, the water will be turned back on earlier. Thank you in advance for your cooperation.

↘ 듣기 필수 표현
· fill up ~을 채우다
· in advance 미리

2

M Honey, how was yoga class?

W Great, but I might need to buy my own mat.

M Don't they have mats you can use at the studio?

W Well, I want to practice at home. Stretching is 1)_____ _____ _____ _____ if you do it every day.

M Oh, did your instructor recommend that?

W Right. She said the benefits would increase if I stretched on my own for a few minutes daily.

M Is that so?

W Yeah, and it's 2)_____ _____ to build up your flexibility slowly. It reduces the chance of injury.

M That makes sense.

W She also mentioned that it helped increase blood flow, so my muscles will recover from workouts faster.

M Then, why don't you order a yoga mat online so you can 3)_____ _____ _____ _____ ?

W Yeah. I think I'll do that now.

↘ 듣기 필수 표현
· on one's own 자기 스스로
· build up 강화하다

3

M Good evening, Lisa. Are you looking for a new book of poetry to read?

W Not today, Andy. Actually, I wanted to speak with you.

M What did you want to talk about?

W 1)_____ _____ _____ hands out an annual award to the best local businesses. Our readers selected your shop as their favorite.

M What's the award?

W It's the Business of the Year Award. And I'm not surprised you won! Your shop has always been the best place to find 2)_____ _____ _____ _____.

M Thanks for saying that. So are you going to write an article about the store?

W Exactly. We'd like to interview you about how you 3)_____ _____ _____ and take some pictures.

M Would this be posted on your site's front page?

W That's right! It would be 4)_____ _____ _____ our readers would see.

M That's exciting! I'd be happy to give an interview. Can you come by the shop tomorrow around 9 a.m.?

W Sure. I'll see you then!

↘ 듣기 필수 표현
· hand out ~을 나눠주다
· be happy to 기꺼이 ~하다
· give an interview 인터뷰를 하다
· come by 잠깐 들르다

4

W How is the redecoration work in the hotel lounge going, Mr. Mendes?

M I think we're almost finished, Ms. Thompson. Here, I can show you. *[Pause]* I just installed the two-tone curtain you requested.

W They make the room look 1)_____ _____ _____ _____. The chandelier is gorgeous, too.

M Thanks! I think your guests will really appreciate these armchairs.

W Those do 2)_____ _____ _____ . But will they be able to eat and drink here?

M We can move the vase with the flowers 3)_____ _____ _____ _____ to make more room.

W Yes, let's do that.

M I will. What do you think of 4)_____ _____ _____ there in the corner?

W That's perfect. We're planning to have jazz music performances here.

M Would you like to see what we've done with the spa as well?

W Certainly. Let's go.

↘ 듣기 필수 표현
· as well ~도, 또한

5

M Joyce, you're studying here, too! When did you get to the library?

W Early this morning. I'm working on the social studies report. Did you finish yours?

M I turned it in yesterday. It's 1)_____ _____ , right?

W Yes, but I still have a lot of work to do on it.

M Do you want me to help you with the report?

W No, thanks. It will be faster to 2)_____ _____ _____ .

M I understand. Well, it's time for lunch. Did you bring anything to eat?

W No. I didn't pack anything.

M I'm heading to the cafeteria now. Should I pick something up for you?

W It would be really nice if I had 3)_____ _____ _____ _____ , like a salad or a sandwich.

M Sure. I can do that now.

W One second, let me get you some money.

M Don't worry about it. You can pay me back later.

W Thanks!

↘ 듣기 필수 표현
· turn ~ in ~을 제출하다
· head to ~로 가다
· pick ~ up ~을 사다
· pay back 갚다

6

[Telephone rings.]

W Deluxe Airways. How can I help you?

M Hi. I'd like to book 1)_____ _____ to Kansas City for March 5th.

W Will that be economy class, sir?

M Yes, please. I 2)_____ _____ _____ my son who is seven years old. Can you tell me how much his ticket will be discounted?

W It's $160 for a round-trip ticket for an adult and 50% off that rate for a child under eight.

M Alright. I'll take one adult ticket and 3)_____ _____ _____ _____ . And I'd like to use my frequent flyer miles.

W Sure. Can I ask for your name?

M It's Samuel Mann. M-A-N-N.

W Okay. *[Typing sound]* It looks like you can save $50 4)_____ _____ _____ if you use all of them.

M Sure. That's fine.

W I'll need your ID number to book the ticket.

M Just a moment. I'll get my passport.

↘ 듣기 필수 표현
· Just a moment. 잠깐만요.

7

W Hey, George. I didn't see you at the robotics club meeting. Are you doing okay?

M I'm fine, Melanie. Actually, I've decided to leave the club.

W Oh, did you 1)_____ _____ _____ _____ _____ for the college entrance exam? I know the club takes up a lot of time.

M That wasn't really a factor for me.

W So you're just not interested in robots anymore?

M No! I really enjoy making robots. But I'm going to volunteer at 2)_____ _____ _____ _____ after school instead.

W Oh, that's cool. I know you want to be a vet one day.

M Exactly. The work is more important to me.

W I see. Well, will you still 3)_____ _____ _____ the school band?

M Certainly! The schedules won't conflict.

W Okay, that's good to hear.

↘ 듣기 필수 표현
· take up (시간·공간을) 차지하다

8

M Do you have any plans for the weekend, Cheryl?

W Hey, Karl. Actually, I was planning to go to the International Food Festival. Do you want to come along?

M Oh, when is that?

W It takes place on 1)_____ _____ _____ _____ through the afternoon and early evening. I'm going on the 10th.

M Haven't you been to that before?

W Yeah, I try to go every year! They always have a wide variety of 2)_____ _____. I want to try the dumplings from Uzbekistan this time.

M Nice. How much is it to get in?

W Tickets are free, but you have to 3)_____ _____ _____ _____.

M Other than food, is there any entertainment?

W Yeah. There will be dance performances and a magic show.

M That sounds fun. Alright, I'm coming! Why don't we meet there at noon?

W Sounds like a plan.

↘ 듣기 필수 표현
· come along 함께 가다
· a wide variety of 매우 다양한
· other than ~ 외에
· Sounds like a plan. 좋은 생각이야

9

W Hello, KESP Radio listeners. Local charities are putting together an event called Relay for Life to raise funds 1)_____ _____ of last month's flood. Many residents in the area lost their homes and possessions. We hope to help them 2)_____ _____ _____ _____. The event will be held on September 7th, starting at 10 a.m. It will include both a 10-kilometer race and 5-kilometer walk. While only adults can take part in the 10-kilometer race, the 5-kilometer walk doesn't have 3)_____ _____ _____. A map showing the routes for both is posted on our website. Several local companies have generously agreed to donate $100 for 4)_____ _____ _____ _____. So the more people that participate, the more help we can provide. We expect you to sign up. Thank you.

↘ 듣기 필수 표현
· raise funds 기금을 모으다
· take part in ~에 참가하다

10

W I've been shopping for a new gaming mouse, but I can't make up my mind. Can you help me, Paul?

M Sure. Do you 1)_____ _____ _____ _____ you're interested in?

W Yeah. Here's what I've been looking at.

M Do you have strong preference about color?

W I'd love a red mouse, but white will be good, too.

M Okay, then you should consider whether you want 2)_____ _____ _____. So do you really dislike having a cord?

W It does get annoying. I want my desk to have a cleaner look.

M Well, then you should get a mouse that doesn't have one.

W I agree. Then, there are three options left.

M Let's consider side buttons.

W I'd like mine to have 3)_____ _____ _____.

M I see. Now, price seems like the final deciding factor.

W Yeah, that's a big difference. I'll go with the cheaper one.

↘ 듣기 필수 표현
· make up one's mind 결단을 내리다
· go with ~을 선택하다

11

W Daniel, you're joining the swim team next year, right? Do you know when 1)_____ _____ _____?

M It's before school. So I'll have to be at the pool by 6:30 a.m.

W Wow. You must have to 2)_____ _____ _____ to do that!

12

M Jenny, do you want to go for a walk in the park this afternoon?

W I'd love to, but I have 1)_____ _____ _____ at 2 p.m.

M Oh, are you 2)_____ _____ _____ your driver's license?

↘ 듣기 필수 표현
· go for a walk 산책하다
· would love to ~하고 싶다

13

[Doorbell rings.]

W Are you ready to head out?

M To 1)_____ _____ _____? Doesn't it start at 7?

W Yeah, but I was planning to drop by Debra's house first.

M What for? That's pretty out of the way.

W I want to 2)_____ _____ _____ to take pictures of the fireworks.

M Why don't you use your phone?

W It's hard to take good photos of fireworks with a phone.

M Then, you can borrow my camera.

W Don't you want to 3)_____ _____ _____?

M I wasn't planning to.

W Thanks!

M So I guess we don't have to rush out, right?

W Well, I still want to get there early so that we can get a good place to sit.

M Alright. Just 4)_____ _____ _____ _____ _____ to get dressed and grab my camera.

14

[Telephone rings.]

M Hello. You've reached Burton Travel Agency.

W Hi. I'm considering going to France for the first week of October.

M 1)_____ _____ _____ _____ are you interested in?

W I want a tour that visits places that people don't really know about.

M Ah, you mean, the hidden France. That's our specialty!

W Great. Can you recommend 2)_____ _____ _____?

M We have two popular package tours. One involves visiting wineries. The other involves hiking in the countryside.

W Both sound interesting. Is it possible to try both of them?

M Sure. We also 3)_____ _____ _____.

W Interesting. But can I get some more information about the package tours beforehand?

M Certainly. If you give me your e-mail address, I can 4)_____ _____ _____.

W Of course. It's jdbaker@softmail.com. Should I call again to book a tour?

15

W Martin and Jean are classmates in a high school chemistry class. Each student 1)_____ _____ _____ a partner during experiments. Today, however, Martin's lab partner was feeling sick and did not come to school. As the teacher explains the experiment of the day, Jean notices that Martin has no one to work with. He looks a little worried about doing the 2)_____ _____ _____. She knows that it will be difficult for Martin to do the assignment by himself. So she wants to suggest that Martin ask for the teacher's 3)_____ _____ _____ her and her partner during today's class. In this situation, what would Jean most likely say to Martin?

16~17

M Welcome back, everyone. Last time, I mentioned that the way hosts treat their guests is changing. Today, I want to discuss some of the ways that dining etiquette 1)_____ _____ _____ _____. First, in China, guests always leave a small amount of food on their plate. Eating everything would suggest that the host did not provide enough food, which would be considered quite rude. Second, people in India famously eat with their right hand only. This etiquette rule began because of 2)_____ _____ _____ that the left hand was dirty. Third, table manners in Chile are quite formal. People there use a knife and fork to eat everything. Even finger foods like tacos and pizza are often eaten with utensils. Lastly, people of Spain 3)_____ _____ _____ that the meal last a long time. Eating too quickly or trying to rush out of a restaurant after finishing a meal is considered bad manners. Now, does anyone have any other examples they'd like to share with the class?

09회

제3교시

대학수학능력시험 문제지
영어듣기 모의고사

▲ 문제 음성
바로 듣기
▲ 고사장 버전
바로 듣기

정답 및 해설 p.50

1번부터 17번까지는 듣고 답하는 문제입니다. 1번부터 15번까지는 한 번만 들려주고, 16번부터 17번까지는 두 번 들려줍니다. 방송을 잘 듣고 답을 하시기 바랍니다.

1. 다음을 듣고, 여자가 하는 말의 목적으로 가장 적절한 것을 고르시오.

① 예정된 바닥 교체 작업을 통지하려고
② 사무실 임시 폐쇄 조치를 예고하려고
③ 화재 안전 점검 일정을 안내하려고
④ 엘리베이터가 수리 중임을 공지하려고
⑤ 새로 추가된 방문객 출입 절차를 설명하려고

2. 대화를 듣고, 여자의 의견으로 가장 적절한 것을 고르시오.

① 교과서를 깨끗이 사용하는 습관을 길러야 한다.
② 급우들과 자유롭게 토론하는 시간을 늘려야 한다.
③ 공부할 때 틈틈이 휴식 시간을 갖는 것은 중요하다.
④ 약간의 소음은 집중하는 데 도움이 될 수 있다.
⑤ 카페에서 공부하기에는 여러 어려움이 있다.

3. 대화를 듣고, 두 사람의 관계를 가장 잘 나타낸 것을 고르시오.

① 전자기기 판매원 — 대학생
② 프로그래머 — 사업 의뢰인
③ 컴퓨터 수리기사 — 대학 교수
④ 게임 개발자 — 그래픽 디자이너
⑤ TV 판매점 직원 — 관리자

4. 대화를 듣고, 그림에서 대화의 내용과 일치하지 않는 것을 고르시오.

5. 대화를 듣고, 남자가 할 일로 가장 적절한 것을 고르시오.

① 기념일 선물 구입하기
② 백화점 쿠폰 발급 받기
③ 마사지 가게 예약하기
④ 레스토랑 검색하기
⑤ 아빠에게 전화하기

6. 대화를 듣고, 여자가 지불할 금액을 고르시오. [3점]

① $27 　② $30 　③ $33 　④ $36 　⑤ $39

7. 대화를 듣고, 남자가 스노보드를 타러 갈 수 없는 이유를 고르시오.

① 2월 주말 일정이 꽉 차서
② 겨울철 운동을 즐기지 않아서
③ 이미 많은 돈을 여행에 써서
④ 발목을 삐는 부상을 당해서
⑤ 함께 가는 사람들과 친하지 않아서

8. 대화를 듣고, Little Italy에 관해 언급되지 않은 것을 고르시오.

① 위치 　　② 배달료 　　③ 종업원 수
④ 개점 시간 　⑤ 인기 메뉴

9. Dottie's Dresses에 관한 다음 내용을 듣고, 일치하지 않는 것을 고르시오.

① 내년 상품의 진열 공간을 마련하려고 할인 행사를 한다.
② 행사 동안 90%까지 할인이 가능하다.
③ 유명 디자이너들의 옷도 할인 품목에 포함된다.
④ 할인 품목이 다 팔릴 때까지 행사가 이어질 것이다.
⑤ 영업시간이 할인 행사 때문에 연장되었다.

10. 다음 표를 보면서 대화를 듣고, 여자가 구입할 이북 리더기를 고르시오.

E-book Readers

	Model	Price	Wireless Charging	Battery Life (days)	Color
①	A	$85	X	6	White
②	B	$95	O	12	Black
③	C	$105	O	8	Silver
④	D	$120	O	10	White
⑤	E	$135	X	14	Black

11. 대화를 듣고, 남자의 마지막 말에 대한 여자의 응답으로 가장 적절한 것을 고르시오.

① Oh, sorry. I'll set my phone on silent.

② Good idea. Do you have my phone number?

③ I don't know. I'm worried she won't pick up when I call.

④ No, I can't. Is it okay to call you back in a few minutes?

⑤ What was that? I thought I heard a loud sound outside.

12. 대화를 듣고, 여자의 마지막 말에 대한 남자의 응답으로 가장 적절한 것을 고르시오.

① I'll send him an email today.

② The neighborhood is great for kids.

③ I'll be free all day Monday and Tuesday.

④ The real estate agent said the rent is $900.

⑤ The apartment needs at least two bedrooms.

13. 대화를 듣고, 여자의 마지막 말에 대한 남자의 응답으로 가장 적절한 것을 고르시오. [3점]

Man: _____

① I'll tell the class what the answers are next week.

② We will cover that chapter during Friday's class.

③ The essay should be at least 200 words long.

④ Is it going to be due before class tomorrow?

⑤ I'll write it on the chalkboard for everyone.

14. 대화를 듣고, 남자의 마지막 말에 대한 여자의 응답으로 가장 적절한 것을 고르시오.

Woman: _____

① Okay. I'll take good care of the plants for you.

② Thanks a lot. I really appreciate you doing this.

③ That's the problem. You've been watering it too much.

④ I understand. I'll come by to plant it on Monday morning.

⑤ Sure. I will put the plant by the window so it gets enough light.

15. 다음 상황 설명을 듣고, Richard가 Amy에게 할 말로 가장 적절한 것을 고르시오. [3점]

Richard: _____

① Did you plan a class party for the end of the year?

② Are you interested in taking a class on video editing?

③ Can you show me how to edit the video I'm making?

④ Could you send me some clips of class events from this year?

⑤ Would you make a video for your channel about a high school event?

[16~17] 다음을 듣고, 물음에 답하시오.

16. 남자가 하는 말의 주제로 가장 적절한 것은?

① organs that are most affected by daily exercise

② activities that you can easily do outside of a gym

③ various exercises that can prevent heart problems

④ ideal workout durations for different physical activities

⑤ importance of regular activity for people with heart problems

17. 언급된 운동이 아닌 것은?

① walking   ② swimming   ③ running

④ climbing   ⑤ cycling

이제 듣기 문제가 끝났습니다. 채점을 마친 후 다음 페이지에서 방송을 다시 들으며 딕테이션 연습을 하시기 바랍니다.

* 채점 결과: 맞은 개수 _____ 개 / 17개   정답 및 해설 p.50

Dictation 정답 p.50

09회 영어듣기 모의고사 Dictation 음성을 들으며 빈칸에 알맞은 단어를 채워 넣으시기 바랍니다.

1

W Hi. I'm Gloria Osterberg, vice president of operations here at GloboChem. 1)_____ _____ _____, we will begin replacing the tiles on the floor of the lobby next Monday. This means the main entrance of our headquarters will be temporarily inaccessible. As such, all employees and visitors will be 2)_____ _____ _____ _____ the rear entrance. Also, since the elevator will not be available, you will need to 3)_____ _____ _____ for the time being. The work is planned to take three days, so things will return to normal by Thursday morning. We appreciate your patience and understanding with this matter.

↘ 듣기 필수 표현
· as such 그런 이유로
· for the time being 당분간
· return to normal 정상으로 돌아오다

2

W Alex, do you know where you and your classmate are going to study this evening?

M Gerard wants to meet up at a café.

W That might not be a good idea.

M Why not?

W I think it's too hard to 1)_____ _____ _____ at a café.

M Really? A lot of people do it.

W Cafés are usually noisy, though. So you may have difficulty focusing.

M I don't know about that. I like some noise. If people are talking, I feel free to 2)_____ _____ _____ _____ out loud.

W Maybe so. But it doesn't seem wise to have your textbook open around food and drinks.

M I guess I have 3)_____ _____ on my work before.

W Well, that's a good reason not to study there!

M Okay. I'll keep that in mind.

↘ 듣기 필수 표현
· meet up 만나다
· feel free to 마음대로 ~하다
· keep in mind 명심하다

3

M Good afternoon. May I help you?

W Hi. I'm looking for a laptop to do some programming and graphic design with.

M Sure thing. Is there 1)_____ _____ _____ you have your eye on?

W Not really. Something powerful but not too expensive.

M I see. Do you play any computer games?

W No. I need it 2)_____ _____ _____. I'm majoring in computer science.

M Okay. In that case, I'd recommend either a Phoenix or a SurTech model.

W *[Pause]* These 3)_____ _____ _____ to me. They have the same screen size, too. What's the difference?

M The SurTech one is lighter but a little more expensive, while the Phoenix is cheaper but 4)_____ _____.

W Is there a discount for students?

M We do have one. It's 10% off.

W Can I try out the SurTech one?

M Go right ahead.

↘ 듣기 필수 표현
· have one's eye on 눈여겨보다
· major in ~을 전공하다
· in that case 그렇다면
· either A or B A나 B 중 하나
· try out 시험 삼아 써 보다

4

W Tony, have you thought about places for us to stay during the holiday weekend?

M Yeah. I think I found one by Lake Morris. Take a look at this cabin.

W It's so cozy. I love 1)_____ _____ _____ _____ _____.

M Me too. And with the two couches close by, we could all sit by the fire together.

W Sounds great. It's beautifully decorated, too.

M Isn't it? That star pattern on the rug looks nice. Most cabins 2)_____ _____ _____.

W Exactly. I was admiring the antique square table. It fits well with the mirror above it.

M I agree. Apparently, the owner likes to collect old furniture.

W That's cool!

M And I believe the 3)_____ _____ _____ _____ by the door were picked from his garden.

W This place has a lot of character. Let's book it!

M Okay, I'll do that now.

5

M Hey, Penny. Mom and Dad's 30th wedding anniversary is coming up soon. Shouldn't we 1)_____ _____ _____ for them?

W I was thinking of getting them a present. I have a department store coupon.

M Hmm... wouldn't it be better to plan something romantic?

W You're right. What about making reservations at 2)_____ _____ _____ _____?

M I think they already have dinner plans.

W Maybe a couples massage would be good?

M Oh, I know a place that does good massages downtown!

W You mean the spa on 6th Street? That would be perfect.

M Then, it's settled. I'll 3)_____ _____ _____ online and put it on my credit card.

W Sounds like a plan.

M Why don't you call Dad and let him know about it so that they don't 4)_____ _____ _____?

W I'll do that now.

6

W Excuse me. How much is this medium-sized cake? I'm getting some desserts to share with my friends.

M Well, that one is $30, but you can also get it by the piece. If you 1)_____ _____ _____ five pieces at one time, you can get a 10% discount on them.

W Oh, that might be better. Then, I can pick the flavors my friends like. How much is it for a piece?

M It's $6 per piece.

W Are all the cakes 2)_____ _____ _____?

M Yes, that's right.

W Okay. Then, I'll take two pieces of this chocolate cake and three pieces of cheesecake.

M Got it. Can I get you anything else?

W Hmm... How much are these vanilla macaroons?

M They are $3 each.

W Great. I'll take 3)_____ _____ _____ _____ _____.

M So... that's five slices of cake and three macaroons.

W That's right. Here's my credit card.

7

M Hi, Mary. How's it going?

W I'm doing well, Ted. Hey, do you 1)_____ _____ _____ for the first week of February?

M For February? No, not really.

W Well, I'm organizing a snowboarding trip. Would you like to come along?

M I don't think I'll be able to make it.

W Really? I thought you loved snowboarding.

M I used to do it a lot.

W Did you get injured or something?

M I 2)_____ _____ _____ a couple of times. But nothing serious.

W I'm only planning on inviting Lana and Bob. So you would know everyone.

M I like all of them, but I 3)_____ _____ _____ _____ during my trip this month. I can't afford to go traveling again.

W I get it. Next time, then!

8

W Ross, have you tried Little Italy?

M Do you mean the restaurant 1)_____ _____ Main Street, across from the Stardust Theater? If so, I wouldn't recommend it.

W Yeah, that's the one I mean. What was wrong with it?

M There was only one waiter working, so it took forever to get our food.

W Oh, then I'll just go early. Do you know 2)_____ _____ _____?

M It opens at 11 a.m. But I have another reason for not liking it. The food was really bland.

W What did you order? I've heard people say that their pasta is good.

M I had the spaghetti with meatballs, which is their 3)_____ _____ _____.

W That's too bad. I was looking forward to trying it.

M Yeah, so was I.

W Maybe I'll try the new Thai place instead.

M Good idea. Tell me how it is.

↘ 듣기 필수 표현
· across from ~ 맞은편에
· take forever 엄청난 시간이 걸리다

9

M Dottie's Dresses shoppers, may I have your attention, please? The new year is coming up, which means that it's time for 1)_____ _____ _____. To make room for next year's designs, all clothing from the past season is being discounted by 50% to 90%. Every dress in our inventory is included in 2)_____ _____ _____, which means that even clothing from the most famous designers will be available. The sale begins December 9th and will continue until every last discounted item is sold. We've also 3)_____ _____ _____ because of the upcoming Christmas holiday, so we're open until 10 p.m. nightly now. For the finest fashions at the fairest prices, come to Dottie's!

↘ 듣기 필수 표현
· come up 다가오다

10

M Jenny, what are you looking at?

W I'm trying to buy a new e-book reader. These are the options I'm considering now.

M Good idea! You always read books 1)_____ _____ _____ _____ to and from school. What's your price range?

W My budget is $130 or less, so I guess this one's out.

M What about wireless charging? Do you think you'll 2)_____ _____ _____?

W Definitely. I hate having to plug my devices in.

M I agree. That'll be much more convenient. Then, you have to think about the battery life.

W I guess more is better. Let's say it should have a battery life of 3)_____ _____ _____ _____.

M Then, you just need to decide which color you want.

W I don't like the white one, so I'll go with black.

M Perfect. You're all set to order it now.

↘ 듣기 필수 표현
· plug ~ in ~에 플러그를 꽂다
· Let's say 이를테면
· all set 만반의 준비가 된

11

M Samantha, is everything all right? You 1)_____ _____ _____ _____.

W I can't find my phone anywhere. Have you seen it by any chance?

M No, I haven't. But I could 2)_____ _____ _____ _____. We'll hear it ring if it's somewhere close by.

↘ 듣기 필수 표현
· by any chance 혹시

12

W Honey, I just 1)_____ _____ _____ from the real estate agent. He found a beautiful apartment for us to go see.

M Really? That's great. I hope it's in a nice neighborhood.

W It is. We just need to set a date to see it. 2)_____ _____ _____ _____?

↘ 듣기 필수 표현
· set a date 날짜를 정하다

13

M Well, that finishes up our discussion for today. Is everyone ready for Friday's test?

W Mr. Jackson, I have a question.

M Yes, Tanya?

W What topics is the test [1]_____ _____ _____?

M Everything in our history book from pages 198 to 310.

W Okay. Is there an essay question on the exam, or are all of them multiple choice questions?

M [2]_____ _____ will appear. I plan on putting in one essay question at the end.

W What's it going to be on?

M I can't tell you the subject, but I can tell you that the essay [3]_____ _____ _____ 25% of your exam grade.

W Mr. Jackson, one last thing before the bell rings.

M Sure. What is it?

W I didn't catch today's homework assignment. Can you repeat it?

↘ 듣기 필수 표현
· finish up 마무리하다

14

[Cell phone rings.]

W Hey, Aaron. What's up?

M Hi, Nicole. Can I ask you a favor?

W Sure. What is it?

M I need someone to look after my plants.

W I'd be happy to help if I can, but I'm planning to [1]_____ _____.

M It's next week. I'll be out of town visiting my relatives for a few days.

W That's good. I'm leaving [2]_____ _____ _____ _____.

M Great. So you don't mind watering the plants?

W Of course not. Is there anything else you need me to do? I can move the plants to make sure they get enough sunlight.

M No, that's not necessary. All of them are [3]_____ _____ _____ _____.

W Okay. Please let me know the door code in that case.

M I'll send the code by text message.

↘ 듣기 필수 표현
· ask a favor 부탁하다
· look after ~을 돌보다

15

W Richard is a high school student. He is making a video for his class's end-of-the-year ceremony that will [1]_____ _____ in a few weeks. He wants it to be memorable for his classmates, so he has worked on the video for a long time. He added lots of clips of events that happened throughout the year, and he tried to make the video [2]_____ _____ with cool transitions and effects. But he's not very skilled at video editing. Then, he remembers that his friend Amy makes interesting videos for her online channel all the time. So he wants to ask her to teach him [3]_____ _____ _____ _____ _____. In this situation, what would Richard most likely say to Amy?

↘ 듣기 필수 표현
· be skilled at ~에 능숙하다
· all the time 항상

16~17

M Hello, everyone. In our last health session, we talked about the importance of heart health. Today, we're going to talk about [1]_____ _____ that are good for heart health. First, let's talk about walking. Walking is a great form of exercise and one of the easiest ways to improve heart health. With just two and a half hours of walking a week, a person can [2]_____ _____ _____ of heart disease. Next, we have swimming. Swimming is an effective way to work the heart and lungs. This activity trains the body to use oxygen in a more efficient way, which benefits your heart. Running is also an excellent activity for taking care of your heart. Regularly running improves blood flow throughout your body. As a result, your heart is easily able [3]_____ _____ _____. Finally, cycling can strengthen heart muscles and reduce blood fat levels. Any of these are great methods for boosting your heart health. Be sure to exercise as much as you can for the best results!

↘ 듣기 필수 표현
· take care of ~을 돌보다
· as a result 결과적으로

10 회

제3교시

대학수학능력시험 문제지
영어듣기 모의고사

▲ 문제 음성
바로 듣기

▲ 고사장 버전
바로 듣기

정답 및 해설 p.56

1번부터 17번까지는 듣고 답하는 문제입니다. 1번부터 15번까지는 한 번만 들려주고, 16번부터 17번까지는 두 번 들려줍니다. 방송을 잘 듣고 답을 하시기 바랍니다.

1. 다음을 듣고, 남자가 하는 말의 목적으로 가장 적절한 것을 고르시오.

① 자전거 도난 사고 위험을 경고하려고
② 등하교 시 자전거 이용을 권장하려고
③ 자전거 거치대 추가 설치를 공지하려고
④ 후문 임시 폐쇄 조치를 안내하려고
⑤ 자전거 안전 수칙을 설명하려고

2. 대화를 듣고, 여자의 의견으로 가장 적절한 것을 고르시오.

① 카페인은 다이어트에 도움이 된다.
② 오후에 커피를 마시면 수면의 질이 떨어진다.
③ 저녁에 과식하면 악몽을 꿀 가능성이 커진다.
④ 충분한 수분 섭취는 기억력과 집중력을 좋게 만든다.
⑤ 공복에 마시는 커피는 위장 장애를 유발할 수 있다.

3. 대화를 듣고, 두 사람의 관계를 가장 잘 나타낸 것을 고르시오.

① 여행사 직원 ― 작사가
② 사진작가 ― 영화배우
③ 방송 기자 ― 야구 선수
④ 토크쇼 진행자 ― 가수
⑤ 승무원 ― 탑승객

4. 대화를 듣고, 그림에서 대화의 내용과 일치하지 않는 것을 고르시오.

5. 대화를 듣고, 남자가 할 일로 가장 적절한 것을 고르시오.

① 무대 제작하기
② 안전 점검하기
③ 음향 확인하기
④ 밴드와 연락하기
⑤ 공연 일정표 보내기

6. 대화를 듣고, 여자가 지불할 금액을 고르시오.

① $30   ② $34   ③ $36   ④ $38   ⑤ $40

7. 대화를 듣고, 남자가 백화점을 방문하려는 이유를 고르시오.

① 여동생을 데리러 가야 해서
② 크리스마스 선물을 구매해야 해서
③ 만화가의 사인회에 참석하고 싶어서
④ 은행에서 금융 상담을 받아야 해서
⑤ 친구들과 만나기로 약속해서

8. 대화를 듣고, Newberry Market에 관해 언급되지 않은 것을 고르시오.

① 주최 기관   ② 날짜   ③ 신청 마감일
④ 참가비   ⑤ 장소

9. National Youth Chess Championship에 관한 다음 내용을 듣고, 일치하지 않는 것을 고르시오.

① 32명의 고등학생들이 대회에 참가할 것이다.
② 6일 동안 경기를 치를 것이다.
③ 결승전은 대회 마지막 이틀 동안 치러질 것이다.
④ 대회의 주요 장면이 매일 밤 방송될 것이다.
⑤ 우승자는 상금 대신 세계 챔피언의 가르침을 받을 수 있다.

10. 다음 표를 보면서 대화를 듣고, 남자가 구매할 겨울 장갑을 고르시오.

Winter Gloves

	Model	Material	Color	Waterproof	Price
①	A	Synthetic	White	O	$75
②	B	Leather	Black	O	$135
③	C	Wool	Black	X	$95
④	D	Wool	Brown	X	$40
⑤	E	Synthetic	Brown	O	$125

11. 대화를 듣고, 여자의 마지막 말에 대한 남자의 응답으로 가장 적절한 것을 고르시오.

① Yes. I'm looking for the non-fiction section.
② Never mind. I think I found a copy for you.
③ No problem. I'll stop back on Monday.
④ I see. I'll order the book right away.
⑤ Great. I really enjoyed that novel.

12. 대화를 듣고, 남자의 마지막 말에 대한 여자의 응답으로 가장 적절한 것을 고르시오.

① Good. Either of them works for me.
② Too bad. You should have exercised every day.
③ Don't worry. I'll teach you how to play badminton.
④ Sorry. I'm exhausted after working out.
⑤ I agree. Working out outdoors is always the best.

13. 대화를 듣고, 여자의 마지막 말에 대한 남자의 응답으로 가장 적절한 것을 고르시오. [3점]

Man: _____

① Can you tell the taxi driver to go faster?
② Ask the other group if they will do us a favor.
③ Just briefly mention what it's about and press play.
④ Inform the professor that I'll be there in 10 minutes.
⑤ See if we can practice the presentation together before class.

14. 대화를 듣고, 남자의 마지막 말에 대한 여자의 응답으로 가장 적절한 것을 고르시오. [3점]

Woman: _____

① No, I can do the exercise by myself.
② The doctor told me not to stretch it too often.
③ I think eating a good dinner will help me heal.
④ It's difficult to stretch my hands properly with the cast.
⑤ It's been hurting a lot, but my wrist is getting stronger.

15. 다음 상황 설명을 듣고, Mike가 Wendy에게 할 말로 가장 적절한 것을 고르시오. [3점]

Mike: _____

① What did you think of today's lunch menu?
② How about inviting her to our geography study group?
③ When should we get together to work on the assignment?
④ Do you mind if I join you in the cafeteria later?
⑤ Why don't you come eat with us if you like?

[16~17] 다음을 듣고, 물음에 답하시오.

16. 여자가 하는 말의 주제로 가장 적절한 것은?

① surprising origins of different foods
② reasons cooking styles change over time
③ how various cooking utensils were invented
④ different countries famous for their cuisine
⑤ the importance of using local ingredients

17. 언급된 음식이 아닌 것은?

① pasta
② fish and chips
③ French toast
④ Swedish meatball
⑤ ice cream

이제 듣기 문제가 끝났습니다. 채점을 마친 후 다음 페이지에서 방송을 다시 들으며 딕테이션 연습을 하시기 바랍니다.

* 채점 결과: 맞은 개수 _____ 개 / 17개   정답 및 해설 p.56

10회 Dictation

Dictation 정답 p.56

10회 영어듣기 모의고사 Dictation 음성을 들으며 빈칸에 알맞은 단어를 채워 넣으시기 바랍니다.

1

M Good morning, Linton High School students. This is your principal, Mr. Henderson. It has come to my attention that some students have been leaving their bikes near the rear entrance. This has caused a lot of problems because it has ¹⁾ _____ _____ _____ _____ to the school. However, I understand that you have been doing this because there is a ²⁾ _____ _____ _____ to store your bikes. So we have decided to add two ³⁾ _____ _____ _____ next to the outdoor basketball courts. These will be available for use starting next week. But do note that, starting Monday, any bike blocking an entrance ⁴⁾ _____ _____ _____ by school staff. Okay, everyone, have a great school day!

↘ **듣기 필수 표현**
· come to one's attention ~을 알게 되다

2

M Tracy, I'm making coffee. Do you want some?

W No, thanks. It's 5 p.m. Isn't it late for that?

M I need energy. I can't ¹⁾ _____ _____ _____ _____ .

W I've read that drinking coffee in the afternoon lowers the quality of your sleep.

M Not me. I can always get to sleep.

W Maybe so, but coffee ²⁾ _____ _____ in your brain, so it prevents deep sleep.

M Interesting. I may wake up tired even if I sleep for a long time, then?

W That's it! Also, caffeine ³⁾ _____ _____ for dinner.

M Why is that a bad thing?

W Well, you still get hungry, but later on.

M So coffee makes you feel like eating a big snack later in the night.

W Exactly. We know it's ⁴⁾ _____ _____ _____ right after eating.

M Then, I'd better have ice water instead.

3

M Marianne Smith, thank you so much for coming on our program tonight.

W It's my pleasure, Larry. I'm a big fan of your ¹⁾ _____ _____ .

M I appreciate that. Now, I understand that you've been on tour for several months.

W I've been flying around the world for almost a year.

M How does this tour differ from ones you've ²⁾ _____ _____ _____ _____ ?

W Well, the venues are bigger. We had 60,000 fans at our last concert, which was in a baseball stadium.

M That must be an amazing feeling.

W It is. But I'm almost ready to ³⁾ _____ _____ _____ the studio.

M Have you written material for your next album?

W Yes, actually. I have several new songs already.

M Would you be able to play one for us?

W Sure! I'd be ⁴⁾ _____ _____ _____ one with my fans.

M Fantastic. We'll be back with Marianne Smith after a quick commercial break.

↘ **듣기 필수 표현**
· It's my pleasure. 천만에요.
· on tour 순회공연 중인
· differ from ~와 다르다

4

W Honey, whose backyard is it in that picture?

M Oh, this is where my friend Robert spent the holiday.

W He must ¹⁾ _____ _____ _____ _____ . Aren't those two palm trees near the fence?

M Yeah. It's in Florida. Don't you think ²⁾ _____ _____ in front of the fence is stylish?

W It's really nice. I'd like to relax by that square table.

M Me too. The striped umbrella over it would keep the sun out of our eyes during the day.

W It's ³⁾ _____ _____ _____ _____ . Oh, look at that cat sleeping next to the chair.

M It's so cute! And do you see that barbecue grill over 4)_____ _____ _____ _____?

W Yeah. It would be great to cook outside.

M Looking at this picture makes me want to go on a trip soon!

W Me too! Let's go next month.

↘ 듣기 필수 표현
· keep A out of B A가 B에 못 들어오게 하다
· go on a trip 여행을 가다

5

M Abbey, is everything going to be ready for the fundraiser concert?

W I think so, John. We finished 1)_____ _____ _____ this morning.

M And what about the safety check? Isn't an inspector from the city government supposed to come?

W He was just here. Everything's approved.

M Great. How about the sound system?

W We're 2)_____ _____ _____, and it sounds good to me.

M Now we just need to contact the bands to let them know what times they'll be playing.

W I already made a timetable. Do you want to take a look at it?

M I do. Can you e-mail it to me? I'm 3)_____ _____ _____ _____ myself.

W Do you have their contact information?

M Yes. I have the musicians' phone numbers.

W Okay. I'll send over that timetable now.

M I appreciate it.

6

M Welcome to Bob's Sandwiches. What can I do for you?

W Hi. Do you still have that 10% off special on ham and cheese sandwiches?

M Sorry, but 1)_____ _____ _____ last week.

W Oh, I see. Well, what specials do you have right now?

M At the moment, we have discounts on a couple of our most popular sandwiches. The turkey sandwich is $14, and the roast beef sandwich is only $10.

W Okay. 2)_____ _____ _____. Let's go with two roast beef sandwiches and one turkey.

M Got it. Do you want those to be meal combos?

W What does that include?

M You get a small soda and regular fries. That costs an extra $2 per sandwich.

W Sure. I'll take that 3)_____ _____ _____ _____.

M So I have three sandwich meal combos. Does that complete your order?

W Yes, that's everything. Here's my credit card.

↘ 듣기 필수 표현
· at the moment 현재

7

W Hey, David. Can you pick your sister up after her music lesson this afternoon?

M I can't, Mom. I 1)_____ _____. I'm heading over to the department store in a few minutes.

W Oh, I see. Do you still need to do some Christmas shopping?

M No. I already bought all of my Christmas presents.

W Well, are you meeting up with your friends?

M Don't you remember? My favorite cartoonist is going to 2)_____ _____ _____ _____ at the department store.

W Oh, right. You mentioned that you wanted to 3)_____ _____ _____.

M Exactly. I'm so excited.

W Well... I'll see if your father can do it. I need to go 4)_____ _____ _____ _____.

M Sorry I couldn't help.

W Don't worry about it. Go have fun!

M Okay, see you later.

↘ 듣기 필수 표현
· pick up ~를 데리러 가다
· head over ~로 가다
· meet up ~와 만나다

8

M Honey, did you see the flyer for the Newberry Market?

W No. What's that?

M It's a huge ¹⁾_____ _____ _____ _____ the Newberry Community Center. Everyone in the neighborhood can sell stuff there.

W Interesting. ²⁾_____ _____ is it being held on?

M Let me check... Oh, it will be on June 15th. That's next weekend.

W I've got a bunch of collectibles I'd like to sell. Would I need to pay a ³⁾_____ _____ _____?

M Yeah, but it is only $10 to use one of the stalls all day.

W Wow. That's very reasonable. Where will the market be located?

M It will take place in Wilson Park, which is just ⁴⁾_____ _____ _____.

W Then, I am going to sign up for it. Thanks for letting me know!

↘ 듣기 필수 표현
· a bunch of 많은
· take place ~에서 열리다

9

M Welcome to the National Youth Chess Championship! We have 32 students competing from high schools all over the country. They ¹⁾_____ _____ _____ for six days. Every day, each player will take part in a single match against another competitor. Competitors must win or ²⁾_____ _____ _____ the tournament. These daily matches will continue until the last two competitors remain. Then, the grand final will be held over the last two days. Highlights of these games ³⁾_____ _____ _____ on the CBN Sports channel nightly. This year's national youth champion will not only receive a $10,000 award but also a lesson from world champion Boris Budanov. It's sure to be an exciting tournament. Good luck, everyone.

↘ 듣기 필수 표현
· not only A but also B A뿐만 아니라 B도

10

W Hi. Can I help you?

M Yes, actually. I'm looking for a pair of gloves for the winter.

W Sure. Well, what do you think of this pair? These gloves are ¹⁾_____ _____ _____.

M I don't really want leather ones.

W Okay. That's a good start. Is there a certain color you want?

M Hmm... I ²⁾_____ _____ _____ gloves. So let's focus on the other pairs.

W Fair enough. Do you want a pair that is waterproof? This can make a big difference.

M Yeah, I definitely need that. Waterproof gloves will ³⁾_____ _____ _____ warm and dry.

W Good choice. That leaves two options. Is there one you like more?

M Both pairs have everything I need, so there's ⁴⁾_____ _____ _____ _____ the more expensive option.

W Do you want me to ring these up?

M Yes, please. Thanks for your help.

↘ 듣기 필수 표현
· make a difference 차이를 낳다
· ring up 계산하다

11

W Welcome to Books World. How may I help you?

M I'm looking for the ¹⁾_____ _____ _____ *My Dream*. I heard it hit the best-seller list.

W I'm afraid it's sold out now. Could you ²⁾_____ _____ _____ next week?

↘ 듣기 필수 표현
· hit the best-seller list 베스트셀러에 오르다
· sold out 품절인

12

M Honey, I'd like to start working out with you. What ¹⁾_____ _____ _____?

W That's a good idea. What exercise do you want to do?

M I'm thinking of playing badminton or squash ²⁾_____ _____ _____.

↘ 듣기 필수 표현
· work out 운동하다

13

[Cell phone rings.]

W Philip, where are you?

M I'm on my way. There was a problem with the subway.

W Well, please hurry. We have to 1)_____ _____ _____ soon!

M I'm just getting in a taxi now.

W When are you going to be here?

M Give me 15 minutes.

W It's scheduled to start in 10 minutes. You're going to be late!

M I'm sorry. Can you ask Professor Benson if another group can present first? I'll get there 2)_____ _____ _____ _____.

W That's not going to work. He's so strict. He won't make an exception for us.

M Okay, well... Can you 3)_____ _____ _____ at the beginning?

W But that's supposed to come at the end!

M I know, but it will buy us some time. I'll be there before 4)_____ _____ _____ _____.

W Okay. I need to introduce it. What should I say?

14

W Honey, can I ask you a favor?

M Sure, what is it?

W Do you mind opening this jar for me?

M No problem. [Pause] Here you go. Does your 1)_____ _____ _____?

W Sadly, yes. I was hoping that it would be stronger by now.

M It's only been two weeks since you got the cast taken off your wrist. Healing takes time.

W Yeah, the doctor said it would be weak 2)_____ _____ _____ _____, but it's annoying that my wrist still doesn't work properly.

M I understand. But I'm happy to help in the meantime. It's really no problem.

W Well, thanks for saying that.

M But you should keep doing those wrist exercises. They're supposed to help.

W I already did those stretches this afternoon. I shouldn't do them again 3)_____ _____ _____.

M Why can't you do them now?

15

M Wendy recently moved to a new city and started going to a different high school. So far, she has not made many friends with her fellow students. Mike is 1)_____ _____ _____ _____ in geography class. During the class this morning, the two of them were assigned to work together on a group report. They got along well and had fun 2)_____ _____ _____ _____. Later, during the lunch hour, Mike sees Wendy sitting all by herself in the cafeteria reading a book. He thinks that she 3)_____ _____. Therefore, Mike wants to suggest that Wendy join him and his group of friends. In this situation, what would Mike most likely say to Wendy?

16~17

W Good afternoon, class. We discussed the invention of different cooking utensils in our last class. Today, I'd like to talk about the unexpected places that 1)_____ _____ _____ _____. First off, we have pasta. Most people assume this is from Italy, but this is not true. History shows us that Italians learned to 2)_____ _____ _____ _____ Chinese noodle dishes during the middle ages. The second food I'll tell you about is fish and chips. This typical English dish was actually invented in Spain. It was brought to England by Jewish refugees in the 15th century. Next, let's consider the Swedish meatball. As you might guess, this is 3)_____ _____ _____ _____. The dish actually traces its origins back to Turkey. Lastly, ice cream also comes from an unexpected place. It's actually Mongolian. The dessert was probably first made by accident by horsemen who were 4)_____ _____ in cold weather. Now, let's take a quick look at a video on this subject.

대학수학능력시험 문제지
영어듣기 모의고사

▲ 문제 음성
바로 듣기
▲ 고사장 버전
바로 듣기

정답 및 해설 p.62

1번부터 17번까지는 듣고 답하는 문제입니다. 1번부터 15번까지는 한 번만 들려주고, 16번부터 17번까지는 두 번 들려줍니다. 방송을 잘 듣고 답을 하시기 바랍니다.

1. 다음을 듣고, 여자가 하는 말의 목적으로 가장 적절한 것을 고르시오.

① 도서 교환 행사 참여를 독려하려고
② 어린이 도서관 운영 시간을 안내하려고
③ 아파트 관리비 인상을 공지하려고
④ 이웃 간 교류의 중요성을 당부하려고
⑤ 도서관 자원봉사자를 모집하려고

2. 대화를 듣고, 남자의 의견으로 가장 적절한 것을 고르시오.

① 조리 방식에 따라 알맞은 기름을 사용해야 한다.
② 건강한 식습관을 위해 염분 섭취를 줄여야 한다.
③ 튀긴 음식을 자주 먹는 것은 건강에 좋지 않다.
④ 심장병을 예방하려면 규칙적으로 운동해야 한다.
⑤ 샐러드의 칼로리는 생각보다 높다.

3. 대화를 듣고, 두 사람의 관계를 가장 잘 나타낸 것을 고르시오.

① 기상 캐스터 – 뉴스 리포터
② 투자 자문위원 – 전문 경영인
③ 식품 연구개발원 – 시식단 일원
④ 매점 직원 – 식료품 배달원
⑤ 은행원 – 아이스크림 가게 사장

4. 대화를 듣고, 그림에서 대화의 내용과 일치하지 않는 것을 고르시오.

5. 대화를 듣고, 남자가 할 일로 가장 적절한 것을 고르시오.

① 체육관 등록하기
② 러닝머신 이용하기
③ 탁구 수업 신청하기
④ 운동복으로 갈아입기
⑤ 아이스크림 얼리기

6. 대화를 듣고, 남자가 지불할 금액을 고르시오. [3점]

① $10 ② $15 ③ $20 ④ $25 ⑤ $30

7. 대화를 듣고, 여자가 중간에 영화관을 나온 이유를 고르시오.

① 영화가 몹시 지루해서
② 화장실이 급해서
③ 갑자기 두통이 너무 심해져서
④ 버스 막차를 타야 해서
⑤ 수의사에게 개를 데려가야 해서

8. 대화를 듣고, Adams Library 재개관 기념식에 관해 언급되지 않은 것을 고르시오.

① 날짜 ② 식순 ③ 식사 주문량
④ 식사 시작 시간 ⑤ 위치

9. Herbert Town Hotdog Festival에 관한 다음 내용을 듣고, 일치하지 않는 것을 고르시오.

① 방문객들은 많은 종류의 핫도그를 맛볼 수 있다.
② 전국 각지의 노점상들이 참여할 것이다.
③ 요리 대회가 오전에 열릴 것이다.
④ 요리 대회의 심사위원은 작년 대회의 우승자들이다.
⑤ 어린이를 위한 활동이 계획되어 있다.

10. 다음 표를 보면서 대화를 듣고, 남자가 구매할 휴대용 스피커를 고르시오.

Bluetooth Speakers

	Model	Price	Waterproof	Playing Time (hours)	Color
①	A	$125	X	24	Red
②	B	$85	O	16	Black
③	C	$80	O	18	Yellow
④	D	$65	X	20	White
⑤	E	$50	O	12	Blue

11. 대화를 듣고, 여자의 마지막 말에 대한 남자의 응답으로 가장 적절한 것을 고르시오.

① No problem. I'll call your company.

② You're right. I didn't get to sleep until dawn.

③ Of course. I'll prescribe medicine for food poisoning.

④ I'm sorry to hear that. I hope you get better soon.

⑤ Definitely. You should see a doctor right now.

12. 대화를 듣고, 남자의 마지막 말에 대한 여자의 응답으로 가장 적절한 것을 고르시오.

① The pears are fresh and taste sweet.

② You had better call to see what is going on.

③ Unfortunately, it looks like the mailman dropped the package.

④ I remember putting it in the mailbox this morning.

⑤ I was too busy to reply to your text message.

13. 대화를 듣고, 여자의 마지막 말에 대한 남자의 응답으로 가장 적절한 것을 고르시오. [3점]

Man: _____

① Yes. I will spend extra time studying the materials.

② Correct. I want you to show me the notes you took.

③ Right. I think doing so would help you understand.

④ It's disappointing. I expected your answer to be longer.

⑤ I know. Math is a difficult subject, but you are doing your best.

14. 대화를 듣고, 남자의 마지막 말에 대한 여자의 응답으로 가장 적절한 것을 고르시오.

Woman: _____

① That's fine. I would prefer a blue one.

② I understand. Thanks for the explanation.

③ I see. Narrow tires are probably a better choice.

④ Is that right? I didn't know they were so expensive.

⑤ Sorry. I'm not sure if that's the size you're looking for.

15. 다음 상황 설명을 듣고, Olivia가 Michael에게 할 말로 가장 적절한 것을 고르시오. [3점]

Olivia: _____

① What would you say is your favorite painting style?

② Why don't you ask your art teacher for more details?

③ Would you recommend this sort of brush for a beginner?

④ Can you tell me more about the kind of painting you will do?

⑤ Is there a discount on art supplies for students?

[16~17] 다음을 듣고, 물음에 답하시오.

16. 남자가 하는 말의 주제로 가장 적절한 것은?

① why traditional stories feature animals

② idioms that are essential to language learning

③ where various international proverbs come from

④ how common expressions change over time

⑤ different old sayings based on animals

17. 언급된 나라가 <u>아닌</u> 것은?

① Greece　　② Australia　　③ Mexico
④ Egypt　　⑤ China

이제 듣기 문제가 끝났습니다. 채점을 마친 후 다음 페이지에서 방송을 다시 들으며 딕테이션 연습을 하시기 바랍니다.

* 채점 결과: 맞은 개수 _____ 개 / 17개　　　　정답 및 해설 p.62

11회 영어듣기 모의고사 Dictation 음성을 들으며 빈칸에 알맞은 단어를 채워 넣으시기 바랍니다.

1

W Good morning, Sunrise Apartments residents! This announcement is a reminder about our upcoming book exchange event. I'd like to 1)_____ _____ _____ to take part. The event will take place tomorrow from 9 a.m. to 7 p.m. We'll set up tables near the front gate, so come and 2)_____ _____ _____ that you'd like to exchange. Participants may take books on a first-come-first-served basis. Beverages and light snacks will also be served. It will be a perfect way to find something new to read and 3)_____ _____ _____ your neighbors. I hope to see you all there!

↘ 듣기 필수 표현
· take part 참여하다
· set up ~을 설치하다
· on a first-come-first-served basis 선착순으로

2

W Jerry, do you want to order some fries with our meal?
M No, thanks.
W Oh, I thought you loved eating them.
M I still like them. But 1)_____ _____ _____ often can be dangerous.
W Yeah? Are they really that bad?
M According to some articles I've been reading, yes. Since fried foods are cooked with so much oil and salt, they 2)_____ _____ _____ _____ a heart attack.
W Yeah, fair point.
M They are also harmful to your blood vessels, which 3)_____ _____ _____ _____ heart problems.
W Oh, I only knew that fried foods were high in calories. The health effects sound scarier than I thought.
M Yeah, that's why I try not to 4)_____ _____ _____.
W Well, why don't we just get a salad, then?
M That's a good idea.

↘ 듣기 필수 표현
· according to ~에 따르면

3

M Hi. How can I assist you today, Ms. Wilson?
W I'm here to apply for a loan.
M I see. I can help you 1)_____ _____ _____ that. First of all, would this be a personal or business loan?
W I'd like to borrow the money to 2)_____ _____ _____ to my business.
M Okay, just a moment. I need to find the relevant form.
W Take your time.
M What kind of business is this for?
W I own an ice cream shop in the Monroe Park area.
M I see. What are you planning to 3)_____ _____ _____ _____?
W We need a new sign because the old one was badly damaged in the recent typhoon.
M Great, I'll pass the form on to the bank manager 4)_____ _____. Please fill it out now.
W Will do. Thanks.

↘ 듣기 필수 표현
· apply for ~을 신청하다
· take one's time 천천히 하다
· pass A on to B A를 B에게 넘기다
· fill out ~을 작성하다

4

M This is the restaurant's private event room, ma'am.
W It will be perfect for my daughter's birthday party.
M I think so. The two paintings of clowns 1)_____ _____ _____ _____.
W I agree. I see there is a microphone set up in the back of the room. Is that usually there?
M No. That was brought in for another event, but I'll put it away if you want.
W Yes, please. Would I be able to get a projector?
M Actually, there's one attached to the ceiling.
W Oh, I see it. Would we be able to 2)_____ _____ _____ by the window?

M That shouldn't be a problem.

W And one last thing. Do you mind if I request another 3)_____ _____? One isn't going to be enough.

M Not at all.

W Great. I'll 4)_____ _____ _____!

5

W It's raining cats and dogs again, Phil. Why doesn't it stop?

M This 1)_____ _____ _____. I'm sure you know that.

W I haven't gone jogging in two weeks now. It's really frustrating.

M Why don't you go to the gym? You can run on the treadmill.

W There is always a long line to use the machine.

M Maybe you could 2)_____ _____ _____ for a couple of weeks.

W But I love running, and it's good for the body.

M You could try table tennis. There's also a pool, so you could swim.

W Actually, table tennis sounds like great fun! Let's 3)_____ _____ _____ _____ and play a few games!

M Give me a few minutes. I just need to change into my sweats.

W Okay! We can go out for ice cream afterwards.

M That's perfect.

↘ 듣기 필수 표현
· rain cats and dogs 비가 억수같이 쏟아지다
· change into ~으로 갈아입다

6

W Good afternoon, sir. Are you having a good time at the festival?

M I am! But it's hot out there. My friends and I are thirsty.

W Well, we have water for $2 per bottle and soft drinks for $3 per can.

M I'll take 1)_____ _____ _____.

W Got it. Did you want anything 2)_____ _____ _____ _____?

M Do you have ice cream?

W Yes. We have chocolate and strawberry ice cream. Cups and cones are both $5 apiece.

M In that case, I'd like three cups of strawberry ice cream.

W I've got two waters, two sodas, and three cups of strawberry ice cream. Does that 3)_____ _____ _____?

M Yes, but can I use this coupon? I'm supposed to get $5 off a purchase.

W Oh, I'm sorry, sir. This coupon is 4)_____ _____ _____ clothing items and souvenirs.

M I understand. I'll pay with cash.

7

M Hi, Kelly. It was good running into you at the theater last weekend.

W 1)_____ _____ _____ we chose the same showing! I might have to go see that movie again, though.

M You 2)_____ _____ _____ _____, right? I noticed you were gone when I came back from the bathroom.

W Yeah. I left in the middle.

M Did you have to catch the last bus? The movie was pretty long.

W No. I 3)_____ _____.

M Then, were you feeling sick? I know you get bad headaches sometimes.

W No. Actually, I got a text message saying that our dog was sick. So I left to 4)_____ _____ _____ _____ _____.

M Oh, no! Is he okay?

W He's doing fine.

M Good. But to be honest, the ending of the movie was pretty boring.

W Then, it sounds like I didn't miss much.

↘ 듣기 필수 표현
· run into ~와 우연히 만나다
· to be honest 솔직히 말해서

8

[Telephone rings.]

M Brooks Catering. This is Dominic speaking. How may I help you?

W Hi. I'm Monica Simms from Adams Library. I want to 1) _____ _____ _____ about the catering for our reopening celebration.

M Sure. Let me pull up our records for that.

W It's scheduled for May 10th.

M Just a second... *[Typing sound]* I've got it. You need 2) _____ _____ _____ _____, correct?

W Right.

M What did you want to check?

W I was 3) _____ _____ _____ _____ you would need to set up before the event.

M We need an hour. Since the dinner starts at 7, we will be there a little before 6.

W Got it. I'll be there to let you in. And do you know 4) _____ _____ _____ _____ _____?

M Yes. The library is on Main Street, next to city hall, right?

W Exactly. I'll see you on that day.

↘ 듣기 필수 표현
· pull up ~을 찾아보다, (기록을) 확인하다
· be scheduled for ~으로 일정이 잡히다

9

M Hello, everyone. I'd like to welcome you all to the Herbert Town Hotdog Festival. Here, hotdog lovers will get the chance to taste as many different hotdogs 1) _____ _____ _____. We've got vendors from all over the country offering delicious hotdogs. So enjoy yourselves. As always, we'll be having a hotdog cooking competition. It will 2) _____ _____ _____ _____ to 2 p.m. All the hotdogs will be prepared by amateur cooks. The judges are the winners of the previous year's competition. May the best cook win! We have a bunch of other programs 3) _____ _____ _____ as well. These include face painting and a race on hotdog carts. Thank you, and enjoy the festival.

↘ 듣기 필수 표현
· enjoy oneself 마음껏 즐기다
· as always 언제나처럼
· a bunch of 많은

10

W Is that an electronics store website? What are you shopping for, Tom?

M I'm looking at portable speakers. I don't know which one to buy, though.

W What's your 1) _____ _____?

M I want to buy one with this $100 store gift card.

W That would eliminate one option if you don't want to spend any of your money.

M That's what I was thinking. I also want 2) _____ _____ _____. I'd like to listen to music outside.

W Then, you should get one that is waterproof.

M Sure. That helps narrow things down.

W What about battery life? You probably want a speaker that can play music for a long time.

M I want 3) _____ _____ _____ of playing time.

W That leaves two. But isn't this one the best choice?

M Hmm... I don't really want a 4) _____ _____.

W In that case, I think the decision is made for you!

↘ 듣기 필수 표현
· narrow down ~을 좁히다

11

W Honey, please wake up. I'm not feeling good.

M Oh, you 1) _____ _____. Tell me what's wrong.

W I'm feeling sick to my stomach. I've been dizzy and throwing up since dawn. Could you 2) _____ _____ _____ _____ _____?

↘ 듣기 필수 표현
· feel sick to one's stomach 메슥거리다
· throw up 토하다

12

M Mom, the 1) _____ _____ _____ _____ drop off a box of pears in front of our house this morning. Did you bring it inside?

W I didn't see anything like that. Are you sure the package arrived?

M Yeah. I got a text message that 2) _____ _____ _____ _____. That's really weird.

↘ 듣기 필수 표현
· drop off ~을 배달하다

13

W You wanted to see me, Mr. Madison?

M Yes. Have a seat. Let's talk about your score on the last math test.

W I was really disappointed.

M I understand. I think you'd better 1)_____ _____ _____ you study.

W Is there anything that you would recommend?

M Yes. You don't show how you 2)_____ _____ _____ in your homework.

W Does that matter?

M When I check your homework, I can't see where you made mistakes. So it's hard to give you the right feedback.

W I see. Then, I should 3)_____ _____ _____ in the process.

M Exactly. Also, you can do more in the classroom.

W I don't know what you mean.

M I see that sometimes you are a little confused and you don't say anything.

W So you're saying that I should 4)_____ _____ _____ _____?

↘ 듣기 필수 표현
· have a seat 자리에 앉다
· make a mistake 실수를 하다

14

M What can I do for you?

W I'd like to buy a women's bicycle.

M Sure, I can help. If you come this way, I'll show you a few different models.

W [Pause] I don't want one with 1)_____ _____ _____ _____. It looks like it would be uncomfortable to ride.

M I see. So you're looking for comfort.

W That's right. I plan to ride it 2)_____ _____ _____ _____ each day, so it needs to be comfortable.

M That makes sense. [Pause] What about this one with big tires?

W That looks better.

M Oh, and how tall are you?

W 160 centimeters. Why?

M It'll help me pick the 3)_____ _____ _____ for you. If you buy a bike with the wrong height, it will be uncomfortable.

↘ 듣기 필수 표현
· make sense 일리가 있다

15

W Michael is a high school student whose favorite subject is art. This year, during the summer break, he 1)_____ _____ _____ _____ _____. To prepare for the class, he needs to buy a few supplies, so he decided to visit an art supply shop. However, he is not sure which paintbrushes he should buy. So he asks Olivia, an employee at the store, to help him 2)_____ _____ _____ _____. Olivia thinks that her recommendation will depend on the art class's requirements. Therefore, she wants to ask Michael 3)_____ _____ _____ about the type of painting he will be making. In this situation, what would Olivia most likely say to Michael?

↘ 듣기 필수 표현
· depend on ~에 따라 달라지다

16~17

M Good afternoon, students. Yesterday, we discussed the origins of several idioms. Today, I want to 1)_____ _____ _____ related to animals. First, let's consider one from Greece. As the saying goes, "every dog has its day." It suggests that lucky situations can come up for anyone. In other words, we all 2)_____ _____ _____ to be successful from time to time. Another common proverb comes from Australia. It is, "Don't count your chickens before they're hatched." This expression warns us not to make plans based on potential alone. After all, not every egg will become a bird. Third, we can look at one from Egypt, "Repetition teaches even a donkey." It suggests that practicing something many times is 3)_____ _____ _____. Lastly, there's an expression from China I want to mention. "Big fish eat small fish." This proverb suggests that the powerful always 4)_____ _____ _____. All right, now I'd like you all to open your textbooks to Page 323.

↘ 듣기 필수 표현
· related to ~과 관련된
· as the saying goes 이른바, 속담에 있듯이
· in other words 다시 말해서
· from time to time 때때로

대학수학능력시험 문제지
영어듣기 모의고사

▲ 문제 음성
바로 듣기

▲ 고사장 버전
바로 듣기

정답 및 해설 p.68

1번부터 17번까지는 듣고 답하는 문제입니다. 1번부터 15번까지는 한 번만 들려주고, 16번부터 17번까지는 두 번 들려줍니다. 방송을 잘 듣고 답을 하시기 바랍니다.

1. 다음을 듣고, 여자가 하는 말의 목적으로 가장 적절한 것을 고르시오.

① 퍼레이드 시작 시간 변경을 공지하려고
② 독립기념관 개관 행사를 안내하려고
③ 도로 통제 조치를 예고하려고
④ 버스 노선을 조회하는 방법을 설명하려고
⑤ 출퇴근 시 대중교통을 이용할 것을 독려하려고

2. 대화를 듣고, 여자의 의견으로 가장 적절한 것을 고르시오.

① 아이들이 심부름하는 것은 교육적 효과가 뛰어나다.
② 어린 아이에게는 과자를 먹게 하면 안 된다.
③ 암산 연습을 하면 수학적 능력을 키울 수 있다.
④ 어린 아이를 홀로 방치하는 것은 위험한 일이다.
⑤ 부모는 자녀가 스스로 집안일을 하도록 교육해야 한다.

3. 대화를 듣고, 두 사람의 관계를 가장 잘 나타낸 것을 고르시오.

① 조명 수리기사 — 경비원
② 사진작가 — 교사
③ 잡지 기자 — 인쇄소 직원
④ 화가 — 미술관 관장
⑤ 체육관 관리인 — 회원

4. 대화를 듣고, 그림에서 대화의 내용과 일치하지 <u>않는</u> 것을 고르시오.

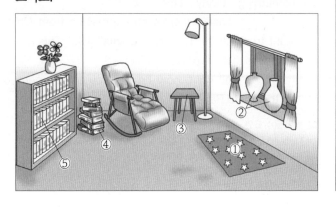

5. 대화를 듣고, 남자가 할 일로 가장 적절한 것을 고르시오.

① 농구팀 지도하기
② 꽃 옮겨심기
③ 체육관 청소하기
④ 운동 장비 정리하기
⑤ 박스 포장하기

6. 대화를 듣고, 남자가 지불할 금액을 고르시오. [3점]

① $72   ② $90   ③ $92   ④ $100   ⑤ $108

7. 대화를 듣고, 남자가 약속을 취소하려는 이유를 고르시오.

① 테니스 수업에 가야 해서
② 일찍 잠자리에 들어야 해서
③ 보드게임을 하고 싶지 않아서
④ 가족과 외식하기로 해서
⑤ 기념품을 사러 가야 해서

8. 대화를 듣고, 돌잔치에 관해 언급되지 <u>않은</u> 것을 고르시오.

① 참석 인원 수   ② 장소   ③ 시작 시간
④ 음식 메뉴   ⑤ 사회자

9. Nature Bicycle Tour of Hungary에 관한 다음 내용을 듣고, 일치하지 <u>않는</u> 것을 고르시오.

① 전체 여정에는 3일이 소요될 것이다.
② 참가자들은 오늘 30킬로미터를 이동할 것이다.
③ 강을 따라 북동쪽으로 자전거를 탈 것이다.
④ 오늘 밤에는 Hotel Citadel에서 묵을 예정이다.
⑤ 자전거에 부착할 위치 감지기가 제공되었다.

10. 다음 표를 보면서 대화를 듣고, 두 사람이 주문할 소파를 고르시오.

Sofa Models

	Model	Seating Capacity	Price	Cushions	Material
①	A	3	$525	O	Polyester
②	B	2	$645	X	Polyester
③	C	4	$650	X	Cotton
④	D	3	$725	O	Leather
⑤	E	4	$900	O	Leather

11. 대화를 듣고, 여자의 마지막 말에 대한 남자의 응답으로 가장 적절한 것을 고르시오.

① All right. Come out when I call you.
② No way. You always lose your umbrellas.
③ You're right. Let's wait for the rain to stop.
④ Sure. What else do you want me to pick up?
⑤ Okay. Remember to come home right after school.

12. 대화를 듣고, 남자의 마지막 말에 대한 여자의 응답으로 가장 적절한 것을 고르시오.

① Sure. I usually prefer swimming to hiking.
② Of course. I enjoyed mountain climbing with him.
③ Why not? It would be nice to have some company.
④ I'm sorry. The summer bus tour is already fully booked.
⑤ Don't worry. I'm sure you'll make a memorable vacation plan.

13. 대화를 듣고, 여자의 마지막 말에 대한 남자의 응답으로 가장 적절한 것을 고르시오.

Man: _____

① I don't think that sounds like my ring tone.
② Where were you when you last used it?
③ I must have left it there when I washed my hands!
④ It was running out of battery when we were at the beach.
⑤ We should call the front desk and mention it's missing.

14. 대화를 듣고, 남자의 마지막 말에 대한 여자의 응답으로 가장 적절한 것을 고르시오. [3점]

Woman: _____

① Sure. That's not too far away from here.
② Great. Let me know when you're heading out.
③ No worries. I brought along a ball to play fetch with.
④ I totally understand. I'll just walk the dog by myself.
⑤ I'm sorry. I really better stay here and study for the test.

15. 다음 상황 설명을 듣고, Amanda가 Barry에게 할 말로 가장 적절한 것을 고르시오. [3점]

Amanda: _____

① You should grow your hair long to change your hairstyle.
② How about getting a perm like you wanted the last time?
③ You can take a seat anywhere you like while you wait.
④ You'd better cut your hair before it gets any longer.
⑤ Why don't we try coloring your hair brown?

[16~17] 다음을 듣고, 물음에 답하시오.

16. 남자가 하는 말의 주제로 가장 적절한 것은?

① advantages of natural energy sources
② reasons that humans started using power
③ ways that various power sources affected civilization
④ effects of energy on ancient farming methods
⑤ how energy sources have become cleaner

17. 언급된 에너지원이 아닌 것은?

① wood　　② water　　③ coal
④ oil　　⑤ sun

> 이제 듣기 문제가 끝났습니다. 채점을 마친 후 다음 페이지에서 방송을 다시 들으며 딕테이션 연습을 하시기 바랍니다.
>
> * 채점 결과: 맞은 개수 _____ 개 / 17개　　　　정답 및 해설 p.68

12회 영어듣기 모의고사 Dictation 음성을 들으며 빈칸에 알맞은 단어를 채워 넣으시기 바랍니다.

1

W Hello, listeners. Here's a quick reminder for you about tomorrow's Independence Day parade. The parade will be taking place from 9 a.m. to noon. The parade will 1)_____ _____ 1st Avenue, so the street will be closed throughout the morning. Many bus routes will also be altered. Therefore, 2)_____ _____ _____ _____ for information on alternative routes before you hop on. Details can be found on the city's website. Traffic in nearby areas will be heavy. I recommend you 3)_____ _____ _____ at home. If you want to come and see the parade, please take the subway. I hope you enjoy the parade.

↘ 듣기 필수 표현
· hop on ~에 탑승하다

2

M Good afternoon, Patricia. What are you doing here?

W I'm waiting for my daughter. She is shopping in this supermarket.

M Isn't she 1)_____ _____ _____ _____ alone?

W No. She's already nine. And I think 2)_____ _____ _____ _____ has great educational effects.

M Why do you think so?

W By remembering the number of items to buy and calculating the total cost, my daughter can 3)_____ _____ _____ .

M Yeah, that makes sense.

W Also, she can develop a sense of responsibility by overcoming the temptation to buy snacks.

M It sounds like asking children to do errands teaches them a lot.

W Seriously! That's why I'm trying to 4)_____ _____ _____ to my daughter.

M I should get my son to help me with the chores, then.

3

W Hi. It's nice to meet you, Mr. Williams.

M You too, Ms. Kelley. Have a seat. You have experience with photo shoots like this, correct?

W That's right. Mainly I do portraits. I can show you 1)_____ _____ _____ _____ _____ .

M Yes. [Pause] Oh, these are excellent.

W Thanks. So you need me to take pictures of students 2)_____ _____ _____ _____ .

M That's correct. Please be here on the 6th of the month.

W Will I be taking the photos in your classroom?

M No. You'll be in the school gym. I'll start bringing students in at 10.

W Good. What time do you want me to 3)_____ _____ _____ that day?

M Come to the teachers' office at 9 in the morning. Since I don't have a class that morning, I'll 4)_____ _____ _____ the gym.

W Perfect. I think I'll have enough time to set up the lighting.

↘ 듣기 필수 표현
· have a seat 자리에 앉다
· take a picture 사진을 찍다
· set up 설치하다

4

W Reece, this is my favorite place in the house. I spend 1)_____ _____ _____ _____ _____ reading books here.

M Everything looks new. Have you been redecorating?

W Yeah! I just got this rug last week.

M The star pattern on it looks great.

W Thanks. What do you think of the two plain vases by the window?

M Those are a nice touch, too.

W I'm 2)_____ _____ _____ the square table next to the armchair, though.

M Don't you need a place to put your coffee when reading?

W Yeah, I'd better not move it, then.

M It looks like you need some more bookshelves. There's
3) _____ _____ _____ _____ on the floor in the corner.

W Oh, we can put those books back on the book shelf. Could you help me?

M Sure. I see the 4) _____ _____ _____ _____.

W Right. Please put them there.

M I see.

5

W Good morning, Liam. Thanks for coming back to volunteer at the community center.

M Hi, Ms. Robinson. I'm 1) _____ _____ _____ _____ again.

W You did a great job coaching the girls' basketball team.

M Thanks. What do you need me to do this time? I saw that you were 2) _____ _____ _____ _____ by the entrance.

W We already have someone taking care of the gardening.

M Then, I could clean up at the gym.

W 3) _____ _____ _____ finished that yesterday. Hold on, let me find something else for you.

M Take your time.

W Okay. A big shipment of 4) _____ _____ _____ _____. So I need you to organize it for us.

M I'd be happy to do it.

W Perfect. The equipment is packed in boxes at the back of the office. Here, I'll show you.

↘ 듣기 필수 표현
· take care of ~을 처리하다
· take one's time 천천히 하다

6

W Hi. How can I help you, sir?

M I'm looking for some jeans.

W Then, I'd like to recommend these two. The blue jeans cost $40, and the black pair costs $50.

M Good. Do you have 1) _____ _____ _____ in a size eight?

W Yes. Here you are. You can try them on in the fitting room.

M Thank you. *[Pause]* Great recommendation. I like the blue ones more. I'll 2) _____ _____ _____ _____.

W Great. I'll ring up two pairs. And you're aware that we're having a sale this week, right?

M Oh, I didn't know that.

W Some of our products are 10% off. You can 3) _____ _____ _____ on the jeans.

M I'm glad I went shopping today. Also, I want to buy that belt displayed beside the fitting room.

W It's $20. But the discount doesn't 4) _____ _____ _____.

M That's okay. I'll take it. Here's my credit card.

↘ 듣기 필수 표현
· try on ~을 입어보다
· ring up 계산하다

7

[Cell phone rings.]

M Hey, Brenda. How's it going?

W Good. I just got back from a tennis lesson.

M I need to talk to you about our plans to play board games at your house tonight.

W You can come later, right?

M I'm sorry, but I have to 1) _____ _____ _____.

W Oh, right. You're leaving on a trip tomorrow. You probably need to go to bed early.

M The flight leaves in the evening. That's not the issue.

W I see. Well, don't you want to play board games? We could 2) _____ _____ _____.

M Board games would be fun. Actually, I forgot that I made plans to go out to eat with my family.

W I see. Well, have fun. Let's hang out when you get back from the trip.

M For sure. I'll 3) _____ _____ _____.

↘ 듣기 필수 표현
· get back from ~에서 돌아오다
· hang out 같이 놀다

8

M Honey, is everything ready for our son's first-birthday party?

W I think so, but we can go over the to-do list one last time.

M Okay. Did you send out the invitations?

W Yes. I sent them last Friday.

M Did you make sure to 1)_____ _____ _____ _____ and friends?

W I did. I'm expecting at least 50 people there. I also mentioned the 2)_____ _____ _____ on the invitation.

M It's beginning at 4 p.m., right?

W That's correct. What about the food? Is everything ready with the caterer?

M Yeah, 3)_____ _____ _____. There's going to be rice cakes, noodles, and a dessert.

W That should work. Did you hire someone 4)_____ _____ _____ _____?

M Of course. I booked a comedian to be the MC.

W I think it's going to be a great party.

M I hope so!

↘ 듣기 필수 표현
· go over ~을 검토하다
· send out ~을 발송하다
· make sure to 확실히 ~하다

9

W Welcome to our Nature Bicycle Tour of Hungary. I'm Claire, your guide for the three-day journey. Today, we are going to 1)_____ _____ 30 kilometers of beautiful landscape where you will see lovely villages and some landmarks. As you can see on your map, we will be 2)_____ _____ along the Danube River. We will enjoy Hungarian cuisine at local restaurants along the way. Tonight, we'll be staying at a place called the Hotel Citadel. Keep in mind that Hungary's summer is very hot and sunny, so you'd better put on sunscreen. Also, 3)_____ _____ _____, the group must stay together. Please attach the GPS sensor that we gave you to your bicycle. Thank you, and enjoy the ride!

↘ 듣기 필수 표현
· keep in mind 명심하다
· put on ~을 바르다

10

M Are you still looking at sofas online, honey?

W Yeah... Actually, do you mind giving me your opinion? It might help me make up my mind.

M Sure. Let me have a look.

W What about this one that seats two people?

M I thought we needed 1)_____ _____ _____ _____ three people.

W Oh, I didn't think about that. You're right. Well, the other ones are the right size.

M Yeah, these are big enough. What about our budget?

W Um, we probably shouldn't 2)_____ _____ _____ $750.

M I agree. What's another option that we should consider?

W What about cushions? Do we need those?

M Yes. I think 3)_____ _____.

W Then, what do you think of the polyester couch?

M I don't like the material. Let's go with a leather one.

↘ 듣기 필수 표현
· give one's opinion ~의 의견을 말하다
· make up one's mind 결정을 내리다
· go with 선택하다

11

[Cell phone rings.]

W Dad, it looks like it's about to rain, and I forgot to 1)_____ _____ _____.

M It's already raining here. Do you want me to come pick you up?

W Yes. I'll 2)_____ _____ _____ inside the school entrance.

↘ 듣기 필수 표현
· be about to 곧 ~할 것이다
· pick up ~를 데리러 가다; 사다 주다

12

M Jessica, do you 1)_____ _____ _____ _____ for summer vacation?

W I'm planning to go hiking in the mountains. It'll be 2)_____ _____ _____.

M Wow. That sounds like a fun plan! Can I join you?

13

M Honey, have you seen my smartphone?

W Um, I don't think so.

M Hmm... I'm worried that I [1)]_____ _____ _____ it at the beach.

W Weren't you using it right when we got back to the hotel room?

M Oh, you're right. I was looking at the weather forecast for tomorrow. But where is it?

W Have you checked your jacket pocket?

M Yeah, I have. It's not there.

W What about under the bed? Maybe you [2)]_____ _____ _____ there.

M One second. *[Pause]* No, I don't see it.

W Okay, do you want me to try calling it for you?

M Good idea. I just hope I didn't set it [3)]_____ _____.

W It's ringing now. Listen out for it.

M I don't hear anything. Do you?

W Wait... I think I hear something buzzing [4)]_____ _____ _____.

↘ 듣기 필수 표현
· listen out 잘 듣다

14

M Clara, I brought you a glass of the apple juice that Mom made. Oh... are you still studying?

W Yeah, I'm a little stressed out about my math exam on Monday.

M Maybe it would be good to take a break [1)]_____ _____ _____.

W I still have a lot of material to get through.

M You might have more energy when you get back to it.

W That's [2)]_____ _____ _____. Well, what are you up to?

M I need to finish some chores. Afterward, I'm planning to go out and walk our dog.

W Where are you going? Is it just a quick walk [3)]_____ _____ _____?

M I want to go over to Logan Park and play with our dog there.

W Oh, that sounds fun. Do you mind if I tag along?

M Not at all. I [4)]_____ _____ _____ _____ in 30 minutes.

↘ 듣기 필수 표현
· take a break 잠시 휴식을 취하다
· get through ~을 끝내다
· go over to (장소)로 넘어가다
· tag along ~를 따라가다

15

W Barry is a regular customer at Amanda's hair salon. He thinks Amanda is a great hairdresser. One day, he notices that his hair is [1)]_____ _____ _____. So he goes to the hair salon to get a haircut. While waiting for his turn, he sees other customers getting a perm or coloring their hair. Suddenly, he thinks that he has stuck with the same hairstyle [2)]_____ _____ _____ _____ and wants to change it. At the same time, he doesn't want to stick out too much. After hearing Barry's explanation, Amanda thinks he should [3)]_____ _____ _____ _____ a lighter color. So Amanda wants to suggest that he get his hair dyed brown. In this situation, what would Amanda most likely say to Barry?

↘ 듣기 필수 표현
· get a haircut 머리를 자르다
· stick with ~을 고수하다
· stick out 눈에 띄다

16~17

M Hello, students. Long before electricity, humans were using other power sources to improve their lives. Today, let's discuss how different sources of energy have [1)]_____ _____ _____ throughout history. First, we have wood. Thousands of years ago, our ancestors learned how to make fires with wood. It allowed people to cook and made it possible to live in colder climates. Second, water is another power source with an ancient history. Waterwheels [2)]_____ _____ _____ since at least 4,000 BC. They were used to grind grain and made farming a more efficient source of food. Third, we need to talk about coal. Coal, which became popular in the 1700s, [3)]_____ _____ _____ than wood. It allowed for the creation of effective steam engines. Finally, the sun may be the most important energy source of our current time period. Solar energy is clean and eco-friendly. Therefore, using it more widely would be an effective way of slowing down [4)]_____ _____. Now, let's watch a related video.

↘ 듣기 필수 표현
· slow down ~을 늦추다

대학수학능력시험 문제지
영어듣기 모의고사

정답 및 해설 p.74

1번부터 17번까지는 듣고 답하는 문제입니다. 1번부터 15번까지는 한 번만 들려주고, 16번부터 17번까지는 두 번 들려줍니다. 방송을 잘 듣고 답을 하시기 바랍니다.

1. 다음을 듣고, 남자가 하는 말의 목적으로 가장 적절한 것을 고르시오.

① 노숙자를 위한 무료 급식소 운영 취지를 알리려고
② 식당 개업 행사를 위한 추가 인력을 모집하려고
③ 배부된 초대장에 잘못 인쇄된 내용을 정정하려고
④ 자원봉사자들을 위해 열리는 만찬회를 공지하려고
⑤ 불우이웃 돕기 행사를 위한 기금을 모금하려고

2. 대화를 듣고, 여자의 의견으로 가장 적절한 것을 고르시오.

① 낮잠을 자면 밤에 깊은 잠을 자기 어렵다.
② 충분한 수면은 우울증 치료에 효과적이다.
③ 일찍 자고 일찍 일어나는 습관이 중요하다.
④ 만성 피로와 수면의 질 사이에는 밀접한 관련이 있다.
⑤ 규칙적인 기상 시간을 유지하는 것이 건강에 좋다.

3. 대화를 듣고, 두 사람의 관계를 가장 잘 나타낸 것을 고르시오.

① 대학생 ― 건축사무소 직원
② 구직자 ― 편집 디자이너
③ 대입 지원생 ― 면접관
④ 컴퓨터 공학자 ― 건설 노동자
⑤ 일러스트레이터 ― 대학 교수

4. 대화를 듣고, 그림에서 대화의 내용과 일치하지 <u>않는</u> 것을 고르시오.

5. 대화를 듣고, 남자가 여자에게 부탁한 일로 가장 적절한 것을 고르시오.

① 과일 자르기
② 청소기 돌리기
③ 접시 꺼내기
④ 대걸레질하기
⑤ 아이스티 만들기

6. 대화를 듣고, 여자가 지불할 금액을 고르시오.

① $50 ② $75 ③ $80 ④ $85 ⑤ $90

7. 대화를 듣고, 남자가 요리 수업을 신청하지 <u>않은</u> 이유를 고르시오.

① 물리학 공부에 전념해야 해서
② 삼촌 병문안을 매주 가야 해서
③ 요리에 더 이상 흥미가 없어서
④ 스케이트보드 연습을 시작해서
⑤ 병원에 입원해야 해서

8. 대화를 듣고, Venice Tour Package에 관해 언급되지 <u>않은</u> 것을 고르시오.

① 잔여석 수 ② 기간 ③ 추천 복장
④ 출발 장소 ⑤ 총비용

9. Annual Guitar-Playing Contest에 관한 다음 내용을 듣고, 일치하지 <u>않는</u> 것을 고르시오.

① 30명의 기타리스트가 대회에 참가했다.
② 참가자들은 세 그룹으로 나뉘었다.
③ 참가자들은 각자 무대에서 한 곡씩 연주할 것이다.
④ 프로 연주자들이 심사위원을 맡았다.
⑤ 수상자가 발표된 후 특별 공연이 이어질 것이다.

10. 다음 표를 보면서 대화를 듣고, 여자가 구입할 소프트볼 배트를 고르시오.

Softball Bats

	Model	Material	Leather Handle	Cost	Length (inches)
①	A	Aluminum	O	$140	28
②	B	Hybrid	O	$145	30
③	C	Aluminum	O	$155	26
④	D	Wood	X	$160	28
⑤	E	Hybrid	X	$170	26

11. 대화를 듣고, 여자의 마지막 말에 대한 남자의 응답으로 가장 적절한 것을 고르시오.

① Oh, no! You are all sweaty now.
② No way! I thought I was hopelessly late.
③ Thanks. It's so kind of you to wait for me.
④ Okay. But you should leave earlier next time.
⑤ My apologies. I'll come back at another time.

12. 대화를 듣고, 남자의 마지막 말에 대한 여자의 응답으로 가장 적절한 것을 고르시오.

① Great. I'd like to reserve a table for six.
② I'm sorry. You should have called us earlier.
③ Too bad. Then, can I cancel the reservation?
④ That's okay. It'll be just me and my husband.
⑤ You can't. We are fully booked this Saturday.

13. 대화를 듣고, 남자의 마지막 말에 대한 여자의 응답으로 가장 적절한 것을 고르시오. [3점]

Woman: _____

① I think it would be smart to hold another promotion.
② Why don't you put the cookie recipe on your website?
③ How about posting a picture of the cookie and mentioning our bakery?
④ What about lowering the price of the peanut butter cookies?
⑤ You can start making more of the most popular cookies.

14. 대화를 듣고, 여자의 마지막 말에 대한 남자의 응답으로 가장 적절한 것을 고르시오. [3점]

Man: _____

① Comedy movies are fun because you hear other people laughing.
② You can come over and watch the film at my house.
③ The theater isn't far from here, so we can take a taxi.
④ Yes, the tickets to the movie will sell out fast.
⑤ Okay, I'll check the movie times right now.

15. 다음 상황 설명을 듣고, Russell이 Mary에게 할 말로 가장 적절한 것을 고르시오. [3점]

Russell: _____

① I am confident you will win the next time.
② Why don't you analyze the previous games?
③ I can teach you a strategy if you want to learn.
④ Let's play again with a different tactic this time.
⑤ What about checking out a chess book from the library?

[16~17] 다음을 듣고, 물음에 답하시오.

16. 여자가 하는 말의 주제로 가장 적절한 것은?

① different trees that can pollinate themselves
② plant survival strategies in harsh conditions
③ various ways that seeds travel to new places
④ why there is such a wide variety of seed types
⑤ how climate affects the growth of young plants

17. 언급된 나무가 <u>아닌</u> 것은?

① oak tree　　　　② maple tree
③ coconut tree　　④ blackberry tree
⑤ pine tree

이제 듣기 문제가 끝났습니다. 채점을 마친 후 다음 페이지에서 방송을 다시 들으며 딕테이션 연습을 하시기 바랍니다.

* 채점 결과: 맞은 개수 _____개 / 17개　　　　정답 및 해설 p.74

13회 Dictation

Dictation 정답 p.74

13회 영어듣기 모의고사 Dictation 음성을 들으며 빈칸에 알맞은 단어를 채워 넣으시기 바랍니다.

1

M Excuse me. I'd like to make an announcement. I want to thank all of you 1)_____ _____ here at Buckington Cares. Our charity organization could not exist without your time and hard work. You have helped the 2)_____ _____ _____ _____. We want to show our appreciation in our own small way by holding a dinner party for you at Jerry's Restaurant. The dinner will be held on December 3rd at 7 p.m. Feel free to 3)_____ _____ _____, and don't forget to bring your invitation. I hope you'll all be able to attend. Once again, thank you so much for your dedication.

↘ 듣기 필수 표현
· feel free to 자유롭게 ~하다

2

M Are you feeling okay, honey?

W I'm just tired. I had a long week.

M Why don't you 1)_____ _____ _____ _____? It is Saturday morning after all.

W Well, I want to start keeping a more 2)_____ _____ _____. I think there are a lot of health benefits to waking up at the same time every day.

M Even if you're feeling tired?

W Yeah. I've read that it really helps your overall health.

M Interesting. What are some of the benefits?

W A steady sleep schedule 3)_____ _____ _____ _____. It makes you less likely to get sad or upset.

M I can see that. I get a bit depressed when I oversleep.

W Me too. Most importantly, getting up at a regular time makes it easier to get a good night's sleep consistently.

M Well, then you'd better stay awake.

↘ 듣기 필수 표현
· after all 어쨌든
· likely to ~할 가능성이 있는, ~할 것 같은

3

M Thanks for meeting with me today, Ms. Lincoln.

W Of course. I understand that you're interested in an internship here at our company.

M That's right. I want to 1)_____ _____ _____ myself one day, so I need as much work experience as possible.

W That's good to hear. And you're majoring in architecture, right?

M Correct. I'm 2)_____ _____ in the fall.

W Have you used computer programs to make architectural designs before?

M Sure. I use them regularly in my courses.

W Okay. That's essential to the work you would do for us. You would 3)_____ _____ _____ _____ construction drawings.

M I think I can do that.

W All right. I hope you have a good experience here at our company.

M Thank you. I'll do my best.

↘ 듣기 필수 표현
· as ~ as possible 가능한 한 ~한/하게
· major in ~을 전공하다
· do one's best 최선을 다하다

4

M Thanks for recommending this dentist's office, Lisa. The lobby is beautiful.

W Right? It makes 1)_____ _____ _____ _____ nicer.

M Exactly. The three potted plants give it a pleasant atmosphere. I don't think I'll go back to my old dentist after coming here.

W That fish tank looks great, too. Do you want to sit in the two chairs in front of it?

M They look pretty uncomfortable. How about that 2)_____ _____ _____ _____ _____ _____?

W Sure. Can you hand me one of those magazines?

M Oh, where are they?

W 3)_____ _____ _____ _____ _____.

M Right. Here you go. *[Pause]* I still have some time before my appointment, right?

W It's in 15 minutes. Mine is right after.

M That's enough time for coffee. Can we use the coffee machine on the cabinet?

W Of course. Would you mind getting some coffee for me?

M No problem. I'll make two cups.

5

W Honey, it's 6 o'clock already. I don't think we'll ever be ready for the party.

M Relax. The house looks fine. It just needs a few more finishing touches.

W Do we have enough snacks?

M Yes. I'm 1)_____ _____ and making a cheese plate.

W Okay. What about the drinks?

M I have some iced tea chilling out back. There's also plenty of soda.

W How about the 2)_____ _____ _____?

M It's all taken care of. We just need to do some last-minute cleaning.

W I already mopped and dusted in the dining room.

M Great. Can you also take care of the living room floor? It needs 3)_____ _____ _____.

W Okay. I'll do it while you keep working on the snacks.

M Sounds like a plan.

↘ 듣기 필수 표현
· be ready for ~할 준비가 되다
· chill out 차게 식히다
· plenty of 많은

6

M Welcome to the National Science Museum. How can I help you?

W Hi. is it right that there's a special offer on tickets today?

M I'm sorry. It's 1)_____ _____ _____. We only offer the 10% discount on tickets sold in the evening.

W Okay. Well, I'm here with my grandparents. You have a 2)_____ _____ _____ _____ _____, right?

M Yes. Tickets are $20 for adults and $15 for seniors.

W Okay. I'll take two senior tickets and one adult.

M Did you want to attend the special exhibition? It's 3)_____ _____ _____ _____.

W Is there a senior price for that?

M I'm afraid not.

W That's fine. I'll take three tickets for that as well.

M Got it. So I've got three general admissions tickets, two with the senior rate, and three special exhibit tickets. Is that correct?

W That's everything. Thanks.

7

W Hey, Nathan. How are your classes going?

M I'm 1)_____ _____ this semester, and it's tough!

W You must be so busy. Didn't you start taking a cooking course on Saturdays?

M Actually, I decided not to sign up for it.

W Ah, you probably need more time to study, right?

M Not really. I'm still free on the weekends usually.

W Are you 2)_____ _____ _____ _____ anymore?

M Oh, no. I still cook whenever I can. Actually, my uncle 3)_____ _____ _____ _____. I've been visiting him on Saturdays.

W How is he doing?

M He's feeling better. But his recovery will take a long time.

W It sounds like he needs your help, then. Well, 4)_____ _____ _____ when you are free. We can go skateboarding while the weather is still nice.

M That's a good idea. I will.

↘ 듣기 필수 표현
· sign up for ~을 신청하다
· take time 시간이 걸리다

8

[Telephone rings.]

M Watford Travel, this is William speaking.

W Hi, William. This is Elizabeth Bowers. I left a message earlier about the Venice Tour Package.

M I was just going to call you. We still have 1)_____ _____ _____ for the trip.

W Great. I'm interested in taking my family, but I wanted to confirm a few things first.

M Sure. What did you want to ask?

W The tour takes place from September 14th to September 20th, right?

M That's correct.

W 2)_____ _____ _____ _____ in Venice at that time of year?

M It's lovely, but it gets cool in the evening. You'll want to pack a light jacket.

W I'll keep that in mind. And does the travel package on your website 3)_____ _____?

M It does. The total cost of $900 includes airfare, accommodations, and boat tours of the city.

W Fantastic. Let's book it.

↘ 듣기 필수 표현
· take place 진행되다
· keep in mind 명심하다

9

W Welcome to the city's second Annual Guitar-Playing Contest. This year we have 30 participants. As you know, our participants are amateur guitarists. I know all of them have been 1)_____ _____ _____ the contest. You won't want to miss any of their performances today. The participants have been 2)_____ _____ _____ _____, which will be judged separately. These are junior, young adult, and adult. Each performer will play a single song on stage. Our judging panel consists of 3)_____ _____ and will be selecting winners from each group. Awards will be given after all of the contestants have performed. While the judges are deciding on the winners, we'll 4)_____ _____ _____ _____ by the city choir.

↘ 듣기 필수 표현
· consist of ~로 구성되다, 이루어지다

10

W Hi, I need to get a bat for my daughter. She's joining a softball league, but I'm 1)_____ _____ _____ _____ to get.

M Of course. Let's start with material. I wouldn't recommend a wooden bat.

W Why not?

M Well, they're generally 2)_____ _____ _____.

W Okay. I'll get one made from some other material. I want her to use this for a while.

M Has your daughter played before?

W Only a month. Why?

M Well, she may need one with a leather handle. It's 3)_____ _____ _____, especially for beginners.

W Sure. I think that's right for her. That leaves only three good options.

M How much were you thinking of spending?

W Not more than $150.

M Got it. Okay... length is another thing to consider.

W Right. I think 4)_____ _____ _____ will fit her better. I'll take it.

M Great choice.

↘ 듣기 필수 표현
· not more than 많아야 ~인

11

W David, 1)_____ _____ a lot. What happened?

M I ran all the way over here, and now I'm late anyway. I'm so sorry.

W But you're 10 minutes early! I think you 2)_____ _____ _____ _____ _____.

↘ 듣기 필수 표현
· all the way 줄곧, 처음부터 끝까지

12

[Telephone rings.]

M Hello, this is Noah's Restaurant.

W Hi. 1)_____ _____ _____ make a reservation for 6 p.m. this Saturday.

M Let me see. *[Pause]* How many guests will there be? We only have 2)_____ _____ _____ _____ on that day.

↘ 듣기 필수 표현
· make a reservation 예약하다

13

W Welcome back, Thomas. How can I help you this morning?

M Hi, Taylor. I'd like a croissant. Oh, and are those new peanut butter cookies?

W Yeah! They're made with [1]_____ _____ _____ I've been working on for a while. Would you like to try a sample?

M I'd love to. *[Pause]* It's really good. This is going to be a popular item at your bakery.

W I thought so too, but so far the [2]_____ _____ _____ _____ _____.

M Are you doing some kind of promotion?

W Right now, if you buy two, you get a third one free.

M Perfect. I'm sure business will pick up soon, then.

W I hope so, but I'm getting a little worried.

M It might help to [3]_____ _____ _____ _____.

W Actually, would you mind spreading the word on social media?

M No problem. What do you [4]_____ _____ _____ _____?

↘ 듣기 필수 표현
· work on ~에 공을 들이다   · pick up (장사가) 잘되다

14

M Hey, Hannah. How was your weekend?

W Good. I went to see a comedy movie called *Noisy Neighbors*.

M Oh, yeah? I've been meaning to watch that.

W [1]_____ _____. I really recommend it.

M Where did you see it? It wasn't playing at the theater near my house.

W I had to take the subway over to West End Village. It's only playing in a few places.

M Were there many people in the theater?

W Yes. It was almost full. But I don't think the movie will be in theaters [2]_____ _____.

M Yeah... It came out a month ago. I'm worried that I [3]_____ _____ _____ _____.

W In any event, it should be on streaming services pretty soon.

M I don't know... It's not the same when you watch a movie at home.

W You can still [4]_____ _____ at the theater I went to, but you'd better hurry.

↘ 듣기 필수 표현
· mean to ~할 셈이다   · come out 개봉하다
· in any event 어쨌든, 아무튼

15

M Mary is a member of her town's chess club. She is [1]_____ _____ _____ and beats most of the other members of the club. Last week, she played several games against a chess master online. Unfortunately, she lost every match they played. As a result, she is [2]_____ _____. One experienced member of the chess club, Russel, notices that she seems very disappointed. Russel thinks that Mary still has a lot to learn from the way that [3]_____ _____ _____. If she wants to reach her full potential as a player, she needs to learn the strategies the master used against her. Therefore, Russell wants to suggest that she [4]_____ _____ _____ she lost last week. In this situation, what would Russell most likely say to Mary?

↘ 듣기 필수 표현
· as a result 결과적으로
· reach one's full potential ~의 잠재력을 최대한 발휘하다

16~17

W Good morning, everyone. In the previous unit, I gave some background information about different methods of plant pollination. Today, I want to discuss how different seeds can [1]_____ _____ _____ _____ to another. First of all, let's consider maple trees. Maple tree seeds have wings that spin. These make them fly like a helicopter and [2]_____ _____ _____ in the wind. The second example is the coconut tree. Its seeds are [3]_____ _____ _____ quite easily in the ocean. Thus, they move through the water to new places. Next, there's the blackberry tree. Tiny blackberry seeds are spread by animals who eat them, travel elsewhere, and then leave the seeds in droppings. Finally, and most unusually, we have the pine tree. Certain pine seeds don't drop off the tree. These are covered in a thick material that only [4]_____ _____ _____ _____ _____. In other words, these seeds can only be spread by forest fires. Let's look at some photos comparing the seeds I've mentioned.

↘ 듣기 필수 표현
· be covered in ~으로 덮여 있다
· in other words 다시 말해서

대학수학능력시험 문제지
영어듣기 모의고사

정답 및 해설 p.80

1번부터 17번까지는 듣고 답하는 문제입니다. 1번부터 15번까지는 한 번만 들려주고, 16번부터 17번까지는 두 번 들려줍니다. 방송을 잘 듣고 답을 하시기 바랍니다.

1. 다음을 듣고, 여자가 하는 말의 목적으로 가장 적절한 것을 고르시오.

① 쇼핑몰 영업시간 변경을 공지하려고
② 쇼핑객 매장 만족도 설문 응답을 요청하려고
③ 쇼핑몰 폐장 전까지 쇼핑 마치기를 재촉하려고
④ 셀프 무인 계산대가 설치된 곳을 안내하려고
⑤ 쇼핑몰의 환불 정책을 설명하려고

2. 대화를 듣고, 남자의 의견으로 가장 적절한 것을 고르시오.

① 운동이 아이들의 건강에 좋지 않을 수 있다.
② 축구는 아이들의 협동심을 키워 준다.
③ 적절한 연습으로 부상의 위험을 줄일 수 있다.
④ 부모는 자녀의 결정을 지지해 주어야 한다.
⑤ 경쟁을 통해 아이들의 의욕을 고취시킬 수 있다.

3. 대화를 듣고, 두 사람의 관계를 가장 잘 나타낸 것을 고르시오.

① 신문 기자 — 경찰관
② TV쇼 진행자 — 소방관
③ 방송 작가 — 외과 의사
④ 라디오 진행자 — 구급대원
⑤ 카메라 감독 — 애니메이션 성우

4. 대화를 듣고, 그림에서 대화의 내용과 일치하지 않는 것을 고르시오.

5. 대화를 듣고, 남자가 할 일로 가장 적절한 것을 고르시오.

① 택시 부르기
② 아내 데리러 가기
③ 보고서 제출하기
④ 세탁물 찾아오기
⑤ 학부모 상담 신청하기

6. 대화를 듣고, 여자가 지불할 금액을 고르시오.

① $160 ② $210 ③ $225 ④ $250 ⑤ $260

7. 대화를 듣고, 남자가 비행기에서 계속 깨어 있었던 이유를 고르시오.

① 낮잠을 충분히 자서
② 다리를 뻗을 공간이 부족해서
③ 난기류로 비행기가 흔들거려서
④ 다른 승객이 너무 시끄러워서
⑤ 커피를 너무 많이 마셔서

8. 대화를 듣고, Heather의 생일 파티에 관해 언급되지 않은 것을 고르시오.

① 날짜 ② 장소 ③ 복장
④ 제공 간식 ⑤ 선물

9. Parkwood Dance Program에 관한 다음 내용을 듣고, 일치하지 않는 것을 고르시오.

① 4명의 댄스 강사가 수업을 지도한다.
② 매일 오전 8시부터 오후 6시까지 진행된다.
③ 초보자들을 대상으로 열리는 수업이다.
④ 프로그램 내내 강사들이 피드백을 줄 것이다.
⑤ 프로그램의 말미에 공연이 있을 것이다.

10. 다음 표를 보면서 대화를 듣고, 남자가 구매할 셔츠를 고르시오.

Shirt Styles

	Style	Size	Price	Fabric Type	Sleeve-length
①	A	Large	$16	polyester	half-sleeve
②	B	Large	$18	100% cotton	full-length
③	C	Medium	$20	cotton blend	half-sleeve
④	D	Large	$24	100% cotton	half-sleeve
⑤	E	Large	$29	cotton blend	full-length

11. 대화를 듣고, 여자의 마지막 말에 대한 남자의 응답으로 가장 적절한 것을 고르시오.

① I hope we can sit together on the bus.
② Did you already pay for the bus tickets?
③ It won't take us long to get there by taxi.
④ Do you need help carrying your suitcases?
⑤ I've been waiting at the station for an hour.

12. 대화를 듣고, 남자의 마지막 말에 대한 여자의 응답으로 가장 적절한 것을 고르시오.

① Thanks for buying the movie tickets last night.
② What did you think of the movie we watched?
③ It's great that we hang out together so much.
④ I'm free tomorrow if you want to go then.
⑤ My yoga class has a lot of new members.

13. 대화를 듣고, 여자의 마지막 말에 대한 남자의 응답으로 가장 적절한 것을 고르시오. [3점]

Man: _____

① I almost forgot to turn on the dishwasher.
② Then, make sure to use lots of dish soap.
③ I'm glad you liked the food I prepared.
④ I haven't finished doing the dishes yet.
⑤ Please send me a copy of the recipe.

14. 대화를 듣고, 남자의 마지막 말에 대한 여자의 응답으로 가장 적절한 것을 고르시오. [3점]

Woman: _____

① Great. I'll go get the book for you.
② Look here. She signed it on the first page.
③ I agree. I think the book has an exciting story.
④ Okay. Let's ask the librarian if it was returned yet.
⑤ No, thanks. I don't have enough time to read these days.

15. 다음 상황 설명을 듣고, Marcus가 Emma에게 할 말로 가장 적절한 것을 고르시오. [3점]

Marcus: _____

① I'm afraid we don't have any openings for the receptionist position.
② You will need to complete an online form in order to volunteer here.
③ Why don't you offer to help at the other shelter in the neighborhood?
④ Please write down your personal information in pen.
⑤ I'll ask a volunteer to help with your pet.

[16~17] 다음을 듣고, 물음에 답하시오.

16. 남자가 하는 말의 주제로 가장 적절한 것은?

① the origins of a music genre
② ways that music affects economies
③ how various cities attract musicians
④ a comparison of different musical styles
⑤ why certain areas generate popular music

17. 언급된 도시가 <u>아닌</u> 것은?

① Nashville   ② Seoul
③ New Orleans   ④ Vienna
⑤ Sydney

이제 듣기 문제가 끝났습니다. 채점을 마친 후 다음 페이지에서 방송을 다시 들으며 딕테이션 연습을 하시기 바랍니다.

* 채점 결과: 맞은 개수 _____ 개 / 17개   정답 및 해설 p.80

Dictation 정답 p.80

14회 영어듣기 모의고사 Dictation 음성을 들으며 빈칸에 알맞은 단어를 채워 넣으시기 바랍니다.

1

W Attention, shoppers. We would like to remind you that the Waterford Mall will be closing at 8 p.m. Therefore, I'd like to recommend that you ¹⁾_____ _____ _____ within the next 15 minutes. Please make your final selections soon. If you have chosen all the items you want to buy, please bring them to the checkout counter right now. We may not be able to assist you with ²⁾_____ _____ _____ after 8. Keep in mind that our self-checkout kiosks are available, which will let you skip the line at the cash register. Thank you for ³⁾_____ _____, and enjoy the rest of your evening.

↘ 듣기 필수 표현
· make a selection 선택하다
· keep in mind 명심하다
· skip a line 줄을 서지 않다

2

W Hey, Terry. Your son wasn't at soccer practice this morning. Is he still on the team?

M Actually, he's decided not to play, Michelle.

W Is there anything wrong?

M He wasn't enjoying soccer anymore. Besides, I don't think sports are ¹⁾_____ _____ _____ _____.

W Really? Isn't it a great way to learn teamwork?

M I'm worried that he might get hurt. Head injuries in particular can ²⁾_____ _____ _____ _____.

W You have a point. There are a lot of fitness benefits, though.

M Sure, but the competition has negative emotional effects. The pressure to win creates too much stress.

W Hmm... it seems like you've made up your mind.

M Yeah. I ³⁾_____ _____ _____ _____ _____.

W Well, I hope he finds an activity that he enjoys more.

M That would be great.

↘ 듣기 필수 표현
· in particular 특히
· You have a point. 일리가 있는 말이야.
· make up one's mind 결단을 내리다

3

W My name is Sara Porter, and I will be interviewing Brandon Harper today. Welcome to the show, Mr. Harper.

M Thanks. I'm a little nervous. I've never been on TV before.

W ¹⁾_____ _____ _____ isn't so scary, especially compared to the work you usually do.

M Well... I have training for that.

W You're doing fine. Let's talk about what happened on May 15th. You saved three people ²⁾_____ _____ _____ _____, right?

M Yes. I'm just glad that I rescued everyone.

W Was anyone injured?

M One person had some scratches, but nothing serious.

W So how does it feel to be a hero?

M I don't think I'm a hero. I did what ³⁾_____ _____ _____ _____ would do. I'm just glad I was able to help.

W You are so humble! I'm sure most of my viewers think what you did was amazing.

M Thanks. I really appreciate that.

↘ 듣기 필수 표현
· compared to ~에 비하면, ~에 비해

4

M Hi, Emily!

W Hey, Luke. What's all this outside the library?

M It's an event to ¹⁾_____ _____ _____ _____.

W Oh, I love the balloons over the entrance.

M Yeah. It seems like a fun event.

W Why is that table set up on the pathway?

M That's where they have books recommended for kids.

W I see. And they must have set up those ²⁾_____ _____ _____ _____ so people could read outside, right?

M Yeah! They're open to anyone. Why don't we go sit down?

W Absolutely! Just let me return my books first. Do you want to meet up at the bench ³)_____ _____ _____?

M Sure. Oh, I'm going to get one of those drinks they're selling over at that booth with the ⁴)_____ _____. Do you want anything?

W Yeah. Could you get me a lemonade?

M Of course! See you in a minute.

↘ 듣기 필수 표현
· set up ~을 설치하다

5

[Cell phone rings.]

W Honey, will you be home soon? We're supposed to be at the parent-teacher conference in an hour.

M I'll be leaving the office in a minute.

W Don't forget to get the dry cleaning on the way home.

M Sorry, but I don't think I can. And honestly, I'm not sure if I have enough time to ¹)_____ _____ _____, either.

W Okay, never mind. We can do that later. I'll head over to the school myself.

M Are you taking your car there?

W No. It'll be easier to just call a taxi.

M Okay, that makes sense. We can go home in my car.

W Great. Let's meet ²)_____ _____ _____ _____ of the school in 30 minutes.

M Sure. I just need to turn in a report to my manager, and then I'll be out of here.

W Got it. Call me if ³)_____ _____ _____.

↘ 듣기 필수 표현
· head over to ~로 가다, 향하다
· turn in ~을 제출하다

6

M Welcome to the Delta Baseball Stadium. How can I help you?

W Hi, I was wondering if you ¹)_____ _____ _____ _____ for tonight's game.

M Sure. We have seats on the upper level for $30 and seats on the lower level for $50.

W Okay, great. I'll take five tickets in ²)_____ _____ _____ of the stadium.

M We also have a special offer this afternoon. You can buy a baseball player figure for only $5.

W Those are cute. Why not? I'll take two of those.

M Great. You should see the total price on your screen.

W Oh, just a moment. Is there ³)_____ _____ _____ for the tickets?

M I'm sorry. You need to buy more than 10 tickets to ⁴)_____ _____ the 20% group discount.

W Ah, that's fine. Here's my credit card.

M Great. Enjoy the game, tonight!

W Thank you.

↘ 듣기 필수 표현
· Why not? 그거 좋죠.

7

W Welcome back to Toronto, Tom!

M It's good to finally be back home, Liz.

W How was your flight? Did you get any sleep?

M No. I was ¹)_____ _____ _____ _____.

W Did you watch some movies?

M No. I didn't really feel like doing that.

W Were the other ²)_____ _____ _____? That's the worst.

M Actually, it was pretty quiet, and it wasn't a bumpy flight.

W Did you drink too much coffee? That always keeps me awake.

M No. It was because I didn't have enough ³)_____ _____ _____ _____. I couldn't stretch my legs out at all.

W You'll need some rest, then. How about taking a nap this afternoon?

M I'd better try to stay awake so I can avoid jet lag.

W That's a good idea.

↘ 듣기 필수 표현
· feel like (doing) ~할 기분이다
· stretch one's legs out 다리를 쭉 뻗다
· take a nap 낮잠 자다
· stay awake 깨어 있다
· avoid jet lag 시차 적응을 하다

8

W Chris, are you going to Heather's birthday party?

M I was planning to. What about you?

W Of course. It's going to be ¹⁾_____ _____ _____ _____ _____, right?

M Yeah. And the party will be held at Heather's house.

W She said that her house was going to be decorated for the party.

M Right. It's going to have ²⁾_____ _____ _____.

W Oh, that sounds fun. So, should I wear a costume or something?

M I don't think so. We can just wear casual clothes.

W Okay. One other thing, ³⁾_____ _____ _____ _____ are you going to get her?

M I'm thinking of buying her a ticket to the musical *Captain Hook*. She is a huge fan of it.

W Oh, right! I'm sure she'll like your present.

M Yeah. I hope so. This party will be a lot of fun, anyway.

↘ 듣기 필수 표현
· be a huge fan of ~의 엄청난 팬이다

9

W Welcome to the Parkwood Dance Program. My name is Marilyn Higgins, and I'll be one of the ¹⁾_____ _____ who will guide you for the next two weeks of intensive practice. The classes are held from 8 a.m. to 6 p.m. every day. Obviously, this will require a lot of energy. But considering that ²⁾_____ _____ _____ are allowed to join our program, all of you will be fine. Throughout the program, you'll have lots of time to practice, and you'll get feedback from the instructors. So you'll really improve if you work hard. At the end of the program, we'll ³⁾_____ _____ _____ for your friends and family. It'll be a perfect opportunity to show off what you've learned. Okay, let's get to it!

↘ 듣기 필수 표현
· show off ~을 뽐내다, 자랑하다
· Let's get to it! 시작해봅시다!

10

M Jennifer, can you help me choose a shirt?

W Sure, but there are a lot of options. Is there one you had your eye on in particular?

M Not really. But I want a bigger one than what I got last time.

W You ¹⁾_____ _____ _____ _____, right? We should look at large shirts, then.

M Oh, and I shouldn't spend more than $25 on a shirt.

W That's helpful. What do you think of this one?

M Hmm... It ²⁾_____ _____ _____ _____ when I touch it. It wouldn't be comfortable.

W In that case, I'd recommend getting something that's made of 100% cotton. It will be the softest choice.

M I agree. That still leaves a couple of options.

W Do you want ³⁾_____ _____?

M No. I'm planning to wear the shirt during the summer.

W Okay, then this half-sleeve shirt should be perfect for you.

M You're right. I'll take it.

↘ 듣기 필수 표현
· have one's eye on 눈여겨보다

11

W Are you almost ¹⁾_____ _____ _____ _____ the bus station, Jamie?

M I just need to put a few things in my suitcase, Mom. Give me five more minutes.

W I'm a little worried. Our bus leaves in 40 minutes. Do you think we'll ²⁾_____ _____ _____ _____ on time?

12

[Cell phone rings.]

M Hi, Beth. I was thinking of ¹⁾_____ _____ _____ _____ this evening. Are you interested?

W I'd love to, but I have a yoga class. It won't finish until 9.

M Oh, that's too bad. I haven't ²⁾_____ _____ _____ _____ _____, and I want to spend some time with you.

↘ 듣기 필수 표현
· not A until B B는 되어야 A하다
· That's too bad. 유감이다.

13

W Thanks for making dinner, Grandpa. That was delicious.
M I'm glad you liked it. It's a very old recipe that I [1)]_____ _____ _____ .
W It was very tasty. Do you need some help cleaning up?
M That would be great. Could you do the dishes?
W Sure. I'll [2)]_____ _____ _____ that right now.
M Thanks. You can just put everything into the dishwasher.
W That seems easy. Cleaning up won't take long at all.
M Oh, hold on... Those pans have a lot of oil on them. I don't think they can [3)]_____ _____ _____ the dishwasher.
W Should I rinse them out first?
M That's right. And maybe wipe them with the cloth.
W Hmm... If I am going to do that, I might as well [4)]_____ _____ _____ _____ _____ .

14

M Hi, Natalie. Did you go to the book signing last night?
W I did! I also [1)]_____ _____ _____ to speak with the author, Kate Snow.
M You've been reading her books for years. That must have been exciting.
W You can say that again! She gave me some advice about [2)]_____ _____ _____ _____ , too.
M Wow. That was very kind of her.
W I know. She's great. Have you ever read any of her books?
M No, I haven't. But I am planning to soon.
W You should start with *The Golden Coral*. It's one of my favorite books.
M Let me write down the title. I'll get a copy next time I'm at the library.
W [3)]_____ _____ _____ _____ if you like.
M That would be great. I want to find out why you're such a big fan.

15

W Emma is a high school student who wants to [1)]_____ _____ _____ one day. She is eager to know as much as she can, so she has been thinking about volunteering at [2)]_____ _____ . Today, she finally visited the shelter in her neighborhood. Unfortunately, Emma learns that she cannot volunteer today. As Marcus, the receptionist, explains, the shelter [3)]_____ _____ _____ _____ working at the moment. Furthermore, all volunteers are required to register online in advance, which she has not done. Therefore, Marcus wants to suggest that Emma fill out [4)]_____ _____ _____ on the shelter's website so that she can volunteer later. In this situation, what would Marcus most likely say to Emma?

16~17

M Hello, everyone. Last Friday, we discussed the [1)]_____ _____ _____ _____ _____ . I want to discuss how music can have a major impact on an economy this time. First, let's look at Nashville, the center of country music. Nashville is famous for hundreds of music venues. Live music here is a true industry. It contributes $5 billion annually to the small city's economy. Another notable example is Seoul. K-pop albums and concerts [2)]_____ _____ _____ on their own. But the genre has also boosted the city's tourism. Next up is New Orleans, which is considered one of the jazz capitals of the world. [3)]_____ _____ _____ visit the city every year to hear jazz music. The money they spend on concerts, hotels, and restaurants are an important part of the city's economy. Finally, I'll mention Vienna. During the time of Mozart and Beethoven, it was the center of the music world. Publishers in the city generated [4)]_____ _____ selling copies of their sheet music. Now, let's have a quick look at a video.

15회

제3교시

대학수학능력시험 문제지
영어듣기 모의고사

▲ 문제 음성
바로 듣기

▲ 고사장 버전
바로 듣기

정답 및 해설 p.86

1번부터 17번까지는 듣고 답하는 문제입니다. 1번부터 15번까지는 한 번만 들려주고, 16번부터 17번까지는 두 번 들려줍니다. 방송을 잘 듣고 답을 하시기 바랍니다.

1. 다음을 듣고, 여자가 하는 말의 목적으로 가장 적절한 것을 고르시오.

① 봉사활동과 물품 기부 참여를 요청하려고
② 화재 사고 예방 캠페인을 홍보하려고
③ 구호 단체의 설립 목적을 설명하려고
④ 자연재해의 위력에 대해 경고하려고
⑤ 이재민 대피소를 공지하려고

2. 대화를 듣고, 여자의 의견으로 가장 적절한 것을 고르시오.

① 저녁에 고열량 음식을 먹는 것은 건강에 해롭다.
② 식욕 억제제에 대한 경각심을 키워야 한다.
③ 일부 식당에서는 몸에 좋지 않은 음식을 제공한다.
④ 식전 디저트가 건강한 식사를 위한 방법일 수 있다.
⑤ 식사 순서를 바꾸는 것은 혈당 관리에 효과적이다.

3. 대화를 듣고, 두 사람의 관계를 가장 잘 나타낸 것을 고르시오.

① 손님 — 약사
② 문병객 — 간호사
③ 환자 — 접수원
④ 테니스 선수 — 의사
⑤ 투숙객 — 호텔 지배인

4. 대화를 듣고, 그림에서 대화의 내용과 일치하지 않는 것을 고르시오.

5. 대화를 듣고, 남자가 여자를 위해 할 일로 가장 적절한 것을 고르시오.

① 음반 녹음하기
② 밴드 가입하기
③ 멤버 모집 돕기
④ 연습 시간 정하기
⑤ 기타 수업 듣기

6. 대화를 듣고, 여자가 지불할 금액을 고르시오. [3점]

① $90   ② $100   ③ $110   ④ $120   ⑤ $130

7. 대화를 듣고, 남자가 여행을 미루려는 이유를 고르시오.

① 기차표를 못 구해서
② 가족 간에 원하는 날짜가 달라서
③ 휴가 신청이 승인되지 않아서
④ 가족 모두가 함께 모이기를 원해서
⑤ 출장 일정이 잡혀서

8. 대화를 듣고, Artists Convention에 관해 언급되지 않은 것을 고르시오.

① 날짜   ② 준비물   ③ 장소
④ 참가자 수   ⑤ 신청 방법

9. Teen Readers Week에 관한 다음 내용을 듣고, 일치하지 않는 것을 고르시오.

① 9월 21일부터 27일까지 진행된다.
② 십 대들의 독서를 장려하는 것을 목표로 한다.
③ 금요일과 토요일에는 약식 토론이 열릴 것이다.
④ 참가자들은 최근 읽은 책에 관해 이야기할 수 있다.
⑤ 웹사이트에 참가자들이 읽은 책 목록이 게시된다.

10. 다음 표를 보면서 대화를 듣고, 남자가 구매할 어항을 고르시오.

Fish Tanks

	Model	Material	Size	Cost	Stand
①	A	Glass	20L	$45	X
②	B	Glass	25L	$30	X
③	C	Glass	30L	$55	O
④	D	Plastic	35L	$60	O
⑤	E	Glass	40L	$65	X

11. 대화를 듣고, 남자의 마지막 말에 대한 여자의 응답으로 가장 적절한 것을 고르시오.

① We should call someone to fix it.
② Please leave your dishes in the sink.
③ We just need to do repairs on the floor.
④ Make sure to turn off the faucet next time.
⑤ The sink hasn't been cleaned since yesterday.

12. 대화를 듣고, 여자의 마지막 말에 대한 남자의 응답으로 가장 적절한 것을 고르시오.

① I think so. I'm in need of a new car.
② No problem. Just give me a moment.
③ Don't worry. I'll wait for you to move.
④ It's okay. You can park there if you want.
⑤ Of course not. I can get the door for you.

13. 대화를 듣고, 남자의 마지막 말에 대한 여자의 응답으로 가장 적절한 것을 고르시오.

Woman: _____

① Take it easy. It's a lot easier than you think.
② I don't know. I've never played it before.
③ Don't give up. You haven't even tried it.
④ Me too. I had a great time at college.
⑤ Not really. But I enjoy playing.

14. 대화를 듣고, 여자의 마지막 말에 대한 남자의 응답으로 가장 적절한 것을 고르시오. [3점]

Man: _____

① Of course. I just need your email address.
② What a relief. I thought it might take too long.
③ Oh, dear. I'm not sure I can afford a trip to Turkey.
④ Great! So when can you give me your feedback?
⑤ Thank you. I'll send you the ticket by e-mail.

15. 다음 상황 설명을 듣고, Abigail이 그녀의 오빠에게 할 말로 가장 적절한 것을 고르시오. [3점]

Abigail: _____

① That's okay. We should just order food next week instead.
② I understand. I can find someone else to move in to the apartment.
③ I'm sorry. I didn't know you were planning to go on a trip next week.
④ That's great. I'll call the cleaner and see if she's available next week.
⑤ Don't worry. I'll take care of all the household chores next week.

[16~17] 다음을 듣고, 물음에 답하시오.

16. 남자가 하는 말의 주제로 가장 적절한 것은?

① ways that ants work together
② differences between ant species
③ why ants live in large communities
④ special characteristics of ants' bodies
⑤ the reason for ants' incredible strength

17. 언급된 부위가 아닌 것은?

① feet   ② necks   ③ stomachs
④ eyes   ⑤ antennae

이제 듣기 문제가 끝났습니다. 채점을 마친 후 다음 페이지에서 방송을 다시 들으며 딕테이션 연습을 하시기 바랍니다.

* 채점 결과: 맞은 개수 _____개 / 17개   정답 및 해설 p.86

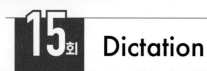

Dictation 정답 p.86

15회 영어듣기 모의고사 Dictation 음성을 들으며 빈칸에 알맞은 단어를 채워 넣으시기 바랍니다.

1

W May I have your attention, please? The Emergency Care Club is asking for volunteers to help with the 1)_____ _____ _____ _____. Our club needs volunteers to prepare and serve meals for those whose homes were burned. If you do not have 2)_____ _____ _____, we can provide training. Please visit the club at the corner of Main and Fifth Streets. Our club is also looking to receive donations of cash, old clothes, bottled water, and canned goods. You may 3)_____ _____ _____ at any time. We ask that volunteers not donate fruit, vegetables, or other food items that can go bad quickly.

↘ **듣기 필수 표현**
· ask for ~를 찾다; 요청하다
· look to ~하기를 기대하다
· go bad 상하다, 썩다

2

M Shelly, our reservation is for 7 p.m. Let's head to the restaurant.

W Sure, but I want to stop by the convenience store here to get a candy bar.

M Right now? Won't that 1)_____ _____ _____ for dinner?

W Actually, eating a little dessert first is a good way to eat healthier.

M You're going to have to explain this to me.

W Well, let me ask you this. What were you thinking of ordering for dinner?

M I wanted tacos with some nachos on the side.

W Right, nachos are a rather unhealthy side dish. But if you have a 2)_____ _____ _____, you might want something healthier instead.

M Oh, I see. So it 3)_____ _____ _____ for something unhealthy.

W Exactly. So you'll end up ordering a salad afterward.

↘ **듣기 필수 표현**
· stop by 들르다
· end up 결국 ~하게 되다

3

W Hello. Can I ask you a favor?

M Sure. What is it?

W I'm looking for a patient who was admitted to this hospital two days ago. I think he's on this floor.

M Can you tell me his name, please?

W It's Kyle Bradley.

M Okay, just give me a moment. *[Pause]* I'm sorry, but I don't see that name on 1)_____ _____ _____ _____. Are you sure you have the right floor?

W Well, I'm not absolutely sure. He injured his elbow playing tennis, and he is supposed to 2)_____ _____ tomorrow.

M I see. I'll check the full list of the patients in our hospital. So please hold on a second.

W All right.

M *[Typing sound]* Ma'am, he's on the sixth floor. That's Room 614. You can 3)_____ _____ _____ down the hall.

W Thank you so much.

↘ **듣기 필수 표현**
· be admitted to hospital 병원에 입원하다
· hold on 기다리다

4

M Hi, Louise. I heard you're going to have a garage sale. How are your preparations for it going?

W Great. These two tables that I'm selling were the last things I 1)_____ _____ _____ _____.

M I see you have some children's toys in a bin to the right of the tables.

W Yes, since my kids are all grown up, we don't need them anymore.

M Are you also selling that 2)_____ _____ _____ the bin?

W I'm not selling it, but I want to clean it before any customers come.

M What about the 3)_____ _____ _____ _____?

W It needs to be fixed, so I'm not charging a lot of money for it.

M You've 4)_____ _____ _____ on the shelf to the left really well.

W They're mostly out of fashion.

M Well, they look great. I bet lots of people will want them.

W Thanks! I hope you're right.

↘ 듣기 필수 표현
· out of fashion 유행이 지난

5

W Alex, I'm planning to 1)_____ _____ _____.

M Really? Are you going to record an album?

W No, nothing like that. I'm looking for friends who are interested in playing music 2)_____ _____ _____.

M You're a singer, right? So I suppose you're looking for people to play instruments.

W Yeah, I am. I'd love to recruit three or four other people.

M Have you found anyone yet?

W Not yet. But I know you have been taking guitar lessons. 3)_____ _____ _____ _____ _____?

M Well, I'm pretty busy these days. I would only be able to practice on Saturday afternoons.

W That's fine. I can schedule our rehearsals for then.

M Okay, I'll be 4)_____ _____ _____.

W Great! This is going to be fun!

6

M Welcome to the Harborview Amusement Park. What can I do for you today?

W Hi. How much is the entrance fee?

M It is $40 for adults and $20 for children.

W Okay. I'd like to pay for two adults and one child, please.

M Of course. Oh, I just realized it is after 4 p.m. That means you get 20% 1)_____ _____ _____ _____.

W Oh, that's great. Thanks for letting me know.

M No problem. Do you want to buy any 2)_____ _____ _____ _____?

W How much do they cost?

M A set of 10 tickets is $15.

W I'll get 3)_____ _____, please. Can I pay with credit card?

M Of course. Let me confirm your purchases.

W Sure, go ahead.

M Entrance tickets for two adults and 4)_____ _____ with a 20% discount, and two sets of ride tickets. Is it correct?

W Yes. Here is my card.

↘ 듣기 필수 표현
· in advance 미리

7

W Jim, you must be excited about your trip to your hometown in December.

M Actually, I may need to 1)_____ _____ _____ by a month.

W Oh, no. Was your leave request rejected by your manager?

M No. He was very understanding and 2)_____ _____ _____ _____.

W Are there no more train tickets available?

M That doesn't seem to be an issue yet. There are many seats left.

W Then, 3)_____ _____ _____ for the delay?

M Well, my sister has to go on a business trip that month and won't be back until January.

W Oh, so you want to visit when all your family can be together, right?

M That's it. We're trying to find the dates when 4)_____ _____ _____ _____.

W I hope everything works out for you.

8

M Hi, Jill. Are you going to the Artists Convention?

W Oh, I hadn't heard about it. Please tell me more.

M It's an event where people can show their work to
1)_____ _____ and get feedback.

W That would be really useful for me. Is it happening soon?

M It's being held on April 28th.

W Great. I think I can make it.

M If you want to come, you would just need to 2)_____
_____ _____ _____ you've been working on.

W I can do that. Where is it being held?

M It's going to be at Parker Community College.

W Okay. Do I just show up, or do I need to register?

M 3)_____ _____ _____. There's a website for
it. I'll send a link to it in an email.

W Thanks for letting me know about this event!

↘ **듣기 필수 표현**
· make it 가다, 참석하다
· show up 가다, 나타나다

9

M Good morning, students. I'm the head librarian at
Monroe Public Library. We are holding a special event
1)_____ _____ _____ _____ _____.
It's called Teen Readers Week, and it's aimed at
encouraging teenagers to read more. Teenagers usually
associate reading with preparing for a class or studying
for an exam. But reading can be enjoyable, too! From
Monday through Friday, teenagers who sign up for this
event will 2)_____ _____ _____ _____.
They can talk about their favorite books or books they
have read recently. Participants can also share lists
of books they've 3)_____ _____ _____
_____. These lists will be posted on the Teen
Readers' board on our website. Sign up, and read for
fun!

↘ **듣기 필수 표현**
· be aimed at ~을 목표로 하다
· associate A with B A를 B와 연관시키다

10

W What are you looking at, Josh?

M I'm getting some fish to keep as pets. But first I need to
buy a fish tank for them.

W This one looks really nice. I like its unique shape.

M It caught my eye as well. But it's 1)_____ _____
_____, and I don't like that material.

W How big of a tank do you need?

M It has to hold at least 2)_____ _____ _____
_____. I'm planning to get three fish.

W Well, that leaves you with a few options.

M Yeah, but I think I can eliminate this one. I don't want to
spend more than $60 on the tank.

W Oh, look! One of the remaining tanks comes with a
stand.

M I definitely want one with a stand. That will make it
3)_____ _____ _____ _____ _____
on my table.

W Then, I guess your choice is clear.

↘ **듣기 필수 표현**
· catch one's eye 눈길을 끌다
· at least 최소한
· come with ~이 딸려 있다

11

M What's the matter, honey? There's water 1)_____
_____ _____ _____ here.

W I'm not sure. 2)_____ _____ is turned off. I just
checked it!

M Let me see. *[Pause]* Oh, the pipe under the kitchen sink
is leaking.

↘ **듣기 필수 표현**
· turn off ~을 잠그다

12

W Hi. I'm 1)_____ _____ _____ you, but is this
your car?

M It is. Oh, it seems I've parked too close to yours.

W Would you 2)_____ _____ _____ _____ _____ a
bit so I can open my door?

13

M It's raining again, Christine.

W That's too bad. It's been raining so much these days.

M I know! I <u>1)_____ _____ _____</u> basketball with my friends. We were going to play in the park.

W You can always play on an indoor court.

M I wasn't <u>2)_____ _____ _____</u> the one at the gym. Some other group is using it.

W You could do another <u>3)_____ _____ _____ _____ _____</u>.

M My friends and I aren't into table tennis.

W You could also go bowling. A new place just opened on Pine Street.

M That sounds like a good idea. I think I'll do that.

W Could I go with you?

M Do you know how to bowl?

W I <u>4)_____ _____ _____</u> in my first year of college.

M I didn't know that. Are you good at bowling?

↘ 듣기 필수 표현
· be into ~을 좋아하다
· be good at ~을 잘하다

14

[Phone rings.]

M Golden Travel Agency. May I help you?

W Hi. Can you recommend a Southeast Asian country to visit at this time of year?

M Actually, it's now the <u>1)_____ _____</u> in Southeast Asia.

W Oh, I didn't know that. Hmm... Where can I go instead?

M May I suggest Turkey? It has a nice Mediterranean climate.

W Is there anything to do there?

M Absolutely! Aside from its many <u>2)_____ _____</u>, there are excellent seaside resorts.

W Well, other countries also have resorts on the beach.

M Turkey also has stunning natural scenery. There are many reasons why it's the sixth <u>3)_____ _____ _____ _____</u> in the world.

W I didn't realize that. I'd like to know more about the country.

M Well, I can send you an electronic brochure about Turkey if you want.

W That would be great. Can you <u>4)_____ _____ _____</u> today?

↘ 듣기 필수 표현
· aside from ~외에도

15

W Abigail and her brother are university students. They live together in an apartment during the school year and <u>1)_____ _____ _____</u>. Abigail buys groceries and does the laundry. Her brother does the dishes and cleans the house. This week, Abigail has to travel out of town. She will not be able to buy groceries or clean their clothes. Her brother will have to do all the chores by himself. But he has been busy lately, and having more chores will <u>2)_____ _____ _____</u> for him. Abigail doesn't want her brother to feel stressed. So she wants to tell him that she will do all the grocery shopping, laundry, and cleaning <u>3)_____ _____ _____</u> instead. In this situation, what would Abigail most likely say to her brother?

↘ 듣기 필수 표현
· do the laundry 빨래하다
· do the dishes 설거지하다
· by oneself 혼자서

16~17

M Good afternoon, class. Last time we discussed insects that live in large communities. Today, we are going to discuss the <u>1)_____ _____ _____</u> of ants. First off, their feet have special sticky pads on them. These allow ants to <u>2)_____ _____ _____</u>, which is why it is easy for them to climb up walls and even walk while upside down. Second, ants have amazingly strong necks. These make it easy for ants to carry heavy loads and allow them to lift weights <u>3)_____ _____ _____ _____ _____</u> than their bodies. Third, ants have two stomachs. One of these is used for digesting food as you would expect. The other is capable of carrying food so that it can be <u>4)_____ _____ _____</u> and shared with other ants. Lastly, there is a pair of long, thin antennae on their heads. They use these antennae to smell scents. They help ants find food and their way back home. Now, let's take a quick look at a video on ants.

↘ 듣기 필수 표현
· upside down 거꾸로 뒤집혀
· be capable of ~하는 기능이 있다, 능력이 있다

대학수학능력시험 문제지
영어듣기 모의고사

정답 및 해설 p.92

1번부터 17번까지는 듣고 답하는 문제입니다. 1번부터 15번까지는 한 번만 들려주고, 16번부터 17번까지는 두 번 들려줍니다. 방송을 잘 듣고 답을 하시기 바랍니다.

1. 다음을 듣고, 남자가 하는 말의 목적으로 가장 적절한 것을 고르시오.

① 과학 상식을 쌓을 것을 권장하려고
② 대학 입시 일정을 안내하려고
③ 학교에서 열릴 설명회를 홍보하려고
④ 과학 경진 대회의 결과를 발표하려고
⑤ 과학 대학의 다양한 전공을 소개하려고

2. 대화를 듣고, 여자의 의견으로 가장 적절한 것을 고르시오.

① 거리 공연을 하는 예술가에게 돈을 기부해야 한다.
② 불법적인 수단을 통해 음악을 공짜로 들어서는 안 된다.
③ 가난한 예술가를 지원하는 복지 정책을 늘려야 한다.
④ 예술적 재능이 부족해도 연습으로 극복할 수 있다.
⑤ 거리 공연 문화는 지역 경제에 도움이 된다.

3. 대화를 듣고, 두 사람의 관계를 가장 잘 나타낸 것을 고르시오.

① 투숙객 — 호텔 직원
② 시민 — 경찰관
③ 수의사 — 앵무새 주인
④ 아파트 주민 — 관리소 직원
⑤ 조류 사육사 — 동물원 방문객

4. 대화를 듣고, 그림에서 대화의 내용과 일치하지 <u>않는</u> 것을 고르시오.

5. 대화를 듣고, 여자가 남자를 위해 할 일로 가장 적절한 것을 고르시오.

① 케이블 TV 장비 설치하기
② 사용 설명서 링크 전달하기
③ 채널 설정 변경하기
④ 리모컨 버튼 조작하기
⑤ 다시 전화 걸기

6. 대화를 듣고, 여자가 지불할 금액을 고르시오.
① $99 ② $110 ③ $120 ④ $126 ⑤ $140

7. 대화를 듣고, 남자가 머리를 염색한 이유를 고르시오.

① 검은색에 싫증이 나서
② 록 밴드에 들어가고 싶어서
③ 맡은 배역을 연기할 때 필요해서
④ 좋아하는 연예인을 따라 하고 싶어서
⑤ 유행에 뒤처지고 싶지 않아서

8. 대화를 듣고, Central Science Museum에 관해 언급되지 <u>않은</u> 것을 고르시오.

① 개관 시기　② 전시 주제　③ 체험 활동
④ 취식 공간　⑤ 단체 할인

9. Graphic Design Competition에 관한 다음 내용을 듣고, 일치하지 <u>않는</u> 것을 고르시오.

① 대회는 9월 12일에 열릴 예정이다.
② 학원 강좌를 등록한 수강생을 대상으로 한다.
③ 참가자들은 제품의 3D 로고를 만들어야 한다.
④ 5명의 그래픽 디자인 업계 전문가들이 심사한다.
⑤ 참가 신청 마감일은 8월 31일이다.

10. 다음 표를 보면서 대화를 듣고, 남자가 구매할 여행 가방을 고르시오.

Suitcases

	Model	Color	Cost	Size	Lock
①	A	Blue	$80	Medium	X
②	B	Silver	$100	Small	O
③	C	Red	$120	Medium	X
④	D	Silver	$140	Large	X
⑤	E	Blue	$180	Large	O

11. 대화를 듣고, 남자의 마지막 말에 대한 여자의 응답으로 가장 적절한 것을 고르시오.

① I may be home a little bit late tonight.
② I'll invite my friends over for dinner next week.
③ I will leave some food for you in the fridge, then.
④ I think you need to focus more on your studying.
⑤ I'm sure you'll learn a lot from the after-school programs.

12. 대화를 듣고, 여자의 마지막 말에 대한 남자의 응답으로 가장 적절한 것을 고르시오.

① No. The receptionist didn't call me back.
② Sure. I'll ask the dentist what toothpaste to use.
③ Yes. My appointment for tomorrow is confirmed.
④ You're right. Now, I've got all my cavities treated.
⑤ Too bad. You should have brushed your teeth more carefully.

13. 대화를 듣고, 여자의 마지막 말에 대한 남자의 응답으로 가장 적절한 것을 고르시오. [3점]

Man: _____

① I disagree. I'd rather go to another bakery.
② Great. Let's buy some cookies for the family.
③ I don't think so. Cupcakes can be hard to bake.
④ Not yet. I'm still developing my own cupcake recipe.
⑤ It's really tasty. I think you could open your own bakery.

14. 대화를 듣고, 남자의 마지막 말에 대한 여자의 응답으로 가장 적절한 것을 고르시오. [3점]

Woman: _____

① I'd better look for a club to join, then.
② I keep forgetting the vocabulary words.
③ It's too late to sign up for the class now.
④ The club doesn't take any new members.
⑤ All of my studying was worth it in the end.

15. 다음 상황 설명을 듣고, Charles가 Abby에게 할 말로 가장 적절한 것을 고르시오. [3점]

Charles: _____

① Relax. Our exam isn't until next month.
② It's okay. I didn't do well on the test, either.
③ Stop worrying! Our new teacher is really nice.
④ Me too. Global history is my weakest subject.
⑤ Take it easy. We've studied all of this bcforc.

[16~17] 다음을 듣고, 물음에 답하시오.

16. 남자가 하는 말의 주제로 가장 적절한 것은?

① reasons to avoid eating junk food
② foods that worsen a sore stomach
③ how to cook food in a healthy way
④ relationship between diet and health
⑤ why it is important to have balanced diet

17. 언급된 음식이 <u>아닌</u> 것은?

① coffee   ② nuts   ③ milk
④ chocolate   ⑤ French fries

이제 듣기 문제가 끝났습니다. 채점을 마친 후 다음 페이지에서 방송을 다시 들으며 딕테이션 연습을 하시기 바랍니다.

* 채점 결과: 맞은 개수 _____ 개 / 17개   정답 및 해설 p.92

16회 Dictation

Dictation 정답 p.92

16회 영어듣기 모의고사 Dictation 음성을 들으며 빈칸에 알맞은 단어를 채워 넣으시기 바랍니다.

1

M Attention, students. This is a message for anyone who is interested in a career in science. Next Monday, our school will host a special 1)_____ _____ _____ _____ _____ from the science department of Chester University. They will be setting up promotional booths, where you can find out about science-related jobs. Professors of 2)_____, _____, _____ _____ will be at the booths to answer any questions you might have. There will also be a talk by Professor Tess Harrison about her work 3)_____ _____. This event will be held in the school gym from 5 to 7 p.m. If you're interested, just drop by after school. Thank you.

↘ 듣기 필수 표현
· find out ~을 알게 되다
· drop by 들르다

2

M Susan, did you give money to that violinist performing on the street?

W Yes. Her playing was beautiful, so I gave her $5.

M That's a lot, isn't it?

W I think people ought to 1)_____ _____ _____ _____ who perform on the street. It can help them launch their careers.

M Do you think she's talented enough to be a professional?

W It's possible. And every artist needs support if they are going to succeed.

M I guess earning money lets them practice more.

W Exactly. It encourages them to 2)_____ _____ _____.

M I just don't feel comfortable giving away money.

W Well, she provided that music to us for free. Giving something back seemed fair.

M I see what you mean.

W And if my money helps her start a professional career, it 3)_____ _____ _____.

↘ 듣기 필수 표현
· give away ~을 거저 주다
· give back ~을 되돌려주다

3

W Excuse me. I have a complaint.

M Sure. Do you live here in the apartment complex?

W Yes. I live in Unit 901.

M What seems to be the problem?

W A bird has 1)_____ _____ _____ outside of my bedroom window, and I'd like you to remove it.

M Is it causing you problems?

W Yes! I 2)_____ _____ _____ _____, and it disturbs my sleep. Why do you ask?

M There are rules protecting wildlife, so we need to make sure it's necessary.

W I also can't open my window because of where the nest is located.

M Okay. I will get in touch with 3)_____ _____ _____ _____.

W Thanks. Also, someone will need to clean the window after it's removed.

M Of course. I'll take care of that for you. Thank you for reporting the problem, ma'am.

↘ 듣기 필수 표현
· get in touch with ~와 연락하다

4

M I see you remodeled the dance studio, Laura.

W That's right. What do you think?

M The 1)_____ _____ _____ _____ wall makes the room look much bigger.

W It does, but it's also important because students can watch themselves.

M Are those two big speakers on the table?

W Yes. Now, I can play the music loudly.

M I notice you installed a flower-shaped light on the ceiling.

W Yes, it's to change the mood of the studio.

M Why do you need the 2)_____ _____ _____ on the floor?

W When students learn difficult dances, they sometimes fall and hurt themselves. It is safer to practice on the mat.

M And I see that you ³)_____ _____ _____ _____ by the door, too.

W Yeah, I'd been meaning to do that for a while.

M Well, everything looks great.

W Thanks. I hope my students like the changes.

↘ 듣기 필수 표현
· mean to ~하려 하다

5

[Phone rings.]

W Smile Broadband. How may I help you?

M Hi. I had cable TV installed yesterday, but some channels don't work.

W Have you checked whether your television is ¹)_____ _____ _____ _____?

M I'm not sure how to do that.

W That's okay. I can help you ²)_____ _____ _____ now. Do you see the Mode button on your remote control?

M Yes. I just pressed it. Now, there are three mode options on the screen.

W Then, select cable mode. It's the second option.

M Okay. That worked. But it would be useful to have more information in case I have any other problems.

W Of course. I'll ³)_____ _____ _____ _____ _____ the user's manual on our website.

M Please do. But what if there is something I don't understand?

W Just call us back at this number, and we can help.

M All right. Thanks a lot.

6

M Welcome to Wilson Jewelry. How may I help you?

W Hi. Can I see your ¹)_____ _____ _____ _____?

M Of course. I have some options in this display over here.

W How much is this ring? It's beautiful.

M It's $45 in silver. If you'd like a gold one, it will be $60.

W Okay, I'd like two of the ²)_____ _____.

M Perfect. We also offer an engraving service. It's $10 per ring.

W Great! I want to put both my name and my friend's name on each ring.

M Okay, so you'd like two gold engraved rings. Do you need anything else?

W No, that will be all. Oh, isn't there a 10% off sale at the moment?

M Actually, that ³)_____ _____ _____.

W That's okay. Can I pay in cash?

M Certainly. Let me ring that up for you.

↘ 듣기 필수 표현
· ring ~ up ~을 계산해주다

7

W Hey, Mark. When did you ¹)_____ _____ _____ _____?

M I got it done last weekend.

W I love it. Were you tired of having black hair?

M Thanks. The bright color is nice, but I like my natural black hair color, too.

W It makes you look like a singer. Did you join a rock band?

M No. I'm not very musical.

W Well, were you trying to ²)_____ _____ _____ _____? It's a trendy style right now.

M Actually, I dyed it for ³)_____ _____ _____ _____ _____. My character has pink hair.

W That makes sense. When is the performance?

M It's next weekend. You should come see it!

W I'll be there. Do you think you'll keep your pink hair afterwards?

M I think so. It's fun to have a new look.

↘ 듣기 필수 표현
· be tired of ~에 싫증 나다
· have a ~ look ~한 스타일을 해보다

8

M I want to take my kids somewhere interesting this summer, Rosa.

W How about bringing them to the Central Science Museum?

M Oh, right. That just opened last year. Have you been there?

W Yes, and my kids really enjoyed it. It has many exhibits that teach kids about 1)_____ _____ _____.

M Are there any hands-on activities?

W The museum has a chemistry room. The staff help kids 2)_____ _____ _____, like making colorful bubbles.

M That sounds great. Do they have any food options at the Museum?

W There's a cafeteria that sells some snacks.

M That's perfect. If your kids are interested in going back there, maybe we could go together.

W That works. In fact, the museum also has 3)_____ _____ _____ _____.

M Even better.

W Let's pick a day to go soon.

9

W Attention, please. I'd like to inform you about an upcoming Graphic Design Competition. It will be hosted by Super Tech Academy on September 12th. The contest is 1)_____ _____ _____ who has enrolled in one of the academy's courses. Participants must design a 3D logo for any type of product. The logo must be attractive and 2)_____ _____ _____ that it represents. There will be one grand prize winner and three consolation prizes. 3)_____ _____ _____ will be composed of three professionals from the graphic design industry. If you're interested, please sign up for the competition by the August 31st deadline. Details about the competition are available on posters at the academy and on its website.

↘ 듣기 필수 표현
· enroll in ~에 등록하다
· be composed of ~로 구성되다

10

W Tony, why are you looking up suitcases? Are you going somewhere?

M Yeah. I have plans to take a trip to Rocky Island. However, my old suitcase has 1)_____ _____ _____, so I need to buy a new suitcase. Can you help me pick one?

W Oh, I like that one. The red color is nice.

M It's not bad, but I don't want a red suitcase. It's too bright.

W That's fair. Do you have a budget in mind?

M I'd like to 2)_____ _____ _____ $150.

W What about size? Do you need something large?

M Not really. I'll only be there for a few days.

W Then, you can get a 3)_____ _____ _____ _____ that you can bring on the plane. Do you need a lock?

M No, I 4)_____ _____ _____. I always worry I'll forget the combination to the lock.

W Then, I think the decision is made for you.

M Right. There's only one good option.

↘ 듣기 필수 표현
· look up ~을 찾아보다, 검색하다

11

M Mom, I think I'll be 1)_____ _____ _____ for dinner this evening.

W Are you doing something after school?

M My friends and I 2)_____ _____ _____ _____. We're going to get together at the library after class.

↘ 듣기 필수 표현
· get together 모이다

12

W Ted, who was it you were 1)_____ _____ _____ _____ _____ just now?

M It was a receptionist from my dentist's office.

W Oh? What was the 2)_____ _____? Are you finally getting that cavity filled?

↘ 듣기 필수 표현
· fill a cavity 충치를 때우다

13

W Wow, this cookie tastes really good. Where did you get it, Neal?

M I bought it at the bakery on Green Street.

W There's always a long line in front of that place, right?

M Yeah, exactly. Mr. and Mrs. Nelson, the owners of the bakery, have 1)_____ _____ _____. Apparently, they spent two years developing it.

W Well, their efforts really paid off. This cookie is delicious.

M I was thinking of opening a bakery like theirs one day.

W You are a really talented baker. I bet your business would be successful.

M Maybe, but I'll need to create my own 2)_____ _____ first.

W Yeah, every good bakery has something they specialize in. What would you make?

M Well, cupcakes are my favorite. So I want to sell those.

W Do you have 3)_____ _____ _____ of making them?

↘ 듣기 필수 표현
· pay off 성과가 있다
· I bet 분명 ~하다
· specialize in ~에 특화되다

14

M Hey, Mandy. What are you up to?

W I'm just looking through a Spanish dictionary.

M Oh, it's so cool that you're 1)_____ _____ _____!

W Yeah, but it's tough! I've been studying Spanish for years, but I feel like I'm still a beginner.

M What makes you say that? Do you have 2)_____ _____ _____ _____?

W No. I can understand most of the words used in everyday conversation.

M Then, it sounds like you're not a beginner.

W I'm having trouble with speaking. Whenever I have to say something, my mind goes blank.

M Have you tried studying with a tutor?

W No, because I always 3)_____ _____ _____ in front of a teacher.

M How about joining a club for Spanish learners?

W I don't know. Would that be helpful?

M Other students may have the same problems you do, so you may feel 4)_____ _____ _____ Spanish with them.

↘ 듣기 필수 표현
· look through ~을 훑어보다
· go blank 새하얗게 되다

15

W Charles and Abby are classmates in a global history class. Today, their teacher explained the final exam for the course. The exam will 1)_____ _____ the entire school year and test each student's knowledge of global history over the past 100 years. Charles and Abby are now studying hard for the test, but Abby is 2)_____ _____. She feels that there is too much to study for, so it will be almost impossible to be fully prepared. However, Charles 3)_____ _____ _____ because the test will only review topics they have already studied. So he wants to tell Abby that she is familiar with the material on the exam and that she should not worry. In this situation, what would Charles most likely say to Abby?

↘ 듣기 필수 표현
· be familiar with ~을 잘 알고 있다, 친숙하다

16~17

M Good afternoon, everyone. Yesterday, we briefly talked about the importance of a balanced diet. Today, I'd like to look at foods you should never eat when you 1)_____ _____ _____ because they will make it worse. First, try not to drink any coffee. It is 2)_____ _____ and will likely make your stomach hurt more. Another type of food you should avoid is nuts. These contain a lot of fiber, which can 3)_____ _____ _____ stomach too much. This stimulation can lead to a number of digestive problems, including diarrhea. Next, you should not drink milk or eat any food that contains it. Milk is hard for the body to digest, and it can cause 4)_____ _____ _____ _____. Finally, greasy foods such as French fries should obviously not be eaten if you have a stomachache. In fact, they are often the cause of a stomachache. I hope this lesson has given information that will be helpful if you ever have an upset stomach.

↘ 듣기 필수 표현
· have an upset stomach 배탈이 나다

대학수학능력시험 문제지
영어듣기 모의고사

▲ 문제 음성
바로 듣기

▲ 고사장 버전
바로 듣기

정답 및 해설 p.98

1번부터 17번까지는 듣고 답하는 문제입니다. 1번부터 15번까지는 한 번만 들려주고, 16번부터 17번까지는 두 번 들려줍니다. 방송을 잘 듣고 답을 하시기 바랍니다.

1. 다음을 듣고, 남자가 하는 말의 목적으로 가장 적절한 것을 고르시오.

① 병원의 암 센터 완공을 발표하려고
② 새로 설치된 주차장 위치를 안내하려고
③ 입원실 부족에 따른 입원 지연을 사과하려고
④ 암 검사 및 수술 절차를 설명하려고
⑤ 전문 간호 인력을 추가로 모집하려고

2. 대화를 듣고, 여자의 의견으로 가장 적절한 것을 고르시오.

① 멍을 빨리 없애는 데는 마사지가 효과적이다.
② 염좌를 당한 직후에는 냉찜질을 해야 한다.
③ 계단에서는 넘어지지 않도록 조심해야 한다.
④ 핫팩을 부주의하게 사용하면 화상을 입을 수 있다.
⑤ 과다한 나트륨 섭취가 몸이 붓는 가장 큰 이유이다.

3. 대화를 듣고, 두 사람의 관계를 가장 잘 나타낸 것을 고르시오.

① 고속버스 운전사 — 여행객
② 조경사 — 미술관 직원
③ 큐레이터 — 조각가
④ 정원사 — 공원 관리인
⑤ 인테리어 디자이너 — 건축가

4. 대화를 듣고, 그림에서 대화의 내용과 일치하지 않는 것을 고르시오.

5. 대화를 듣고, 여자가 할 일로 가장 적절한 것을 고르시오.

① 도서 구매하기
② 서점에 연락하기
③ 잔액 확인하기
④ 환불 신청서 작성하기
⑤ 카드 교체해주기

6. 대화를 듣고, 남자가 지불할 금액을 고르시오. [3점]

① $180 ② $210 ③ $220 ④ $230 ⑤ $250

7. 대화를 듣고, 남자가 휴대폰을 해지하려는 이유를 고르시오.

① 유학을 가게 돼서
② 통화 품질이 좋지 않아서
③ 휴대폰을 바꿔야 해서
④ 학업에 열중하려 해서
⑤ 다른 통신사에 가입하고 싶어서

8. 대화를 듣고, 피아노 수업에 관해 언급되지 않은 것을 고르시오.

① 수업 요일   ② 수업 대상   ③ 수업료
④ 수업 장소   ⑤ 가르치는 음악

9. English Speaking Competition에 관한 다음 내용을 듣고, 일치하지 않는 것을 고르시오.

① 4월 5일에 열릴 것이다.
② 참가 신청 시 동영상을 제출해야 한다.
③ 경연자들은 영어 실력에 따라 세 단계로 나뉜다.
④ 우승자는 대회 당일에 발표된다.
⑤ 우승 상품에는 무료 수강권이 포함되어 있다.

10. 다음 표를 보면서 대화를 듣고, 남자가 구매할 식탁을 고르시오.

Kitchen Tables

	Model	Seating Capacity	Material	Price	Foldable
①	A	5	Plastic	$200	X
②	B	6	Wood	$230	O
③	C	8	Plastic	$210	X
④	D	10	Wood	$260	O
⑤	E	12	Wood	$240	X

11. 대화를 듣고, 남자의 마지막 말에 대한 여자의 응답으로 가장 적절한 것을 고르시오.

① I'll turn the TV off if it is distracting you.

② She has lived in that apartment for about a year.

③ There's nothing interesting to watch on TV tonight.

④ We should complain to the building manager instead.

⑤ I'll lend you this book after I have finished reading it.

12. 대화를 듣고, 여자의 마지막 말에 대한 남자의 응답으로 가장 적절한 것을 고르시오.

① Of course. It sounds like it'll be fun.

② Really? What did you do on Saturday night?

③ Me neither. I'm not interested in going on rides.

④ That's okay. The tickets to the park are all sold out.

⑤ You're right. Let me check out the advertisement again.

13. 대화를 듣고, 남자의 마지막 말에 대한 여자의 응답으로 가장 적절한 것을 고르시오.

Woman: _____

① Parrot food can be a little expensive.

② Are you sure you don't want a cat instead?

③ Do you want to head over there this weekend?

④ Don't forget to let the bird out of its cage.

⑤ I've been reading a lot about birds.

14. 대화를 듣고, 여자의 마지막 말에 대한 남자의 응답으로 가장 적절한 것을 고르시오. [3점]

Man: _____

① All right. I guess I don't have any other choice.

② Good idea. I'll stop by the pharmacy later today.

③ Why not? I don't need to take medicine right now.

④ Are you sure? You should try taking some medicine.

⑤ I don't know. My headache seems to be getting worse.

15. 다음 상황 설명을 듣고, George가 Teresa에게 할 말로 가장 적절한 것을 고르시오. [3점]

George: _____

① You can only use the telescope effectively at night.

② The weather will be a lot better later in the evening.

③ We should check the forecast before we make a reservation.

④ I think we'd better move our reservation to another week.

⑤ We should see if the observatory is open on Saturdays.

[16~17] 다음을 듣고, 물음에 답하시오.

16. 남자가 하는 말의 주제로 가장 적절한 것은?

① how the invention of writing changed history

② importance of storytelling in ancient cultures

③ how communication influenced human culture

④ musical instruments as communication devices

⑤ different ways that early humans communicated

17. 언급된 통신 수단이 아닌 것은?

① storytelling   ② cave paintings

③ writing systems   ④ drumming

⑤ smoke signals

> 이제 듣기 문제가 끝났습니다. 채점을 마친 후 다음 페이지에서 방송을 다시 들으며 딕테이션 연습을 하시기 바랍니다.
>
> * 채점 결과: 맞은 개수 _____ 개 / 17개   정답 및 해설 p.98

17회 Dictation

Dictation 정답 p.98

17회 영어듣기 모의고사 Dictation 음성을 들으며 빈칸에 알맞은 단어를 채워 넣으시기 바랍니다.

1

M Good morning, everyone. Thank you for coming. I'm the director of the Greenwich Hospital. I'm happy to announce that the construction of our 1)_____ _____ _____ has just finished. It is located next to the hospital's parking facilities. The center includes a number of new patient rooms and surgery areas. It also has 2)_____ _____ equipped with state-of-the-art medical devices. We recently hired 20 new staff members who specialize in cancer treatment. We hope this will demonstrate the hospital's 3)_____ _____ _____ our patients with excellent medical service. Now, I'll take a few minutes to answer any questions you might have.

↘ 듣기 필수 표현
· a number of 많은
· equipped with ~을 갖춘
· specialize in ~을 전문으로 하다

2

W Greg, why are you lying on the couch?
M Hi, Mom. I 1)_____ _____ _____ on the stairs.
W Oh, no. How are you treating it?
M I heated up this towel and put it on my ankle.
W You shouldn't do that. When you have a sprain, you need to apply an ice pack to the area immediately. A hot pack doesn't help.
M Are you sure?
W Yes. After getting a sprain, the 2)_____ _____ _____ _____. Ice reduces the blood flow there, which prevents swelling.
M But I thought heat was useful for healing.
W It isn't at the moment. Swelling is the main problem now. The ice will reduce your pain and 3)_____ _____.
M I didn't realize that.
W Just take that off your ankle. I'll get you some ice.
M Thanks, Mom.

↘ 듣기 필수 표현
· heat up ~을 데우다
· apply an ice pack 냉찜질을 하다
· at the moment 지금, 마침

3

M Sorry I'm late. There was 1)_____ _____ on the highway.
W That's fine. But we should get started right away. Our art gallery has an exhibition opening next Tuesday.
M No problem. You need some work done on the garden, right?
W Yes. And I'd like you to 2)_____ _____ _____ _____ _____ by the front gate, too.
M Sure. They will look nice there.
W Mainly I want you to focus on the garden, though. It needs to be more attractive for visitors.
M I've been 3)_____ _____ _____ for years, so I'm sure I can come up with some good ideas.
W I'm glad to hear that.
M Is there anything in particular that I should be aware of?
W Yes. There are a few 4)_____ _____ _____ _____ that I'd like to display in the garden.
M Could I see them?
W Of course. Let's go take a look at them.

↘ 듣기 필수 표현
· get started 시작하다
· focus on ~에 집중하다
· come up with ~을 생각해 내다
· in particular 특별히
· be aware of ~을 알고 있다
· take a look at ~을 살펴보다

4

M Lisa, is everything ready for the 1)_____ _____ _____?
W Yes, I think so. What do you think of the field decorations?
M They're perfect. I love the two logos painted on the grass.
W As the teams are called The Dragons and The Tigers, I put the letters D and T there.
M Is that person in front of the fence 2)_____ _____ _____?
W That's right. It's our team's mascot.
M And that banner on the fence looks good. The design with the bat and ball turned out well.

W I'm glad you like it.

M Oh, is there water available for the players?

W Yes. It's in the cooler on the right side of the field.

M Ah, I see it. And the two players 3)_____ _____ _____ are already on the field.

W I think they're stretching to get ready for the game.

M Yeah. I can't wait to get started!

↘ 듣기 필수 표현
· turn out well 잘 되다
· can't wait to 빨리 ~하면 좋겠다

5

W Welcome to Pearson Mall's customer service desk. How can I help you?

M I tried to use this gift card to buy some books at the mall's bookstore, but it didn't work.

W I'm sorry about that. Did you check if there was 1)_____ _____ _____ on the card?

M Yes. There is still $50 left.

W Hmm... Maybe the store's 2)_____ _____ _____ _____ properly. In that case, I'll contact the bookstore.

M You don't have to. I saw other customers using their cards there.

W That's strange. Could I take a look at it?

M Here you go.

W Well, the card doesn't 3)_____ _____ _____ _____.

M What can I do, then? Should I fill out a refund request form?

W No. I'll just replace the card with one that has the same amount of money.

M Thanks. I really appreciate that.

↘ 듣기 필수 표현
· fill out ~을 작성하다
· replace A with B A를 B로 교체하다

6

M Hi. I'm looking for a new printer.

W I'd recommend a laser printer. They 1)_____ _____ _____ _____ with a single cartridge of ink.

M I heard that some brands can print 9,000 pages.

W Our models can print about 10,000 pages with just one cartridge.

M That's impressive. How much does this one cost?

W It's normally $250, but we're having a sale this week, so it's now 20% off.

M Do you have other models?

W We have another model which normally costs $200. You will 2)_____ _____ _____ at the moment, though.

M In that case, I'll go for the cheaper model.

W That's a good choice, sir.

M Oh, I also need to buy some A4 printer paper.

W Sure. A box of 500 sheets is $10. How many do you need?

M I'll take 3)_____ _____ _____ _____. Here's my credit card.

7

W Hi, Drake. What are you looking at?

M I'm searching for a way to 1)_____ _____ _____ _____ online.

W Didn't you sign up for it a couple of weeks ago?

M It was last month, actually.

W What happened? Is there a problem with the call quality?

M No. The calls sound great, and I never 2)_____ _____.

W Ah, I guess you want a new phone. Some companies offer discounts if you sign a new contract.

M I'm not planning to replace my current phone.

W Oh, does another phone company have 3)_____ _____ _____?

M That's not it. This is the cheapest option available.

W Then, what's the problem?

M Do you remember I applied for a 4)_____ _____ _____? I got accepted, so I won't need my phone service anymore.

W That's great. Good luck with your studies!

↘ 듣기 필수 표현
· search for ~을 찾다
· apply for ~에 지원하다
· good luck with ~을 잘하길 바라다

8

M Julie, are you interested in learning how to play the piano?

W Not really. I don't have much free time these days. Why do you ask?

M My sister gives piano lessons 1)_____ _____ _____ _____, and she's looking for more students.

W Oh, I can see if my friends want to learn. Does she mainly teach 2)_____ _____ _____ _____?

M She works with students of all levels.

W Oh, that's good. Where does she teach? I know some piano teachers visit the students' houses.

M Normally, she asks students to 3)_____ _____ _____ _____.

W What about the type of music?

M She gives lessons in both classical and jazz styles.

W Okay. I'll make sure to share that information with my friends.

M Thanks. She will really appreciate your help.

↘ 듣기 필수 표현
· look for ~을 찾다

9

M Attention, please. The Global Language Institute is holding an English Speaking Competition. If you're studying English 1)_____ _____ _____ _____, this contest will give you a chance to use your speaking skills! It will be held on April 5th, but the deadline for signing up is March 10th. If you're interested in participating, please 2)_____ _____ _____ _____ of yourself speaking in English when you sign up. The video should be less than five minutes long. We will divide the competitors into three levels based on their English ability. The winners of each level will be announced the day after the contest. Prizes 3)_____ _____ _____ _____ _____ at our institute. For more details, visit our website or call 555-3333.

↘ 듣기 필수 표현
· based on ~에 따라

10

W Peter, is that a furniture catalog you're reading?

M Yes. I'm thinking of buying a table. Since I enjoy cooking, I'd like to invite people over for dinner.

W That's a great idea. How many 1)_____ _____ _____ _____?

M It should be big enough for at least six people.

W Do you have any preference between wood and plastic?

M Oh, I definitely want wood. Wood is stronger than plastic.

W Okay. How much are you willing to spend?

M I can 2)_____ _____ _____ $250.

W Then, it looks like you have two choices left. Do you prefer a table you can fold and put away?

M Yeah, that would be ideal.

W I think you've made your decision, then.

M Yes, I'd 3)_____ _____ _____ _____ _____.

↘ 듣기 필수 표현
· invite A over B A를 B에 초대하다
· be willing to ~할 의향이 있다
· put away ~을 넣어두다

11

M Honey, our upstairs neighbor's TV is 1)_____ _____.

W I know. I'm trying to read a book, but the noise is 2)_____ _____.

M Maybe I should go up and ask her to turn down the volume.

↘ 듣기 필수 표현
· turn down ~을 줄이다

12

W I'm really excited, Justin. A new amusement park just opened in our city. It is 1)_____ _____ _____.

M Yeah. I've seen several advertisements for it already.

W I really want to check it out. Do you want to 2)_____ _____ _____ on Saturday?

↘ 듣기 필수 표현
· check out ~에 가보다; ~을 확인하다

13

W Honey, I was thinking of adopting a pet. What do you think?

M Really? I thought you [1]_____ _____ _____.

W Cats and dogs make me sneeze. But what about getting a bird?

M That's an interesting choice. What kind of bird?

W Actually, my friend is looking for someone to [2]_____ _____ _____. I want to get one of them.

M Well, I've never had a pet bird before. Is taking care of them difficult?

W I think it's pretty easy. You just need to feed them, clean their cages, and let them have some exercise.

M Exercise? What do you mean by that?

W You let them [3]_____ _____ _____ _____ for a couple of hours every day.

M You've really done your research.

W I have. I'm excited about getting a parrot.

M In that case, we should visit your friend to see her parrots soon.

↘ 듣기 필수 표현
· What do you mean by that? 그게 무슨 말이야?

14

W Hey, Andrew. What's wrong?

M I have a splitting headache, and [1]_____ _____ _____ makes it go away.

W What have you tried so far?

M I've tried taking a nap, going for a walk, and drinking some water.

W I think you [2]_____ _____ _____. How about taking medicine?

M Actually, I like to avoid taking medicine. I'm worried about [3]_____ _____ _____.

W But it will ease your pain. And unless you take it too often, there is nothing to worry about.

M You're right. But it will be better if I can recover through other means.

W Well, you said you've tried other methods, and you still have that headache.

M That's true. I'm not sure what else I can do about it.

W I have some aspirin right here. You should [4]_____ _____ _____.

↘ 듣기 필수 표현
· have a splitting headache 머리가 깨질 듯이 아프다
· go away 사라지다　　　　· so far 지금까지
· take a nap 낮잠 자다　　· go for a walk 산책 가다

15

W George and Teresa are looking for a good place to bring their children on a weekend evening. They think that the kids will enjoy looking at [1]_____ _____ _____. They check the schedule of an observatory, which is open to the public on Fridays and Saturdays only. However, the schedule mentions that it is [2]_____ _____ _____, _____ _____. George and Teresa make a reservation for the following Saturday evening. However, on Saturday morning, the sky is cloudy, so George checks the weather forecast. It says there is a 90% chance of rain that night. So he wants to suggest to Teresa that they should [3]_____ _____ _____ _____ to a different week. In this situation, what would George most likely say to Teresa?

16~17

M Good afternoon, everyone. As we discussed last week, communication was important for the survival of early humans. But how did people do this without modern communication devices? Today, we'll discuss some of the [1]_____ _____ _____. First, storytelling was a common form of passing on information. Through stories, humans could share knowledge with each other and [2]_____ _____. Then, communication became easier with the creation of early writing systems. The ancient Egyptians developed a type of writing that was made up of symbols. Ancient people also found ways of communicating [3]_____ _____ _____. Drumming was the first example of this. The sound could act as a warning signal or announce certain events. Similarly, smoke signals were used to send messages to people who were far away. For example, people made smoke to inform of [4]_____ _____ _____. Now, let's watch a video about some of these early forms of communication.

↘ 듣기 필수 표현
· pass on ~을 전달하다
· be made up of ~으로 구성되다
· act as ~의 역할을 하다
· inform of ~을 알리다

정답 및 해설 p.104

1번부터 17번까지는 듣고 답하는 문제입니다. 1번부터 15번까지는 한 번만 들려주고, 16번부터 17번까지는 두 번 들려줍니다. 방송을 잘 듣고 답을 하시기 바랍니다.

1. 다음을 듣고, 남자가 하는 말의 목적으로 가장 적절한 것을 고르시오.

① 비평문 작성 방법을 설명하려고
② 도서 출판 전시회를 홍보하려고
③ 출판사의 연간 출간 일정을 안내하려고
④ 전자책과 종이책의 장단점을 비교하려고
⑤ 월간 독서 목표 세우기를 권장하려고

2. 대화를 듣고, 여자의 의견으로 가장 적절한 것을 고르시오.

① 제품은 현장에서 직접 본 후 구매해야 한다.
② 빠른 배송을 위해 추가 금액은 지불할 만하다.
③ 제품을 구매하기 전에 가격을 비교해야 한다.
④ 구매 전에 제품의 모든 요소를 따져봐야 한다.
⑤ 할인 기간을 기다리는 것이 가장 현명한 쇼핑 방법이다.

3. 대화를 듣고, 두 사람의 관계를 가장 잘 나타낸 것을 고르시오.

① 자선 사업가 ─ 학생 기자
② 보육원 교사 ─ 기부자
③ 의사 ─ 자원봉사자
④ 사회 운동가 ─ 대학교수
⑤ 펀드 매니저 ─ 편집자

4. 대화를 듣고, 그림에서 대화의 내용과 일치하지 <u>않는</u> 것을 고르시오.

5. 대화를 듣고, 남자가 할 일로 가장 적절한 것을 고르시오.

① 건조기 돌리기
② 셔츠 다림질하기
③ 케이스에 악기 넣기
④ 바이올린 연습하기
⑤ 찬물에 손빨래하기

6. 대화를 듣고, 여자가 지불할 금액을 고르시오. [3점]

① $54   ② $72   ③ $81   ④ $90   ⑤ $94

7. 대화를 듣고, 여자가 점심을 함께 할 수 <u>없는</u> 이유를 고르시오.

① 태국 음식을 좋아하지 않아서
② 시험공부를 해야 해서
③ 외식할 돈이 부족해서
④ 점심 선약이 있어서
⑤ 지갑을 잃어버려서

8. 대화를 듣고, 채소 배송 서비스에 관해 언급되지 <u>않은</u> 것을 고르시오.

① 배송 주기   ② 서비스명   ③ 채소 종류
④ 채소 원산지   ⑤ 서비스 가격

9. Milton Community Center Health Run에 관한 다음 내용을 듣고, 일치하지 <u>않는</u> 것을 고르시오.

① 8월 25일 일요일에 열릴 것이다.
② 참가하려면 16세 이상이어야 한다.
③ 신분증을 지참해서 와야 한다.
④ 자원봉사자들이 생수병을 나눠줄 것이다.
⑤ 최초 완주자 3명에게만 기념 가방이 주어진다.

10. 다음 표를 보면서 대화를 듣고, 여자가 구매할 침대 시트를 고르시오.

Bedsheets

	Model	Price	Color	Number	Fabric
①	A	$95	Blue	1	Cotton
②	B	$115	White	2	Cotton
③	C	$125	Gray	1	Polyester
④	D	$130	White	2	Polyester
⑤	E	$175	Blue	1	Cotton

11. 대화를 듣고, 여자의 마지막 말에 대한 남자의 응답으로 가장 적절한 것을 고르시오.

① Yes, I wrote you a short letter.
② Luckily, there's no pain at all.
③ No, I should go visit the hospital.
④ I need to buy some more bandages.
⑤ I prepared some onion soup for you.

12. 대화를 듣고, 남자의 마지막 말에 대한 여자의 응답으로 가장 적절한 것을 고르시오.

① That's fine. The jacket will dry off soon.
② I'm sorry. I was feeling cold and decided to wear it.
③ Don't worry. You can find it in the closet by the door.
④ You're right. I left my keys in the front pocket.
⑤ Hold on. It's with the rest of the laundry.

13. 대화를 듣고, 여자의 마지막 말에 대한 남자의 응답으로 가장 적절한 것을 고르시오. [3점]

Man: _____

① That sounds tough. But I'll try to cut it down.
② Thanks a lot. I will include that detail in my video.
③ Great idea. I'll share my film with other club members.
④ I don't think so. The film festival only accepts documentaries.
⑤ I'm not sure. I still need to film the students in the forest.

14. 대화를 듣고, 남자의 마지막 말에 대한 여자의 응답으로 가장 적절한 것을 고르시오.

Woman: _____

① We'll drive to the dentist's office after work.
② But I dropped the kids off at the dentist.
③ You'll just have to pay the penalty fee.
④ I'll call and see what he says, then.
⑤ We should play tennis more often.

15. 다음 상황 설명을 듣고, Brad가 Allison에게 할 말로 가장 적절한 것을 고르시오. [3점]

Brad: _____

① Which recipes are you interested in learning?
② Why don't you check in our used books section?
③ I can order a copy of the book for you if you like.
④ How about looking it up in our store inventory system?
⑤ I can recommend a different cookbook by the same author.

[16~17] 다음을 듣고, 물음에 답하시오.

16. 여자가 하는 말의 주제로 가장 적절한 것은?

① what happened after people began trading goods
② how farming changed in early human civilization
③ different jobs that emerged in early human civilization
④ special skills required for professions in early human history
⑤ why humans began to live together in larger settlements

17. 언급된 직업이 아닌 것은?

① farmers ② bakers ③ soldiers
④ merchants ⑤ priests

이제 듣기 문제가 끝났습니다. 채점을 마친 후 다음 페이지에서 방송을 다시 들으며 딕테이션 연습을 하시기 바랍니다.

* 채점 결과: 맞은 개수 _____ 개 / 17개   정답 및 해설 p.104

18회 영어듣기 모의고사 Dictation 음성을 들으며 빈칸에 알맞은 단어를 채워 넣으시기 바랍니다.

1

M Hello, everyone. I have good news for those who are looking for some new books to read. A ¹)_____ _____ _____ will be held at the Gilman Center next month. The participating publishers will display the books they published over the course of the year. They will also give ²)_____ _____ _____ of their upcoming books. These will include e-books, which are popular among readers these days. The exhibition will also include ³)_____ _____ _____ and talks by authors. Make sure to be there, and start making a list of the books you want to read in the future. Thank you.

↘ 듣기 필수 표현
· over the course of ~ 동안

2

M Honey, let's buy this coffee machine.

W We do need to ¹)_____ _____ _____ _____, but let's wait a little.

M Why should we wait? Our current coffee machine hardly works!

W I think it's always better to ²)_____ _____ before buying something.

M This coffee machine is pretty cheap, though. And it's on sale.

W There are frequently better deals online. We need to look.

M But isn't it worth a little more money to have it right away?

W Sometimes. But it doesn't ³)_____ _____ _____ _____, and shipping is fast these days.

M Maybe we could compare prices on my phone.

W Great idea. Why don't we look up prices right now, then? If we don't see a better deal, we'll buy this one.

M Okay, let's check.

↘ 듣기 필수 표현
· look up ~을 찾아보다

3

W Hello, Mr. Harrison. Thanks for coming.

M I appreciate you meeting with me. I've ¹)_____ _____ _____ to ask from my classmates.

W I'm glad to hear that. Go ahead.

M What made you dedicate your life to helping others?

W I was born in a poor family and received help from the community. So I always felt that I needed to give back.

M I see. When did you start volunteering?

W I helped out ²)_____ _____ _____ when I was still a CEO. But it became my full-time job after I sold my investment company.

M What is your focus nowadays?

W These days, I run an organization that ³)_____ _____ _____ _____ and trains doctors.

M I think many of our readers will want to volunteer after they see my article.

W I hope they do!

M Thank you for your time. I'll send you a copy of the school newspaper later.

↘ 듣기 필수 표현
· dedicate A to B A를 B에 바치다
· be born in ~에서 태어나다
· help out 일을 돕다

4

M Mary, look at this photo of the living room in our old house.

W Whoa... I haven't thought about that place in a while, Dad.

M I forgot that we had that ¹)_____ _____ _____ _____ _____ on it.

W Mom threw it out when we moved. We still have that dolphin poster on the wall, though.

M Exactly. It's in storage now.

W Oh, right. Hmm... I like how our furniture was set up.

M Yeah, we had a ²)_____ _____ _____ the TV, so we spent some time reading books instead of watching TV.

W Right. And it was nice to have that ³⁾_____ _____ the couch and the chair.

M That tall floor lamp in the back-left corner was useful, too.

W This brings back so many memories!

M Let's take a picture of this room so we can remember it.

W Good idea! I'll go get my camera.

↘ 듣기 필수 표현
· throw out ~을 버리다
· bring back ~을 떠올리게 하다

5

W Simon, why are you still awake? Your violin performance is tomorrow.

M I know, Mom. But I couldn't sleep. I'm feeling nervous.

W I'm sure it will go well. You've been practicing so much.

M Yes. I can play all the songs in my sleep.

W Then, maybe you just need to go over all the things you need. That always helps.

M Okay. I already put my violin and ¹⁾_____ _____ _____ _____ _____.

W Great. Do you know what you're going to wear? Maybe you need to iron your clothes.

M Let me check. [Pause] Oh, no! There's a ²⁾_____ _____ _____ _____.

W Hmm... You should wash it by hand with cold water.

M All right, I'll go do that now.

W When you're done, ³⁾_____ _____ _____ in baking soda. I'll put it in the dryer tomorrow morning.

M Thanks, Mom.

↘ 듣기 필수 표현
· go over ~을 점검하다

6

M Hello. May I help you?

W Yes. How much are these scarves in the display window?

M They're normally $20, but our store is selling them at 10% off right now.

W Are they on sale because they are older designs?

M That's right. But if you'd like the latest designs, we have some with very nice ¹⁾_____ _____ $24.

W How about those long knitted scarves?

M Those are really warm. They go for $30.

W Hmm... I don't know which one I should choose for my brother.

M If he would like something simple, the knitted one would be a good choice.

W Yeah, that red ²⁾_____ _____ _____ _____ him. And I'll take a checkered one for myself.

M So you want two full-priced scarves.

W Oh, wait. I'll also get two more with the older design.

M No problem. ³⁾_____ _____ _____ _____?

W That's everything! Here's my credit card.

↘ 듣기 필수 표현
· go for ~의 가격에 팔리다

7

M Hey, Charlotte. Did you find your lost wallet?

W Yes, I did. It had fallen behind my couch.

M That's a relief. Do you want to ¹⁾_____ _____ _____ _____ at the Thai restaurant?

W Actually, I can't do that today.

M Why not? If you don't have enough money, I can treat.

W I just got paid on Friday, so that's not an issue.

M Don't you like the food there? We could go somewhere else.

W I like the Thai place. There are a lot of good ²⁾_____ _____ _____ _____.

M Do you have a test coming up you need to prepare for?

W I took the last of my tests yesterday.

M Then, what's the issue?

W I ³⁾_____ _____ _____ _____ with someone else. I'm sorry!

M That's okay. Let's meet another day.

↘ 듣기 필수 표현
· That's a relief. 다행이다.
· get paid 월급을 받다
· have ~ coming up 곧 ~가 있다

8

W Hey, Paul. What do you have in that large box?

M It's full of vegetables. I ¹⁾_____ _____ a vegetable delivery service.

W Oh, so they send them straight to your house?

M Yeah. I get a box of ²⁾_____ _____ _____ _____.

W That's convenient. What's the service called?

M It's called Lilly's Veggies. I really recommend it.

W Where do the vegetables come from?

M Everything is ³⁾_____ _____ _____ _____ of Greenford County.

W Wow. The produce must be really fresh.

M It is. And it's a pretty good deal too. It's $20 per week.

W I think I might be interested in subscribing. Can anyone sign up online?

M Yes, but they only ⁴⁾_____ _____ _____ on Mondays.

W Oh, I guess I missed out this time.

M That's true, but you should try it next week!

↘ **듣기 필수 표현**
· be full of ~으로 가득 차 있다
· miss out 놓치다

9

W May I have your attention, please? I'd like to invite you all to join the Milton Community Center Health Run. It will be held on Sunday, August 25th. This five-kilometer race is open to local residents. However, you must be ¹⁾_____ _____ _____ to enter. If you'd like to participate, please sign up on our center's website by August 18th. On the morning of the race, you will need to register with event staff. So remember to ²⁾_____ _____ _____ _____ such as a school ID or a driver's license. There will be volunteers passing out bottles of water along the course of the race. The first three finishers will be given awards, and all participants will get ³⁾_____ _____ _____.

↘ **듣기 필수 표현**
· pass out ~을 나눠주다

10

M Welcome to Wallace Home Store. Can I help you?

W Yes, thanks. I just got a new bed, and I'm looking for sheets.

M What is your price range?

W Hmm... I want something nice, but I don't want to ¹⁾_____ _____ _____ $150.

M Okay, sure. Is there a color you prefer?

W The walls of my bedroom are blue, so I'd prefer to get a color, ²⁾_____ _____ _____.

M Did you want only one set of bedsheets? Some of our sheets are sold in a pack of two.

W I think it would be better to get sheets that ³⁾_____ _____ _____ _____ _____ _____ so I have an extra set.

M That makes sense. All that's left is the fabric.

W Cotton is not warm enough in the winter. I prefer the other type.

M It looks like you've made your choice.

11

W Hey, Walter. What is the bandage on your hand for?

M I ¹⁾_____ _____ _____ chopping some onions last night. I should have been more careful.

W Does it hurt when you write or ²⁾_____ _____ _____?

12

M Emma, have you seen the leather jacket I ¹⁾_____ _____ _____? I thought I left it in the living room.

W Yeah. It was on the floor, Dad. So I ²⁾_____ _____ _____. Why do you ask?

M I need to get my keys out of one of the pockets.

13

M Hi, Ms. Fielder. Can I ask for your advice?

W Sure, Nathan. I'm always happy to help a member of the film club.

M Well, I was considering 1)_____ _____ _____ to the Neo City Film Festival.

W That's great. What is it about?

M It's about a group of students who helped prevent a local forest from being cut down.

W That sounds really interesting. Have you edited it yet?

M Not yet. I wanted to 2)_____ _____ _____ _____, actually.

W I see. It can be one of the hardest parts of filmmaking.

M Yeah, I don't know which parts to use in the film. I have a few hours of good video.

W Hmm... That's too long. You should 3)_____ _____ _____.

M Why do you think so?

W The organizers of that festival don't often accept movies that are more than 30 minutes long.

↘ 듣기 필수 표현
· prevent A from B A가 B하는 것을 막다
· cut down a forest 삼림을 벌목하다

14

W Honey, can you take the kids to their 1)_____ _____ tomorrow afternoon? You get off work early on Fridays, right?

M Sorry, but I can't do it. I have a meeting with a client at 5 tomorrow.

W Hmm... I see. But I'm not quite sure what to do, then.

M I don't understand the problem. Why can't you take them there?

W I have a tennis lesson, and it's too late to cancel 2)_____ _____ _____ _____.

M Isn't that normally on Sundays?

W It used to be, but the schedule changed recently.

M What is the fee for canceling?

W If you cancel less than 24 hours beforehand, you should pay for the whole lesson.

M Oh, that doesn't sound fair.

W Yeah, that's why I don't think canceling is a good option.

M I think you should contact your tennis coach. Why don't you try 3)_____ _____ _____ _____ to him?

↘ 듣기 필수 표현
· get off work 퇴근하다

15

M Allison has recently gotten into cooking. She finds it 1)_____ _____ _____ to make new dishes every week and is constantly searching for recipes. Today, Allison is at a bookstore looking for 2)_____ _____ _____ _____ she read good reviews about online. However, she can't find it in the cooking section. So she approaches Brad, one of the store employees, for help. Allison tells Brad what the title of the book is. Brad knows that the store does not have 3)_____ _____ _____ _____ _____, but he thinks it may have a used one. Therefore, Brad wants to suggest to Allison that she should search in the 4)_____ _____ _____ of the bookstore. In this situation, what would Brad most likely say to Allison?

↘ 듣기 필수 표현
· get into ~을 시작하다

16~17

W Welcome back, class. Earlier, we discussed how human settlements first formed. Now, I'd like to talk about the 1)_____ _____ that began to appear in early human civilizations. First off, farmers made up the largest group of people in this era. Farming 2)_____ _____ _____ _____ of work back then, so most people worked in the fields to produce grain. Next up, we have bakers. Their special skills were essential for turning grain into food that could 3)_____ _____ _____ _____ and cities. Soldiers are the third distinct group that emerged at this time. They were able to fight and train for fighting full-time because, for the first time in history, there was a 4)_____ _____ _____. And they became necessary to protect the city's resources from attack. Lastly, merchants were another class that began to appear at this time. They were needed to trade the extra resources of one town or city for those of another. Now, let's watch a video on early civilizations in the Middle East.

↘ 듣기 필수 표현
· make up ~을 이루다
· turn A into B A를 B로 바꾸다

19회
제3교시
대학수학능력시험 문제지
영어듣기 모의고사

▲ 문제 음성 바로 듣기
▲ 고사장 버전 바로 듣기

정답 및 해설 p.110

1번부터 17번까지는 듣고 답하는 문제입니다. 1번부터 15번까지는 한 번만 들려주고, 16번부터 17번까지는 두 번 들려줍니다. 방송을 잘 듣고 답을 하시기 바랍니다.

1. 다음을 듣고, 남자가 하는 말의 목적으로 가장 적절한 것을 고르시오.

① 반려동물 관찰 카메라를 광고하려고
② 새로운 반려동물 훈련법을 소개하려고
③ 반려동물을 방치하지 말 것을 경고하려고
④ 주의할 반려동물의 이상 행동을 설명하려고
⑤ 주문한 스피커의 배송 지연을 사과하려고

2. 대화를 듣고, 남자의 의견으로 가장 적절한 것을 고르시오.

① 불을 켜고 자는 것은 숙면을 방해한다.
② 밤늦게까지 게임을 하면 피로도가 심하다.
③ 자기 전에는 휴대폰을 보지 말아야 한다.
④ 시력 보호를 위해 블루라이트를 차단해야 한다.
⑤ 잠들기 전 독서하는 습관은 뇌에 좋다.

3. 대화를 듣고, 두 사람의 관계를 가장 잘 나타낸 것을 고르시오.

① 세미나 관계자 — 취재 기자
② 숙박업소 사장 — 경제학 교수
③ 카페 주인 — 다국적 기업 직원
④ 여행사 직원 — 관광객
⑤ 박물관장 — 미술 교사

4. 대화를 듣고, 그림에서 대화의 내용과 일치하지 않는 것을 고르시오.

5. 대화를 듣고, 남자가 할 일로 가장 적절한 것을 고르시오.

① 단체 채팅방에 파일 올리기
② 관광 안내 지도 다운받기
③ 잠수 장비 구매하기
④ 식당 검색하기
⑤ 호텔 예약하기

6. 대화를 듣고, 여자가 지불할 금액을 고르시오. [3점]
① $12   ② $16   ③ $18   ④ $20   ⑤ $24

7. 대화를 듣고, 여자가 캠핑을 갈 수 없는 이유를 고르시오.

① 다리가 계속 뻐근하고 아파서
② 아버지 생신 잔치에 가야 해서
③ 과학 수행평가가 밀려서
④ 버스표를 구하지 못해서
⑤ 스터디 모임이 있어서

8. 대화를 듣고, Public Speaking Club에 관해 언급되지 않은 것을 고르시오.

① 모임 장소   ② 활동 내용   ③ 가입 방법
④ 회원 수   ⑤ 모임 요일

9. Digital Drawing Course에 관한 다음 내용을 듣고, 일치하지 않는 것을 고르시오.

① 65세 이상의 주민이면 누구나 참가할 수 있다.
② Parker Community Center에서 수업이 진행될 것이다.
③ 6주간 수강료는 20달러이다.
④ 수업에 개인 태블릿 PC를 따로 가져올 필요는 없다.
⑤ 수강생을 위해 셔틀버스가 운행될 것이다.

10. 다음 표를 보면서 대화를 듣고, 남자가 구매할 샴푸를 고르시오.

Shampoo

	Model	Size	Hair Type	Price	Scent
①	A	200 ml	Dry	$11	Fruity
②	B	500 ml	Oily	$14	Minty
③	C	500 ml	Normal	$22	Minty
④	D	1,000 ml	Normal	$19	Flowery
⑤	E	1,000 ml	Normal	$17	Fruity

11. 대화를 듣고, 여자의 마지막 말에 대한 남자의 응답으로 가장 적절한 것을 고르시오.

① Really? The time really flew by.
② I bet! I'm sure you'd like that story.
③ That's right. The movie is one hour long.
④ Sure. Let's watch the next movie together.
⑤ So do I. The lawyer was my favorite character.

12. 대화를 듣고, 남자의 마지막 말에 대한 여자의 응답으로 가장 적절한 것을 고르시오.

① Perfect. That swimsuit is so cute on her.
② Sure. That's a good price for six lessons.
③ No problem. I'm not busy tomorrow morning.
④ Yes. One of us has to hold her the entire time.
⑤ Maybe. She has taken lessons for two months.

13. 대화를 듣고, 여자의 마지막 말에 대한 남자의 응답으로 가장 적절한 것을 고르시오. [3점]

Man: _____

① All right. I'll read through the text message.
② Don't worry. I plan to have a large breakfast.
③ You should. Otherwise, you'll get tested again.
④ That's right. I already checked my blood test results.
⑤ It's true. I will need to change my appointment time.

14. 대화를 듣고, 남자의 마지막 말에 대한 여자의 응답으로 가장 적절한 것을 고르시오.

Woman: _____

① I'll get started on the pasta.
② I'll call now to check if we do.
③ I put in an order five minutes ago.
④ I didn't have anything to eat today.
⑤ I don't feel like Indian food anyway.

15. 다음 상황 설명을 듣고, Celine이 Thomas에게 할 말로 가장 적절한 것을 고르시오. [3점]

Celine: _____

① I didn't know the contest had a cash prize.
② I'll search for more recycled materials to use.
③ Let's give it away to a non-profit organization.
④ We ought to look for a buyer for our sculpture.
⑤ Don't you think our art piece is good enough to win?

[16~17] 다음을 듣고, 물음에 답하시오.

16. 여자가 하는 말의 주제로 가장 적절한 것은?

① how virtual reality was first invented
② examples of successful metaverse products
③ why virtual reality will be adopted in the future
④ future ways that the metaverse may be used
⑤ ways that media has changed over time

17. 언급된 분야가 아닌 것은?

① medicine   ② fashion
③ education   ④ entertainment
⑤ tourism

이제 듣기 문제가 끝났습니다. 채점을 마친 후 다음 페이지에서 방송을 다시 들으며 딕테이션 연습을 하시기 바랍니다.

* 채점 결과: 맞은 개수 _____ 개 / 17개   정답 및 해설 p.110

19회 Dictation

Dictation 정답 p.110

19회 영어듣기 모의고사 Dictation 음성을 들으며 빈칸에 알맞은 단어를 채워 넣으시기 바랍니다.

1

M Hello, pet owners. Do you ever worry about your pet when you're out of the house? Then, you should consider ¹⁾_____ _____ _____ _____, Pet Viewer. This is an Internet-connected camera that can be used to ²⁾_____ _____ _____ _____ your pet. You can watch your pet through the camera at any time by connecting it to an app on your phone. It has 360-degree views and can detect both sound and motion. These features allow it to ³⁾_____ _____ if anything is wrong with your pet. The camera also includes a speaker. This will allow you to give your pet commands while you're away. So place an order for your pet today.

↘ 듣기 필수 표현
· at any time 언제든지　　　　· connect A to B A를 B에 연결하다
· place an order 주문하다

2

M Hey, Jasmine. You look tired. Did you stay up late last night?

W Yeah. I couldn't fall asleep.

M Let me guess. Were you using your phone before bedtime?

W Yes. I didn't feel sleepy, so I was playing a game and waiting until I got tired.

M That's probably why you couldn't sleep. You shouldn't ¹⁾_____ _____ _____ _____ before bedtime.

W But doesn't everyone do it?

M Maybe so. But the blue light from the screen ²⁾_____ _____ _____.

W My phone wasn't very bright, though. Why would it be a problem?

M Blue light is like the light from the sun. Seeing it makes your brain ³⁾_____ _____ _____.

W Really? What should I do instead of looking at my phone?

M You should try reading a book. Drinking milk could help, too.

W Okay. I'll try that.

↘ 듣기 필수 표현
· stay up late 늦게까지 깨어 있다　　　· fall asleep 잠들다
· instead of ~ 대신

3

M Good morning, Ms. Miller. Did you sleep well?

W Yes. The room was quite comfortable. I'm really satisfied with your inn.

M That's good to hear. I made some coffee. Would you like some?

W Yes. That would be lovely.

M Ms. Miller, you're in our town for a conference, aren't you? Are you doing a presentation?

W Well, it's something like that. I'm participating in a seminar on ¹⁾_____ _____ _____.

M Oh, are you studying economics?

W Actually, I teach economics at Kensington University.

M Wow, that's impressive!

W Thanks. Oh, I had a question for you. I was thinking of seeing some of the museums in the area after the conference. Could I ²⁾_____ _____ _____ by one night?

M Certainly! There are plenty of great sights around here. I can give you ³⁾_____ _____ _____ _____ if you like.

W Yes, I'd really appreciate that.

↘ 듣기 필수 표현
· be satisfied with ~에 만족하다

4

W Honey, is that the new playground you were talking about?

M Yes. I think it's opening next week.

W It looks so nice. That's a really big slide in the back of the playground.

M Yes, but it's a bit high for small children. They can use the ¹⁾_____ _____ _____ _____ _____ of it.

W The two swings next to the smaller slide look fun, too. Our kids are going to love those.

M They look well-built, too. So even if the kids get a little wild, the ²⁾_____ _____ _____.

W Is that a sandbox over on the left?

M Yes. Small children can bring buckets and shovels to play in the sand.

W Where can parents sit while the children are playing?

M On 3)_____ _____ _____ in the front of the sandbox.

W Oh, it looks pretty comfortable.

5

W Are we ready for our family trip, Dad?

M We should be. But let's check one last time to make sure.

W Mom told me that she finished booking a room at a hotel near the beach.

M And I 1)_____ _____ _____ _____ including masks and wetsuits for our family to go snorkeling.

W Perfect. Did you download a 2)_____ _____ _____ on your phone? We can look around if we have extra time.

M Yes. I got it already. Do you want me to upload it on our group chat room?

W No. I don't think it's necessary.

M Okay. Is that everything? It sounds like we're ready.

W Oh, one more thing. Did you decide where to eat dinner after snorkeling? Maybe we should 3)_____ _____ _____ _____.

M Good point. Then, I'll search for some good restaurants first.

W Thanks. I'm really looking forward to our trip!

↘ 듣기 필수 표현
· Good point. 좋은 지적이야.
· search for ~을 찾다

6

M Welcome to Dalton's Highway Snack Stand. How can I help you?

W Hi. I'd like some 1)_____ _____ for my kids, please.

M No problem. Would you like the regular or large size?

W How much are they?

M The regular one is $4, and the large is $6.

W I'll take 2)_____ _____ _____ _____ _____, please. I don't want the kids fighting over their food.

M Sure. Will there be anything else for you today?

W I'll get 3)_____ _____ as well. How much are those?

M They're $4 each. So that'll be two regular-sized grilled potatoes and three hotdogs. Is it correct?

W That's right. And can I use this coupon for a 10% discount?

M Sure. But it's only valid if you pay 4)_____ _____.

W Let's see... *[Pause]* Ah, yes, I've got some. Here you go.

7

M Danielle, you look exhausted.

W Hi, Tyler. I just went jogging along the river. My 1)_____ _____ _____ _____.

M Oh, I see. I'm planning to go camping this weekend. Do you want to come?

W I'd love to, but I can't make it.

M That's too bad. Do you think you'll 2)_____ _____ _____?

W No. I'll feel fine once I get some rest.

M Are you behind on your science project, then?

W No. I'm almost done with it. Actually, my father 3)_____ _____ on Saturday. So I'm going to his birthday party.

M I didn't know! Send him my best wishes!

W I will. Are you going to be back on Sunday afternoon for our study group?

M No. I couldn't get a bus ticket 4)_____ _____ _____ _____. I'll be back around 10 p.m.

W Alright. Have fun!

↘ 듣기 필수 표현
· be behind on ~이 밀리다
· be done with ~을 다 하다
· send ~ one's best wishes ~에게 안부를 전하다

8

W Zack, where did you go last night?

M I was at the Public Speaking Club meeting. I joined it a couple weeks ago.

W That club meets at the Lincoln library, right?

M Exactly. It's [1]_____ _____ _____ our school.

W What do you do during club meetings? Do you give speeches every time?

M Yes. Everyone [2]_____ _____ _____ _____ the other members for two minutes about a chosen topic.

W Is there usually a big audience?

M Yeah. The club has over 50 members. So there are usually a lot of people.

W I see. I was thinking of joining myself, but I'm not sure I can.

M What's the problem?

W Doesn't the club always meet on Wednesdays?

M That's right. Do you [3]_____ _____ _____ _____?

W I'm busy with my part-time job on those nights.

M Well, if your schedule changes, you should sign up.

9

W Attention, residents. The city government has recently begun offering the Digital Drawing Course for seniors. Any resident of our city who is 65 or older is [1]_____ _____ _____ in this course. Classes will be held at Parker Community Center. During the course, our instructors' goal is to teach seniors how to make drawings of people on a tablet computer. Students will practice [2]_____ _____ _____ on this digital device. The entire six-week course will cost only $20. But please make sure to [3]_____ _____ _____ tablet computer to the classes. To make the program easier to attend, a shuttle bus will be available to take students to and from classes. If you're interested, you can register online or in person at the community center.

↘ 듣기 필수 표현
· in person 직접

10

W Good afternoon. Please let me know if you need help finding anything.

M I'd like to buy some shampoo. Can you help me choose?

W Sure. [1]_____ _____ _____ _____ _____? We have three different sizes.

M I think a 200-milliliter one will run out too quickly. So 500 milliliters or more would be good.

W Okay. Do you know what hair type you have?

M I would say it's normal. It's not too [2]_____ _____ _____.

W And do you have a price range in mind?

M It should be no more than $20.

W Then, here are a couple of options. What kind of scent would you prefer?

M Hmm... I'm not picky. But I don't want it to [3]_____ _____ _____.

W All right. Then, this one would be perfect for you.

M Yeah, I'll take that. Thanks for your help.

↘ 듣기 필수 표현
· run out 다 떨어지다

11

W Andy, I can't believe the movie ended like that. I feel like the story isn't finished.

M Yeah. The story isn't over. The next film in the series will [1]_____ _____ _____ character's story in detail. But the movie was pretty short, wasn't it?

W Actually, it was [2]_____ _____ _____ _____.

12

M Honey, when is our daughter's first swimming lesson?

W It's tomorrow morning. I [1]_____ _____ _____ _____ how she reacts to the water.

M Me too. She might need some help, though. Should we [2]_____ _____ _____ _____ with her?

13

[Phone rings.]

M You've reached Jake Larsen.

W Hi. I'm calling to remind you about your appointment at Dr. Carter's office for 11 a.m. tomorrow.

M Thanks! Um... the doctor mentioned that I would need to ¹⁾_____ _____ _____ _____. Do I need to do anything special?

W Yes. Please follow the guidelines that we sent you through text message.

M I was ²⁾_____ _____ _____ _____. Is that right?

W Correct. You shouldn't eat anything for 12 hours beforehand.

M Well, I don't like to skip breakfast.

W Is there a medical reason that requires you to eat?

M No, but that's a long time to go without eating.

W I understand this requirement can cause difficulty. But we won't get accurate results from the blood test if you eat.

M ³⁾_____ _____ I get thirsty?

W You are allowed to drink water. The instructions we sent you ⁴⁾_____ _____ _____.

14

W Honey, do you want me to make pasta tonight?

M You ¹⁾_____ _____ _____ _____ dinner again. You've cooked every night this week.

W I suppose it would be nice to have a night off. Maybe we could order some food?

M Sure. You can decide on the place.

W Hmm... I don't really like the delivery options.

M We don't have to stay at home and get delivery.

W Do you want to ²⁾_____ _____ _____ _____ somewhere downtown?

M Yes! It would be nice to get out of the house.

W Do you know if the Indian restaurant on Main Street is open?

M It is, but the service is so slow there.

W Then, maybe we should try that new barbecue place ³⁾_____ _____ _____ from it.

M Perfect! We've been talking about going there for a while. But do we have to ⁴⁾_____ _____ _____?

❯ 듣기 필수 표현
· have a night off 하룻밤 (일을) 쉬다
· get out of ~에서 나가다

15

M Thomas and Celine are artists who frequently work together. They recently heard about a local contest in which all of the art has to be made out of ¹⁾_____ _____. They thought it sounded fun, so they decided to make their own recycled art piece. Thomas and Celine made a sculpture together using old cans, plastic, and cardboard. Both of them feel certain they will ²⁾_____ _____ _____. However, the prize for winning is only $100. Celine thinks that they can make more money ³⁾_____ _____ _____ themselves, so they shouldn't just give it away. Therefore, she wants to tell Thomas that they should find someone to ⁴⁾_____ _____ _____. In this situation, what would Celine most likely say to Thomas?

❯ 듣기 필수 표현
· feel certain ~을 확신하다
· give away ~을 거저 주다, 기부하다

16~17

W Good morning, class. Last time, I talked about the invention of ¹⁾_____ _____ _____. Today, I want to discuss how the metaverse may be used in the future. First, the field of medicine could be transformed by the metaverse. Doctors will have access to 3D simulations of the inside of their patients' bodies. These accurate simulations will make surgeries ²⁾_____ _____ _____ _____. Next, fashion may work differently. Instead of making clothes by hand, designers can create them virtually and ³⁾_____ _____ _____ avatars, which would save time and money. Third, education has the potential to be very different in the metaverse. Students will have more chances for "hands-on" learning. Instead of reading about a famous historic site, they could walk around it. Lastly, ⁴⁾_____ _____ _____ _____ the most. In the metaverse, people will be able to attend live concerts remotely. Interactive movies could also become possible, where the viewer plays a part in the story. Now, let's watch a brief video on this topic.

❯ 듣기 필수 표현
· have access to ~할 수 있다, 접할 수 있다
· by hand 손으로, 수동으로
· play a part in ~에 일조하다

대학수학능력시험 문제지
영어듣기 모의고사

제3교시

정답 및 해설 p.116

1번부터 17번까지는 듣고 답하는 문제입니다. 1번부터 15번까지는 한 번만 들려주고, 16번부터 17번까지는 두 번 들려줍니다. 방송을 잘 듣고 답을 하시기 바랍니다.

1. 다음을 듣고, 여자가 하는 말의 목적으로 가장 적절한 것을 고르시오.

① 의류별 어울리는 색상 조합을 설명하려고
② 출시된 아동복 라인을 소개하려고
③ 유기농 소재의 안전성을 강조하려고
④ 패션쇼 참석을 요청하려고
⑤ 어린이집 개원을 알리려고

2. 대화를 듣고, 남자의 의견으로 가장 적절한 것을 고르시오.

① 무지는 부끄러워해야 할 일이 아니다.
② 수업이 끝나면 바로 복습하는 것이 효과적이다.
③ 교과서를 통해 개념을 먼저 확실히 이해해야 한다.
④ 질문을 너무 많이 하면 상대를 곤란하게 만들 수 있다.
⑤ 모르는 것에 대해 질문하는 것을 두려워하면 안 된다.

3. 대화를 듣고, 두 사람의 관계를 가장 잘 나타낸 것을 고르시오.

① TV쇼 진행자 — 수의사
② 학부모 — 영양사
③ 식당 주인 — 식품 안전 감독관
④ 라디오 진행자 — 반려동물 주인
⑤ 의사 — 환자 보호자

4. 대화를 듣고, 그림에서 대화의 내용과 일치하지 않는 것을 고르시오.

5. 대화를 듣고, 남자가 할 일로 가장 적절한 것을 고르시오.

① 옷 기장 줄이기
② 가격표 제거하기
③ 바지 수선 맡기기
④ 쇼핑하러 가기
⑤ 세탁물 찾아오기

6. 대화를 듣고, 남자가 지불할 금액을 고르시오. [3점]

① $46 　② $56 　③ $60 　④ $61 　⑤ $65

7. 대화를 듣고, 여자가 보고서 작성을 시작하지 못한 이유를 고르시오.

① 주제를 정하지 못해서
② 사촌 집을 방문해야 해서
③ 다른 숙제가 많아서
④ 오케스트라 연습으로 바빠서
⑤ 필요한 책을 빌리지 못해서

8. 대화를 듣고, Classic Cars Motor Show에 관해 언급되지 않은 것을 고르시오.

① 기간 　　② 장소 　　③ 전시 차량
④ 입장료 　⑤ 종료 시각

9. Oldfield Harbor Fishing Competition에 관한 다음 내용을 듣고, 일치하지 않는 것을 고르시오.

① 5월 28일에 열린다.
② 참가자들은 오전 7시 전에 항구로 와야 한다.
③ 오후 5시까지 모든 배가 귀항해야 한다.
④ 참가 가능 인원은 총 20명이다.
⑤ 2명의 우승자에게 상금이 수여된다.

10. 다음 표를 보면서 대화를 듣고, 남자가 구매할 쌀을 고르시오.

Bags of Rice

	Variety	Size	Type	Grain Size	Price
①	A	4 kg	Brown	Medium	$20
②	B	5 kg	Brown	Long	$25
③	C	5 kg	White	Short	$15
④	D	10 kg	Brown	Long	$30
⑤	E	12 kg	White	Medium	$25

11. 대화를 듣고, 여자의 마지막 말에 대한 남자의 응답으로 가장 적절한 것을 고르시오.

① That's why I took a shortcut down this quiet road.
② There is a lot of road construction at the moment.
③ I'm going to take the subway instead of the bus.
④ We will arrive at our destination on time.
⑤ I hope we don't run into any traffic.

12. 대화를 듣고, 남자의 마지막 말에 대한 여자의 응답으로 가장 적절한 것을 고르시오.

① Certainly. I'll find the owner.
② Why not? I'll issue a new ID card.
③ Sorry. The restroom is under repair.
④ Of course. Be sure to return it on time.
⑤ Thank you. I was looking for my wallet!

13. 대화를 듣고, 여자의 마지막 말에 대한 남자의 응답으로 가장 적절한 것을 고르시오. [3점]

Man: _____

① Can I project my photos onto the TV screen?
② I have to go out of town in a few days, unfortunately.
③ I'll ask her to come listen to my stories about Antarctica.
④ I'd be happy to write a college recommendation letter.
⑤ Very few scientists get a chance to visit Antarctica.

14. 대화를 듣고, 남자의 마지막 말에 대한 여자의 응답으로 가장 적절한 것을 고르시오.

Woman: _____

① Good. Your cooking skills really improved a lot.
② Not exactly. You don't have to follow the recipes.
③ You're right. You should make a dish every night.
④ I'm sure of it. That was the worst dish I ever tried.
⑤ Definitely. I'll help you avoid cooking it for too long.

15. 다음 상황 설명을 듣고, Brandon이 Alice에게 할 말로 가장 적절한 것을 고르시오. [3점]

Brandon: _____

① I would like the design finished by the end of the month.
② These signs need to be made of eco-friendly materials.
③ We need different designs for different parts of the trail.
④ I'd like you to remake this sign according to my directions.
⑤ The red color emphasizes the danger of breaking this rule.

[16~17] 다음을 듣고, 물음에 답하시오.

16. 남자가 하는 말의 주제로 가장 적절한 것은?

① old animal-related sayings from Korea
② what animals stand for in traditional Korean art
③ depictions of animal characters in Korean literature
④ common animals known to bring luck in Korea
⑤ mythical creatures in ancient Korean paintings

17. 언급된 동물이 아닌 것은?

① pig   ② bat   ③ turtle
④ chicken   ⑤ tiger

이제 듣기 문제가 끝났습니다. 채점을 마친 후 다음 페이지에서 방송을 다시 들으며 딕테이션 연습을 하시기 바랍니다.

* 채점 결과: 맞은 개수 _____ 개 / 17개   정답 및 해설 p.116

20회 Dictation

Dictation 정답 p.116

20회 영어듣기 모의고사 Dictation 음성을 들으며 빈칸에 알맞은 단어를 채워 넣으시기 바랍니다.

1

W Good evening, and welcome to the Luna Kidswear fashion show. I'm designer Chloe Levine. It's an honor for me to be here this evening to introduce my 1)_____ _____ _____ _____. I was inspired to create it after having my own kids. All the pieces are soft, light, and comfortable, making them perfect for active children. They come in neutral colors that can be easily 2)_____ _____ _____. And everything is made of 100% organic cotton or other natural materials that are easy to care for. To 3)_____ _____ _____ _____ _____ shown here today, please visit the Luna Kidswear pop-up store in London. You can also check out our online shop at www.lunakids.com. Thank you.

↘ 듣기 필수 표현
· come in ~으로 출시되다, 나오다
· care for ~을 관리하다

2

M Caroline, are you still studying for your physics class?

W Yeah, Dad. I'm having trouble.

M Don't get worked up. Physics is a tough subject.

W But even when I review the chapter several times, I still don't 1)_____ _____ _____ _____.

M Have you been asking questions in class when you don't understand something?

W Not really. I'm too shy to speak up in front of everyone.

M In my opinion, you should 2)_____ _____ _____ _____ _____ questions. That's the best way to learn.

W Sometimes I don't know what to ask, though.

M You need to try. If nothing else, it will help you figure out what you don't know.

W That make sense, but I 3)_____ _____ _____ when I talk in class.

M Then, why don't you speak with your teacher after class?

W That's a good idea. Thanks, Dad.

↘ 듣기 필수 표현
· get worked up 속상해하다
· speak up 크게 말하다
· in one's opinion ~의 생각에
· if nothing else 적어도
· figure out ~을 알아내다

3

W Dr. Carson, it's great to have you back on *Morning Talk*.

M I'm happy to be on the show, Laura.

W I understand that you want to tell our viewers about food safety.

M Yes. Many people come to my clinic because their pets have 1)_____ _____ _____.

W What are some foods that animals shouldn't eat?

M Not every animal is the same. But, for instance, chocolate is dangerous for dogs.

W I see. What would you recommend that people do to protect their pets?

M 2)_____ _____ _____ _____ pet foods. And put anything dangerous in the refrigerator or a cabinet.

W But what should they do if their pet eats something dangerous?

M You need to act fast. 3)_____ _____ _____ _____ or call the pet help hotline right away.

W We'll display that phone number on the screen now. Okay, let's discuss this topic more after a quick commercial break.

4

M Hi, Maria. It looks like you've changed the setup of your art supply shop.

W Yes. I think it'll be easier for customers to find what they need.

M What's inside those two big boxes on the left?

W The paints are in those. I should organize them later on.

M And all the 1)_____ _____ _____ on the back wall now.

W Yeah. I displayed them to show all the different styles. The diamond-shaped one is the most popular.

M What's the easel in the front for?

W Customers can try out the paint samples there.

M Oh, I see. So that must be why you put the brushes and paint samples on the 2)_____ _____ _____ _____ it.

W That's right. And what do you think of the poster of an 3)_____ _____ _____ _____?

M Oh, I like that. It reminds customers of your store's name, Elephant Paints.

W Thank you.

↘ **듣기 필수 표현**
· try out ~을 테스트해 보다
· remind A of B A에게 B를 떠올리게 하다

5

W Steven, did you go shopping today? What's in that shopping bag?

M These are my pants. I just picked them up 1)_____ _____ _____.

W What did you bring them in for? Was there a problem with them?

M They were too long, so I needed to 2)_____ _____ _____.

W Did the tailor do a good job?

M Let me check. [Pause] Oh, he didn't fix the hole in the back.

W Huh? Why is there a hole in your pants?

M I accidentally cut them when I was removing the tags. I asked the tailor to fix the hole, but he 3)_____ _____ _____.

W You should take them back to the tailor. The hole is small, so it shouldn't take him too long to fix.

M Yeah. I should 4)_____ _____ _____ _____ now.

↘ **듣기 필수 표현**
· pick up (맡긴 물건을) 찾아오다

6

W Welcome to Green Valley Campground. How can I help you?

M Hi. I'd like to stay at this campground with my family tonight.

W Okay. All of our sites cost $40 1)_____ _____.

M Oh, I have this coupon. Can I use it?

W Let me see. [Pause] Yes. You'll get 10% off the campsite itself, but not on additional purchases.

M That's fine. We will need to buy some 2)_____ _____ _____ _____ tonight. How much are your packs of firewood?

W Those are $10 each.

M Okay, then I'll take two. Please add that to my bill.

W And would you also like to buy some marshmallows? We sell a 3)_____ _____ _____ _____. It's great for kids.

M How much is a set?

W It's $5.

M No. I think we'll be fine. We have plenty of food.

W All right. Then, I'll take your card for the payment now.

7

W Hi, Brent. Did you start your earth science report?

M Yeah. I'm almost done. I'll be finished by Friday.

W Really? It's due next Monday. Why are you in such a hurry?

M I'm visiting my cousin this weekend. 1)_____ _____ _____ is your report?

W Actually, I haven't started yet.

M Are you having trouble coming up with a topic?

W No. I've already decided what I'll write about.

M Then, you must be occupied with your other classes.

W Not really. My other classes haven't 2)_____ _____ _____.

M Is it because you are busy with practice for the school orchestra?

W It's not that. Actually, I 3)_____ _____ _____ _____ for my report from the library. They were checked out.

M Oh no. So, what are you going to do?

W I'll go back tomorrow. They should be available by then.

↘ **듣기 필수 표현**
· be in a hurry 서두르다
· come up with ~을 생각해내다
· be occupied with ~으로 바쁘다
· check out ~을 대출하다

8

M Honey, I don't want to waste our Sunday afternoon. We should do something fun!

W How about going to the Classic Cars Motor Show?

M I'd love that! I didn't even know it was running right now.

W Yes. It started on March 10th and will 1)_____ _____ _____ _____ _____.

M Where is it being held?

W At the Clifton Convention Center.

M That's pretty close to us. We should buy tickets in advance, though. That way, we won't have to wait in the ticket line.

W I agree. Tickets are $20 2)_____ _____.

M Okay. What time should we go?

W Well, it 3)_____ _____ _____ p.m. So I think we should be there by 4 p.m.

M All right. And let's go out for dinner afterwards.

W Sounds good.

↘ 듣기 필수 표현
· in advance 미리
· wait in line 줄 서서 기다리다

9

W Hello, everyone. The Oldfield Harbor Fishing Competition will take place again this year. It'll be held on May 28th. The fishing boats will 1)_____ _____ the Oldfield Harbor at 8 a.m., so everyone who wants to enter the competition will need to arrive at the harbor before 7 a.m. All boats must 2)_____ _____ _____ _____ by 5 p.m., which is when the competition officially ends. This year, 3)_____ _____ _____ of boats will be 20, but five participants are allowed per boat, so there are 100 places available in total. Prizes of $1,000 will be awarded to both the person who catches the most fish and the person who catches the biggest fish. Visit our website to register now for this exciting event.

10

W Hey, Ron, what are you shopping for?

M I want to buy a bag of rice. I recently bought a rice cooker, so I want to use it.

W That sounds good. How much are you looking to buy?

M Well, I don't want to buy too 1)_____ _____ _____ _____, so I don't want more than 10 kilograms.

W That makes sense. Do you prefer white rice or brown rice?

M They say that 2)_____ _____ _____ _____, so I'll get that.

W What about grain size? That's an important factor.

M I'm going to make Indian curry. So I better go with the long-grain rice.

W That leaves you with two good options.

M Hmm... The $25 one is cheaper, but I'd 3)_____ _____ _____ _____ the $30 bag considering its size.

W So do you want the more expensive one?

M Yes, I think so. I'll order it now.

11

W Excuse me, sir. Is the traffic here usually this slow? I'm worried our bus won't 1)_____ _____ _____.

M I've been driving buses in this area for 10 years, and I've never seen it this bad.

W Really? Do you know what is 2)_____ _____ _____ _____?

12

M Ms. Brown, I 1)_____ _____ _____ left in the school restroom.

W Oh, how kind of you! Is there a student ID card in it?

M Luckily, there is. But I don't know him. I 2)_____ _____ _____ you might return this to him.

13

W Harold! It's so good to see you! How was ¹⁾_____ _____ _____ in Antarctica?

M Incredible, but I'm happy to be back.

W I'll bet. By the way, you've become my daughter's hero. She really looks up to her Uncle Harold.

M Does she still want to major in science when she ²⁾_____ _____ _____?

W Yes! And now she wants to explore Antarctica.

M I'm sure she can do it! Is she at home now?

W No. She's out with some friends.

M That's too bad. I have a lot of great photos I think she would be interested in.

W Oh, I'm sure she would. Are you going to be in town for long?

M I'll be staying at Mom and Dad's house for a couple of weeks.

W My daughter would love it if you ³⁾_____ _____ _____ there to tell her about your experience.

↘ 듣기 필수 표현
· I'll bet. 틀림없이 그렇겠어.
· by the way 그런데
· look up to ~를 존경하다
· major in ~을 전공하다

14

M Mom, can I ask you something?

W Sure, Paul. What is it?

M How did you learn to cook so well?

W Well, I followed a lot of recipes at first. Once I knew the basics, I started experimenting more.

M I see. I've been watching some cooking videos online. But I've failed each time I ¹⁾_____ _____ _____ them.

W What's the hardest part about cooking for you?

M Well, I don't know how long to cook things. The dishes I make are usually overcooked.

W I think that's something you have to learn from experience. ²⁾_____ _____ _____.

M But I don't get a chance to cook very often.

W Then, why don't you start helping me when I make dinner? You can make a dish tonight.

M Great! But can you let me know when to ³⁾_____ _____ _____ _____?

↘ 듣기 필수 표현
· get a chance to ~할 기회를 얻다

15

W Brandon is a park ranger at a national park. Recently, many visitors have been ¹⁾_____ _____ _____ _____ and walking through off-limits parts of the forest. This is harming the forest environment. So Brandon has decided to post signs that warn visitors not to leave the trails. Last week, he went to a sign maker, Alice, and asked her to make a design. However, when Alice showed him the design today, Brandon was not pleased. He requested that the word *trail* be ²⁾_____ _____ _____ _____ on the sign, but instead it is written in black. Therefore, he wants to ask that she redesign the sign ³⁾_____ _____ _____. In this situation, what would Brandon most likely say to Alice?

↘ 듣기 필수 표현
· post a sign 표지판을 세우다

16~17

M Good afternoon, class. In the last lecture, we looked at plants that appear in Korean paintings throughout history. Today, we will examine the ¹⁾_____ _____ of animals in traditional Korean art. First, there's the pig, which most people associate with wealth. This idea is so common that there is a saying that when you see a ²⁾_____ _____ _____ _____, you'll have good luck. Similarly, the bat is a traditional symbol of good fortune. Therefore, the pattern of bats' wings was carved on furniture and buildings in the past to ³⁾_____ _____ _____. Next, there is the long-lived turtle. Many of them can live for centuries. Not surprisingly, this animal symbolizes longevity in Korean artwork. Lastly, the tiger is a familiar symbol. These animals ⁴⁾_____ _____ _____ _____, so paintings of them were often hung on gates to keep away evil. Now, please turn your attention to the screen. I'll show you some examples of these creatures in traditional paintings.

↘ 듣기 필수 표현
· associate A with B A를 B와 연결 지어 생각하다
· keep away ~을 물리치다
· turn one's attention to ~으로 주의를 돌리다

고난도
21회

제3교시

대학수학능력시험 문제지
영어듣기 모의고사

▲ 문제 음성
바로 듣기

▲ 고사장 버전
바로 듣기

정답 및 해설 p.122

1번부터 17번까지는 듣고 답하는 문제입니다. 1번부터 15번까지는 한 번만 들려주고, 16번부터 17번까지는 두 번 들려줍니다. 방송을 잘 듣고 답을 하시기 바랍니다.

1. 다음을 듣고, 여자가 하는 말의 목적으로 가장 적절한 것을 고르시오.

① 대기질 개선 운동 동참에 감사하려고
② 대중교통 요금 인상을 예고하려고
③ 고농도 미세먼지 대응 요령을 설명하려고
④ 잦은 실내 환기를 당부하려고
⑤ 올바른 마스크 착용법을 알려주려고

2. 대화를 듣고, 여자의 의견으로 가장 적절한 것을 고르시오.

① 동영상은 정보 전달에 효과적이다.
② 온라인 검색 능력을 발전시켜야 한다.
③ 참고 자료의 출처 표시를 누락하면 안 된다.
④ 자료 조사 시 학술서나 학술지를 참고해야 한다.
⑤ 보고서의 주제는 누구에게나 흥미로워야 한다.

3. 대화를 듣고, 두 사람의 관계를 가장 잘 나타낸 것을 고르시오.

① 영양사 — 골프 선수
② 약사 — 환자 보호자
③ 헬스장 트레이너 — 회원
④ 물리치료사 — 육상 선수
⑤ 요리사 — 대회 관계자

4. 대화를 듣고, 그림에서 대화의 내용과 일치하지 <u>않는</u> 것을 고르시오.

5. 대화를 듣고, 여자가 할 일로 가장 적절한 것을 고르시오.

① 고양이를 위한 여행 가방 싸기
② 기차 출발 시간 확인하기
③ 자외선 차단제 구매하기
④ 쓰레기 밖에 내놓기
⑤ 택시 예약 취소하기

6. 대화를 듣고, 남자가 지불할 금액을 고르시오. [3점]

① $72   ② $77   ③ $81   ④ $86   ⑤ $95

7. 대화를 듣고, 여자가 테니스 수업을 신청하지 <u>않은</u> 이유를 고르시오.

① 허리가 계속 아파서
② 수업 인원이 다 차서
③ 피아노 수업과 시간이 겹쳐서
④ 수업 장소가 너무 멀어서
⑤ 이사 준비를 하느라 바빠서

8. 대화를 듣고, Wiltshire Vintage Market에 관해 언급되지 <u>않은</u> 것을 고르시오.

① 장소   ② 날짜   ③ 노점상 수
④ 운영 시간   ⑤ 준비물

9. Edwards City Film Festival에 관한 다음 내용을 듣고, 일치하지 <u>않는</u> 것을 고르시오.

① 일주일 동안 진행된다.
② 추가 요금을 내야 하는 강연도 열린다.
③ 웹사이트에서 축제 관련 정보를 확인할 수 있다.
④ 50편 이상의 데뷔작이 상영될 것이다.
⑤ 감독이 개막작 영화를 소개할 예정이다.

10. 다음 표를 보면서 대화를 듣고, 남자가 구매할 커피 메이커를 고르시오.

Coffee Makers

	Model	Max Cups Brewed	Price	Built-in Grinder	Free Gift
①	A	4	$120	X	Coffee Beans
②	B	2	$160	X	Coffee Beans
③	C	6	$180	O	Tumbler
④	D	4	$140	O	Coffee Beans
⑤	E	6	$220	O	Tumbler

11. 대화를 듣고, 여자의 마지막 말에 대한 남자의 응답으로 가장 적절한 것을 고르시오.

① I will be back in my office after lunch.
② The politics lecture ended around 2 p.m.
③ I can come back to ask about the essay later.
④ I have to turn in my assignment this morning.
⑤ I'm going to send you the essay file this afternoon.

12. 대화를 듣고, 남자의 마지막 말에 대한 여자의 응답으로 가장 적절한 것을 고르시오.

① The painting style of impressionists is not my taste.
② Let's check if the gallery sells the paintings.
③ In that case, we'd better get a move on!
④ The gallery's hours are posted online.
⑤ My painting class starts in an hour.

13. 대화를 듣고, 남자의 마지막 말에 대한 여자의 응답으로 가장 적절한 것을 고르시오.

Woman: _____

① I told her that she had to eat it to go to the zoo.
② We asked a zoo employee to take a photo of us.
③ We'll see the monkeys after you finish your lunch.
④ There are still some leftovers if you are still hungry.
⑤ I chopped up the broccoli and mixed it with the chicken.

14. 대화를 듣고, 여자의 마지막 말에 대한 남자의 응답으로 가장 적절한 것을 고르시오. [3점]

Man: _____

① I thought so. In the video, you can see the thief's face.
② I'm afraid not. Some of the necklaces were badly damaged.
③ What a relief. I was worried I wouldn't get them back.
④ That's right. The man probably stole several other items.
⑤ It's okay. Our jewelry store has a good insurance policy.

15. 다음 상황 설명을 듣고, Mary가 Jared에게 할 말로 가장 적절한 것을 고르시오. [3점]

Mary: _____

① I'd be happy to rewrite this part for you.
② You ought to come audition for the musical.
③ I'm sure your voice sounded great in that song.
④ I will tell the club members about your acting skills.
⑤ Congratulations on getting the lead role in the musical!

[16~17] 다음을 듣고, 물음에 답하시오.

16. 남자가 하는 말의 주제로 가장 적절한 것은?

① why threats to biodiversity harm the environment
② how to increase predator populations in nature
③ causes of deadly animal-borne diseases
④ ways that predators aid other species
⑤ how to prevent the overpopulation of a species

17. 언급된 동물이 아닌 것은?

① bats   ② bears   ③ buffaloes
④ eagles   ⑤ wolves

이제 듣기 문제가 끝났습니다. 채점을 마친 후 다음 페이지에서 방송을 다시 들으며 딕테이션 연습을 하시기 바랍니다.

* 채점 결과: 맞은 개수 _____ 개 / 17개   정답 및 해설 p.122

Dictation 정답 p.122

21회 고난도 영어듣기 모의고사 Dictation 음성을 들으며 빈칸에 알맞은 단어를 채워 넣으시기 바랍니다.

1

W Attention, listeners. This is Melinda Kim with a news update. Air quality in the Central City area is expected to be very poor for the next few days, with ¹⁾_____ _____ _____ _____ _____. So please remain indoors as much as you can for the time being. As physical activities in these conditions can be dangerous, it is ²⁾_____ _____ _____ a mask if you need to do work outside. To improve air quality, the city council has decided to limit the number of cars on the road and make public transportation ³⁾_____ _____ _____ _____ _____. These policies are expected to remain in place until at least Friday. Stay tuned for more updates.

❯ 듣기 필수 표현
· for the time being 당분간
· remain in place 계속 유지되다
· stay tuned 채널을 고정하다

2

W What are you watching, Charles?
M I'm watching a short video about the Industrial Revolution. It's for my history report.
W Well, it doesn't seem like it ¹⁾_____ _____ _____ for a report.
M I'll watch a few more videos, though. I find them more interesting than other ways of researching.
W I understand, but you should refer to academic books or journals ²⁾_____ _____ _____.
M But that sounds more difficult and boring.
W It is, but you'll find they have much more information.
M I guess that's true.
W You'll get a better grade if you don't cut corners. Plus, those materials are ³⁾_____ _____ _____.
M Yeah, I would hate for anything in my report to be incorrect.
W You can even find many books and journals online nowadays.
M You're right. I'll start doing some research now.

❯ 듣기 필수 표현
· refer to ~을 참고하다
· cut corners (쉽게 하려고) 원칙을 무시하다

3

W Hi, Mr. Davis. How are you feeling today?
M I'm okay. But my ¹⁾_____ _____ _____ _____.
W I see. You suffered your injury during a recent golf tournament, right?
M That's correct. It was ²⁾_____ _____ _____ _____ I've experienced playing sports.
W My husband was watching the golf tournament, actually. He was cheering for you.
M That's good to hear, but is there anything you recommend eating that would speed up my recovery? I know you've helped other ³⁾_____ _____ _____ in the past.
W The most important thing is to increase your protein intake.
M Does that mean eating more meat?
W Not exactly. You'll need to avoid food that is high in fat. Fish is a better choice.
M I can do that. Is there anything else you'd recommend?
W I'll make a ⁴⁾_____ _____ _____ for you, with all the vitamins and minerals you need.
M I see. That sounds helpful.

❯ 듣기 필수 표현
· cheer for ~를 응원하다

4

W Hey, Ian. What are you looking at on your phone?
M Hi, Morgan. It's a picture my dad took by the lake last weekend.
W Can I see? [Pause] Oh, it looks beautiful. That tree next to you is huge.
M Yeah, it provided a lot of shade.
W Is that why you ¹⁾_____ _____ _____ _____ there?
M Right. We sat on it and looked out at the lake.
W I like ²⁾_____ _____ _____ you're wearing.

How was the weather there?

M It was perfect. But the path was in the sun, so I sweated a bit while walking.

W Those three flowers 3)_____ _____ _____ are also lovely.

M Yeah. And did you notice the duck floating on the water?

W That's so cute. It seems like you had a great time.

M We did. You should try to go there soon, too.

5

W Honey, are you ready for our trip tomorrow?

M I just 1)_____ _____ _____ _____. But I need to check a few things. Do we have any sunscreen?

W Yeah! I bought some this afternoon. It's in my bag.

M Okay. And you arranged for a cat sitter, right?

W Yes. My cousin is 2)_____ _____ _____ our cat.

M And what about transportation to the airport? Did you arrange for a taxi?

W Oh, I canceled that. Instead, I booked express train tickets.

M Yeah, that will be much faster. When does it leave?

W I can't remember off the top of my head. I will check 3)_____ _____ _____ on the website right away.

M Thanks. Why don't I take out the trash in the meantime?

W Good idea. That's something we don't want to forget!

�“ 듣기 필수 표현
· arrange for ~을 준비하다, 마련하다
· off the top of one's head 당장 생각나는 대로, 즉석에서
· in the meantime 그동안에

6

W I see you've found 1)_____ _____ _____ _____.

M Yes. This one looks nice. I was thinking of buying it with 2)_____ _____ _____ blue ink.

W Great! I should mention that there's a discount. It's 10% off the original price of both.

M Okay, and how much is that?

W Normally, the pen would be $80, and the ink would be another $10.

M That works for me. My son is going to love this.

W Oh, is it a present for your son?

M Yes. He's graduating this weekend, so I need it to be wrapped.

W There is an additional fee for wrapping.

M How much 3)_____ _____ _____?

W It's $5 on top of the discounted total.

M That sounds reasonable. It wouldn't look good if I tried to 4)_____ _____ _____.

W I'll have it ready for you in a couple of minutes.

↘ 듣기 필수 표현
· That works for me. 괜찮네요.
· on top of ~ 외에

7

W Hey, Steven. Did you sign up for those tennis lessons I told you about?

M I did. I was surprised the class 1)_____ _____ _____ when I signed up.

W Yeah. I actually ended up not registering for them.

M Why? Is your back still bothering you?

W No. I've had some physical therapy, and it's much better now.

M Then, 2)_____ _____ _____ _____ _____ a scheduling conflict? I know you also have piano classes.

W Those usually take place on different days.

M Then, why didn't you sign up?

W Well, we're moving to another area near my mother's new office. The problem is that it's 3)_____ _____ _____ _____ where the lessons are held.

M Oh, I see. I'm sorry you'll miss the lessons, but I'm sure you're looking forward to moving.

W Definitely. I hope you enjoy them, though.

M Thanks. I'm sure I will.

↘ 듣기 필수 표현
· sign up for ~을 신청하다
· end up 결국 ~하게 되다
· look forward to ~을 기대하다

8

M Lily, do you still want to get together on Sunday?

W Yes, Mark. I'd love to.

M Well, the Wiltshire Vintage Market ¹⁾_____ _____ _____ _____ in front of city hall if you want to go.

W Oh, that sounds great. Is it a big market?

M Yes. Apparently there will be around ²⁾_____ _____ _____ there selling secondhand clothes.

W Wow. I bet they'll have some high-quality items, then. What time should we go?

M The market opens at 9 a.m. and closes at 3 p.m., so maybe we could go in the morning?

W Yeah. I don't want to miss out on anything.

M Oh, and the website says we should bring ³⁾_____ _____ _____ _____ _____. It's a sustainable market.

W All right. I've never heard of this market, though. Does it happen every week?

M No. It's just a one-time event. It'll end next month.

↘ 듣기 필수 표현
· get together 만나다
· I bet 분명 ~이다
· miss out on ~을 놓치다

9

M Good evening, everyone. I'm honored to be here at ¹⁾_____ _____ _____ of the Edwards City Film Festival. From today, the city's theaters will ²⁾_____ _____ _____ great new films for one week. If you have purchased a festival pass, you will be able to attend these movies. However, some events and lectures may have an extra charge. For more information on these events, check the festival's website. As always, we are committed to showing the work of exciting up-and-coming filmmakers. This year, we'll show more than 50 debut movies by ³⁾_____ _____ _____.
In addition, we have more international films than ever, including this opening film, *The Clockwork Canary*. To introduce the film, here is ⁴⁾_____ _____ _____, Carlos Forman. Everyone, please give him a warm welcome!

↘ 듣기 필수 표현
· be committed to ~하는 데 최선을 다하다, 전념하다
· give ~ a warm welcome ~를 따뜻하게 맞이하다

10

M Hi, Sarah. Could I ¹⁾_____ _____ _____ _____ on coffee makers? I've found some recommendations online.

W These all look good, but how much coffee do you usually brew?

M I usually make about four cups at once for me and my family.

W I don't think you want anything smaller than that, then.

M Very true! That rules out one of the coffee makers.

W What kind of budget are you working with?

M I want to ²⁾_____ _____ _____ $200.

W That sounds reasonable. Do you have a coffee grinder?

M No, I don't. Is that important?

W ³⁾_____ _____ _____ always tastes better.

M All right. I'd better get one with that built-in, then.

W That still leaves two options.

M Hmm... I think I'll go with the one that offers a free tumbler in that case.

W I think that's a good choice.

↘ 듣기 필수 표현
· at once 한 번에
· rule out 제외시키다

11

W Professor Mathews, can I ask you a question about ¹⁾_____ _____ _____ for your politics course?

M I'm busy right now, Matilda. I ²⁾_____ _____ _____ this morning. Can you come back later today?

W Sure. Will you be around this afternoon?

↘ 듣기 필수 표현
· be around (부근에) 있다, 체재하다

12

M Did you want to ¹⁾_____ _____ _____ in the gallery, Tanya?

W Let's check out the East Wing. I heard they have some great impressionist paintings there.

M That's fine with me, but the gallery closes ²⁾_____ _____ _____ _____.

↘ 듣기 필수 표현
· check out 살펴보다

13

M Thanks for looking after the kids, Mom. They really
¹⁾_____ _____ _____ with you.

W No problem. It's always nice to see my grandchildren.

M What did you do with them today?

W We went to the zoo in the morning, and then we came home and had lunch.

M Were they well-behaved?

W Mostly. Benji got ²⁾_____ _____ _____ at the zoo, but I think he was just hungry. Both of the kids loved seeing the monkeys, though.

M That's so cute. I hope you got some photos!

W I took a few. I'll send them to you.

M Thanks. What did you do for lunch?

W I just heated up the leftover chicken and broccoli.

M Oh, wait... Did Laura ³⁾_____ _____ _____? She's been refusing to eat them lately.

W That's right. I tricked her into eating everything.

M How did you do that?

↘ **듣기 필수 표현**
· look after ~를 돌보다
· trick A into B A가 B하도록 꾀어내다

14

[Cell phone rings.]

W You've reached the Easton Police Department. This is Officer Philips speaking.

M Hi. I'm Neal Sanchez. I'm calling to follow up on a ¹⁾_____ _____ _____ last week.

W Ah, yes. I remember your case. Some items were stolen from your jewelry store, correct?

M That's right. A thief took ²⁾_____ _____ _____.

W Let me check our files. *[Typing sound]* So it looks like our officers arrested the man who did it this morning.

M How do you know it's the right person?

W Actually, we identified him from your CCTV video.

M Great! I'm glad that helped.

W He also had stolen items from several local stores, including the necklaces you mentioned.

M I see. Will we be able to ³⁾_____ _____ _____?

W We have to hold the stolen items for now, but yes. We will return them to you ⁴⁾_____ _____ _____ _____ _____.

↘ **듣기 필수 표현**
· follow up on ~에 대해 더 알아보다

15

W Mary is a very talented student who loves to ¹⁾_____ _____. Recently, her school drama club decided to put on a musical that she wrote. However, her play has 15 different characters and the drama club only has 10 actors. So the club needs to ²⁾_____ _____ _____ to fill the extra parts. Mary knows that her friend Jared has a ³⁾_____ _____ _____. He hasn't acted before, but she thinks that he would be ⁴⁾_____ _____ _____ one of the parts in the play. So Mary wants to suggest to Jared that he should try out for the drama club's musical. In this situation, what would Mary most likely say to Jared?

↘ **듣기 필수 표현**
· put on 상연하다
· try out for (오디션 등에) 도전하다

16~17

M Hello, class. Last week we discussed threats to biodiversity. This afternoon, I'd like to show how predators help other ¹⁾_____ _____ _____ _____. First off, they prevent harmful insect populations from becoming too large. Bats, for instance, play a big role in ²⁾_____ _____ _____ of insects that spread deadly diseases. Second, predators can actually increase a prey species' population. For buffaloes and other herd species, this is especially true. Since predators generally hunt ³⁾_____ _____ _____ _____, healthier animals have access to more food and are more likely to reproduce. Third, larger predators are vital to the existence of scavengers. Eagles and other scavengers rely on the meat large predators ⁴⁾_____ _____. Lastly, predators can protect plant life by influencing the behavior of their prey. Wolves are a perfect example of this. They scare away animals that eat young trees. With these grazing animals gone, the trees are free to grow again. Now, let's open our books to page 232.

↘ **듣기 필수 표현**
· play a role in ~에 역할을 하다
· have access to ~에 접근할 수 있다
· rely on ~에 의존하다
· scare away 겁주어 쫓아내다

대학수학능력시험 문제지
영어듣기 모의고사

▲ 문제 음성
바로 듣기
▲ 고사장 버전
바로 듣기

정답 및 해설 p.128

1번부터 17번까지는 듣고 답하는 문제입니다. 1번부터 15번까지는 한 번만 들려주고, 16번부터 17번까지는 두 번 들려줍니다. 방송을 잘 듣고 답을 하시기 바랍니다.

1. 다음을 듣고, 남자가 하는 말의 목적으로 가장 적절한 것을 고르시오.

① 축제 부스 제안서 제출을 재촉하려고
② 봄 소풍 날짜가 변경됨을 안내하려고
③ 학교 웹사이트 개설을 홍보하려고
④ 게임 동아리 가입 방법을 설명하려고
⑤ 다양한 미술 공예 작품들을 소개하려고

2. 대화를 듣고, 여자의 의견으로 가장 적절한 것을 고르시오.

① 단체 운동이 개인 운동보다 효과가 크다.
② 고강도 운동 후에는 휴식을 취해야 한다.
③ 짧지만 격한 운동은 효율적인 신체 관리법이다.
④ 근육을 키우려면 정확한 자세로 운동해야 한다.
⑤ 저강도의 운동을 하면 열량 소모가 천천히 이루어진다.

3. 대화를 듣고, 두 사람의 관계를 가장 잘 나타낸 것을 고르시오.

① 신문 기자 — 의사
② 소설가 — 천문학자
③ 카페 주인 — 바리스타
④ 사서 — 대학 교수
⑤ 과학자 — 삽화가

4. 대화를 듣고, 그림에서 대화의 내용과 일치하지 <u>않는</u> 것을 고르시오.

5. 대화를 듣고, 남자가 할 일로 가장 적절한 것을 고르시오.

① 승합차 예약하기
② 단백질 바 구비하기
③ 등산 코스 설문 조사하기
④ 단체 문자 메시지 보내기
⑤ 호텔 예약 확인하기

6. 대화를 듣고, 여자가 지불할 금액을 고르시오. [3점]

① $54   ② $56   ③ $60   ④ $63   ⑤ $66

7. 대화를 듣고, 남자가 달리기 대회에 참여하지 <u>못한</u> 이유를 고르시오.

① 다친 무릎이 낫지 않아서
② 예선전 기록이 좋지 못해서
③ 아침에 일찍 일어나지 못해서
④ 할머니를 병원에 모셔다드려야 해서
⑤ 가벼운 감기 기운이 있어서

8. 대화를 듣고, Junior Robotics Class에 관해 언급되지 <u>않은</u> 것을 고르시오.

① 수업 요일   ② 수업 장소   ③ 수업료
④ 소요 시간   ⑤ 대상 연령

9. Winslow Christmas Food Donation Event에 관한 다음 내용을 듣고, 일치하지 <u>않는</u> 것을 고르시오.

① 시에서 최초로 개최하는 행사이다.
② 12월 1일부터 한 달간 진행된다.
③ 현장에 기부 물품을 받을 직원이 있을 것이다.
④ 현금 기부도 받아줄 것이다.
⑤ 기부된 식품은 다섯 곳의 보육원에 전달될 것이다.

10. 다음 표를 보면서 대화를 듣고, 남자가 구매할 중고 자전거를 고르시오.

Used Bike Models

	Model	Price	Material	Foldable	Color
①	A	$200	Aluminum	X	Black
②	B	$250	Steel	X	Blue
③	C	$260	Steel	O	Red
④	D	$300	Titanium	O	Green
⑤	E	$320	Titanium	O	Yellow

11. 대화를 듣고, 여자의 마지막 말에 대한 남자의 응답으로 가장 적절한 것을 고르시오.

① No. I haven't bought a gift yet.

② Yes. We're booked for dinner at 7 p.m.

③ Alright. I'll make steaks and a salad, then.

④ It's okay. You can return the gift if you don't like it.

⑤ I did. The presentation should be finished for work tomorrow.

12. 대화를 듣고, 남자의 마지막 말에 대한 여자의 응답으로 가장 적절한 것을 고르시오.

① I know. He stars in many action movies.

② That's too bad. I won't be 18 for a few months.

③ You're all set, then. Your movie is in Theater 3.

④ I'm sorry. Then, you can't buy a ticket for this movie.

⑤ That's fine. There are still tickets for the later showing.

13. 대화를 듣고, 여자의 마지막 말에 대한 남자의 응답으로 가장 적절한 것을 고르시오. [3점]

Man: _____

① Let's aim to head out at 12 p.m.

② I'll pack a few T-shirts and shorts then.

③ I'll leave in 10 minutes to visit my parents.

④ I can change my appointment to an earlier time.

⑤ The train will be faster considering the heavy traffic.

14. 대화를 듣고, 남자의 마지막 말에 대한 여자의 응답으로 가장 적절한 것을 고르시오.

Woman: _____

① Okay. You can use my parking spot.

② No. Just turn right instead of left at the café.

③ Sure. People with dogs must sit outside, though.

④ Don't worry. I'll walk there instead.

⑤ Yes. But parking costs $2 per hour.

15. 다음 상황 설명을 듣고, Albert가 Jessica에게 할 말로 가장 적절한 것을 고르시오. [3점]

Albert: _____

① Why don't you come up with the words for the song yourself?

② I was really impressed with your performance last time.

③ I'm positive that your concert will be a great success.

④ Could you tell me if these lyrics express your ideas?

⑤ I think that your fans will love your latest song.

[16~17] 다음을 듣고, 물음에 답하시오.

16. 남자가 하는 말의 주제로 가장 적절한 것은?

① how ancient cities expanded in size

② importance of durable structures to civilizations

③ various ways buildings were made in ancient times

④ misconceptions about Roman architecture

⑤ how cities were planned in ancient times

17. 언급된 자재가 아닌 것은?

① wood　　② bricks　　③ glass

④ stone　　⑤ concrete

이제 듣기 문제가 끝났습니다. 채점을 마친 후 다음 페이지에서 방송을 다시 들으며 딕테이션 연습을 하시기 바랍니다.

* 채점 결과: 맞은 개수 _____개 / 17개　　　정답 및 해설 p.128

Dictation 정답 p.128

22회 고난도 영어듣기 모의고사 Dictation 음성을 들으며 빈칸에 알맞은 단어를 채워 넣으시기 바랍니다.

1

M Good morning, Trafford High School students. This is your principal, Mr. Burns, speaking. As most of you know, our school's Spring Festival will take place in a matter of weeks. Therefore, any last-minute booth proposals from school clubs 1)_____ _____ _____ _____ noon this Friday at the latest. After that, any new applications will not be accepted. Before submitting an idea, check the 2)_____ _____ _____ that have already been confirmed for the festival on our school's website. We currently have clubs running booths that will serve food, host games, and 3)_____ _____ _____ _____ _____. I hope to see many more new ideas in the coming days, and I look forward to celebrating at the Spring Festival with you all.

↘ **듣기 필수 표현**
· a matter of 약, 대충; ~의 문제
· at the latest 늦어도

2

M Are you already leaving the gym, Carla?

W Yeah. I'm all done with my 30-minute group class.

M Is that enough time for a good workout?

W It is! The class is 1)_____ _____ _____. Such workouts are the most efficient way to get in shape.

M Why do you say that?

W Your body keeps burning calories for several hours after a high-intensity session.

M Are you saying that you 2)_____ _____ _____ _____ _____ while you're recovering?

W Yes. The after-burn effect can last up to 16 hours. And when you exercise like that, you quickly build muscles.

M I can see why that would be. You can't take it easy in an intense class.

W Also, the short period helps you 3)_____ _____ _____ your workout.

M I want to try that. When is your next group class?

W It's at 7 p.m. on Tuesday. You should come!

↘ **듣기 필수 표현**
· be done with ~을 끝내다, 마치다
· get in shape 좋은 몸 상태를 유지하다
· burn calories 열량을 소모하다
· take it easy (일을) 쉬엄쉬엄하다

3

M Hi, Dr. Williams! It's a pleasure to meet you.

W Likewise. I hope I 1)_____ _____ _____ _____.

M No, problem. The cappuccino at this café is very good. Do you want to try one?

W No, thanks. Let's get straight into the interview.

M Sure. 2)_____ _____ _____ _____ I take notes?

W Go ahead. I imagine you'll need them when you're writing.

M That's right. I want to be as accurate as possible 3)_____ _____ _____ when it comes to science.

W I admire that in your books. I just read your last one.

M Wow, thank you! Now, I want to ask you about black holes first.

W Sure. I've been studying them 4)_____ _____ _____.

M I'm wondering how you do that.

W Just a moment. Let me draw you a picture. I think it will illustrate this point well.

↘ **듣기 필수 표현**
· get straight into 바로 ~으로 들어가다
· take notes 메모하다, 필기하다
· when it comes to ~에 관해서라면

4

M Hey, April. Would you help me get ready to paint your sister's room?

W Sure, Dad. What do you need me to do?

M Let's move a few things into the hallway. Can you 1)_____ _____ _____ in front of the window?

W Got it. What about the round mirror between the bookcase and the window?

M I'll take care of that.

W And we'd better leave the bookcase where it is. It's too big and heavy.

M You're right. Then, just move the two plant pots 2)_____ _____ _____ _____ _____.

W Okay. What about this rainbow-shaped rug?

M Can you take that downstairs? We'd better replace it.

W No problem. Is there anything else?

M We need to remove the 3)_____ _____ _____.

W It will be easier to peel off if we heat it up a little bit first.

M Good thinking. I'll try using a hair dryer. Let's get started!

↘ 듣기 필수 표현
· take care of ~을 처리하다
· peel off 벗기다
· heat up 열을 가하다, 데우다

5

M Annie, I'm looking forward to our club trip to Mount Helens National Park this weekend.

W Me too. Everyone in the hiking club 1)_____ _____ _____ _____ it, so I hope it goes well.

M Should we check our preparations, then?

W Sure. I booked a van yesterday.

M Perfect. And what about snacks for the hike?

W I've got some protein bars and fruit already.

M Okay. I also 2)_____ _____ _____ about which trails they want to do.

W What was the result?

M Most of them want to go up the north peak of the mountain.

W Okay. We'll need to leave around 6:30 a.m., then. Let's send everyone a text message 3)_____ _____.

M Can you take care of that? I don't have everyone's number.

W Sure. And I'd better call the hotel and make sure that our booking is all set.

M Don't worry about it. I'll do that later today.

↘ 듣기 필수 표현
· be all set 준비가 되어 있다

6

M Welcome to Office Supply World. May I help you?

W Hello. I need a new planner for work.

M Our planners are over here. Do you have 1)_____ _____ _____?

W I'd like a small one.

M Then, I would consider these two. This blue one here is $20, and the pink one is $30.

W Oh, I like the 2)_____ _____. I'll take it.

M Great. And do you need anything else?

W Yes. I'd also like some good pens.

M Well, this three-piece set here is our bestseller. It's $20.

W I'll 3)_____ _____ _____ _____, then. I think my husband also needs a set.

M Okay, great. So you're getting the blue planner and two sets of pens. Is that right?

W Yes. Also, I have this 10% discount coupon. Does that apply to these items?

M It applies to the pen sets, but 4)_____ _____ _____.

W That's fine. Here's my card.

↘ 듣기 필수 표현
· apply to ~에 적용되다

7

M Hi, Rachel. How was your weekend?

W It was good, but 1)_____ _____ _____ at the five-kilometer race on Saturday.

M I know. I'm sad I missed it. I wanted to set a new personal record.

W Yeah, you cut a few seconds off your record at the last practice. But why couldn't you come? Was it that injury you had last month?

M No. My 2)_____ _____ _____ _____.

W Then, did you not wake up on time? I know it was early in the morning.

M I was up early. I actually couldn't go because I had to take my grandmother to the hospital.

W Oh, I'm sorry. I hope she's feeling better now.

M Thanks. Luckily, she just had 3)_____ _____ _____, and she's fine.

W Glad to hear that.

M I'll be sure to run in the next race. See you at the next practice!

↘ 듣기 필수 표현
· set a record 기록을 세우다
· cut off ~을 줄이다
· be sure to 꼭 ~하다

8

W Hi, Joseph. Did your son enjoy Junior Robotics Class last weekend?

M He loved it. Were you 1)_____ _____ _____ _____ your son Ryan for the next one?

W Oh, I didn't realize there was another class scheduled.

M Yeah, the robotics class is held on the 2)_____ _____ _____ _____ _____.

W Oh, interesting. Is it always held in the Bluemont Community Center?

M That's right. So it's just a quick walk from our apartment complex.

W I heard the class is 3)_____ _____ _____. Is that correct?

M It is. The class lasts from 11 a.m. to 3 p.m.

W Are you sure Ryan can sign up? He's a sixth-grader now.

M Sure! It's open to kids who are 4)_____ _____ _____ of 8 and 14.

W I'll see if he's interested. It sounds like a good opportunity.

M I think he'd like it!

9

W Hello, listeners. This is Mayor Janet Harrison. I'm glad to announce that our city government has decided to 1)_____ _____ _____ _____ Winslow Christmas Food Donation Event. The event will run for a month beginning on December 1st. We will set up the event booths by city hall and have 2)_____ _____ _____ to collect any donations that you bring. We will accept food donations and monetary contributions. If you want to donate food, only canned or dry food is acceptable. The collected food and funds will be given to five local institutions, including 3)_____ _____ _____ _____ _____. We thank you so much for your time and any help you can offer. I hope all of you enjoy the holiday season!

10

W Hey, Jasper. Have you picked out a bike yet?

M No, but I went to the used bike shop yesterday, and I've narrowed it down to a few options. Do you want to 1)_____ _____ _____ _____ one?

W Sure. What is the most you want to spend on it?

M I want to pay $300 2)_____ _____. That seems reasonable for a used bike.

W Okay, so not this one. And what about the material of the bike?

M Steel and titanium are fine, but I don't want to deal with aluminum. It's 3)_____ _____ _____ _____.

W Okay, then does the bike have to be foldable?

M I think that would be more convenient for storing it, so yeah.

W Then, all you have to do is pick a color. These are the ones left.

M The 4)_____ _____ looks nicer, so I'll go for that.

↘ **듣기 필수 표현**
· pick out 고르다, 선택하다
· narrow down to ~으로 좁히다
· deal with ~을 취급하다, 다루다

11

W Honey, I'm so excited that it's 1)_____ _____ _____ this Friday.

M Me too. It was really hard to pick out your gift, but I think you're going to love it.

W I'm sure I will. I also can't wait to go to a nice dinner after a long day of work. Did you 2)_____ _____ _____ yesterday?

↘ **듣기 필수 표현**
· can't wait to ~이 너무 기대되다, 빨리 ~하고 싶다

12

M Hello, I'd like a ticket to see the new action movie starring Harry Golding.

W Well, the movie 1)_____ _____ _____ _____, so those under 18 years are not allowed to watch it. May I ask how 2)_____ _____ _____?

M Oh, I didn't know that. I'm only 17.

13

W Honey, are you done packing for the trip to my parents' house tomorrow?

M Not yet. I can start right now.

W My parents said it's been really hot, so be sure to 1)_____ _____ _____ _____ _____ .

M Got it. And we'd better take our sunglasses, too.

W Okay. I also looked up the 2)_____ _____ _____ for tomorrow. Apparently, the roads will be very busy since everyone's going out of town.

M I guess that's not a surprise.

W Yeah, so we should leave early tomorrow to beat traffic.

M Well, we can't leave until after 11:30 a.m. because of 3)_____ _____ _____ .

W Oh, I totally forgot about that.

M Yeah, it's just a checkup, but it's the only time I could get an appointment in the next few weeks.

W That's okay. So 4)_____ _____ _____ _____ _____ we can leave for my parents' house, then?

↘ 듣기 필수 표현
· look up (정보를) 찾아보다
· beat traffic 교통 체증을 피하다
· not A until B B가 되어서야 A하다

14

[Cell phone rings.]

W Hi, Justin. Are we still meeting this afternoon?

M Of course. I was 1)_____ _____ _____ _____ I could bring my dog. It would be nice to get him out of the house.

W Sure! There's actually a great dog park inside the park we're going to.

M Oh, perfect. What else is in that area?

W There's a really nice café nearby. We can walk there from the park for a coffee.

M Is it 2)_____ _____ ?

W It is. I see dogs there all the time.

M Then, I'd love to check it out. But I have to think about parking.

W Oh, right. You'll need to drive if you're bringing your dog.

M Would I be able to leave my car in your building's garage?

W I don't think that would be helpful. It's a long walk from my place.

M Well, is there 3)_____ _____ _____ at the park?

15

W Jessica is a singer, and Albert is a songwriter. She asked him to write a new song that she will perform at her next concert. She wants the song to 1)_____ _____ to her fans. Albert has finished creating the music for the song. It has a very 2)_____ _____ _____ . But he is having difficulties writing the lyrics. He is finding it hard to express 3)_____ _____ _____ _____ . He also thinks that Jessica's fans would appreciate it if she was involved in the songwriting process. So he wants to suggest to Jessica that she 4)_____ _____ _____ _____ . In this situation, what would Albert most likely say to Jessica?

↘ 듣기 필수 표현
· be involved in ~에 참여하다, 관련되다

16~17

M Good morning, everyone. Last time, we discussed reasons why city planning became necessary in ancient civilizations. Today, I want to give you a brief overview of 1)_____ _____ _____ . At first, builders could only create simple structures 2)_____ _____ _____ . These homes did not protect people from rain and wind well because of the gaps between the sticks or logs. Eventually, builders found ways to make 3)_____ _____ _____ _____ . They started to use bricks that fit together tightly. This method is at least 9,000 years old. Later, ancient builders began to make beautiful and durable structures from stone. However, the material was difficult to work with, so it was only used for special structures like temples or monuments. The last example I want to look at is the surprising use of concrete in Roman times. Concrete's strength and cost-effectiveness allowed builders to create structures 4)_____ _____ _____ _____ , so it became the go-to material for public buildings. Now, let's take a look at some pictures of ancient buildings.

↘ 듣기 필수 표현
· give an overview of ~의 개요를 설명하다
· fit together 꼭 들어맞다

대학수학능력시험 문제지

영어듣기 모의고사

▲ 문제 음성
바로 듣기

▲ 고사장 버전
바로 듣기

정답 및 해설 p.134

1번부터 17번까지는 듣고 답하는 문제입니다. 1번부터 15번까지는 한 번만 들려주고, 16번부터 17번까지는 두 번 들려줍니다. 방송을 잘 듣고 답을 하시기 바랍니다.

1. 다음을 듣고, 여자가 하는 말의 목적으로 가장 적절한 것을 고르시오.

① 연극부 운영 회의 안건을 발표하려고
② 동아리 회의 장소 변경을 공지하려고
③ 학생회장 입후보 절차를 설명하려고
④ 극단 가입 신청 기간을 안내하려고
⑤ 정기 공연에 출연할 배우를 모집하려고

2. 대화를 듣고, 여자의 의견으로 가장 적절한 것을 고르시오.

① 바다는 많은 해양생물에 은신처를 제공한다.
② 야생동물에 너무 가까이 다가가지 말아야 한다.
③ 해변에서 조개껍데기 같은 것을 함부로 가져오면 안 된다.
④ 외래종의 유입은 생태계 균형 파괴의 주요 원인이다.
⑤ 놀러 갔을 때 사진을 찍는 대신 눈으로 풍경을 즐겨야 한다.

3. 대화를 듣고, 두 사람의 관계를 가장 잘 나타낸 것을 고르시오.

① 방송 기자 — 경찰관
② 여론 조사원 — 정치학 교수
③ 기상 캐스터 — 시청 공무원
④ 프로듀서 — 환경운동가
⑤ 뉴스 앵커 — 정치인

4. 대화를 듣고, 그림에서 대화의 내용과 일치하지 않는 것을 고르시오.

5. 대화를 듣고, 남자가 할 일로 가장 적절한 것을 고르시오.

① 책 추가 주문하기
② 작가에게 전화하기
③ 고객에게 이메일 보내기
④ 현수막 찾아오기
⑤ 책꽂이 옮기기

6. 대화를 듣고, 여자가 지불할 금액을 고르시오. [3점]

① $32 ② $34 ③ $36 ④ $40 ⑤ $46

7. 대화를 듣고, 남자가 시험에서 좋은 성적을 받지 못한 이유를 고르시오.

① 공부할 시간이 부족해서
② 배탈 때문에 집중을 못 해서
③ 수학 시험과 날짜를 착각해서
④ 시험 본다는 사실을 잊어버려서
⑤ 보고서를 쓰는 데 더 치중해서

8. 대화를 듣고, Junior Bowling Tournament에 관해 언급되지 않은 것을 고르시오.

① 일시   ② 참가팀 인원   ③ 신청 방법
④ 참가비   ⑤ 장소

9. Winter Computer Camp에 관한 다음 내용을 듣고, 일치하지 않는 것을 고르시오.

① 강사진은 컴퓨터 공학 교수들이다.
② 12세 이상부터 참여할 수 있다.
③ 2주 동안 매일 진행된다.
④ 등록 모집 인원은 20명이다.
⑤ 금요일 오후 5시부터 등록 신청을 받는다.

10. 다음 표를 보면서 대화를 듣고, 두 사람이 대여할 부스를 고르시오.

Booth Rentals

	Booth	Space	Price	Rental Time	Premium Spot
①	A	4m²	$85	9 a.m.-1 p.m.	X
②	B	6m²	$100	8 a.m.-12 p.m.	X
③	C	8m²	$150	8 a.m.-12 p.m.	O
④	D	10m²	$165	1 p.m.-5 p.m.	O
⑤	E	12m²	$200	9 a.m.-1 p.m.	O

11. 대화를 듣고, 여자의 마지막 말에 대한 남자의 응답으로 가장 적절한 것을 고르시오.

① The plumber's number is on that notepad.
② Let's try to get it fixed as soon as possible.
③ I just brushed my teeth a few minutes ago.
④ Let me just wash my hands in the sink first.
⑤ I actually cleaned the bathroom this morning.

12. 대화를 듣고, 남자의 마지막 말에 대한 여자의 응답으로 가장 적절한 것을 고르시오.

① Sure. I'll take an iced latte, please.
② Okay. I'll send the address of the café.
③ You're right. The traffic is from an accident.
④ Please hurry. Your coffee will get cold.
⑤ Don't worry. I'll take my car instead.

13. 대화를 듣고, 여자의 마지막 말에 대한 남자의 응답으로 가장 적절한 것을 고르시오. [3점]

Man: _____

① The history essay is only due next week.
② I'm sure he would love to talk with you.
③ I think I need to check my article again.
④ I'll see you tomorrow for the interview.
⑤ It should be a very interesting lecture.

14. 대화를 듣고, 남자의 마지막 말에 대한 여자의 응답으로 가장 적절한 것을 고르시오.

Woman: _____

① Exactly. You'll need to wear sunscreen there in the summer.
② You're right. The prices are higher during the peak season.
③ Definitely. We had a wonderful vacation in Europe last year.
④ That's true. I'll start looking at flights and hotels now.
⑤ That's fine. We can just go to the beach next time.

15. 다음 상황 설명을 듣고, Steve가 Diana에게 할 말로 가장 적절한 것을 고르시오. [3점]

Steve: _____

① I think I can find another good space topic.
② Do you think we can both write about asteroids?
③ Can you share your paper on the solar system with me?
④ Wow, I didn't realize that asteroids were so interesting.
⑤ Why don't we team up to work on the class presentation?

[16~17] 다음을 듣고, 물음에 답하시오.

16. 여자가 하는 말의 주제로 가장 적절한 것은?

① reasons people don't vote
② ways of motivating people to vote
③ how to choose someone to vote for
④ consequences of low voting rates
⑤ results of international elections

17. 언급된 나라가 아닌 것은?

① Switzerland ② Argentina ③ Belgium
④ France ⑤ Australia

이제 듣기 문제가 끝났습니다. 채점을 마친 후 다음 페이지에서 방송을 다시 들으며 딕테이션 연습을 하시기 바랍니다.

* 채점 결과: 맞은 개수 _____개 / 17개　　　　정답 및 해설 p.134

23회 Dictation

Dictation 정답 p.134

23회 고난도 영어듣기 모의고사 Dictation 음성을 들으며 빈칸에 알맞은 단어를 채워 넣으시기 바랍니다.

1

W Good morning, everyone. This is Drama Club President, Sally Howard. As you know, the Drama Club's first meeting of the year will be held today at 5 p.m. We will start by 1)_____ _____ _____ _____ _____, and then we will begin planning this year's performances. Since we accepted so many students into our club this semester, our group will have 2)_____ _____ _____ members as before. That's why we've decided to change the location of our meeting to 3)_____ _____ _____ _____. Instead of taking place in the student council room, it will now be held in the auditorium so that we'll have plenty of space. I look forward to seeing all of you there and hope you have a great rest of the day!

2

M Sarah, it's such a nice day. Isn't this beach beautiful?

W Yes. The water is so blue, and there aren't any clouds in the sky.

M Oh, look! There's a pretty seashell. I want to take it home with me.

W Hmm... You shouldn't 1)_____ _____ _____ _____ like seashells and stones from the beach.

M I disagree. It's not a living creature.

W Sure, but removing those things from a habitat can 2)_____ _____ _____ _____.

M Really? I had no idea that they were so important.

W Many animals and plants need these objects for specific purposes. For example, a crab could use that shell for shelter.

M Well, I definitely don't want to 3)_____ _____ _____ here.

W You can take a picture of it instead or just enjoy looking at it now.

M You're right. Thanks for letting me know.

3

W Mr. Dillon, thank you for your time today.

M You're welcome, Ms. Charles. I'm happy to talk to you and your viewers.

W I want to first congratulate you 1)_____ _____ _____ _____.

M Thank you. I'm honored to represent our city's residents.

W Many claim they voted for you due to your crime prevention policies. Can you give us more details?

M Sure. I want to increase the budget of local police departments.

W Why is that necessary?

M Well, with more money, we'll 2)_____ _____ _____ _____ being used by our police.

W Do you have any other future plans for the city?

M Yes. I also hope to provide more public transportation options. This is necessary to 3)_____ _____ _____ and traffic jams.

W And do you have any final messages for our viewers today?

M I do. I appreciate your votes, and I won't let you down.

W Great. Now, it's time for the weekly weather report.

↘ 듣기 필수 표현
· due to ~ 때문에
· let ~ down ~를 실망시키다

4

M Wow, honey. I love how you decorated the backyard for our son's birthday party.

W Thank you. But do you think he will like it?

M Definitely. That soccer goal 1)_____ _____ _____ _____ is perfect. I'm sure the kids will enjoy that.

W That's what I thought. Our dog is already playing with the ball on the grass.

M I saw that. But what's that table 2)_____ _____ _____ for?

W That's for face painting.

M I see. It's nice that there will be so many activities.

W Yes. And I've also put some heart-shaped balloons next to the table.

M They look good. 3)_____ _____ _____ you have his gifts in are unique.

W Do you think they're okay next to the balloons there?

M Yes. Everything is perfect just as it is.

W Thanks. I really hope our son has a wonderful time.

↘ 듣기 필수 표현
· just as it is 있는 그대로

5

W Hey, Eric. Is everything ready for our bookstore's signing event next week?

M Almost. I actually just emailed all our customers about it.

W And did you pick up that banner we're hanging in the store?

M I did. It looks great.

W Excellent. I 1)_____ _____ _____ this morning to confirm all of the event details.

M Does he have any requests?

W He said he'd appreciate it if we put his other books on display.

M Do we have 2)_____ _____ _____ _____ in the store?

W I think so, but I ordered a few more just in case.

M I guess the only thing we have to worry about is 3)_____ _____ _____ for the event.

W Yeah, we'll need more open space. I'll get here early that day to handle it.

M No, I'll take care of that now. You've done enough.

W Thanks. That's very kind of you.

↘ 듣기 필수 표현
· pick up ~을 찾아오다, 찾다
· put ~ on display ~을 진열하다, 전시하다
· just in case 만약을 위해서

6

M Welcome to Carter Movie Theater. How can I help you?

W Do you have 1)_____ _____ _____ for *Future Seems Good*?

M We have tickets for both 11 a.m. and 1 p.m. The 11 a.m. showing has an early-bird price.

W Oh, what's 2)_____ _____ _____?

M It's $10 for a ticket instead of $12.

W In that case, I'd like three tickets for 11 o'clock.

M Great. And would you be interested in buying a mini movie poster? They're $5 each.

W Oh, I like those. Um, I'll take 3)_____ _____ _____. And can I use my VIP membership card?

M Yes. You're actually entitled to a 20% discount. However, that will 4)_____ _____ _____ _____.

W Sure. That's fine.

M Okay. Your total is on the screen, ma'am.

W Here you go.

M Enjoy the movie!

↘ 듣기 필수 표현
· be entitled to ~을 받을 자격이 있다, ~이 주어지다

7

W Hi, Adam. Come in.

M Is there something wrong, Ms. Barnes?

W I just graded your English test from last week. Your score was 1)_____ _____ _____ _____.

M I see.

W Did you forget about the test?

M Not at all. I had a math test last week, too. So I 2)_____ _____ about both test dates every day.

W Then, did you run out of time to study?

M No. It wasn't that, either. It was actually because I 3)_____ _____ _____ on the exam day. I couldn't focus on the exam.

W Oh, I'm very sorry that happened. Are you feeling better now?

M Yes. I'm okay now. I'll work hard on 4)_____ _____ _____ to make up for it.

↘ 듣기 필수 표현
· run out of ~이 부족하다, ~을 다 써버리다
· make up for ~을 만회하다, 보충하다

8

W Rick, what are you looking at on your phone?

M Hi, Angela. I'm reading about this year's Junior Bowling Tournament.

W Oh, I heard it was fun last year. When is it?

M It starts at 5 p.m. on November 23rd.

W Wow, that's soon. Are you 1)_____ _____ _____?

M Yes, but it requires participants to register as part of a four-person team. So do you want to 2)_____ _____ _____? I'll also ask some other friends to join.

W Hmm... Is there any entry fee?

M Yeah. It costs $20 to enter. Is that too much?

W No. It's fine. Count me in. 3)_____ _____ _____ _____?

M It will be at the Astro Bowling Center downtown.

W Perfect. I hope we have a great time together.

↘ 듣기 필수 표현
· count ~ in ~를 끼워주다

9

W Hello, parents. As you know, technology is becoming 1)_____ _____ _____ _____ to our world. So why don't you give your kids a head start at mastering it? Sign them up for Winter Computer Camp to provide them with the skills they need for their future. Our instructors are 2)_____ _____ _____ who will help your children learn about different computer programs and features. This course is open to children who are 12 or older. Classes will be held from 9 a.m. to 4 p.m. 3)_____ _____ _____ _____ on the campus of Andersen College. And only 20 students can register. Registration is open online 4)_____ _____ _____ _____ p.m. Don't let this opportunity pass you by, and register today. We hope to see you soon!

↘ 듣기 필수 표현
· provide A with B A에게 B를 제공하다

10

W Robert, did you 1)_____ _____ _____ to sell our photographs at the art market next Saturday yet?

M I'm looking at the website to book a booth now.

W Oh, let's see. [Pause] Well, this one is too small. I think it should be over five square meters.

M Okay, and 2)_____ _____ _____ _____?

W Let's try to keep it under $200.

M Good idea. That still leaves us with a few options.

W Right. What about the rental time?

M I don't think the afternoon will be as busy, so let's book a booth 3)_____ _____ _____.

W Then, this one won't work.

M And I don't think we need a premium spot at the market.

W I disagree. By 4)_____ _____ _____ _____, we will have a booth right by the entrance. People will see us easily.

M Okay. Let's go for it, then.

W That sounds good.

11

W Honey, there's 1)_____ _____ _____ the bathroom sink. When I brush my teeth, the water doesn't drain.

M Oh, no. The pipe must be blocked. I guess we have to 2)_____ _____ _____.

W I can do it. When should I ask him to come?

↘ 듣기 필수 표현
· brush one's teeth 양치질하다

12

[Cell phone rings.]

M Hey, Julie. Are you on your way to the café? Did you forget we are supposed to meet here today?

W Hi, Mark. I'm stuck in traffic, so I'm running a little late. I'm sorry 1)_____ _____ _____.

M No, it's okay. If you want, I can go ahead and 2)_____ _____ _____.

↘ 듣기 필수 표현
· be one's way to ~로 오는[가는] 중이다
· be supposed to ~하기로 하다
· stuck in traffic 차가 막히는, 교통이 정체된
· be running late 늦어지다

13

M Hey, Tina. 1)_____ _____ _____ your history essay.

W Thank you, Mr. Roberts.

M It was very well written. It seems like your writing has improved a lot this year.

W Yes, I joined the student newspaper a couple months ago and 2)_____ _____ _____. It's taught me a lot about how to be an effective writer.

M I bet. Are you interested in journalism as a career?

W I think so. I really love telling stories and interviewing people.

M So what article are you working on right now?

W I'm writing an 3)_____ _____ _____ _____ that's going to take place at the local museum next week.

M Do you mean the one about the founding of our city?

W That's right!

M Well, I know the lecturer. If you want, I can put you in touch with him.

W Thank you! That would help. Do you think he would 4)_____ _____ _____?

↘ 듣기 필수 표현
· put A in touch with B A를 B와 연락이 닿게 하다

14

M Where do you want to go for a vacation this year, honey?

W We went to the beach last year, so let's visit a place 1)_____ _____ _____ this time.

M We could rent a cabin by a lake. There are many good places nearby.

W I'd rather go abroad.

M Okay. Then, maybe we should visit a city in Europe.

W I really want to be close to nature, too. I don't want to just be in a city the whole time.

M Hmm... How about going to Finland? Then, we can stay in a place close to 2)_____ _____ _____ _____ _____.

W That sounds perfect.

M Great. So we should decide when we want to go.

W I think summer would be best. It's too cold there at other times of the year.

M That makes sense. But summer is peak season, so we better hurry to get all of 3)_____ _____ _____.

↘ 듣기 필수 표현
· would rather 차라리 ~하고 싶다
· the whole time 내내

15

M Steve and Diana are 1)_____ _____ _____. They both spend their free time reading books about it. So both of them were excited when their science class started studying the solar system this week. Today, they were given a group project. The students were 2)_____ _____ _____ a space-related topic for a class presentation. Each student submitted a piece of paper with their choice of topic written on it. Since both Steve and Diana have been reading about asteroids in their spare time, they both wrote "asteroids." After Steve finds out that he and Diana have the same idea, he wants to suggest to her that they 3)_____ _____ _____ _____ _____. In this situation, what would Steve most likely say to Diana?

16~17

W Hello, class. In today's lecture, I'm going to talk about elections. Specifically, I'd like to look at some successful methods 1)_____ _____ _____. The first one is mandatory voting. For example, people in Switzerland have to 2)_____ _____ _____ if they don't vote. According to one study, this increased voting by around 10%. Next, in Argentina, there is a 3)_____ _____ _____ _____ _____ _____. If people do not go to the polls, they are prohibited from holding government positions for three years. Another effective approach is to make election day a national holiday. Belgium is one such country. Thanks to its holiday, the country has a voting rate of nearly 75%. 4)_____ _____ _____ is to make voting a fun and welcoming experience. We can see one example of this in Australia. Its people often host barbecues outside of its polling places and cook so-called "democracy sausages." Nine out of ten people there vote. Now, let's take a look at a quick video clip on this subject.

↘ 듣기 필수 표현
· go to the poll 투표소에 가다
· be prohibited from ~하는 것이 금지되다
· thanks to ~ 덕분에

고난도
24회

제3교시

대학수학능력시험 문제지
영어듣기 모의고사

▲ 문제 음성
바로 듣기
▲ 고사장 버전
바로 듣기

정답 및 해설 p.140

1번부터 17번까지는 듣고 답하는 문제입니다. 1번부터 15번까지는 한 번만 들려주고, 16번부터 17번까지는 두 번 들려줍니다. 방송을 잘 듣고 답을 하시기 바랍니다.

1. 다음을 듣고, 남자가 하는 말의 목적으로 가장 적절한 것을 고르시오.

① 미술용품 구입처를 소개하려고
② 온라인 미술 강의를 홍보하려고
③ 강의 시간 변경을 공지하려고
④ 미술 학원의 신규 강사를 모집하려고
⑤ 실시간 강의 수강 방법을 설명하려고

2. 대화를 듣고, 여자의 의견으로 가장 적절한 것을 고르시오.

① 감기 치료제로 항생제를 쓰면 안 된다.
② 아플 때 빨리 나으려면 병원에 바로 가야 한다.
③ 의약품을 함부로 아무 데나 버리면 안 된다.
④ 처방 없이 항생제를 복용하는 것은 안전하지 않다.
⑤ 영양제를 꾸준히 먹으면 감기 예방 효과를 볼 수 있다.

3. 대화를 듣고, 두 사람의 관계를 가장 잘 나타낸 것을 고르시오.

① 편집장 — 탐험가
② 소설가 — 환경운동가
③ 사진작가 — 동물 조련사
④ 잡지 기자 — 해양 생물학자
⑤ 영화감독 — 아쿠아리움 직원

4. 대화를 듣고, 그림에서 대화의 내용과 일치하지 않는 것을 고르시오.

5. 대화를 듣고, 여자가 할 일로 가장 적절한 것을 고르시오.

① 잉크 사 오기
② 디자인 작업하기
③ 광고지 배포하기
④ 친구에게 연락하기
⑤ 할인 행사 준비하기

6. 대화를 듣고, 남자가 지불할 금액을 고르시오. [3점]

① $36　② $48　③ $60　④ $78　⑤ $96

7. 대화를 듣고, 여자가 축제 무대에 서지 못한 이유를 고르시오.

① 강풍으로 무대가 취소돼서
② 유행 중인 독감에 걸려서
③ 조명 장치에 문제가 생겨서
④ 가게 일을 거들어야 해서
⑤ 춤을 연습하다가 다리가 부러져서

8. 대화를 듣고, The Poetry Night에 관해 언급되지 않은 것을 고르시오.

① 변경 장소　　　　② 행사 날짜
③ 참여 시인 수　　 ④ 리허설 시작 시간
⑤ 기념품

9. Earth All Together 콘서트에 관한 다음 내용을 듣고, 일치하지 않는 것을 고르시오.

① 지난주에 Griffith Park에서 열렸다.
② 환경 보호의 중요성을 강조하려는 취지에서 개최되었다.
③ Green Planet Network의 전임 회장에게 영감을 받았다.
④ 1969년에 최초로 개최된 이후 계속되어왔다.
⑤ 1,200만 달러를 모을 수 있었다.

10. 다음 표를 보면서 대화를 듣고, 두 사람이 예매할 열차 편을 고르시오.

Train Tickets from Paris to Marseille

	Train	Departure Time	Train Type	Number of changes	Price
①	A	3:30 p.m.	High Speed	0	€90
②	B	4:30 p.m.	Standard	1	€50
③	C	4:30 p.m.	Standard	2	€30
④	D	5:45 p.m.	Standard	1	€75
⑤	E	5:45 p.m.	High Speed	2	€80

11. 대화를 듣고, 남자의 마지막 말에 대한 여자의 응답으로 가장 적절한 것을 고르시오.

① No way. That service is too expensive.

② Don't worry. Take as much time as you need.

③ Oh, wait. Then, we won't close until late tonight.

④ Great. I'll come by around 6 o'clock then.

⑤ Thank you. My car looks amazing.

12. 대화를 듣고, 여자의 마지막 말에 대한 남자의 응답으로 가장 적절한 것을 고르시오.

① It's a 45-minute bus ride both ways.

② Do you want to walk over there now?

③ I will know when we move next week.

④ My dad can drive us there if we ask him.

⑤ That's pretty far from my work, actually.

13. 대화를 듣고, 여자의 마지막 말에 대한 남자의 응답으로 가장 적절한 것을 고르시오. [3점]

Man: _____

① Don't wait. Just send it to a phone repairperson now.

② Of course not. I've saved a lot of money already.

③ No, I don't. I couldn't find it on the website.

④ I'm sorry. My phone broke last night.

⑤ Not at all. I'll text them to you now.

14. 대화를 듣고, 남자의 마지막 말에 대한 여자의 응답으로 가장 적절한 것을 고르시오.

Woman: _____

① This album looks nice. And it's only $20.

② That's a great idea. I bet they'd both love that.

③ Not at all. You can keep the photos if you want.

④ That's right. We'll leave for their house around 3 p.m.

⑤ Everyone, get together. I want to take a quick picture.

15. 다음 상황 설명을 듣고, Max가 Katie에게 할 말로 가장 적절한 것을 고르시오. [3점]

Max: _____

① Don't forget to prepare for the next writing workshop.

② I think you should focus on your writing goals right now.

③ You should join the workshop to make your book better.

④ How about reading each other's books and giving feedback?

⑤ You'd better spend more time writing in order to finish your book.

[16~17] 다음을 듣고, 물음에 답하시오.

16. 여자가 하는 말의 주제로 가장 적절한 것은?

① why Pluto is not classified as a planet

② planets that are unable to support life

③ various features of our solar system's planets

④ why some planets are much larger than others

⑤ how the planets in our solar system were formed

17. 언급된 행성이 아닌 것은?

① Mercury ② Venus ③ Mars

④ Jupiter ⑤ Saturn

이제 듣기 문제가 끝났습니다. 채점을 마친 후 다음 페이지에서 방송을 다시 들으며 딕테이션 연습을 하시기 바랍니다.

* 채점 결과: 맞은 개수 _____개 / 17개   정답 및 해설 p.140

Dictation 정답 p.140

24회 고난도 영어듣기 모의고사 Dictation 음성을 들으며 빈칸에 알맞은 단어를 채워 넣으시기 바랍니다.

1

M Hello, listeners. Do you want to create art from the comfort of your home? Then, 1)_____ _____ _____ an Easy Art online course and make beautiful pieces where you live! With Easy Art courses, you don't need to go out and 2)_____ _____ _____. Instead, we send kits including paintbrushes, paints, and canvases right to your door. Make your own work and learn about art with the help of our professional instructors online in either live streaming classes or recorded sessions. To register, just visit our website at www.easyart.com. We can't wait to 3)_____ _____ _____ _____!

↘ 듣기 필수 표현
· from the comfort of ~에서 편안하게
· right to one's door (~의) 바로 현관 앞까지

2

W Ron, what is that medicine you're taking?

M I have a slight cold, so I'm 1)_____ _____ _____.

W I don't think that's a good idea. You shouldn't use them to treat a cold.

M Why not?

W Every time you use antibiotics, it can 2)_____ _____ _____.

M But I need to get better fast. Aren't antibiotics helpful for that?

W Actually, no. They can't cure a cold.

M Really? I thought antibiotics would kill the cold virus.

W That's a common misunderstanding. Antibiotics are only effective at getting rid of bacteria. They have no effect on viruses.

M Oh, I didn't realize that. So antibiotics won't help me at all.

W Exactly! You'll 3)_____ _____ _____, and the drug may be less effective when you actually need it.

M Okay. I'll stop taking it. Thanks for the advice.

↘ 듣기 필수 표현
· have a slight cold 감기 기운이 있다
· get rid of ~을 없애다
· have an effect on ~에 영향을 주다
· not ~ at all 전혀 ~ 아니다

3

M Thank you for meeting with me, Ms. Michaels.

W Of course. I'm 1)_____ _____ _____ of your magazine articles, so I'm excited to be featured in one.

M I'm happy to hear it. So you've recently been 2)_____ _____ _____ _____ _____ on sea turtles. Can you tell me more about that?

W Yes. I've been tracking different species of sea turtles to get a better idea of their movements.

M Why is this data helpful?

W Well, 3)_____ _____ _____ _____ about their movements, the easier they are to protect.

M Why is their protection so important?

W Sea turtles are critical to the health of our oceans. They keep our reefs 4)_____ _____ _____ and transport nutrients from the water to land.

M That's amazing. What's your next goal, then?

W I'm going to examine fish that live in and around reefs.

M I see. I hope your studies go well. And thank you so much for your time.

↘ 듣기 필수 표현
· be featured in (신문, 잡지 등에) 실리다
· get a better idea of ~을 더 잘 알다
· go well 순조롭게 진행되다

4

W Well, it looks as if everything is ready for the school's band auditions, Kevin.

M I think so. What catches your eye the most?

W I really love the banner with "Good Luck" on it above the stage.

M Thanks. I thought it might help the students feel more comfortable.

W Why did you set up a chair 1)_____ _____ _____ _____?

M Each participant will sit there and play.

W I see the microphone is already set up 2)_____ _____ _____ _____. Did you test the sound system?

M I did that this morning. We're all good to go.

W Great! What is the rectangular table facing the stage for?

M That's where the senior band members will sit.

W I see. And did you put the 3)_____ _____ _____ ?

M Yeah, but I brought only two. I should find out who brought the other one.

W Maybe it's one of the senior members.

↘ 듣기 필수 표현
· catch one's eye 눈길을 끌다
· set up 설치하다
· good to go 시작할 준비가 된

5

W Honey, you seem really stressed. Is everything okay?

M Well, our clothing shop's 1)_____ _____ _____ this month. I'm so worried about it.

W I think it's because of the cold weather. It'll be all right soon.

M I still think we should find a way to bring in more customers.

W Do you have any ideas?

M Why don't we have a sale? If we 2)_____ _____ _____ _____ new arrivals, more shoppers might stop by.

W I think we would lose money from that. How about handing out flyers instead?

M Good idea. I can make a design on the computer today.

W No, let me 3)_____ _____ _____ . She's a great designer, so she can create an impressive flyer.

M That sounds great. Then, I'll buy some ink for the printer so we can just print them out here.

W All right. I hope it helps with business!

↘ 듣기 필수 표현
· bring in ~를 끌어들이다, 유치하다
· stop by 들르다
· lose money 손해를 보다
· hand out ~을 나눠주다, 배포하다

6

W Good afternoon. Is there anything in particular you're looking for?

M Yes. I need to 1)_____ _____ _____ , please.

W Okay. Well, we have yellow bulbs and white bulbs.

M How much are they?

W The yellow bulbs are $3 each, and the white ones are $5 each.

M I see. Do they 2)_____ _____ _____ of time?

W Yes. Now that you mention it, we also have an LED bulb that's $8.

M That's expensive compared to the others.

W It is, but it's very long-lasting. It also uses 3)_____ _____ , so it's cheaper in the long run.

M Got it. Then, I'll take six LED bulbs and six yellow bulbs.

W All right. *[Pause]* Oh, I'm sorry. It looks like the yellow bulbs are out of stock.

M In that case, I'll get 4)_____ _____ _____ _____ _____ instead.

W No problem. Here you go.

↘ 듣기 필수 표현
· Now that you mention it 그 말을 듣고 보니
· compared to ~에 비해
· in the long run 장기적으로
· out of stock 재고가 떨어진

7

M Hi, Angela. How was your performance at the festival last Friday?

W Hey, Mark. Do you mean my dance group performance?

M Yeah! I was looking forward to seeing you, but I had to help out at my family's shop that evening.

W We actually didn't end up 1)_____ _____ _____ .

M Was someone in your group sick? The flu is going around.

W That's true. But everyone was feeling good that day.

M Oh, wasn't there a problem with the lighting? I heard that 2)_____ _____ _____ _____ during the magic show.

W You are right about the lighting problem, but we couldn't perform because of the weather. There were 3)_____ _____ , so the whole event ended early.

M That's bad luck! Is it going to be rescheduled?

W No. It's canceled, but we'll have another show next week.

M Break a leg! I'll definitely be there!

↘ 듣기 필수 표현
· help out 거들다, 돕다
· end up 끝내 ~하게 되다
· go around 유행하다, 퍼지다
· Break a leg! 행운을 빌어!

8

[Telephone rings.]

W Hi. This is Cheryl Williams. I wanted to talk to you about The Poetry Night.

M Oh, do you mean the poetry-reading event I'm hosting?

W Yeah. We've had to make a few changes.

M Go on.

W Well, there has been ¹⁾_____ _____ _____ _____ _____. We're moving the event to the Hampton Center.

M Will it still be on the same night?

W Yeah. It will ²⁾_____ _____ _____ _____ on September 12th.

M Okay, good. And will I be introducing the same poets?

W Yes. All ³⁾_____ _____ _____ _____ will be participating.

M Is there anything else I need to know?

W Oh, make sure to be there by 6. That's when we will begin rehearsing.

M No problem. I'll be there then.

W That's perfect. Thanks.

↘ 듣기 필수 표현
· make sure to 꼭 ~하다

9

W Good evening. I'm here to discuss an event that I organize every year. Last week, we held the most recent Earth All Together concert in Griffith Park. As always, the purpose of the concert was to ¹⁾_____ _____ _____ of protecting the environment. We were inspired by John Graham, ²⁾_____ _____ _____ _____ of Green Planet Network, who was dedicated to protecting our planet. We have carried on his mission with Earth All Together ever since our first concert in 1969. Thanks to our close collaboration with musicians and activists, we've been ³⁾_____ _____ _____ _____ $12 million and spread awareness about key issues. I really appreciate your support and interest in our concert. We'll be back with even better performances next year.

↘ 듣기 필수 표현
· be dedicated to ~에 전념하다
· carry on 계속하다

10

M After visiting Paris, we're planning to get to Marseille by train, right?

W I was thinking of heading down on the 26th.

M Have you booked train tickets, yet? It looks like there are quite a few options on the schedule.

W Oh! Let me see that. *[Pause]* Leaving before 4 p.m. seems too early.

M Okay. What about taking the high-speed train? That could ¹⁾_____ _____ _____ _____.

W It's not really important one way or the other. So let's take a standard one. It should be quick enough.

M Yeah, maybe it's ²⁾_____ _____ to look at the number of times we would have to change trains.

W Good point. We don't want to stop twice if we can avoid it.

M It looks like there are still a couple of good choices, then.

W Let's just go with ³⁾_____ _____ _____.

↘ 듣기 필수 표현
· change trains 열차를 갈아타다

11

[Telephone rings.]

M Hi, this is Jack's Car Wash Service. How can I help you?

W Hello. I'm just calling to see ¹⁾_____ _____ _____ _____ today. I want to visit later this afternoon.

M We close at 8 p.m., but you should ²⁾_____ _____ _____ if you want your car to be washed today.

12

W Hey, Chris. I heard you ¹⁾_____ _____ a new apartment recently. How do you like it?

M It could be better. It is closer to my dad's work, but I can't walk to school anymore.

W ²⁾_____ _____ _____ is it now?

↘ 듣기 필수 표현
· It could be better. 그저 그래.

13

M What's wrong with your phone, Daisy?

W What do you mean?

M I called you, but ¹⁾_____ _____ _____
_____ again.

W Oh, sometimes it just turns off randomly. It's a really old phone.

M How long have you had it?

W About five years. It's probably time for me to get a new one, but I ²⁾_____ _____ _____ at the moment.

M I see. Well, maybe you could buy a secondhand phone instead of a new one. It wouldn't be so expensive that way.

W But I'm worried a ³⁾_____ _____
_____ _____.

M Don't worry. Some of them are in perfect condition. You just need to check them carefully. Plus, many sellers offer money-back guarantees.

W I'll go online and look then.

M I know some really good websites where you can find them.

W Really? Do you ⁴⁾_____ _____ _____
to me?

↘ 듣기 필수 표현
· turn off 꺼지다

14

M What are you looking at, Jane?

W Dad, I found some old photographs in a box. ¹⁾_____
_____ _____ when my brother and I were kids.

M Wow, I forgot about these. I remember this day, though. We were at your grandparents' house.

W I don't remember it at all.

M That's natural. You were only four at the time.

W I wish we went to see grandmother and grandfather more often like we used to.

M I know. But your schedules became busier on the weekends ²⁾_____ _____ _____
_____.

W I guess that's true. It makes these pictures very special to me.

M Then, why don't you put them in a nice album?

W Like a photo album? ³⁾_____ _____ _____
_____?

M We don't, but we can go buy one. Then, you could take it to your grandparents' house the next time we go.

15

M Katie is an aspiring author who is writing her first book. Recently, she was invited to join a weekly writer's workshop in which people critique one another's work. Katie is worried that she will ¹⁾_____ _____
_____. She discusses the issue with her friend Max, who also writes stories, and asks for his advice about joining the workshop. Max believes that Katie should ²⁾_____ _____ _____ other writers as it can highlight what parts of her story to work on. He thinks that this can benefit the overall quality of her work. So Max wants to tell Katie that she should consider joining the group in order to ³⁾_____ _____ _____. In this situation, what would Max most likely say to Katie?

↘ 듣기 필수 표현
· work on ~에 공을 들이다, 애쓰다

16~17

W Good morning, students. Last class, we talked about why Pluto is no longer considered a planet. Today, we'll learn about the ¹⁾_____ _____ of planets in our solar system. First, we have Mercury. Not only is this the smallest planet, but it is also closest to the sun. This planet has a rocky surface that ²⁾_____
_____ that of our own moon. Next, there is Venus. Venus is the hottest planet in our solar system with a surface temperature of around 475 degrees Celsius. It's ³⁾_____ _____ _____ volcanoes, which might be still active. Thirdly, Mars is a unique planet with seasons, canyons, and even polar ice caps. It's also been explored extensively because scientists believe that ⁴⁾_____ _____ _____ there. Lastly, Jupiter is the largest planet in our solar system. The Great Red Spot of Jupiter is visible from space. This is actually a vast storm that's larger than some planets, and it's been brewing for hundreds of years. Now, let's watch a video about these planets.

↘ 듣기 필수 표현
· no longer 더 이상 ~이 아닌
· not only A but also B A뿐만 아니라 B도

수능 1등급을 위한 **완벽한 실전 대비서**

해커스

수능영어듣기 모의고사 20+4회

실전

초판 2쇄 발행 2023년 8월 14일

초판 1쇄 발행 2023년 5월 9일

지은이	해커스 어학연구소
펴낸곳	㈜해커스 어학연구소
펴낸이	해커스 어학연구소 출판팀

주소	서울특별시 서초구 강남대로61길 23 ㈜해커스 어학연구소
고객센터	02-537-5000
교재 관련 문의	publishing@hackers.com
	해커스북 사이트(HackersBook.com) 고객센터 Q&A 게시판
동영상강의	star.Hackers.com

ISBN	978-89-6542-588-5 (53740)
Serial Number	01-02-01

중고등영어 1위,
해커스북 HackersBook.com

· 여러 가지 버전으로 실전에 대비할 수 있는 **기본 속도 MP3, 고속 버전 MP3, 고사장 버전 MP3**
· 복습이 간편해지는 **딕테이션 MP3 및 문항별 MP3**
· 학습한 단어의 암기 여부를 쉽게 점검할 수 있는 **어휘 리스트 및 어휘 테스트**

한경비즈니스 선정 2020 한국품질만족도 교육(온·오프라인 중·고등영어) 부문 1위 해커스

중·고등영어도 역시 1위 해커스

중·고등

해커스 young star

중·고등영어의 압도적인 점수 상승,
해커스 영스타 중·고등에서 현실이 됩니다.

해커스 영스타 중·고등 강의 무료체험

내게 맞는 공부법 체크! 학습전략검사

해커스 중·고등교재 무료 학습자료

보카 강의 수강생 수
1위 박가은

수능 1등급을 위한
완벽한 실전 대비서

해커스

수능영어듣기
모의고사 20+4회 ^{고난도}

실전

정답 및 해설

해커스

수능영어듣기 모의고사 20+4회
실전

정답 및 해설

해커스 어학연구소

1	③	2	①	3	①	4	④	5	⑤	6	③	7	②	8	③	9	④	10	③
11	⑤	12	①	13	④	14	④	15	②	16	②	17	③						

• 각 문제의 정답 근거는 굵은 글씨로, Dictation 정답은 밑줄로 표시되어 있습니다.

---

1 목적 파악
정답 ③

M Thank you for listening to the *Ghost Stories* podcast. Today's episode ¹⁾is sponsored by EZ Safe. **If you're looking for a great way to protect your home, you should try EZ Safe. For a low monthly fee, EZ Safe ²⁾offers a security service that includes state-of-the-art alarms, cameras, and smoke detectors.** All of ³⁾these devices are monitored by a team that works around the clock. And for a limited time, EZ Safe is offering free installation for first-time customers. To take advantage of this offer, visit www.ezsafe.com. Don't forget to enter our discount code "ghost stories" at checkout.

남 <Ghost Stories> 팟캐스트를 들어주셔서 감사합니다. 오늘의 에피소드는 EZ Safe로부터 후원받았습니다. 여러분의 집을 보호할 훌륭한 방법을 찾고 계신다면, EZ Safe를 사용해보십시오. 낮은 월 사용료로, EZ Safe는 최신식의 경보 장치, 카메라, 화재 탐지기를 포함한 보안 서비스를 제공합니다. 이 모든 기기들은 24시간 내내 근무 중인 팀에 의해 모니터링됩니다. 그리고 한시적으로, EZ Safe는 첫 구매 고객들에게 무료 설치를 제공합니다. 이 할인 혜택을 받으시려면, www.ezsafe.com에 방문하십시오. 결제 시 할인 코드인 'ghost stories'를 입력하는 것 잊지 마십시오.

남자가 팟캐스트의 후원사인 EZ Safe의 가정용 보안 서비스를 사용해보라고 하면서, 무료 설치 혜택 등을 설명하고 있다. 따라서, 남자가 하는 말의 목적으로 ③ '후원사의 가정용 보안 서비스를 홍보하려고'가 가장 적절하다.

어휘 sponsor 통 후원하다 look for ~을 찾다 offer 통 제공하다 명 할인; 제안 security 명 보안 state-of-the-art 형 최신식의 smoke detector 명 화재 탐지기 around the clock 24시간 내내 for a limited time 한시적으로 installation 명 설치 take advantage of ~의 혜택을 받다

---

2 의견 파악
정답 ①

W Hi, Derek. Are you going to the farm again?
M Yeah! My daughter and I go every Saturday.
W It must be nice to share a hobby together.
M It is, **and I think farming is a great way for kids to learn ¹⁾how to solve problems.**
W Isn't most of the work pretty simple like planting and watering crops?
M Not really. Farming is complicated.
W Well, ²⁾what kind of issues do you have to solve?
M For example, when we noticed that our lettuce was turning yellow, we had to figure out why.
W Did the plants need water?
M No. They were exposed to too much sunlight. So we moved them into the shade. **Kids ³⁾can learn problem solving by encountering situations like this.**
W Oh, I never considered all the critical thinking involved.
M It's hard to picture unless you've tried it yourself.

여 안녕, Derek. 농장에 또 가는 거야?
남 응! 우리 딸이랑 나는 매주 토요일에 가.
여 취미를 함께 공유한다는 건 분명 멋진 일이야.
남 맞아, 그리고 나는 농사가 아이들이 어떻게 문제를 해결해야 하는지 익힐 수 있는 좋은 방법이라고 생각해.
여 대부분의 일이 농작물을 심고 물을 주는 것처럼 꽤 단순하지 않아?
남 그렇지만은 않아. 농사는 복잡해.
여 음, 어떤 종류의 문제들을 해결해야 하는데?
남 예를 들어, 상추가 노란색으로 변하는 걸 알아차렸을 때, 왜 그런지 알아내야 했어.
여 상추에 물이 필요했던 거야?
남 아니. 너무 많은 햇빛에 노출된 거였어. 그래서 우리는 그걸 그늘로 옮겼어. 아이들은 이러한 상황을 맞닥뜨리면서 문제 해결을 배울 수 있어.
여 오, 난 이런 모든 비판적 사고가 수반되는지 전혀 생각지 못했네.
남 스스로 시도해보지 않으면 상상하기 어렵지.

농사일이 단순하다고 생각하는 여자에게 남자가 농사는 해결해야 하는 복잡한 문제가 있어서 아이들이 이런 상황을 맞닥뜨리며 문제 해결을 배울 수 있다고 했다. 따라서, 남자의 의견으로 ① '농사는 아이들이 문제 해결을 익히기에 좋은 방법이다.'가 가장 적절하다.

어휘 farming 명 농사 plant 통 심다 명 식물 water 통 물을 주다 명 물 crop 명 농작물 figure out ~을 알아내다 be exposed to ~에 노출되다 shade 명 그늘 encounter 통 맞닥뜨리다, 부딪히다 critical thinking 비판적 사고 involve 통 수반하다, 포함하다

---

3 관계 파악
정답 ①

M I'm excited to talk about my future plans.
W **Oh, before we get started, do you mind if I ¹⁾record our interview? I want to make sure that I get your quotes right when I ²⁾write my article.**
M That's fine.

남 제 미래 계획에 관해 얘기하게 되어서 신나네요.
여 오, 시작하기 전에, 제가 우리 인터뷰를 녹음해도 될까요? 기사를 쓸 때 당신의 말을 확실하게 인용하고 싶거든요.
남 괜찮습니다.

W Oh, and my photographer will be here soon. We want to ³⁾<u>get</u> <u>a</u> <u>shot</u> <u>of</u> <u>you</u> in the kitchen for the front page of the Food Section.	여 오, 그리고 저희 사진작가도 곧 여기 올 거예요. 저희는 식도락 섹션의 1면에 넣을 사진으로 당신이 주방에 있는 걸 찍고 싶어요.
M Perfect. Should we get started?	남 좋아요. 시작해볼까요?
W Certainly. **So Mr. Barton, how will the Knife's Edge Bistro differ from other dining establishments you've run in the past?**	여 물론이지요. 그럼 Barton 씨, Knife's Edge Bistro가 과거에 당신이 경영했던 음식점과 어떻게 다를까요?
M Well, it will ⁴⁾<u>focus</u> <u>on</u> <u>seafood</u>. Crab soup will be our specialty.	남 음, 해산물에 중점을 둘 거예요. 게살수프가 저희의 특선 요리가 되겠죠.
W And what inspired you to make seafood such an important part of the menu?	여 그럼 무엇이 당신에게 해산물을 메뉴의 중요 요소로 만들도록 영감을 주었나요?
M There is a large seafood market in the area.	남 이 지역에는 큰 수산물 시장이 있거든요.
W Sorry. Just a moment. The photographer is here. Can we take your photo during the interview?	여 죄송해요. 잠깐만 기다려 주세요. 사진작가가 여기 왔어요. 인터뷰하는 동안 사진을 찍어도 될까요?
M No problem. Go ahead.	남 문제없습니다. 계속하세요.

두 사람이 남자의 미래 계획에 관해 이야기하고 있다. 남자는 Knife's Edge Bistro가 과거에 본인이 경영했던 음식점과 다른 점을 설명하고 있고, 여자는 인터뷰 녹음에 동의를 구하는 등 기사 작성을 위한 준비를 하는 것으로 보아 두 사람의 관계로 ① '식당 주인 — 기자'가 가장 적절하다.

어휘 Do you mind if ~? ~해도 될까요? quote 명 인용문 동 인용하다 dining establishment 음식점 run 동 경영하다; 달리다 past 명 과거 형 지나간 inspire 동 영감을 주다

4 그림 내용 불일치 파악   정답 ④

M Is this a photo from your family's trip last summer, Judy?	남 이게 지난여름 가족 여행에서 찍은 사진이니, Judy?
W Yeah, Alan. That was our campsite by Wolf National Park.	여 그래, Alan. 그곳은 울프 국립공원에 있는 야영장이었어.
M It looks lovely there.	남 거기 정말 멋져 보인다.
W It was great. I wish we'd brought more folding chairs, though. We ¹⁾<u>only</u> <u>had</u> <u>those</u> <u>two</u>.	여 정말 좋았어. 그렇지만 접이식 의자를 더 가져갔다면 좋았을 텐데. 저 두 개만 있었거든.
M I see. But it looks like there's plenty of room to sit on that striped mat.	남 그렇구나. 하지만 저 줄무늬 돗자리에는 앉을 자리가 많아 보여.
W That's true. We often lay down on it and watched birds fly in the sky.	여 맞아. 우리는 종종 그 위에 누워서 하늘을 나는 새들을 봤어.
M Oh, you can see them in this photo, too. **Is that your triangle-shaped ²⁾tent in front of the big tree?**	남 오, 이 사진에서도 그것들을 볼 수 있네. 큰 나무 앞에 있는 건 네 삼각형 모양의 텐트니?
W Yeah. I've had that one for years.	여 응. 난 그걸 몇 년째 갖고 있어.
M I thought I recognized it. And it's good to see that you were able to make a fire. A lot of campsites don't ³⁾<u>let</u> <u>you</u> <u>do</u> <u>that</u>.	남 내가 알아봤을 줄 알았어. 그리고 네가 모닥불을 피울 수 있었던 걸 알게 돼서 좋아. 많은 야영장들이 그렇게 하도록 두지 않거든.
W Yeah! I had so much fun roasting marshmallows.	여 맞아! 나는 마시멜로를 굽는 게 너무 재미있었어.
M Oh, wow. That sounds perfect. I need to go there.	남 오, 우와. 완벽하다. 그곳에 가봐야겠어.

대화에서 남자가 큰 나무 앞에 삼각형 모양의 텐트가 있다고 말했는데, ④에는 사각형 모양의 텐트가 그려져 있다.

어휘 campsite 명 야영장 folding chair 접이식 의자 plenty of 많은 striped 형 줄무늬의 lie down 눕다 recognize 알아보다, 식별하다 make a fire 모닥불을 피우다 roast 동 굽다

5 할 일 파악   정답 ⑤

M Let's make a plan for our class presentation, Mary.	남 우리 수업 발표 계획을 세워보자, Mary.
W Good idea. Ms. Garcia says that we need to make a slide show.	여 좋은 생각이야. Garcia 선생님께서 슬라이드를 만들어야 한다고 말씀하셨어.
M Okay. Why don't we make that ¹⁾<u>as</u> <u>we</u> <u>prepare</u> our speech?	남 그래. 우리 발표를 준비하면서 만들어보는 게 어때?
W That's smart. It will help us keep our ideas organized.	여 현명한 방법이야. 그건 우리의 생각을 정리하는 데 도움이 될 거야.
M What about photos? Since our topic is butterflies, there should be plenty of great photos.	남 사진은 어떻게 할까? 우리 주제가 나비이기 때문에, 멋진 사진들이 많이 있을 거야.
W Don't worry. I've ²⁾<u>already</u> <u>chosen</u> <u>some</u> <u>pictures</u> to include.	여 걱정하지 마. 이미 포함시킬 사진들 몇 장을 골라놨어.
M We should include some important graphs, too. I'll search for them.	남 중요한 그래프들도 포함시켜야 해. 내가 찾아볼게.
W Thank you. Oh, how about ³⁾<u>making</u> <u>a</u> <u>handout</u> with the most important information?	여 고마워. 오, 가장 중요한 정보를 가지고 유인물을 만드는 건 어때?
M Good thinking. That would help people follow along. I'd be happy to create that.	남 좋은 생각이야. 그건 사람들이 내용을 따라잡는 데 도움이 될 거야. 내가 그걸 만들고 싶어.
W Before that, let's do some research. Why don't we head over to the library now?	여 그 전에, 조사를 좀 해보자. 우리 지금 도서관으로 가는 게 어때?
M Sorry, I can't. **But I'll read the materials if ⁴⁾you check them out.**	남 미안, 난 못해. 하지만 네가 자료를 대출해주면 읽을게.
W **No problem. I'll do that.** See you tomorrow!	여 문제없어. 내가 할게. 내일 봐!

수업 발표 계획에 관해 이야기하고 있다. 남자가 도서관에서 자료를 대출해달라고 하자, 여자가 하겠다고 했으므로 여자가 할 일로 ⑤ '자료 대출하기'가 가장 적절하다.

어휘 make a plan 계획을 세우다 organize 동 정리하다 include 동 ~을 포함시키다 handout 명 유인물 follow 동 내용을 따라잡다; 따라가다 head over to ~으로 가다, 향하다

6 금액 정보 파악

정답 ③

W Welcome to Florence's Flowers. How may I help you?	여 Florence's Flowers에 오신 것을 환영합니다. 무엇을 도와드릴까요?
M Hi, I'm looking for some flowers for my friend. She's been sick, but she's finally getting out of the hospital tomorrow.	남 안녕하세요, 친구에게 줄 꽃을 좀 찾고 있어요. 친구가 계속 아프다가, 내일 드디어 퇴원할 예정이거든요.
W That's great! You must want ¹⁾<u>some flowers</u> to <u>celebrate</u>.	여 잘됐네요! 축하할 꽃이 필요하시겠어요.
M What would you recommend?	남 어떤 걸 추천해 주시겠어요?
W I'd get something bright and cheerful. How about sunflowers and pink tulips?	여 저라면 밝고 경쾌한 것으로 하겠어요. 해바라기와 분홍색 튤립은 어때요?
M That would be lovely. How much are they?	남 그거 좋겠네요. 얼마예요?
W **The sunflowers are $6, and the tulips are $8 per flower.**	여 한 송이에 해바라기는 6달러이고, 튤립은 8달러예요.
M **Okay. I'd like ²⁾five of each.**	남 네. 각각 5송이씩 주세요.
W Great. Would you like to purchase a basket to put them in? It's an additional $10.	여 좋아요. 그것들을 넣을 바구니를 구매하시겠어요? 10달러가 추가돼요.
M No, thanks. It's fine to just ³⁾<u>wrap</u> them <u>in</u> <u>paper</u>.	남 아니요, 괜찮아요. 그냥 종이에 싸주셔도 괜찮아요.
W **And would you like to join our loyalty program? You'd get a 10% discount on your purchase.**	여 저희 로열티 프로그램에 가입하시겠어요? 구매 시 10% 할인받으실 수 있어요.
M **Why not?** What information do you need?	남 물론이죠. 어떤 정보가 필요하세요?
W Just a moment. I'll get the form.	여 잠깐만요. 제가 양식을 가져올게요.

남자가 해바라기와 튤립을 각각 5송이씩($6×5+$8×5=$70) 구매했고, 로열티 프로그램에 가입하여 10% 할인($70×0.9=$63)을 받겠다고 했으므로 정답은 ③ '$63'이다.

[어휘] get out of the hospital 퇴원하다 celebrate 통 축하하다 cheerful 형 경쾌한 purchase 통 구매하다 additional 형 추가의 wrap 통 싸다, 포장하다 Why not? 물론이죠.
form 명 (문서) 양식; 형태

7 이유 파악

정답 ②

M Are you going to the Spanish club meeting this afternoon, Tanya?	남 오늘 오후에 스페인어 동아리 모임에 갈 거야, Tanya?
W I'll be there. We're going to discuss the fundraising event, right?	여 난 갈 거야. 우리 모금 행사에 관해 논의할 거잖아, 그렇지?
M Exactly. It's an important meeting. So it ¹⁾<u>may run a little long</u>. Last year, I think it took two hours.	남 맞아. 중요한 회의야. 그래서 조금 오래 진행될 수도 있어. 작년에는, 두 시간이 걸렸던 것 같아.
W I have a few ideas to share, but I don't know if I can stay the whole time.	여 몇 가지 아이디어를 공유하고 싶은데, 내가 끝까지 있을 수 있을지 모르겠어.
M Oh, is that because ²⁾<u>it interferes</u> with your school orchestra practice?	남 오, 그게 학교 오케스트라 연습에 지장을 주기 때문이니?
W No. That's next Tuesday.	여 아니. 그건 다음 주 화요일이야.
M Then, do you need some time to work on the Spanish assignment?	남 그럼, 스페인어 과제를 하는 데 시간이 좀 필요한 거야?
W I already finished it. Actually, I need to ³⁾<u>go to the dentist</u>. **I have a toothache that I should get checked out.**	여 이미 다 끝냈어. 사실, 난 치과에 가야 해. 치통이 있어서 검진을 받아야 하거든.
M That's really too bad.	남 정말 안됐다.
W I know. I hope you understand why I need to leave early.	여 그러게. 왜 내가 일찍 떠나야만 하는지 네가 이해해주면 좋겠어.
M It's okay. See you later.	남 괜찮아. 나중에 보자.

여자는 스페인어 동아리 모임에 끝까지 있을 수 없겠다고 하면서 치통 때문에 검진받으러 치과에 가야 한다고 말했으므로, 여자가 모임에 끝까지 있을 수 없는 이유는 ② '치과에서 검진을 받아야 해서'이다.

[어휘] fundraising 명 모금 Is that because ~? ~하기 때문이니? interfere 통 지장을 주다, 방해하다 assignment 명 과제, 숙제 get ~ checked out 검진을 받다

8 언급 유무 파악

정답 ③

M Hey, Gina. Did you see that a new mall is opening up near us?	남 안녕, Gina. 우리 근처에 새로운 쇼핑몰이 개점하는 것 알았니?
W I did. I keep seeing ads about the Marina Mall Grand Opening Sale.	여 알고 있었어. Marina Mall Grand Opening Sale에 관한 광고를 계속 보고 있거든.
M Yeah, do you want to go on Saturday? It ¹⁾<u>starts on</u> **the 20th.**	남 응, 이번 토요일에 가고 싶니? 20일에 시작해.
W I guess. But won't it be too busy?	여 그래. 하지만 너무 붐비지 않을까?
M Probably so, but there are discounts of **up to 50%** at a bunch of stores.	남 그럴 수도 있지만, 많은 매장에서 50%까지 할인을 해 줘.
W Wow, that's great. Do you know ²⁾<u>which stores will participate</u>?	여 와, 그거 대단하네. 어떤 매장이 참여할지 알고 있어?
M Hmm... I only remember that **Lana's Boutique** will. You love their clothes, right?	남 흠... Lana's Boutique가 참여할 거라는 것만 기억하고 있어. 네가 그곳 옷을 좋아하잖아, 그렇지?
W Yes, I do. I used to drive 30 minutes to shop at one of their locations.	여 응, 맞아. 나는 거기 점포 중 한 곳에서 쇼핑하기 위해 30분을 운전하곤 했었지.
M And I heard that ³⁾<u>a mug</u> will <u>be given</u> as a special gift to the first 500 customers.	남 그리고 선착순 500명에게 머그컵을 특별 선물로 줄 거라고 들었어.
W Well, we better get there early, then.	여 음, 그렇다면 그곳에 일찍 도착하는 게 좋겠어.
M I'll pick you up at 8?	남 내가 8시에 데리러 갈까?
W Okay, sure!	여 그래, 물론이지!

시작일(20일), 할인율(50%까지), 참여 매장(Lana's Boutique), 증정품(머그컵)에 대해 언급했고, ③ '행사 기간'은 언급하지 않았다.

어휘 ad(advertisement) 圐 광고 up to ~까지 a bunch of 많은 participate 图 참여하다 pick up ~를 (차로) 데리러 가다

---

9 내용 불일치 파악   정답 ④

W Welcome back to *Jazz Night* on K-BRMC Radio. Before we get back to the music, I'd like to let you know about the upcoming Clearbrook City Art Fair. It will be held at Somerset Auditorium from May 8th to May 10th. This annual event features artwork made right here in Clearbrook City by some of our ¹⁾most talented local artists. This year, in addition to paintings, the festival will include photography and sculpture exhibits. **Starting things off on the 8th, there will be a ceremony ²⁾announcing the winner of this year's student art contest.** The winning piece will be displayed throughout the festival. Tickets for the event ³⁾can be purchased from the city government's website or in person at Clearbrook Gallery. They will cost $25.	여 K-BRMC 라디오의 <Jazz Night>로 잘 돌아오셨습니다. 음악으로 돌아가기 전에, 곧 있을 Clearbrook City Art Fair에 대해 알려드리고 싶습니다. 그것은 5월 8일부터 5월 10일까지 서머셋 회관에서 열릴 것입니다. 매년 열리는 이 행사는 가장 재능 있는 우리 지역의 예술가들이 바로 이곳 클리어브룩시에서 만든 예술작품을 다룹니다. 올해에는, 그림뿐만 아니라, 사진과 조각 전시회가 축제에 포함될 것입니다. 8일에 행사를 시작하며, 올해 학생미술대회의 수상자를 발표하는 시상식이 있을 것입니다. 수상작은 축제 기간 내내 전시될 것입니다. 이 행사의 티켓은 시 정부의 웹사이트나 클리어브룩 미술관에서 직접 구매할 수 있습니다. 가격은 25달러입니다.

클리어브룩시의 예술 박람회에 대한 안내 방송이다. 여자가 8일에 행사를 시작하며 학생미술대회의 수상자를 발표하는 시상식이 있겠다고 했으므로 ④ '마지막 날 학생미술대회 시상식이 진행될 것이다.'는 내용과 일치하지 않는다.

어휘 upcoming 圐 곧 있을, 다가오는 artwork 圐 예술작품 in addition to ~뿐만 아니라 sculpture 圐 조각 start ~ off ~을 시작하다 in person 직접

---

10 도표 정보 파악   정답 ③

M Melissa, did you get a new phone?	남 Melissa, 새 휴대폰 샀어?
W Hi, Fred. I did. This is the latest model.	여 안녕, Fred. 그랬어. 최신 모델이야.
M I've been thinking of getting a new phone, but I can't make up my mind about which one.	남 나 새 휴대폰을 살까 생각 중인데, 어떤 휴대폰으로 할지 결정을 못 하겠어.
W Maybe one of the first things to consider is the size of the device.	여 아마도 가장 먼저 고려해야 할 것 중 하나는 기기의 크기일 거야.
M The one you have looks ¹⁾too big for my taste.	남 네가 가지고 있는 건 내 취향에는 너무 커 보여.
W Fair enough. **Mine has a 6.8-inch screen, so you should ²⁾pick a smaller model.** And what's your price range?	여 좋아. 내 것은 화면이 6.8인치니까, 너는 더 작은 모델을 선택해야 해. 그리고 네가 생각하는 가격대는 어떻게 돼?
M **I can spend up to $900.**	남 난 900달러까지 쓸 수 있어.
W That narrows it down a little. Is memory a big factor?	여 그럼 범위가 좀 좁혀지네. 용량이 중요한 요인이니?
M It's ³⁾not especially important. **I'm fine with anything over 200 gigabytes.**	남 특별히 중요한 건 아니야. 200기가가 넘는 건 아무거나 괜찮아.
W I see. **And do you care if it comes with a wireless charger?**	여 그렇구나. 그리고 무선 충전기가 딸려 있는지가 상관이 있니?
M **Yes.** That's very important to me.	남 응. 그건 내게 아주 중요해.
W In that case, I think there's only one good option for you.	여 그렇다면, 네게 딱 한 가지의 좋은 선택지가 있는 것 같아.

남자는 6.8인치 화면보다는 크기가 작으면서, 900달러 이하의, 용량이 200기가가 넘는 것 중에서, 무선 충전기가 딸린 휴대폰 기종을 골랐다.

어휘 make up one's mind 결정하다 taste 圐 취향; 맛 range 圐 -대, 범위 narrow down 좁히다 factor 圐 요인 care 图 상관하다; 돌보다 come with ~이 딸려 있다 wireless 圐 무선의 charger 圐 충전기

---

11 짧은 대화의 응답 파악   정답 ⑤

W Excuse me, sir. You ¹⁾can't bring your bicycle inside.	여 실례합니다, 선생님. 자전거를 안으로 가지고 들어가실 수 없어요.
M I'll just be here for a minute. I'm delivering something to Mr. Jensen.	남 여기 잠깐만 있을 거예요. Jensen 씨에게 뭔가를 배달하고 있어요.
W **I'm afraid ²⁾there are no exceptions. You can lock up your bike at the rack next to the building.**	여 죄송하지만, 예외는 없어요. 자전거는 건물 옆에 있는 자전거 보관대에 잠가놓을 수 있어요.
M Got it. In that case, I'll be right back.	남 <u>알겠어요. 그렇다면, 바로 다시 올게요.</u>
	선택지 ① 정말 감사합니다. 배송 서비스가 정말 맘에 드는군요.
	② 그건 필요하지 않아요. 전 제 자전거가 있어요.
	③ 정말요? 전 그곳이 지금 잠겨있었는지 몰랐어요.
	④ 네. 당신의 경우에는 제가 예외를 두죠.
	⑤ 알겠어요. 그렇다면, 바로 다시 올게요.

여자가 예외 없이 모든 자전거는 건물 옆 자전거 보관대에 둬야 한다고 했으므로, 이에 대한 응답으로는 알겠다고 대답하는 ⑤ 'Got it. In that case, I'll be right back.'이 가장 적절하다.

어휘 exception 圐 예외 lock up (자물쇠, 문 등을) 잠그다 rack 圐 자전거 보관대; 선반

[Cell phone rings.]
M Hey, Chloe? This is Alex. **I'll be able to** ¹⁾come pick you up at the airport tomorrow.
W Thanks! I have a lot of luggage, so that'll be very helpful. I'll be on Flight ZE 281.
M ²⁾It's the least I can do. **When is it scheduled to land?**
W It's supposed to get there at 11:30 a.m.

[휴대폰이 울린다.]
남 안녕, Chloe? 나 Alex야. 내가 내일 공항으로 널 데리러 갈 수 있겠어.
여 고마워! 내가 짐이 많아서, 정말 도움이 많이 될 거야. 나는 ZE 281편에 탈 거야.
남 내가 할 수 있는 최소한의 일인걸. 언제 도착할 예정이니?
여 그곳에 오전 11시 30분에 도착하기로 되어있어.

선택지 ① 그곳에 오전 11시 30분에 도착하기로 되어있어.
② 내가 짐을 찾으면 네게 전화할게.
③ 유감스럽게도, 내가 탄 비행기가 제때 도착하지 않았어.
④ 내가 예약하고 나서 항공편 번호를 확인해줄게.
⑤ 공항에 도착하기까지 몇 분 더 걸릴 거야.

남자가 여자를 데리러 공항에 가겠다면서 언제 도착 예정인지 물었으므로, 이에 대한 응답으로는 도착 예정 시간을 말하는 ① 'It's supposed to get there at 11:30 a.m.'이 가장 적절하다.

어휘 luggage 몡 짐, 수하물   be scheduled to ~할 예정이다   be supposed to ~하기로 되어있다   on time 제때   make a booking 예약을 하다

W Hi, Mr. Miller. I'm Emily. **I wanted to ask about joining the high school jazz band.**
M To join, you'll have to ¹⁾pass an audition. The auditions are being held next week.
W Sure, that's fine.
M Great. So what instrument do you play?
W I'm a singer, actually.
M **The audition for singers is on Tuesday, but I should warn you.** There are a lot of ²⁾talented students trying out, and only one will be selected.
W I understand. I'd still like to sign up.
M Also, most of the students auditioning have been performing for years. And almost all of them are seniors.
W I realize that. But I have a lot of experience, and I think ³⁾you'll be impressed.
M I love your confidence! **Here's the sign-up sheet.**
W Thanks. I hope ⁴⁾my confidence will help with my audition.
M I'm looking forward to hearing you sing on Tuesday.

여 안녕하세요, Miller 선생님. 전 Emily예요. 고등학교 재즈 밴드에 가입하는 것에 대해 여쭤보고 싶었어요.
남 가입하려면, 오디션을 통과해야 한단다. 다음 주에 오디션이 열릴 예정이야.
여 네, 그건 괜찮아요.
남 좋아. 그래서 어떤 악기를 연주하니?
여 저는 가수예요, 사실.
남 가수 오디션은 화요일에 있는데, 미리 알려줘야겠구나. 많은 재능 있는 학생들이 도전하고 있고, 단 한 명만 선발될 거야.
여 이해해요. 그래도 신청하고 싶어요.
남 또한, 오디션을 보는 대부분의 학생들은 수년 동안 공연을 해왔단다. 그리고 그들은 거의 모두 3학년이지.
여 알고 있어요. 하지만 저는 경험이 많고, 선생님께서 깊은 인상을 받으실 거라고 생각해요.
남 자신감이 정말 맘에 드는구나! 여기 신청서가 있단다.
여 감사합니다. 제 자신감이 오디션에 도움이 되면 좋겠어요.
남 화요일에 네 노래를 듣길 기대할게.

선택지 ① 재즈 피아노는 치기 쉽지 않다고 생각한단다.
② 그러면 보조 가수로 신청하겠구나.
③ 밴드에 있는 내 친구가 오디션을 보라고 추천했지.
④ 화요일에 네 노래를 듣길 기대할게.
⑤ 오디션을 보려면 내년까지 기다리는 것을 고려해야 한단다.

고등학교 재즈 밴드 가입 방법을 묻는 상황이다. 남자가 가수 오디션을 앞두고 자신감을 보이는 여자에게 주의 사항을 전달하며 신청서를 건네주자 여자가 본인의 자신감이 오디션에 도움이 되면 좋겠다고 했으므로, 이에 대한 응답으로는 여자를 오디션장에서 보길 기대한다고 말하는 ④ 'I'm looking forward to hearing you sing on Tuesday.'가 가장 적절하다.

어휘 pass 통 통과하다   audition 몡 오디션 통 오디션을 보다   instrument 몡 악기   warn 통 미리 알려주다; 경고하다   try out (오디션에) 도전하다   sign up 신청하다
    impress 통 깊은 인상을 주다, 감명을 받다   confidence 몡 자신감

[Cell phone rings.]
W Hello?
M Hi, Jessica. This is Adam Kim from biology class.
W Hey, Adam. What's up?
M I'm just calling to say that I ¹⁾found your textbook.
W Oh, wow! I had almost given up looking. Where did you find it?
M I saw it in the library's lost and found when I was collecting an umbrella I left there.
W Hmm... That's weird. I ²⁾haven't visited the library recently. Are you sure it's mine?
M It has your name in it!
W I wonder if someone moved it. In any case, thanks for letting me know.
M Of course. I bet you were pretty worried.
W I was! Well, would you mind ³⁾bringing it to class tomorrow?

[휴대폰이 울린다.]
여 여보세요?
남 안녕, Jessica. 나 생물 수업 듣는 Adam Kim이야.
여 안녕, Adam. 무슨 일이야?
남 네 교과서를 찾았다고 말해주려고 전화했어.
여 오, 우와! 난 찾는 것을 거의 포기했었어. 어디서 찾았니?
남 도서관의 분실물 보관소에 내가 두고 온 우산을 가지러 갔을 때 그걸 봤어.
여 흠... 이상하다. 난 최근에 도서관을 방문하지 않았거든. 내 것이 확실해?
남 거기에 네 이름이 있어!
여 누가 갖다 놓았는지 의문이네. 어쨌든, 알려줘서 고마워.
남 물론이지. 네가 꽤 걱정했을 것 같아.
여 그랬어! 음, 내일 수업에 가져와 주겠니?

M Don't you need it for your homework tonight? **I can take it to your house now if you want.**

W It's okay. I'll come collect it from you.

남 오늘 밤 숙제할 때 이게 필요하지 않아? 네가 원하면 지금 너희 집에 가져다줄 수 있어.

여 괜찮아. 내가 네 쪽으로 가지러 갈게.

[선택지] ① 좋은 생각이야. 우리 수업 같이 듣잖아.

② 완벽해. 네 책상으로 가져갈게.

③ 어떻게 된 거야? 난 도서관을 온통 다 찾아봤어.

④ 괜찮아. 내가 네 쪽으로 가지러 갈게.

⑤ 물론이야. 그냥 네 우편함에 넣어둘게.

여사의 잃어버린 교과서를 남자가 찾아주는 상황이다. 남자가 원한다면 교과서를 지금 여자의 집에 가져다줄 수 있다고 말했으므로, 이에 대한 응답으로는 반대로 본인이 찾으러 가겠다고 대답하는 ④ 'It's okay. I'll come collect it from you.'가 가장 적절하다.

[어휘] biology 명 생물(학) give up 포기하다 lost and found 분실물 보관소 wonder 통 의문이다, 의아하다; 궁금하다

---

15 상황에 적절한 말 파악

정답 ②

M Henry and Esther are friends who live in the same apartment building. Henry is leaving for a summer vacation next week, and he needs someone [1]to take care of his cat. Esther knows about his plans and offers to come feed it. However, Henry wants someone who can visit his house and look after his cat every day. He thinks that Esther is [2]too busy to do this, so he plans to hire a cat sitter. Esther believes that she has [3]enough time to help. **Therefore, she wants to tell Henry that she can come by to cat-sit daily, so he can leave it to her.** In this situation, what would Esther most likely say to Henry?

남 Henry와 Esther는 같은 아파트에 사는 친구입니다. Henry는 다음 주에 여름휴가를 떠나서, 그는 자기 고양이를 돌봐줄 누군가가 필요합니다. Esther는 그의 계획을 알고 있고 자신이 먹이를 주러 오겠다고 제안합니다. 하지만, Henry는 그의 집을 방문해서 매일 그의 고양이를 돌볼 수 있는 누군가를 원합니다. 그는 Esther가 너무 바빠 이것을 할 수 없다고 생각해서, 고양이 돌보미를 고용할 계획입니다. Esther는 그녀가 도와줄 시간이 충분하다고 생각합니다. 그래서, 그녀는 Henry에게 매일 고양이를 돌보러 갈 수 있으니, 그녀에게 맡기면 된다고 말하고 싶습니다. 이러한 상황에서, Esther가 Henry에게 가장 할 것 같은 말은 무엇입니까?

[선택지] ① 알겠어. 오늘 밤 8시에 들를게.

② 걱정하지 마. 난 매일 짬을 낼 수 있어.

③ 고마워. 난 고양이 사료를 살 시간이 없었어.

④ 미안해. 내가 고양이 알레르기가 있어서 도움이 못 되겠어.

⑤ 안됐다. 넌 지금 해야 할 일이 산더미네.

Henry가 여름휴가 동안 자기 고양이를 돌봐줄 사람을 찾는 것을 보고, Esther는 본인이 매일 고양이를 돌보러 갈 수 있으니 맡겨 달라고 제안하려 한다. 따라서, Esther가 할 말로 ② 'Don't worry. I can make time every day.'가 가장 적절하다.

[어휘] feed 통 먹이를 주다 look after 돌보다 cat sitter 고양이 돌보미 come by 들르다 leave A to B A를 B에게 맡기다 stop by 들르다 make time 짬을 내다 be allergic to ~에 알레르기가 있다 have a lot on one's plate 해야 할 일이 산더미다

16-17 세트 문항

정답 16 ② 17 ③

W Good morning, everyone. In our class on Friday we discussed the history of space flight. **Today, I want to talk about how journeys to space [1]harm astronauts' bodies.** First, let's consider the effect on their **bones**. Studies show that in low gravity conditions, the body mostly stops building up bones. So they will often [2]be much weaker when astronauts get back to Earth. Second, the **heart** can be hurt by space travel. This is due to radiation, which can damage and harden the heart's tissues. The **eyes** are also [3]affected by spending time in space. In fact, 80% of astronauts experience some difficulty seeing. For some, this damage becomes permanent. Lastly, the **brain** can change shape in zero-gravity conditions. As a consequence, astronauts' mental abilities get worse the longer [4]they are in space. This can affect astronauts' judgment and problem-solving skills. Now, let's take a look at an interview with an astronaut about her space travels.

여 안녕하십니까, 여러분. 금요일 수업에서, 우리는 우주 비행의 역사에 대해 논의했습니다. 오늘은 우주여행이 우주 비행사들의 신체에 어떻게 해를 끼치는지에 대해 이야기하고 싶습니다. 첫째, 그들의 뼈에 미치는 영향을 고려해 봅시다. 연구에서는 저중력 조건에서, 신체는 뼈를 강하게 만들기를 대체로 멈춘다는 것을 보여줍니다. 그래서 우주 비행사들이 지구로 돌아왔을 때 뼈는 종종 훨씬 더 약해질 것입니다. 둘째, 우주여행으로 인해 심장이 손상될 수 있습니다. 이것은 방사선 때문인데, 이것은 심장 조직을 손상시키고 굳게 만들 수 있습니다. 눈 또한 우주에서 시간을 보내는 것에 의한 영향을 받습니다. 사실, 우주비행사들의 80%가 시력 장애를 겪습니다. 어떤 사람들에게, 이 손상은 영구적으로 남습니다. 마지막으로, 무중력 상태에서 뇌의 모양이 바뀔 수 있습니다. 그 결과, 우주 비행사들이 우주에 오래 있을수록 지적 능력이 나빠집니다. 이는 우주 비행사들의 판단력과 문제 해결 능력에 영향을 미칠 수 있습니다. 이제, 한 우주 비행사와 나눈 그녀의 우주여행에 대한 인터뷰를 살펴봅시다.

[선택지] **16** ① 우주 비행사를 계속 동기 부여하게 하는 방법

② 우주로 가는 것의 부정적인 건강상의 영향

③ 우주 비행의 발전에 대한 역사적 회고

④ 우주와 연관된 건강에 대한 연구의 발전

⑤ 우주 비행사가 되기 위한 신체적 필요조건

17 ① 뼈 ② 심장 ③ 폐 ④ 눈 ⑤ 뇌

16 우주여행이 우주 비행사들의 신체에 어떻게 해를 끼치는지에 관해 이야기하고 있으므로 여자가 하는 말의 주제로 ② 'negative health effects of going to space'가 가장 적절하다.

17 뼈, 심장, 눈, 뇌는 언급했지만 ③ 'lungs'는 언급하지 않았다.

[어휘] harm 통 해를 끼치다, 손상시키다 astronaut 명 우주 비행사 gravity 명 중력 build up 강하게 만들다 due to ~ 때문인 radiation 명 방사선 tissue 명 조직 difficulty 명 장애, 어려움 permanent 형 영구적인 zero-gravity condition 무중력 상태 as a consequence 그 결과 mental ability 지적 능력 judgment 명 판단 take a look 살펴보다

| 1 | ① | 2 | ⑤ | 3 | ② | 4 | ④ | 5 | ③ | 6 | ② | 7 | ③ | 8 | ③ | 9 | ⑤ | 10 | ⑤ |
| 11 | ⑤ | 12 | ② | 13 | ① | 14 | ⑤ | 15 | ② | 16 | ③ | 17 | ④ | | | | | | |

• 각 문제의 정답 근거는 굵은 글씨로, Dictation 정답은 밑줄로 표시되어 있습니다.

1 목적 파악

정답 ①

W Attention, please. This is an announcement for all visitors to the Parkview Tennis Center. **Due to ongoing renovations to our outdoor courts, all beginner and intermediate tennis lessons** 1)have been moved indoors **today.** Beginners will meet with their coaches on Courts 3 and 4, while intermediate students will play on Courts 5 and 6. As a result, our indoor courts will not be open 2)for general play until classes have ended for the day. Any reservations made during class times or for our outdoor courts 3)will be refunded. We expect to reopen our outdoor facility by next week. Our apologies for any inconvenience this may cause.

여 주목해 주십시오. Parkview Tennis Center의 모든 방문객 여러분께 안내 말씀 드립니다. 진행 중인 야외 코트의 보수 공사로 인해, 오늘 모든 초급 및 중급 테니스 수업이 실내로 옮겨졌습니다. 초급반은 3번과 4번 코트에서 코치와 만날 것이고, 중급반 수강생들은 5번과 6번 코트에서 경기를 할 것입니다. 결과적으로, 실내 코트는 그날 수업이 끝날 때까지 일반 경기에는 개방되지 않을 예정입니다. 수업 시간 동안의 사용 예약이나 야외 코트의 예약은 모두 환불될 것입니다. 저희는 다음 주까지는 야외 시설을 다시 열 것으로 예상하고 있습니다. 이로 인한 불편을 드려 죄송합니다.

여자가 Parkview Tennis Center의 야외 코트 보수 공사가 진행 중임에 따라, 센터의 모든 수업 장소가 실내로 옮겨졌음을 말해 주고 있다. 따라서, 여자가 하는 말의 목적으로 ① '테니스 수업 장소 변경을 공지하려고'가 가장 적절하다.

어휘 ongoing 혱 진행 중인 renovation 몡 보수 공사, 보수 intermediate 몡 중급(자) indoors 븬 실내로 refund 동 환불하다 facility 몡 시설 inconvenience 몡 불편

2 의견 파악

정답 ⑤

M Do you want to take a quick break, Jessica?

W I'd prefer to keep going. We still have a lot of work to do on the group project, and it's getting late.

M True, **but I think** 1)quick breaks boost productivity.

W How do you figure? I don't want to waste any time.

M It would give us more energy, which would 2)help us finish faster.

W Oh, that makes sense.

M Also, a break tends to make you more creative. If we come back to our work with a fresh perspective, it might be easier 3)to think of new solutions.

W Yeah. I do feel like we're stuck.

M Exactly. **Don't you think we should take a few minutes to reset?**

W I suppose so.

M See you back here at 4:30?

W Sounds good.

남 짧은 휴식 시간을 가지고 싶니, Jessica?

여 난 계속하고 싶어. 우리 조별 과제에 아직 해야 할 일이 많고, 시간은 늦어지고 있잖아.

남 맞아, 하지만 난 짧은 휴식이 생산성을 높여 준다고 생각해.

여 왜 그렇게 생각하니? 난 시간 낭비하고 싶지 않아.

남 휴식은 우리에게 더 많은 에너지를 주고, 우리가 더 빨리 끝낼 수 있도록 도울 거야.

여 오, 일리가 있네.

남 또한, 휴식은 우리를 더 창의적으로 만드는 경향이 있어. 산뜻한 관점을 가지고 작업을 다시 시작하면, 새로운 해결책을 생각하는 것이 더 쉬울 수 있지.

여 그래. 우리가 막혔다는 느낌이 들어.

남 맞아. 몇 분 정도 재정비할 시간을 가져야 한다고 생각하지 않아?

여 그런 것 같아.

남 4시 30분에 여기서 다시 볼까?

여 좋아.

조별 과제를 계속하고 싶어 하는 여자에게 남자가 짧은 휴식이 생산성을 높여 주니 몇 분 정도 재정비할 시간을 갖자고 했다. 따라서, 남자의 의견으로 ⑤ '짧게 휴식을 취하면 생산성이 높아진다.'가 가장 적절하다.

어휘 take a break 휴식 시간을 가지다 boost 동 높이다; 밀어 올리다 productivity 몡 생산성 waste time 시간 낭비하다 make sense 일리가 있다 perspective 몡 관점 be stuck 막혀 있다

3 관계 파악

정답 ②

M Dr. Brown, thank you for meeting with me.

W I always enjoy a chance to visit the Museum of Archeology. What did you want to speak about?

M Well, I wanted to 1)discuss an exhibit that I'm planning here.

W What did you have in mind?

M I'd like you to write an audio guide 2)giving background information on some of the artifacts in the exhibit.

W I see. I presume these are famous pieces of Greek pottery?

M Right. **You** 3)were involved in discovering **several of them, so you have unique insights.**

남 Brown 박사님, 만나주셔서 감사합니다.

여 전 항상 고고학 박물관을 방문할 기회를 즐기는걸요. 무슨 얘기를 하고 싶으셨나요?

남 음, 제가 여기서 계획하고 있는 전시회에 대해 논의하고 싶었어요.

여 어떤 것들을 생각하셨나요?

남 전시회에 있는 몇몇 유물에 대한 배경 정보를 제공하는 오디오 가이드를 작성해 주셨으면 합니다.

여 그렇군요. 제가 짐작하기로는 이것들이 유명한 그리스 도자기 작품들이죠?

남 맞아요. 박사님께서 그것들 중 몇몇을 발견하는 데 관여하셨으니까, 특별한 통찰력을 갖고 계시잖아요.

W Great. It would be my pleasure.	여 좋아요. 기쁜 마음으로 할게요.
M We'd also like to invite you to come speak at an event when the exhibit opens.	남 그리고 전시회가 열리면 행사에 와서 강연해주시기를 요청하고 싶어요.
W When would that be?	여 그게 언제죠?
M Sometime next May.	남 내년 5월쯤이요.
W Let me check my schedule. If I'm not out of the country ⁴⁾on a dig, I'll be there.	여 제 스케줄을 확인해 볼게요. 제가 발굴하러 해외에 나가 있지 않다면, 강연하러 가겠습니다.

두 사람이 전시회의 오디오 가이드 제작에 관해 이야기하고 있다. 남자는 고고학 박물관에서 전시를 계획하고 있다고 했고, 여자는 그리스 도자기를 발견하는 데 관여했다고 하는 것으로 보아 두 사람의 관계로 ② '박물관 큐레이터 — 고고학자'가 가장 적절하다.

어휘 archeology 몡 고고학 have ~ in mind ~을 생각하다, 계획하다 background 몡 배경 artifact 몡 유물 presume 동 짐작하다, 추정하다 involve 동 관여하다 insight 몡 통찰력 speak 동 강연하다, 연설하다; 말하다 out of the country 해외에, 국외에 dig 몡 발굴 동 (땅을) 파다

---

4 그림 내용 불일치 파악   정답 ④

W Welcome to Greenwich High School, Mr. Walker. I'll show you around.	여 그리니치 고등학교에 오신 것을 환영해요, Walker 선생님. 제가 안내해 드릴게요.
M I appreciate that.	남 감사합니다.
W Let's drop by the teacher's office first. You'll prepare ¹⁾for your classes here.	여 우선 교무실에 들르죠. 선생님께선 여기서 수업을 준비하실 거예요.
M Which one is my desk?	남 어느 것이 제 책상인가요?
W It's in the front of the room, ²⁾with the two books next to the keyboard.	여 교무실 앞쪽의, 키보드 옆에 책 두 권이 있는 것이에요.
M I see it.	남 알겠어요.
W My desk is to the left of yours. It's the one with the cactus plant on it.	여 제 책상은 선생님 책상 왼쪽에 있어요. 선인장 화분이 올려져 있는 것입니다.
M What's that whiteboard in the back of the room for?	남 교무실 뒤쪽에 있는 화이트보드는 뭐예요?
W We use it for reminders. If we have a teachers' meeting, I'll ³⁾post the time there.	여 저희는 그걸 알림판으로 사용해요. 만약 교무 회의가 있다면, 제가 그곳에 시간을 게시하죠.
M It's blank right now, so there's no meeting today, right?	남 지금은 비어 있으니, 오늘은 회의가 없는 거네요, 그렇죠?
W Correct.	여 맞아요.
M Oh, is there a printer I could use?	남 아, 제가 쓸 수 있는 프린터기가 있나요?
W It's ⁴⁾underneath the round poster of a light bulb. If you need more paper, there's some in the drawers on its right.	여 전구가 그려진 둥근 모양의 포스터 아래에 있어요. 종이가 더 필요하시면, 오른쪽 서랍 안에 있습니다.
M Thanks!	남 고마워요!

대화에서 여자가 전구가 그려진 둥근 모양의 포스터 아래 프린터기가 있다고 말했는데, ④에는 사각형의 포스터가 그려져 있다.

어휘 show ~ around ~를 안내하다 drop by 들르다 teacher's office 교무실 cactus 몡 선인장 post 동 게시하다 light bulb 전구

---

5 할 일 파악   정답 ③

W Okay, let's get to it, Daniel. We have a lot of cleaning to do before Mom and Dad get back home.	여 좋아, 시작하자, Daniel. 엄마 아빠가 집에 돌아오시기 전에 청소해야 할 것 많아.
M Right. We ¹⁾should have started earlier. We don't have much time.	남 맞아. 좀 더 일찍 시작했어야 했어. 시간이 별로 없어.
W Let's get organized. How does the kitchen look?	여 정리 좀 하자. 부엌은 어때 보여?
M Well, I already washed and put away the dishes.	남 음, 내가 벌써 설거지하고 그릇들을 넣어뒀어.
W What about wiping down the dining table? Did you do that?	여 식탁을 닦는 건 어때? 네가 했어?
M They look pretty clean, actually. We can probably ²⁾skip that for now.	남 꽤 깨끗해 보여, 사실. 지금은 생략해도 될 것 같아.
W Great. That makes things easier. I'll ³⁾start vacuuming.	여 좋아. 그러면 일이 더 쉬워지네. 내가 청소기를 돌릴게.
M Should I dust the bookshelves?	남 나는 책장 먼지를 털까?
W I think we need to take out the trash first.	여 내 생각에 우리는 먼저 쓰레기를 버려야 할 것 같아.
M Okay, ⁴⁾I'm on it.	남 알겠어, 내가 할게.
W Mom and Dad will be happy to see that the house is in good shape.	여 엄마 아빠께서 집 상태가 좋은 것을 보고 기뻐하실 거야.

부모님이 돌아오시기 전에 해야 할 청소에 관해 이야기하고 있다. 여자가 쓰레기를 먼저 버려야 할 것 같다고 하자, 남자가 자신이 하겠다고 했으므로 남자가 할 일로 ③ '쓰레기 버리기'가 가장 적절하다.

어휘 get organized 정리하다 put away 넣어두다, 치우다 wipe down (걸레, 행주로) 닦다 dining table 식탁 skip 동 생략하다 vacuum 동 청소기를 돌리다 몡 진공 dust 동 먼지를 털다 take out the trash 쓰레기를 버리다 in good shape 상태가 좋은

6 금액 정보 파악

정답 ②

M Welcome to Sam's Home Décors. Can I help you?	남 Sam's Home Décors에 오신 것을 환영합니다. 도와 드릴까요?
W Hi, I'm wondering about these two picture frames. Do they have the same price?	여 안녕하세요, 이 두 액자에 관해 궁금한 점이 있어요. 이 둘의 가격이 같은가요?
M Actually, no. **The gold one is $10 while the brown one is $15.**	남 사실, 아니에요. 갈색 액자는 15달러인 반면에 금색은 10달러예요.
W Hmm... **I prefer** ¹⁾the brown one. **I'll take four of those, please.**	여 흠... 저는 갈색이 더 좋아요. 그것들로 4개 주세요.
M Do you need anything else?	남 더 필요한 것은 없으세요?
W I'd like to buy a table lamp, too.	여 테이블 램프도 사고 싶어요.
M This is our most popular model, and it's on sale right now.	남 이게 가장 인기 있는 모델이고, 지금 할인 중이에요.
W That's perfect. I'll ²⁾take it.	여 완벽해요. 이걸 살게요.
M I can ring you up now if you like.	남 원하시면 지금 계산해드릴 수 있어요.
W Sure. **And I have this coupon for 10% off. Can I use it?**	여 물론이죠. 그리고 저는 10% 할인해주는 쿠폰을 갖고 있어요. 이걸 쓸 수 있나요?
M Certainly. I'll apply it ³⁾to your total. So... you have four brown picture frames and the lamp. Is that right?	남 물론이죠. 총액에 적용할게요. 그러면... 네 개의 갈색 액자와 이 램프를 사시는 거죠. 맞나요?
W Wait! **The lamp is $30?** That's more expensive than I thought. I ⁴⁾don't think I'll buy it.	여 잠깐만요! 램프가 30달러라고요? 제 생각보다 비싸네요. 전 그걸 사지 않겠어요.
M No problem.	남 문제없습니다.

여자가 갈색 액자 4개($15×4=$60)를 구매했고, 램프는 사지 않겠다고 했으며, 10% 할인($60×0.9=$54)을 받았으므로 정답은 ② '$54'이다.

[어휘] picture frame 액자 on sale 할인 중인 ring up 계산해주다 certainly (대답으로) 물론이죠; 확실히 apply ⑧ 적용하다

7 이유 파악

정답 ③

W Honey, are you almost ready to leave?	여 여보, 떠날 준비 거의 다 했어?
M Give me 10 minutes. I have to return a phone call. One of my clients has a quick question.	남 10분만 줘. 전화 한 통 다시 해야 해. 고객 중 한 명이 간단한 질문이 있대.
W Okay. But are you sure we're not going to be late to Marcia's science fair?	여 알았어. 하지만 Marcia의 과학 박람회에 늦지 않는 건 확실하지?
M We should be fine. The building where it's ¹⁾being held is only a 15-minute drive away.	남 괜찮을 거야. 행사가 열리는 건물은 차로 단 15분 거리에 있거든.
W But remember, we can't use the car.	여 그렇지만 기억해, 우리는 차를 사용할 수 없어.
M Really? Is it ²⁾getting repaired at the shop?	남 정말? 가게에서 수리 중이야?
W You really don't remember?	여 당신 정말 기억 안 나?
M Is traffic blocked off downtown? I thought the parade on Main Street was tomorrow.	남 시내에 교통이 차단되어 있어? 메인가에서 있을 퍼레이드가 내일인 줄 알았는데.
W Honey, my brother ³⁾is borrowing the car this weekend.	여 여보, 내 동생이 이번 주말에 차를 빌려 가서 쓰고 있잖아.
M Oh! Of course... Well, we better call a cab soon.	남 아! 그렇지... 음, 빨리 택시를 부르는 게 좋겠네.
W I'll get the taxi. Can you be ready to leave in five minutes?	여 내가 택시를 잡을게. 5분 후에 떠날 준비를 할 수 있겠어?
M Yes, I'll be ready!	남 응, 준비될 거야!

여자가 박람회에 가는 데 차를 사용할 수 없다고 하면서 여자의 동생이 차를 빌려 가서 쓰고 있다고 했으므로, 두 사람이 승용차로 이동할 수 없는 이유는 ③ '동생에게 차를 빌려주어서'이다.

[어휘] be ready to ~할 준비를 하다 client ⑲ 고객, 의뢰인 block off 차단하다 cab ⑲ 택시

8 언급 유무 파악

정답 ③

M Hey, Carla. Have you attended the Mayfield Woodcraft Program?	남 안녕, Carla. 너 Mayfield Woodcraft Program에 다녀본 적 있어?
W I have. And I'm going back this year, actually. It's a great summer program.	여 다녀봤어. 그리고 난 사실 올해도 갈 거야. 정말 좋은 여름 프로그램이거든.
M My art teacher recommended it to me, so I was thinking of ¹⁾going there in **July**.	남 미술 선생님께서 내게 추천해 주셔서, 7월에 거기 갈까 생각 중이었어.
W You should definitely come! You'd love it.	여 꼭 와야 해! 마음에 들 거야.
M It's a **two-week-long** program, right?	남 2주간의 프로그램이지, 그렇지?
W That's right.	여 맞아.
M And all of the participants are ²⁾high school students?	남 그리고 참가자들은 모두 고등학생들이야?
W Yes. You have to be **between 15 and 17 years old** to attend.	여 응. 참석하려면 15세에서 17세 사이여야 해.
M Okay, great. I might sign up for the furniture-making course in that case.	남 그래, 좋아. 그렇다면 난 가구 제작 과정에 등록하는 게 좋겠어.
W Just make sure that you apply soon. The application deadline is coming up ³⁾on **Friday**.	여 빨리 신청하도록 해. 신청 마감일이 금요일로 다가오고 있어.
M Okay. I'll make up my mind soon.	남 알았어. 빨리 결정할게.
W Hope to see you there!	여 거기서 만나길 바랄게!

행사 시기(7월), 행사 기간(2주), 연령 제한(15세에서 17세 사이), 신청 마감일(금요일)에 대해 언급했고, ③ '참가자 수'는 언급하지 않았다.

어휘 attend 통 다니다, 참석하다 definitely 부 꼭, 분명히 sign up for ~에 등록하다 come up (날짜가) 다가오다 make up one's mind 결정하다

9 내용 불일치 파악
정답 ⑤

M Hello, everyone. Thanks for tuning into *All Things Boston*. Today, we have some exciting news for you. Our city will hold the annual Chef Conference from March 3rd to 6th. ¹⁾Over 200 chefs from all over the country will participate in this event. The conference aims to introduce the trendiest dishes and provide information about new ingredients. This year, the conference will be open to the public. Celebrity chefs ²⁾will treat attendees to their signature dishes in addition to leading cooking workshops. If you want to visit, purchase a ticket for $30 on the conference website. **Please note that tickets ³⁾will not be sold on-site.** Do you like to try delicious foods? Then, make sure to come!	남 안녕하십니까, 여러분. <All Things Boston>을 들어주셔서 감사합니다. 오늘, 여러분을 위한 흥미로운 소식을 가져왔습니다. 우리 시에서 3월 3일부터 6일까지 연례 Chef Conference를 개최할 예정입니다. 전국에서 온 200명 이상의 요리사들이 이 행사에 참여할 것입니다. 콘퍼런스에서는 최신 유행하는 요리를 소개하고 새로운 재료에 대한 정보를 제공하는 것을 목표로 합니다. 올해, 이 콘퍼런스는 대중에게 공개될 것입니다. 유명 요리사들은 요리 워크숍을 진행하는 것뿐만 아니라 참석자들에게 그들의 대표 요리를 대접할 것입니다. 방문하고 싶으시다면, 콘퍼런스 웹사이트에서 30달러에 티켓을 구매하십시오. 티켓은 현장에서 판매되지 않는 점 부디 유의해 주십시오. 맛있는 음식을 맛보고 싶으십니까? 그렇다면, 꼭 오십시오!

시에서 열리는 셰프 콘퍼런스 행사에 대한 안내 방송이다. 남자가 티켓은 현장에서 판매되지 않는다고 했으므로 ⑤ '티켓은 현장에서 구입할 수 있다.'는 내용과 일치하지 않는다.

어휘 tune into (라디오를) 듣다 annual 형 연례의 aim to ~하는 것을 목표로 하다 trendy 형 최신 유행의 ingredient 명 재료 treat 통 대접하다; 치료하다 attendee 명 참석자 in addition to ~뿐만 아니라 on-site 현장에서, 현장의

10 도표 정보 파악
정답 ⑤

W Honey, we need a tent for our vacation.	여 여보, 우리 휴가 때 텐트가 필요해.
M I know. I've been looking online. I found a site that lists some good ones. Here, take a look.	남 그러게. 내가 인터넷으로 찾아보고 있었어. 좋은 물건들을 내놓은 사이트를 찾았지. 자, 한번 봐봐.
W Oh, interesting. *[Pause]* Well, ¹⁾all four of us would need to sleep in it, so **this one isn't going to be a good option.**	여 오, 흥미롭네. [잠시 멈춤] 음, 우리 4명 모두가 안에서 잠을 자야 하니까, 이건 좋은 선택이 아닐 거야.
M That's true.	남 맞아.
W The weather is expected to be chilly for this season. **So how about ²⁾buying a winter tent?**	여 이 계절에는 날씨가 쌀쌀할 것으로 예상돼. 그렇다면 겨울용 텐트를 사는 것은 어떨까?
M **I think it's the safer choice.**	남 그게 더 안전한 선택인 것 같아.
W All right. That makes picking one a little bit easier. Is weight going to be a big factor?	여 좋아. 그러면 하나를 고르기가 조금 더 쉬워지는군. 무게가 중요한 요인이 될까?
M **Um... anything under six kilograms would be fine for backpacking.**	남 음... 배낭여행을 위해서는 6kg 이하면 아무거나 괜찮아.
W That leaves us with two choices.	여 두 가지 선택지가 남았네.
M I don't mind ³⁾spending a little more for a better tent. **We should get the more expensive one.**	남 더 좋은 텐트를 사기 위해서라면 난 돈을 좀 더 써도 상관없어. 더 비싼 걸로 사야겠어.
W **That's fine with me.**	여 그렇게 해도 난 괜찮아.
M Great. I'll go ahead and buy it.	남 좋아. 내가 곧바로 그걸 구매할게.

두 사람은 4명이 안에서 잘 수 있고, 겨울용 텐트이면서, 무게가 6kg 이하인 것 중, 더 비싼 텐트를 골랐다.

어휘 Take a look. 한번 봐봐. be expected to ~일 것으로 예상되다 chilly 형 쌀쌀한 pick 통 고르다 weight 명 무게 I don't mind ~해도 상관없다

11 짧은 대화의 응답 파악
정답 ⑤

W Excuse me. Are you headed to Wentworth Train Station?	여 실례합니다. 웬트워스 기차역으로 가시나요?
M No, ma'am. This bus is ¹⁾going across the river, toward downtown. Wentworth Station is on this side of the river.	남 아뇨, 선생님. 이 버스는 강을 건너, 시내로 갑니다. 웬트워스 역은 강을 기준으로 이쪽 편에 있습니다.
W **If you don't mind me asking, ²⁾where could I catch a bus going in the right direction?**	여 여쭤봐도 괜찮다면, 맞는 방향으로 가는 버스를 어디서 탈 수 있나요?
M **Cross the street. Then, you'll see a bus stop.**	남 길을 건너세요. 그럼, 버스 정류장이 보일 거예요.
	선택지 ① 맞아요. 버스 요금은 단 2달러예요.
	② 물론이죠. 차를 세우고 길을 물어봅시다.
	③ 서둘러야 해요. 기차가 몇 분 후에 떠나요.
	④ 잠깐만요. 역에 도착하면 알려드릴게요.
	⑤ 길을 건너세요. 그럼, 버스 정류장이 보일 거예요.

여자가 맞는 방향으로 가는 버스를 어디서 탈 수 있는지 물었으므로, 이에 대한 응답으로는 버스 정류장의 위치를 알려주는 ⑤ 'Cross the street. Then, you'll see a bus stop.'이 가장 적절하다.

어휘 be headed to ~으로 가다, 향하다 catch a bus 버스를 타다 fare 명 요금 pull over (길 한 쪽에) 차를 세우다

12 짧은 대화의 응답 파악   정답 ②

M Gina, I need a favor. **Can you ¹⁾switch seats with me?**	남 Gina, 부탁이 있어. 나랑 자리를 바꿔줄 수 있어?
W Why? I always sit here during class.	여 왜? 난 수업 시간에 항상 여기 앉아.
M I know, but I ²⁾forgot my glasses today. I won't be able to see the whiteboard from the back.	남 알아, 그런데 내가 오늘 안경을 까먹고 안 가져왔어. 뒷자리에서는 칠판이 안 보일 거야.
W I understand. I'll move to your desk.	여 알겠어. 네 책상으로 옮길게.

선택지 ① 미안한데 말이야. 앉아 줄래?
② 알겠어. 네 책상으로 옮길게.
③ 물론이지. 내가 나가서 칠판에 그걸 쓸게.
④ 좋아. 뒷자리에 계속 있으면서 불을 켜줘.
⑤ 그건 사실이 아니야. 나는 보통 안경 대신에 콘택트렌즈를 껴.

남자가 여자에게 자리를 바꿔 달라고 부탁하며, 그 이유로 안경을 안 가져와서 뒷자리에서는 칠판이 안 보일 거라고 했으므로, 이에 대한 응답으로는 부탁을 수락하는 ② 'I understand. I'll move to your desk.'가 가장 적절하다.

어휘 I need a favor. 부탁이 있어. switch 통 바꾸다 switch the lights on 불(전등)을 켜다 wear contacts 콘택트렌즈를 끼다

---

13 긴 대화의 응답 파악   정답 ①

[Phone rings.]	*[전화기가 울린다.]*
W You've reached the Sampson County Library help desk.	여 샘슨 카운티 도서관 안내데스크입니다.
M Hi, **I want to request that the library ¹⁾purchase a book.**	남 안녕하세요, 도서관에 책을 구매해달라고 요청하고 싶은데요.
W I may be able to help. What's the title of the book?	여 제가 도울 수 있을 것 같네요. 책 제목이 뭔가요?
M It's called *The Understanding of Diabetes*. It was not in the library's online catalog.	남 <The Understanding of Diabetes>라고 해요. 도서관 온라인 카탈로그에는 없더라고요.
W Let's see… Yes, I can confirm that we ²⁾don't have a copy.	여 어디 볼까요… 네, 한 권도 없다는 걸 확인할 수 있네요.
M I need it for a class research project.	남 전 이게 수업 연구 과제 때문에 필요해요.
W Let me see what I can do. *[Typing sound]* Hmm, ordering the book may not be the best option for you.	여 제가 뭘 할 수 있는지 볼게요. *[타자 치는 소리]* 흠, 책을 주문하는 게 최선의 선택이 아닐 수도 있겠어요.
M Oh, really? Is it not available?	남 아, 정말요? 구할 수 없나요?
W It's available for purchase, but this process ³⁾is slow. The book would arrive in six to eight weeks.	여 구매할 수는 있지만, 이 과정이 느리게 진행돼요. 그 책은 6주에서 8주 후에 도착할 거예요.
M That won't help! My project is due at the end of the month.	남 그건 도움이 안 돼요! 제 과제는 이번 달 말까지예요.
W **Then, we could borrow it ⁴⁾from another library. You just need to fill out an application.**	여 그럼, 다른 도서관으로부터 책을 빌려올 수 있어요. 신청서만 작성하시면 돼요.
M If I do that, when will I be able to get the book?	남 만약 그렇게 하면, 언제 그 책을 받을 수 있나요?

선택지 ① 만약 그렇게 하면, 언제 그 책을 받을 수 있나요?
② 유감스럽게도, 그 주제에 대한 다른 책을 찾을 수 없어요.
③ 온라인 카탈로그에서 '다른 옵션'을 클릭해주세요.
④ 도서관 웹사이트에서 이용 가능한지 확인할 수 있어요.
⑤ 당뇨병에 대한 정보를 사방으로 찾아 다녔어요.

도서관에 도서 구매 요청을 하는 상황이다. 여자가 도서관에서 구매할 수는 있지만 과정이 느리게 진행된다면서 다른 도서관으로부터 책을 빌려오는 방법을 제안하고 있으므로, 이에 대한 응답으로는 그렇게 할 경우 시간이 얼마나 걸릴지 묻는 ① 'If I do that, when will I be able to get the book?'이 가장 적절하다.

어휘 purchase 통 구매하다 명 구매 diabetes 명 당뇨병 confirm 통 확인하다 copy 명 (책, 잡지의) 권, 부 process 명 과정 fill out (양식을) 작성하다, 기입하다
application 명 신청서; 지원

---

14 긴 대화의 응답 파악   정답 ⑤

M What's in the bag? Did someone give you a gift?	남 가방 안에 그건 뭐야? 누가 네게 선물을 줬어?
W No. **I bought this bracelet ¹⁾for my best friend.**	여 아니. 가장 친한 친구에게 주려고 이 팔찌를 산 거야.
M Do you mean Grace?	남 Grace 말하는 거야?
W Yes. She is moving to Phoenix tomorrow.	여 응. 그녀는 내일 피닉스로 이사 가.
M It's a nice present. I'm sure she'll love it.	남 좋은 선물이네. 걔가 좋아할 게 확실해.
W I'm not so sure. **In the store, ²⁾the bracelet looked like a light yellow-gold. But in this light, it looks silver.**	여 난 잘 모르겠어. 가게에서, 팔찌는 밝은 노란 빛의 금색으로 보였어. 하지만 이 불빛에서 보면, 은색으로 보여.
M Is there anything wrong with that?	남 그게 무슨 문제가 돼?
W **She doesn't like silver.** I should have known better than to buy this on impulse.	여 걘 은색을 좋아하지 않아. 이걸 충동적으로 사지 말았어야 했는데.
M Why don't you exchange it for another piece of jewelry?	남 그걸 다른 장신구로 바꾸는 게 어때?
W The shop won't let me. The receipt says "No returns, no exchanges."	여 가게에서 그렇게 해주지 않을 거야. 영수증에 '반품 및 교환 불가'라고 적혀 있거든.

M Oh, dear. **What if you keep the bracelet for yourself, and ³⁾buy her another one?**

W That's not possible. The bracelet cost me a lot of money.

남 오, 이런. 그러면 이 팔찌는 네가 가지고, 그 애에게 다른 팔찌를 사주는 건 어때?

여 <u>그건 불가능해. 그 팔찌 사는 데 돈이 많이 들었어.</u>

선택지 ① 아니. 이건 내가 착용하기 좋아하는 종류의 팔찌야.

② 모르겠어. 그녀에게 팔찌가 두 개나 필요할 것 같지 않아.

③ 좋은 생각이야. 우리 같이 가서 교환해오는 게 어때?

④ 신경 쓰지 마. 그녀가 내게 블라우스나 스웨터를 사줄 계획이야.

⑤ 그건 불가능해. 그 팔찌 사는 데 돈이 많이 들었어.

친구에게 줄 선물을 두고 고민하는 상황이다. 여자가 친구는 은색을 좋아하지 않는다면서 은색으로도 보이는 팔찌를 어떻게 할지 고민하자 남자가 이미 산 팔찌는 여자가 가지고 다른 팔찌를 새로 사라고 제안했으므로, 이에 대한 응답으로는 제안을 거절하는 ⑤ 'That's not possible. The bracelet cost me a lot of money.'가 가장 적절하다.

어휘 bracelet 몡 팔찌 move to ~로 이사 가다 should have known better than to ~하지 말았어야 했다 on impulse 충동적으로 return 몡 반품 exchange 몡 교환
cost money 돈이 들다

15 상황에 적절한 말 파악

정답 ②

M Steve invited Jennifer over for a meal at his apartment. He just learned ¹⁾some new recipes and wanted to try them out. He grilled some shrimp, put together a salad, and even made his own fish soup. All of the food was already prepared when Jennifer arrived. She was excited to try the food that Steve had cooked, but when he handed her a plate, she noticed that it had ²⁾shrimp on it. **Since Jennifer has a shrimp allergy, she knows that she would get ill if she ate it.** Even though she doesn't want to make Steve feel bad, **she has to tell him that she must ³⁾decline the food.** In this situation, what would Jennifer most likely say to Steve?

남 Steve는 식사 대접을 위해 Jennifer를 아파트로 초대했습니다. 그는 막 몇 가지 새로운 요리법을 배웠고 그것들을 시도해보고 싶었습니다. 그는 새우를 굽고, 샐러드를 만들고, 심지어 자신만의 생선 수프를 만들었습니다. Jennifer가 도착했을 때 모든 음식은 이미 준비되어 있었습니다. 그녀는 Steve가 요리한 음식을 먹어볼 생각에 신이 났지만, 그가 그녀에게 접시를 건네주었을 때, 그녀는 그 위에 새우가 있다는 것을 알아차렸습니다. Jennifer는 새우 알레르기가 있기 때문에, 그것을 먹으면 탈이 날 것이라는 것을 알고 있습니다. 비록 그녀가 Steve의 기분을 상하게 하고 싶지는 않지만, 그녀는 그에게 음식을 거절할 수밖에 없다고 말해야 합니다. 이러한 상황에서, Jennifer가 Steve에게 가장 할 것 같은 말은 무엇입니까?

선택지 ① 이 샐러드 포장 주문할 수 있어?

② 정말 미안하지만, 나는 새우를 못 먹어.

③ 네게 새우 알레르기가 있다는 걸 잊어버렸어.

④ 너 아직 내가 가장 좋아하는 음식을 기억하고 있구나.

⑤ 유감이지만, 오늘 밤에 너희 집에 못 놀러 갈 것 같아.

Steve가 요리한 음식에 새우가 있는 것을 보고, Jennifer는 새우 알레르기 때문에 음식을 거절할 수밖에 없다고 말하려 한다. 따라서, Jennifer가 할 말로 ② 'I'm so sorry, but I can't eat shrimp.'가 가장 적절하다.

어휘 grill 통 굽다 put together 만들다; 조립하다 hand 통 건네주다 allergy 몡 알레르기 get ill 탈이 나다, 병들다 decline 통 거절하다; 줄어들다 come over 놀러 가다; 건너가다

16-17 세트 문항

정답 16 ③ 17 ④

W Good morning, everyone. Last time we talked about the importance of diet to maintain a high level of fitness. **In today's class, I'd like to discuss ¹⁾various exercises throughout history.** First off, **weightlifting** has been an essential workout for thousands of years. Stone weights have been found that were used in the ancient Olympics. **Running** is another exercise that is present ²⁾throughout recorded history. For instance, the gymnasiums all over the Roman empire usually included tracks where joggers could run. Next, let's talk about **dancing**. Dancing has been used to improve physical fitness since at least the medieval period. Some records show that knights ³⁾used dance steps to get used to wearing their armor. Finally, we can take a recent example, **Pilates**. This is indeed a modern invention, which was created by a German physical trainer. People who practice it ⁴⁾improve their balance and learn breathing techniques. Now, let's take a look at a brief video.

여 안녕하십니까, 여러분. 지난 시간에 우리는 높은 수준의 건강을 유지하기 위한 식습관의 중요성에 대해 이야기했습니다. 오늘 수업에서는, 역사 속 다양한 운동에 관해 이야기하려고 합니다. 첫 번째로, 역도는 수천 년 동안 필수적인 운동이었습니다. 고대 올림픽에서 사용되었던 돌로 만든 역기가 발견되기도 했습니다. 육상은 기록된 역사 속에 존재하는 또 다른 운동입니다. 예를 들어, 로마 제국 전역의 체육관에는 보통 조깅하는 사람들이 뛸 수 있는 트랙이 포함되었습니다. 다음으로는, 무용에 대해 이야기해봅시다. 무용은 적어도 중세 시대부터 신체 건강을 향상시키기 위해 사용되어 왔습니다. 어떤 기록들은 기사들이 갑옷을 입는 것에 익숙해지기 위해 무용 스텝을 사용했다는 것을 보여줍니다. 마지막으로, 최근의 예시로 필라테스를 들 수 있습니다. 이것은 정말로 현대의 발명품인데, 독일의 트레이너에 의해 만들어졌습니다. 이 운동을 연습한 사람들은 몸의 균형감을 향상시키고 호흡법을 배웁니다. 자, 이제 간단한 영상을 보시겠습니다.

선택지 **16** ① 전통적인 운동의 이점

② 식습관과 신체 단련 방법의 발전

③ 역사 속 신체 훈련의 다양한 형태

④ 특정 체육 활동이 인기를 얻은 방식

⑤ 다양한 스포츠에서 훈련을 위해 사용된 방법

17 ① 역도 ② 육상 ③ 무용 ④ 복싱 ⑤ 필라테스

16 역사 속 다양한 운동에 관해 이야기하고 있으므로 여자가 하는 말의 주제로 ③ 'different forms of fitness training in history'가 가장 적절하다.

17 역도, 육상, 무용, 필라테스는 언급했지만 ④ 'boxing'은 언급하지 않았다.

어휘 diet 몡 식습관 fitness 몡 건강, 신체 단련 weightlifting 몡 역도 weight 몡 역기; 무게 ancient 톙 고대의 recorded 톙 기록된 gymnasium 몡 체육관 jogger 몡 조깅하는 사람들
physical 톙 신체의, 육체의 medieval 톙 중세의 knight 몡 (중세의) 기사 get used to ~에 익숙해지다 armor 몡 갑옷 indeed 悍 정말로 invention 몡 발명품 breathing 몡 호흡

1	④	2	③	3	①	4	④	5	③	6	①	7	①	8	⑤	9	②	10	④
11	①	12	④	13	①	14	④	15	⑤	16	①	17	②						

• 각 문제의 정답 근거는 굵은 글씨로, Dictation 정답은 밑줄로 표시되어 있습니다.

1 목적 파악
정답 ④

W Attention, Brook High School students. As you may know, the flu is going around right now. **This viral disease is spread through human contact** ¹⁾in crowded spaces. Consequently, schools are often a place where the flu spreads quickly. **Therefore, we would like to advise students to take preventive measures to** ²⁾avoid catching this disease **and spreading it.** Wash your hands often and use your sleeve if you need to sneeze or cough. It is also a good idea to wear a mask. Free vaccinations against this disease are offered by local hospitals and community health centers. Vaccinations are ³⁾not mandatory, but students are strongly advised to get vaccinated. Thank you.

여 주목해 주십시오, 브룩 고등학교 학생 여러분. 여러분도 알다시피, 지금 독감이 유행하고 있습니다. 이 바이러스성 질병은 붐비는 공간에서 사람들의 접촉을 통해 퍼집니다. 결과적으로, 학교는 종종 독감이 빠르게 퍼지는 장소가 됩니다. 따라서, 우리는 학생들에게 이 질병에 걸려서 전파시키는 것을 방지하기 위해 예방 조치를 취할 것을 권고하고 싶습니다. 손을 자주 씻고 재채기나 기침이 나면 옷소매를 이용하십시오. 마스크를 쓰는 것도 좋은 생각입니다. 이 질병에 대한 무료 예방 접종은 지역 병원과 지역 보건소에서 제공됩니다. 예방 접종이 의무적인 것은 아니지만, 학생들에게는 예방 접종을 받는 것이 강력히 권고됩니다. 감사합니다.

여자가 독감이 유행하고 있다고 말하면서, 학생들에게 예방 조치를 취하고 예방 접종을 받으라고 권고하고 있다. 따라서, 여자가 하는 말의 목적으로 ④ '독감 예방 수칙 준수를 권고하려고'가 가장 적절하다.

[어휘] flu 몡 독감 go around (질병이) 유행하다 viral 휑 바이러스성의 spread 통 퍼지다 crowded 휑 붐비는 advise A to B A에게 B하기를 권고하다 take a measure 조치를 취하다 sneeze 통 재채기하다 mandatory 휑 의무적인 strongly 뷔 강력히 get vaccinated 예방 접종을 받다

2 의견 파악
정답 ③

W Hi, Carl. Did you book a hotel for your trip to Paris?
M Hey, Sheila. Not yet.
W Where do you want to stay?
M I was thinking of getting a hotel ¹⁾in the suburbs. Then, I could take a train in to Paris to go sightseeing.
W Hmm... **I think it's better to find accommodations in** ²⁾the city center **when you're traveling.**
M Really? I could save 50 euros per night.
W Maybe so, but then you'll have to spend a lot of time going back and forth.
M It's 45 minutes each way. I guess that will get tiring.
W Exactly. That's why you need a place to stay in the middle of the city. You'll have ³⁾more energy to explore the attractions.
M Yeah... I want to have a special experience there.
W Then, keep looking!
M I will.

여 안녕, Carl. 너 파리 여행 때 묵을 호텔을 예약했니?
남 안녕, Sheila. 아직 안 했어.
여 어디에 머물고 싶어?
남 교외에 호텔을 잡을 생각이었어. 그러면, 기차를 타고 파리로 관광하러 갈 수 있거든.
여 흠... 여행할 때는 도심에 있는 숙소를 찾는 게 더 나은 것 같아.
남 정말? 하룻밤에 50유로를 절약할 수도 있는데.
여 그럴지도 모르지만, 그러면 왔다 갔다 하는 데 많은 시간을 써야 할 거야.
남 편도 45분 거리야. 그러면 피곤할 것 같네.
여 정확해. 그게 바로 네가 도시 중심에 머물 곳이 필요한 이유야. 넌 관광지를 탐방할 기운을 더 많이 갖게 될 거야.
남 응... 난 거기서 특별한 경험을 하고 싶어.
여 그럼, 계속 찾아봐!
남 그럴게.

여행 계획을 세우며 숙소를 교외로 잡으려 하는 남자에게 여자가 여행할 때는 도심에 있는 숙소를 찾는 것이 더 낫다고 했다. 따라서, 여자의 의견으로 ③ '여행 시 숙소는 도심에 위치한 곳이 좋다.'가 가장 적절하다.

[어휘] suburb 몡 교외 go sightseeing 관광하러 가다 accommodation 몡 숙소 go back and forth 왔다 갔다 하다 That's why ~. 그게 바로 ~한 이유이다. attraction 몡 관광지, 명소; 매력

3 관계 파악
정답 ①

W Hi. Welcome to the studio!
M It's nice to meet you, Lauren.
W It's my pleasure. I'm a big fan of yours. **I've watched all the movies** ¹⁾you've acted in.
M Thanks. **I've wanted to work with you since I saw your last collection of photos.**
W Then, you're going to like today's shoot. **It'll be based on the same theme.**
M You mean we'll ²⁾take pictures using flowers?

여 안녕하세요. 작업실에 오신 걸 환영해요!
남 만나서 반가워요, Lauren.
여 천만에요. 전 당신의 열렬한 팬이에요. 당신이 연기했던 모든 영화를 봤어요.
남 고마워요. 저는 당신의 마지막 사진집을 본 이후로 당신과 함께 일하고 싶었어요.
여 그럼, 오늘 촬영이 마음에 드실 거예요. 같은 주제를 기반으로 할 거거든요.
남 꽃을 이용해서 사진을 찍겠다는 말씀이신가요?

W	Yeah. I'm sure you're eager to begin. **I know you have a meeting with the director of your new movie later.**	여	맞아요. 일을 몹시 시작하고 싶으시겠죠. 이후에 새로 들어가는 영화의 감독님과 미팅이 있다는 걸 알고 있거든요.
M	No rush. Is there anything in particular you want me to wear in the pictures?	남	서두르지 마세요. 사진에서 제게 특별히 착용하게 하고 싶은 것이 있으세요?
W	The stylist has a few choices for you.	여	스타일리스트가 당신을 위해 몇 가지 선택지를 갖춰 뒀어요.
M	Great. And we'll take the pictures in this room?	남	좋아요. 그리고 이 방에서 사진을 찍을 거죠?
W	That's right. I have the ³⁾lighting all set up. I think this magazine cover is going to look great!	여	맞아요. 조명은 다 설치해 뒀어요. 잡지 표지가 정말 멋지게 나올 것 같네요!
M	I hope so! I'll go ahead and get ready.	남	그랬으면 좋겠어요! 가서 준비할게요.

두 사람이 작업실에서 사진 촬영에 관해 이야기하고 있다. 여자는 그녀의 마지막 사진집 때처럼 꽃을 이용해서 사진을 찍겠다고 했으며, 남자는 영화에서 연기한 적이 있고 사진 촬영 이후 새로 들어가는 영화의 감독과 미팅이 있다고 하는 것으로 보아 두 사람의 관계로 ① '사진작가 — 배우'가 가장 적절하다.

어휘 shoot 명 사진 촬영, 영화 촬영 통 쏘다 be based on ~을 기반으로 하다 be eager to 몹시 ~하고 싶다 No rush. 서두르지 마세요. in particular 특별히 lighting 명 조명

4 그림 내용 불일치 파악   정답 ④

W	Honey, do you mind taking a look at the room setup? I want to check if we're forgetting anything for Jake's graduation party.	여	여보, 방 배치 좀 봐주겠어? Jake의 졸업 파티에 잊어버린 것이 있는지 확인하고 싶어.
M	No problem. I love the balloon arch ¹⁾above the door.	남	문제없어. 문 위에 있는 풍선 아치가 너무 맘에 들어.
W	Thanks.	여	고마워.
M	Is there enough seating? I only see three tables.	남	자리는 충분해? 테이블이 세 개밖에 안 보이는걸.
W	We're expecting 20 people, so I think everyone will have ²⁾a place to sit.	여	20명이 올 예정이라, 모두 앉을 자리가 있을 것 같아.
M	You've already put a stack of square plates on the table in the front.	남	이미 앞쪽 테이블에는 네모난 접시를 쌓아 놓았네.
W	Right. We'll serve the snacks and cake on those plates.	여	맞아. 그 접시에 간식과 케이크를 담아서 제공할 거야.
M	**What about that photo of Jake ³⁾playing basketball?** Is that the one you want to display?	남	Jake가 농구하는 저 사진은 어때? 당신이 전시해놓고 싶은 거야?
W	Yes. He wanted a sports-themed one.	여	응. Jake가 스포츠를 주제로 한 사진을 원했어.
M	That makes sense. I see you have ⁴⁾a pair of speakers in the back of the room.	남	이해가 되네. 방 뒤쪽에 스피커 한 쌍이 있는 게 보여.
W	Right, we'll have music playing.	여	응, 음악을 틀어둘 거야.
M	I think everything is good to go.	남	모든 게 준비가 된 것 같아.

대화에서 남자가 Jake의 농구하는 사진이 있다고 말했는데, ④에는 Jake의 졸업 사진이 그려져 있다.

어휘 take a look at ~을 보다 arch 명 아치 stack 명 쌓아올린 것 serve 통 제공하다 display 통 전시하다, 보여주다 good to go 준비가 된, 순조로운

5 할 일 파악   정답 ③

M	Hey, Alison. What are you working on?	남	안녕, Alison. 지금 무슨 일을 하고 있니?
W	I just finished revising the end of my speech, Uncle Steve.	여	방금 연설 마지막 부분 수정을 끝마쳤어요, Steve 삼촌.
M	Oh, right. You're in a speech competition. When is it?	남	아, 맞아. 넌 웅변대회에 나가지. 그게 언제니?
W	It's next Friday afternoon.	여	다음 주 금요일 오후예요.
M	That's perfect. I'll be able to watch it.	남	완벽하군. 내가 볼 수 있겠다.
W	Do you want to come? I know you're ¹⁾busy coaching your basketball team.	여	오실래요? 삼촌이 농구팀을 지도하느라 바쁘신 것 알아요.
M	No worries. Our team is taking a break. So I'll be free for a while.	남	걱정 없어. 우리 팀은 휴식을 취하고 있어. 그래서 당분간은 한가할 거야.
W	Really? Then, please help me with my speech. I'm nervous about it.	여	정말요? 그럼, 제 연설을 도와주세요. 긴장돼요.
M	Sure. **Why don't you read it out loud for me? I'd be happy to listen to your speech and ²⁾give you some feedback.**	남	물론이지. 내 앞에서 큰 소리로 읽어보는 것은 어떠니? 기꺼이 네 연설을 듣고 의견을 줄게.
W	That would be really helpful. Give me just a second to ³⁾print the script for you.	여	그거 정말 도움이 될 거예요. 대본을 인쇄할 시간을 잠깐 주세요.
M	Sure! Take your time. Oh, and please bring me a pen, too.	남	물론이지! 천천히 해. 오, 그리고 펜도 가져다주렴.
W	Alright. One moment.	여	알았어요. 잠깐만요.

여자가 나갈 웅변대회 준비에 대해 이야기하고 있다. 남자가 여자에게 연설문을 큰 소리로 읽어보라고 하며 그것을 듣고 의견을 주겠다고 했으므로 남자가 할 일로 ③ '연설 듣고 의견 주기'가 가장 적절하다.

어휘 revise 통 수정하다 coach 통 지도하다, 코치하다 take a break 휴식을 취하다 for a while 당분간, 잠시 read out loud 큰 소리로 읽다 I'd be happy to ~. 기꺼이 ~할게.
Take your time. 천천히 해.

6 금액 정보 파악

정답 ①

M Welcome to the Hotel Marigold, ma'am. May I help you?	남 Hotel Marigold에 오신 것을 환영합니다, 손님. 도와드릴까요?
W Yes, thanks. I need a room for the next couple of nights. Do you ¹⁾have any available?	여 네, 고마워요. 앞으로 이틀 밤 묵을 방이 필요해요. 빈방이 있나요?
M We do have a few rooms available. [Typing sound] It looks like you have two options. **There's one room with a queen-sized bed for $100 per night, and one with a king-sized bed for $120 per night.**	남 빈방이 몇 개 있어요. [타자 치는 소리] 두 가지 선택지가 있는 것 같네요. 퀸사이즈 침대가 있는 방은 1박에 100달러이고, 킹사이즈 침대가 있는 방은 1박에 120달러입니다.
W I'll take the one with the queen-sized bed.	여 퀸사이즈 침대가 있는 걸로 할게요.
M And that's ²⁾for two nights?	남 그리고 이틀 밤 동안 묵으시는 거죠?
W Right. Also, I have this discount voucher.	여 맞아요. 또, 저는 이 할인권을 가지고 있어요.
M Ah, sure. **This would give you $20 off of the total on your bill.**	남 아, 네. 계산서의 총액에서 20달러를 할인해 드릴 거예요.
W Great. And is breakfast included?	여 좋아요. 그리고 조식도 포함되어 있나요?
M There's an ³⁾additional charge of $15 per person for our breakfast buffet.	남 조식 뷔페는 1인당 15달러의 추가 요금이 있습니다.
W Well, it's just me, but I would like it both mornings.	여 음, 저 혼자이고, 이틀간의 아침에 다 이용하고 싶어요.
M All right, then. I just need an ID and credit card.	남 좋아요, 그럼. 신분증과 신용카드만 있으면 됩니다.
W I've got those right here.	여 바로 여기 있어요.

여자가 퀸사이즈 침대가 있는 방을 이틀 묵기로 하고($100×2=$200), 조식 이틀 치($15×2=$30)를 추가했다. 이때 총액에서 20달러 할인($230-$20=$210)을 받았으므로 정답은 ① '$210'이다.

어휘 per night 1박에 voucher 명 할인권, 쿠폰 buffet 명 뷔페

7 이유 파악

정답 ①

W Hi, David. I heard you started a computer programming course. How is that going?	여 안녕, David. 네가 컴퓨터 프로그래밍 과정을 시작했다고 들었어. 어떻게 되어가고 있니?
M It's really fun, Lisa. I practiced coding a website today.	남 정말 재미있어, Lisa. 나는 오늘 웹사이트 코딩을 연습했어.
W That's really interesting. Oh, I needed to ask you something. Can you bring your laptop for our class presentation tomorrow?	여 정말 흥미롭다. 오, 나 물어볼 게 있었는데. 내일 수업 발표를 위해 노트북을 가지고 올 수 있어?
M I ¹⁾don't think that's going to be possible.	남 그건 불가능할 것 같아.
W Did you lend it to your sister?	여 여동생한테 빌려줬니?
M Yes, but she gave it back to me already.	남 응, 하지만 그녀는 이미 내게 그것을 돌려줬어.
W Then, I guess you're not comfortable bringing it to school, right? That's understandable.	여 그럼, 학교에 가져오는 게 불편한 것 같네, 그렇지? 이해할 수 있어.
M I normally take mine to school. **Actually, I have to take it to the shop ²⁾for repairs.**	남 난 보통 학교에 내 것을 가지고 가. 사실, 수리를 위해 가게에 가져가야 해.
W Oh... I see. Well, what are we going to do?	여 오... 그렇구나. 이런, 어떻게 해야 할까?
M We can use our smartphones to project the slideshow. Let me look up ³⁾how to do that.	남 스마트폰으로 슬라이드 쇼를 보여줄 수 있어. 내가 어떻게 하는지 찾아볼게.
W Great! That should work.	여 좋아! 그러면 되겠네.

남자는 내일 발표에 노트북을 가져올 수 없다고 하면서 수리를 위해 가게에 가져가야 한다고 대답했으므로, 남자가 노트북을 가져올 수 없는 이유는 ① '수리를 맡겨야 해서'이다.

어휘 laptop 명 노트북 presentation 명 발표 understandable 형 이해할 수 있는 slideshow 명 (발표에 사용하는) 슬라이드 쇼 look up 찾아보다

8 언급 유무 파악

정답 ⑤

W Hey, Patrick. How was the performance of *Swan Lake*?	여 안녕, Patrick. <백조의 호수> 공연은 어땠어?
M It was wonderful, Carrie! What a great ballet performance!	남 훌륭했어, Carrie! 정말 멋진 발레 공연이었어!
W Aren't the dancers ¹⁾from Germany?	여 무용수들이 독일 출신 아니니?
M That's right. The lead ballerina is one of the best dancers in the world.	남 맞아. 수석 발레리나가 세계 최고의 무용수 중 한 명이야.
W Wow. Is there still time to get tickets?	여 우와. 아직 표를 살 수 있는 시간이 있어?
M Yeah, I think so. There are performances ²⁾until June 28th.	남 응, 그런 것 같아. 6월 28일까지 공연이 있거든.
W How much are they?	여 얼마야?
M Well, it's different depending on where you sit. The one I bought was $25, though.	남 음, 어디에 앉느냐에 따라 달라. 그렇지만 내가 샀던 것은 25달러였어.
W That's not so bad. Where are the performances being held?	여 그렇게 나쁘진 않네. 공연은 어디서 열려?
M The shows are at the **Sheldon Auditorium.**	남 쉘든 회관에서 해.
W That's perfect. That's close to my house. I'll ³⁾definitely go.	여 완벽하네. 거긴 우리 집에서 가까워. 꼭 가야겠다.
M Well, let me know your plan. I'd be happy to go see it again.	남 그럼, 네 계획을 알려줘. 나 그 공연 다시 보러 가고 싶거든.
W I will!	여 그럴게!

무용단 국적(독일), 마지막 공연일(6월 28일), 티켓 가격(25달러), 공연 장소(쉘든 회관)에 대해 언급했고, ⑤ '공연 길이'는 언급하지 않았다.

어휘 ballet 명 발레   depending on ~에 따라   close to ~에서 가까운

---

9 내용 불일치 파악

정답 ②

W Hello, WBBZ Radio listeners. Before we get to the next program, I want to remind listeners about our radio station's 10th Annual Charity Concert. During this event, which is 1)held each February, our station raises money for charity with the help of our loyal listeners. **This year, 2)all the money raised will be donated to several local pet shelters.** The event, which will take place on the sixth, will be held downtown at the Logan Ballroom on 1st Avenue. Jennifer Haley, the city's most popular radio DJ, will 3)host the event. Food and beverages will be provided by Winston Catering Services. Tickets are $50 each and available on our website. Okay, now let's get back to your regularly scheduled program.	여 안녕하십니까, WBBZ 라디오 청취자 여러분. 다음 프로그램에 들어가기 전에, 청취자 여러분께 우리 라디오 방송국의 열 번째 연례 자선 콘서트에 대해 다시 말씀드리고 싶습니다. 매년 2월에 열리는 이 행사 동안, 우리 방송국은 애청자님들의 도움을 받아 자선기금을 모금합니다. 올해, 모금된 모든 돈은 지역 동물 보호소 몇 군데에 기부될 것입니다. 6일에 열리는 이 행사는 시내 1번가의 로건 무도회장에서 개최될 예정입니다. 이 도시에서 가장 인기 있는 라디오 DJ인 Jennifer Haley가 이 행사의 사회를 맡을 것입니다. 음식과 음료는 Winston Catering Services에서 제공합니다. 입장권은 인당 50달러이며, 저희 웹사이트에서 구입하실 수 있습니다. 좋습니다. 이제 정규 편성된 프로그램으로 돌아가 봅시다.

라디오 방송국의 연례 자선 콘서트에 대한 홍보 방송이다. 여자가 모금된 모든 돈이 지역 동물 보호소에 기부된다고 했으므로 ② '모금액의 일부만 동물 보호소에 기부될 것이다.'는 내용과 일치하지 않는다.

어휘 raise money for charity 자선기금을 모금하다   pet shelter 동물 보호소   take place (행사가) 열리다, 개최되다   host 통 사회를 맡다 명 사회자   beverage 명 음료

---

10 도표 정보 파악

정답 ④

W Honey, shouldn't we get something for the bedroom? I think these dressers look good.	여 여보, 우리 침실에 놓을 것 좀 사야 하지 않을까? 이 서랍장들이 좋아 보이는 것 같아.
M Yeah, definitely. It would be nice to have a new dresser next to the bed.	남 응, 물론이지. 침대 옆에 새 서랍장이 있으면 좋겠어.
W The problem is that there are so many choices in this showroom.	여 문제는 이 전시장에 선택지가 너무 많다는 거야.
M Maybe we should 1)decide on our budget first.	남 우선 예산을 결정하는 게 좋을지도 모르겠어.
W **We can't spend more than $800.**	여 우리 800달러 이상은 못 써.
M That's fair. Well, what about this one? It looks pretty nice.	남 적당해. 음, 이건 어때? 꽤 좋아 보이네.
W Yeah, I like the style, **but it only has four drawers. That 2)won't be enough.**	여 응, 그 스타일이 마음에 드는데, 서랍이 네 개밖에 없어. 그걸로는 충분하지 않을 거야.
M Right, we need it to store a lot of clothes.	남 맞아, 많은 옷을 보관할 수 있는 게 필요해.
W Does the color make a big difference to you?	여 색상이 당신에게 크게 중요해?
M **I think any of these colors could work except for white.**	남 흰색을 제외하고는 이 색상들 중 어떤 것이라도 어울리겠어.
W Okay. How about the material?	여 알았어. 소재는 어때?
M I 3)like walnut. It lasts a long time.	남 월넛이 좋아. 오래 가거든.
W That's exactly what I was thinking.	여 그게 바로 내가 생각하고 있던 거야.
M Well, I think the decision is made for us, then.	남 음, 그럼, 결정이 내려진 것 같네.

두 사람은 800달러 이하의 예산 내에서, 서랍이 네 개보다 많고, 흰색을 제외한 색상 중에서, 월넛 소재로 된 서랍장을 골랐다.

어휘 dresser 명 서랍장   showroom 명 전시장   budget 명 예산   store 통 보관하다   except for ~을 제외하고는   last 통 오래 가다

---

11 짧은 대화의 응답 파악

정답 ①

W Peter, I'm really 1)eager to go somewhere this weekend. **How about heading to the beach?**	여 Peter, 난 진짜 이번 주말에 어딘가 너무 가고 싶어. 해변으로 가는 게 어때?
M I'd like to, but I'm worried it will be crowded and the traffic will be awful.	남 그러고 싶지만, 사람들로 붐비고 교통 상황이 아주 나쁠까 봐 걱정돼.
W **But if we stay at home, we'll 2)regret it later.**	여 하지만 집에 있으면, 나중에 후회할 거야.
M Good point. But let's visit somewhere quieter.	남 좋은 지적이야. 하지만 좀 더 조용한 곳으로 가자.
	선택지 ① 좋은 지적이야. 하지만 좀 더 조용한 곳으로 가자.
	② 말도 안 돼. 난 주말 내내 여행하길 기대하고 있었어.
	③ 알겠어. 나중에 후회하지 않도록 최선을 다할게.
	④ 걱정 마. 우리가 일찍 출발하면 교통 상황이 더 나을 거야.
	⑤ 동의해. 우리는 집에서 쉬면서 더 즐겁게 지낼 거야.

주말에 해변에 가자는 여자의 제안을 남자가 완곡히 거절하자 여자가 집에 있으면 나중에 후회할 거라고 회유했으므로, 이에 대한 응답으로는 제안을 승낙하는 ① 'Good point. But let's visit somewhere quieter.'가 가장 적절하다.

어휘 head to ~으로 가다   awful 형 아주 나쁜, 끔찍한   regret 통 후회하다   Good point. 좋은 지적이야.   look forward to ~하길 기대하다   do one's best 최선을 다하다

12 짧은 대화의 응답 파악   정답 ④

M Jane! What a coincidence running into you here! I ¹⁾haven't seen you in years.	남 Jane! 여기서 우연히 널 만나다니 이런 우연이! 몇 년 동안 널 못 봤잖아.
W It's great to see you, Mark! Are you leaving the modern art exhibit?	여 만나서 반가워, Mark! 현대 미술 전시회에서 나가는 중이니?
M Yeah, I was about to go home. **But why don't we go somewhere and ²⁾chat for a bit?**	남 응, 집에 막 가려던 참이었어. 그렇지만 우리 어디 가서 잠깐 얘기하는 건 어때?
W Sure. How about getting some coffee at a nearby café?	여 물론이지. 근처 카페에서 커피 마시는 게 어때?

	선택지 ① 네 말에 동의해. 그 전시회는 정말 훌륭했어.
	② 응. 난 여길 여가 시간에 친구들과 자주 와.
	③ 정말? 우리가 마지막으로 본 지 그렇게 오래되었다는 게 믿기지 않아.
	④ 물론이지. 근처 카페에서 커피 마시는 게 어때?
	⑤ 미안. 일찍 나가야 해서 수다를 못 떨었네.

남자와 여자가 오랜만에 우연히 만난 상황에서 남자가 어디 가서 잠깐 얘기하자고 제안했으므로, 이에 대한 응답으로는 제안을 승낙하는 ④ 'Sure. How about getting some coffee at a nearby café?'가 가장 적절하다.

어휘 What a coincidence ~! ~하다니 이런 우연이! run into ~를 우연히 만나다 be about to 막 ~하려던 참이다 chat 통 이야기하다, 수다 떨다 brilliant 형 훌륭한, 눈부신 nearby 형 근처의

13 긴 대화의 응답 파악   정답 ①

M Hi! What can I do for you?	남 안녕하세요! 무엇을 도와드릴까요?
W I'd like to have these clothes dry-cleaned.	여 이 옷들을 드라이클리닝 받고 싶어요.
M Please set your items down here.	남 여기에 옷을 넣어 주세요.
W Here they are.	여 여기 있어요.
M So I've got a woman's jacket, a short-sleeved dress, and a coat.	남 그러니까 여성용 재킷, 반소매 원피스, 그리고 코트를 받았습니다.
W **Oh, I also have this shirt. Can you ¹⁾mend it?**	여 아, 이 셔츠도 있어요. 수선 가능한가요?
M What's wrong with it?	남 무슨 문제가 있나요?
W There's a small tear down the back. You can hardly see it.	여 뒤쪽에 작은 찢어진 곳이 있어요. 거의 보이지는 않아요.
M Ma'am... **I don't think I'll be ²⁾able to fix this.**	남 손님... 이건 고칠 수 없을 것 같아요.
W Why not? It doesn't look too badly damaged. This is one of my favorite shirts.	여 왜요? 엄청 심하게 손상된 것 같아 보이진 않아요. 이건 제가 가장 좋아하는 셔츠 중 하나거든요.
M The material is too fine and fragile. I'm certain it will ³⁾rip again even if I mend it.	남 옷감이 너무 섬세하고 손상되기 쉬워요. 제가 수선해도 또 찢어질 거라고 확신해요.
W I ⁴⁾won't blame you if that happens. Can you please try mending it for me?	여 그런 일이 있어도 당신을 탓하지 않겠어요. 부디 절 위해 이걸 한번 수선해주실 수 있나요?
M I'll do my best. But I can't promise a perfect result.	남 최선을 다할게요. 하지만 완벽한 결과를 장담할 수는 없어요.

	선택지 ① 최선을 다할게요. 하지만 완벽한 결과를 장담할 수는 없어요.
	② 알겠습니다. 음, 그렇게 빨리 다시 찢어진 것도 놀랍지 않네요.
	③ 정말 감사합니다. 언제 옷을 찾으러 오면 되나요?
	④ 유감스럽게도 안 됩니다. 이런 제품은 세탁이 안 돼요.
	⑤ 아뇨. 겉보기보다 옷감이 훨씬 튼튼하네요.

세탁소에 옷을 맡기는 상황에서 남자가 여자의 셔츠 수선을 거절하자 여자가 그럼에도 불구하고 수선해달라고 부탁했으므로, 이에 대한 응답으로는 부탁을 수락하는 ① 'I'll do my best. But I can't promise a perfect result.'가 가장 적절하다.

어휘 have ~ dry-cleaned ~을 드라이클리닝 받다 short-sleeved 형 반소매의, 짧은 소매의 mend 통 수선하다 tear 명 찢어진 곳, 구멍 badly 부 심하게 fine 형 섬세한, 미세한 fragile 형 손상되기 쉬운, 취약한 rip 통 찢어지다, 찢다 I can't promise ~. ~을 장담할 수는 없어요. no wonder that ~한 것도 놀랍지 않다 pick up 찾으러 오다

14 긴 대화의 응답 파악   정답 ④

M Hey, Samantha. What's wrong?	남 얘, Samantha. 무슨 문제 있어?
W **Well, I think there's a ¹⁾fly in my soup.**	여 음, 수프에 파리가 들어간 것 같아.
M Are you sure? Can I take a look?	남 확실해? 내가 한번 봐도 돼?
W It's right there on the side of the bowl.	여 그릇 가장자리 바로 그쪽에 있어.
M That doesn't look like a fly to me. I think it's probably a small piece of onion that's turned a little black from frying.	남 내게는 파리처럼 보이지 않는걸. 아마 튀겨서 약간 까맣게 변한 작은 양파 조각일 거야.
W Then, do you mind ²⁾taking it out of the soup to check? I can't do it myself.	여 그럼, 수프에서 꺼내서 확인해 줄 수 있어? 내가 스스로 못 하겠어.
M Not at all. I'm going to ³⁾put it on this napkin.	남 그럼. 이 냅킨 위에 올려놓을게.
W Go ahead. [Pause] Ah, maybe I was wrong.	여 그렇게 해. [잠시 멈춤] 아, 내가 틀렸나 봐.
M Yeah, that's not a fly. But it's not an onion either. I'm not sure if it's a part of your dish or not.	남 응, 파리가 아니네. 하지만 양파도 아니야. 이게 요리의 일부인지 아닌지 확신이 안 서.
W Me neither. **I should call over a manager to check it.**	여 나도 그래. 확인하기 위해서 매니저를 불러야겠어.
M **You'd better ⁴⁾ask for another bowl of soup or something else.**	남 수프나 다른 뭔가를 하나 더 달라고 하는 게 낫겠어.

W Yeah. I can't eat this, so I'll ask for a salad instead.	여 응. 이건 못 먹겠으니, 대신 샐러드를 시킬게.
	선택지 ① 네 말이 맞아. 매니저가 참 친절했어.
	② 왜 안 돼? 난 여기서 수프를 먹어본 적이 없어.
	③ 아니, 괜찮아. 원한다면 내 냅킨을 사용해도 돼.
	④ 응. 이건 못 먹겠으니, 대신 샐러드를 시킬게.
	⑤ 이건 용납할 수 없어. 종업원이 요리를 잘못 가져왔어!

수프에 이물질이 들어간 상황에서 여자가 이물질 확인을 위해 매니저를 부르겠다고 하자 남자가 수프나 다른 요리를 하나 더 달라고 하는 게 낫겠다고 했으므로, 이에 대한 응답으로는 대신 시킬 요리를 언급하는 ④ 'Yeah. I can't eat this, so I'll ask for a salad instead.'가 가장 적절하다.

어휘 fly 명 파리   take a look 힐끗 보다   turn 통 번하나; 돌다   take A out of B B에서 A를 꺼내다   Go ahead. 그렇게 해.   unacceptable 형 용납할 수 없는

15   상황에 적절한 말 파악   정답 ⑤

W Kendra and Hank are friends who recently enrolled in an advanced physics class at an after-school program. Both of them are quite 1)interested in physics. However, Hank is finding the class more difficult than he thought it would be, so he has to spend extra time studying the course materials every night. Today, everyone in the class 2)got the results of the first quiz of the semester. Despite his hard work, Hank was very disappointed with his score. However, he noticed that Kendra 3)looked pleased when she saw her grade. **So he wants to ask her if she can 4)share any advice to help him improve his grade on the next test.** In this situation, what would Hank most likely say to Kendra?	여 Kendra와 Hank는 최근 방과 후 프로그램의 상급 물리학 수업에 등록한 친구입니다. 그들 둘 다 물리학에 꽤 관심이 있습니다. 하지만 Hank는 수업이 생각했던 것보다 어렵다는 것을 알게 되어, 매일 밤 수업 자료를 공부하는 데 추가 시간을 써야 합니다. 오늘은, 학급 모두가 이번 학기 첫 번째 퀴즈의 결과를 받았습니다. 힘들게 노력했음에도 불구하고, Hank는 그의 점수에 매우 실망했습니다. 하지만, 그는 Kendra가 그녀의 성적을 보고 기뻐하는 것을 알아차렸습니다. 그래서, 그는 그녀에게 다음 시험에서 그의 성적을 올리는 데 도움이 될 조언을 공유해 줄 수 있는지 요청하고 싶습니다. 이러한 상황에서, Hank가 Kendra에게 가장 할 것 같은 말은 무엇입니까?
	선택지 ① 몇 점 받았는지 물어봐도 될까?
	② 사실, 스터디 그룹에 가입할까 생각 중이야.
	③ 공식을 공부하는 데 더 많은 시간을 투자하면 된다고 생각해.
	④ 이 수업은 너무 어려워서, 수강한 것을 후회하기 시작했어.
	⑤ 다음에 어떻게 하면 더 좋은 점수를 받을 수 있는지 팁 좀 알려줄 수 있어?

퀴즈 성적에 기뻐하는 Kendra를 보고 Hank는 다음 시험에서 성적을 올리는 데 도움이 될 조언을 공유해달라고 요청하려 한다. 따라서, Hank가 할 말로 ⑤ 'Could you give me some tips on how I can get a better score next time?'이 가장 적절하다.

어휘 advanced 형 상급의   after-school program 방과 후 프로그램   extra 형 추가의   semester 명 학기   despite 전 ~에도 불구하고   be disappointed with ~에 실망하다   pleased 형 기뻐하는   formula 명 공식

16-17   세트 문항   정답 16 ① 17 ②

M Good afternoon, everyone. We previously learned about what kinds of animals lay eggs. **Today, I want to talk about some of the unique ways that animals 1)raise their young.** To begin, let's think about **sea turtles** that skip parenting entirely. When young turtles hatch, they have to get to the ocean 2)on their own. Predictably, this means that very few of them survive to adulthood. In contrast, we have **emperor penguins**, who make a great effort to 3)protect their young. After laying an egg, the female penguin returns to the sea to look for food while its father holds on to it. Next up, **elephants** raise their young together. For them, parenting is a community-wide activity. Along with help from their mothers, baby elephants are fed, protected, and taught by elder females in the herd. Finally, we can consider **kangaroos**. Their babies are born tiny and underdeveloped. So kangaroos 4)spend their first months in a pouch under their mothers' skin for warmth and protection. Now, let's take a look at a quick video.	남 안녕하세요, 여러분. 우리는 이전에 어떤 종류의 동물이 알을 낳는지에 대해 배웠습니다. 오늘은, 동물들이 새끼를 기르는 독특한 방법에 대해 이야기하고 싶습니다. 우선, 육아를 완전히 생략하는 바다거북에 대해 생각해 보죠. 어린 거북들이 부화하면, 그들은 스스로 바다에 도착해야 합니다. 예상대로, 이는 그들 중 극소수만이 성체가 될 때까지 생존한다는 것을 의미합니다. 대조적으로, 황제펭귄이 있는데, 그들은 새끼들을 보호하기 위해 많은 노력을 합니다. 알을 낳은 후, 아빠 펭귄이 그것을 계속 품고 있는 동안 암컷 펭귄은 먹이를 찾기 위해 바다로 돌아갑니다. 다음으로, 코끼리는 새끼를 함께 기릅니다. 그들에게, 육아는 지역 사회 전체의 활동입니다. 어미들의 도움과 함께, 새끼 코끼리들은 무리 내 원로 암컷에게 먹이를 받고, 보호받으며, 가르침을 받습니다. 마지막으로, 우리는 캥거루를 생각할 수 있습니다. 캥거루의 새끼들은 작고 미성숙한 상태로 태어납니다. 그래서 캥거루는 온기와 보호를 위해 어미의 피부 밑에 있는 주머니에서 첫 몇 달을 보냅니다. 이제, 짧은 비디오를 보겠습니다.
	선택지 16 ① 다양한 동물들의 특이한 양육 방법
	② 바다에 사는 조류의 진화
	③ 동물이 알에서 부화하는 독특한 방법
	④ 협력적 육아가 포유류에게 필수적인 이유
	⑤ 야생동물에게 있어 높은 생존율의 중요성
	17 ① 바다거북 ② 악어 ③ 황제펭귄 ④ 코끼리 ⑤ 캥거루

16 동물들이 새끼를 기르는 독특한 방법에 대해 이야기하고 있으므로 남자가 하는 말의 주제로 ① 'unusual parenting methods of various animals'가 가장 적절하다.
17 바다거북, 황제펭귄, 코끼리, 캥거루는 언급했지만 ② 'alligators'는 언급하지 않았다.

어휘 lay 통 (알을) 낳다; 놓다   raise 통 기르다, 키우다   parenting 명 육아   predictably 부 예상대로   adulthood 명 성체, 성인   in contrast 대조적으로   hold on to ~을 계속 품다, 잡다   along with ~과 함께   feed 통 먹이를 주다   herd 명 무리   underdeveloped 형 미성숙한, 발육이 덜 된; 저개발의   pouch 명 주머니

1	③	2	⑤	3	④	4	④	5	③	6	②	7	③	8	⑤	9	③	10	①
11	④	12	①	13	⑤	14	②	15	③	16	①	17	③						

• 각 문제의 정답 근거는 굵은 글씨로, Dictation 정답은 밑줄로 표시되어 있습니다.

---

1 목적 파악

정답 ③

W Attention, Channel 15 viewers. Is there a musician inside you wanting to come out? **Then, call Harmony Music Academy at 555-9283, and let us help you** ¹⁾**achieve your dreams!** We offer a great variety of music classes for both beginners and more advanced students. Our classes will not only provide you with theoretical and historical knowledge of ²⁾different musical genres, from classical music to rock music, but will also give you the practice you need to develop and ³⁾improve your musical skills. Our academy is located next to city hall, in front of the bus terminal. Call or stop by.	여 주목해주세요, Channel 15번 시청자 여러분. 여러분 내면에서 나오고 싶어 하는 음악가가 있나요? 그렇다면, Harmony Music Academy에 555-9283으로 전화해서, 저희가 여러분이 꿈을 이루는 것을 도울 수 있게 해주세요! 저희는 초급자와 상급자 모두를 위한 매우 다양한 음악 수업을 제공합니다. 저희 수업은, 클래식부터 록까지, 다양한 음악 장르에 대한 이론적, 역사적 지식을 제공할 뿐만 아니라, 음악 실력을 키우고 향상시키는 데 필요한 연습도 제공하겠습니다. 저희 학원은 시청 옆, 버스 터미널 앞에 있습니다. 전화하거나 들러주세요.

여자가 Harmony Music Academy에 관심이 있으면 전화하면서, 커리큘럼 및 위치 등 정보를 주고 있다. 따라서, 여자가 하는 말의 목적으로 ③ '음악 학원을 홍보하려고'가 가장 적절하다.

어휘 come out 나오다 a variety of 다양한 theoretical 혱 이론적인 genre 몡 장르 stop by 들르다

---

2 의견 파악

정답 ⑤

M Kaylie, what are you working on? Are you finished with your chemistry homework? **W** Oh, I was getting bored with chemistry, so I started an essay for my English class. **M** I'm not sure that's a good idea. **W** Why not? I have to ¹⁾do both of them. **M** I think it's better to finish one task ²⁾before starting on another. **W** I was having trouble focusing. **M** I understand. But switching back and forth between different assignments wastes time. **W** Maybe you're right. **M** And finishing one thing always feels better. Doing another assignment only adds something else ³⁾to worry about. **W** Yeah, now I'm worrying about both assignments. **M** That's why you should stick to one thing at a time! **W** Okay, I'll get back to my chemistry homework so I don't have to think about it anymore.	남 Kaylie, 뭘 하고 있니? 화학 숙제는 다 했니? 여 오, 화학 숙제에 신물이 나서, 영어 수업의 에세이를 쓰기 시작했어. 남 난 그게 좋은 생각인지 잘 모르겠어. 여 왜? 난 둘 다 해야 되는걸. 남 나는 다른 일을 시작하기 전에 한 가지 일을 끝내는 게 더 좋다고 생각해. 여 난 집중하는 데 어려움이 있었어. 남 이해해. 그렇지만 다른 과제를 왔다 갔다 하며 바꾸는 건 시간을 낭비하게 해. 여 네 말이 맞을 수도 있겠어. 남 그리고 한 가지 일을 끝내면 항상 기분이 더 좋아져. 다른 과제를 하는 것은 단지 걱정거리를 추가할 뿐이야. 여 응, 이제 두 과제 모두 걱정 중이야. 남 그게 바로 한 번에 한 가지만 고수해야 하는 이유야! 여 알았어, 화학 숙제로 다시 돌아가서 더 이상 그것에 대해 생각하지 않아도 되게 할게.

여러 일을 동시에 하려는 여자에게 남자가 다른 일을 시작하기 전에 한 가지 일을 끝내는 것이 더 좋다고 했다. 따라서, 남자의 의견으로 ⑤ '시작한 과제를 끝마친 후에 다른 과제를 하는 것이 좋다.'가 가장 적절하다.

어휘 get bored with ~에 신물이 나다 task 몡 일, 과업 switch 통 바꾸다, 전환하다 back and forth 왔다 갔다 stick to ~을 고수하다

---

3 관계 파악

정답 ④

M Hi, Ms. Williams. **Did you see my draft of** ¹⁾**the lobby design?** **W** It looks good, but it's a big change from the old lobby, don't you think? **M** That's true. **But considering your company is an advertising agency, the change should** ²⁾**work well.** **W** I guess. Maybe I'm not used to the bold colors. **M** This is just a prospective design. If there are some things that you want to tone down, we can do that. **W** It needs a carpet that stands out less. **M** Sure, Ms. Williams. You can choose ³⁾any style you want.	남 안녕하세요, Williams 씨. 제 로비 디자인 도면 보셨어요? 여 보기엔 좋은데, 예전 로비에서 큰 변화가 있죠, 그렇게 생각하지 않나요? 남 맞아요. 하지만 선생님의 회사가 광고 대행사라는 점을 고려하면, 이러한 변화가 효과적일 겁니다. 여 그렇겠죠. 아마도 전 이런 선명한 색깔에 익숙하지 않은 것 같아요. 남 이것은 단지 예상 디자인일 뿐입니다. 색상을 은은하게 하고 싶은 게 있으면 그렇게 해드릴 수 있어요. 여 눈에 덜 띄는 카펫이 필요해요. 남 물론이죠, Williams 씨. 원하는 어떤 스타일도 선택하실 수 있어요.

W I also think we should go with different furniture. Those chairs don't look comfortable.	여 또한 다른 가구들을 골라야 한다고 생각해요. 저 의자들은 편안해 보이지 않아요.
M Got it. I'll show you some different samples.	남 알았어요. 몇 가지 다른 샘플을 보여드리겠습니다.
W Good. Can I also see your design of the area near the elevators?	여 좋아요. 엘리베이터 근처의 디자인도 볼 수 있을까요?
M Of course. You'll see I included a mirror across from each elevator, ⁴⁾<u>as you requested</u>.	남 그럼요. 요청하신 대로, 각 엘리베이터 바로 맞은편에 거울을 둔 걸 확인하실 수 있어요.

두 사람이 인테리어 계획에 관해 이야기하고 있다. 남자는 여자에게 도면을 보여주며 의견을 받고 있고, 여자는 원하는 가구 등을 요청하는 것으로 보아 두 사람의 관계로 ④ '인테리어 디자이너 — 고객'이 가장 적절하다.

[어휘] draft ⑲ 도면 advertising agency 광고 대행사 bold ⑲ 선명한, 대담한 be used to ~에 익숙하다 prospective ⑲ 예상된; 장래의 tone ~ down ~의 색상을 은은하게 하다
stand out 눈에 띄다 across from 바로 맞은편에

4 그림 내용 불일치 파악   정답 ④

W Nathan, is the auditorium ready for the speech contest?	여 Nathan, 강당에 강연회 준비 다 됐니?
M I think so, Principal Hill. I just finished setting up the judges' table in front of the stage.	남 그런 것 같아요, Hill 교장 선생님. 저는 방금 무대 앞에 심사위원석을 설치했어요.
W Did you lower the projector screen at the ¹⁾<u>back of the stage</u> yet?	여 무대 뒤쪽에 있는 프로젝터 스크린을 내려놓았니?
M I did. And I placed two microphones on the podium on the right side of the stage.	남 내렸어요. 그리고 무대 오른쪽에 있는 단상에 마이크 두 개를 두었어요.
W By the way, **did you replace the old curtains?**	여 그나저나, 오래된 커튼은 교체했니?
M Yes. I installed the ²⁾<u>new striped ones</u> a few days ago. Do you want me to do anything with the piano?	남 네. 며칠 전에 줄무늬가 있는 새 커튼을 설치했어요. 피아노에도 뭔가 하길 원하시나요?
W Is it in the way?	여 그게 방해가 될까?
M No. I pushed it to ³⁾<u>the left</u> corner.	남 아뇨. 왼쪽 구석으로 밀어놨어요.
W Let's leave it there, then. It's not worth the trouble of moving it off the stage.	여 거기에 두자, 그럼. 그걸 무대 밖으로 옮기는 수고를 할 가치는 없어.
M Sounds good.	남 좋아요.
W I think we're all set. Thanks, Nathan.	여 다 된 것 같네. 고맙구나, Nathan.

대화에서 남자가 며칠 전에 줄무늬가 있는 새 커튼을 설치했다고 말했는데, ④에는 무늬가 없는 커튼이 그려져 있다.

[어휘] auditorium ⑲ 강당 judge ⑲ 심사위원, 심판 place ⑧ 두다, 놓다 podium ⑲ 단상 by the way 그나저나, 그런데 install ⑧ 설치하다 a few days ago 며칠 전에
be in the way 방해가 되다 be worth ~의 가치가 있다 the trouble of ~하는 수고

5 할 일 파악   정답 ③

M Did you hear? Jennifer is getting married!	남 소식 들었어? Jennifer가 결혼한대!
W Really? I can't believe that! I didn't even know she was in a relationship.	여 정말? 믿기지가 않아! 난 그녀가 누굴 사귀고 있는 줄도 몰랐어.
M She told me that the wedding will be in September. The ceremony ¹⁾<u>is being held</u> at St. Mary's Church downtown.	남 결혼식이 9월에 있을 거라고 말해줬어. 식은 시내에 있는 성 마리아 성당에서 열릴 거야.
W That's so great. It'll be fun to visit the city then. The weather in September is beautiful.	여 너무 잘 됐다. 그때 그 도시를 방문하는 건 재미있을 거야. 9월의 날씨가 아름답거든.
M Anyway, I think we should ²⁾<u>prepare a surprise</u> for her at the wedding.	남 어쨌든, 우리 결혼식에서 그녀를 위한 깜짝 선물을 준비해야 할 것 같아.
W Sure. What should we do?	여 물론이지. 뭘 하면 좋을까?
M How about performing a dance at the reception?	남 피로연에서 춤을 추는 건 어때?
W Oh, you know I'm a bad dancer!	여 오, 나 춤 잘 못 추는 거 알잖아!
M Then, what about a song? You can play the piano, and I will sing.	남 그럼, 노래는 어때? 넌 피아노를 칠 수 있고, 난 노래를 부를래.
W That sounds better. Do you have a song in mind?	여 그게 더 낫겠다. 염두에 둔 노래가 있어?
M I do, actually! **Let me ³⁾<u>play the music</u> for you on my phone.**	남 실은 있어! 휴대폰으로 그 노래를 틀어줄게.
W You've already worked everything out!	여 넌 이미 모든 걸 해결해 두었구나!

친구의 결혼식에서 할 깜짝 공연 계획에 대해 이야기하고 있다. 여자가 남자에게 염두에 둔 노래가 있는지 묻자, 남자가 있다고 하면서 휴대폰으로 노래를 틀어주겠다고 했으므로 남자가 할 일로 ③ '노래 재생하기'가 가장 적절하다.

[어휘] in a relationship (연인으로) 사귀는, 만나는 ceremony ⑲ 식, 의식 reception ⑲ 피로연, 연회; (호텔의) 접수처 have ~ in mind ~을 염두에 두다 work out 해결하다

W	Good afternoon, sir.	여	안녕하세요, 손님.
M	Hi. I'd like to buy some tickets for the art museum.	남	안녕하세요. 미술관 티켓을 좀 사고 싶은데요.
W	It's $10 per person for ¹⁾the audio tour and $20 per person for the guided tour.	여	오디오 투어는 1인당 10달러, 가이드 투어는 1인당 20달러입니다.
M	Okay. When does the next guided tour start?	남	네. 다음 가이드 투어는 언제 시작하나요?
W	Let's see. [Pause] The next one leaves at 2 p.m.	여	한번 볼게요. [잠시 멈춤] 다음 시간은 오후 2시에 시작해요.
M	Hmm... That's ²⁾a long wait. I'll stick with the audio tour. Three tickets, please.	남	음... 오래 기다려야 하네요. 오디오 투어로 할게요. 티켓 세 장 주세요.
W	Got it. And are you a student?	여	알겠습니다. 그리고 학생이신가요?
M	Yes. Is there a discount?	남	네. 할인이 있나요?
W	It's 20% off the ticket price if you have a ³⁾valid student ID.	여	유효한 학생증이 있으면 티켓 값의 20%가 할인됩니다.
M	Thanks for mentioning it. Here you go.	남	말씀해 주셔서 감사해요. 여기 있어요.
W	Okay, that's three audio tour tickets at the student rate. And would you like a copy of our exhibition catalog? It's a great souvenir, and it's only $5.	여	네, 학생 요금으로 오디오 투어 티켓 세 장입니다. 그리고 저희 전시회 도록을 한 권 드릴까요? 좋은 기념품인데, 5달러밖에 안 해요.
M	Sure, I'll ⁴⁾take one.	남	네, 하나 주세요.
W	Great. Here you are. I hope you enjoy the exhibit today.	여	좋아요. 여기 있습니다. 오늘 전시회 즐겁게 보시길 바랍니다.

남자가 오디오 투어 티켓 세 장($10×3=$30)과 전시회 카탈로그 1권($5)을 구매했고, 20% 할인을 티켓에만 받았으므로($30×0.8=$24) 정답은 ② '$29'이다.

어휘 leave 통 시작하다, 출발하다　valid 형 유효한　rate 명 요금, 가격; 비율　copy 명 (책, 잡지의) 권, 부　catalog 명 도록, 카탈로그　souvenir 명 기념품

W	Tom, are you coming to the book club meeting?	여	Tom, 독서 동아리 모임에 올 거니?
M	Hi, Marta. I can't make it.	남	안녕, Marta. 못 갈 것 같아.
W	Oh, no. Again? You don't like the novel we're reading, do you?	여	오, 이런. 또? 우리가 읽고 있는 소설이 마음에 안 드는 거지, 그렇지?
M	It's ¹⁾nothing like that. I'm enjoying the book.	남	그런 게 아니야. 그 책 재미있게 읽고 있어.
W	It must be the meeting place, then. I could have scheduled it at a café closer to the school.	여	그러면 틀림없이 약속 장소 때문이겠구나. 학교에 좀 더 가까운 카페에서 일정을 잡을 수도 있었을 텐데.
M	No. I've just been busy with the end of the semester. I need to focus on studying ²⁾for my exams at the moment.	남	아니야. 학기 말이라 좀 바빴을 뿐이야. 지금은 시험공부에 집중해야 해.
W	Got it. It's too bad that you can't come this time. I haven't seen you there since you went to ³⁾visit your aunt in December.	여	알았어. 이번에 올 수 없다니 유감이네. 네가 12월에 고모님 댁을 방문한 이후로 그곳에서 널 만나지 못했어.
M	Yeah, I wish I could go. But I'll be back soon.	남	응, 갈 수 있으면 좋을 텐데. 하지만 곧 돌아갈 거야.
W	When do you think you can come to a club meeting again?	여	동아리 모임에 언제 다시 올 수 있을 것 같아?
M	I'll return in January. See you soon!	남	1월에 돌아갈 거야. 곧 만나!

남자는 독서 동아리 모임에 못 간다고 하면서 지금은 시험 공부에 집중해야 한다고 말했으므로, 남자가 모임에 참석할 수 없는 이유는 ③ '시험공부를 해야 해서'이다.

어휘 I can't make it. 못 갈 것 같아.　schedule 통 일정을 잡다 명 일정　focus on ~에 집중하다　at the moment 지금은　I wish ~. ~하면 좋을 텐데.

W	Hey, Alex. Do you have special plans for next week?	여	안녕, Alex. 다음 주에 특별한 계획이 있니?
M	Yeah. I'm going to Maple Campsite! I've been looking forward to this for a long time.	남	응. 메이플 야영장에 갈 거야! 난 오랫동안 이걸 기대해 왔어.
W	Oh, was it closed for a while?	여	아, 그곳이 한동안 문을 닫았었나?
M	Yes. Visitors are only allowed there ¹⁾during the fall.	남	응. 방문객들은 가을에만 그곳 출입이 허락돼.
W	And the campsite is in Maple Forest, right? Doesn't it get cold there in the autumn?	여	그리고 야영장은 메이플 숲속에 있잖아, 맞지? 가을에는 거기 춥지지 않니?
M	You're right. But don't worry. I think I'm well prepared.	남	맞아. 그런데 걱정하지 마. 내 생각엔 준비된 것 같아.
W	Really? You'll have to ²⁾make a campfire to stay warm.	여	정말? 따뜻하게 있으려면 모닥불을 피워야 할 거야.
M	No, actually. That's against campsite rules. The rangers won't let us build one.	남	아니야, 사실은. 그건 야영장 규칙을 거스르는 거야. 삼림 관리원들이 피우지 못하게 할 거야.
W	Oh, that must be to prevent forest fires.	여	아, 분명 산불을 예방하기 위해서겠구나.
M	Right. But they ³⁾provide visitors with a tent, so I just have to bring a thick sleeping bag.	남	맞아. 하지만 방문객들에게 텐트를 제공하기 때문에, 난 그저 두꺼운 침낭을 가져가기만 하면 돼.
W	I see. Well, it sounds like you've got everything covered. Have a nice trip!	여	그렇구나. 음, 네가 모든 것을 해결한 것 같네. 여행 잘 다녀와!

개장 기간(가을), 위치(메이플 숲속), 운영 규칙(모닥불 금지), 제공 용품(텐트)에 대해 언급했고, ⑤ '이용 요금'은 언급하지 않았다.

9 내용 불일치 파악   정답 ③

M Hi. I'm Michael Jacobs, owner of Jacobs Department Store. I want to invite everyone in the Peterville area to our Reopening Sale on October 24th. To celebrate our [1]newly renovated facility on Madison Street, we're cutting prices throughout the store. On the second floor, where women's casual wear has been relocated, summer dresses are marked 25% off. **In the men's fashion section, which is now on the third floor, [2]all our winter coats are discounted.** Kids' clothing can now be found [3]on the top floor, along with a supervised playground area for your children. Also, make sure to stop by our food court in the basement. We have over a dozen different restaurants that will be offering free samples from their new menus. I hope you'll join us.	남 안녕하세요. 저는 제이콥스 백화점의 소유주인 Michael Jacobs입니다. 피터빌 지역의 모든 분들을 10월 24일에 열리는 재개장 세일에 초대하고 싶습니다. 매디슨가에 새로 단장한 시설을 기념하기 위해, 매장 전체에 걸쳐 가격을 인하하려고 합니다. 여성용 평상복이 이동한 곳인 2층에는 여름 원피스가 25% 할인된 가격으로 표시돼 있습니다. 지금은 3층에 있는 남성용 패션 코너의 모든 겨울 코트가 할인됩니다. 아동복은 이제 최상층에서 여러분의 자녀를 위한 감독관이 있는 놀이 공간과 함께 찾아보실 수 있습니다. 그리고 지하에 있는 저희 푸드 코트에도 꼭 들러주십시오. 새로운 메뉴의 무료 시식을 제공하는 12개가 넘는 다양한 식당들이 있습니다. 여러분께서 와주시길 바랍니다.

백화점 재개장 세일에 대한 안내 방송이다. 남자가 남성용 패션 코너의 모든 겨울 코트가 할인된다고 했으므로 ③ '남성용 겨울 코트는 할인 대상에서 제외된다.'는 내용과 일치하지 않는다.

10 도표 정보 파악   정답 ①

W Patrick's birthday party is coming up. We need to order a cake soon.	여 Patrick의 생일 파티가 다가오고 있네. 우리 빨리 케이크를 주문해야겠어.
M Why don't we get one from that new bakery on the corner?	남 길모퉁이에 새로 생긴 베이커리에서 하나 사는 게 어때?
W Right! Red Panther Bakery. I'll open their website.	여 맞아! Red Panther Bakery야. 거기 웹사이트 열어볼게.
M **Let's make sure [1]not to get a carrot cake.** Patrick wasn't happy with the one we got last year.	남 당근 케이크는 확실하게 사지 않도록 하자. Patrick은 작년에 우리가 사준 당근 케이크에 만족하지 않았어.
W Fair enough. Well, there are still plenty of good options here.	여 일리가 있어. 음, 여기 아직 좋은 선택지들이 많이 있어.
M Should we get one with a custom message?	남 주문 제작 메시지를 넣을 수 있는 것으로 할까?
W Yeah. I think that would be cute.	여 응. 그게 귀여울 것 같아.
M But I don't want to [2]spend too much. Some of these are expensive.	남 하지만 너무 많이 지출하고 싶지는 않아. 이것들 중 몇 개는 비싸네.
W No problem. **We can go up to $60.**	여 좋아. 60달러까지 감당할 수 있겠어.
M Perfect.	남 완벽해.
W What about size? We're expecting five people, and some will want an extra serving.	여 사이즈는? 5명이 올 예정이고, 일부는 1인분 이상을 추가로 원할 거야.
M Let's not get something too small. But at the same time, we don't need to overdo it. [3]More than 10 pieces is probably excessive.	남 너무 작은 것은 사지 말자. 그렇지만 동시에, 지나치게 할 필요는 없어. 10조각보다 많은 건 아마 과할 거야.
W I agree.	여 동의해.

두 사람은 당근 케이크가 아니면서, 주문 제작 메시지를 넣을 수 있고, 60달러 이하의 가격대의, 10조각보다 많지 않은 케이크를 골랐다.

11 짧은 대화의 응답 파악   정답 ④

M Excuse me. Do you know [1]how to get to the Foster Center Basketball Arena from here?	남 실례합니다. 여기서 포스터 센터 농구 경기장까지 어떻게 가는지 아세요?
W Just turn right at the corner, and then go straight. **But are you sure you want to walk there? I [2]wouldn't recommend doing that.**	여 모퉁이에서 그냥 우회전하시고, 그 다음 직진하세요. 그런데 거기까지 걸어가고 싶으신 게 확실하세요? 그렇게 하는 것은 추천하지 않아요.
M No? Why not?	남 안 하신다고요? 왜요?
W It's about a 30-minute walk from here.	여 여기서 걸어서 30분 정도 걸려요.
	선택지 ① 걷기에 좋은 날이에요.
	② 그 코너에는 아무 가게도 없어요.
	③ 그 경기장에서 제가 가장 좋아하는 팀이 경기해요.
	④ 여기서 걸어서 30분 정도 걸려요.
	⑤ 전 농구 경기 티켓을 가지고 있지 않아요.

여자가 농구 경기장까지 걸어가는 것은 추천하지 않는다고 하자 남자가 왜냐고 물었으므로, 이에 대한 응답으로는 그 이유를 말하는 ④ 'It's about a 30-minute walk from here.'가 가장 적절하다.

12 짧은 대화의 응답 파악

정답 ①

W Toby, I'm [1)]feeling tired from all this studying. Should we call it a night?	여 Toby, 이거 다 공부하느라 피곤하다. 오늘 밤은 여기서 끝낼까?
M We've covered almost everything that will be on the exam. Is [2)]one more hour okay?	남 우리는 시험에 나올 거의 모든 것을 다 다뤘어. 한 시간만 더 해도 돼?
W I can manage that. **I need to run over to the convenience store, though.**	여 그건 해낼 수 있어. 하지만 편의점에 잠시 들러야겠어.
M Oh, could you pick me up a snack?	남 오, 나 간식 좀 사다 줄래?

선택지 ① 오, 나 간식 좀 사다 줄래?
② 그 부분은 오전에 다룰 수 있어.
③ 그건 시험에 안 나올 것 같아.
④ 난 피곤해서 일찍 잘 거야.
⑤ 내가 시간을 관리하는 데 어려움을 겪고 있다는 걸 알았어.

늦게까지 공부를 하는 상황에서 여자가 피곤하다면서 편의점에 잠시 들러야겠다고 했으므로, 이에 대한 응답으로는 편의점 심부름을 부탁하는 ① 'Oh, could you pick me up a snack?' 이 가장 적절하다.

어휘 **call it a night** (이날 밤의 일을) 여기서 끝내다, 중지하다 **cover** 图 다루다; 덮다 **manage** 图 해내다; 관리하다 **run over to** ~에 잠시 들르다 **convenience store** 편의점
pick up ~을 사다 주다

13 긴 대화의 응답 파악

정답 ⑤

M Welcome to Antonio's Restaurant. What will you be having this afternoon?	남 Antonio's Restaurant에 오신 것을 환영합니다. 오늘 오후에 어떤 걸 드실 건가요?
W I'd like to [1)]start with the shrimp salad.	여 새우 샐러드로 시작할게요.
M Fantastic. Would you like cocktail sauce or the chef's special dressing?	남 환상적이에요. 칵테일소스를 드릴까요, 아니면 주방장 특선 드레싱을 드릴까요?
W The special dressing is fine. I'd also like a bowl of soup.	여 특선 드레싱이 좋겠어요. 수프 한 그릇도 주세요.
M Okay. We have tomato, potato, and clam chowder.	남 네. 토마토, 감자, 클램 차우더가 있습니다.
W I'm in the mood for seafood. Clam chowder, please.	여 해산물이 먹고 싶네요. 클램 차우더로 부탁합니다.
M Excellent choice. Now, [2)]what would you like for the main course?	남 훌륭한 선택입니다. 이제, 메인 요리는 무엇으로 하시겠습니까?
W I'm thinking about the fried octopus. How is that served?	여 문어 튀김을 생각 중이에요. 이건 어떻게 나오나요?
M It's served with a fresh herb sauce. It's also our special of the day, which means it's half off.	남 신선한 허브 소스와 함께 나옵니다. 그것은 또한 오늘의 특별 요리인데요, 즉 반값이라는 의미죠.
W Oh, that sounds lovely.	여 오, 참 좋군요.
M So that's a clam chowder, a shrimp salad, and the fried octopus?	남 그럼 클램 차우더, 새우 샐러드, 그리고 문어 튀김이 맞으시죠?
W Correct. **Can you bring everything [3)]at the same time?**	여 맞습니다. 전부 동시에 가져다주실 수 있나요?
M No problem. I'll be back with your order in about 15 minutes.	남 문제없죠. 약 15분 후에 주문하신 것을 가지고 오겠습니다.

선택지 ① 아마도요. 이따 다시 불러주시겠어요?
② 아뇨. 문어 튀김은 추천하지 않습니다.
③ 네. 곧 계산서를 가져다 드리겠습니다.
④ 상황에 따라 달라요. 혼자 식사하세요, 아니면 누군가와 함께이신가요?
⑤ 문제없죠. 약 15분 후에 주문하신 것을 가지고 오겠습니다.

레스토랑에서 주문을 하는 상황에서 여자가 주문한 요리를 전부 동시에 가져다줄 수 있는지 물었으므로, 이에 대한 응답으로는 가능하다고 대답하는 ⑤ 'No problem. I'll be back with your order in about 15 minutes.'가 가장 적절하다.

어휘 **clam chowder** 클램 차우더, 조개 수프 **be in the mood for** ~하고 싶다 **main course** 메인 요리 **half off** 반값의 **in a moment** 곧, 바로 **That depends.** 상황에 따라 달라요.

14 긴 대화의 응답 파악

정답 ②

M Sally, do you have plans tonight?	남 Sally, 오늘 밤에 약속 있어?
W I'm going to the Street Dance Battle.	여 나 Street Dance Battle에 갈 거야.
M Oh, I heard about that event. Don't the performers dance to hip-hop music?	남 오, 그 행사에 대해 들었어. 공연자들이 힙합 음악에 맞춰 춤을 추지 않니?
W Yeah. There's a famous DJ doing the music, and the dancers are supposed to be spectacular.	여 응. 유명한 DJ가 음악을 트는데, 댄서들이 굉장할 거야.
M Why do they [1)]call it a battle?	남 왜 배틀이라고 하는 거야?
W It is a competition, with a winner and loser after each performance.	여 매 공연 후에 승자와 패자가 있는 대회거든.
M I see. But who judges the dancers?	남 그렇구나. 하지만 누가 댄서들을 평가해?
W The fans pick the winners. It's based on [2)]how loudly the crowd cheers.	여 팬들이 우승자를 뽑아. 관중이 얼마나 크게 환호하는지를 근거로 해.
M Wow. That sounds like a lot of fun.	남 우와. 그거 정말 재미있을 것 같다.
W Do you want to come? It starts at 8:30 in Central Park.	여 너도 올래? 센트럴 공원에서 8시 30분에 시작해.
M Sure! Where should we meet?	남 물론이지! 어디서 만날까?
W **I was going to take the subway to Murray Station. See you there at 7:30?**	여 머레이역으로 가는 지하철을 타려고 했어. 7시 30분에 거기서 만날까?
M Okay, but let's pick a [3)]more specific spot.	남 좋아, 하지만 좀 더 구체적인 장소를 정하자.
W How about the water fountain next to Exit 2?	여 2번 출구 옆에 있는 분수대 어때?

① 누가 승자가 될지 보는 게 기대돼.

② 2번 출구 옆에 있는 분수대 어때?

③ 물론 나와 함께 댄스 배틀을 보러 가도 돼.

④ 최대한 큰 소리로 댄서들을 응원하자.

⑤ 공연이 시작되기 한 시간 전에 거기 도착할 거야.

공연을 함께 보러 갈 약속을 하는 상황이다. 여자가 약속 장소를 모호하게 말하자 남자가 좀 더 구체적인 장소를 정하자고 했으므로, 이에 대한 응답으로는 정확한 장소가 언급되는 ② 'How about the water fountain next to Exit 2?'가 가장 적절하다.

[어휘] performer 몡 공연자, 연기자 spectacular 휑 굉장한, 장관인 competition 몡 대회, 경쟁 judge 통 평가하다, 판단하다 be based on ~을 근거로 하다 cheer 통 환호하다, 응원하다
specific 휑 구체적인 spot 몡 장소; 점 fountain 몡 분수대, 분수

15 상황에 적절한 말 파악 정답 ③

W Harry is a high school student who wants to become a film director. Recently, his mother 1)bought him a video camera to support his dream. Since then, he has been filming almost everywhere he goes. This includes in his school, where Harry often makes videos of 2)his classmates. Then, he posts nearly all of these on his website without asking for permission. Now, Harry's mother has begun to worry. She thinks that he is filming and sharing 3)too many private scenes. She is concerned that this will upset or embarrass someone. **So she wants to tell Harry that he should be careful 4)not to violate other people's privacy.** In this situation, what would Harry's mother most likely say to Harry?

여 Harry는 영화감독이 되고 싶은 고등학생입니다. 최근, 그의 어머니는 그의 꿈을 응원하기 위해 그에게 비디오카메라를 사주었습니다. 그 이후로, 그는 그가 가는 거의 모든 곳에서 촬영하고 있습니다. 여기에는 Harry가 종종 학교 반 친구들의 영상을 찍는 학교도 포함됩니다. 그리고 나서, 그는 허락을 구하지 않고 거의 모든 것을 그의 웹사이트에 올립니다. 이제, Harry의 어머니는 걱정하기 시작했습니다. 그녀는 그가 너무 많은 사적인 장면을 촬영하고 공유하고 있다고 생각합니다. 그녀는 이것이 누군가를 화나게 하거나 난처하게 할까 봐 염려합니다. 그래서 그녀는 Harry에게 다른 사람들의 사생활을 침해하지 않도록 조심해야 한다고 말하고 싶습니다. 이러한 상황에서, Harry의 어머니가 Harry에게 가장 할 것 같은 말은 무엇입니까?

① 솔직히, 네가 날 촬영하지 않으면 좋겠구나.

② 다른 웹사이트에 영상을 올리는 게 어때?

③ 사적인 장면을 찍을 때는 좀 더 신중해야 한단다.

④ 그건 네 영화에서 별로 좋은 장면으로 만들어지지 않을 거야.

⑤ 난 항상 영화감독이 되려는 너의 꿈을 응원할 거야.

Harry가 허락을 구하지 않고 친구들을 찍어 웹사이트에 올리는 것을 보고, Harry의 어머니는 사생활 침해에 대해 주의를 주려 한다. 따라서, Harry의 어머니가 할 말로 ③ 'You should be more cautious when shooting private scenes.'가 가장 적절하다.

[어휘] support 통 응원하다, 지지하다 ask for ~을 구하다, 요청하다 permission 몡 허락, 허가 private 휑 사적인 (privacy 몡 사생활) embarrass 통 난처하게 하다, 당황하게 하다
violate 통 침해하다, 위반하다 cautious 휑 신중한, 조심스러운 to be honest 솔직히

16-17 세트 문항 정답 16 ① 17 ③

M Good afternoon, everyone. We've been discussing the effects of jogging on the body lately. **But today I want to look at some of the effects yoga has 1)on the body's health.** First of all, the **heart** does benefit from such exercise. High levels of stress-related chemicals are a major cause of heart disease. Since the practice of yoga 2)reduces stress, it lowers the chances of a heart attack. Next, we see a notable improvement in **spine** health. This is because deep stretching helps to maintain good posture and strengthens core muscle groups. However, there are some downsides. For example, a sprained **wrist** is a 3)common injury among people who practice yoga. This occurs when people put too much weight on the wrist, and it can be painful. Also, the **legs** can be put under 4)a large amount of pressure when people do yoga poses inappropriately. Stretching too deeply can lead to pulled and torn muscles. But these risks are minimal with proper technique. Now, we'll see some examples of yoga poses for beginners.

남 안녕하십니까, 여러분. 우리는 최근에 조깅이 신체에 끼치는 영향에 대해 논의해왔습니다. 하지만 오늘은 요가가 신체 건강에 끼치는 영향을 살펴보려고 합니다. 첫 번째로, 심장은 정말 이 운동으로부터 이득을 봅니다. 고농도의 스트레스 관련 화학물질은 심장병의 주요 원인입니다. 요가 수련이 스트레스를 줄이기 때문에, 그것은 심장마비의 가능성을 낮춥니다. 다음으로, 척추 건강의 눈에 띄는 개선을 확인할 수 있습니다. 깊은 스트레칭은 좋은 자세를 유지하고 코어 근육군을 강화하는 데 도움이 되기 때문입니다. 하지만, 단점도 있습니다. 예를 들어, 손목 염좌는 요가를 하는 사람들 사이에서 흔한 부상입니다. 이는 사람들이 손목에 너무 많은 무게를 실을 때 발생하며, 고통스러울 수 있습니다. 또한, 사람들이 요가 자세를 부적절하게 취할 때 다리가 큰 압박을 받을 수 있습니다. 너무 깊게 스트레칭을 하는 것은 근육 당김과 파열로 이어질 수 있습니다. 하지만 이러한 위험요소는 적절한 기술을 사용하면 최소화됩니다. 이제, 초보자를 위한 요가 자세의 예시를 보겠습니다.

16 ① 요가가 사람들의 건강에 영향을 끼치는 방식

② 매일 조깅하는 것의 문제점

③ 건강 이상의 원인

④ 스트레스 수준을 줄이기 위한 전략

⑤ 사람들이 운동 중 부상을 당하는 방식

17 ① 심장 ② 척추 ③ 어깨 ④ 손목 ⑤ 다리

16 요가가 신체 건강에 끼치는 영향을 살펴보고 있으므로 남자가 하는 말의 주제로 ① 'how yoga influences people's health'가 가장 적절하다.
17 심장, 척추, 손목, 다리는 언급했지만 ③ 'shoulder'는 언급하지 않았다.

[어휘] benefit 통 이득을 보다 몡 이득, 이익 chemical 몡 화학물질 reduce 통 줄이다, 낮추다 lower 통 낮추다, 내리다 heart attack 심장마비 notable 휑 눈에 띄는 spine 몡 척추
This is because ~. ~하기 때문이다. strengthen 통 강화하다 downside 몡 단점, 불리한 면 sprained 휑 염좌의, (관절을) 삔 inappropriately 閈 부적절하게 lead to ~으로 이어지다
minimal 휑 최소한의 drawback 몡 문제점 disorder 몡 이상, 장애 strategy 몡 전략

| 1 | ④ | 2 | ② | 3 | ① | 4 | ④ | 5 | ③ | 6 | ⑤ | 7 | ④ | 8 | ③ | 9 | ⑤ | 10 | ④ |
| 11 | ① | 12 | ② | 13 | ② | 14 | ① | 15 | ⑤ | 16 | ⑤ | 17 | ③ | | | | |

• 각 문제의 정답 근거는 굵은 글씨로, Dictation 정답은 밑줄로 표시되어 있습니다.

---

1 목적 파악

정답 ④

W Hello, Radio 602 listeners. It's time for the 5 o'clock news. **Local officials have announced new restrictions at Herald Lake.** The lake has long been [1)]a beloved attraction among both locals and visitors. However, recent diving accidents have created worries about its safety. The problem is, people who jump in from nearby rocks are not [2)]usually aware that the lake is less than two meters deep in spots. As a consequence, they risk injuries to their heads or necks on the bottom of the lake, which can be fatal. **Thus, to [3)]prevent future accidents, the city government has decided to ban all diving at the lake.** For more information, visit the city government's website.

여 안녕하십니까, 라디오 602 청취자 여러분. 5시 뉴스 시간입니다. 지역 공무원들이 헤럴드 호수에 새로운 규제를 발표했습니다. 이 호수는 오랫동안 현지인들과 방문객들 모두에게 사랑받는 명소였습니다. 하지만, 최근의 다이빙 사고는 그것의 안전에 대한 우려를 불러일으켰습니다. 문제는 근처 바위에서 뛰어드는 사람들은 호수의 수심이 군데군데 2m 미만이라는 점을 보통 인식하지 못한다는 것입니다. 결과적으로, 그들은 호수 바닥에 부딪혀 머리나 목을 다칠 위험이 있는데, 이는 죽음을 초래할 수도 있습니다. 따라서, 미래의 사고를 막기 위해, 시 정부는 호수에서의 모든 다이빙을 금지하기로 했습니다. 더 많은 정보를 원하시면, 시 정부의 웹사이트를 방문하십시오.

여자가 헤럴드 호수에 새로운 규제가 발표됐다고 하면서, 미래의 사고를 막기 위해 호수에서의 모든 다이빙을 금지하기로 했다고 알려주고 있다. 따라서, 여자가 하는 말의 목적으로 ④ '호숫가에서의 다이빙 금지 조치를 안내하려고'가 가장 적절하다.

어휘 official 圈 공무원 restriction 圈 규제, 제한 beloved 圈 사랑받는, 사랑하는 attraction 圈 명소; 매력 recent 圈 최근의 accident 圈 사고 aware 圈 인식하는 in spots 군데군데 as a consequence 결과적으로 risk 圄 ~할 위험이 있다 圈 위험 bottom 圈 바닥 fatal 圈 죽음을 초래하는, 치명적인 prevent 圄 막다, 방지하다 ban 圄 금지하다

---

2 의견 파악

정답 ②

M Claire, can I borrow your laptop charger?

W I don't have it. Do you need it during class?

M Yeah. **I usually use my laptop for note-taking. I think typing my notes makes it [1)]easier to remember lessons.**

W Why don't you just use pen and paper?

M I can type a lot faster than I can write by hand, so using a laptop [2)]lets me include more detailed information.

W But don't you get distracted?

M Not really. I only use apps relevant to the class.

W Oh, good thinking.

M The best part is that I have [3)]everything saved digitally, so I can quickly search through my notes when I study later.

W Yeah, typing on a laptop is helpful for studying. See if one of our classmates has a charger.

M Okay. I better go do that now.

남 Claire, 노트북 충전기 좀 빌릴 수 있을까?

여 내겐 없어. 수업 중에 필요한 거야?

남 응. 노트 필기할 때 주로 노트북을 사용하거든. 필기 내용을 타이핑하면 수업을 기억하기가 더 쉬워지는 것 같아.

여 그냥 펜과 종이를 사용하는 게 어때?

남 손으로 쓰는 것보다 타이핑이 훨씬 더 빨라서, 노트북을 사용하면 더 자세한 정보를 포함시킬 수 있어.

여 하지만 정신이 산만해지지는 않아?

남 그렇지 않아. 나는 수업과 관련된 앱만 사용하거든.

여 오, 좋은 생각이야.

남 가장 좋은 점은 모든 것을 디지털로 저장했기 때문에, 나중에 공부할 때 필기한 걸 빠르게 검색할 수 있다는 거야.

여 그래, 노트북으로 타이핑하는 건 공부하는 데 도움이 되는구나. 우리 반 친구 중에 충전기를 가진 사람이 있는지 확인해 봐.

남 알겠어. 지금 하러 가야겠어.

노트 필기를 할 때 펜과 종이를 사용하는 것을 제안하는 여자에게 남자가 노트북으로 필기 내용을 타이핑하면 수업을 기억하기가 더 쉽고, 나중에 공부할 때 빨리 검색할 수도 있다고 했다. 따라서, 남자의 의견으로 ② '노트북으로 필기하는 것은 학습에 도움이 되는 방법이다.'가 가장 적절하다.

어휘 charger 圈 충전기 note-taking 圈 필기 detailed 圈 자세한 get distracted 정신이 산만해지다 relevant to ~에 관련된

---

3 관계 파악

정답 ①

M Hello, Ms. Simmons. **Welcome to *Music and People*.**

W Thank you for having me on your show.

M I wanted to discuss your recent win in *The National Talent Competition* that [1)]aired on our channel last week. How did you prepare for it?

W It took a lot of preparation. I began rehearsing my dance months ago.

M Wow, really?

W Yes. I wanted my performance to be perfect.

M It was really incredible. Can you tell our viewers how you created your [2)]unique dancing style?

남 안녕하세요, Simmons 씨. <Music and People>에 오신 것을 환영합니다.

여 쇼에 초대해 주셔서 감사합니다.

남 지난주 저희 채널에서 방송된 <The National Talent Competition>에서 당신이 거둔 최근 우승에 관해 이야기하고 싶었어요. 어떻게 준비하셨나요?

여 많은 준비가 필요했어요. 저는 몇 달 전부터 춤 예행연습을 시작했어요.

남 와, 정말요?

여 네. 저는 제 공연이 완벽하기를 원했거든요.

남 정말 대단했습니다. 우리 시청자분들께 당신의 독특한 춤 스타일을 어떻게 만드셨는지 말씀해주시겠어요?

W I've been taking ballet and tap-dancing lessons for a long time. So I tried to combine those two styles.
M Were you nervous when you finally ³⁾<u>got on stage</u>?
W Absolutely. I was so scared I'd mess up one of my moves.
M Well, it ended up going well for you after all. Thank you so much for talking about it with us today.
W You're welcome.

여 저는 발레와 탭댄스 수업을 오랫동안 들었어요. 그래서 그 두 가지 스타일을 합치려고 노력했죠.
남 드디어 무대에 서게 됐을 때 긴장하셨나요?
여 물론이죠. 동작 중 하나라도 망칠까 봐 엄청 겁먹었답니다.
남 음, 결국에는 잘 끝나게 됐잖아요. 오늘 이렇게 얘기해주셔서 정말 감사합니다.
여 천만에요.

두 사람이 지난주에 방송된 경연 프로그램에서 여자가 거둔 우승에 관해 이야기하고 있다. 남자는 여자에게 <Music and People> 쇼에 온 것을 환영한다고 했고, 여자는 몇 달 전부터 춤 연습을 하며 많은 준비를 했다고 말하는 것으로 보아 두 사람의 관계로 ① 'TV쇼 진행자 — 댄서'가 가장 적절하다.

어휘 air 통 방송되다 명 공기 rehearse 통 예행연습하다 incredible 형 대단한, 믿을 수 없는 for a long time 오랫동안 combine 통 합치다 mess up 망치다 move 명 동작 통 움직이다 end up ~으로 끝나게 되다 after all 결국

---

4 그림 내용 불일치 파악   정답 ④

M Julia, come and see! This is my bedroom.
W It's beautiful. Did you ¹⁾<u>hire</u> the <u>interior designer</u> I introduced you to?
M Yes, I did. He picked out the floral print on the rug.
W I love it. What about the striped chair by the window?
M Yeah, he recommended that, too.
W I thought so. The ²⁾<u>photo of the mountain</u> is a nice touch, too.
M Thanks.
W **Do you normally keep all ³⁾<u>four of those pillows</u> on the bed like that?**
M Honestly, no. They're just for decoration. I usually put them in that box by the foot of the bed right before I go to sleep.
W Good idea. They would get in the way while you are sleeping.
M You're telling me. Now, why don't we go downstairs and take a look at the kitchen?
W Sounds good.

남 Julia, 와서 봐! 여기가 내 침실이야.
여 아름답다. 내가 소개해 준 인테리어 디자이너를 고용한 거야?
남 응, 그랬어. 디자이너가 카펫에 꽃무늬를 골랐어.
여 너무 좋네. 창가에 있는 줄무늬 의자는 어때?
남 응, 그것도 추천했어.
여 그럴 줄 알았어. 산 사진도 멋진 느낌이네.
남 고마워.
여 보통 침대 위에 저렇게 베개 네 개를 놓아두니?
남 솔직하게 말하면, 아니야. 그것들은 단지 장식용이야. 평소에는 잠들기 직전에 침대 발치에 있는 저 상자에 넣어둬.
여 좋은 생각이야. 네가 자는 동안 방해가 되겠구나.
남 내 말이 바로 그 말이야. 이제 아래층으로 내려가서 부엌을 보는 게 어때?
여 좋아.

대화에서 여자가 보통 침대 위에 저렇게 베개 네 개를 놓아두는지 물었는데, ④에는 베개 두 개가 그려져 있다.

어휘 hire 통 고용하다 pick out ~을 고르다 floral 형 꽃무늬의 touch 명 느낌; 손질 통 만지다 normally 부 보통 pillow 명 베개 get in the way 방해가 되다 You're telling me. 내 말이 바로 그 말이야. take a look at ~을 보다

---

5 할 일 파악   정답 ③

M Jess, is everything okay?
W Oh, I'm a little stressed out, Dad.
M Are you looking for something?
W Yeah. I can't ¹⁾<u>find my textbook anywhere</u>. I thought it was in my bag, but it's not there.
M Which one is it?
W It's my ethics textbook. I need it for my exam on Tuesday.
M Let's retrace your steps. Where did you go ²⁾<u>before you went home</u>?
W Well, I had biology class in the last period. After school, I met with my English teacher. Then, I went to a German club meeting with my friend Jill.
M Does that help you remember?
W Actually, yes! I showed Jill something in the book while we were waiting for the meeting to begin. Maybe she took it by accident!
M ³⁾**You'd better call** her to see if she has it.
W **I'll do that.**

남 Jess, 무슨 일이니?
여 아, 스트레스를 좀 받고 있어요, 아빠.
남 뭐 찾는 중이니?
여 네. 제 교과서를 어디에서도 찾을 수가 없어요. 가방 안에 있는 줄 알았는데, 없네요.
남 어떤 거니?
여 윤리 교과서예요. 화요일 시험에 필요하거든요.
남 왔던 길을 되짚어 보자. 집에 오기 전에 어디에 갔니?
여 음, 마지막 시간에 생물 수업이 있었어요. 방과 후에는, 영어 선생님을 만났고요. 그러고 나서, Jill과 함께 독일어 동아리 모임에 갔어요.
남 기억하는 데 도움이 되니?
여 사실, 그래요! 동아리 모임이 시작되기를 기다리는 동안 제가 Jill에게 교과서 속의 무언가를 보여줬어요. 그녀가 실수로 그걸 가져갔을지도 모르겠어요!
남 그녀에게 전화해서 가지고 있는지 알아보는 게 좋겠다.
여 그렇게 할게요.

여자가 교과서를 잃어버려 찾고 있다. 여자가 그녀의 친구 Jill이 무심코 가져갔을지도 모른다고 하자 남자가 그녀에게 전화해서 가지고 있는지 알아보는 게 좋겠다고 했으므로 여자가 할 일로 ③ '친구에게 전화하기'가 가장 적절하다.

어휘 be stressed out 스트레스를 받다 textbook 명 교과서 ethics 명 윤리 retrace one's steps 왔던 길을 되짚다 by accident 실수로

6 금액 정보 파악　　　　　　　　　　　　　　　　　　　　　　　정답 ⑤

M	Welcome to Barry's Burgers. What can we make for you today?	남	Barry's Burgers에 오신 것을 환영합니다. 오늘은 무엇을 만들어 드릴까요?
W	Hi. I was wondering 1)what was included in the combo meal.	여	안녕하세요. 세트 메뉴에 뭐가 포함되는지 궁금해서요.
M	**The combo meal includes a burger, fries, and a soda for $9.** If you just want the burger, it's $6.	남	9달러에 햄버거, 감자튀김, 탄산음료가 포함된 세트 메뉴입니다. 햄버거만 드시면 6달러예요.
W	Oh, so I can't get a milkshake with a combo?	여	아, 그럼 세트로는 밀크셰이크를 살 수 없나요?
M	**Actually, you can 2)upgrade your combo for an additional $2.**	남	사실, 2달러를 추가로 더 내시면 세트를 업그레이드할 수 있어요.
W	I see. **Well, I'll take three combo meals. I'd like two with sodas, and one with a vanilla milkshake.**	여	그렇군요. 음, 세트 3개로 할게요. 세트 두 개는 탄산음료로 주시고, 하나는 바닐라 밀크셰이크로 주세요.
M	So you want three combos, one with a shake upgrade. Does that complete your order?	남	그럼 세트 세 개에, 하나는 밀크셰이크 업그레이드하시는 거군요. 주문을 완료하신 걸까요?
W	Yes. That's all. **But I do have a discount coupon for $2 off.**	여	네. 그게 다예요. 그런데 저 2달러 할인 쿠폰을 가지고 있어요.
M	[Pause] **I'm afraid this coupon is 3)not valid here.**	남	[잠시 멈춤] 죄송하지만 이 쿠폰은 이곳에서는 유효하지 않습니다.
W	Why not?	여	왜 안 되나요?
M	This is 4)only usable at our downtown location.	남	저희 시내 지점에서만 쓸 수 있어요.
W	Ah, well. I understand. Here's my credit card.	여	아, 그래요. 알겠습니다. 여기 제 신용카드요.

여자가 탄산음료를 포함한 세트 메뉴 두 개($9×2 =$18)와, 바닐라 밀크셰이크를 포함하도록 업그레이드한 세트 메뉴 하나($9+$2=$11)를 주문했으므로 정답은 ⑤ '$29'이다.

[어휘] combo meal 세트 메뉴　additional 휑 추가의　complete one's order 주문을 완료하다　valid 휑 유효한

7 이유 파악　　　　　　　　　　　　　　　　　　　　　　　정답 ④

W	Terry, did you get your driver's license yet?	여	Terry, 이제 운전면허증은 땄니?
M	No, Grandma, I haven't gotten it.	남	아니요, 할머니, 안 땄어요.
W	Oh, that's right. You're 1)not old enough yet.	여	아, 맞아. 너는 아직 나이가 충분히 들지 않았지.
M	No, I am eligible to get one. I turned 18 in January.	남	아니요, 저는 딸 수 있는 자격이 돼요. 1월에 18살이 되었거든요.
W	Oh, did you fail the test? I know it is a little tricky. But you can 2)take it again!	여	아, 시험에 떨어진 거니? 그게 조금 까다롭다는 걸 알고 있단다. 하지만 다시 치를 수 있어!
M	I haven't taken the test. And to be honest, I don't think I'm ever going to.	남	시험 본 적 없어요. 그리고 솔직히 말해서, 절대 안 볼 것 같아요.
W	You're concerned about the environment, right?	여	환경이 걱정돼서 그런 거구나, 그렇지?
M	That's not it. I think it's eco-friendly to 3)drive an electric car. **I'm just worried that I would get in an accident.**	남	그게 아니에요. 전기 자동차를 모는 건 친환경적이라고 생각하거든요. 저는 그냥 사고를 당할까 봐 걱정되는 거예요.
W	Hmm... You may change your mind about that when you're older.	여	흠... 나이가 더 들면 생각이 바뀔지도 모른단다.
M	We'll see.	남	두고 보죠.

남자는 절대 운전면허 시험을 안 볼 것 같다고 하면서 사고를 당할까 봐 걱정된다고 말했으므로, 남자가 운전면허증이 없는 이유는 ④ '사고가 날까 봐 염려되어서'이다.

[어휘] driver's license 운전면허증　be eligible to ~할 자격이 되다　fail the test 시험에 떨어지다　tricky 휑 까다로운　to be honest 솔직히 말해서　eco-friendly 휑 친환경적인
get in an accident 사고를 당하다

8 언급 유무 파악　　　　　　　　　　　　　　　　　　　　　　　정답 ③

M	Hailey, didn't you mention something about a class trip on Monday?	남	Hailey, 월요일에 가는 현장학습에 관해 뭔가 말하지 않았었니?
W	Yeah. We're going to the Greenhills Apple Picking Festival, Dad.	여	네. Greenhills Apple Picking Festival에 갈 거예요, 아빠.
M	Oh, where 1)will that be held?	남	아, 그건 어디서 열리니?
W	The event is in **Parkerville.** I think it's about 25 kilometers from my high school.	여	파커빌에서 열려요. 저희 고등학교에서 25km 정도 떨어져 있는 것 같아요.
M	Ah, okay. When are you supposed to leave?	남	아, 그렇구나. 언제 출발해야 하니?
W	The festival begins at **10 a.m.,** so we'll leave at 9:30.	여	축제가 오전 10시에 시작하니까, 9시 30분에 출발할 거예요.
M	Good. Are there 2)any activities other than **picking apples**?	남	좋아. 사과 따는 것 외에 다른 활동이 있니?
W	Yes. We'll have a chance to **bake some apple cinnamon cookies.** They also have a gift shop I want to visit. Could I borrow some money?	여	네. 사과 시나몬 쿠키를 구울 기회가 있을 거예요. 제가 방문하고 싶은 기념품 가게도 있어요. 돈 좀 빌려주실 수 있어요?
M	Why not? Here's $50. Buy 3)yourself a souvenir. And can you get one for our family?	남	물론이지. 여기 50달러. 널 위한 기념품을 사렴. 그리고 우리 가족을 위해서도 하나 사 오겠니?
W	Sure. I heard that **the apple-shaped magnets** are popular. I'll buy one.	여	물론이죠. 사과 모양 자석이 인기가 좋다고 들었어요. 그걸 살게요.
M	Thanks. Your mom will love it.	남	고맙구나. 네 엄마가 좋아할 거야.

개최 장소(파커빌), 시작 시간(오전 10시), 참가 활동(사과 따기, 사과 시나몬 쿠키 굽기), 기념품(사과 모양 자석)에 대해 언급했고, ③ '입장료'는 언급하지 않았다.

[어휘] mention 통 말하다; 언급하다　be supposed to ~해야 한다　activity 휑 활동　other than ~외에　souvenir 휑 기념품　magnet 휑 자석

9 내용 불일치 파악

정답 ⑤

W Welcome to Falcon Crest National Park. For your safety, the following guidelines are in place. First of all, we recommend that you ¹⁾do not hike alone. In the event of an accident, you would not have someone with you to call for help. We also ask that you only ²⁾follow the trails that have signs posted. Going off the trails may damage precious wildlife. There are water fountains, but there is no guarantee the water is clean. Therefore, we strongly recommend bringing drinking water with you. Lastly, because of recent dry weather, lighters and portable burners are prohibited. **Those caught with ³⁾these restricted items will be removed from the park.** Thank you for your cooperation, and I hope you all have a great visit.	여 팔콘 크레스트 국립공원에 오신 것을 환영합니다. 여러분의 안전을 위해 다음 지침이 준비되어 있습니다. 우선, 혼자 등산하지 않기를 권합니다. 만약 사고가 날 경우, 도움을 요청할 사람이 함께 있지 않을 것입니다. 또한 표지판이 붙어 있는 등산로만 따라가시길 부탁합니다. 등산로를 벗어나는 것은 소중한 야생 동물들에게 피해를 줄 수 있습니다. 식수대는 있지만, 물이 깨끗하다는 보장은 없습니다. 그러므로, 마실 물을 가지고 가시는 것을 강력하게 추천합니다. 마지막으로, 최근 건조한 날씨 때문에 라이터와 휴대용 버너가 금지되었습니다. 이 금지 물품이 적발되어 잡힌 사람들은 공원에서 쫓겨날 것입니다. 협조해주셔서 감사하며, 모두 즐거운 방문이 되길 바랍니다.

팔콘 크레스트 국립공원의 안전 지침에 대한 안내 방송이다. 여자가 금지 물품이 적발되어 잡힌 사람들은 공원에서 쫓겨날 것이라고 했으므로 ⑤ '반입 금지 물품은 적발되는 즉시 압수 조치된다.'는 내용과 일치하지 않는다.

어휘 safety 명 안전 guideline 명 지침 be in place 준비되다 in the event of 만약 ~할 경우 trail 명 등산로; 흔적 water fountain 식수대 guarantee 명 보장 portable 형 휴대용의 prohibit 통 금지하다 restrict 통 금지하다, 제한하다 cooperation 명 협조

10 도표 정보 파악

정답 ④

W Okay, we've got the hotel and plane tickets for Rome. What else do we need to plan, Mike?	여 좋아, 우리 로마로 가는 호텔과 비행기 표는 있어. 우리가 또 무엇을 계획해야 할까, Mike?
M What about a guided tour? It would be a good way to learn more about ¹⁾the historical sites.	남 가이드 투어는 어때? 그건 유적지에 대해 더 많이 배울 수 있는 좋은 방법일 거야.
W Sure. Let's look up some tour options.	여 물론이지. 몇 가지 투어 옵션을 검색해보자.
M Okay... well, this website lists a few. What do you think?	남 좋아... 음, 이 웹사이트에 몇 가지가 실려 있어. 어떻게 생각해?
W I don't want to go on a bus tour. Let's do ²⁾something more active!	여 버스 투어는 가고 싶지 않아. 좀 더 활동적인 걸 하자!
M Fair enough. We can rule this one out.	남 좋아. 이건 제외할 수 있겠어.
W Let's keep it short, too. We need plenty of time to explore on our own.	여 투어를 짧게 하자. 우리는 우리 스스로 탐방할 충분한 시간이 필요해.
M Alright. **Anything ³⁾longer than three hours would be too much.**	남 알겠어. 3시간보다 긴 건 무리겠어.
W That leaves us with a couple of options. Is price a factor?	여 몇 가지 선택지가 남아있어. 가격이 중요한 요인이겠지?
M I'm okay as long as we ⁴⁾don't spend more than $40 on it.	남 40달러보다 많이만 안 쓴다면 나는 괜찮아.
W I agree. **And let's go with the one that includes a meal.**	여 동의해. 그리고 식사가 포함된 걸로 하자.
M I'll book it!	남 그걸로 예약할게!

두 사람은 버스 투어가 아니면서, 3시간보다 짧으며, 40달러 이하인 것 중에서, 식사가 포함된 가이드 투어를 골랐다.

어휘 historical site 유적지 look up 검색하다, 찾다 list 통 싣다, 기재하다 Fair enough. 좋아. rule out 제외하다 as long as ~하기만 한다면

11 짧은 대화의 응답 파악

정답 ①

W Carl, I'm headed down to the convenience store. Should I pick anything up for you?	여 Carl, 나 편의점에 갈 거야. 뭐 좀 사다 줄까?
M Yes, please. **Do you mind ¹⁾grabbing a sandwich for me?** Here's my card.	남 응, 부탁해. 샌드위치 좀 집어 줄래? 여기 내 카드야.
W Sure. Is there ²⁾any particular type that you wanted?	여 물론이지. 원하는 특별한 종류가 있니?
M Roast beef would be good.	남 로스트비프가 좋겠어.

선택지 ① 로스트비프가 좋겠어.
② 나는 까다롭지 않아서 어느 가게든 좋아.
③ 그래, 내가 샌드위치를 가져다줄게.
④ 신용카드로 결제하는 게 더 좋아.
⑤ 나는 편의점에서 우유를 샀어.

남자가 샌드위치를 사다 달라고 부탁하자 여자가 원하는 특별한 종류가 있는지 물었으므로, 이에 대한 응답으로는 그 종류를 말하는 ① 'Roast beef would be good.'이 가장 적절하다.

어휘 head 통 가다, 향하다 convenience store 편의점 pick up ~을 사다 grab 통 집다 particular 형 특별한; 특정한 picky 형 까다로운

12 짧은 대화의 응답 파악   정답 ②

M   Kate, do you need a ride to your doctor's appointment tomorrow afternoon?
W   No. I'm okay, Dad. The hospital is ¹⁾<u>close to my school</u>, so I was thinking of walking there after soccer practice.
M   Sounds good. **Call me if you change your mind, though. I'll be** ²⁾<u>in the area</u>.
W   Thanks, and I'll let you know if I do.
	남 Kate, 내일 오후 진료 예약에 태워다 줄까?
	여 아뇨. 괜찮아요, 아빠. 병원이 학교와 가까워서 축구 연습이 끝나면 걸어갈까 생각 중이었어요.
	남 좋아. 그래도 생각이 바뀌면 전화하렴. 나는 그 지역에 있을 거란다.
	여 감사해요, 만약 그러면 알려 드릴게요.
	
	선택지 ① 내일 거기서 자전거를 탈 거예요.
	       ② 감사해요, 만약 그러면 알려 드릴게요.
	       ③ 지금 당장 병원에 전화할 수 있어요.
	       ④ 축구 경기장까지는 한참 운전해야 해요.
	       ⑤ 의사가 당분간 축구하지 말라고 했어요.

여자가 병원이 학교와 가까워서 걸어가겠다고 하자 남자가 생각이 바뀌면 전화하라고 했으므로, 이에 대한 응답으로는 그러겠다고 답하는 ② 'Thanks, and I'll let you know if I do.'가 가장 적절하다.

어휘   doctor's appointment 진료 예약   change one's mind 생각을 바꾸다   stadium 몡 경기장

13 긴 대화의 응답 파악   정답 ②

W   Hi. I'm looking for a gift for my father.
M   We have some great leather jackets. I think you could find one that your dad would love.
W   Yeah, I think this ¹⁾<u>style really suits him</u>. How much are they?
M   They're priced at $160 to $200 each.
W   Whoa! That's way ²⁾<u>outside my budget</u>. Could you suggest something else?
M   Well, what about something practical?
W   You mean like some underwear or socks? That doesn't seem very exciting.
M   Maybe not, but he might appreciate something like that. Wool socks really come in handy this time of year.
W   Hmm... I don't think he needs socks, but something warm could be good. Can I see ³⁾<u>your wool sweaters</u>?
M   They're right over here. Most of them are $30 to $40.
W   Perfect. **Do you have a red and black one?**
M   <u>Sure. Do you know what size your dad wears?</u>
	여 안녕하세요. 저는 아버지께 드릴 선물을 찾고 있어요.
	남 저희에겐 멋진 가죽 재킷이 몇 벌 있어요. 아버님이 좋아하실 만한 걸 찾을 수 있을 것 같군요.
	여 네, 이 스타일이 정말 아버지께 어울리는 것 같아요. 얼마예요?
	남 하나에 160달러에서 200달러예요.
	여 와! 제 예산 범위 훨씬 밖이네요. 다른 것을 제안해 주시겠어요?
	남 그럼 실용적인 건 어때요?
	여 속옷이나 양말 같은 거 말씀이신가요? 별로 감동적이지 않아 보이는데요.
	남 아닐 수도 있지만, 그런 걸 고마워하실지도 몰라요. 매년 이맘때면 양모 양말이 정말 유용하거든요.
	여 흠... 양말은 필요 없을 것 같은데, 따뜻한 건 좋을 것 같아요. 양모 스웨터를 볼 수 있을까요?
	남 바로 여기 있어요. 대부분 30달러에서 40달러입니다.
	여 완벽해요. 빨간색과 검은색이 있나요?
	남 <u>물론이죠. 아버님이 어떤 사이즈를 입는지 아시나요?</u>
	
	선택지 ① 좋은 생각이에요. 양말은 매우 실용적이에요.
	       ② 물론이죠. 아버님이 어떤 사이즈를 입는지 아시나요?
	       ③ 여기 좀 보세요. 이 재킷은 어떠신가요?
	       ④ 모르겠네요. 여전히 조금 비싼 것 같아요.
	       ⑤ 물론이죠. 창고에서 양말 한 켤레 갖다 드릴게요.

가게에서 선물을 고르는 상황이다. 남자가 스웨터를 보여주며 가격을 말해주자 여자가 빨간색과 검은색이 있는지 물었으므로, 이에 대한 응답으로는 있다고 답하며 사이즈를 물어보는 ② 'Sure. Do you know what size your dad wears?'가 가장 적절하다.

어휘   suit 통 ~에게 어울리다   outside 젠 (~의 범위) 밖의   budget 몡 예산   practical 혱 실용적인   underwear 몡 속옷   appreciate 통 고마워하다   come in handy 유용하다

14 긴 대화의 응답 파악   정답 ①

M Hey, Sally. I'm going to a film festival tonight with some friends. Do you care to join us? **W** What are they showing? **M** Some ¹⁾<u>classic horror movies</u> from the 1980s. **W** Oh, I read about that. That's at the Jacobson Theater, right? **M** That's the one. I can give you a ride to it if you want. **W** Thanks, but I don't think I can make it. **M** I thought you loved scary movies. **W** I do, but I stayed up too late studying for my history exam last night. **M** Oh, you ²⁾<u>must be very tired</u>. **W** Yeah, so I'm not sure I'd be able to stay awake the whole time. **M** How about coming for only the first movie? **W** When does it start?	남 안녕, Sally. 나는 오늘 밤 친구들과 영화제에 갈 거야. 같이 갈래? 여 뭘 상영해주는 거야? 남 1980년대 고전 공포 영화들이야. 여 아, 그것에 관해 읽었어. 제이콥슨 극장에서 하는 거지, 그렇지? 남 바로 그거야. 원하면 내가 태워다 줄 수 있어. 여 고마워, 하지만 못 갈 것 같아. 남 나는 네가 무서운 영화를 좋아하는 줄 알았는데. 여 좋아해, 하지만 어젯밤에 역사 시험공부를 하느라 너무 늦게까지 깨어있었거든. 남 아, 많이 피곤하겠네. 여 응, 그래서 계속 자지 않고 깨어있을 수 있을지 모르겠어. 남 첫 번째 영화만 보러 오는 건 어때? 여 언제 시작하는데?

M 8 p.m. There are three movies, ³⁾with short breaks in between. **You can just get a ticket for the first one.**

W That's a good idea. Then, I'll join you.

남 저녁 8시에. 세 편의 영화가 나오고, 중간에 짧은 휴식 시간이 있어. 넌 그냥 첫 번째 영화표만 구매할 수도 있어.

여 좋은 생각이야. 그럼, 나도 같이 갈게.

선택지 ① 좋은 생각이야. 그럼, 나도 같이 갈게.
② 그래. 우리 같이 시험공부 하자.
③ 좋아! 그렇다면, 저녁 8시에 데리러 갈게.
④ 맞아. 축제는 자정 이후까지 계속돼.
⑤ 나는 됐어. 사실, 난 공포 영화를 별로 좋아하지 않아.

남자가 여자에게 영화제에 함께 가자고 설득하는 상황이다. 여자가 시험공부를 하느라 피곤하다고 거절하자 남자가 저녁 8시에 시작하는 첫 번째 영화표만 구매할 수도 있다고 했으므로, 이에 대한 응답으로는 영화제에 가겠다고 하는 ① 'That's a good idea. Then, I'll join you.'가 가장 적절하다.

어휘 Do you care to ~? ~할래? make it (모임 등에) 가다 stay up late 늦게까지 깨어있다 awake 형 깨어있는 break 명 휴식 시간 동 깨다

---

15 상황에 적절한 말 파악

정답 ⑤

W Billy and Erica are best friends who love jazz music. They always go to jazz concerts together. So when either Billy or Erica buys tickets ¹⁾for a concert, he or she takes it for granted that the other will go, too. This is why they always buy two tickets. Unfortunately, they ²⁾accidentally bought tickets for two different shows scheduled on Saturday at the same time. When Billy realizes the problem, it is already too late to get a refund for his tickets. However, he knows that the band Erica wants to see is playing again on Sunday. **Therefore, Billy wants to suggest that Erica ³⁾trade her tickets for ones on Sunday so that they can go together.** In this situation, what would Billy most likely say to Erica?

여 Billy와 Erica는 재즈 음악을 사랑하는 절친입니다. 그들은 항상 함께 재즈 콘서트에 갑니다. 그래서, Billy나 Erica 중 한 명이 콘서트 표를 사면, 다른 한 명도 가는 것을 당연하게 여깁니다. 이것이 그들이 항상 두 장의 티켓을 사는 이유입니다. 불행하게도, 그들은 우연히 이번 주 토요일 같은 시간에 예정된 두 장이 다른 공연의 티켓을 동시에 구입했습니다. Billy가 그 문제를 깨달았을 때, 그의 티켓을 환불받기에는 이미 너무 늦었습니다. 하지만, 그는 Erica가 보고 싶어 하는 밴드가 일요일에 다시 공연한다는 것을 알고 있습니다. 그래서 Billy는 Erica에게 그들이 함께 갈 수 있도록 티켓을 일요일 것으로 교환하라고 제안하고 싶습니다. 이러한 상황에서, Billy가 Erica에게 가장 할 것 같은 말은 무엇입니까?

선택지 ① 토요일에 나와 같이 갈 다른 사람을 초대할게.
② 만약 돈을 돌려받고 싶다면, 환불 정책을 확인해.
③ 그 밴드가 더 잘하니까 우리는 첫 번째 공연에 가야 해.
④ 다른 공연 티켓을 구했는데, 둘 다 갈래?
⑤ 대신 다음 날 갈 수 있도록 네 것을 교환해 줄 수 있어?

Erica가 토요일 같은 시간의 공연 티켓을 구매한 것을 보고, Billy는 그들이 함께 보러 갈 수 있도록 Erica의 공연 티켓을 일요일 것으로 교환하라고 제안하려고 한다. 따라서, Billy가 할 말로 ⑤ 'Can you exchange yours so we can go on the next day instead?'가 가장 적절하다.

어휘 either A or B A나 B 중 하나 take ~ for granted ~을 당연하게 여기다 unfortunately 뷔 불행하게도 accidentally 뷔 우연히 at the same time 동시에 realize 동 깨닫다 get a refund 환불받다 trade 동 교환하다 명 거래 policy 명 정책

16-17 세트 문항

정답 16 ⑤ 17 ③

M Hi, class. We've been talking about the importance of a healthy diet lately. **Today, I'll point out some of ¹⁾the surprising disadvantages associated with having too much of any healthy food.** First, what about **tuna**? It's wonderful in many ways, with lots of protein and fatty acids. But it also ²⁾contains high levels of mercury. So if you eat it every day, it can eventually damage your brain. Next, we have pineapples. **Pineapples** have a large amount of vitamin C, but they are slightly toxic when uncooked. If you eat too many, they'll make your mouth sore or give you a rash. Thirdly, **avocados** can ³⁾become problematic in large amounts. Their high fiber content is great for you, but it can cause diarrhea when avocados are overeaten. Last, we need to talk about **broccoli**. It helps keep your heart healthy. But when you eat too much, it can lower your energy level and even cause you ⁴⁾to gain weight. I hope you'll take more care from now on when eating these foods.

남 안녕하십니까, 학생 여러분. 우리는 최근에 건강한 식단의 중요성에 관해 이야기해 왔습니다. 오늘은, 건강에 좋은 어떤 음식이든 너무 많이 먹는 것과 관련된 몇 가지 놀라운 단점들을 지목해 보려고 합니다. 먼저, 참치는 어떨까요? 그것은 많은 단백질과 지방산이 함유되어 있어, 여러 가지 면에서 훌륭합니다. 하지만 그것은 또한 높은 수준의 수은을 포함하고 있습니다. 그래서 만약 매일 그것을 먹는다면, 결국 뇌를 손상시킬 수 있습니다. 다음으로 파인애플이 있습니다. 파인애플에는 많은 양의 비타민 C가 있지만, 날것일 때 약간 독성이 있습니다. 너무 많이 먹으면 입을 아프게 하거나 발진이 생길 수 있습니다. 셋째로, 아보카도는 많은 양일 때 문제가 될 수 있습니다. 그것의 높은 섬유질 함량은 여러분에게 좋지만, 과식하면 설사를 일으킬 수 있습니다. 마지막으로 브로콜리에 관해 이야기해 보겠습니다. 그것은 심장을 건강하게 유지하도록 도와줍니다. 하지만 너무 많이 먹으면, 그것은 에너지 수치를 낮추고 심지어 살이 찌게 할 수도 있습니다. 앞으로 이 음식들을 먹을 때 더 조심하시기를 바랍니다.

선택지 16 ① 다양한 과일을 먹는 것의 효과
② 다양한 종류의 음식에 들어 있는 비타민
③ 적절한 영양을 섭취하는 것의 이점
④ 더 건강한 식단을 선택하는 방법
⑤ 건강에 좋은 음식을 과식하면 일어나는 문제
17 ① 참치 ② 파인애플 ③ 시금치 ④ 아보카도 ⑤ 브로콜리

16 건강에 좋은 음식을 너무 많이 먹는 것과 관련된 단점들을 지목하고 있으므로 남자가 하는 말의 주제로 ⑤ 'problems caused by overeating healthy foods'가 가장 적절하다.
17 참치, 파인애플, 아보카도, 브로콜리는 언급되었지만 ③ 'spinach'는 언급하지 않았다.

어휘 diet 명 식단 point out 지목하다 disadvantage 명 단점, 불리한 점 associated with ~과 관련된 protein 명 단백질 fatty acid 지방산 mercury 명 수은 slightly 뷔 약간 toxic 형 독성이 있는 uncooked 형 날것의 sore 형 아픈 rash 명 발진 fiber 명 섬유질 content 명 함량 diarrhea 명 설사 gain weight 살이 찌다 from now on 앞으로

1	③	2	①	3	②	4	④	5	③	6	④	7	⑤	8	②	9	③	10	②
11	④	12	③	13	①	14	④	15	⑤	16	④	17	②						

• 각 문제의 정답 근거는 굵은 글씨로, Dictation 정답은 밑줄로 표시되어 있습니다.

---

1 목적 파악

정답 ③

M Good afternoon, students. This is Principal Simmons. I have an announcement regarding the school sports day. Unfortunately, tomorrow's forecast calls for a severe thunderstorm and hail. In these conditions, it would be dangerous to be outside on the school field. **So in the interest of safety, tomorrow's ¹⁾event is canceled.** I know this is disappointing. However, we do have another sports day scheduled this fall. You'll still get a ²⁾chance to participate in the relay race and jump rope competition this year. The school will send out messages informing your parents about this cancellation, but please ³⁾remind them not to come. Enjoy your evening, and we'll see you back in school tomorrow.

남 안녕하십니까, 학생 여러분. 저는 교장 Simmons입니다. 학교 체육대회와 관련하여 공지사항이 있습니다. 유감스럽게도, 내일 일기예보상 심한 뇌우와 우박이 예상됩니다. 이런 상황에서, 학교 운동장에 나가는 것은 위험할 것입니다. 그러므로 안전을 위하여 내일 행사는 취소됩니다. 실망스러우리라는 점은 압니다. 하지만 우리는 이번 가을에 또 한 번의 체육대회가 예정되어 있습니다. 여러분에게 아직 올해에 계주와 줄넘기 대회에 참가할 기회가 있을 것입니다. 학교에서 여러분의 부모님께 취소를 알리는 메시지를 보내겠지만, 그들에게 다시 한번 오지 말라고 알려 주십시오. 저녁 시간을 즐겁게 보내고, 내일 학교에서 봅시다.

남자가 내일 일기예보상 심한 뇌우와 우박이 예상된다고 하면서, 안전을 위해 체육대회가 취소되는 점을 알려주고 있다. 따라서, 남자가 하는 말의 목적으로 ③ '학교 체육대회 취소를 공지하려고'가 가장 적절하다.

어휘 regarding 전 ~에 관하여 call for (날씨를) 예상하다 severe 형 심한, 가혹한 thunderstorm 명 뇌우 hail 명 우박 in the interest of ~을 위하여 relay race 계주 send out ~을 보내다 inform 통 알리다 cancellation 명 취소 remind 명 다시 한번 알려주다, 상기시키다

---

2 의견 파악

정답 ①

W How are you feeling today, Mark?
M Much better, Abbey. I got some good rest for the first time since I broke my arm.
W That's good to hear!
M I'm really happy about it. **I think the best way to ¹⁾heal an injury is to get enough sleep.**
W Is it better than taking medicine?
M That's important, too. But your body ²⁾builds more tissues when you sleep.
W Is that right? Please tell me more.
M Your body produces a lot of extra hormones when you sleep. They are called human growth hormones, and they help ³⁾rebuild your muscles faster.
W Wow. I didn't know that. Well, let me know if I can do anything to help. And make sure to eat healthy as well.
M Thanks. I will!

여 오늘은 컨디션이 어때, Mark?
남 훨씬 나아졌어, Abbey. 팔이 부러진 이래 처음으로 푹 쉬었거든.
여 다행이다!
남 정말 만족스러워. 내 생각에 부상을 낫게 하는 가장 좋은 방법은 충분한 수면을 취하는 것 같아.
여 약 먹는 것보다 더 좋아?
남 그것도 중요하지. 하지만 몸은 잠을 잘 때 더 많은 세포 조직을 만들어.
여 그래? 좀 더 말해 줘.
남 몸에서 잘 때 많은 여분의 호르몬을 만들어 내. 사람의 성장 호르몬이라고 불리는 건데, 그게 근육을 더 빨리 회복하도록 도와줘.
여 와. 그건 몰랐네. 그럼, 내가 도울 일이 있으면 알려줘. 그리고 꼭 식사도 건강하게 하도록 해.
남 고마워. 그럴게!

팔을 다친 남자가 부상을 낫게 하는 가장 좋은 방법은 충분한 수면을 취하는 것이라고 했다. 따라서, 남자의 의견으로 ① '숙면은 부상 회복을 돕는 가장 좋은 방법이다.'가 가장 적절하다.

어휘 for the first time 처음으로 That's good to hear! 다행이다! heal 통 낫게 하다, 치료하다 injury 명 부상, 상처 tissue 명 (세포들로 이뤄진) 조직 growth 명 성장 hormone 명 호르몬 rebuild 통 회복하다; 재건하다

---

3 관계 파악

정답 ②

M Hello, Julia Michaels. **Welcome to The Morning Break.**
W Thanks for inviting me. I ¹⁾listen to your program every morning.
M We're always happy to have a fan on the show! **So Julia, I hear you're opening a new coffee shop.**
W **That's right. Fresh Beans Coffee is ²⁾opening a new branch right here in Murton.**
M This will be on Main Street?
W That's correct. To celebrate, I've organized a grand-opening event there on the 23rd.

남 안녕하세요, Julia Michaels 씨. <The Morning Break>에 오신 것을 환영합니다.
여 초대해 주셔서 감사합니다. 저는 매일 아침 당신의 프로그램을 들어요.
남 저희 쇼에 팬 여러분을 모시는 일은 언제나 기쁘군요! Julia, 새 커피숍을 연다고 들었어요.
여 맞아요. Fresh Beans Coffee가 바로 여기 머튼에 새로운 지점을 열 예정이에요.
남 메인가에 생기는 건가요?
여 정확해요. 기념으로, 그곳에서 23일에 개업 행사를 준비했어요.

M	I'm sure many of our listeners will be interested in attending. Isn't this ³⁾your 10th location?	남	많은 청취자들이 참석할 의향이 있을 거예요. 여기가 10번째 지점 아닌가요?
W	Actually, this will be the 11th.	여	사실, 이번이 11번째가 될 거예요.
M	Wow. **When you founded Fresh Beans Coffee, did you imagine it would become a successful chain?**	남	와. 당신이 Fresh Beans Coffee를 창업했을 때, 성공적인 체인 사업이 될 것이라고 상상했나요?
W	I just wanted to make sure ⁴⁾we sold great coffee.	여	전 그냥 꼭 좋은 커피를 팔고 싶었을 뿐이었어요.
M	Well, I think you've achieved that. Now, for a brief word from our sponsors. We'll be right back.	남	음, 그건 이룬 것 같군요. 이제 후원사들의 짧은 광고가 있겠습니다. 금방 돌아올게요.

두 사람이 커피숍의 새로운 지점 개업에 관해 이야기하고 있다. 남자는 청취자들이 매일 아침 듣는 프로그램을 진행하고 있고, 여자는 자기가 창업한 커피숍의 새로운 지점을 연다고 말하는 것으로 보아 두 사람의 관계로 ② '라디오 쇼 진행자 — 창업주'가 가장 적절하다.

어휘 celebrate 동 기념하다 organize 동 준비하다, 조직하다 be interested in ~할 의향이 있다 found 동 창업하다; 설립하다 make sure (that) 꼭 ~하다 achieve 동 이루다, 성취하다
brief 형 짧은, 간단한

---

4 | 그림 내용 불일치 파악

정답 ④

W	Honey, what's this framed photograph? Are you planning to hang it up?	여	여보, 이 액자에 넣은 사진은 뭐야? 그걸 걸어 놓을 계획이야?
M	Yeah. That's my grandfather's farm about 20 years ago.	남	응. 그건 약 20년 전 우리 할아버지의 농장이야.
W	So is that your grandfather wearing ¹⁾the striped shirt?	여	그럼, 줄무늬 셔츠를 입고 있는 지분이 당신 할아버님이서?
M	Exactly. And those are his two old dogs walking alongside him.	남	맞아. 그리고 저기 할아버지와 나란히 걷고 있는 건 그분의 오래된 노견 두 마리야.
W	Is that the farmhouse down at the ²⁾end of the road with the triangle-shaped roof?	여	길 끝에 삼각형 모양의 지붕이 있는 게 농장의 본채야?
M	Yeah. It looks totally different now.	남	맞아. 지금은 완전히 달라 보이지.
W	Oh, I didn't realize he used to ³⁾**raise horses. It looks like there's a group of them in that field next to the farmhouse.**	여	아, 할아버님이 말을 기르셨던 걸 몰랐네. 본채 옆 들판에 말 떼가 있는 것 같아.
M	Yeah, he sold them 10 years ago.	남	응, 10년 전에 파셨어.
W	What about the tree on the right? Is that still there?	여	오른쪽에 있는 나무는 어때? 아직도 거기에 있어?
M	It is. It's just ⁴⁾a lot taller these days.	남	있어. 요즘은 키가 훨씬 더 커졌지.
W	We should go visit your grandfather soon.	여	곧 할아버님을 뵈러 가야겠어.
M	We should. I miss him.	남	그래야지. 할아버지가 그립다.

대화에서 여자가 농장의 본채 옆에 있는 들판에 말 떼가 있는 것 같다고 말했는데, ④에는 소 떼가 그려져 있다.

어휘 framed 형 액자에 넣은 hang up (그림 등을) 걸다 alongside 전 ~와 나란히 totally 부 완전히 used to (과거에) ~했다 raise 동 기르다; 올리다 field 명 들판, 밭

---

5 | 할 일 파악

정답 ③

W	What happened, Eric? Your face is scratched.	여	무슨 일이야, Eric? 네 얼굴이 긁혔는데.
M	I fell off my electric scooter ¹⁾on the way to school.	남	학교 오는 길에 전동 킥보드에서 넘어졌어.
W	Maybe you should go to the doctor.	여	병원에 가봐야 할 것 같아.
M	No need. I feel more embarrassed than anything else. A bunch of people saw me fall.	남	그럴 필요 없어. 난 무엇보다도 부끄러워. 많은 사람이 내가 넘어지는 것을 봤어.
W	I think you'd better put a bandage on your face, though.	여	그래도 얼굴에 반창고를 붙이는 게 좋을 것 같아.
M	I'm okay. It's just a few scratches.	남	괜찮아. 약간의 긁힌 상처일 뿐이야.
W	Then, how about applying some medicine so that you don't get an infection?	여	그럼, 감염되지 않도록 약을 바르는 건 어때?
M	It'll be fine. [Pause] But... do you think ²⁾my glasses look bent? I dropped them in the crash.	남	괜찮을 거라도. [잠시 멈춤] 그런데... 내 안경이 휜 것처럼 보이니? 사고 날 때 떨어뜨렸거든.
W	Yeah. I think you'll need to bring them to the shop to get them fixed.	여	그러게. 가게에 가져가서 수리받아야 할 것 같아.
M	Hmm... I better not wear them. **Do you mind ³⁾switching desks with me so I can see the board better?**	남	흠... 안경 안 쓰는 게 좋겠네. 칠판을 더 잘 볼 수 있도록 나랑 책상을 바꿔줄 수 있어?
W	**Of course.** Let me know if you need anything else.	여	물론이지. 더 필요한 게 있으면 말해 줘.
M	I will.	남	그럴게.

남자가 전동 킥보드에서 넘어진 것에 관해 이야기하고 있다. 남자가 안경이 휘어져서 못 쓴다며 칠판을 더 잘 볼 수 있도록 책상을 바꿔줄 수 있는지 묻자, 여자가 물론이라고 했으므로 여자가 할 일로 ③ '자리 바꿔주기'가 가장 적절하다.

어휘 scratch 동 긁다 electric scooter 전동 킥보드 embarrassed 형 부끄러운 more than anything else 무엇보다도 a bunch of 많은 bandage 명 반창고
apply 동 바르다; 신청하다 infection 명 감염 bent 형 휜, 구부러진 crash 명 사고; 충돌 switch 동 바꾸다

6 금액 정보 파악

정답 ④

M	Good evening. Welcome to Celebration Cinema.	남	안녕하세요. Celebration Cinema에 오신 것을 환영합니다.
W	Hi. We'd like three tickets to the animated film, *Space Cadets*. **Two for my husband and I, and one for our son.**	여	안녕하세요. 애니메이션 영화 <Space Cadets> 표 세 장 주세요. 남편과 저 두 장, 아들 한 장이요.
M	Sure. **Adult tickets are $8.** By the way, how old is your son?	남	물론이죠. 성인 표는 8달러입니다. 그런데 손님 아드님은 몇 살인가요?
W	Oh, he's only six.	여	아, 겨우 여섯 살이에요.
M	Well, you're in luck. **Tickets for children under age seven are** ¹⁾half price.	남	음, 운이 좋으시네요. 7세 미만 어린이들의 표는 반값이에요.
W	I wasn't expecting that. It saves us a few dollars.	여	그건 예상 못 했네요. 몇 달러를 절약해 주는군요.
M	Yes, it certainly does. **And did you park your car in the mall parking garage? We can give you** ²⁾a discounted rate.	남	네, 물론 그래요. 그리고 쇼핑몰 주차장에 차를 주차하셨나요? 할인해 드릴 수 있어요.
W	We did.	여	주차했어요.
M	**It's only $5 if you pay here.**	남	여기서 계산하면 5달러밖에 안 됩니다.
W	Okay, let's do that.	여	네, 그렇게 할게요.
M	Great. I'll ring you up now.	남	좋아요. 지금 계산해 드리겠습니다.
W	Thanks. My son has been looking forward to seeing this movie for weeks.	여	고마워요. 제 아들이 몇 주 동안 이 영화 보기를 기대했어요.
M	That's ³⁾good to hear. Here are your tickets. You'll be in Theater 6.	남	잘됐네요. 여기 표 드리겠습니다. 6관으로 가시면 됩니다.

여자가 영화표를 성인으로 두 장($8×2 =$16), 7세 미만 어린이 표로 한 장($8×0.5 =$4) 구매했고, 쇼핑몰 주차 요금($5)을 함께 지불했으므로 정답은 ④ '$25'이다.

[어휘] animated film 애니메이션 영화 by the way 그런데 You're in luck. 운이 좋으시네요. parking garage 주차장 ring up 계산하다 look forward to ~을 기대하다

7 이유 파악

정답 ⑤

W	Hey, Justin. Are you still interested in going to the baseball game on Saturday?	여	안녕, Justin. 너 아직 토요일에 야구 경기 보러 갈 의향이 있니?
M	Oh! It's the first ¹⁾game of the season on Saturday. I forgot about that!	남	아! 토요일에 시즌 첫 경기가 열리지. 잊고 있었어!
W	So... you can't make it?	여	그래서... 못 가니?
M	I'm afraid not.	남	안 될 것 같아.
W	That's too bad. You have your part-time job on the weekends, right?	여	유감이야. 주말마다 아르바이트가 있구나, 그렇지?
M	Actually, that was ²⁾only over the winter. The job ended in February.	남	사실, 그건 겨울 동안만이었어. 그 일은 2월에 끝났어.
W	Then, are you worried about the weather? I haven't checked the forecast yet.	여	그럼, 날씨가 걱정되니? 내가 아직 예보를 확인하지 않았어.
M	No. It's supposed to be warm and sunny on Saturday.	남	아니. 토요일은 따뜻하고 화창할 거야.
W	Then, what's the problem?	여	그러면 뭐가 문제야?
M	I'll be out of town. I ³⁾have to drive my brother to St. Louis. He's in a speech contest.	남	난 동네에 없을 거야. 내 동생을 세인트루이스까지 태워다 줘야 해. 동생이 말하기 대회에 나가거든.
W	That makes sense. Well, let's go to a game soon, then.	여	이해가 됐어. 음, 그럼 조만간 경기 보러 가자.
M	For sure.	남	물론이야.

남자는 토요일 야구 경기에 못 간다고 하면서 말하기 대회에 나가는 동생을 태워다 줘야 한다고 말했으므로, 남자가 경기를 보러 갈 수 없는 이유는 ⑤ '동생을 대회장에 데려다줘야 해서'이다.

[어휘] I'm afraid not. 안 될 것 같아. That's too bad. 유감이야. part-time job 아르바이트 speech contest 말하기 대회

8 언급 유무 파악

정답 ②

W	Hey, Billy. What are you watching?	여	안녕, Billy. 뭐 보고 있어?
M	It's a reality show about young musicians. It's called *Elite Singer*.	남	젊은 음악가들에 대한 리얼리티 쇼야. <Elite Singer>라고 불려.
W	Oh, I wanted to see that. I didn't realize it had started.	여	아, 그거 보고 싶었는데. 시작된 줄 몰랐네.
M	Yeah. The ¹⁾first episode aired **last week, on the 19th.** They're going to come out **every Tuesday at 7 p.m.**	남	응. 첫 회는 지난주 19일에 방송됐어. 매주 화요일 오후 7시에 나올 거야.
W	I see. Doesn't the whole show take place in **Los Angeles**?	여	그렇구나. 쇼 전체가 로스앤젤레스에서 촬영되지 않니?
M	Yeah. All of the participants ²⁾moved there and live in a house together.	남	그래. 모든 참가자들이 그곳으로 이동해서 한 집에서 같이 살아.
W	I didn't know that. *[Pause]* Oh, is that **Tina Sanders**?	여	그건 몰랐어. *[잠시 멈춤]* 저 사람 Tina Sanders야?
M	Yeah! She is a special guest star. She's ³⁾mentoring the musicians.	남	응! 그녀는 특별 출연자로 나온 스타야. 음악가들을 지도하고 있지.
W	Cool! I love her singing.	여	멋지다! 나는 그녀가 노래하는 걸 좋아해.
M	Me too. Why don't you sit down and watch it with me?	남	나도. 앉아서 나랑 같이 보는 게 어때?
W	Okay. I think I will.	여	그래. 그럴게.

첫 방영일(지난주 19일), 정규 방송 시간(매주 화요일 오후 7시), 촬영 장소(로스앤젤레스), 특별 출연자(Tina Sanders)에 대해 언급했고, ② '담당 프로듀서'는 언급하지 않았다.

[어휘] air ⑧ 방송되다 ⑲ 공기 come out 나오다 participant ⑲ 참가자 mentor ⑧ 지도하다

9 내용 불일치 파악

정답 ③

M Hello, visitors. I'd like to remind you that the Natural History Museum is holding a special hands-on program. It's for children aged 11 to 13 who are interested in ¹⁾becoming an archaeologist for a day. The four-hour program will be held for three days only. It ²⁾will begin with a presentation on basic digging techniques. The group will then participate in a simulation of an archeological dig. If you're interested, please apply soon. **Each day, the group of participants will be ³⁾limited to 10 children, so there will only be 30 in all.** The last day for signing up is April 15th, and the fee is $10 per student. Adults who ⁴⁾wish to accompany their children will not be charged. Thank you.	남 안녕하십니까, 방문객 여러분. 자연사 박물관에서 특별 실습 프로그램을 개최한다는 것을 다시 한번 알려드리고 싶습니다. 하루 동안 고고학자가 되고 싶은 의향이 있는 11세에서 13세 사이의 어린이를 대상으로 한 것입니다. 이 4시간짜리 프로그램은 3일 동안만 열릴 것입니다. 기초적인 발굴 기술에 대한 발표로 시작할 예정입니다. 그런 다음 고고학 발굴 모의실험에 참여할 것입니다. 관심 있으신 분들은 빨리 신청하십시오. 매일 참가자는 10명의 어린이로 제한될 것이기 때문에, 총 30명만 참가할 것입니다. 신청 마지막 날은 4월 15일이며, 학생 1인당 요금은 10달러입니다. 자녀와 동행하고자 하는 성인에게는 참가비가 청구되지 않습니다. 감사합니다.

박물관 실습 프로그램 개회에 대한 안내 방송이다. 남자가 매일 참가자의 수는 10명의 어린이로 제한될 것이라고 했으므로 ③ '하루에 30명의 어린이만 참가할 수 있다.'는 내용과 일치하지 않는다.

어휘 hands-on 혱 실습의 archaeologist 몡 고고학자 dig 동 발굴하다 몡 발굴 technique 몡 기술 participate in ~에 참여하다 simulation 몡 모의실험 limit 동 제한하다 몡 한계 fee 몡 요금; 수수료 accompany 동 동행하다 charge 동 청구하다

10 도표 정보 파악

정답 ②

M Carrie, you need a backpack for the new school year, right?	남 Carrie, 새 학기에 쓸 책가방이 필요하겠구나, 그렇지?
W I do, Dad.	여 그래요, 아빠.
M Well, I found a website with a few good options. What do you think of this one?	남 음, 몇 가지 좋은 선택지가 있는 웹사이트를 찾았어. 이건 어떠니?
W Hmm... I like the style, but it's ¹⁾way too big!	여 흠... 스타일은 좋은데, 너무 커요!
M Right, **a capacity of 25 liters should be plenty.**	남 그래, 25L 용량이면 충분하겠지.
W Okay, so there are four to look at.	여 좋아요, 살펴볼 것이 4개가 있네요.
M **Do you usually bring your laptop to school? If so, you should get one ²⁾with a special pocket for it.**	남 보통 학교에 노트북을 가지고 가니? 만약 그렇다면, 노트북을 넣을 특별한 주머니가 있는 걸 사야 해.
W Good point. I'll definitely need one of those.	여 좋은 지적이에요. 저 책가방 중 하나가 꼭 필요하겠어요.
M Okay, but let's keep the price down. Some of these are too expensive.	남 좋아, 하지만 가격은 좀 낮추렴. 이것들 중 몇 개는 너무 비싸구나.
W How much can we spend?	여 얼마나 쓸 수 있어요?
M Let's ³⁾keep it under $100. *[Pause]* What about the color?	남 100달러 미만으로 하자. *[잠시 멈춤]* 색깔은 어떠니?
W I really like this green one.	여 이 초록색 책가방이 정말 마음에 들어요.
M Why don't I order it?	남 내가 주문할까?
W Okay! Thanks, Dad.	여 좋아요! 고마워요, 아빠.

여자는 25L 용량 이하이면서, 노트북을 넣을 특별한 주머니가 있고, 100달러 미만인 것 중에서, 초록색인 책가방을 골랐다.

어휘 capacity 몡 용량 Good point. 좋은 지적이에요. keep ~ down ~을 낮추다

11 짧은 대화의 응답 파악

정답 ④

W Jason, there you are! Can you lend me a hand ¹⁾for a second?	여 Jason, 여기 있었구나! 날 잠깐 도와줄 수 있니?
M Sure, Mom. What do you need me to help you with?	남 그럼요, 엄마. 뭘 도와드릴까요?
W There's a box down in the basement with Christmas decorations in it. **Please ²⁾carry it up to the living room.**	여 지하실에 크리스마스 장식이 들어 있는 상자가 있어. 그걸 거실로 옮겨 주렴.
M Okay. I'll go down there now and get it.	남 알았어요. 지금 내려가서 가져올게요.

선택지 ① 죄송해요. 지금은 빌려드릴 수 없어요.
② 괜찮아요. 다시 상자 안에 넣을게요.
③ 그건 좀 무거워요. 조심해서 옮기세요.
④ 알았어요. 지금 내려가서 가져올게요.
⑤ 네. 크리스마스트리 바로 옆에 있어요.

남자가 뭘 도와줄지 물어보자 여자가 지하실에서 크리스마스 장식이 들어 있는 상자를 거실로 옮겨달라고 했으므로, 이에 대한 응답으로는 지금 내려가서 가져오겠다고 말하는 ④ 'Okay. I'll go down there now and get it.'이 가장 적절하다.

어휘 lend ~ a hand ~를 도와주다 basement 몡 지하 carry 동 옮기다

12 짧은 대화의 응답 파악 — 정답 ③

[Phone rings.]	[전화기가 울린다.]
M BBM Electronics customer service, this is Liam speaking. How may I help you?	남 BBM Electronics 고객 서비스의 Liam입니다. 무엇을 도와드릴까요?
W Hi. ¹⁾I'm calling about the headphones I ordered recently. I think they were supposed to arrive yesterday.	여 안녕하세요. 최근에 주문한 헤드폰 때문에 전화 드렸어요. 어제 도착하기로 되어 있는 줄 알았는데요.
M Okay. **Have you checked ²⁾the delivery status on our website?**	남 알겠습니다. 저희 웹사이트에서 배송 상태를 확인하셨나요?
W I have. And it shows that they haven't shipped yet.	여 했어요. 그리고 아직 배송되지 않은 것으로 나오네요.
	선택지 ① 물론이죠. 하지만 현재 아직 재고가 없네요.
	② 초조하네요. 지금쯤 환불을 받기로 되어 있었거든요.
	③ 했어요. 그리고 아직 배송되지 않은 것으로 나오네요.
	④ 아뇨. 온라인 매장에서 주문했어요.
	⑤ 죄송해요. 지금 바로 보내드릴게요.

여자가 주문한 헤드폰이 도착하지 않았다고 하자 남자가 웹사이트에서 배송 상태를 확인했는지 물었으므로, 이에 대한 응답으로는 확인 여부를 말하는 ③ 'I have. And it shows that they haven't shipped yet.'이 가장 적절하다.

어휘 be supposed to ~하기로 되어 있다 status ⑲ 상태 out of stock 재고가 없는 ship ⑧ 배송하다 ⑲ 배

13 긴 대화의 응답 파악 — 정답 ①

W Mr. Robinson, can you step into my office?	여 Robinson 씨, 제 사무실로 들어와 주시겠어요?
M Sure, Ms. Porter. I hope you have positive feedback ¹⁾on my recent article.	남 물론이죠, Porter 씨. 최근 제 기사에 대해 긍정적인 의견이시길 바랍니다.
W I think you did a fine job.	여 잘 하신 것 같아요.
M Thanks. I worked hard on that story about the construction of wind farms.	남 감사합니다. 풍력 발전소 건설에 관한 기사를 열심히 썼거든요.
W I can tell. That's why I'd like to give you another ²⁾important assignment.	여 그래 보여요. 그래서 제가 중요한 과제를 하나 더 주려고 해요.
M What's that?	남 그게 뭔가요?
W I'd like you to write an article on the government's upcoming clean energy program.	여 곧 있을 정부의 청정에너지 프로그램에 대한 기사를 써주면 좋겠어요.
M They're ³⁾planning to invest a lot of money in solar energy, right?	남 정부에서 태양 에너지에 많은 돈을 투자할 계획이죠, 그렇죠?
W That's what I hear, but I want you to do some hard reporting and get all the details.	여 제가 듣기로는 그런데, 좀 더 열심히 취재해서 모든 세부 사항을 알아내 주면 좋겠어요.
M Okay, I'll call my contacts in the energy department and do some interviews.	남 네, 에너지 부서에 있는 아는 사람들에게 전화해서 인터뷰를 좀 해볼게요.
W I think this will be a front-page story, so make it your ⁴⁾top priority.	여 이게 1면 기사가 될 것 같으니, 우선순위로 삼으세요.
M You have my word. I'll surely give it my all.	남 약속 드려요. 반드시 최선을 다하겠습니다.
	선택지 ① 약속드려요. 반드시 최선을 다하겠습니다.
	② 물론이죠. 풍력 발전소에 대한 정보도 포함시켰어요.
	③ 맞아요. 당신의 인터뷰를 정치란에 실었어요.
	④ 네. 의견 주신 것들로 수정하겠습니다.
	⑤ 아뇨. 건설은 일찍 완료될 겁니다.

새로운 기사를 써 달라고 요청하는 상황에서 여자가 요청한 기사가 1면 기사가 될 것 같으니 우선 순위로 삼으라고 당부했으므로, 이에 대한 응답으로는 최선을 다하겠다고 약속하는 ① 'You have my word. I'll surely give it my all.'이 가장 적절하다.

어휘 article ⑲ 기사 construction ⑲ 건설 wind farm 풍력 발전소 I can tell. 그래 보여요. government ⑲ 정부 upcoming ⑳ 곧 있을 invest ⑧ 투자하다 solar energy 태양 에너지 front-page ⑲ (신문의) 1면 priority ⑲ 우선순위 You have my word. 약속드려요. give it one's all 최선을 다하다 correction ⑲ 수정

14 긴 대화의 응답 파악 — 정답 ④

W I felt embarrassed when Mr. Wallace called on me last class. I hope he doesn't do that again today.	여 지난 수업 시간에 Wallace 선생님이 날 부르셨을 때 당황스럽더라. 오늘도 그러시지는 않기를 바라고 있어.
M He probably will. ¹⁾Participating in discussions is required.	남 아마 그렇게 하실걸. 토론에 참여하는 건 필수잖아.
W I know, but the discussions seem unnecessary and stressful.	여 알아, 하지만 토론은 불필요하고 스트레스를 많이 주는 것 같아.
M I don't agree. Having a discussion is a great way to learn.	남 나는 동의하지 않아. 토론을 하는 건 훌륭한 학습 방법이야.
W Really? I'm not an expert. Why are my thoughts so important?	여 정말? 난 전문가가 아니잖아. 내 생각이 왜 그렇게 중요한 거야?
M By putting our thoughts into words, we can ²⁾evaluate our own ideas.	남 생각을 말로 나타냄으로써, 우리 자신의 생각을 평가할 수 있잖아.
W And what if those ideas are totally wrong?	여 그런 생각들이 완전히 틀렸다면?
M That can be good! Another student has to explain why they're wrong.	남 그것도 좋을 수 있지! 다른 학생이 왜 그 생각이 틀렸는지 설명해야 하잖아.
W That sounds time consuming.	여 시간 소모가 큰 것 같은걸.
M It can be. But if you can make a good argument, you'll ³⁾understand the topic on a deeper level.	남 그럴 수도 있지. 하지만 만약 네가 좋은 주장을 펼칠 수 있다면, 너는 그 주제를 더 깊이 이해하게 될 거야.
W I see what you mean, **but I'm not very good at that.**	여 무슨 말인지 알겠지만, 난 그런 건 잘 못해.

M Then you should practice by speaking more often during class!
W You're right. I need to participate in discussions more.

남 그러면 수업 시간에 더 자주 말을 해서 연습을 해야겠네!
여 네 말이 맞아. 토론에 더 많이 참여해야겠어.

선택지 ① 걱정하지 마. 난 말하기 연습을 많이 했어.
② 알겠어. 그 주제에 대해 심도 있는 토론을 해 볼게.
③ 물론이지. 그게 네 생각을 평가하는 데 도움이 될 것 같아.
④ 네 말이 맞아. 토론에 더 많이 참여해야겠어.
⑤ 고마워. 내가 과제를 제때 끝내도록 도와주다니.

수업 시간에 토론하는 것에 관해 이야기하는 상황이다. 여자가 토론을 잘하지 못한다며 불만을 토로하자 남자가 수업 시간에 더 자주 말을 해서 연습해야겠다고 여자에게 충고했으므로, 이에 대한 응답으로는 충고를 받아들이는 ④ 'You're right. I need to participate in discussions more.'이 가장 적질하다.

어휘 required 형 필수의 unnecessary 형 불필요한 expert 명 전문가 put ~ into words ~을 말로 나타내다 evaluate 동 평가하다 time consuming 시간 소모가 큰
argument 명 주장; 논쟁 be good at ~을 잘 하다

---

15 상황에 적절한 말 파악

정답 ⑤

M Christine is planning to buy a used car. She recently found one she was interested in online. But she ¹⁾was not sure whether it was a good buy. So she called her friend Rick who knows a lot about cars. He advised her not to buy the car. Even though the ²⁾vehicle was listed for a low price, he thought Christine would have to spend a lot of money to repair it. He recommended that she look for ³⁾a different model. Thanks to his advice, Christine found a good car. **Therefore, she wants to tell Rick that she will ⁴⁾treat him to a great dinner to return the favor.** In this situation, what would Christine most likely say to Rick?

남 Christine은 중고차를 살 계획입니다. 그녀는 최근에 온라인에서 관심 있는 것을 발견했습니다. 하지만 그녀는 그것이 좋은 구매인지 확신하지 못했습니다. 그래서 그녀는 자동차에 대해 많이 아는 그녀의 친구 Rick에게 전화했습니다. 그는 그녀에게 그 차를 사지 말라고 충고했습니다. 비록 그 차량이 낮은 가격으로 나와 있었지만, 그는 Christine이 그것을 수리하기 위해 많은 돈을 써야 할 것이라고 생각했습니다. 그는 그녀에게 다른 모델을 찾아보라고 권했습니다. 그의 충고 덕분에, Christine은 좋은 차를 찾았습니다. 그래서 그녀는 Rick에게 그 호의에 보답하기 위해 멋진 저녁 식사를 대접하겠다고 말하고 싶습니다. 이러한 상황에서, Christine이 Rick에게 가장 할 것 같은 말은 무엇입니까?

선택지 ① 내 차 고치는 것 좀 도와줄래?
② 다른 의견을 물어볼게.
③ 엔진이 손상되었으니 조심히 다뤄 줘.
④ 이 차를 추천해 줘서 고마워.
⑤ 감사의 표시로 네게 저녁을 사 줘도 될까?

Rick이 충고를 해준 것에 보답하기 위해 Christine은 멋진 저녁 식사를 대접하려고 한다. 따라서, Christine이 할 말로 ⑤ 'Can I take you out to dinner to thank you?'가 가장 적절하다.

어휘 used 형 중고의 advise 동 충고하다 vehicle 명 차량, 자동차 repair 동 수리하다 thanks to ~ 덕분에 treat A to B A에게 B를 대접하다 return favor 호의에 보답하다

16-17 세트 문항

정답 16 ④ 17 ②

W Good afternoon, everyone. Last week, we discussed parasites that harm the animals they are attached to. **This week, we'll discuss ways in which ¹⁾species can cooperate with one another.** First off, let's take the **rhino bird**. It sits on the back of large mammals and eats the ²⁾small insects that collect in their fur. This helps to keep the large animal clean. Another example is the **white-eye bird**. It lives on the nectar of flowers. It helps the plants to reproduce ³⁾by spreading pollen. Third, we have the **woolly bat**. These winged animals use an insect-eating plant as their nest. At the same time, their droppings provide the nitrogen that the plant needs. Finally, let's consider the **clownfish**. It is provided shelter by sea anemones that are poisonous to other fish. While there, the clownfish's bright colors ⁴⁾attract prey to the anemone. So the clownfish gets a place to stay while the anemone gets some food. Now, let's take a moment to watch a brief video describing how this process works.

여 안녕하십니까, 여러분. 지난주에 우리는 달라붙은 동물들에게 해를 끼치는 기생충에 대해 논의했습니다. 이번 주에는 여러 종이 서로서로 협력할 수 있는 방법에 대해 논의할 것입니다. 먼저, 코뿔소 새를 봅시다. 이것은 큰 포유류의 등에 앉아 털에 모인 작은 곤충들을 먹습니다. 이것은 그 동물이 깨끗함을 유지하는 데 도움을 줍니다. 또 다른 예는 동박새입니다. 그것은 꽃의 꿀을 먹고 삽니다. 이는 꽃가루를 퍼뜨림으로써 식물이 번식하는 것을 돕습니다. 셋째, 양털 박쥐가 있습니다. 이 날개 달린 동물들은 곤충을 잡아먹는 식물을 둥지로 사용합니다. 동시에, 그들의 배설물은 그 식물이 필요로 하는 질소를 제공합니다. 마지막으로, 흰동가리에 대해 생각해 봅시다. 그것은 다른 물고기들에게는 유독한 말미잘에게 은신처를 제공 받습니다. 그곳에 있는 동안, 흰동가리의 밝은색은 먹이를 말미잘로 끌어들입니다. 그래서, 흰동가리는 말미잘이 음식을 얻는 동안 머물 곳을 얻습니다. 이제 이 과정이 어떻게 진행되는지 보여주는 짧은 동영상을 잠시 보도록 하겠습니다.

선택지 16 ① 동물의 진화 역사
② 동물의 번식을 돕는 적응
③ 다양한 기생충의 생존 전략
④ 여러 동물이 다른 종을 돕는 방법
⑤ 식물이 동물로부터 스스로를 보호하는 방법
17 ① 코뿔소 새 ② 악어새 ③ 동박새 ④ 양털 박쥐 ⑤ 흰동가리

16 여러 종이 서로서로 협력할 수 있는 방법에 대해 논의하고 있으므로 여자가 하는 말의 주제로 ④ 'how different animals aid other species'가 가장 적절하다.
17 코뿔소 새, 동박새, 양털 박쥐, 흰동가리는 언급했지만 ② 'crocodile bird'는 언급하지 않았다.

어휘 parasite 명 기생충 attach 동 달라붙다 cooperate 동 협력하다 with one another 서로서로 mammal 명 포유류 live on ~을 먹고 살다 nectar 명 꿀 reproduce 동 번식하다
pollen 명 꽃가루 dropping 명 배설물; 낙하 nitrogen 명 질소 anemone 명 말미잘 poisonous 형 유독한, 독성이 있는 evolutionary 형 진화의 aid 동 돕다

1	①	2	③	3	①	4	⑤	5	⑤	6	④	7	④	8	①	9	④	10	④
11	③	12	②	13	⑤	14	④	15	②	16	①	17	③						

• 각 문제의 정답 근거는 굵은 글씨로, Dictation 정답은 밑줄로 표시되어 있습니다.

1 목적 파악

정답 ①

| M | Attention, visitors. Thanks for coming to today's recording of *The Angela Ross Comedy Hour*. **I'm Jeff Bennett, chief security manager at this studio. Before it begins, I want to remind you that certain items** ¹⁾are not allowed in the television studio. These include any ²⁾unauthorized recording equipment and outside beverages. **Also, we will ask that you keep your smartphones turned off during your time in the studio. And don't forget that children under the age of 16 must be accompanied by a parent or guardian at all times.** Any visitors caught breaking these rules will be asked to ³⁾leave at once. Does anyone have any questions? | 남 | 주목해 주십시오, 방문객 여러분. 오늘 <The Angela Ross Comedy Hour>의 녹화에 와주셔서 감사합니다. 저는 이 촬영장의 보안 관리 책임자인 Jeff Bennett입니다. 시작하기 전에, 촬영장에서 특정 물품은 허용되지 않는다는 점을 다시 한번 알려드리고 싶습니다. 여기에는 허가받지 않은 녹음 장비 및 외부 음료가 포함됩니다. 또한, 촬영장에 머무는 동안에는 스마트폰 전원을 꺼주시길 바랍니다. 그리고 16세 미만의 어린이는 항상 부모님이나 보호자를 동반해야 한다는 것을 잊지 마십시오. 이러한 규칙을 어기다 적발된 방문객은 즉시 퇴장해야 합니다. 질문 있으신 분 계십니까? |

남자가 촬영장의 보안 관리 책임자임을 밝히면서, 반입이 허용되지 않는 물품과 그 외 촬영장에서 지켜야 하는 규칙들을 알려주고 있다. 따라서, 남자가 하는 말의 목적으로 ① '촬영장 내 보안 규칙을 안내하려고'가 가장 적절하다.

어휘 chief manager 관리 책임자 certain ⑱ 특정한; 확신하는 unauthorized ⑱ 허가 받지 않은, 권한이 없는 equipment ⑲ 장비, 설비 beverage ⑲ 음료 turn off (전원을) 끄다 be accompanied by ~을 동반하다 guardian ⑲ 보호자 break a rule 규칙을 어기다

2 의견 파악

정답 ③

M	Amy, are you doing okay?	남	Amy, 괜찮니?
W	I'm fine, Dad. But I am still disappointed about my team losing the championship soccer match on Saturday.	여	괜찮아요, 아빠. 하지만 아직도 토요일 축구 결승전에서 우리 팀이 진 게 실망스러워요.
M	You don't need to be. You played well.	남	그럴 필요 없어. 넌 경기를 잘했단다.
W	Thanks. But it was ¹⁾such a close game. I thought we were going to win.	여	감사해요. 하지만 정말 접전이었잖아요. 전 우리가 이길 거라고 생각했어요.
M	I understand. **But I don't think feeling bad about the past will help you win.**	남	이해해. 그래도 지난 일을 후회하는 게 이기는 데 도움이 될 것 같지는 않구나.
W	What do you mean?	여	무슨 말씀이세요?
M	You ²⁾can't change the past. So when you think that way, you feel powerless. It's a very negative mindset.	남	과거는 바꿀 수 없어. 그러니 그런 식으로 생각하면, 무력함을 느끼게 된단다. 그건 매우 부정적인 마음가짐이지.
W	But I care about my team. Should I feel nothing?	여	하지만 우리 팀이 신경 쓰이는걸요. 제가 아무것도 생각하지 말아야 하나요?
M	No! **I just mean that it's hard to** ³⁾improve your own abilities if you keep thinking about the past.	남	아니! 내 말은 지난 일을 계속 생각한다면, 너 자신의 능력을 향상시키기 어렵다는 거야.
W	I see.	여	그렇군요.
M	Maybe it would help to set some new goals for yourself.	남	어쩌면 널 위한 새로운 목표를 세우는 게 도움이 될지도 모르겠구나.
W	I'll think about it.	여	생각해 볼게요.

축구 경기에서 진 것을 계속 후회하고 있는 여자에게 남자가 지난 일을 계속 생각한다면 자신의 능력을 향상시키기 어렵다고 했다. 따라서, 남자의 의견으로 ③ '지나간 과거를 곱씹다 보면 능력을 발전시키기 어렵다.'가 가장 적절하다.

어휘 disappointed ⑱ 실망스러운 a close game 접전 feel bad about ~을 후회하다 powerless ⑱ 무력한 negative ⑱ 부정적인 mindset ⑲ 마음가짐, 사고방식 set a goal 목표를 세우다

3 관계 파악

정답 ①

	[Phone rings.]		[전화기가 울린다.]
M	You've reached Bruno's Auto. This is Bruno speaking.	남	Bruno's Auto입니다. 저는 Bruno입니다.
W	Hi. It's Rachel Miller. I brought in a motorbike for repairs this morning.	여	안녕하세요. Rachel Miller인데요. 오늘 아침에 수리받으러 오토바이를 가지고 갔었어요.
M	Oh, you ¹⁾had a problem with your brakes, correct?	남	아, 브레이크에 문제가 있으셨죠, 맞죠?
W	That's right. I was wondering how much the repairs would cost.	여	그래요. 수리 비용이 얼마나 들까 궁금해서요.
M	**I'd estimate they** ²⁾will cost about $100.	남	100달러 정도 들 거라고 예상되네요.
W	That's more than I expected.	여	생각했던 것보다 더 비싸네요.

M That includes ³⁾a tire replacement. **I found your tire was flat while inspecting your brakes.**	남 타이어 교체가 포함되었어요. 브레이크 점검 중에 타이어가 펑크 난 걸 발견했거든요.
W I see. And how long will that take? **I use the bike to deliver pizzas, so I'd like to have it back as soon as possible.**	여 그렇군요. 그리고 얼마나 걸릴까요? 피자 배달하는 데 오토바이를 써서, 가능한 한 빨리 가져오고 싶어요.
M Not to worry. I ordered a new part, and it should be here by tomorrow.	남 걱정하지 마세요. 새 부품을 주문했는데, 내일이면 도착할 거예요.
W So will it ⁴⁾be ready on Thursday?	여 그러면 목요일에는 준비가 되는 거죠?
M It should be. I will call you if there's any delay.	남 그럴 거예요. 지연되면 전화 드리겠습니다.
W Okay. I really appreciate that.	여 알겠습니다. 정말 감사해요.

두 사람이 오토바이 수리에 관해 이야기하고 있다. 남자는 여자가 수리를 맡긴 오토바이를 점검했다고 하면서 비용 등을 말해주고 했고, 여자는 피자 배달하는 데 오토바이를 쓰고 있다고 하는 것으로 보아 두 사람의 관계로 ① '오토바이 수리공 — 배달 기사'가 가장 적절하다.

[어휘] estimate 통 예상하다; 추정하다 replacement 명 교체 flat 형 바람이 빠진; 평평한 inspect 통 점검하다, 검사하다 as soon as possible 가능한 한 빨리 delay 명 지연 통 연기하다

4 그림 내용 불일치 파악

정답 ⑤

M Thanks for letting me sleep here in your home office, Aunt Roberts.	남 여기 고모가 재택 근무하는 방에서 자게 해줘서 고마워요, Roberts 고모.
W Certainly! The weather is terrible. It's not safe to go out in this storm.	여 당연한걸! 날씨가 안 좋잖니. 이런 폭풍우 속에서 외출하는 건 안전하지 않아.
M It must be nice to do remote work here. It's lovely. I really like that poster ¹⁾with a tiger on it.	남 여기서 원격 근무하는 건 분명 근사할 거예요. 아주 멋져요. 호랑이가 그려진 저 포스터가 정말 마음에 드는걸요.
W Thanks.	여 고맙구나.
M Should I sleep on the couch ²⁾underneath the window?	남 제가 창문 밑에 있는 소파에서 자면 될까요?
W It's a bit short for you. I'll bring in an air mattress.	여 너한테는 좀 짧겠구나. 에어 매트리스를 가져올게.
M Is it okay if I place it here on the striped rug?	남 그것을 여기 줄무늬 러그 위에 둬도 될까요?
W Of course. And if you need ³⁾a little more room, you can move that computer chair by my desk out into the hall.	여 물론이지. 그리고 조금 더 공간이 필요하면, 내 책상 옆에 있는 컴퓨터 의자를 복도로 옮기면 된단다.
M Okay.	남 좋아요.
W **Just be careful that you don't bump into the round table by the door.**	여 문가의 둥근 탁자에 부딪치지 않도록만 조심하렴.
M Got it. The vase on top of it ⁴⁾looks fragile.	남 알겠어요. 그 위에 있는 꽃병이 깨지기 쉬워 보이네요.
W I'll be right back with that air mattress.	여 난 에어 매트리스 가시러 금방 놀아올게.
M Thanks again!	남 다시 한번 감사해요!

대화에서 여자가 문가의 둥근 탁자에 부딪치지 않도록 조심하라고 말했는데, ⑤에는 사각 탁자가 그려져 있다.

[어휘] storm 명 폭풍우 remote work 원격 근무 underneath 전 ~ 밑에 있는 bump into ~에 부딪치다 fragile 형 깨지기 쉬운, 부서지기 쉬운

5 할 일 파악

정답 ⑤

W Hello, Mr. Brown. Can I ask a question about the essay assignment?	여 안녕하세요, Brown 선생님. 에세이 과제에 관해 질문해도 될까요?
M Sure. You mean the poetry analysis essay?	남 물론이란다. 시 분석 에세이를 말하는 거지?
W Right. You mentioned that we should ¹⁾discuss three poems by a single poet.	여 맞아요. 한 시인이 쓴 세 편의 시에 관해 논해야 한다고 말씀하셨잖아요.
M Yes, that's correct.	남 그래, 맞아.
W Well, the poet is Russian, and only one of her poems has been ²⁾translated into English. So I couldn't find three poems to use.	여 음, 시인이 러시아 사람이고, 그 사람의 시 중에서 단 한 편만 영어로 번역됐어요. 그래서 저는 에세이에 쓸 세 편의 시를 찾지 못했어요.
M I see. Why did you pick this poet?	남 그렇구나. 왜 그 시인을 선택했니?
W Her poem inspired me to write my own poetry.	여 그 시인의 시는 제게 직접 시를 쓰도록 영감을 줬어요.
M **Then, you could do ³⁾a thorough analysis of that single poem using the critical approach I taught in class.**	남 그러면 내가 수업 시간에 가르쳤던 비판적 접근법을 사용해서 그 한 편의 시에 대해 철저한 분석을 하면 되겠구나.
W I didn't think you'd accept an essay on only one poem.	여 시 한편만으로 쓴 에세이를 받아주실 줄 몰랐네요.
M Under the circumstances, it would be fine.	남 사정이 그러니 괜찮단다.
W Great!	여 잘됐네요!
M **But remember your essay will be the same length. I expect you to ⁴⁾research the subject more thoroughly so you have a deep enough analysis.**	남 하지만 에세이는 같은 분량이어야 한다는 점을 기억하렴. 네가 충분히 심도 있는 분석을 할 수 있도록 주제 조사를 더 철저히 하길 기대하고 있으마.
W **Okay, I will.**	여 알겠습니다, 그럴게요.

시 분석 에세이 과제에 관해 이야기하고 있다. 남자가 충분히 심도 있는 분석을 할 수 있도록 주제 조사를 더 철저히 하길 기대하고 있겠다고 하자, 여자가 그러겠다고 했으므로 여자가 할 일로 ⑤ '작품 심층 조사하기'가 가장 적절하다.

[어휘] poetry 명 시 analysis 명 분석 thorough 형 철저한 critical 형 비판적인 approach 명 접근법; 접근 under the circumstances 사정이 그러니 length 명 분량, 길이

6 금액 정보 파악

정답 ④

W	Welcome to Keith's Stationery. May I help you?
M	Hi. I'm looking for a small-sized photo album.
W	Sure. Those are right over here.
M	How much is this photo album ¹⁾with the red cover?
W	That's $20. **We also have that in a blue leather version for $30.**
M	**I'll take the blue one. Oh... and I should mention that I have a 10% discount coupon for this item.**
W	Great. ²⁾I can apply that when you check out. Do you need some paper?
M	Yes. **I'd like two packs of thick white paper.**
W	**Those are $12 each.**
M	Sure, that's fine.
W	Anything else, sir?
M	**I'll also take a pack of those silver stickers. It's $2, right?**
W	It is. Okay, so all I need is the coupon for that album, and I'll ³⁾add up the total.
M	Here you go.

여	Keith's Stationery에 오신 것을 환영합니다. 도와드릴까요?
남	안녕하세요. 전 작은 크기의 사진첩을 찾고 있어요.
여	그럼요. 그것들은 바로 여기에 있어요.
남	이 빨간 표지의 사진첩은 얼마인가요?
여	20달러예요. 30달러짜리 파란색 가죽으로 된 것도 있어요.
남	파란색으로 할게요. 아... 그리고 제가 이 상품에 대해 10% 할인 쿠폰을 가지고 있다는 것을 말씀드려야겠네요.
여	좋습니다. 계산하실 때 적용하면 돼요. 용지도 좀 필요하신가요?
남	네. 두꺼운 흰 용지로 두 묶음 주세요.
여	그건 하나에 12달러예요.
남	네, 괜찮습니다.
여	다른 건 없으세요, 손님?
남	저기 은색 스티커도 한 묶음 살게요. 2달러, 맞죠?
여	그렇습니다. 좋아요, 그러니까 그 앨범에 쓸 쿠폰만 주시면, 합산해 드릴게요.
남	여기 있습니다.

남자가 파란색 가죽으로 된 사진첩 1개에 대해 10% 할인($30×0.9 =$27)을 받았고, 두꺼운 흰 용지 두 묶음($12×2 =$24)과, 은색 스티커 한 묶음($2)을 구매했으므로 정답은 ④ '$53'이다.

[어휘] cover 몡 표지 툉 덮다　leather 몡 가죽　apply 툉 적용하다; 신청하다　check out 계산하다

7 이유 파악

정답 ④

	[Cell phone rings.]
W	Hey, Jonathan.
M	Hi, Mary. How are you feeling?
W	I'm ¹⁾all better. I'll be back at school tomorrow.
M	That's great. Well, I was calling to see if you could still go to the school musical on Saturday.
W	I don't think I can make it.
M	You must still be feeling a little under the weather, right?
W	No. I'm fine.
M	Ah, well, is it because you don't like musicals? Some people don't like that ²⁾type of play.
W	No. I was excited to see it, and the actors in it are really talented. **Actually, I promised my dad I would ³⁾go on a weekend trip with him.**
M	Oh, I see.
W	We're going birdwatching together. Sorry I forgot to ⁴⁾mention it before.
M	It's okay.
W	Well, let's do something fun together soon.

	[휴대폰이 울린다.]
여	안녕, Jonathan.
남	안녕, Mary. 몸은 좀 어때?
여	다 나았어. 내일 학교로 돌아갈 거야.
남	잘됐어. 음, 토요일에 학교 뮤지컬을 보러 갈 수 있는지 알아보려고 전화했어.
여	난 못 갈 것 같아.
남	여전히 몸이 좀 안 좋은 거구나, 그렇지?
여	아니야. 난 괜찮아.
남	아, 음, 뮤지컬을 안 좋아해서 그래? 어떤 사람들은 그런 종류의 극은 좋아하지 않더라.
여	아니. 그걸 보게 돼서 신났고, 거기 출연하는 배우들은 정말 실력 있잖아. 사실, 아빠와 주말여행을 가기로 약속했어.
남	아, 그렇구나.
여	함께 조류 관찰을 하러 갈 거야. 전에 말해준다는 걸 잊어버려서 미안.
남	괜찮아.
여	음, 조만간 같이 재미있는 거 하자.

여자는 학교 뮤지컬에 못 갈 것 같다고 하면서 아빠와 주말여행을 가기로 약속했다고 말했으므로, 여자가 뮤지컬을 관람하러 갈 수 없는 이유는 ④ '아버지와 여행을 가기로 해서'이다.

[어휘] make it (모임 등에) 가다　under the weather 몸이 좀 안 좋은　birdwatching 몡 조류 관찰, 들새 관찰

8 언급 유무 파악

정답 ①

W	Nick, are you still working on that ¹⁾chemistry experiment? I thought you were finished.
M	Well, I'm going to be participating in the National Science Fair.
W	Whoa, really?
M	Yeah. My project won first prize, so I ²⁾was invited to the nationwide competition in **Pinesburg City**.
W	That's so cool. Do you think you can win ³⁾the national competition, too?
M	I hope so. The winner gets a cash prize. It's **$5,000** this year.
W	Wow. But I bet it's not easy. There must be a lot of people competing.
M	Right. **A ⁴⁾total of 200 people** are going to be presenting their projects.
W	How is it evaluated?
M	**It's decided by the science fair judges. They walk around the fair filling out score sheets and asking questions.**

여	Nick, 아직 그 화학 실험을 하고 있니? 끝난 줄 알았는데.
남	음, 난 National Science Fair에 참가할 거야.
여	와, 정말?
남	응. 내 프로젝트가 1등을 해서, 파인즈버그시에서 열리는 전국 대회에 초청됐어.
여	정말 멋지다. 전국 대회에서도 우승할 수 있을 것 같아?
남	그러면 좋겠지. 우승자는 상금을 받거든. 올해는 5,000달러야.
여	우와. 하지만 분명 쉽지 않겠지. 출전하는 사람들이 분명 많을 거야.
남	맞아. 총 200명의 사람들이 프로젝트를 발표할 거야.
여	평가는 어떻게 되는 거야?
남	과학 박람회 심사위원들이 결정해. 박람회장을 돌아다니며 질문을 하고 점수표를 작성하거든.

| W | That sounds a little stressful. But I bet you'll do really well! | 여 | 스트레스를 좀 받을 것 같네. 하지만 분명 넌 정말 잘할 거야! |
| M | Thanks so much. | 남 | 정말 고마워. |

개최 장소(파인즈버그시), 우승 상금(5,000달러), 참가자 수(200명), 평가 방식(심사위원이 돌아다니며 질문하고 점수표를 작성함)에 대해 언급했고, ① '프로젝트 주제'는 언급하지 않았다.

[어휘] chemistry 몡 화학 win first prize 1등을 하다 nationwide 혱 전국적인 compete 동 출전하다; 경쟁하다 evaluate 동 평가하다 fill out 작성하다

9 내용 불일치 파악 정답 ④

| W | Welcome to the Merkel Park Tree-Planting Event. I'm Michelle Bach from the Greenwood Community Center. My organization put together today's event. Over the course of the afternoon, we're planning to plant around 350 trees ¹⁾to transform the park into a more beautiful and eco-friendly space. This is only possible because so many members of our local community have volunteered to do this hard work. Give yourself ²⁾a round of applause. *[Pause]* **I also want to thank Wilson Garden Store for ³⁾donating the young trees we'll be using today.** And I should remind you of one more thing. As you're working today, remember to ⁴⁾take regular breaks. Water and snacks will be provided when you need them. Okay? Let's get started! | 여 | Merkel Park Tree-Planting Event에 오신 것을 환영합니다. 저는 그린우드 주민 센터의 Michelle Bach입니다. 저희 기관이 오늘의 행사를 종합하여 만들었습니다. 오후 동안, 우리는 공원을 더 아름답고 친환경적인 공간으로 탈바꿈시키기 위해 350여 그루의 나무를 심을 계획입니다. 이것이 가능한 이유는 지역 사회의 많은 구성원분들이 이 힘든 일에 자원해주셨기 때문입니다. 여러분 스스로에게 한 차례의 박수를 보내주세요. *[잠시 멈춤]* 또한 오늘 사용할 묘목을 기증해 주신 Wilson Garden Store에도 감사드립니다. 그리고 한 가지 더 말씀드리겠습니다. 오늘 작업하실 때, 규칙적으로 휴식을 취하는 것을 기억하세요. 물과 간식이 필요할 때에 제공될 예정입니다. 됐나요? 시작합시다! |

주민 센터에서 열리는 나무 심기 행사에 대한 안내 방송이다. 여자가 오늘 사용할 묘목을 Wilson Garden Store에서 기증해 줬다고 했으므로 ④ '행사에 쓸 묘목을 대량 구매했다.'는 내용과 일치하지 않는다.

[어휘] organization 몡 기관, 조직 put together 종합하여 만들다 over the course of ~ 동안 plant 동 심다 몡 식물 transform 동 탈바꿈시키다, 변형하다 a round of 한 차례의 applause 몡 박수 donate 동 기증하다, 기부하다 regular 혱 규칙적인 Let's get started! 시작합시다!

10 도표 정보 파악 정답 ④

W	Honey, we need to ¹⁾book a hotel room in San Diego. The prices are already going up.	여	여보, 샌디에이고에 있는 호텔 객실을 예약해야 해. 가격이 벌써 오르고 있어.
M	I found one, but I wanted to check with you about which room to reserve. I'll send you a link.	남	호텔은 하나 찾았는데, 어떤 객실을 예약해야 할지 당신과 확인하고 싶었어. 링크를 보내줄게.
W	Hmm... all of these look good.	여	흠... 모두 좋아 보이는걸.
M	I thought so! How much can we spend?	남	나도 그렇게 생각했어! 우리 얼마를 쓸 수 있지?
W	Let's ²⁾keep it under $200.	여	200달러 미만으로 하자.
M	Sounds good. And I don't think our room needs to be too big.	남	좋아. 그리고 우리 객실이 너무 클 필요는 없을 것 같아.
W	True. It's just the two of us, so **we don't need a room that can accommodate four.**	여	맞아. 그냥 우리 둘뿐이니까, 네 명을 수용할 수 있는 객실은 필요 없어.
M	Also, don't forget we are traveling with our dog, which ³⁾limits our options a little.	남	또, 우리 개랑 함께 여행한다는 걸 잊지 마, 이건 우리 선택지를 약간 제한해.
W	**Right, we need a room where pets are allowed.** And we can choose what kind of view the room has.	여	맞아, 반려동물이 허용되는 객실이 필요해. 그리고 객실을 어떤 종류의 뷰로 할지 고르면 돼.
M	**Oh, I'd ⁴⁾prefer a mountain view.**	남	아, 난 산이 보이는 뷰가 좋아.
W	Sure. That's probably nicer.	여	그래. 어쩌면 그게 더 좋겠어.
M	Okay, we're all set.	남	알겠어, 준비가 다 됐네.

두 사람은 가격이 200달러 미만인 것 중에서, 네 명을 수용할 수 있는 객실이 아니며, 반려동물이 허용되고, 산이 보이는 뷰의 호텔 객실을 골랐다.

[어휘] go up (가격 등이) 오르다 reserve 동 예약하다 accommodate 동 수용하다, 공간을 제공하다 be all set 준비가 다 되어 있다

11 짧은 대화의 응답 파악 정답 ③

[Door knocks.]	*[문을 똑똑 두드린다.]*
W Hello, Jeremy? Are you in the bedroom?	여 안녕, Jeremy? 너 침실에 있니?
M Yes, Liz. I was just reading. Is ¹⁾there something wrong?	남 응, Liz. 그냥 책을 읽고 있었어. 무슨 일 있어?
W **Mom was just trying to call you, but she ²⁾couldn't reach you. Is your phone turned off?**	여 엄마가 방금 너한테 전화하려고 했는데, 너랑 연락이 안 됐대. 휴대폰 꺼져 있는 거야?
M Oh, I didn't realize that it was out of power.	남 아, 전원이 나갔는지 몰랐어.
	[선택지] ① 엄마는 네가 지금 당장 침실을 청소하길 원하셔.
	② 방해해서 미안, 휴대폰 끌게.
	③ 아, 전원이 나갔는지 몰랐어.
	④ 무슨 책을 읽고 있는지 물어봐도 돼?
	⑤ 내가 너무 늦게까지 잤나 봐.

여자가 남자에게 엄마가 전화하려 했는데 연락이 안 됐다고 한 소식을 전하면서 남자의 휴대폰이 꺼져 있는지 물었으므로, 이에 대한 응답으로는 휴대폰이 꺼져 있는지 몰랐다고 말하는 ③ 'Oh, I didn't realize that it was out of power.'가 가장 적절하다.

어휘 reach 통 ~와 연락하다; 닿다 interrupt 통 방해하다 out of power 전원이 나간

12 짧은 대화의 응답 파악
정답 ②

M How may I help you? W Is this where I can ¹⁾buy tickets for the express train to the airport? M No, ma'am. This is just ²⁾an information office. You need to go up to the top floor for that. W Can you point me to the elevator?	남 무엇을 도와드릴까요? 여 여기가 공항으로 가는 급행열차 표를 살 수 있는 곳인가요? 남 아니요, 손님. 이곳은 그냥 안내소입니다. 그러시려면 맨 위층으로 올라가셔야 해요. 여 엘리베이터로 가는 길을 알려 주시겠어요? 선택지 ① 제 비행기는 오후 2시 15분에 출발해요. ② 엘리베이터로 가는 길을 알려 주시겠어요? ③ 음, 제 표를 찾을 수 있을 것 같지 않네요. ④ 공항에 관한 정보를 찾고 있어요. ⑤ 지금 바닥이 미끄러우니 조심하세요.

여자가 급행열차 표를 구매하려고 하는 상황에서 남자가 표를 구매하기 위해서는 맨 위층으로 올라가야 한다고 했으므로, 이에 대한 응답으로는 엘리베이터가 있는 곳을 묻는 ② 'Can you point me to the elevator?'가 가장 적절하다.

어휘 express 형 급행의 동 표현하다 point A to B B로 가는 길을 A에게 알려주다 can't seem to ~할 수 있을 것 같지 않다 slippery 형 미끄러운

13 긴 대화의 응답 파악
정답 ⑤

M Mom said we haven't been keeping up with our chores lately, Elena. W I've been really busy lately, but I try my best! M You forgot ¹⁾to wash the dishes last night. I had to do them this morning. W Are you sure about that? Wasn't it your turn last night? M Go check the schedule on the fridge. W Oh, you're right. I thought yesterday was Tuesday. M How did that happen? W I don't know... I was all mixed up. M Okay. My point is that you're ²⁾making a problem for someone else when you don't do your chores. W You're right. But I have trouble keeping track of things. Do you have any ideas? M I suggest that you ³⁾set a reminder alarm on your phone before each task. W That's a good idea. Thank you for the tip! M Don't mention it. Mom will be happy that you remembered.	남 엄마가 우리 요즘 집안일을 제때 안 한다고 말씀하셨어, Elena. 여 요즘 정말 바빴는데도, 난 최선을 다하고 있는걸! 남 어젯밤에 설거지하는 걸 잊었잖아. 오늘 아침에 내가 해야 했어. 여 그게 확실해? 어젯밤에 네 차례 아니었어? 남 가서 냉장고에 있는 일정표를 확인해 봐. 여 아, 네 말이 맞네. 어제가 화요일인 줄 알았어. 남 어떻게 이런 일이 일어난 거야? 여 모르겠어... 완전히 헷갈렸어. 남 알겠어. 내 요점은 네가 해야 할 집안일을 하지 않으면 다른 사람에게 문제를 일으킨다는 거야. 여 맞아. 그런데 난 할 일을 기억하는 데 어려움을 겪고 있어. 좋은 생각 있니? 남 각각의 일에 앞서 미리 알림을 설정하는 걸 추천할게. 여 좋은 생각이야. 조언해줘서 고마워! 남 천만에. 엄마는 네가 기억하고 있으면 좋아하실 거야. 선택지 ① 정말 고마워. 난 쓰레기를 밖에 갖다 버리는 걸 좋아하지 않거든. ② 나도 바빴어. 그건 좋은 변명이 아니야. ③ 걱정하지 마. 내가 아침에 처리할게. ④ 못하겠어. 난 그때 전화를 받아야 할 것 같아. ⑤ 천만에. 엄마는 네가 기억하고 있으면 좋아하실 거야.

여자가 바빠서 해야 할 일을 잊어버리는 문제를 겪는 상황이다. 남자가 미리 알림을 설정할 것을 추천하자 여자가 조언해줘서 고맙다고 했으므로, 이에 대한 응답으로는 감사 표현에 답하는 ⑤ 'Don't mention it. Mom will be happy that you remembered.'가 가장 적절하다.

어휘 keep up with ~을 제때 하다 chore 명 집안일 try one's best 최선을 다하다 be mixed up 헷갈리다, 혼란해지다 keep track of ~을 기억하다 excuse 명 변명

14 긴 대화의 응답 파악
정답 ④

W Excuse me. I bought these shirts yesterday. M Is there ¹⁾something wrong with them? W They were supposed to be a gift for my nephew, and I asked the clerk to wrap them. But when he opened the box, we discovered they were the wrong size. M Are you sure you didn't buy ²⁾the wrong size by mistake? W Yes, I double-checked before giving them to the clerk. M Do you have the receipt? W Here. It says "S" for small, but these are large. M You're right. Well, it looks like we gift-wrapped the wrong package. W Can I just exchange these for shirts in the correct size?	여 실례합니다. 어제 이 셔츠들을 샀는데요. 남 셔츠에 무슨 문제라도 있나요? 여 조카에게 줄 선물이었거든요, 그래서 점원에게 포장해 달라고 부탁했어요. 그런데 조카가 선물 상자를 열어봤을 때, 사이즈가 잘못됐다는 걸 알게 됐어요. 남 실수로 사이즈를 잘못 구매하신 건 아니신 거죠? 여 네, 점원에게 주기 전에 두 번이나 확인했어요. 남 영수증 가지고 계세요? 여 여기요. 영수증에는 스몰 사이즈라고 'S'가 쓰여 있지만, 셔츠는 라지 사이즈예요. 남 맞네요. 음, 저희가 선물 포장을 잘못한 것 같네요. 여 사이즈가 맞는 셔츠로 교환할 수 있을까요?

M	One moment. I need to ³⁾check the inventory. [Typing sound] I'm afraid we're all sold out of small shirts in this style.	남	잠깐만요. 재고를 확인해야 해요. [타자 치는 소리] 유감스럽지만, 이 스타일의 스몰 사이즈 셔츠는 다 팔렸네요.
W	That's very disappointing.	여	정말 실망스럽네요.
M	I'm sorry, ma'am. **But we do have other similar styles available.**	남	죄송합니다, 손님. 하지만 다른 비슷한 스타일은 구매하실 수 있습니다.
W	No, thanks. I'd like to ask for a refund.	여	됐어요. 환불을 요청하고 싶어요.

선택지 ① 그렇군요. 셔츠를 잘못된 상자에 넣은 것 같네요.
② 아, 정말요? 다 팔렸다고 하신 줄 알았는데요.
③ 괜찮아요. 그냥 포장만 제대로 해주시면 좋겠어요.
④ 됐어요. 환불을 요청하고 싶네유
⑤ 좋습니다. 라지 사이즈로 주세요.

잘못된 사이즈의 셔츠가 포장되어 손님이 가게로 찾아온 상황이다. 남자가 같은 스타일의 사이즈가 맞는 셔츠는 다 팔렸지만, 다른 비슷한 스타일은 구매할 수 있다고 말했으므로, 이에 대한 응답으로는 환불받겠다고 말하는 ④ 'No, thanks. I'd like to ask for a refund.'가 가장 적절하다.

어휘 clerk 뗑 점원 by mistake 실수로 receipt 뗑 영수증 say 통 ~이라고 쓰여 있다; 말하다 exchange 통 교환하다 inventory 뗑 재고 sold out 다 팔린

15 상황에 적절한 말 파악   정답 ②

| M | Jackie and Scott live in the same area. They are in different grades at school, so they don't know each other very well. However, Jackie recognizes Scott because they ¹⁾ride the same bus every day. She even knows that Scott gets off the bus at the stop right before hers. One afternoon ²⁾on the way home from school, Jackie notices that Scott has fallen asleep in his seat. Because she is about to get off the bus, she realizes that Scott has probably ³⁾missed his stop. **So Jackie wants to wake him up and tell him that he should exit the bus right away.** In this situation, what would Jackie most likely say to Scott? | 남 | Jackie와 Scott은 같은 지역에 살고 있습니다. 그들은 학년이 달라서, 서로를 잘 알지는 못합니다. 하지만 매일 같은 버스를 타기 때문에 Jackie는 Scott을 알아보기는 합니다. 그녀는 심지어 Scott이 그녀가 내리는 곳 바로 앞 정류장에서 내린다는 것도 알고 있습니다. 어느 날 오후 학교에서 집으로 돌아오는 길에, Jackie는 Scott이 앉은 자리에서 잠이 든 것을 알아차립니다. 그녀가 버스에서 막 내리려는 참이었기 때문에, 그녀는 Scott이 아마 그의 정류장을 지나쳤을 것임을 깨닫습니다. 그래서 Jackie는 그를 깨워서 당장 버스에서 내려야 한다고 말하고 싶습니다. 이러한 상황에서, Jackie가 Scott에게 가장 할 것 같은 말은 무엇입니까? |

선택지 ① 잠깐만! 난 지금 당장 내려야 해!
② 일어나! 넌 버스에서 내려야 해.
③ 걱정하지 마. 우리 여기서 집까지 걸어가는 건 어때?
④ 알겠어. 넌 어젯밤에 잠을 잘 못 잤나 보구나.
⑤ 실례할게. 우리 같은 학교에 다니지 않니?

Scott이 잠이 들어 버스에서 못 내린 것을 보고, Jackie는 그를 깨워서 당장 버스에서 내려야 한다고 알려주려 한다. 따라서, Jackie가 할 말로 ② 'Wake up! You need to get off the bus.'가 가장 적절하다.

어휘 recognize 통 알아보다 get off 내리다 fall asleep 잠이 들다 be about to 막 ~하려는 참이다 wake ~ up ~를 깨우다 exit 통 내리다, 나가다 뗑 출구

16-17 세트 문항   정답 16 ① 17 ③

| W | Hello, students. Although we usually think of colors as merely decorative, many have meanings tied to them. **So today, we're going to discuss the symbolic meanings of ¹⁾various colors in cultures around the world.** First, **purple** has been connected with wealth and power for centuries. This is because purple dye was ²⁾difficult to get in the past. Therefore, the dye was very expensive and was used for the clothes worn by royalty in places like ancient Rome. Next, **white** has different meanings depending on what part of the world you're in. In Western cultures, white is associated with ³⁾weddings and new beginnings since it is seen as pure. However, it is tied to funerals and death in many Eastern cultures. Thirdly, **brown** is often connected with the earth. It symbolizes safety and reliability as the earth supports living things. Lastly, there is **red**. This color stands for ⁴⁾passion and love in many cultures. But it's also used as a warning color since it catches attention easily. Now, let's watch a short related video. | 여 | 안녕하십니까, 학생 여러분. 우리는 보통 색깔을 단지 장식적인 것으로만 생각하지만, 많은 색깔에 그것과 관련된 의미가 있습니다. 그래서 오늘은 전 세계 문화권에서 다양한 색깔이 가지는 상징적 의미에 관해 논의할 것입니다. 첫째, 보라색은 수 세기 동안 부와 권력에 연관되어 왔습니다. 이는 과거엔 보라색 염료를 구하기 어려웠기 때문입니다. 그러므로 이 염료는 매우 비쌌고 고대 로마와 같은 곳에서는 왕족들이 입는 옷에 쓰였습니다. 다음으로, 흰색은 여러분이 어느 지역에 있는지에 따라 다른 의미를 가집니다. 서양의 문화권에서, 흰색은 순수한 것으로 여겨지기 때문에 결혼식 및 새로운 시작과 관련지어집니다. 하지만, 많은 동양의 문화권에서는 장례식 및 죽음과 관련됩니다. 세 번째로, 갈색은 종종 대지와 연관됩니다. 그것은 대지가 생명체를 지탱하듯이 안전과 신뢰성을 상징합니다. 마지막으로 빨간색이 있습니다. 이 색깔은 많은 문화권에서 열정과 사랑을 나타냅니다. 하지만 쉽게 주의를 끌기 때문에 경고하는 색깔로도 사용됩니다. 이제, 그럼 관련된 짧은 동영상을 보도록 하겠습니다. |

선택지 16 ① 다양한 색깔이 나타내는 것
② 색깔이 사람들의 감정에 끼치는 영향
③ 색깔 있는 옷이 개발된 방식
④ 문화적 의식에 있어서 색깔의 중요성
⑤ 어떤 색깔이 다른 색깔보다 인기가 많은 이유
17 ① 보라색 ② 흰색 ③ 검은색 ④ 갈색 ⑤ 빨간색

16 전 세계 문화권에서 다양한 색깔이 가지는 상징적 의미에 관해 논의하고 있으므로 여자가 하는 말의 주제로 ① 'what different colors stand for'가 가장 적절하다.
17 보라색, 흰색, 갈색, 빨간색은 언급했지만 ③ 'black'은 언급하지 않았다.

어휘 merely 뷰 단지 decorative 혱 장식적인, 장식의 tied to ~과 관련된 symbolic 혱 상징적인 be connected with ~에 연관되다 dye 뗑 염료 통 염색하다 royalty 뗑 왕족
depending on ~에 따라 be associated with ~과 관련지어지다 funeral 뗑 장례식 reliability 뗑 신뢰성 stand for ~을 나타내다 catch attention 주의를 끌다

1	④	2	①	3	②	4	⑤	5	②	6	③	7	①	8	②	9	②	10	③
11	⑤	12	①	13	③	14	⑤	15	①	16	④	17	④						

• 각 문제의 정답 근거는 굵은 글씨로, Dictation 정답은 밑줄로 표시되어 있습니다.

---

1 목적 파악

정답 ④

M Hello, residents! This is an announcement from the Riverside Hill Apartment Committee. We have discovered a damaged pipe in the basement, which needs to 1)be replaced immediately. **So please be aware that the water will be turned off from 10 a.m. to 1 p.m. today.** We are sorry that we didn't announce this earlier. However, the leak will 2)reduce water pressure throughout the complex if we don't replace the pipe right away. Anyone who will need water during those hours should fill up their sink or bathtub beforehand. If the work takes 3)less time than expected to finish, the water will be turned back on earlier. Thank you in advance for your cooperation.

남 안녕하십니까, 주민 여러분! 리버사이드 힐 아파트 위원회에서 안내 말씀드립니다. 지하실에서 파손된 파이프를 발견했으며, 즉시 교체해야 합니다. 그러므로 오늘 오전 10시부터 오후 1시까지 단수되는 점을 알아두시기 바랍니다. 더 일찍 알리지 못해서 죄송합니다. 하지만 파이프를 바로 교체하지 않으면 누수로 인해 단지 전체의 수압이 감소할 것입니다. 그 시간 동안 물이 필요하신 분은 싱크대나 욕조에 미리 물을 채워 두셔야 합니다. 만약 작업을 끝내는 데 예상보다 시간이 덜 걸린다면, 더 일찍 물이 다시 나올 것입니다. 여러분의 협조에 미리 감사드립니다.

남자가 지하실에서 파손된 파이프를 발견하여 즉시 교체해야 한다면서, 오늘 오전 10시부터 오후 1시까지 단수가 된다는 점을 안내하고 있다. 따라서, 남자가 하는 말의 목적으로 ④ '긴급 단수 조치를 공지하려고'가 가장 적절하다.

어휘 resident 휑 주민, 거주자 aware 휑 알고 있는 immediately 휑 즉시 leak 휑 누수 reduce 통 감소하다 water pressure 수압 complex 휑 단지 휑 복잡한 fill up ~을 채우다 beforehand 휑 미리 in advance 미리 cooperation 휑 협조

---

2 의견 파악

정답 ①

M Honey, how was yoga class?
W Great, but I might need to buy my own mat.
M Don't they have mats you can use at the studio?
W Well, I want to practice at home. **Stretching is 1)better for your health if you do it every day.**
M Oh, did your instructor recommend that?
W Right. She said the benefits would increase if I stretched on my own for a few minutes daily.
M Is that so?
W Yeah, and it's 2)more effective to build up your flexibility slowly. It reduces the chance of injury.
M That makes sense.
W She also mentioned that it helped increase blood flow, so my muscles will recover from workouts faster.
M Then, why don't you order a yoga mat online so you can 3)start stretching more often?
W Yeah. I think I'll do that now.

남 여보, 요가 강습은 어땠어?
여 좋았어, 그런데 내 매트를 사야 할지도 몰라.
남 강습실에서 쓸 수 있는 매트가 있지 않아?
여 음, 집에서 연습하고 싶거든. 스트레칭은 매일 하는 게 더 건강에 좋아.
남 아, 강사님이 그걸 추천해줬어?
여 맞아. 매일 몇 분씩 스스로 스트레칭을 하면 더 이득이라고 했어.
남 정말 그래?
여 응, 그리고 유연성을 천천히 강화하는 게 더 효과적이야. 부상의 가능성을 줄여주거든.
남 일리가 있네.
여 또한 그게 혈류를 증가시키는 데 도움이 되어서, 내 근육이 운동 후에 더 빨리 회복될 거라고도 했어.
남 그렇다면, 스트레칭을 더 자주 할 수 있도록 온라인으로 요가 매트를 주문하는 게 어때?
여 응. 지금 해야 할 것 같아.

왜 요가 매트를 사려고 하는지 묻는 남자에게 여자가 집에서 요가를 연습하고 싶고, 스트레칭은 매일 하는 것이 건강에 좋다고 했다. 따라서, 여자의 의견으로 ① '매일 스트레칭을 하면 건강에 좋다.'가 가장 적절하다.

어휘 studio 휑 강습실, 연습실 benefit 휑 이득, 이익 on one's own 자기 스스로 build up 강화하다 flexibility 휑 유연성 chance 휑 가능성 injury 휑 부상; 손상 blood flow 혈류 recover 통 회복하다 workout 휑 운동

---

3 관계 파악

정답 ②

M Good evening, Lisa. Are you looking for a new book of poetry to read?
W Not today, Andy. Actually, I wanted to speak with you.
M What did you want to talk about?
W 1)My news website hands out an annual award to the best local businesses. Our readers selected your shop as their favorite.
M What's the award?

남 좋은 밤이에요, Lisa. 읽을 만한 새로운 시집을 찾고 있나요?
여 오늘은 아니에요, Andy. 사실, 당신과 이야기하고 싶었어요.
남 무슨 이야기를 하고 싶으셨나요?
여 저희 뉴스 웹사이트는 매년 최고의 지역 기업에게 상을 나눠줘요. 독자들이 당신의 가게를 가장 좋아하는 가게로 선택했어요.
남 상이 뭔가요?

W	It's the Business of the Year Award. And I'm not surprised you won! **Your shop has always been the best place to find** 2)**new and used books**.	여	올해의 비즈니스상이에요. 그리고 당신이 수상한 게 놀랍지는 않아요! 당신의 가게는 항상 새 책과 중고 책을 찾기 위한 최고의 장소였어요.
M	Thanks for saying that. So are you going to write an article about the store?	남	그렇게 말해줘서 고마워요. 그럼 가게에 대한 기사를 쓰실 건가요?
W	Exactly. **We'd like to interview you about how you** 3)**run the store and take some pictures.**	여	정확해요. 가게 운영 방식에 대해 인터뷰를 하고 사진을 좀 찍고 싶어요.
M	Would this be posted on your site's front page?	남	이게 사이트의 첫 페이지에 게시되나요?
W	That's right! **It would be** 4)**the first thing our readers would see.**	여	맞아요! 우리 독자들이 가장 처음으로 볼 기사가 될 거예요.
M	That's exciting! I'd be happy to give an interview. Can you come by the shop tomorrow around 9 a.m.?	남	신나는 일이네요! 기꺼이 인터뷰를 하겠습니다. 내일 오전 9시쯤 잠깐 가게에 들를 수 있나요?
W	Sure. I'll see you then!	여	물론이죠. 그럼 그때 봬요!

두 사람이 올해의 비즈니스상을 받게 된 남자의 가게에 관해 이야기하고 있다. 남자의 가게는 새 책과 중고 책을 찾기 위한 최고의 장소라고 했고, 여자는 인터뷰를 기사로 써서 뉴스 웹사이트에 게시할 것이라고 하는 것으로 보아 두 사람의 관계로 ② '서점 주인 — 인터넷 신문 기자'가 가장 적절하다.

[어휘] hand out ~을 나눠주다 local 웹 지역의 select 통 선택하다 be happy to 기꺼이 ~하다 give an interview 인터뷰를 하다 come by 잠깐 들르다

---

4 그림 내용 불일치 파악 　　　　　　　　　　　　　　정답 ⑤

W	How is the redecoration work in the hotel lounge going, Mr. Mendes?	여	호텔 라운지 재단장 작업은 어떻게 진행되고 있나요, Mendes 씨?
M	I think we're almost finished, Ms. Thompson. Here, I can show you. [Pause] I just installed the two-tone curtain you requested.	남	거의 끝난 것 같아요, Thompson 씨. 여기, 보여드릴 수 있어요. [잠시 멈춤] 요청하신 두 가지 색으로 된 커튼을 방금 설치했어요.
W	They make the room look 1)a lot more modern. The chandelier is gorgeous, too.	여	공간을 훨씬 더 현대적으로 보이게 하네요. 샹들리에도 아주 멋져요.
M	Thanks! I think your guests will really appreciate these armchairs.	남	감사합니다! 투숙객들이 이 안락의자를 정말 높이 평가할 거예요.
W	Those do 2)look quite comfortable. But will they be able to eat and drink here?	여	꽤 편안해 보이네요. 하지만 그들이 여기서 먹고 마실 수 있을까요?
M	We can move the vase with the flowers 3)off the round table to make more room.	남	원탁에서 꽃이 있는 꽃병을 옮겨서 더 많은 공간을 만들 수 있어요.
W	Yes, let's do that.	여	네, 그렇게 합시다.
M	I will. **What do you think of** 4)**having the piano there in the corner?**	남	그럴게요. 저기 구석에 피아노가 있는 건 어떻게 생각하세요?
W	That's perfect. We're planning to have jazz music performances here.	여	완벽해요. 이곳에서 재즈 음악 공연을 할 계획이거든요.
M	Would you like to see what we've done with the spa as well?	남	스파도 어떻게 했는지 보시겠어요?
W	Certainly. Let's go.	여	물론이죠. 갑시다.

대화에서 남자가 구석에 피아노가 있는 건 어떻게 생각하는지를 물었는데, ⑤에는 드럼이 그려져 있다.

[어휘] install 통 설치하다 two-tone 웹 두 가지 색으로 된 room 명 공간; 방 modern 웹 현대적인 gorgeous 웹 아주 멋진 appreciate 통 ~을 높이 평가하다; 진가를 인정하다
armchair 명 안락의자 as well ~도, 또한

---

5 할 일 파악 　　　　　　　　　　　　　　　　　정답 ②

M	Joyce, you're studying here, too! When did you get to the library?	남	Joyce, 너도 여기서 공부하고 있었구나! 도서관에 언제 도착했어?
W	Early this morning. I'm working on the social studies report. Did you finish yours?	여	오늘 아침 일찍. 난 사회학 보고서를 작성하고 있는데. 넌 끝냈니?
M	I turned it in yesterday. It's 1)due tomorrow, right?	남	어제 제출했어. 내일까지잖아, 그렇지?
W	Yes, but I still have a lot of work to do on it.	여	응, 하지만 난 아직 할 게 많아.
M	Do you want me to help you with the report?	남	내가 보고서 작성하는 거 도와줄까?
W	No, thanks. It will be faster to 2)do it myself.	여	됐어. 내가 직접 하는 게 더 빠를 거야.
M	I understand. Well, it's time for lunch. Did you bring anything to eat?	남	이해해. 음, 점심 먹을 시간이야. 뭐 먹을 거 가지고 왔어?
W	No. I didn't pack anything.	여	아니. 아무것도 안 챙겼어.
M	**I'm heading to the cafeteria now. Should I pick something up for you?**	남	지금 구내식당으로 갈 건데. 뭐 좀 사다 줄까?
W	**It would be really nice if I had** 3)**something light to eat**, like a salad or a sandwich.	여	샐러드나 샌드위치 같은 가벼운 걸 먹으면 정말 좋을 것 같아.
M	Sure. I can do that now.	남	물론이지. 지금 사다 줄 수 있어.
W	One second, let me get you some money.	여	잠시만, 돈 좀 줄게.
M	Don't worry about it. You can pay me back later.	남	그건 걱정하지 마. 나중에 갚아도 돼.
W	Thanks!	여	고마워!

도서관에서 우연히 만난 두 사람이 점심을 어떻게 할지에 대해 이야기하고 있다. 구내식당에서 먹을거리를 사다 줄지 묻는 남자에게 여자가 샐러드나 샌드위치 같은 가벼운 것을 먹으면 정말 좋을 것 같다고 하자, 남자가 지금 사다 줄 수 있다고 했으므로 남자가 할 일로 ② '먹을거리 사 오기'가 가장 적절하다.

[어휘] social studies 사회학 turn ~ in ~을 제출하다 pack 통 챙기다, 싸다 head to ~로 가다 pick ~ up ~을 사다 pay back 갚다

6 금액 정보 파악

정답 ③

[Telephone rings.]	[전화기가 울린다.]

W Deluxe Airways. How can I help you?

M Hi. I'd like to book [1)]two round-trip tickets to Kansas City for March 5th.

W Will that be economy class, sir?

M Yes, please. I [2)]am traveling with my son who is seven years old. Can you tell me how much his ticket will be discounted?

W It's $160 for a round-trip ticket for an adult and 50% off that rate for a child under eight.

M Alright. I'll take one adult ticket and [3)]one for a child. And I'd like to use my frequent flyer miles.

W Sure. Can I ask for your name?

M It's Samuel Mann. M-A-N-N.

W Okay. [Typing sound] It looks like you can save $50 [4)]on the total if you use all of them.

M Sure. That's fine.

W I'll need your ID number to book the ticket.

M Just a moment. I'll get my passport.

여 Deluxe Airways입니다. 무엇을 도와드릴까요?

남 안녕하세요. 3월 5일 캔자스시티행 왕복표 두 장을 예약하고 싶은데요.

여 이코노미 클래스로 하시겠습니까?

남 네, 부탁합니다. 저는 일곱 살 난 아들과 함께 갈 거예요. 아들의 티켓이 얼마나 할인되는지 알려주실래요?

여 성인 왕복표는 160달러이고 여덟 살 미만 어린이는 그 요금에서 50% 할인됩니다.

남 알겠습니다. 성인 한 장과 어린이 한 장 주세요. 그리고 제 항공 마일리지를 쓰고 싶어요.

여 물론입니다. 성함을 여쭤봐도 될까요?

남 Samuel Mann입니다. M-A-N-N입니다.

여 알겠습니다. [타자 치는 소리] 전부 사용하시면 총 50달러를 아끼실 수 있을 것 같군요.

남 네. 좋아요.

여 표를 예매하려면 신분증 번호가 필요합니다.

남 잠깐만요. 여권을 가져올게요.

남자가 성인 왕복표 한 장($160)과, 반값으로 할인되는 어린이 표 한 장($160×0.5=$80)을 구매했고, 항공 마일리지를 전부 사용($240-$50=$190) 했으므로 정답은 ③ '$190'이다.

어휘 round-trip 형 왕복의 rate 명 요금; 속도 frequent flyer miles 항공 마일리지 Just a moment. 잠깐만요. passport 명 여권

7 이유 파악

정답 ①

W Hey, George. I didn't see you at the robotics club meeting. Are you doing okay?

M I'm fine, Melanie. Actually, I've decided to leave the club.

W Oh, did you [1)]need more time to study for the college entrance exam? I know the club takes up a lot of time.

M That wasn't really a factor for me.

W So you're just not interested in robots anymore?

M No! I really enjoy making robots. But I'm going to volunteer at [2)]the local animal shelter after school instead.

W Oh, that's cool. I know you want to be a vet one day.

M Exactly. The work is more important to me.

W I see. Well, will you still [3)]have time for the school band?

M Certainly! The schedules won't conflict.

W Okay, that's good to hear.

여 안녕, George. 로봇 동아리 모임에서 너를 못 봤네. 잘 지내고 있지?

남 잘 지내, Melanie. 사실, 나는 그 동아리를 탈퇴하기로 결정했어.

여 아, 대학 입학시험을 위해 공부할 시간이 더 필요했니? 그 동아리가 많은 시간을 차지하는 건 알고 있어.

남 그건 나한테는 별로 중요한 요인이 아니었어.

여 그러면 그냥 더 이상 로봇에 관심이 없는 거야?

남 아니! 나는 로봇 만드는 걸 정말 좋아해. 하지만 방과 후에 대신 지역 동물 보호소에서 자원봉사를 할 거야.

여 오, 멋지다. 내가 알기로 넌 언젠가 수의사가 되고 싶어 하잖아.

남 맞아. 나에게는 그 일이 더 중요해.

여 그렇구나. 음, 그런데도 학교 밴드를 할 시간은 있어?

남 물론이지! 일정이 겹치지 않을 거야.

여 알겠어, 잘됐네.

남자는 로봇 동아리를 탈퇴하려고 결정했다고 하면서 대신 지역 동물 보호소에서 자원봉사를 할 것이라고 말했으므로, 남자가 동아리를 탈퇴하려는 이유는 ① '동물 보호소에서 봉사활동을 하기로 해서'이다.

어휘 college entrance exam 대학 입학시험 take up (시간·공간을) 차지하다 animal shelter 동물 보호소 vet 명 수의사 still 부 그런데도; 아직 conflict 동 겹치다; 충돌하다

8 언급 유무 파악

정답 ②

M Do you have any plans for the weekend, Cheryl?

W Hey, Karl. Actually, I was planning to go to the International Food Festival. Do you want to come along?

M Oh, when is that?

W It takes place on [1)]October 10th and 11th through the afternoon and early evening. I'm going on the 10th.

M Haven't you been to that before?

W Yeah, I try to go every year! They always have a wide variety of [2)]food options. I want to try the dumplings from Uzbekistan this time.

M Nice. How much is it to get in?

W Tickets are free, but you have to [3)]pay for the food.

M Other than food, is there any entertainment?

W Yeah. There will be dance performances and a magic show.

남 주말에 계획 있니, Cheryl?

여 안녕, Karl. 실은, International Food Festival에 갈 계획이었어. 함께 갈래?

남 아, 그게 언제야?

여 10월 10일과 11일 오후와 초저녁 내내 열릴 거야. 나는 10일에 가려고.

남 전에 가본 적 있지 않아?

여 응, 매년 가려고 해! 항상 매우 다양한 음식 선택지가 있거든. 나는 이번에 우즈베키스탄의 만두를 먹어보고 싶어.

남 좋은걸. 입장료는 얼마야?

여 표는 무료지만, 음식값은 내야 해.

남 음식 외에 오락거리가 있어?

여 응. 춤 공연과 마술 쇼가 있을 거야.

M That sounds fun. Alright, I'm coming! Why don't we meet there at noon?	남 재미있을 것 같아. 좋아, 나도 갈게! 정오에 거기서 만나는 게 어때?
W Sounds like a plan.	여 좋은 생각이야.

행사 기간(10월 10일과 11일), 판매 음식(우즈베키스탄 만두), 입장료(무료), 공연 종류(춤 공연, 마술 쇼)에 대해 언급했고, ② '행사 장소'는 언급하지 않았다.

어휘 come along 함께 가다 a wide variety of 매우 다양한 other than ~ 외에 entertainment 명 오락거리, 환대 Sounds like a plan. 좋은 생각이야

---

9 내용 불일치 파악 　　　　정답 ②

W Hello, KESP Radio listeners. Local charities are putting together an event called Relay for Life to raise funds ¹⁾for <u>victims</u> of last month's flood. Many residents in the area lost their homes and possessions. We hope to help them ²⁾<u>get</u> <u>a</u> <u>new</u> <u>start</u>. **The event will be held on September 7th, starting at 10 a.m.** It will include both a 10-kilometer race and 5-kilometer walk. While only adults can take part in the 10-kilometer race, the 5-kilometer walk doesn't have ³⁾<u>an</u> <u>age</u> <u>limit</u>. A map showing the routes for both is posted on our website. Several local companies have generously agreed to donate $100 for ⁴⁾<u>every</u> <u>person</u> <u>that</u> <u>joins</u>. So the more people that participate, the more help we can provide. We expect you to sign up. Thank you.	여 안녕하세요, KESP 라디오 청취자 여러분. 지역 자선 단체에서 지난달 홍수 이재민들을 위한 기금을 모으기 위해 Relay for Life라는 행사를 준비하고 있습니다. 이 지역의 많은 주민들이 집과 재산을 잃었습니다. 저희는 그들이 새로운 시작을 할 수 있도록 돕고 싶습니다. 행사는 9월 7일 오전 10시에 시작될 예정입니다. 10km 달리기와 5km 걷기가 모두 포함됩니다. 성인만 10km 달리기에 참가할 수 있는 것에 반해, 5km 걷기에는 연령 제한이 없습니다. 두 경주의 경로를 보여주는 지도가 저희 웹사이트에 게시되어 있습니다. 몇몇 지역 기업들은 참가하는 사람 한 명당 100달러를 기부하기로 관대하게 합의했습니다. 그래서 참여하는 사람이 더 많을수록, 저희는 더 많은 도움을 줄 수 있습니다. 여러분이 등록해 주시길 바랍니다. 감사합니다.

홍수 이재민을 위한 기금을 모으기 위해 열리는 달리기와 걷기 행사에 대한 라디오 방송이다. 여자가 행사는 9월 7일 오전 10시에 시작될 예정이라고 했으므로 ② '9월 7일 오전 9시에 시작될 예정이다.'는 내용과 일치하지 않는다.

어휘 charity 명 자선 단체; 자선 raise funds 기금을 모으다 possession 명 재산; 소유 race 명 달리기; 경주 while 접 ~에 반하여, ~하는 동안 take part in ~에 참가하다 route 명 경로, 길 generously 부 관대하게 donate 동 기부하다

---

10 도표 정보 파악 　　　　정답 ③

W I've been shopping for a new gaming mouse, but I can't make up my mind. Can you help me, Paul?	여 새 게임용 마우스를 사려고 쇼핑을 하고 있는데, 결단을 못 내리겠어. 나 좀 도와줄래, Paul?
M Sure. Do you ¹⁾<u>have</u> <u>a</u> <u>list</u> <u>of</u> <u>models</u> you're interested in?	남 물론이지. 관심 있는 제품들 목록이 있니?
W Yeah. Here's what I've been looking at.	여 응. 여기 내가 보고 있던 거야.
M Do you have strong preference about color?	남 색깔에 대한 확실한 선호가 있니?
W **I'd love a red mouse, but white will be good, too.**	여 빨간색 마우스가 좋지만, 흰색도 좋을 것 같아.
M Okay, then you should consider whether you want ²⁾<u>a</u> <u>wireless</u> <u>mouse</u>. So do you really dislike having a cord?	남 좋아, 그럼 무선 마우스를 원하는지 생각해봐야 해. 그러니까 줄이 있는 건 정말 싫으니?
W It does get annoying. I want my desk to have a cleaner look.	여 그건 진짜 성가셔. 내 책상이 좀 더 깨끗해 보이면 좋겠고.
M **Well, then you should get a mouse that doesn't have one.**	남 음, 그러면 줄이 없는 마우스를 사야겠네.
W I agree. Then, there are three options left.	여 동의해. 그러면 세 가지 선택지가 남아 있어.
M **Let's consider side buttons.**	남 측면 버튼을 생각해 보자.
W **I'd like mine to have ³⁾<u>two</u> <u>of</u> <u>them</u>.**	여 그게 두 개가 있으면 좋겠어.
M I see. Now, price seems like the final deciding factor.	남 그렇구나. 이제 가격이 마지막 결정 요소인 것 같아.
W Yeah, that's a big difference. **I'll go with the cheaper one.**	여 맞아, 차이가 많이 나네. 좀 더 저렴한 걸 선택할래.

여자는 색깔이 빨간색이나 흰색이면서, 무선이고, 측면 버튼이 2개가 있는 것 중에서, 더 저렴한 게임용 마우스를 골랐다.

어휘 make up one's mind 결단을 내리다 strong 형 확실한; 강한 preference 명 선호 wireless 형 무선의 cord 명 줄 dislike 동 싫어하다 annoying 형 성가신 go with ~을 선택하다

---

11 짧은 대화의 응답 파악 　　　　정답 ⑤

W Daniel, you're joining the swim team next year, right? Do you know when ¹⁾<u>the</u> <u>team</u> <u>practices</u>?	여 Daniel, 내년에 수영 팀에 들어가는 거지, 그렇지? 팀 연습이 언제인지 아니?
M It's before school. **So I'll have to be at the pool by 6:30 a.m.**	남 학교 가기 전이야. 그래서 오전 6시 30분까지 수영장에 도착해야 할 거야.
W **Wow. You must have to ²⁾<u>wake</u> <u>up</u> <u>early</u> to do that!**	여 우와. 그러기 위해서는 틀림없이 일찍 일어나야겠다!
M <u>Seriously. I won't be able to stay up late like I usually do.</u>	남 정말. 평소처럼 늦게까지 깨어 있을 수 없을 거야.
	선택지 ① 알았어. 그럼 일찍 출발하는 게 좋겠어.
	② 그렇지 않아. 우리는 보통 오후에 연습해.
	③ 고마워. 너는 수영을 꽤 잘하는구나.
	④ 아니. 너는 사실 거의 비슷한 시간에 일어나도 돼.
	⑤ 정말. 평소처럼 늦게까지 깨어 있을 수 없을 거야.

남자가 오전 6시 30분까지 수영장에 도착해야 한다고 하자 여자가 그러기 위해서는 일찍 일어나야겠다고 했으므로, 이에 대한 응답으로는 공감하는 말을 하는 ⑤ 'Seriously. I won't be able to stay up late like I usually do.'가 가장 적절하다.

어휘 pool 명 수영장 stay up late 늦게까지 깨어 있다

12 짧은 대화의 응답 파악

정답 ①

M Jenny, do you want to go for a walk in the park this afternoon?	남 Jenny, 오늘 오후에 공원으로 산책하러 갈래?
W I'd love to, but I have 1)a driving lesson at 2 p.m.	여 그러고 싶지만, 오후 2시에 운전 강습이 있어.
M **Oh, are you** 2)**planning to get your driver's license?**	남 아, 운전면허증을 딸 계획이야?
W Right. My goal is to pass the exam this year.	여 맞아. 내 목표는 올해 시험에 합격하는 거야.

선택지
① 맞아. 내 목표는 올해 시험에 합격하는 거야.
② 물론이지. 하지만 거기는 주차 공간을 찾기가 어려워.
③ 맞아. 거기까지 차로 두 시간 걸릴 거야.
④ 모르겠어. 오늘 오후에는 교통 체증이 매우 심하네.
⑤ 그러고 싶어. 내가 10분 후에 너를 데리러 가는 건 어때?

여자가 운전 강습이 있어서 산책하러 가지 못한다고 하자 남자가 운전면허증을 딸 계획인지 물었으므로, 이에 대한 응답으로는 맞다고 답하는 ① 'Right. My goal is to pass the exam this year.'가 가장 적절하다.

어휘 go for a walk 산책하다 would love to ~하고 싶다 driver's license 운전면허증

13 긴 대화의 응답 파악

정답 ③

[Doorbell rings.]	[초인종이 울린다.]
W Are you ready to head out?	여 출발할 준비 됐어?
M To 1)the fireworks show? Doesn't it start at 7?	남 불꽃놀이 쇼에? 그거 7시에 시작하지 않아?
W Yeah, but I was planning to drop by Debra's house first.	여 응, 하지만 먼저 Debra의 집에 잠깐 들를 계획이었어.
M What for? That's pretty out of the way.	남 뭐 때문에? 꽤 멀잖아.
W I want to 2)borrow her camera to take pictures of the fireworks.	여 불꽃놀이 사진을 찍기 위해 그녀의 카메라를 빌리고 싶거든.
M Why don't you use your phone?	남 네 휴대폰을 쓰는 건 어때?
W It's hard to take good photos of fireworks with a phone.	여 휴대폰으로는 불꽃놀이 사진을 잘 찍기가 어려워.
M Then, you can borrow my camera.	남 그럼 내 카메라를 빌려도 돼.
W Don't you want to 3)take pictures yourself?	여 넌 직접 사진을 찍고 싶지 않니?
M I wasn't planning to.	남 그럴 계획은 없었어.
W Thanks!	여 고마워!
M So I guess we don't have to rush out, right?	남 그럼 서둘러 나갈 필요는 없겠네, 그렇지?
W **Well, I still want to get there early so that we can get a good place to sit.**	여 음, 그래도 우리가 앉을 좋은 자리를 구할 수 있도록 거기에 일찍 도착하고 싶어.
M **Alright. Just** 4)**give me a few minutes to get dressed and grab my camera.**	남 알겠어. 옷을 입고 카메라를 챙기게 잠깐만 기다려줘.
W No worries. I will wait here in the meantime.	여 걱정하지 마. 그동안에 나는 여기서 기다릴게.

선택지
① 그래? 사진 찍으려면 네 휴대폰을 써도 돼.
② 확실해? 네가 집에 있고 싶어 하는 줄 알았어.
③ 걱정하지 마. 그동안에 나는 여기서 기다릴게.
④ 괜찮아. 우리는 거기에 일찍 도착할 필요가 없어.
⑤ 좋은 생각이야. 내가 카메라도 가지고 갈게.

불꽃놀이 쇼에 갈 준비를 하는 상황에서 여자가 좋은 자리를 구할 수 있도록 일찍 도착하고 싶다고 하자 남자가 옷을 입고 카메라를 챙기게 잠시만 기다려달라고 했으므로, 이에 대한 응답으로는 기다리겠다고 말하는 ③ 'No worries. I will wait here in the meantime.'이 가장 적절하다.

어휘 head out 출발하다 firework 명 불꽃놀이 drop by 잠깐 들르다 out of the way (거리가) 먼 rush out 서둘러 나가다 get dressed 옷을 입다 in the meantime 그동안에

14 긴 대화의 응답 파악

정답 ⑤

[Telephone rings.]	[전화기가 울린다.]
M Hello. You've reached Burton Travel Agency.	남 안녕하세요. Burton Travel Agency입니다.
W Hi. I'm considering going to France for the first week of October.	여 안녕하세요. 10월 첫째 주에 프랑스에 갈까 생각 중이에요.
M 1)What kind of tour are you interested in?	남 어떤 유형의 관광에 관심이 있으세요?
W I want a tour that visits places that people don't really know about.	여 사람들이 잘 모르는 곳을 방문하는 관광을 하고 싶어요.
M Ah, you mean, the hidden France. That's our specialty!	남 아, 숨겨진 프랑스 말이군요. 그게 저희 전문입니다!
W Great. Can you recommend 2)specific tour programs?	여 좋아요. 구체적인 관광 프로그램을 추천해 주시겠어요?
M We have two popular package tours. One involves visiting wineries. The other involves hiking in the countryside.	남 인기 있는 패키지 관광이 두 개 있어요. 하나는 포도주 양조장 방문을 포함하고 있고요. 다른 하나는 시골에서 하이킹 하는 것이 포함돼 있어요.
W Both sound interesting. Is it possible to try both of them?	여 둘 다 흥미롭게 들리네요. 둘 다 시도해 볼 수 있나요?
M Sure. We also 3)provide customized tours.	남 물론이죠. 저희는 맞춤형 관광도 제공해요.
W Interesting. But can I get some more information about the package tours beforehand?	여 흥미롭군요. 그런데 패키지 관광에 대한 정보를 미리 좀 더 얻을 수 있을까요?

M Certainly. If you give me your e-mail address, I can ⁴⁾send the itineraries.

W Of course. It's jdbaker@softmail.com. **Should I call again to book a tour?**

M That's fine. Or you can contact me by e-mail.

남 물론이죠. 이메일 주소를 알려주시면 여행 일정표를 보내드릴 수 있어요

여 그럼요. jdbaker@softmail.com입니다. 관광 예약을 하려면 다시 전화해야 하나요?

남 그러면 좋죠. 또는 이메일로 연락하셔도 됩니다.

선택지 ① 좋네요. 패키지 비용은 얼마인가요?

② 물론입니다. 예약 확인 번호는 2827입니다.

③ 확실한가요? 전 아직 여행 일정표를 받지 못했어요.

④ 다시 한번 감사드려요. 지침 주신 게 정말 도움이 됐어요.

⑤ 그러면 좋죠. 또는 이메일로 연락하셔도 됩니다.

프랑스 관광을 하려고 여행사에 전화하여 문의하는 상황이다. 여자가 여행 일정표를 받기 위해 이메일 주소를 알려주면서 관광 예약을 하려면 다시 전화해야 하는지 물었으므로, 이에 대한 응답으로는 전화나 이메일로 연락하라고 말하는 ⑤ 'That's fine. Or you can contact me by e-mail.'이 가장 적절하다.

어휘 specialty 뗑 전문, 본업 specific 휑 구체적인 involve 통 포함하다, 수반하다 winery 뗑 포도주 양조장 countryside 뗑 시골 customized 휑 맞춤형의, 주문 제작의 beforehand 뿐 미리, 전부터 itinerary 뗑 여행 일정표 confirmation 뗑 확인

15 상황에 적절한 말 파악   정답 ①

W Martin and Jean are classmates in a high school chemistry class. Each student ¹⁾normally works with a partner during experiments. Today, however, Martin's lab partner was feeling sick and did not come to school. As the teacher explains the experiment of the day, Jean notices that Martin has no one to work with. He looks a little worried about doing the ²⁾complicated experiment alone. She knows that it will be difficult for Martin to do the assignment by himself. **So she wants to suggest that Martin ask for the teacher's ³⁾permission to join her and her partner during today's class.** In this situation, what would Jean most likely say to Martin?

여 Martin과 Jean은 고등학교 화학 수업을 같이 듣는 반 친구입니다. 실험하는 동안에는 각 학생은 보통 파트너와 함께 작업합니다. 하지만 오늘 Martin의 실험 파트너는 몸이 아파서 학교에 오지 않았습니다. 선생님이 오늘의 실험에 대해 설명할 때, Jean은 Martin이 함께 작업할 사람이 없다는 것을 알아차립니다. 그는 복잡한 실험을 혼자 하는 것에 대해 약간 걱정하는 것처럼 보입니다. 그녀는 Martin이 혼자서 그 과제를 하는 것이 어려우리라는 것을 알고 있습니다. 그래서, 그녀는 Martin에게 오늘 수업 동안 그녀랑 그녀의 파트너와 함께 할 수 있도록 선생님께 허락을 구하라고 제안하고 싶습니다. 이러한 상황에서, Jean이 Martin에게 가장 할 것 같은 말은 무엇입니까?

선택지 ① 오늘 선생님께 우리 같이 작업하게 해 달라고 부탁하는 게 어때?

② 보통, 화학 문제는 보기만큼 어렵지 않아.

③ 선생님의 지시 사항을 다시 한번 말해줄래?

④ 몸이 안 좋으면 언제든지 보건실에 가도 돼.

⑤ 우리가 그에게 함께 실험을 하자고 요청해야 한다고 생각하니?

Martin이 실험 파트너가 없어 혼자 복잡한 실험을 해야 함을 걱정하는 것을 보고, Jean은 수업 동안 함께 실험할 수 있도록 선생님께 허락을 구하라고 제안하려 한다. 따라서, Jean이 할 말로 ① 'How about asking our teacher to let us work together today?'가 가장 적절하다.

어휘 normally 뿐 보통, 보통 때는 experiment 뗑 실험 lab 뗑 실험; 연구실 complicated 휑 복잡한 by oneself 혼자서 permission 뗑 허락 instruction 뗑 지시 사항; 가르침

16-17 세트 문항   정답 16 ④ 17 ④

M Welcome back, everyone. Last time, I mentioned that the way hosts treat their guests is changing. **Today, I want to discuss some of the ways that dining etiquette ¹⁾varies in different cultures.** First, in **China**, guests always leave a small amount of food on their plate. Eating everything would suggest that the host did not provide enough food, which would be considered quite rude. Second, people in **India** famously eat with their right hand only. This etiquette rule began because of ²⁾a traditional belief that the left hand was dirty. Third, table manners in **Chile** are quite formal. People there use a knife and fork to eat everything. Even finger foods like tacos and pizza are often eaten with utensils. Lastly, people of **Spain** ³⁾consider it important that the meal last a long time. Eating too quickly or trying to rush out of a restaurant after finishing a meal is considered bad manners. Now, does anyone have any other examples they'd like to share with the class?

남 돌아오신 걸 환영합니다, 여러분. 지난번에 저는 주인이 손님을 대접하는 방식이 바뀌고 있다고 말했습니다. 오늘은 문화권에 따라 달라지는 몇몇 식사 예절에 대해 논의하고자 합니다. 첫째, 중국에서 손님들은 항상 접시에 소량의 음식을 남깁니다. 다 먹는 것은 주인이 충분한 음식을 제공하지 않았다는 것을 암시할 것이고, 이는 꽤 무례하게 여겨질 것입니다. 둘째, 인도 사람들은 오른손으로만 먹는 것으로 유명합니다. 이 예절 원칙은 왼손이 불결하다는 전통적인 믿음 때문에 시작되었습니다. 셋째, 칠레의 식사 예절은 상당히 격식을 차립니다. 그곳 사람들은 모든 것을 먹는 데에 나이프와 포크를 사용합니다. 심지어 타코와 피자 같은 손으로 집어먹는 음식도 종종 식기로 먹습니다. 마지막으로, 스페인 사람들은 식사가 오래 지속되는 것을 중요하게 생각합니다. 음식을 너무 빨리 먹거나 식사를 마친 후에 식당에서 서둘러 나가려고 하는 것은 나쁜 예절로 여겨집니다. 자, 학급 학생들과 공유하고 싶은 다른 사례가 있는 사람이 있나요?

선택지 16 ① 사람들이 음식을 제공하는 독특한 방식

② 음식과 관련된 다양한 관습이 시작된 방식

③ 식사 예절이 바뀌는 이유

④ 문화 간 식사 예절의 차이

⑤ 해외여행을 할 때 공손하게 행동해야 하는 이유

17 ① 중국 ② 인도 ③ 칠레 ④ 멕시코 ⑤ 스페인

16 문화권에 따라 달라지는 몇몇 식사 예절에 대해 논의하고 있으므로 남자가 하는 말의 주제로 ④ 'differences in table manners across cultures'가 가장 적절하다.

17 중국, 인도, 칠레, 스페인은 언급했지만 ④ 'Mexico'는 언급하지 않았다.

어휘 dining etiquette 식사 예절 host 뗑 (손님을 초대한) 주인 vary 통 달라지다; 서로 다르다 suggest 통 암시하다; 제안하다 rude 휑 무례한 belief 뗑 믿음 table manners 식사 예절 formal 휑 격식을 차린, 정중한 utensil 뗑 식기, 도구 last 통 지속되다; 계속되다 custom 뗑 관습 politely 뿐 공손하게

1	①	2	⑤	3	①	4	⑤	5	③	6	④	7	③	8	②	9	⑤	10	②
11	②	12	③	13	⑤	14	①	15	③	16	③	17	④						

• 각 문제의 정답 근거는 굵은 글씨로, Dictation 정답은 밑줄로 표시되어 있습니다.

---

1 목적 파악

정답 ①

W Hi. I'm Gloria Osterberg, vice president of operations here at GloboChem. **1)As previously announced, we will begin replacing the tiles on the floor of the lobby next Monday.** This means the main entrance of our headquarters will be temporarily inaccessible. As such, all employees and visitors will be **2)required to enter through** the rear entrance. Also, since the elevator will not be available, you will need to **3)take the stairs** for the time being. The work is planned to take three days, so things will return to normal by Thursday morning. We appreciate your patience and understanding with this matter.

여 안녕하십니까. 이곳 GloboChem의 운영 담당 부사장인 Gloria Osterberg입니다. 이전에 공지한 대로 다음 주 월요일부터 로비 바닥 타일 교체 작업을 시작할 것입니다. 이는 본사 정문을 일시적으로 이용하실 수 없다는 말입니다. 그런 이유로 모든 직원과 방문객은 후문을 통해 출입하셔야 합니다. 또한 엘리베이터를 이용하실 수 없기 때문에 당분간 계단을 이용하셔야 합니다. 작업에는 3일이 소요될 예정이므로, 목요일 오전까지는 정상으로 돌아올 것입니다. 이 문제에 대한 여러분의 인내와 이해에 감사드립니다.

여자가 다음 주 월요일부터 본사 건물 로비 바닥 타일 교체 작업을 시작할 것이라고 하면서, 건물 이용 시 참고 사항을 안내하고 있다. 따라서, 여자가 하는 말의 목적으로 ① '예정된 바닥 교체 작업을 통지하려고'가 가장 적절하다.

어휘 vice president 부사장 previously 凰 이전에 headquarters 圀 본사, 본부 temporarily 凰 일시적으로 inaccessible 圀 이용할 수 없는, 입장이 허락되지 않는 as such 그런 이유로 rear entrance 후문 for the time being 당분간 return to normal 정상으로 돌아오다 patience 圀 인내, 참을성

---

2 의견 파악

정답 ⑤

W Alex, do you know where you and your classmate are going to study this evening?
M Gerard wants to meet up at a café.
W That might not be a good idea.
M Why not?
W **I think it's too hard to 1)get schoolwork done at a café.**
M Really? A lot of people do it.
W Cafés are usually noisy, though. So you may have difficulty focusing.
M I don't know about that. I like some noise. If people are talking, I feel free to **2)discuss the class materials** out loud.
W Maybe so. But it doesn't seem wise to have your textbook open around food and drinks.
M I guess I have **3)spilled coffee** on my work before.
W Well, that's a good reason not to study there!
M Okay. I'll keep that in mind.

여 Alex, 오늘 저녁에 너와 반 친구들이 어디서 공부할 건지 아니?
남 Gerard가 카페에서 만나고 싶어 해.
여 그건 좋은 생각이 아닐 수도 있어.
남 왜?
여 카페에서 학교 공부를 하는 건 너무 어려운 것 같아.
남 정말? 많은 사람들이 그러잖아.
여 하지만 카페는 보통 시끄러워. 그래서 집중하는 데 곤란을 겪을 지도 몰라.
남 그건 잘 모르겠어. 나는 소음이 좀 있는 게 좋거든. 사람들이 이야기를 하고 있으면, 내 마음대로 크게 소리 내어 수업 자료에 대해 토론할 수 있잖아.
여 그럴지도 모르지. 하지만 음식과 음료 주변에 교재를 펴놓는 건 현명하지 않아 보여.
남 전에 공부하던 것 위에 커피를 쏟은 적이 있었던 것 같아.
여 음, 그게 거기서 공부하지 말아야 할 타당한 이유야!
남 알겠어. 명심할게.

반 친구들과 카페에서 만나 공부하려는 남자에게 여자가 카페에서 공부하면 집중이 어렵고, 교재에 뭔가를 쏟을 수 있어서 너무 힘들다고 했다. 따라서, 여자의 의견으로 ⑤ '카페에서 공부하기에는 여러 어려움이 있다.'가 가장 적절하다.

어휘 meet up 만나다 feel free to 마음대로 ~하다 material 圀 자료; 재료 wise 圀 현명한 spill 图 쏟다, 흘리다 keep in mind 명심하다

---

3 관계 파악

정답 ①

M Good afternoon. May I help you?
W Hi. I'm looking for a laptop to do some programming and graphic design with.
M Sure thing. Is there **1)any particular computer** you have your eye on?
W Not really. Something powerful but not too expensive.
M I see. Do you play any computer games?
W No. **I need it 2)for my courses. I'm majoring in computer science.**
M Okay. **In that case, I'd recommend either a Phoenix or a SurTech model.**
W [Pause] These **3)look the same** to me. They have the same screen size, too. What's the difference?

남 안녕하세요. 도와드릴까요?
여 안녕하세요. 프로그래밍과 그래픽 디자인을 할 노트북을 찾고 있어요.
남 그럼요. 눈여겨보신 특정한 컴퓨터가 있나요?
여 그렇지는 않아요. 성능은 좋은데 너무 비싸지 않은 걸로요.
남 그렇군요. 컴퓨터 게임을 하시나요?
여 아뇨. 수업에 필요한 거예요. 컴퓨터 공학을 전공하고 있거든요.
남 알겠습니다. 그렇다면 Phoenix나 SurTech 모델 중 하나를 추천해 드리고 싶어요.
여 [잠시 멈춤] 제가 보기엔 똑같아 보이는데요. 화면 크기도 똑같고요. 뭐가 다른가요?

M The SurTech one is lighter but a little more expensive, while the Phoenix is cheaper but 4)less portable. **W** Is there a discount for students? **M** We do have one. It's 10% off. **W** Can I try out the SurTech one? **M** Go right ahead.	남 SurTech는 더 가볍지만 조금 더 비싸고, 반면에 Phoenix는 더 저렴하지만 휴대하기 덜 편리해요. 여 학생 할인이 있나요? 남 있습니다. 10% 할인돼요. 여 SurTech를 시험 삼아 써 봐도 될까요? 남 그렇게 하세요.

두 사람이 여자가 구매할 노트북에 대해 이야기하고 있다. 남자는 여자에게 노트북 모델을 추천하고 있고, 여자는 노트북이 수업에 필요하다고 하며 컴퓨터 공학을 전공하고 있다고 말하는 것으로 보아 두 사람의 관계로 ① '전자기기 판매원 — 대학생'이 가장 적절하다.

어휘 particular 형 특정한 have one's eye on 눈여겨보다 course 명 수업; 과정 major in ~을 전공하다 in that case 그렇다면 either A or B A나 B 중 하나
portable 형 휴대하기 편리한, 들고 다닐 수 있는 try out 시험 삼아 써 보다

---

4 그림 내용 불일치 파악   정답 ⑤

W Tony, have you thought about places for us to stay during the holiday weekend? **M** Yeah. I think I found one by Lake Morris. Take a look at this cabin. **W** It's so cozy. I love 1)the fireplace under the window. **M** Me too. And with the two couches close by, we could all sit by the fire together. **W** Sounds great. It's beautifully decorated, too. **M** Isn't it? That star pattern on the rug looks nice. Most cabins 2)are more basic. **W** Exactly. I was admiring the antique square table. It fits well with the mirror above it. **M** I agree. Apparently, the owner likes to collect old furniture. **W** That's cool! **M** And I believe the 3)flowers in the basket by the door were picked from his garden. **W** This place has a lot of character. Let's book it! **M** Okay, I'll do that now.	여 Tony, 우리가 주말 연휴 동안 머물 곳을 생각해 봤니? 남 응. 모리스 호수 옆에 있는 곳을 찾은 것 같아. 이 오두막을 한번 봐. 여 정말 아늑하네. 창문 아래 벽난로가 마음에 들어. 남 나도. 그리고 두 개의 소파가 가까이에 있어서, 우리는 불 옆에 함께 앉을 수 있을 거야. 여 좋아. 장식도 멋지게 되어 있네. 남 그렇지? 러그의 별 무늬가 멋져 보여. 대부분 오두막들은 오히려 기본만 하는 정도잖아. 여 맞아. 고풍스러운 사각 테이블에는 감탄이 나와. 그 위의 거울과도 잘 어울리네. 남 동감이야. 듣자니, 주인이 고가구 수집을 좋아한대. 여 멋지다! 남 그리고 문가의 바구니에 있는 꽃들은 주인의 정원에서 따온 것 같아. 여 이곳은 개성이 풍부해. 여기로 예약하자! 남 좋아, 지금 할게.

대화에서 남자가 문가의 바구니에 있는 꽃들은 주인의 정원에서 따온 것 같다고 말했는데, ⑤에는 식물이 심어진 화분이 그려져 있다.

어휘 cabin 명 오두막 cozy 형 아늑한 fireplace 명 벽난로 close by 가까이에 admire 통 감탄하다; 존경하다 antique 형 고풍스러운, 골동품의 fit with ~과 어울리다
apparently 분 듣자니, 보아하니; 분명히 furniture 명 가구 character 명 개성, 성격

---

5 할 일 파악   정답 ③

M Hey, Penny. Mom and Dad's 30th wedding anniversary is coming up soon. Shouldn't we 1)do something special for them? **W** I was thinking of getting them a present. I have a department store coupon. **M** Hmm... wouldn't it be better to plan something romantic? **W** You're right. What about making reservations at 2)a fancy restaurant? **M** I think they already have dinner plans. **W** Maybe a couples massage would be good? **M** Oh, I know a place that does good massages downtown! **W** You mean the spa on 6th Street? That would be perfect. **M** Then, it's settled. I'll 3)book an appointment online and put it on my credit card. **W** Sounds like a plan. **M** Why don't you call Dad and let him know about it so that they don't 4)make other plans? **W** I'll do that now.	남 있잖아, Penny. 엄마 아빠의 30주년 결혼기념일이 곧 다가와. 부모님을 위해 뭔가 특별한 걸 해야 하지 않을까? 여 선물을 사드릴까 생각 중이야. 내게 백화점 쿠폰이 있거든. 남 음... 뭔가 로맨틱한 사드릴 계획하는 게 낫지 않을까? 여 네 말이 맞아. 고급 레스토랑을 예약하는 건 어때? 남 이미 저녁 계획이 있으신 것 같아. 여 어쩌면 커플 마사지가 좋을까? 남 아, 시내에 마사지 잘하는 곳을 알아! 여 6번가에 있는 스파 말하는 거지? 딱 좋을 것 같아. 남 그럼 해결됐네. 온라인으로 예약하고 내 신용카드로 결제할게. 여 좋은 계획인 것 같아. 남 아빠가 다른 계획을 세우시지 않도록 전화해서 알려주는 게 어때? 여 지금 할게.

부모님의 결혼기념일 준비에 대해 이야기하고 있다. 남자가 스파를 온라인으로 예약하고 본인 신용카드로 결제하겠다고 했으므로 남자가 할 일로 ③ '마사지 가게 예약하기'가 가장 적절하다.

어휘 wedding anniversary 결혼기념일 make a reservation 예약하다 settle 통 해결하다, 합의를 보다 put ~ on one's credit card ~을 신용카드로 결제하다

6 금액 정보 파악

정답 ④

W	Excuse me. How much is this medium-sized cake? I'm getting some desserts to share with my friends.	여	실례합니다. 이 중간 크기 케이크는 얼마인가요? 제 친구들과 나눠 먹을 디저트를 좀 사려고요.
M	Well, that one is $30, but you can also get it by the piece. **If you** ¹⁾**buy more than five pieces at one time, you can get a 10% discount on them.**	남	음, 그건 30달러인데, 조각으로 사실 수도 있어요. 한번에 다섯 조각 이상 사시면, 10% 할인을 받으실 수 있어요.
W	Oh, that might be better. Then, I can pick the flavors my friends like. How much is it for a piece?	여	아, 그게 더 나을 것 같네요. 그러면 친구들이 좋아하는 맛으로 고를 수 있으니까요. 한 조각에 얼마죠?
M	**It's $6 per piece.**	남	6달러입니다.
W	Are all the cakes ²⁾the same price?	여	모든 케이크가 가격이 같나요?
M	Yes, that's right.	남	네, 맞습니다.
W	Okay. **Then, I'll take two pieces of this chocolate cake and three pieces of cheesecake.**	여	네. 그러면 초콜릿 케이크 두 조각과 치즈 케이크 세 조각으로 할게요.
M	Got it. Can I get you anything else?	남	알겠습니다. 다른 것 더 필요하세요?
W	Hmm... **How much are these vanilla macaroons?**	여	흠... 여기 바닐라 마카롱은 얼마예요?
M	**They are $3 each.**	남	개당 3달러예요.
W	Great. I'll take ³⁾three of those as well.	여	좋네요. 그것도 세 개 주세요.
M	So... that's five slices of cake and three macaroons.	남	그러니까, 조각 케이크 다섯 개와 마카롱 세 개인 거군요.
W	That's right. Here's my credit card.	여	맞아요. 여기 제 신용카드요.

여자가 조각 케이크 다섯 개($6×5 =$30)를 구매하여 10% 할인($30×0.9 =$27)을 받았고, 마카롱 세 개($3×3 =$9)를 추가로 더 구매하였으므로 정답은 ④ '$36'이다.

[어휘] at one time 한번에   flavor 뗑 맛, 풍미   slice 뗑 조각

7 이유 파악

정답 ③

M	Hi, Mary. How's it going?	남	안녕, Mary. 어떻게 지내?
W	I'm doing well, Ted. Hey, do you ¹⁾have any plans for the first week of February?	여	잘 지내고 있어, Ted. 있잖아, 2월 첫째 주에 무슨 계획 있니?
M	For February? No, not really.	남	2월에? 아니, 그렇지 않아.
W	Well, I'm organizing a snowboarding trip. Would you like to come along?	여	음, 내가 스노보드 여행을 준비하고 있어. 함께 갈래?
M	I don't think I'll be able to make it.	남	난 못 갈 것 같아.
W	Really? I thought you loved snowboarding.	여	정말? 스노보드를 좋아하는 줄 알았는데.
M	I used to do it a lot.	남	많이 타곤 했었지.
W	Did you get injured or something?	여	부상이나 뭐 그런 걸 당한 거야?
M	I ²⁾twisted my ankle a couple of times. But nothing serious.	남	발목을 몇 번 삐긴 했어. 그런데 심각한 건 아니야.
W	I'm only planning on inviting Lana and Bob. So you would know everyone.	여	Lana와 Bob만 초대할 계획이야. 그러니 넌 일행 모두를 알 거야.
M	I like all of them, **but I** ³⁾**spent too much money during my trip this month. I can't afford to go traveling again.**	남	내가 다들 좋아하는 사람들인데, 이번 달에 여행하면서 돈을 너무 많이 썼어. 다시 여행을 갈 여유가 없어.
W	I get it. Next time, then!	여	알겠어. 그럼, 다음번에 가자!

남자가 스노보드 여행을 함께 가지 못하겠다고 하면서 이번 달 여행 동안 돈을 많이 써서 다시 여행을 갈 여유가 없다고 말했으므로, 남자가 스노보드를 타러 갈 수 없는 이유는 ③ '이미 많은 돈을 여행에 써서'이다.

[어휘] organize 图 준비하다; 조직하다   come along 함께 가다   get injured 부상을 당하다   twist 图 삐다; 왜곡하다   afford 图 (금전적·시간적) 여유가 있다   I get it. 알겠어.

8 언급 유무 파악

정답 ②

W	Ross, have you tried Little Italy?	여	Ross, 너 Little Italy에 가봤니?
M	Do you mean the restaurant ¹⁾located on **Main Street, across from the Stardust Theater**? If so, I wouldn't recommend it.	남	메인가에 위치한, 스타더스트 극장 맞은편에 있는 식당 말하는 거야? 만약 그렇다면 추천하지는 않을게.
W	Yeah, that's the one I mean. What was wrong with it?	여	응, 내가 말하는 곳이 거기야. 뭐가 잘못됐어?
M	There was **only one waiter** working, so it took forever to get our food.	남	일하는 웨이터가 한 명밖에 없어서, 음식을 받는 데 엄청난 시간이 걸렸어.
W	Oh, then I'll just go early. Do you know ²⁾when it opens?	여	아, 그럼 그냥 일찍 갈게. 언제 문 여는지 아니?
M	It opens at **11 a.m.** But I have another reason for not liking it. The food was really bland.	남	오전 11시에 열어. 하지만 거길 좋아하지 않는 또 다른 이유가 있어. 음식이 정말 심심했어.
W	What did you order? I've heard people say that their pasta is good.	여	뭘 주문했는데? 사람들이 파스타가 맛있다고 하는 걸 들었어.
M	I had the **spaghetti with meatballs**, which is their ³⁾most popular dish.	남	미트볼이 들어간 스파게티를 먹었는데, 그게 가장 인기 있는 음식이야.
W	That's too bad. I was looking forward to trying it.	여	이거 곤란하게 됐는데. 먹어볼 것을 기대하고 있었거든.
M	Yeah, so was I.	남	그래, 나도 그랬어.
W	Maybe I'll try the new Thai place instead.	여	어쩌면 대신 새로 생긴 태국 식당에 가보는 게 좋겠어.
M	Good idea. Tell me how it is.	남	좋은 생각이야. 어떤지 말해줘.

위치(메인가 스타더스트 극장 맞은편), 종업원 수(한 명), 개점 시간(오전 11시), 인기 메뉴(미트볼이 들어간 스파게티)에 대해 언급했고, ② '배달료'는 언급하지 않았다.

어휘 across from ~ 맞은편에 take forever 엄청난 시간이 걸리다 bland 웹 (맛이) 심심한, 특별한 맛이 안 나는; 단조로운

---

9 내용 불일치 파악

정답 ⑤

M Dottie's Dresses shoppers, may I have your attention, please? The new year is coming up, which means that it's time for ¹⁾our annual sale. To make room for next year's designs, all clothing from the past season is being discounted by 50% to 90%. Every dress in our inventory is included in ²⁾the clearance sale, which means that even clothing from the most famous designers will be available. The sale begins December 9th and will continue until every last discounted item is sold. **We've also ³⁾extended our hours because of the upcoming Christmas holiday**, so we're open until 10 p.m. nightly now. For the finest fashions at the fairest prices, come to Dottie's!	남 Dottie's Dresses 쇼핑객 여러분, 주목해 주시겠습니까? 새해가 다가오고 있는데요, 이는 즉 연간 세일을 해야 할 때라는 말입니다. 내년 디자인을 둘 공간을 만들기 위해, 지난 시즌의 모든 의류를 50%에서 90%까지 할인하고 있습니다. 재고 목록에 있는 모든 원피스는 재고 정리 세일에 포함되어 있으며, 이는 가장 유명한 디자이너의 옷차조 할인 가능하다는 뜻입니다. 세일은 12월 9일부터 시작되어, 마지막 할인 품목이 모두 판매될 때까지 계속될 것입니다. 다가오는 크리스마스 연휴로 인해 영업시간도 연장되어 현재 매일 밤 10시까지 영업합니다. 가장 합리적인 가격에 가장 멋진 패션을 원한다면, Dottie's로 오십시오!

옷 가게의 연간 세일에 대한 안내 방송이다. 남자가 크리스마스 연휴로 인해 영업 시간이 연장되었다고 했으므로 ⑤ '영업시간이 할인 행사 때문에 연장되었다.'는 내용과 일치하지 않는다.

어휘 come up 다가오다 annual 웹 연간의, 연례의 inventory 명 재고 목록 clearance sale 재고 정리 세일 extend 동 연장하다 upcoming 웹 다가오는 nightly 뷔 매일 밤에 fine 웹 멋진; 질 좋은 fair 웹 합리적인

---

10 도표 정보 파악

정답 ②

M Jenny, what are you looking at?	남 Jenny, 뭘 보고 있어?
W I'm trying to buy a new e-book reader. These are the options I'm considering now.	여 이북 리더기를 새로 사려고 해. 이것들이 내가 지금 고려하고 있는 선택지들이야.
M Good idea! You always read books ¹⁾during your bus ride to and from school. What's your price range?	남 좋은 생각이야! 너는 학교로 오가는 버스 안에서 항상 책을 읽잖아. 가격대가 어떻게 되니?
W **My budget is $130 or less**, so I guess this one's out.	여 내 예산이 130달러 이하이니까, 이건 탈락인 것 같네.
M **What about wireless charging? Do you think you'll ²⁾need that feature?**	남 무선 충전은? 그 기능이 필요할 것 같니?
W **Definitely.** I hate having to plug my devices in.	여 물론이지. 기기에 플러그를 꽂아야 하는 건 싫어.
M I agree. That'll be much more convenient. Then, you have to think about the battery life.	남 동의해. 그게 훨씬 더 편할 거야. 그렇다면, 배터리 수명에 대해 생각해야 해.
W I guess more is better. **Let's say it should have a battery life of ³⁾10 days or more.**	여 많을수록 좋겠지. 이를테면 배터리 수명은 10일 이상이어야 해.
M Then, you just need to decide which color you want.	남 그럼, 어떤 색을 원하는지만 결정하면 돼.
W I don't like the white one, **so I'll go with black.**	여 흰색은 마음에 안 드니까, 검은색으로 고를래.
M Perfect. You're all set to order it now.	남 완벽해. 이제 주문할 만반의 준비가 되었어.

여자는 130달러 이하이면서, 무선 충전이 되고, 배터리 수명은 10일 이상인 것 중에서, 검은색인 이북 리더기를 골랐다.

어휘 price range 가격대 wireless charging 무선 충전 feature 명 기능 plug ~ in ~에 플러그를 꽂다 battery life 배터리 수명 Let's say 이를테면 all set 만반의 준비가 된

---

11 짧은 대화의 응답 파악

정답 ②

M Samantha, is everything all right? You ¹⁾look a little worried.	남 Samantha, 무슨 일 있어? 걱정이 좀 있어 보여.
W I can't find my phone anywhere. Have you seen it by any chance?	여 어디에서도 내 휴대폰을 찾을 수가 없어. 혹시 그걸 본 적 있니?
M No, I haven't. **But I could ²⁾try calling your phone. We'll hear it ring if it's somewhere close by.**	남 아니, 못 봤어. 그런데 내가 네 휴대폰으로 전화해보면 될 거야. 어딘가 가까이에 있으면 울리는 게 들릴 테니까.
W Good idea. Do you have my phone number?	여 좋은 생각이야. 내 휴대폰 번호 있지?
	선택지 ① 아, 미안. 내 휴대폰을 무음으로 해둘게.
	② 좋은 생각이야. 내 휴대폰 번호 있지?
	③ 모르겠어. 내가 전화하면 그녀가 안 받을까 봐 걱정돼.
	④ 아니, 안 되겠어. 몇 분 후에 다시 전화해 줘도 될까?
	⑤ 뭐였어? 밖에서 큰 소리가 들린 것 같았는데.

여자가 휴대폰을 찾을 수 없다고 하자 남자가 가까이에 있으면 울리는 게 들릴 테니 전화해보겠다고 제안했으므로, 이에 대한 응답으로 제안에 동의하는 ② 'Good idea. Do you have my phone number?'가 가장 적절하다.

어휘 by any chance 혹시 set ~ on silent ~을 무음으로 해두다 pick up 전화를 받다

12 짧은 대화의 응답 파악

정답 ③

W Honey, I just ¹⁾<u>got an email</u> from the real estate agent. He found a beautiful apartment for us to go see.	여 여보, 방금 부동산 중개인으로부터 이메일을 받았어. 우리가 보러 갈 멋진 아파트를 찾았대.
M Really? That's great. I hope it's in a nice neighborhood.	남 정말? 잘됐다. 좋은 동네에 있으면 좋겠네.
W It is. **We just need to set a date to see it.** ²⁾**When are you available?**	여 그렇대. 보러 갈 날짜를 정하기만 하면 돼. 당신 언제 시간돼?
M I'll be free all day Monday and Tuesday.	남 <u>월요일과 화요일은 하루 종일 한가할 거야.</u>
	선택지 ① 내가 오늘 그에게 이메일을 보낼게.
	② 그 동네는 아이들에게 아주 좋아.
	③ 월요일과 화요일은 하루 종일 한가할 거야.
	④ 부동산 중개인이 집세가 900달러라고 했어.
	⑤ 아파트에는 적어도 침실 두 개는 필요해.

여자가 부동산 중개인이 찾은 아파트를 보러 갈 날짜를 정하기만 하면 된다고 하며 남자에게 언제 시간이 되는지 물었으므로, 이에 대한 응답으로는 가능한 날을 말하는 ③ 'I'll be free all day Monday and Tuesday.'가 가장 적절하다.

어휘 real estate agent 부동산 중개인 neighborhood 뗑 동네, 이웃 set a date 날짜를 정하다 at least 적어도, 최소한

13 긴 대화의 응답 파악

정답 ⑤

M Well, that finishes up our discussion for today. Is everyone ready for Friday's test?	남 그럼, 오늘의 토론은 이걸로 마무리하자. 모두 금요일 시험 준비는 다 됐지?
W Mr. Jackson, I have a question.	여 Jackson 선생님, 저 질문 있어요.
M Yes, Tanya?	남 그래, Tanya?
W What topics is the test ¹⁾<u>going to cover</u>?	여 이번 시험에서는 어떤 주제를 다루나요?
M Everything in our history book from pages 198 to 310.	남 198쪽부터 310쪽까지 우리 역사책에 있는 모든 것이란다.
W Okay. Is there an essay question on the exam, or are all of them multiple choice questions?	여 알겠어요. 시험에 서술형 문제가 있나요, 아니면 모두 객관식 문제인가요?
M ²⁾<u>Both types</u> will appear. I plan on putting in one essay question at the end.	남 두 가지 유형이 모두 나온단다. 마지막에 서술형 문제를 하나 넣을 계획이야.
W What's it going to be on?	여 무엇에 대한 건가요?
M I can't tell you the subject, but I can tell you that the essay ³⁾<u>will be worth</u> 25% of your exam grade.	남 주제는 말해줄 수 없지만, 그 서술형 문제가 시험 성적의 25%를 차지할 거라는 건 말할 수 있단다.
W Mr. Jackson, one last thing before the bell rings.	여 Jackson 선생님, 수업종이 치기 전에 마지막으로 한 가지 더요.
M Sure. What is it?	남 물론이지. 무엇이니?
W **I didn't catch today's homework assignment. Can you repeat it?**	여 오늘 숙제를 못 알아들었어요. 다시 한번 말씀해 주시겠어요?
M I'll write it on the chalkboard for everyone.	남 <u>모두를 위해 칠판에 써 놓으마.</u>
	선택지 ① 다음 주에 반 학생들에게 답이 뭔지 말해 줄 거란다.
	② 금요일 수업에서 그 챕터를 다룰 거란다.
	③ 서술형 답안은 적어도 200단어는 되어야 한다.
	④ 내일 수업 전까지 내야 하는 거니?
	⑤ 모두를 위해 칠판에 써 놓으마.

수업이 끝나기 전 선생님께 질문하는 상황이다. 여자가 오늘 숙제를 못 알아들었다며 다시 한번 말해 달라고 했으므로, 이에 대한 응답으로는 숙제를 칠판에 써 놓겠다고 하는 ⑤ 'I'll write it on the chalkboard for everyone.'이 가장 적절하다.

어휘 finish up 마무리하다 cover 동 다루다; 덮다 multiple choice question 객관식 문제 appear 동 나오다; ~인 것 같다 catch 동 알아듣다; 잡다 chalk board 뗑 칠판

14 긴 대화의 응답 파악

정답 ①

[Cell phone rings.]	[휴대폰이 울린다.]
W Hey, Aaron. What's up?	여 여보세요, Aaron. 무슨 일이야?
M Hi, Nicole. Can I ask you a favor?	남 안녕, Nicole. 부탁 하나 해도 될까?
W Sure. What is it?	여 물론이지. 뭔데?
M I need someone to look after my plants.	남 내 식물을 돌봐줄 사람이 필요해.
W I'd be happy to help if I can, but I'm planning to ¹⁾<u>travel myself</u>.	여 할 수만 있다면 기꺼이 돕고 싶지만, 혼자 여행을 갈 계획이야.
M It's next week. I'll be out of town visiting my relatives for a few days.	남 다음 주 얘기야. 며칠 동안 친척들을 만나러 가서 동네에 없을 거야.
W That's good. I'm leaving ²⁾<u>the week after that</u>.	여 다행이야. 나는 그보다 한 주 더 뒤에 떠나.
M Great. So you don't mind watering the plants?	남 좋아. 그러니까 식물에 물 주는 거 괜찮은 거지?
W Of course not. Is there anything else you need me to do? I can move the plants to make sure they get enough sunlight.	여 물론이지. 내가 더 해줘야 할 일이 있니? 식물이 충분히 햇볕을 쬐도록 옮겨둘 수도 있어.
M No, that's not necessary. All of them are ³⁾<u>out on the terrace</u>.	남 아니, 그럴 필요 없어. 모두 테라스에 나와 있거든.
W **Okay. Please let me know the door code in that case.**	여 알겠어. 그렇다면 현관문 비밀번호를 알려줘.
M I'll send the code by text message.	남 문자 메시지로 비밀번호 보내줄게.

W Okay. I'll take good care of the plants for you.

여 알겠어. 식물을 잘 보살펴 줄게.

선택지 ① 알겠어. 식물을 잘 보살펴 줄게.
② 고마워. 이렇게 해주다니 정말 고마워.
③ 그게 문제야. 넌 물을 너무 많이 줘 왔어.
④ 이해해. 월요일 아침에 그거 심으러 들를게.
⑤ 물론이지. 식물이 충분히 빛을 받도록 창가에 둘게.

남자가 동네에 없는 동안 식물을 돌봐달라고 부탁하는 상황이다. 여자가 현관문 비밀번호를 알려달라고 하자 남자가 문자 메시지로 보내주겠다고 했으므로, 이에 대한 응답으로는 식물을 잘 돌보겠다고 약속하는 ① 'Okay. I'll take good care of the plants for you.'가 가장 적절하다.

어휘 ask a favor 부탁하다 look after ~을 돌보다 relative 몡 친척 code 몡 비밀번호, 암호

15 상황에 적절한 말 파악   정답 ③

W Richard is a high school student. He is making a video for his class's end-of-the-year ceremony that will ¹⁾take place in a few weeks. He wants it to be memorable for his classmates, so he has worked on the video for a long time. He added lots of clips of events that happened throughout the year, and he tried to make the video ²⁾flow smoothly with cool transitions and effects. But he's not very skilled at video editing. Then, he remembers that his friend Amy makes interesting videos for her online channel all the time. **So he wants to ask her to teach him ³⁾how to edit the videos.** In this situation, what would Richard most likely say to Amy?

여 Richard는 고등학생입니다. 그는 몇 주 후에 있을 학급 연말 기념식을 위한 영상을 만들고 있습니다. 그는 그것이 반 친구들의 기억에 남기를 원해서 오랫동안 영상 작업을 해왔습니다. 그는 한 해 동안 있었던 행사의 많은 영상 클립들을 추가했고, 그는 멋진 장면 전환과 특수 효과로 영상이 매끄럽게 흘러가도록 노력했습니다. 하지만 그는 영상 편집에 그다지 능숙하지 않습니다. 그때 그는 친구 Amy가 그녀의 온라인 채널에 올릴 흥미로운 영상을 항상 만든다는 것을 떠올립니다. 그래서 그는 그녀에게 영상 편집 방법을 가르쳐 달라고 부탁하고 싶습니다. 이러한 상황에서, Richard가 Amy에게 가장 할 것 같은 말은 무엇입니까?

선택지 ① 네가 연말에 학급 파티를 계획했니?
② 너 영상 편집 수업을 들을 의향이 있니?
③ 내가 만들고 있는 영상을 어떻게 편집해야 하는지 알려줄 수 있니?
④ 내게 올해 학급 행사 영상을 좀 보내줄 수 있니?
⑤ 네 채널에 올릴 고등학교 행사에 대한 영상을 만들어 주겠니?

Richard는 영상 편집에 능숙하지 않아서, 항상 흥미로운 영상을 만드는 Amy에게 영상 편집 방법을 가르쳐 달라고 부탁하려고 한다. 따라서, Richard가 할 말로 ③ 'Can you show me how to edit the video I'm making?'이 가장 적절하다.

어휘 ceremony 몡 기념식 memorable 혱 기억에 남을만한 throughout 젠 ~동안 flow 동 흘러가다, 흐르다 smoothly 뷔 매끄럽게, 부드럽게 transition 몡 장면 전환; 이행 effects 몡 특수 효과 be skilled at ~에 능숙하다 edit 동 편집하다 all the time 항상

16-17 세트 문항   정답 16 ③ 17 ④

M Hello, everyone. In our last health session, we talked about the importance of heart health. **Today, we're going to talk about ¹⁾different activities that are good for heart health.** First, let's talk about **walking**. Walking is a great form of exercise and one of the easiest ways to improve heart health. With just two and a half hours of walking a week, a person can ²⁾lower their risk of heart disease. Next, we have **swimming**. Swimming is an effective way to work the heart and lungs. This activity trains the body to use oxygen in a more efficient way, which benefits your heart. **Running** is also an excellent activity for taking care of your heart. Regularly running improves blood flow throughout your body. As a result, your heart is easily able ³⁾to circulate blood. Finally, **cycling** can strengthen heart muscles and reduce blood fat levels. Any of these are great methods for boosting your heart health. Be sure to exercise as much as you can for the best results!

남 안녕하십니까, 여러분. 지난 보건 수업에서, 우리는 심장 건강의 중요성에 대해 이야기했습니다. 오늘은 심장 건강에 좋은 다양한 활동들에 대해 이야기할 것입니다. 먼저, 걷기에 대해 이야기해봅시다. 걷기는 훌륭한 형태의 운동이고 심장 건강을 향상시키는 가장 쉬운 방법들 중 하나입니다. 일주일에 두 시간 반만 걸으면, 심장병의 위험을 낮출 수 있습니다. 다음은 수영입니다. 수영은 심장과 폐를 일하게 하는 효과적인 방법입니다. 이 활동은 몸이 더 효율적인 방식으로 산소를 쓰도록 훈련시키는데, 이는 심장에 이롭습니다. 달리기 또한 심장을 돌보는 데 훌륭한 활동입니다. 규칙적으로 달리는 것은 몸 전체의 혈류를 개선시킵니다. 결과적으로, 심장이 쉽게 혈액을 순환시킬 수 있습니다. 마지막으로, 자전거 타기는 심장 근육을 강화하고 혈중 지방 수치를 줄일 수 있습니다. 이것들 중 어느 것이든 심장 건강을 신장시키기 위한 훌륭한 방법입니다. 최상의 결과를 위해 할 수 있는 한 많이 운동하십시오!

선택지 16 ① 매일 하는 운동에 영향을 가장 많이 받는 신체 기관
② 체육관 밖에서 쉽게 할 수 있는 활동
③ 심장 문제를 예방할 수 있는 다양한 운동
④ 다양한 신체 활동의 이상적인 운동 지속 시간
⑤ 심장 문제가 있는 사람들에게 있어 규칙적인 활동의 중요성
17 ① 걷기 ② 수영 ③ 달리기 ④ 등산 ⑤ 자전거 타기

16 심장 건강에 좋은 다양한 활동들에 대해 이야기하고 있으므로 남자가 하는 말의 주제로 ③ 'various exercises that can prevent heart problems'가 가장 적절하다.
17 걷기, 수영, 달리기, 자전거 타기는 언급했지만 ④ 'climbing'은 언급하지 않았다.

어휘 session 몡 수업; 기간 lung 몡 폐 train 동 훈련하다 oxygen 몡 산소 efficient 혱 효율적인 take care of ~을 돌보다 as a result 결과적으로 circulate 동 순환시키다 strengthen 동 강화하다 boost 동 신장시키다 organ 몡 신체 기관, 장기 ideal 혱 이상적인 duration 몡 지속 시간; 지속

10회 영어듣기 모의고사

1	③	2	②	3	④	4	②	5	④	6	⑤	7	③	8	③	9	⑤	10	①
11	③	12	①	13	③	14	②	15	⑤	16	①	17	③						

• 각 문제의 정답 근거는 굵은 글씨로, Dictation 정답은 밑줄로 표시되어 있습니다.

1 목적 파악

정답 ③

M Good morning, Linton High School students. This is your principal, Mr. Henderson. It has come to my attention that some students have been leaving their bikes near the rear entrance. This has caused a lot of problems because it has 1)blocked an access point to the school. However, I understand that you have been doing this because there is a 2)shortage of places to store your bikes. **So we have decided to add two 3)additional bike racks next to the outdoor basketball courts.** These will be available for use starting next week. But do note that, starting Monday, any bike blocking an entrance 4)will be removed by school staff. Okay, everyone, have a great school day!

남 좋은 아침입니다, 린튼 고등학교 학생 여러분. 저는 교장 Henderson입니다. 저는 몇몇 학생들이 후문 근처에 자전거를 두고 간다는 것을 알게 되었습니다. 이것은 학교로 출입하는 곳을 막아버리기 때문에 많은 문제를 일으킵니다. 하지만, 여러분이 자전거를 보관할 장소가 부족하기 때문에 그렇게 해온 것은 이해가 됩니다. 그래서, 야외 농구장 옆에 자전거 거치대 두 개를 추가하기로 결정했습니다. 그것은 다음 주부터 사용할 수 있습니다. 하지만 월요일부터 입구를 막는 모든 자전거는 학교 직원들이 치울 것이라는 점을 꼭 명심하십시오. 그럼, 여러분, 즐거운 학교생활 보내십시오!

남자가 학교에 자전거 보관 장소가 부족한 것을 이해한다면서, 자전거 거치대 두 개를 추가하기로 결정했다는 것을 알려주고 있다. 따라서, 남자가 하는 말의 목적으로 ③ '자전거 거치대 추가 설치를 공지하려고'가 가장 적절하다.

어휘 come to one's attention ~을 알게 되다 block 통 막다 access 명 출입, 통로 shortage 명 부족 store 통 보관하다; 저장하다 rack 명 거치대, 받침대 outdoor 형 야외의 remove 통 치우다, 제거하다

2 의견 파악

정답 ②

M Tracy, I'm making coffee. Do you want some?
W No, thanks. It's 5 p.m. Isn't it late for that?
M I need energy. I can't 1)keep my eyes open.
W **I've read that drinking coffee in the afternoon lowers the quality of your sleep.**
M Not me. I can always get to sleep.
W Maybe so, but coffee 2)increases activity in your brain, so it prevents deep sleep.
M Interesting. I may wake up tired even if I sleep for a long time, then?
W That's it! Also, caffeine 3)suppresses your appetite for dinner.
M Why is that a bad thing?
W Well, you still get hungry, but later on.
M So coffee makes you feel like eating a big snack later in the night.
W Exactly. We know it's 4)hard to sleep right after eating.
M Then, I'd better have ice water instead.

남 Tracy, 나 커피 탈 건데. 너도 좀 마실래?
여 아니, 괜찮아. 오후 5시잖아. 그러기엔 늦지 않아?
남 에너지가 필요해. 눈을 뜨고 있을 수가 없어.
여 오후에 커피를 마시는 게 수면의 질을 떨어트린다는 것을 읽어봤어.
남 난 아니야. 나는 언제든지 잠을 잘 수 있어.
여 그럴지도 모르지만, 커피는 뇌의 활동을 증가시켜서 깊은 잠을 방해해.
남 흥미롭네. 그러면 오래 자더라도 피곤한 채로 일어날 수도 있다는 거야?
여 바로 그거야! 또한, 카페인이 저녁 식사에 대한 식욕을 억제해.
남 그게 왜 나쁜 거야?
여 음, 배고파지는 건 여전한데, 나중에 고파지는 거야.
남 그래서 커피를 마시면 밤늦게 많은 간식을 먹고 싶은 기분이 드는구나.
여 맞아. 먹은 후에 바로 잠들기 어렵다는 건 알고 있잖아.
남 그럼, 대신 얼음물을 마시는 게 좋겠어.

오후 늦게 커피를 마시려는 남자에게 여자가 오후에 커피를 마시면 수면의 질이 떨어지고 깊은 잠을 방해받는다고 했다. 따라서, 여자의 의견으로 ② '오후에 커피를 마시면 수면의 질이 떨어진다.'가 가장 적절하다.

어휘 lower 통 떨어트리다, ~을 낮추다 increase 통 증가시키다 prevent 통 방해하다; 방지하다 suppress 통 억제하다; 진압하다 appetite 명 식욕

3 관계 파악

정답 ④

M Marianne Smith, **thank you so much for coming on our program tonight.**
W It's my pleasure, Larry. I'm a big fan of your 1)talk show.
M I appreciate that. **Now, I understand that you've been on tour for several months.**
W **I've been flying around the world for almost a year.**
M How does this tour differ from ones you've 2)done in the past?
W Well, the venues are bigger. We had 60,000 fans at our last concert, which was in a baseball stadium.
M That must be an amazing feeling.

남 Marianne Smith, 오늘 밤 저희 프로그램에 나와 주셔서 정말 감사합니다.
여 천만에요, Larry. 전 당신 토크쇼의 열렬한 팬이에요.
남 감사합니다. 자, 몇 달 동안 순회공연 중인 것으로 알고 있는데요.
여 거의 1년 동안 세계 곳곳을 비행했죠.
남 이번 투어는 당신이 과거에 했던 투어와 어떻게 다른가요?
여 음, 공연장이 더 커요. 바로 전에 야구장에서 했던 콘서트에는 6만 명의 팬들이 있었어요.
남 분명 굉장한 느낌이겠군요.

W	It is. But I'm almost ready to ³⁾<u>get back into</u> the studio.	여	맞아요. 하지만 전 녹음실로 돌아갈 준비가 거의 됐어요.
M	Have you written material for your next album?	남	다음 앨범에 실을 내용을 다 썼나요?
W	Yes, actually. **I have several new songs already.**	여	네, 사실은요. 이미 신곡이 몇 곡 있어요.
M	Would you be able to play one for us?	남	저희를 위해 한 곡 들려주시겠어요?
W	Sure! I'd be ⁴⁾<u>excited to share</u> one with my fans.	여	물론이죠! 팬들과 함께 할 수 있으면 너무 좋을 것 같아요.
M	Fantastic. We'll be back with Marianne Smith after a quick commercial break.	남	환상적이에요. Marianne Smith와 함께 잠시 광고 후에 돌아오겠습니다.

두 사람이 토크쇼에서 여자의 근황에 관해 이야기하고 있다. 남자는 토크쇼를 진행하며 여자에게 근황을 묻고 있고, 여자는 몇 달 동안의 순회 공연을 마치고 새 앨범의 신곡을 썼다고 하는 것으로 보아 두 사람의 관계로 ④ '토크쇼 진행자 — 가수'가 가장 적절하다.

어휘 It's my pleasure. 천만에요. on tour 순회공연 중인 differ from ~와 다르다 venue 명 공연장; 현장 commercial break 광고

---

4 그림 내용 불일치 파악   정답 ②

W	Honey, whose backyard is it in that picture?	여	여보, 저 사진 속에 있는 건 누구네 뒤뜰이야?
M	Oh, this is where my friend Robert spent the holiday.	남	아, 내 친구 Robert가 휴가를 보낸 곳이야.
W	He must ¹⁾<u>have gone somewhere</u> warm. Aren't those two palm trees near the fence?	여	따뜻한 곳으로 갔나 보네. 울타리 근처에 있는 저건 두 그루의 야자수 아니야?
M	Yeah. It's in Florida. **Don't you think ²⁾<u>that curved bench</u> in front of the fence is stylish?**	남	맞아. 플로리다거든. 울타리 앞에 있는 곡선 벤치가 세련된 거 같지 않아?
W	It's really nice. I'd like to relax by that square table.	여	정말 멋지네. 저 네모난 테이블 옆에서 쉬고 싶다.
M	Me too. The striped umbrella over it would keep the sun out of our eyes during the day.	남	나도. 그 위에 있는 줄무늬 파라솔이 낮 동안 눈에 햇빛이 못 들어오게 해줄 거야.
W	It's ³⁾<u>such a peaceful scene</u>. Oh, look at that cat sleeping next to the chair.	여	정말 평화로운 장면이다. 아, 의자 옆에서 고양이가 자고 있는 것 좀 봐.
M	It's so cute! And do you see that barbecue grill over ⁴⁾<u>in the right corner</u>?	남	아주 귀엽네! 그리고 오른쪽 구석에 있는 바비큐 그릴 보이니?
W	Yeah. It would be great to cook outside.	여	응. 밖에서 요리하는 것도 좋을 것 같아.
M	Looking at this picture makes me want to go on a trip soon!	남	이 사진을 보니 빨리 여행을 가고 싶어지네!
W	Me too! Let's go next month.	여	나도! 다음 달에 가자.

대화에서 남자가 울타리 앞에 있는 곡선 벤치가 세련된 것 같지 않냐고 물었는데, ②에는 직선형 벤치가 그려져 있다.

어휘 backyard 명 뒤뜰, 뒷마당 palm tree 야자수 fence 명 울타리 curved 형 곡선의 keep A out of B A가 B에 못 들어오게 하다 scene 명 장면 go on a trip 여행을 가다

---

5 할 일 파악   정답 ④

M	Abbey, is everything going to be ready for the fundraiser concert?	남	Abbey, 모금 콘서트를 위한 모든 준비가 다 되었나요?
W	I think so, John. We finished ¹⁾<u>building the stage</u> this morning.	여	그런 것 같아요, John. 오늘 아침에 무대를 다 만들었어요.
M	And what about the safety check? Isn't an inspector from the city government supposed to come?	남	안전 점검은 어때요? 시 정부에서 조사관이 오기로 되어 있지 않나요?
W	He was just here. Everything's approved.	여	방금 여기 있었어요. 모두 승인받았어요.
M	Great. How about the sound system?	남	좋아요. 음향 시스템은 어떤가요?
W	We're ²⁾<u>testing it now</u>, and it sounds good to me.	여	지금 테스트 중인데, 괜찮은 것 같아요.
M	**Now we just need to contact the bands to let them know what times they'll be playing.**	남	이제 밴드들에게 연락해서 몇 시에 연주하는지 알려주기만 하면 되겠네요.
W	I already made a timetable. Do you want to take a look at it?	여	제가 이미 일정표를 짰어요, 한번 볼래요?
M	I do. Can you e-mail it to me? **I'm ³⁾<u>happy to call them</u> myself.**	남	네. 이메일로 보내줄 수 있나요? 그들에게 직접 전화하게 되다니 기쁘네요.
W	Do you have their contact information?	여	그들의 연락처를 알고 있나요?
M	Yes. I have the musicians' phone numbers.	남	네. 그 음악가들의 전화번호를 가지고 있어요.
W	Okay. I'll send over that timetable now.	여	알겠어요. 지금 일정표를 보낼게요.
M	I appreciate it.	남	감사해요.

두 사람이 모금 콘서트 준비 상황을 확인하고 있다. 여자가 밴드들이 연주할 일정표를 짰다고 하자, 남자가 그것을 이메일로 보내달라고 하면서 그들에게 직접 전화하게 되어 기쁘다고 했으므로 남자가 할 일로 ④ '밴드와 연락하기'가 가장 적절하다.

어휘 inspector 명 조사관, 감독관 government 명 정부 approve 동 승인하다 timetable 명 일정표, 시간표 contact information 연락처

6 금액 정보 파악

정답 ⑤

M	Welcome to Bob's Sandwiches. What can I do for you?	남	Bob's Sandwiches에 오신 걸 환영합니다. 뭘 도와 드릴까요?
W	Hi. Do you still have that 10% off special on ham and cheese sandwiches?	여	안녕하세요. 햄치즈 샌드위치 아직도 10% 할인되나요?
M	Sorry, but 1)that promotion ended last week.	남	죄송하지만, 그 판촉 행사는 지난주에 끝났어요.
W	Oh, I see. Well, what specials do you have right now?	여	아, 그렇군요. 음, 지금은 어떤 특가 상품이 있나요?
M	At the moment, we have discounts on a couple of our most popular sandwiches. **The turkey sandwich is $14, and the roast beef sandwich is only $10.**	남	현재 가장 인기 있는 샌드위치 몇 개를 할인해 드리고 있어요. 칠면조 샌드위치는 14달러이고, 로스트비프 샌드위치는 단 10달러예요.
W	Okay. 2)Those would work. **Let's go with two roast beef sandwiches and one turkey.**	여	알겠습니다. 그것들도 좋아요. 로스트비프 샌드위치 두 개랑 칠면조 한 개로 할게요.
M	Got it. Do you want those to be meal combos?	남	알겠습니다. 세트 메뉴를 원하시나요?
W	What does that include?	여	거기에는 뭐가 포함되나요?
M	You get a small soda and regular fries. **That costs an extra $2 per sandwich.**	남	스몰 사이즈 탄산음료와 레귤러 사이즈 감자튀김을 드려요. 샌드위치 하나에 2달러가 추가됩니다.
W	Sure. **I'll take that** 3)for all of them.	여	물론이죠. 모두 세트 메뉴로 할게요.
M	So I have three sandwich meal combos. Does that complete your order?	남	그럼 샌드위치 세트 세 개인 거군요. 주문 끝나신 거죠?
W	Yes, that's everything. Here's my credit card.	여	네, 그게 다예요. 여기 제 신용카드요.

여자가 로스트비프 샌드 위치 두 개($10×2=$20)와 칠면조 샌드위치 한 개($14)를 주문했고, 세 메뉴를 모두 세트 메뉴로 시켜서 각각 2달러씩 추가($2×3=$6)되었으므로 정답은 ⑤ '$40'이다.

어휘 promotion 명 판촉 행사, 홍보; 승진 special 명 특가 상품, 특별 요리 형 특별한 at the moment 현재 turkey 명 칠면조

7 이유 파악

정답 ③

W	Hey, David. Can you pick your sister up after her music lesson this afternoon?	여	얘, David. 오늘 오후에 여동생 음악 수업이 끝나면 걔를 데리러 갈 수 있니?
M	I can't, Mom. I 1)have plans. I'm heading over to the department store in a few minutes.	남	그럴 수 없어요, 엄마. 약속이 있거든요. 잠시 후에 백화점으로 갈 거예요.
W	Oh, I see. Do you still need to do some Christmas shopping?	여	아, 그렇구나. 아직도 크리스마스 쇼핑을 좀 해야 하니?
M	No. I already bought all of my Christmas presents.	남	아니요. 크리스마스 선물은 이미 다 샀어요.
W	Well, are you meeting up with your friends?	여	음, 친구들을 만날 거니?
M	Don't you remember? **My favorite cartoonist is going to** 2)have a fan event **at the department store.**	남	기억 안 나세요? 제가 가장 좋아하는 만화가가 백화점에서 팬 이벤트를 할 거예요.
W	Oh, right. You mentioned that you wanted to 3)get his autograph.	여	아, 맞아. 그의 사인을 받고 싶다고 말했지.
M	Exactly. I'm so excited.	남	맞아요. 너무 신나요.
W	Well... I'll see if your father can do it. I need to go 4)to the bank myself.	여	음... 네 아빠가 데리러 갈 수 있는지 알아볼게. 난 직접 은행에 가야 하거든.
M	Sorry I couldn't help.	남	도와 드리지 못해서 죄송해요.
W	Don't worry about it. Go have fun!	여	걱정하지 마. 가서 즐기렴!
M	Okay, see you later.	남	네, 나중에 봐요.

남자는 잠시 후 백화점에 간다고 하면서 좋아하는 만화가가 그곳에서 팬 이벤트를 할 건데 그의 사인을 받고 싶다고 말했으므로, 남자가 백화점을 방문하려는 이유는 ③ '만화가의 사인회에 참석하고 싶어서'이다.

어휘 pick up ~를 데리러 가다 head over ~로 가다 meet up ~와 만나다 cartoonist 명 만화가 autograph 명 사인, 서명

8 언급 유무 파악

정답 ③

M	Honey, did you see the flyer for the Newberry Market?	남	여보, Newberry Market의 광고지 봤어?
W	No. What's that?	여	아니. 그게 뭐야?
M	It's a huge 1)outdoor market organized by the **Newberry Community Center.** Everyone in the neighborhood can sell stuff there.	남	뉴베리 주민센터에서 주관하는 큰 규모의 야외 마켓이야. 동네 사람들은 모두 그곳에서 물건을 팔 수 있어.
W	Interesting. 2)What day is it being held on?	여	흥미롭네. 무슨 요일에 열려?
M	Let me check... Oh, it will be on **June 15th.** That's next weekend.	남	확인해 볼게... 아, 6월 15일이야. 다음 주말이네.
W	I've got a bunch of collectibles I'd like to sell. Would I need to pay a 3)fee to participate?	여	난 팔고 싶은 수집품이 많이 있어. 참가하려면 돈을 내야 해?
M	Yeah, but it is only **$10** to use one of the stalls all day.	남	응, 하지만 하루 종일 가판대 하나를 사용하는 데 10달러밖에 안 들어.
W	Wow. That's very reasonable. Where will the market be located?	여	우와. 정말 합리적이네. 마켓이 어디에서 열릴 예정이야?
M	It will take place in **Wilson Park,** which is just 4)down the street.	남	길 바로 아래에 있는 윌슨 공원에서 열릴 거야.
W	Then, I am going to sign up for it. Thanks for letting me know!	여	그럼, 나는 참가 신청할래. 알려줘서 고마워!

주최 기관(뉴베리 주민센터), 날짜(6월15일), 참가비(10달러), 장소(윌슨 공원)에 대해 언급했고, ③ '신청 마감일'은 언급하지 않았다.

어휘 flyer 명 광고지, 전단 a bunch of 많은 collectible 명 수집품 형 모을 수 있는 stall 명 가판대 reasonable 형 합리적인 take place ~에서 열리다

9 내용 불일치 파악　　　　　　　정답 ⑤

M Welcome to the National Youth Chess Championship! We have 32 students competing from high schools all over the country. They 1)will be competing for six days. Every day, each player will take part in a single match against another competitor. Competitors must win or 2)be eliminated from the tournament. These daily matches will continue until the last two competitors remain. Then, the grand final will be held over the last two days. Highlights of these games 3)will be aired on the CBN Sports channel nightly. **This year's national youth champion will not only receive a $10,000 award but also a lesson from world champion Boris Budanov.** It's sure to be an exciting tournament. Good luck, everyone.	남 National Youth Chess Championship에 오신 것을 환영합니다! 전국 각지의 고등학교에서 온 32명의 학생들이 출전했습니다. 그들은 6일 동안 경합할 것입니다. 매일, 각 선수들은 다른 경쟁자를 상대하여 단판전을 벌일 것입니다. 출전자는 승리하거나 토너먼트에서 탈락해야 합니다. 이러한 일일 경기는 마지막 두 출전자가 남을 때까지 계속됩니다. 그런 다음, 마지막 이틀 동안 결승전이 열릴 것입니다. 이 경기들의 하이라이트는 CBN 스포츠 채널에서 매일 밤 방송됩니다. 올해의 전국 청소년 챔피언은 1만 달러의 상금뿐만 아니라 세계 챔피언 Boris Budanov로부터 가르침도 받을 것입니다. 분명 흥미로운 토너먼트가 될 것입니다. 행운을 빌겠습니다, 여러분.

전국 청소년 체스 선수권 대회에 대한 안내 방송이다. 남자가 올해의 전국 청소년 챔피언은 1만 달러의 상금뿐만 아니라 세계 챔피언 Boris Budanov로부터 가르침을 받을 것이라고 했으므로 ⑤ '우승자는 상금 대신 세계 챔피언의 가르침을 받을 수 있다.'는 내용과 일치하지 않는다.

어휘 compete 통 출전하다; 경합하다, 경쟁하다　against 전 ~를 상대하여　eliminate 통 탈락시키다　air 통 방송하다 명 공기　not only A but also B A뿐만 아니라 B도　lesson 명 가르침; 수업

10 도표 정보 파악　　　　　　　정답 ①

W Hi. Can I help you?	여 안녕하세요. 도와드릴까요?
M Yes, actually. I'm looking for a pair of gloves for the winter.	남 네, 정말로요. 겨울에 낄 장갑을 찾고 있어요.
W Sure. Well, what do you think of this pair? These gloves are 1)made of leather.	여 그럼요. 음, 이건 어떠세요? 이 장갑은 가죽으로 만들어졌어요.
M I don't really want leather ones.	남 가죽 제품은 별로 갖고 싶지 않아요.
W Okay. That's a good start. Is there a certain color you want?	여 알겠습니다. 시작이 좋네요. 원하시는 특정한 색상이 있으신가요?
M Hmm... I 2)don't like black gloves. So let's focus on the other pairs.	남 음... 저는 검은색 장갑을 좋아하지 않아요. 그러니 다른 것에 집중해보죠.
W Fair enough. Do you want a pair that is waterproof? This can make a big difference.	여 당연하죠. 방수가 되는 걸 원하시나요? 이게 큰 차이를 낳을 수 있어요.
M Yeah, I definitely need that. Waterproof gloves will 3)keep my hands warm and dry.	남 네, 꼭 필요해요. 방수 장갑은 제 손을 따뜻하고 물기가 없게 해줄 거예요.
W Good choice. That leaves two options. Is there one you like more?	여 잘 선택하셨어요. 그러면 두 가지 선택지가 남았는데요. 더 좋아하는 게 있나요?
M Both pairs have everything I need, **so there's 4)no reason to buy the more expensive option.**	남 둘 다 제가 필요로 하는 모든 걸 갖추고 있으니, 더 비싼 걸 살 이유가 없어요.
W Do you want me to ring these up?	여 계산해 드릴까요?
M Yes, please. Thanks for your help.	남 네, 부탁합니다. 도와주셔서 고마워요.

남자는 가죽 제품이 아니면서, 검은색이 아니고, 방수가 되는 것 중에서, 덜 비싼 겨울 장갑을 골랐다.

어휘 be made of (재료로) 만들어지다　leather 명 가죽　certain 형 특정한; 확신하는　make a difference 차이를 낳다　waterproof 형 방수가 되는　ring up 계산하다

11 짧은 대화의 응답 파악　　　　　　　정답 ③

W Welcome to Books World. How may I help you?	여 Books World에 오신 것을 환영합니다. 무엇을 도와드릴까요?
M I'm looking for the 1)newly released novel *My Dream*. I heard it hit the best-seller list.	남 새로 나온 소설 <My Dream>을 찾고 있어요. 베스트셀러에 올랐다고 들었는데요.
W I'm afraid it's sold out now. Could you 2)visit us again next week?	여 유감스럽지만, 지금은 품절이에요. 다음 주에 다시 방문해 주실 수 있나요?
M No problem. I'll stop back on Monday.	남 문제없어요. 월요일에 다시 들를게요.
	선택지 ① 네. 논픽션 코너를 찾고 있어요. ② 신경 쓰지 마세요. 드릴 책을 한 부 찾은 것 같아요. ③ 문제없어요. 월요일에 다시 들를게요. ④ 알겠어요. 지금 바로 책을 주문할게요. ⑤ 잘됐네요. 저는 그 소설을 정말 재미있게 읽었어요.

남자가 새로 나온 소설을 찾자 여자가 지금은 품절이니 다음 주에 다시 방문해 줄 수 있는지 물었으므로, 이에 대한 응답으로는 다시 들르겠다고 말하는 ③ 'No problem. I'll stop back on Monday.'가 가장 적절하다.

어휘 release 통 내다, 출간하다; 풀어주다　novel 명 소설　hit the best-seller list 베스트셀러에 오르다　sold out 품절인

12 짧은 대화의 응답 파악

정답 ①

M Honey, I'd like to start working out with you. What ¹⁾do you think?	남 여보, 당신과 함께 운동을 시작하고 싶어. 어떻게 생각해?
W That's a good idea. What exercise do you want to do?	여 좋은 생각이야. 어떤 운동을 하고 싶은데?
M I'm thinking of playing badminton or squash ²⁾in the gym.	남 체육관에서 배드민턴이나 스쿼시를 할 생각이야.
W Good. Either of them works for me.	여 좋아. 어느 쪽이든 괜찮아.

선택지 ① 좋아. 어느 쪽이든 괜찮아.
　　　② 아쉽네. 당신은 매일 운동을 했어야 했어.
　　　③ 걱정하지 마. 배드민턴 치는 법 가르쳐 줄게.
　　　④ 미안해. 운동을 했더니 녹초가 됐어.
　　　⑤ 동의해. 밖에서 운동하는 것이 언제나 최고지.

운동을 함께 시작하려는 상황에서 여자가 어떤 운동을 하고 싶은지 묻자 남자가 배드민턴이나 스쿼시를 할 생각이라고 했으므로, 이에 대한 응답으로는 둘 중 어느 것이든 괜찮다고 답하는 ① 'Good. Either of them works for me.'가 가장 적절하다.

어휘 work out 운동하다　exhausted 혱 녹초가 된, 기진맥진한

13 긴 대화의 응답 파악

정답 ③

[Cell phone rings.]	[휴대폰이 울린다.]
W Philip, where are you?	여 Philip, 어디야?
M I'm on my way. There was a problem with the subway.	남 가는 중이야. 지하철에 문제가 있었어.
W Well, please hurry. We have to ¹⁾start our presentation soon!	여 음, 서둘러 줘. 우리 곧 발표를 시작해야 해!
M I'm just getting in a taxi now.	남 지금 막 택시를 탔어.
W When are you going to be here?	여 여기 언제 올 거야?
M Give me 15 minutes.	남 15분만 줘.
W It's scheduled to start in 10 minutes. You're going to be late!	여 10분 후에 시작할 예정이야. 늦겠어!
M I'm sorry. Can you ask Professor Benson if another group can present first? I'll get there ²⁾as soon as possible.	남 미안해. Benson 교수님께 다른 조가 먼저 발표를 할 수 있는지 여쭤볼 수 있니? 최대한 빨리 갈게.
W That's not going to work. He's so strict. He won't make an exception for us.	여 그건 안 될 거야. 교수님은 너무 엄격하셔. 우리에게 예외를 허락하지 않으실 거야.
M Okay, well... **Can you ³⁾put on our video at the beginning?**	남 좋아, 음... 시작할 때에 우리 영상 좀 틀어줄 수 있을까?
W But that's supposed to come at the end!	여 하지만 그건 마지막에 순서잖아!
M I know, but it will buy us some time. I'll be there before ⁴⁾the video is finished.	남 알아, 그래도 그게 우리에게 시간을 좀 벌어줄 거야. 영상이 끝나기 전에 갈게.
W Okay. **I need to introduce it. What should I say?**	여 알겠어. 영상 소개를 해야 해. 뭐라고 말해야 할까?
M Just briefly mention what it's about and press play.	남 그냥 어떤 내용에 관한 건지 짧게 말하고 재생 버튼을 눌러.

선택지 ① 택시 기사님에게 더 빨리 가달라고 해줄 수 있니?
　　　② 다른 조한테 호의를 베풀어줄 수 있는지 물어봐.
　　　③ 그냥 어떤 내용에 관한 건지 짧게 말하고 재생 버튼을 눌러.
　　　④ 교수님께 내가 10분 후에 도착한다고 알려드려.
　　　⑤ 수업 전에 함께 발표 연습을 할 수 있을지 확인해 봐.

수업 발표 시간에 남자가 늦은 상황에서, 시간을 벌기 위해 영상을 틀어줄 것을 부탁하자 여자가 뭐라고 영상을 소개해야 할지 물었으므로, 이에 대한 응답으로는 할 말을 알려주는 ③ 'Just briefly mention what it's about and press play.'가 가장 적절하다.

어휘 on one's way 가는 중인　strict 혱 엄격한　make an exception 예외를 허락하다　buy time 시간을 벌다　do a favor 호의를 베풀다　briefly 븟 짧게

14 긴 대화의 응답 파악

정답 ②

W Honey, can I ask you a favor?	여 여보, 부탁 하나 해도 될까?
M Sure, what is it?	남 물론이지, 무슨 일이야?
W Do you mind opening this jar for me?	여 이 병 좀 열어 줄래?
M No problem. [Pause] Here you go. Does your ¹⁾wrist still hurt?	남 문제없어. [잠시 멈춤] 여기 있어. 아직도 손목이 아파?
W Sadly, yes. I was hoping that it would be stronger by now.	여 안타깝게도 그래. 지금쯤엔 더 튼튼해졌으면 싶었는데 말이야.
M It's only been two weeks since you got the cast taken off your wrist. Healing takes time.	남 손목 깁스를 푼 지 2주밖에 안 됐잖아. 낫는 데는 시간이 걸려.
W Yeah, the doctor said it would be weak ²⁾for a while, but it's annoying that my wrist still doesn't work properly.	여 응, 의사 선생님이 당분간 손목이 약할 거라고 하긴 했는데, 아직도 손목이 제대로 움직이지 않는 게 짜증나네.
M I understand. But I'm happy to help in the meantime. It's really no problem.	남 이해해. 그래도 그동안 내가 기꺼이 도와줄게. 정말 아무 문제도 안 돼.
W Well, thanks for saying that.	여 음, 그렇게 말해줘서 고마워.
M But you should keep doing those wrist exercises. They're supposed to help.	남 하지만 당신 손목 운동은 계속 해야 해. 그게 도움이 될 거야.
W **I already did those stretches this afternoon. I shouldn't do them again ³⁾until after dinner.**	여 오늘 오후에 이미 스트레칭 했어. 저녁 식사 후까지는 다시 하면 안 돼.

M Why can't you do them now?

W The doctor told me not to stretch it too often.

남 왜 지금은 못 해?

여 의사 선생님이 너무 자주 스트레칭 하지 말라고 했어.

[선택지] ① 아니, 그 운동은 나 혼자 할 수 있어.

② 의사 선생님이 너무 자주 스트레칭 하지 말라고 했어.

③ 저녁을 든든하게 먹는 게 낫는 데 도움이 될 것 같아.

④ 깁스를 한 채로는 손을 제대로 스트레칭 하기 힘들어.

⑤ 그동안 많이 아프긴 했지만, 손목이 점점 더 튼튼해지고 있어.

여자가 손목을 다친 후 회복 중인 상황이다. 여자가 오후에 이미 손목 스트레칭을 해서 저녁 식사 후까지는 다시 하면 안 된다고 하자 남자가 왜 지금 못 하는지 물었으므로, 이에 대한 응답으로는 이유를 말해주는 ② 'The doctor told me not to stretch it too often.'이 가장 적절하다.

[어휘] jar 명 병, 항아리 wrist 명 손목 cast 명 깁스 heal 동 낫다, 치유되다 properly 부 제대로

15 상황에 적절한 말 파악

정답 ⑤

M Wendy recently moved to a new city and started going to a different high school. So far, she has not made many friends with her fellow students. Mike is ¹⁾one of her classmates in geography class. During the class this morning, the two of them were assigned to work together on a group report. They got along well and had fun ²⁾doing the assignment together. Later, during the lunch hour, Mike sees Wendy sitting all by herself in the cafeteria reading a book. He thinks that she ³⁾looks lonely. **Therefore, Mike wants to suggest that Wendy join him and his group of friends. In this situation, what would Mike most likely say to Wendy?**

남 Wendy는 최근에 새로운 도시로 이사하여 다른 고등학교에 다니기 시작했습니다. 지금까지는, 그녀는 학우들과 많이 친해지지 못했습니다. Mike는 그녀와 지리학 수업을 같이 듣는 친구 중 한 명입니다. 오늘 오전 수업 시간에 두 사람이 조별 보고서를 함께 쓰도록 배정받았습니다. 그들은 서로 마음이 잘 맞았고 함께 과제를 하면서 즐거워했습니다. 이후 점심시간에, Mike는 Wendy가 구내식당에 혼자 앉아 책을 읽고 있는 것을 봅니다. 그는 그녀가 외로워 보인다고 생각합니다. 따라서 Mike는 Wendy가 자신과 그의 친구 무리에 합류할 것을 제안하고 싶습니다. 이러한 상황에서, Mike가 Wendy에게 가장 할 것 같은 말은 무엇입니까?

[선택지] ① 오늘 점심 메뉴는 어땠어?

② 그녀를 우리 지리학 스터디 그룹에 초대하는 게 어때?

③ 우리 언제 모여서 과제해야 할까?

④ 나중에 구내식당에 같이 가도 되니?

⑤ 괜찮으면 와서 우리랑 같이 밥 먹을래?

Mike는 구내식당에 혼자 앉아 책을 읽고 있는 Wendy를 보고 그녀가 외로워 보인다고 생각해서, Wendy에게 그의 친구 무리에 합류할 것을 제안하려고 한다. 따라서, Mike가 할 말로 ⑤ 'Why don't you come eat with us if you like?'가 가장 적절하다.

[어휘] recently 형 최근에 move 동 이사하다; 움직이다 make friends with ~와 친해지다 fellow student 학우 geography 명 지리학 assign 동 배정하다
get along well 마음이 잘 맞다, 사이가 좋다 all by oneself 혼자

16-17 세트 문항

정답 16 ① 17 ③

W Good afternoon, class. We discussed the invention of different cooking utensils in our last class. **Today, I'd like to talk about the unexpected places that ¹⁾famous foods come from.** First off, we have **pasta**. Most people assume this is from Italy, but this is not true. History shows us that Italians learned to ²⁾make it by imitating Chinese noodle dishes during the middle ages. The second food I'll tell you about is **fish and chips**. This typical English dish was actually invented in Spain. It was brought to England by Jewish refugees in the 15th century. Next, let's consider the **Swedish meatball**. As you might guess, this is ³⁾quite a misleading name. The dish actually traces its origins back to Turkey. Lastly, **ice cream** also comes from an unexpected place. It's actually Mongolian. The dessert was probably first made by accident by horsemen who were ⁴⁾delivering milk in cold weather. Now, let's take a quick look at a video on this subject.

여 안녕하십니까, 학생 여러분. 우리는 지난 수업에서 다양한 조리 기구의 발명에 대해 논의했습니다. 오늘은 유명한 음식이 생겨난 뜻밖의 장소들에 대해 이야기하려고 합니다. 우선, 파스타가 있습니다. 대부분의 사람들은 이것이 이탈리아에서 유래했다고 추정하지만, 이는 사실이 아닙니다. 역사는 우리에게 이탈리아인들이 중세 시대에 중국의 국수 요리를 모방함으로써 그것을 만드는 법을 배웠다는 것을 보여줍니다. 두 번째로 말씀드릴 음식은 피시 앤 칩스입니다. 이 대표적인 영국식 요리는 사실 스페인에서 발명되었습니다. 그것은 15세기에 유대인 난민들에 의해 영국으로 전해졌습니다. 다음으로, 스웨덴 미트볼을 생각해 보겠습니다. 짐작하시겠지만, 이것은 꽤 오해의 소지가 있는 이름입니다. 이 요리는 사실 튀르키예에서 기원했습니다. 마지막으로, 아이스크림도 예상치 못한 곳에서 생겨났습니다. 사실은 몽골의 것입니다. 이 디저트는 아마도 추운 날씨에 우유를 배달하던 마부들에 의해 처음으로 우연히 만들어졌을 것입니다. 자, 이 주제에 대한 영상을 간단히 살펴보도록 하겠습니다.

[선택지] 16 ① 다양한 음식의 놀라운 기원

② 시간이 지남에 따라 요리법이 바뀌는 이유

③ 다양한 조리 기구가 발명된 방법

④ 요리로 유명한 다양한 나라

⑤ 현지 재료를 사용하는 것의 중요성

17 ① 파스타 ② 피시 앤 칩스 ③ 프렌치토스트

④ 스웨덴 미트볼 ⑤ 아이스크림

16 유명한 음식이 생겨난 뜻밖의 장소에 대해 이야기하고 있으므로 여자가 하는 말의 주제로 ① 'surprising origins of different foods'가 가장 적절하다.

17 파스타, 피시 앤 칩스, 스웨덴 미트볼, 아이스크림은 언급했지만 ③ 'French toast'는 언급하지 않았다.

[어휘] cooking utensil 조리 기구 unexpected 형 뜻밖의 come from ~에서 생겨나다 assume 동 추정하다 imitate 동 모방하다 typical 형 대표적인 refugee 명 난민
misleading 형 오해의 소지가 있는 trace one's origins back ~에서 기원하다 by accident 우연히 cuisine 명 요리

1	①	2	③	3	⑤	4	④	5	④	6	④	7	⑤	8	②	9	③	10	②
11	⑤	12	②	13	③	14	②	15	④	16	⑤	17	③						

• 각 문제의 정답 근거는 굵은 글씨로, Dictation 정답은 밑줄로 표시되어 있습니다.

1 목적 파악

정답 ①

W	Good morning, Sunrise Apartments residents! **This announcement is a reminder about our upcoming book exchange event. I'd like to** 1)encourage all residents **to take part.** The event will take place tomorrow from 9 a.m. to 7 p.m. We'll set up tables near the front gate, so come and 2)bring any books that you'd like to exchange. Participants may take books on a first-come-first-served basis. Beverages and light snacks will also be served. It will be a perfect way to find something new to read and 3)get to know your neighbors. I hope to see you all there!	여	좋은 아침입니다, 선라이즈 아파트 주민 여러분! 이 공지는 곧 있을 도서 교환 행사에 대한 알림입니다. 모든 주민 여러분에게 참여할 것을 권하고 싶습니다. 행사는 내일 오전 9시부터 오후 7시까지 열릴 것입니다. 정문 근처에 테이블을 설치해 놓을 테니, 교환하고 싶은 책을 가져오십시오. 참가자들은 선착순으로 책을 가져갈 수 있습니다. 음료와 간단한 간식도 제공될 것입니다. 이 행사는 새로운 읽을거리를 찾고 여러분의 이웃들을 알아가는 완벽한 방법이 될 것입니다. 거기서 여러분 모두를 뵙길 바랍니다!

여자가 곧 있을 아파트 도서 교환 행사를 공지하면서, 주민들의 참여를 권하고 있다. 따라서, 여자가 하는 말의 목적으로 ① '도서 교환 행사 참여를 독려하려고'가 가장 적절하다.

어휘 resident 뎽 주민 reminder 뎽 알림 exchange 뎽 교환 동 교환하다 take part 참여하다 set up ~을 설치하다 on a first-come-first-served basis 선착순으로 beverage 뎽 음료

2 의견 파악

정답 ③

W	Jerry, do you want to order some fries with our meal?	여	Jerry, 우리 식사에 감자튀김 주문할래?
M	No, thanks.	남	아니, 됐어.
W	Oh, I thought you loved eating them.	여	오, 네가 감자튀김 먹는 걸 좋아하는 줄 알았는데.
M	I still like them. **But** 1)eating fried foods **often can be dangerous.**	남	아직도 좋아해. 하지만 튀긴 음식을 자주 먹는 건 위험할 수 있어.
W	Yeah? Are they really that bad?	여	응? 정말 그렇게 나빠?
M	According to some articles I've been reading, yes. Since fried foods are cooked with so much oil and salt, they 2)increase the chance of a heart attack.	남	내가 읽은 기사에 따르면 그래. 튀긴 음식은 너무 많은 기름과 소금으로 요리되기 때문에, 심장마비의 가능성을 증가시켜.
W	Yeah, fair point.	여	그래, 타당한 주장이야.
M	They are also harmful to your blood vessels, which 3)raises the risk of heart problems.	남	또한 혈관에도 해로운데, 이것은 심장 문제가 생길 위험을 높여.
W	Oh, I only knew that fried foods were high in calories. The health effects sound scarier than I thought.	여	아, 난 튀긴 음식이 칼로리가 높다는 것만 알았어. 생각보다 건강에 끼치는 영향이 무섭네.
M	Yeah, that's why I try not to 4)eat them frequently.	남	응, 그래서 자주 먹지 않으려 하는 거야.
W	Well, why don't we just get a salad, then?	여	그럼, 그럼 그냥 샐러드를 사는 게 어때?
M	That's a good idea.	남	좋은 생각이야.

감자 튀김을 주문하려는 여자에게 남자가 튀긴 음식을 자주 먹는 것은 건강에 위험할 수 있다고 했다. 따라서, 남자의 의견으로 ③ '튀긴 음식을 자주 먹는 것은 건강에 좋지 않다.'가 가장 적절하다.

어휘 according to ~에 따르면 chance 뎽 가능성, 기회 heart attack 심장 마비 fair 뎽 타당한 harmful 뎽 해로운 blood vessel 혈관 scary 뎽 무서운 frequently 뷛 자주

3 관계 파악

정답 ⑤

M	Hi. How can I assist you today, Ms. Wilson?	남	안녕하세요. 오늘은 무엇을 도와드릴까요, Wilson 씨?
W	**I'm here to apply for a loan.**	여	대출을 신청하러 왔어요.
M	**I see. I can help you** 1)get started with that. First of all, would this be a personal or business loan?	남	그렇군요. 제가 그걸 시작하시는 것을 도와드릴 수 있어요. 우선, 개인 대출인가요, 아니면 사업 대출인가요?
W	I'd like to borrow the money to 2)make some improvements to my business.	여	제 사업을 좀 개선시키기 위해 돈을 빌리고 싶어요.
M	Okay, just a moment. I need to find the relevant form.	남	네, 잠시만요. 관련된 신청서를 찾아야 해서요.
W	Take your time.	여	천천히 하세요.
M	What kind of business is this for?	남	어떤 종류의 사업이죠?
W	**I own an ice cream shop in the Monroe Park area.**	여	저는 먼로 공원 구역에서 아이스크림 가게를 운영하고 있어요.
M	I see. What are you planning to 3)spend the money on?	남	그렇군요. 그 돈을 어디에 쓰실 계획인가요?
W	We need a new sign because the old one was badly damaged in the recent typhoon.	여	오래된 간판이 최근 태풍으로 심하게 파손되어서 새 간판이 필요해요.

M Great, I'll pass the form on to the bank manager ⁴⁾for approval. Please fill it out now.

W Will do. Thanks.

남 좋습니다. 신청서를 은행 지점장님에게 넘겨서 승인을 받도록 할게요. 이걸 지금 작성해 주세요.

여 그러죠. 감사해요.

두 사람이 은행 대출 신청에 대해 이야기하고 있다. 남자는 여자의 대출 신청 절차를 도우며 은행 지점장에게 신청서를 넘기겠다고 했고 여자는 먼로 공원 구역에서 아이스크림 가게를 운영하고 있다고 하는 것으로 보아 두 사람의 관계로 ⑤ '은행원 — 아이스크림 가게 사장'이 가장 적절하다.

어휘 assist 图 돕다 apply for ~을 신청하다 loan 图 대출 personal 图 개인의 relevant 图 관련된 take one's time 천천히 하다 pass A on to B A를 B에게 넘기다 approval 图 승인 fill out ~을 작성하다

---

4 그림 내용 불일치 파악
정답 ④

M This is the restaurant's private event room, ma'am.

W It will be perfect for my daughter's birthday party.

M I think so. The two paintings of clowns ¹⁾create a festive atmosphere.

W I agree. I see there is a microphone set up in the back of the room. Is that usually there?

M No. That was brought in for another event, but I'll put it away if you want.

W Yes, please. Would I be able to get a projector?

M Actually, there's one attached to the ceiling.

W Oh, I see it. Would we be able to ²⁾remove the cactus by the window?

M That shouldn't be a problem.

W And one last thing. Do you mind if I request another ³⁾square table? One isn't going to be enough.

M Not at all.

W Great. I'll ⁴⁾reserve this room!

남 이곳이 식당의 프라이빗 이벤트 룸입니다, 손님.

여 우리 딸 생일 파티에 딱 좋을 것 같네요.

남 저도 그렇게 생각해요. 광대 그림 두 점이 축제 분위기를 만들어요.

여 동의해요. 방 뒤쪽에 마이크가 설치되어 있는 게 보이네요. 보통 저기에 있나요?

남 아뇨. 다른 행사를 위해 들여온 건데, 원하시면 치워드릴게요.

여 네, 부탁드립니다. 제가 프로젝터를 구할 수 있을까요?

남 사실, 천장에 하나 붙어 있어요.

여 아, 보이네요. 창가에 있는 선인장은 치울 수 있을까요?

남 문제없을 거예요.

여 그리고 마지막으로 한 가지 더요. 제가 네모난 테이블을 하나 더 요청해도 될까요? 하나로는 충분하지 않을 거라서요.

남 물론이죠.

여 좋아요. 이 방으로 예약할게요!

대화에서 여자가 창가에 있는 선인장을 치워도 되는지 물어봤는데, ④에는 고양이 조각상이 그려져 있다.

어휘 clown 图 광대 festive 图 축제의 atmosphere 图 분위기; 대기 put away ~을 치우다 attached to ~에 붙어 있는 ceiling 图 천장 cactus 图 선인장

---

5 할 일 파악
정답 ④

W It's raining cats and dogs again, Phil. Why doesn't it stop?

M This ¹⁾happens every summer. I'm sure you know that.

W I haven't gone jogging in two weeks now. It's really frustrating.

M Why don't you go to the gym? You can run on the treadmill.

W There is always a long line to use the machine.

M Maybe you could ²⁾do another exercise for a couple of weeks.

W But I love running, and it's good for the body.

M You could try table tennis. There's also a pool, so you could swim.

W Actually, table tennis sounds like great fun! Let's ³⁾go to the gym and play a few games!

M Give me a few minutes. I just need to change into my sweats.

W Okay! We can go out for ice cream afterwards.

M That's perfect.

여 비가 또 억수같이 쏟아지고 있어, Phil. 왜 안 그치는 거야?

남 여름마다 일어나는 일이잖아. 너도 분명 알고 있을 텐데.

여 지금 조깅하러 2주 동안 못 갔어. 정말 답답해.

남 체육관에 가는 건 어때? 러닝머신에서 뛰면 되잖아.

여 기구를 사용하려면 항상 긴 줄이 서 있어.

남 어쩌면 몇 주 동안 다른 운동을 해도 되고.

여 하지만 나는 달리기를 정말 좋아하고, 그게 몸에 좋은걸.

남 탁구를 한번 쳐봐. 수영장도 있으니 수영을 해도 돼.

여 사실, 탁구는 정말 재미있을 것 같아! 체육관에 가서 몇 게임 치자!

남 잠깐만 기다려 줘. 운동복으로 갈아입기만 하면 돼.

여 알았어! 그 뒤에 아이스크림 먹으러 갈 수도 있겠어.

남 완벽해.

비가 올 때 할 수 있는 운동에 대해 이야기하고 있다. 여자가 남자에게 체육관으로 탁구 치러 가자고 하자, 남자가 운동복으로 갈아입겠다고 했으므로 남자가 할 일로 ④ '운동복으로 갈아입기'가 가장 적절하다.

어휘 rain cats and dogs 비가 억수같이 쏟아지다 frustrating 图 답답하게 하는; 불만스러운 treadmill 图 러닝머신 table tennis 탁구 change into ~으로 갈아입다 sweats 图 운동복 afterwards 图 그 뒤에

6 금액 정보 파악

정답 ④

W Good afternoon, sir. Are you having a good time at the festival?	여 안녕하세요. 축제에서 즐거운 시간 보내고 계신가요?
M I am! But it's hot out there. My friends and I are thirsty.	남 네! 하지만 밖이 덥네요. 친구들과 저는 목이 말라요.
W Well, we have water for $2 per bottle and soft drinks for $3 per can.	여 음, 생수는 한 병에 2달러이고 탄산음료는 한 캔에 3달러예요.
M I'll take ¹⁾two of each.	남 각각 두 개씩 주세요.
W Got it. Did you want anything ²⁾to eat as well?	여 알겠습니다. 드시고 싶은 것도 있으신가요?
M Do you have ice cream?	남 아이스크림 있나요?
W Yes. We have chocolate and strawberry ice cream. **Cups and cones are both $5 apiece.**	여 네. 초콜릿과 딸기 아이스크림이 있어요. 컵과 콘 둘 다 각각 5달러입니다.
M In that case, **I'd like three cups of strawberry ice cream.**	남 그렇다면, 딸기 아이스크림 컵으로 세 개 주세요.
W I've got two waters, two sodas, and three cups of strawberry ice cream. Does that ³⁾complete your order?	여 생수 두 병, 탄산음료 두 캔, 딸기 아이스크림 컵으로 세 개 주문받았습니다. 주문 끝나신 거죠?
M Yes, but can I use this coupon? I'm supposed to get $5 off a purchase.	남 네, 그런데 이 쿠폰 쓸 수 있나요? 구매 시 5달러 할인을 받게 되어있는데요.
W Oh, I'm sorry, sir. This coupon is ⁴⁾only valid for clothing items and souvenirs.	여 아, 죄송합니다, 손님. 이 쿠폰은 의류와 기념품에만 유효해요.
M I understand. I'll pay with cash.	남 알겠습니다. 현금으로 지불할게요.

남자가 생수 두 병($2×2=$4)과 탄산음료 두 캔($3×2=$6), 딸기 아이스크림 컵 세 개($5×3=$15)를 구매했으므로 정답은 ④ '$25'이다.

어휘 thirsty 혱 목이 마른 soft drink 탄산음료 apiece 閉 각각 valid 혱 유효한 souvenir 몡 기념품

7 이유 파악

정답 ⑤

M Hi, Kelly. It was good running into you at the theater last weekend.	남 안녕, Kelly. 지난 주말 극장에서 널 우연히 만나서 좋았어.
W ¹⁾What a coincidence we chose the same showing! I might have to go see that movie again, though.	여 우리가 같은 영화를 골랐다니 이런 우연의 일치! 그런데 난 그 영화를 다시 보러 가야 할지도 몰라.
M You ²⁾left the theater early, right? I noticed you were gone when I came back from the bathroom.	남 넌 극장에서 일찍 나갔잖아, 맞지? 화장실에서 돌아왔을 때 네가 가고 없는 걸 알아차렸어.
W Yeah. I left in the middle.	여 응. 중간에 나갔어.
M Did you have to catch the last bus? The movie was pretty long.	남 마지막 버스를 타야 했었니? 그 영화는 꽤 길었잖아.
W No. I ³⁾drove there.	여 아니. 난 거기 운전해서 갔어.
M Then, were you feeling sick? I know you get bad headaches sometimes.	남 그럼 어디 아팠어? 네가 가끔씩 심한 두통을 앓는다는 걸 알고 있어.
W No. **Actually, I got a text message saying that our dog was sick. So I left to ⁴⁾take him to the vet.**	여 아니. 실은, 우리 개가 아프다는 문자를 받았어. 그래서 수의사에게 데려가려고 나간 거야.
M Oh, no! Is he okay?	남 오, 이런! 그 녀석 괜찮아?
W He's doing fine.	여 잘 지내고 있어.
M Good. But to be honest, the ending of the movie was pretty boring.	남 다행이다. 하지만 솔직히 말해서, 그 영화의 결말은 꽤 지루했어.
W Then, it sounds like I didn't miss much.	여 그럼 별로 놓쳐서 아쉬울 게 없는 것 같네.

여자는 영화 중간에 개가 아프다는 문자를 받고 수의사에게 데려가기 위해 나갔다고 했으므로, 여자가 중간에 영화관을 나온 이유는 ⑤ '수의사에게 개를 데려가야 해서'이다.

어휘 run into ~와 우연히 만나다 coincidence 몡 우연의 일치 headache 몡 두통 vet 몡 수의사 to be honest 솔직히 말해서

8 언급 유무 파악

정답 ②

[Telephone rings.]	*[전화기가 울린다.]*
M Brooks Catering. This is Dominic speaking. How may I help you?	남 Brooks Catering입니다. 저는 Dominic이고요. 무엇을 도와드릴까요?
W Hi. I'm Monica Simms from Adams Library. I want to ¹⁾check some details about the catering for our reopening celebration.	여 안녕하세요, 저는 애덤스 도서관의 Monica Simms입니다. 저희 재개관 기념식을 위한 케이터링의 세부 사항을 확인하고 싶은데요.
M Sure. Let me pull up our records for that.	남 물론이죠. 저희 기록을 찾아볼게요.
W It's scheduled for **May 10th.**	여 5월 10일로 일정이 잡혀있어요.
M Just a second... *[Typing sound]* I've got it. You need ²⁾food for **100 people**, correct?	남 잠깐만요... *[타자 치는 소리]* 알겠습니다. 100인분의 음식이 필요하신 거네요, 맞죠?
W Right.	여 맞아요.
M What did you want to check?	남 무엇을 확인하고 싶으셨나요?
W I was ³⁾wondering how much time you would need to set up before the event.	여 행사 전에 준비하는 데 시간이 얼마나 필요하실지 궁금했어요.
M We need an hour. Since the dinner starts at **7**, we will be there a little before 6.	남 한 시간은 필요해요. 저녁 식사가 7시에 시작하니까, 6시 조금 전에 도착하겠습니다.
W Got it. I'll be there to let you in. And do you know ⁴⁾how to get here?	여 알았어요. 들여보내 드릴 수 있도록 제가 거기에 있을 거예요. 그리고 여기 어떻게 오는지 아시나요?
M Yes. The library is **on Main Street, next to city hall**, right?	남 네. 도서관은 시청 옆 메인가에 있잖아요, 맞죠?
W Exactly. I'll see you on that day.	여 정확해요. 그날 뵐게요.

날짜(5월 10일), 식사 주문량(100인분), 식사 시작 시간(오후 7시), 위치(시청 옆 메인가)에 대해 언급했고, ② '식순'은 언급하지 않았다.

어휘 details 몡 세부 사항 pull up ~을 찾아보다, (기록을) 확인하다 be scheduled for ~으로 일정이 잡히다

---

9 내용 불일치 파악
정답 ③

M Hello, everyone. I'd like to welcome you all to the Herbert Town Hotdog Festival. Here, hotdog lovers will get the chance to taste as many different hotdogs ¹⁾<u>as they want</u>. We've got vendors from all over the country offering delicious hotdogs. So enjoy yourselves. **As always, we'll be having a hotdog cooking competition. It will** ²⁾<u>take place from noon to 2 p.m.</u> All the hotdogs will be prepared by amateur cooks. The judges are the winners of the previous year's competition. May the best cook win! We have a bunch of other programs ³⁾<u>planned for kids</u> as well. These include face painting and a race on hotdog carts. Thank you, and enjoy the festival.	남 안녕하세요, 여러분. Herbert Town Hotdog Festival에 오신 여러분 모두를 환영합니다. 여기서, 핫도그 애호가들은 원하는 만큼 많은 종류의 핫도그를 맛볼 수 있는 기회를 얻게 될 것입니다. 전국 각지에서 온 노점상들이 맛있는 핫도그를 제공할 것입니다. 그러니 마음껏 즐기세요. 언제나처럼 핫도그 요리 대회를 열 것입니다. 대회는 정오부터 오후 2시까지 진행될 예정입니다. 모든 핫도그는 아마추어 요리사들이 준비할 것입니다. 심사위원들은 작년 대회의 우승자들입니다. 최고의 요리사가 이기길 바랍니다! 저희는 어린이들을 위한 많은 다른 프로그램들도 계획하고 있습니다. 여기에는 페이스페인팅과 핫도그 카트 경주가 포함됩니다. 여러분께 감사드리며, 즐거운 축제 되세요.

핫도그 축제에 대한 안내 방송이다. 남자가 핫도그 요리 대회는 정오부터 오후 2시까지 진행될 예정이라고 했으므로 ③ '요리 대회가 오전에 열릴 것이다.'는 내용과 일치하지 않는다.

어휘 vendor 몡 노점상 offer 통 제공하다 enjoy oneself 마음껏 즐기다 as always 언제나처럼 competition 몡 대회 previous year 작년 a bunch of 많은

---

10 도표 정보 파악
정답 ②

W Is that an electronics store website? What are you shopping for, Tom?	여 이거 전자제품 매장 웹사이트니? 뭘 살 거야, Tom?
M I'm looking at portable speakers. I don't know which one to buy, though.	남 휴대용 스피커를 보고 있어. 하지만 어떤 것을 사야 할지 모르겠어.
W What's your ¹⁾<u>price range</u>?	여 가격대가 어떻게 돼?
M I want to buy one with this $100 store gift card.	남 이 100달러짜리 상품권으로 하나 사고 싶어.
W That would eliminate one option if you don't want to spend any of your money.	여 네 돈을 조금도 쓰기 싫은 거라면 한 가지 선택지가 제거되네.
M That's what I was thinking. I also want ²⁾<u>a durable one</u>. I'd like to listen to music outside.	남 나도 그렇게 생각하고 있었어. 또, 나는 내구성이 좋은 걸 원해. 밖에서 음악을 듣고 싶거든.
W **Then, you should get one that is waterproof.**	여 그럼 방수가 되는 걸로 사야겠네.
M Sure. That helps narrow things down.	남 물론이지. 범위를 좁히는 데 도움이 되네.
W What about battery life? You probably want a speaker that can play music for a long time.	여 배터리 수명은? 아마도 오랫동안 음악을 재생할 수 있는 스피커를 원할 텐데.
M I want ³⁾<u>over 15 hours</u> of playing time.	남 재생 시간이 15시간이 넘는 걸 원해.
W That leaves two. But isn't this one the best choice?	여 그럼 두 개 남았어. 하지만 이게 최선의 선택 아니니?
M Hmm... **I don't really want a** ⁴⁾<u>yellow speaker</u>.	남 흠... 나는 노란색 스피커는 별로 갖고 싶지 않은걸.
W In that case, I think the decision is made for you!	여 그렇다면, 결정이 내려진 것 같네!

남자는 100달러짜리 상품권을 이용하여 자신의 돈을 전혀 쓰지 않을 수 있고, 방수가 되고, 재생 시간이 15시간이 넘으며, 노란색이 아닌 휴대용 스피커를 골랐다.

어휘 portable 몡 휴대용의, 휴대가 쉬운 gift card 상품권, 선불카드 eliminate 통 제거하다 durable 몡 내구성이 좋은 waterproof 몡 방수가 되는 narrow down ~을 좁히다

---

11 짧은 대화의 응답 파악
정답 ⑤

W Honey, please wake up. I'm not feeling good.	여 여보, 일어나봐. 나 몸이 안 좋아.
M Oh, you ¹⁾<u>look pale</u>. Tell me what's wrong.	남 아, 얼굴이 창백해 보여. 무엇이 문제인지 말해봐.
W I'm feeling sick to my stomach. I've been dizzy and throwing up since dawn. **Could you** ²⁾<u>take me to the hospital</u>?	여 속이 메슥거려. 새벽부터 어지럽고 토했어. 날 병원에 데려가 줄래?
M Definitely. You should see a doctor right now.	남 <u>물론이지. 지금 당장 병원에 가야겠어.</u>
	선택지 ① 문제없어. 내가 당신 회사에 전화할게.
	② 맞아. 난 새벽까지 잠을 못 잤어.
	③ 물론이지. 식중독 약을 처방해줄게.
	④ 안됐네. 빨리 나으면 좋겠다.
	⑤ 물론이지. 지금 당장 병원에 가야겠어.

남자가 무엇이 문제인지 말해보라고 하자 여자가 속이 메슥거린다고 말하며 병원에 데려가 달라고 부탁했으므로, 이에 대한 응답으로는 당장 병원에 가자고 말하는 ⑤ 'Definitely. You should see a doctor right now.'가 가장 적절하다.

어휘 pale 몡 창백한 feel sick to one's stomach 메슥거리다 dizzy 몡 어지러운 throw up 토하다 dawn 몡 새벽 prescribe 통 처방하다 food poisoning 식중독

12 짧은 대화의 응답 파악

M Mom, the 1)mailman was supposed to drop off a box of pears in front of our house this morning. Did you bring it inside?	**남** 엄마, 오늘 아침에 우체부가 배 한 상자를 우리 집 앞에 배달해 주기로 했는데요. 그걸 안에 들여놓으셨어요?
W I didn't see anything like that. Are you sure the package arrived?	**여** 그런 건 못 봤단다. 택배가 도착한 게 확실하니?
M Yeah. **I got a text message that** 2)**the delivery was completed. That's really weird.**	**남** 네. 배송이 완료되었다는 문자를 받았어요. 정말 이상하네요.
W You had better call to see what is going on.	**여** 무슨 일인지 전화해서 확인하는 게 좋겠어.
	선택지 ① 배가 신선하고 맛이 달콤하구나.
	② 무슨 일인지 전화해서 확인하는 게 좋겠어.
	③ 불행하게도, 우체부가 택배를 떨어뜨린 것 같네.
	④ 오늘 아침에 우체통에 넣어뒀던 게 기억나는구나.
	⑤ 너무 바빠서 네 문자에 답장을 못 했단다.

택배가 오지 않은 상황에서 남자가 택배 배송 완료 문자를 받았다면서 이상하다고 했으므로, 이에 대한 응답으로는 전화해서 확인해보라고 조언하는 ② 'You had better call to see what is going on.'이 가장 적절하다.

어휘 mailman 뎅 우체부, 집배원 drop off ~을 배달하다 package 뎅 택배, 소포 complete 퉁 완료하다 weird 혱 이상한

13 긴 대화의 응답 파악

W You wanted to see me, Mr. Madison?	**여** 절 보자고 하셨나요, Madison 선생님?
M Yes. Have a seat. Let's talk about your score on the last math test.	**남** 그래. 자리에 앉으렴. 지난 수학 시험 점수에 대해 이야기해보자.
W I was really disappointed.	**여** 저 정말 실망했어요.
M I understand. I think you'd better 1)change the way you study.	**남** 이해한다. 내 생각엔 공부하는 방식을 바꾸는 게 좋을 것 같구나.
W Is there anything that you would recommend?	**여** 추천해주실 게 있나요?
M Yes. You don't show how you 2)solve the problems in your homework.	**남** 그래. 넌 숙제에다가 문제 풀이 방식을 보여주지 않잖니.
W Does that matter?	**여** 그게 중요한가요?
M When I check your homework, I can't see where you made mistakes. So it's hard to give you the right feedback.	**남** 숙제를 확인해 볼 때, 네가 어디서 실수를 했는지 난 알 수가 없단다. 그래서 너에게 적절한 피드백을 주기가 어렵구나.
W I see. Then, I should 3)write down every step in the process.	**여** 그렇군요. 그럼 풀이 과정의 모든 단계를 적어야겠네요.
M Exactly. Also, you can do more in the classroom.	**남** 맞아. 또한, 교실에서 더 많은 것을 할 수도 있지.
W I don't know what you mean.	**여** 무슨 말씀이신지 모르겠어요.
M **I see that sometimes you are a little confused and you don't say anything.**	**남** 내가 보기에 넌 가끔 좀 헷갈려도 아무 말도 하지 않더구나.
W **So you're saying that I should** 4)**ask questions more often?**	**여** 그러니까, 제가 질문을 더 자주 해야 한다는 말씀이신가요?
M Right. I think doing so would help you understand.	**남** 맞아. 그렇게 하는 게 네가 이해하는 데 도움이 될 거라고 생각해.
	선택지 ① 그래. 자료를 연구하는 데 시간을 더 쓸 거란다.
	② 정답이야. 네가 필기한 걸 보여주길 바란단다.
	③ 맞아. 그렇게 하는 게 네가 이해하는 데 도움이 될 거라고 생각해.
	④ 아쉽구나. 답변이 더 길 거라고 예상했거든.
	⑤ 그러게. 수학은 어려운 과목이지만, 너는 최선을 다하고 있어.

여자의 수학 공부 방식을 바꾸는 것에 대해 이야기하고 있는 상황이다. 남자가 내용이 헷갈려도 아무 말 하지 않는 여자의 태도를 지적하자 여자가 그 말이 질문을 더 자주 해야 한다는 뜻이 맞는지 되물었으므로, 이에 대한 응답으로는 그렇다고 답하는 ③ 'Right. I think doing so would help you understand.'가 가장 적절하다.

어휘 have a seat 자리에 앉다 score 뎅 점수 matter 퉁 중요하다, 문제가 되다 make a mistake 실수를 하다 confused 혱 헷갈려하는, 혼란스러워하는 take a note 필기하다 do one's best 최선을 다하다

14 긴 대화의 응답 파악

M What can I do for you?	**남** 무엇을 도와드릴까요?
W I'd like to buy a women's bicycle.	**여** 여성용 자전거를 사고 싶은데요.
M Sure, I can help. If you come this way, I'll show you a few different models.	**남** 물론이죠, 도와드릴게요. 이쪽으로 오시면 몇 가지 다른 모델을 보여드릴게요.
W *[Pause]* I don't want one with 1)skinny tires like that. It looks like it would be uncomfortable to ride.	**여** *[잠시 멈춤]* 저런 얇은 타이어는 원하지 않아요. 타기 불편할 것 같아요.
M I see. So you're looking for comfort.	**남** 그렇군요. 그러니까 편안한 걸 찾고 계시는 군요.
W That's right. I plan to ride it 2)to and from work each day, so it needs to be comfortable.	**여** 맞아요. 매일 출퇴근하는 데 탈 예정이라 편해야 해요.
M That makes sense. *[Pause]* What about this one with big tires?	**남** 일리 있는 말이네요. *[잠시 멈춤]* 타이어가 큰 이것은 어떠세요?
W That looks better.	**여** 더 좋아 보이네요.
M Oh, and **how tall are you?**	**남** 아, 그리고 키가 어떻게 되시나요?
W **160 centimeters. Why?**	**여** 160cm요. 왜요?

M It'll help me pick the ³⁾right frame size for you. If you buy a bike with the wrong height, it will be uncomfortable.

W I understand. Thanks for the explanation.

남 고객님께 맞는 프레임 사이즈를 고르는 데 도움이 될 거예요. 잘못된 높이의 자전거를 구매하시면 불편하실 겁니다.

여 알겠습니다. 설명해 주셔서 감사해요.

<u>선택지</u> ① 괜찮아요. 저는 파란색을 선호해요.
② 알겠습니다. 설명해 주셔서 감사해요.
③ 그렇군요. 폭이 좁은 타이어가 더 나은 선택일지도 몰라요.
④ 그게 맞나요? 그렇게 비쌀 줄 몰랐어요.
⑤ 죄송합니다. 저게 찾으시는 사이즈인지 잘 모르겠네요.

출퇴근하는 데 탈 자전거를 고르는 상황이다. 여자가 남자에게 왜 키를 물어봤는지 궁금해하자 남자가 그게 어떻게 자전거 선택에 도움이 되는지 설명했으므로, 이에 대한 응답으로는 설명해줘서 고맙다고 말하는 ② 'I understand. Thanks for the explanation.'이 가장 적절하다.

<u>어휘</u> skinny 혭 얇은, 가는; 마른 uncomfortable 혭 불편한 make sense 일리가 있다 height 몝 높이, 키 explanation 몝 설명 narrow 혭 폭이 좁은

---

15 상황에 적절한 말 파악   정답 ④

W Michael is a high school student whose favorite subject is art. This year, during the summer break, he ¹⁾enrolled in a painting class. To prepare for the class, he needs to buy a few supplies, so he decided to visit an art supply shop. However, he is not sure which paintbrushes he should buy. So he asks Olivia, an employee at the store, to help him ²⁾choose the right paintbrushes. Olivia thinks that her recommendation will depend on the art class's requirements. **Therefore, she wants to ask Michael ³⁾for more information about the type of painting he will be making.** In this situation, what would Olivia most likely say to Michael?

여 Michael은 가장 좋아하는 과목이 미술인 고등학생입니다. 올해 여름 방학 동안 그는 그림 수업에 등록했습니다. 수업을 준비하려면 몇 가지 준비물을 사야 해서, 그는 미술용품 가게를 방문하기로 결정했습니다. 하지만, 그는 어떤 붓을 사야 할지 확신하지 못합니다. 그래서 그는 가게의 직원인 Olivia에게 알맞은 붓을 고르는 것을 도와달라고 부탁합니다. Olivia는 자신의 추천이 미술 수업의 요구 조건에 따라 달라질 것이라고 생각합니다. 따라서, 그녀는 Michael에게 그가 그릴 그림의 종류에 대한 더 많은 정보를 묻고 싶습니다. 이러한 상황에서, Olivia가 Michael에게 가장 할 것 같은 말은 무엇입니까?

<u>선택지</u> ① 가장 좋아하는 화풍이 무엇인가요?
② 미술 선생님께 더 자세한 내용을 물어보는 게 어때요?
③ 초보자에게 이런 종류의 붓을 추천하실 건가요?
④ 어떤 종류의 그림을 그릴 건지 더 말해줄 수 있나요?
⑤ 미술용품에 대한 학생 할인이 있나요?

Michael이 붓 고르는 것을 도와달라고 부탁하자, Olivia는 그가 그릴 그림의 종류에 대한 더 많은 정보를 물어보려고 한다. 따라서, Olivia가 할 말로 ④ 'Can you tell me more about the kind of painting you will do?'가 가장 적절하다.

<u>어휘</u> enroll 툉 등록하다 supplies 몝 준비물, 용품 depend on ~에 따라 달라지다 requirement 몝 요구 조건, 필요조건

16-17 세트 문항   정답 16 ⑤ 17 ③

M Good afternoon, students. Yesterday, we discussed the origins of several idioms. **Today, I want to ¹⁾explain various proverbs related to animals.** First, let's consider one from **Greece**. As the saying goes, "every dog has its day." It suggests that lucky situations can come up for anyone. In other words, we all ²⁾get a chance to be successful from time to time. Another common proverb comes from **Australia**. It is, "Don't count your chickens before they're hatched." This expression warns us not to make plans based on potential alone. After all, not every egg will become a bird. Third, we can look at one from **Egypt**, "Repetition teaches even a donkey." It suggests that practicing something many times is ³⁾a powerful tool. Lastly, there's an expression from **China** I want to mention. "Big fish eat small fish." This proverb suggests that the powerful always ⁴⁾dominate the weak. All right, now I'd like you all to open your textbooks to Page 323.

남 안녕하세요, 학생 여러분. 어제, 우리는 몇 가지 관용구의 기원에 대해 논의했습니다. 오늘은 동물과 관련된 다양한 속담에 대해 설명하려고 합니다. 먼저, 그리스 속담을 하나 생각해봅시다. 이른바 '모든 개는 자신의 날이 있다.(쥐구멍에도 볕들 날 있다.)'라는 속담이 있습니다. 그것은 행운의 상황이 누구에게나 일어날 수 있다는 것을 암시합니다. 다시 말해서, 우리 모두는 때때로 성공할 기회를 얻습니다. 또 다른 흔한 속담은 호주에서 왔습니다. 그것은 '달걀이 부화하기 전에 닭을 세지 마라.(떡 줄 사람은 생각도 없는데 김칫국부터 마신다.)'입니다. 이 표현은 우리에게 가능성 하나만을 바탕으로 계획을 세우지 말라고 경고합니다. 결국, 모든 달걀이 새가 되는 것은 아니니까요. 셋째로, 우리는 이집트 속담인 '반복은 당나귀도 가르친다.(서당 개 삼 년이면 풍월을 읊는다.)'라는 말을 볼 수 있습니다. 그것은 무언가를 여러 번 연습하는 것이 강력한 도구라는 것을 암시합니다. 마지막으로, 제가 언급하고 싶은 중국의 표현이 있습니다. '큰 물고기가 작은 물고기를 먹는다.(약육강식)' 이 속담은 강자가 항상 약자를 지배한다는 것을 암시합니다. 좋습니다. 이제 여러분 모두 교과서 323쪽을 펴세요.

<u>선택지</u> **16** ① 전통적인 이야기에서 특히 동물이 나오는 이유
② 언어 학습에 필수적인 관용구
③ 다양한 국제적인 속담이 생겨난 장소
④ 시간이 지남에 따라 흔히 쓰이는 표현이 바뀌는 방식
⑤ 동물에 근거한 다양한 속담
17 ① 그리스 ② 호주 ③ 멕시코 ④ 이집트 ⑤ 중국

16 동물과 관련된 다양한 속담에 대해 설명하고 있으므로 남자가 하는 말의 주제로 ⑤ 'different old sayings based on animals'가 가장 적절하다.
17 그리스, 호주, 이집트, 중국은 언급했지만 ③ 'Mexico'는 언급하지 않았다.

<u>어휘</u> origin 몝 기원 idiom 몝 관용구, 숙어 proverb 몝 속담 related to ~과 관련된 as the saying goes 이른바, 속담에 있듯이 suggest 툉 암시하다; 제안하다
in other words 다시 말해서 from time to time 때때로 warn 툉 경고하다 potential 몝 가능성, 잠재력 repetition 몝 반복 dominate 툉 지배하다

1	③	2	①	3	②	4	⑤	5	④	6	③	7	④	8	②	9	③	10	④
11	①	12	③	13	③	14	②	15	⑤	16	③	17	④						

• 각 문제의 정답 근거는 굵은 글씨로, Dictation 정답은 밑줄로 표시되어 있습니다.

1 목적 파악
정답 ③

W	Hello, listeners. Here's a quick reminder for you about tomorrow's Independence Day parade. The parade will be taking place from 9 a.m. to noon. **The parade will** 1)run along **1st Avenue, so the street will be closed throughout the morning.** Many bus routes will also be altered. Therefore, 2)make sure to check for information on alternative routes before you hop on. Details can be found on the city's website. Traffic in nearby areas will be heavy. I recommend you 3)keep your vehicle at home. If you want to come and see the parade, please take the subway. I hope you enjoy the parade.	여	안녕하세요, 청취자 여러분. 내일 있을 독립기념일 퍼레이드에 대해 간단히 알려드립니다. 퍼레이드는 오전 9시부터 정오까지 열릴 예정입니다. 퍼레이드가 1번가를 따라 이어질 예정이어서, 오전 내내 그 거리가 폐쇄될 것입니다. 많은 버스 노선들도 바뀔 것입니다. 따라서, 탑승하기 전에 대체 경로에 대한 정보를 반드시 확인하십시오. 자세한 내용은 시의 웹사이트에서 확인하실 수 있습니다. 인근 지역의 교통 체증이 심할 것입니다. 차량은 집에 두고 오시는 것을 추천합니다. 퍼레이드를 보러 오고 싶다면, 지하철을 타십시오. 퍼레이드를 즐기시길 바랍니다.

여자가 독립기념일 퍼레이드가 열릴 예정이라고 하면서, 오전 내내 1번가 거리가 폐쇄될 것이라고 안내했다. 따라서, 여자가 하는 말의 목적으로 ③ '도로 통제 조치를 예고하려고'가 가장 적절하다.

[어휘] run ⑧ 이어지다; 달리다 throughout 웹 ~ 내내 alter ⑧ 바꾸다 hop on ~에 탑승하다 vehicle ⑲ 차량

2 의견 파악
정답 ①

M	Good afternoon, Patricia. What are you doing here?	남	안녕하세요, Patricia. 여기는 어쩐 일이에요?
W	I'm waiting for my daughter. She is shopping in this supermarket.	여	딸을 기다리고 있어요. 이 슈퍼마켓에서 쇼핑을 하고 있어요.
M	Isn't she 1)too young to do that alone?	남	혼자 쇼핑하기에는 너무 어리지 않나요?
W	No. She's already nine. And **I think** 2)giving errands to kids **has great educational effects.**	여	아뇨. 벌써 9살이에요. 그리고 아이들에게 심부름을 시키는 게 교육적인 효과가 크다고 생각해요.
M	Why do you think so?	남	왜 그렇게 생각해요?
W	By remembering the number of items to buy and calculating the total cost, my daughter can 3)learn math skills.	여	구입할 품목의 개수를 기억하고 총 비용을 계산함으로써, 제 딸은 수학 기술을 배울 수 있어요.
M	Yeah, that makes sense.	남	네, 말이 되네요.
W	Also, she can develop a sense of responsibility by overcoming the temptation to buy snacks.	여	또한, 간식을 사고 싶은 유혹을 극복함으로써 책임감을 기를 수도 있죠.
M	It sounds like asking children to do errands teaches them a lot.	남	아이들에게 심부름을 시키는 게 많은 걸 가르쳐 주는 것처럼 들리네요.
W	Seriously! That's why I'm trying to 4)give daily tasks to my daughter.	여	정말이에요! 그래서 저는 딸에게 매일 할 일을 주려고 노력하고 있어요.
M	I should get my son to help me with the chores, then.	남	그러면 제 아들에게 집안일을 도와달라고 해야겠어요.

아이가 혼자 쇼핑하기에는 너무 어리지 않은지 묻는 남자에게 여자는 아이들에게 심부름을 시키는 것은 교육적 효과가 크다고 했다. 따라서, 여자의 의견으로 ① '아이들이 심부름하는 것은 교육적 효과가 뛰어나다.'가 가장 적절하다.

[어휘] errand ⑲ 심부름 educational ⑱ 교육적인 calculate ⑧ 계산하다 a sense of responsibility 책임감 overcome ⑧ 극복하다 temptation ⑲ 유혹

3 관계 파악
정답 ②

W	Hi. It's nice to meet you, Mr. Williams.	여	안녕하세요. 만나서 반가워요, Williams 선생님.
M	You too, Ms. Kelley. Have a seat. You have experience with photo shoots like this, correct?	남	저도요, Kelley 씨. 자리에 앉으시죠. 이런 사진 촬영 경험이 있으시죠, 그렇죠?
W	That's right. **Mainly I do portraits.** I can show you 1)some examples of my work.	여	맞아요. 주로 인물 사진을 찍어요. 제 작업물의 몇 가지 예를 보여드릴 수도 있어요.
M	Yes. [Pause] Oh, these are excellent.	남	네. [잠시 멈춤] 아, 이것들은 훌륭하네요.
W	Thanks. So you need me to take pictures of students 2)for the school yearbook.	여	감사해요. 그래서 학생들의 졸업 앨범 사진을 찍는 데 제가 필요하시다고요.
M	That's correct. Please be here on the 6th of the month.	남	맞아요. 이달 6일에 여기로 와 주세요.
W	Will I be taking the photos in your classroom?	여	선생님 교실에서 사진을 찍는 걸까요?
M	No. You'll be in the school gym. I'll start bringing students in at 10.	남	아뇨. 학교 체육관에서 하실 거예요. 제가 학생들을 10시에 데려오기 시작할 거예요.
W	Good. **What time do you want me to** 3)arrive at school **that day?**	여	좋아요. 제가 그날 학교에 몇 시에 도착하기를 원하세요?

M Come to the teachers' office at 9 in the morning. Since I don't have a class that morning, I'll ⁴⁾take you to the gym.	남 아침 9시에 교무실로 오세요. 제가 그날 아침에 수업이 없으니 체육관으로 데려 다 드릴게요.
W Perfect. I think I'll have enough time to set up the lighting.	여 딱 좋네요. 조명을 설치할 시간이 충분할 것 같아요.

두 사람이 학생들의 졸업 앨범 촬영에 대해 이야기하고 있다. 여자는 주로 인물 사진을 찍는다면서 구체적인 촬영 일정을 묻고 있고, 남자는 촬영 일정을 설명하며 당일 아침에 수업이 없다고 말하는 것으로 보아 두 사람의 관계로 ② '사진작가 ― 교사'가 가장 적절하다.

어휘 have a seat 자리에 앉다 mainly 图 주로 portrait 명 인물 사진; 초상화 take a picture 사진을 찍다 yearbook 명 졸업 앨범 set up 설치하다 lighting 명 조명

4 그림 내용 불일치 파악　　　　　　　　　　　　　　정답 ⑤

W Reece, this is my favorite place in the house. I spend ¹⁾most of my free time reading books here.	여 Reece, 여기가 내가 집에서 제일 좋아하는 곳이야. 난 여가 시간의 대부분을 이곳에서 책을 읽으며 보내.
M Everything looks new. Have you been redecorating?	남 모든 게 새로워 보이네. 실내 장식을 새로 하고 있었어?
W Yeah! I just got this rug last week.	여 응! 지난주에 막 이 러그를 샀어.
M The star pattern on it looks great.	남 별 무늬가 아주 멋져 보여.
W Thanks. What do you think of the two plain vases by the window?	여 고마워. 창가에 있는 두 개의 민무늬 꽃병은 어때?
M Those are a nice touch, too.	남 그것들도 좋은 느낌이야.
W I'm ²⁾thinking of moving the square table next to the armchair, though.	여 그런데 안락의자 옆에 있는 네모난 테이블은 옮길까 생각 중이야.
M Don't you need a place to put your coffee when reading?	남 책을 읽을 때 커피를 놓아둘 곳이 필요하지 않을까?
W Yeah, I'd better not move it, then.	여 그러네. 그럼 안 옮기는 게 좋겠다.
M It looks like you need some more bookshelves. There's ³⁾a stack of books on the floor in the corner.	남 책꽂이가 좀 더 필요한가 봐. 구석 바닥에 책 더미가 쌓여 있어.
W Oh, we can put those books back on the book shelf. Could you help me?	여 아, 그 책들을 책꽂이에 다시 넣으면 돼. 좀 도와줄래?
M Sure. **I see the ⁴⁾second shelf is empty.**	남 물론이야. 두 번째 선반이 비어 있구나.
W Right. Please put them there.	여 맞아. 그것들을 거기에 놓아줘.
M I see.	남 알겠어.

대화에서 남자가 책꽂이의 두 번째 선반이 비어 있다고 말했는데, ⑤에는 선반이 꽉 차게 그려져 있다.

어휘 redecorate 图 실내 장식을 새로 하다 plain 형 민무늬의; 분명한, 명료한 stack 명 더미, 쌓인 것 empty 형 비어 있는

5 할 일 파악　　　　　　　　　　　　　　　　　　정답 ④

W Good morning, Liam. Thanks for coming back to volunteer at the community center.	여 좋은 아침이에요, Liam. 주민센터에 자원봉사 하러 와주셔서 감사합니다.
M Hi, Ms. Robinson. I'm ¹⁾happy to be here again.	남 안녕하세요, Robinson 씨. 다시 이곳에 오게 되어 기쁩니다.
W You did a great job coaching the girls' basketball team.	여 여자 농구팀 지도를 정말 잘 해주셨잖아요.
M Thanks. What do you need me to do this time? I saw that you were ²⁾replanting the flower bed by the entrance.	남 고마워요. 이번에는 제가 뭘 해야 하나요? 입구 옆에서 화단을 옮겨 심고 있는 걸 봤는데요.
W We already have someone taking care of the gardening.	여 정원 가꾸는 일을 처리할 사람은 이미 있어요.
M Then, I could clean up at the gym.	남 그러면, 체육관에서 청소를 할 수 있겠어요.
W ³⁾Some other volunteers finished that yesterday. Hold on, let me find something else for you.	여 다른 자원봉사자들이 어제 그걸 끝냈어요. 잠시만요, 다른 일 찾아 드릴게요.
M Take your time.	남 천천히 하세요.
W Okay. **A big shipment of ⁴⁾sports equipment just arrived. So I need you to organize it for us.**	여 네. 대량의 운동 장비가 방금 도착했어요. 그래서 그걸 정리해주셨으면 해요.
M **I'd be happy to do it.**	남 기꺼이 그렇게 할게요.
W Perfect. The equipment is packed in boxes at the back of the office. Here, I'll show you.	여 아주 좋군요. 장비는 사무실 뒤쪽에 있는 박스에 포장되어 있어요. 여기요, 제가 보여드릴게요.

주민센터에 자원봉사를 하러 온 남자에게 여자가 할 일을 알려주고 있다. 여자가 남자에게 대량의 운동 장비가 도착했으니 정리해 달라고 하자, 남자가 기꺼이 하겠다고 했으므로 남자가 할 일로 ④ '운동 장비 정리하기'가 가장 적절하다.

어휘 volunteer 图 자원봉사하다 명 자원봉사자 coach 图 지도하다 replant 图 옮겨 심다 flower bed 화단 take care of ~을 처리하다 take one's time 천천히 하다 equipment 명 장비 organize 图 정리하다; 조직하다 pack 图 포장하다

6 금액 정보 파악

정답 ③

W Hi. How can I help you, sir?	여 안녕하세요. 무엇을 도와드릴까요, 손님?
M I'm looking for some jeans.	남 청바지를 찾고 있어요.
W Then, I'd like to recommend these two. **The blue jeans cost $40, and the black pair costs $50.**	여 그럼, 이 두 가지를 추천해 드리고 싶어요. 파란색은 40달러이고, 검은색은 50달러입니다.
M Good. Do you have ¹⁾<u>both of them</u> in a size eight?	남 좋아요. 두 벌 다 8사이즈 있나요?
W Yes. Here you are. You can try them on in the fitting room.	여 네. 여기 있습니다. 탈의실에서 입어보실 수 있어요.
M Thank you. *[Pause]* Great recommendation. **I like the blue ones more. I'll** ²⁾<u>take two of them.</u>	남 감사합니다. *[잠시 멈춤]* 좋은 추천이네요. 저는 파란색이 더 좋아요. 이거 두 벌 주세요.
W Great. I'll ring up two pairs. And you're aware that we're having a sale this week, right?	여 좋아요. 두 벌 계산해 드릴게요. 그리고 이번 주에 세일하는 거 알고 계시죠?
M Oh, I didn't know that.	남 아, 몰랐어요.
W **Some of our products are 10% off. You can** ³⁾<u>get a discount</u> on the jeans.	여 저희 제품 중 일부는 10% 할인됩니다. 그 청바지는 할인 받으실 수 있어요.
M I'm glad I went shopping today. **Also, I want to buy that belt displayed beside the fitting room.**	남 오늘 쇼핑하러 와서 다행이네요. 그리고 탈의실 옆에 진열된 벨트도 사고 싶어요.
W **It's $20.** But the discount doesn't ⁴⁾<u>apply to that item</u>.	여 그건 20달러입니다. 하지만 그 품목에는 할인이 적용되지 않아요.
M That's okay. I'll take it. Here's my credit card.	남 괜찮아요. 살게요. 여기 신용카드요.

남자가 파란색 바지 두 벌($40×2=$80)과 벨트 하나($20)를 구매했고, 바지 두 벌에만 10% 할인($80×0.9=$72)을 받았으므로 정답은 ③ '$92'이다.

[어휘] **try on** ~을 입어 보다 **fitting room** 탈의실 **ring up** 계산하다 **aware** 圈 알고 있는 **product** 圐 제품 **display** 图 진열하다

7 이유 파악

정답 ④

[Cell phone rings.]	*[휴대폰이 울린다.]*
M Hey, Brenda. How's it going?	남 안녕, Brenda. 어떻게 지내?
W Good. I just got back from a tennis lesson.	여 잘 지내. 테니스 수업에서 막 돌아왔어.
M I need to talk to you about our plans to play board games at your house tonight.	남 오늘 밤 너희 집에서 보드게임을 하기로 한 계획에 대해 얘기 좀 해야겠어.
W You can come later, right?	여 이따가 올 수 있는 거지, 그렇지?
M I'm sorry, but I have to ¹⁾<u>cancel our plans</u>.	남 미안하지만, 취소해야겠어.
W Oh, right. You're leaving on a trip tomorrow. You probably need to go to bed early.	여 아, 맞아. 너 내일 여행을 떠나지. 아마 일찍 자야겠네.
M The flight leaves in the evening. That's not the issue.	남 비행기는 저녁에 떠나. 그게 문제가 아니야.
W I see. Well, don't you want to play board games? We could ²⁾<u>do something else</u>.	여 그렇구나. 음, 보드게임을 하고 싶지 않은 거야? 다른 걸 해도 되는데.
M Board games would be fun. **Actually, I forgot that I made plans to go out to eat with my family.**	남 보드게임은 재미있을 거야. 사실, 나 가족들과 외식 약속을 했던 걸 잊고 있었어.
W I see. Well, have fun. Let's hang out when you get back from the trip.	여 그렇구나. 음, 재미있게 놀아. 여행에서 돌아오면 같이 놀자.
M For sure. I'll ³⁾<u>buy you some souvenirs</u>.	남 물론이지. 기념품을 사다 줄게.

남자는 보드게임을 하기로 한 계획을 취소하려고 한다면서 가족들과 외식 약속을 했던 것을 잊고 있었다고 말했으므로, 남자가 약속을 취소하려는 이유는 ④ '가족과 외식하기로 해서'이다.

[어휘] **get back from** ~에서 돌아오다 **cancel** 图 취소하다 **probably** 图 아마 **hang out** 같이 놀다 **souvenir** 圐 기념품

8 언급 유무 파악

정답 ②

M Honey, is everything ready for our son's first-birthday party?	남 여보, 우리 아들 돌잔치 준비 다 됐어?
W I think so, but we can go over the to-do list one last time.	여 그런 것 같은데, 할 일 목록을 마지막으로 한 번 더 검토할 수도 있겠어.
M Okay. Did you send out the invitations?	남 그래. 초대장은 발송했어?
W Yes. I sent them last Friday.	여 응. 지난 금요일에 보냈어.
M Did you make sure to ¹⁾<u>invite all our relatives</u> and friends?	남 우리 친척들과 친구들 확실히 전부 초대한 거지?
W I did. I'm expecting **at least 50 people** there. I also mentioned the ²⁾<u>new start time</u> on the invitation.	여 응. 적어도 50명은 거기 올 걸로 예상해. 초대장에 새로운 시작 시간도 말해뒀어.
M It's beginning at **4 p.m.**, right?	남 오후 4시에 시작하는 거, 맞지?
W That's correct. What about the food? Is everything ready with the caterer?	여 맞아. 음식은? 케이터링 업체랑 준비는 다 됐어?
M Yeah, ³⁾<u>everything is arranged</u>. There's going to be **rice cakes, noodles, and a dessert**.	남 응, 다 준비됐어. 떡, 국수, 그리고 후식이 있을 거야.
W That should work. Did you hire someone ⁴⁾<u>to be the host</u>?	여 그거면 될 거야. 사회자는 고용했어?
M Of course. I booked a **comedian** to be the MC.	남 물론이지. 개그맨을 MC로 예약해 뒀어.
W I think it's going to be a great party.	여 멋진 잔치가 될 것 같아.
M I hope so!	남 그러면 좋겠어!

참석 인원 수(적어도 50명), 시작 시간(오후 4시), 음식 메뉴(떡, 국수, 후식), 사회자(개그맨)에 대해 언급했고, ② '장소'는 언급하지 않았다.

[어휘] go over ~을 검토하다 send out ~을 발송하다 make sure to 확실히 ~하다 relative 명 친척 expect 통 예상하다 arrange 통 준비하다 hire 통 고용하다 host 명 사회자

---

9 내용 불일치 파악   정답 ③

W Welcome to our Nature Bicycle Tour of Hungary. I'm Claire, your guide for the three-day journey. Today, we are going to ¹⁾travel through 30 kilometers of beautiful landscape where you will see lovely villages and some landmarks. As you can see on your map, **we will be ²⁾biking northwest along the Danube River.** We will enjoy Hungarian cuisine at local restaurants along the way. Tonight, we'll be staying at a place called the Hotel Citadel. Keep in mind that Hungary's summer is very hot and sunny, so you'd better put on sunscreen. Also, ³⁾for safety purposes, the group must stay together. Please attach the GPS sensor that we gave you to your bicycle. Thank you, and enjoy the ride!	여 Nature Bicycle Tour of Hungary에 오신 것을 환영합니다. 저는 3일간의 여정을 안내해드릴 Claire입니다. 오늘 우리는 멋진 마을들과 몇몇 랜드마크를 볼 수 있는 아름다운 풍경을 거쳐 30km를 이동할 것입니다. 지도에서 볼 수 있듯이, 우리는 다뉴브강을 따라 북서쪽으로 자전거를 탈 것입니다. 가는 길에 현지 식당에서 헝가리 요리를 즐길 것입니다. 오늘 밤에는 호텔 시타델이라는 곳에서 묵을 예정입니다. 헝가리의 여름은 매우 덥고 화창하므로 자외선 차단제를 바르는 것이 낫다는 점을 명심하세요. 또한, 안전 목적으로, 일행은 반드시 함께 있어야 합니다. 여러분에게 드린 GPS 센서를 부디 자전거에 부착해주세요. 감사드리고, 즐거운 여행 되세요!

헝가리 자전거 투어에 대한 안내 방송이다. 여자가 다뉴브강을 따라 북서쪽으로 자전거를 탈 것이라고 했으므로 ③ '강을 따라 북동쪽으로 자전거를 탈 것이다.'는 내용과 일치하지 않는다.

[어휘] journey 명 여정 landscape 명 풍경 cuisine 명 요리 keep in mind 명심하다 put on ~을 바르다 safety 명 안전 purpose 명 목적 attach 통 부착하다

---

10 도표 정보 파악   정답 ④

M Are you still looking at sofas online, honey? **W** Yeah... Actually, do you mind giving me your opinion? It might help me make up my mind. **M** Sure. Let me have a look. **W** What about this one that seats two people? **M** I thought we needed ¹⁾room for at least three people. **W** Oh, I didn't think about that. You're right. Well, the other ones are the right size. **M** Yeah, these are big enough. What about our budget? **W** Um, we probably shouldn't ²⁾spend more than $750. **M** I agree. What's another option that we should consider? **W** What about cushions? Do we need those? **M** Yes. I think ³⁾they're essential. **W** Then, what do you think of the polyester couch? **M** I don't like the material. **Let's go with a leather one.**	남 아직도 온라인으로 소파를 보고 있는 거야, 여보? 여 응... 사실, 당신의 의견을 말해 줄래? 결정을 내리는 데 도움이 될지도 몰라. 남 물론이지. 내가 한번 볼게. 여 2인 좌석이 있는 이건 어때? 남 난 적어도 세 명이 앉을 자리가 필요하다고 생각했어. 여 아, 그런 생각은 못 했네. 맞아. 음, 다른 것들은 사이즈가 적절하네. 남 응, 이것들은 충분히 커. 우리 예산은 어떻게 돼? 여 음, 아마 750달러 이상은 쓰지 말아야 할 것 같아. 남 동의해. 우리가 고려해야 할 또 다른 선택지는 뭐야? 여 쿠션은? 그게 필요할까? 남 응. 꼭 필요한 것 같아. 여 그럼, 폴리에스터 소파는 어때? 남 소재가 마음에 안 들어. 가죽으로 선택하자.

두 사람은 적어도 세 명이 앉을 자리가 있고, 750달러 이하인 것 중에서, 쿠션이 있으며, 가죽 소재인 소파를 골랐다.

[어휘] give one's opinion ~의 의견을 말하다 make up one's mind 결정을 내리다 budget 명 예산 essential 형 꼭 필요한 go with 선택하다 leather 명 가죽

---

11 짧은 대화의 응답 파악   정답 ①

[Cell phone rings.] **W** Dad, it looks like it's about to rain, and I forgot to ¹⁾bring my umbrella. **M** It's already raining here. **Do you want me to come pick you up?** **W** Yes. I'll ²⁾wait for you inside the school entrance. **M** All right. Come out when I call you.	*[휴대폰이 울린다.]* 여 아빠, 곧 비가 올 것 같은데 우산 가져오는 걸 깜빡했어요. 남 여긴 벌써 비가 오고 있단다. 내가 널 데리러 갈까? 여 네. 학교 입구 안에서 기다릴게요. 남 좋아. 내가 전화하면 나오렴. [선택지] ① 좋아. 내가 전화하면 나오렴. ② 말도 안 돼. 너는 항상 우산을 잃어버리잖니. ③ 맞아. 비가 그치기를 기다리자. ④ 그래. 또 뭐 사다 줄까? ⑤ 좋아. 방과 후에 바로 집으로 오는 것을 기억하렴.

남자가 여자에게 데리러 갈지 묻자 여자가 그래 달라고 하면서 학교 입구 안에서 기다리겠다고 했으므로, 이에 대한 응답으로는 전화하면 나오라고 말하는 ① 'All right. Come out when I call you.'가 가장 적절하다.

[어휘] be about to 곧 ~할 것이다 pick up ~를 데리러 가다; 사다 주다 entrance 명 입구

영어듣기 모의고사 해커스 수능영어듣기 모의고사 20+4회 실전

12 짧은 대화의 응답 파악
정답 ③

M	Jessica, do you ¹⁾have any special plans for summer vacation?
W	**I'm planning to go hiking in the mountains.** It'll be ²⁾hard but rewarding.
M	Wow. That sounds like a fun plan! **Can I join you?**
W	Why not? It would be nice to have some company.

남 Jessica, 여름 방학에 특별한 계획 있니?
여 산으로 등산을 갈 계획이야. 힘들겠지만 보람이 있을 거야.
남 우와. 재미있는 계획인 것 같네! 나도 같이 가도 돼?
여 **왜 안 되겠어? 동행이 있으면 좋을 거야.**

선택지 ① 물론이지. 나는 보통 등산보다 수영을 더 좋아해.
② 물론이지. 그와 함께 등산하는 건 즐거웠어.
③ 왜 안 되겠어? 동행이 있으면 좋을 거야.
④ 미안해. 여름 버스 투어는 이미 예약이 꽉 찼어.
⑤ 걱정하지 마. 기억에 남을 만한 휴가 계획을 분명 세우게 될 거야.

여름 방학 계획을 말하는 상황에서 여자가 등산을 갈 계획이라고 하자 남자가 같이 가도 되는지 물었으므로, 이에 대한 응답으로는 된다고 하는 ③ 'Why not? It would be nice to have some company.'가 가장 적절하다.

[어휘] rewarding 형 보람 있는 prefer A to B B보다 A를 더 좋아하다 company 명 동행 memorable 형 기억에 남을만한

13 긴 대화의 응답 파악
정답 ③

M	**Honey, have you seen my smartphone?**
W	Um, I don't think so.
M	Hmm... **I'm worried that I** ¹⁾might have left **it at the beach.**
W	Weren't you using it right when we got back to the hotel room?
M	Oh, you're right. I was looking at the weather forecast for tomorrow. But where is it?
W	Have you checked your jacket pocket?
M	Yeah, I have. It's not there.
W	What about under the bed? Maybe you ²⁾dropped it down there.
M	One second. [Pause] No, I don't see it.
W	Okay, **do you want me to try calling it for you?**
M	Good idea. I just hope I didn't set it ³⁾on silent mode.
W	It's ringing now. Listen out for it.
M	I don't hear anything. Do you?
W	Wait... **I think I hear something buzzing** ⁴⁾from the bathroom.
M	I must have left it there when I washed my hands!

남 여보, 내 스마트폰 봤어?
여 음, 못 본 것 같은데.
남 흠... 해변에 두고 왔을까 봐 걱정되네.
여 우리가 호텔 방으로 돌아왔을 때 바로 그걸 쓰고 있지 않았어?
남 아, 당신 말이 맞아. 내일 일기예보를 보고 있었지. 그런데 어디에 있는 거지?
여 재킷 주머니는 확인해 봤어?
남 응, 해봤어. 거기 없어.
여 침대 밑은? 아마 그 아래로 떨어뜨린 것 같아.
남 잠깐만. [잠시 멈춤] 아니, 안 보여.
여 좋아, 내가 대신 전화 걸어줄까?
남 좋은 생각이야. 무음 모드로 설정하지만 않았으면 좋겠네.
여 이제 울릴 거야. 잘 들어봐.
남 난 아무 소리도 안 들려. 당신은?
여 잠깐만... 화장실에서 뭔가 윙윙거리는 소리가 들리는 것 같아.
남 **손을 씻을 때 그곳에 두고 온 게 틀림없어!**

선택지 ① 그건 내 벨소리 같지 않은데.
② 마지막으로 사용했을 때 어디에 있었어?
③ 손을 씻을 때 그곳에 두고 온 게 틀림없어!
④ 우리가 해변에 있을 때는 배터리가 다 떨어져 가고 있었어.
⑤ 프런트에 전화해서 그걸 잃어버렸다고 말해야겠어.

남자의 스마트폰이 보이지 않는 상황에서 여자가 전화를 걸어본 후 화장실에서 뭔가 윙윙거리는 소리가 들리는 것 같다고 말했으므로, 이에 대한 응답으로는 손을 씻을 때 그곳에 두고 온 것 같다고 대답하는 ③ 'I must have left it there when I washed my hands!'가 가장 적절하다.

[어휘] weather forecast 일기예보 drop 통 떨어뜨리다 silent mode 무음 모드 listen out 잘 듣다 buzz 통 윙윙거리다 ring tone 벨소리 run out of ~이 다 떨어지다

14 긴 대화의 응답 파악
정답 ②

M	Clara, I brought you a glass of the apple juice that Mom made. Oh... are you still studying?
W	Yeah, I'm a little stressed out about my math exam on Monday.
M	Maybe it would be good to take a break ¹⁾for a while.
W	I still have a lot of material to get through.
M	You might have more energy when you get back to it.
W	That's ²⁾a good point. Well, what are you up to?
M	I need to finish some chores. Afterward, I'm planning to go out and walk our dog.
W	Where are you going? Is it just a quick walk ³⁾around the block?
M	**I want to go over to Logan Park and play with our dog there.**
W	Oh, that sounds fun. **Do you mind if I tag along?**
M	**Not at all. I** ⁴⁾will be ready to go **in 30 minutes.**
W	Great. Let me know when you're heading out.

남 Clara, 엄마가 만드신 사과 주스 한 잔 가져왔어. 아... 아직도 공부하고 있어?
여 응, 월요일 수학 시험 때문에 좀 스트레스 받아.
남 아마도 잠시 휴식을 취하는 게 좋을 것 같아.
여 아직 끝내야 할 자료가 많아.
남 쉬고 다시 하면 공부할 기운이 더 생길 수도 있어.
여 좋은 지적이야. 음, 넌 뭐 할 건데?
남 집안일을 좀 끝내야 해. 그 후엔, 나가서 개를 산책시킬 계획이야.
여 어디로 갈 거야? 그냥 한 블록 빨리 도는 거야?
남 로건 공원으로 넘어가서 개랑 놀아주고 싶어.
여 아, 재미있겠는데. 내가 따라가도 돼?
남 당연하지. 30분 후에 갈 준비를 할 거야.
여 **좋아. 나갈 때 알려줘.**

① 물론이지. 여기서 그리 멀지 않아.

② 좋아. 나갈 때 알려줘.

③ 걱정하지 마. 던지기 놀이할 공을 가지고 왔어.

④ 전적으로 이해해. 그냥 나 혼자 개를 산책시킬게.

⑤ 미안해. 나는 여기 남아서 시험공부를 하는 게 정말 좋겠어.

남자가 공부 중인 휴식을 취할 것을 제안하고 있는 상황이다. 공원에 가서 개랑 놀아주려는 남자에게 여자가 따라가도 되는지 묻자 가도 된다며 자신은 30분 후에 갈 준비를 할 것이라고 했으므로, 이에 대한 응답으로는 나갈 때 알려달라고 하는 ② 'Great. Let me know when you're heading out.'이 가장 적절하다.

어휘 take a break 잠시 휴식을 취하다   get through ~을 끝내다   afterward 뿐 그 후에   go over to (장소)로 넘어가다   tag along ~를 따라가다   fetch 뗑 공 던지기 놀이

15 상황에 적절한 말 파악

정답 ⑤

W Barry is a regular customer at Amanda's hair salon. He thinks Amanda is a great hairdresser. One day, he notices that his hair is 1)becoming too long. So he goes to the hair salon to get a haircut. While waiting for his turn, he sees other customers getting a perm or coloring their hair. Suddenly, he thinks that he has stuck with the same hairstyle 2)for a long time and wants to change it. At the same time, he doesn't want to stick out too much. After hearing Barry's explanation, Amanda thinks he should 3)try dyeing his hair a lighter color. **So Amanda wants to suggest that he get his hair dyed brown.** In this situation, what would Amanda most likely say to Barry?

여 Barry는 Amanda의 미용실의 단골손님입니다. 그는 Amanda가 훌륭한 미용사라고 생각합니다. 어느 날, 그는 자신의 머리카락이 너무 길어지고 있다는 것을 알아차립니다. 그래서, 그는 머리를 자르러 미용실에 갑니다. 그의 차례를 기다리는 동안, 그는 다른 손님들이 파마를 하거나 머리를 염색하는 것을 봅니다. 갑자기, 그는 자신이 오랫동안 같은 헤어스타일을 고수해 왔다고 생각하고 헤어스타일을 바꾸고 싶어 합니다. 동시에, 그는 너무 눈에 띄는 것은 원하지 않습니다. Barry의 설명을 들은 후, Amanda는 그가 머리를 좀 더 밝은 색으로 염색해봐야 한다고 생각합니다. 그래서, Amanda는 그에게 갈색으로 염색하라고 제안하고 싶습니다. 이러한 상황에서, Amanda가 Barry에게 가장 할 것 같은 말은 무엇입니까?

선택지 ① 헤어스타일을 바꾸려면 머리를 길게 길러야 해요.

② 저번에 원했던 것처럼 파마하는 건 어때요?

③ 기다리는 동안 원하는 자리 아무 곳에나 앉아도 돼요.

④ 머리가 더 이상 길어지기 전에 자르는 게 좋겠어요.

⑤ 머리를 갈색으로 염색해 보는 게 어때요?

Barry가 헤어스타일을 바꾸되 너무 눈에 띄고 싶어 하지는 않는 것을 보고, Amanda는 갈색으로 염색하는 것을 제안하려고 한다. 따라서, Amanda가 할 말로 ⑤ 'Why don't we try coloring your hair brown?'이 가장 적절하다.

어휘 regular customer 단골손님   hairdresser 뗑 미용사   notice 통 알아차리다   get a haircut 머리를 자르다   turn 뗑 차례 통 돌다   stick with ~을 고수하다   stick out 눈에 띄다   explanation 뗑 설명   dye 통 염색하다   light 톙 밝은; 가벼운

16-17 세트 문항

정답 16 ③ 17 ④

M Hello, students. Long before electricity, humans were using other power sources to improve their lives. **Today, let's discuss how different sources of energy have 1)affected human civilization throughout history.** First, we have **wood**. Thousands of years ago, our ancestors learned how to make fires with wood. It allowed people to cook and made it possible to live in colder climates. Second, **water** is another power source with an ancient history. Waterwheels 2)have been around since at least 4,000 BC. They were used to grind grain and made farming a more efficient source of food. Third, we need to talk about **coal**. Coal, which became popular in the 1700s, 3)burns much hotter than wood. It allowed for the creation of effective steam engines. Finally, the **sun** may be the most important energy source of our current time period. Solar energy is clean and eco-friendly. Therefore, using it more widely would be an effective way of slowing down 4)climate change. Now, let's watch a related video.

남 안녕하십니까, 학생 여러분. 전기를 쓰기 훨씬 전에, 인류는 그들의 삶을 개선하기 위해 다른 에너지원을 사용했습니다. 오늘은, 다양한 종류의 에너지원이 역사를 통틀어 인류 문명에 어떻게 영향을 끼쳤는지에 대해 논의해 보겠습니다. 먼저, 나무가 있습니다. 수천 년 전, 우리 조상들은 나무로 불을 피우는 법을 배웠습니다. 이는 사람들이 요리할 수 있게 했고, 더욱 추운 기후에서 사는 것을 가능하게 했습니다. 둘째, 물은 오랜 역사를 지진 또 다른 에너지원입니다. 물레방아는 적어도 기원전 4,000년부터 있었습니다. 그것은 곡식을 빻는데 사용되었고 농업을 더 효율적인 식량원으로 만들었습니다. 셋째, 우리는 석탄에 대해 이야기해야 합니다. 1700년대에 인기가 많았던 석탄은 나무보다 훨씬 더 뜨겁게 타오릅니다. 이것은 효과적인 증기 기관의 탄생을 가능하게 했습니다. 마지막으로, 태양은 현재 시기에 가장 중요한 에너지원일 것입니다. 태양 에너지는 깨끗하고 친환경적입니다. 그러므로, 그것을 더 널리 사용하는 것은 기후 변화를 늦추는 효과적인 방법이 될 것입니다. 이제 관련 영상을 보도록 하겠습니다.

선택지 16 ① 천연 에너지원의 이점

② 인류가 동력을 사용하기 시작한 이유

③ 다양한 에너지원들이 문명에 영향을 끼친 방법

④ 에너지가 고대 농업 방법에 끼친 영향

⑤ 에너지원이 더 깨끗해진 방법

17 ①나무 ②물 ③석탄 ④석유 ⑤태양

16 다양한 종류의 에너지원이 역사를 통틀어 인류 문명에 어떻게 영향을 끼쳤는지에 대해 논의하고 있으므로 남자가 하는 말의 주제로 ③ 'ways that various power sources affected civilization'이 가장 적절하다.

17 나무, 물, 석탄, 태양은 언급했지만 ④ 'oil'은 언급하지 않았다.

어휘 power source 에너지원   civilization 뗑 문명   ancestor 뗑 조상, 선조   allow 통 ~할 수 있게 하다, 허용하다   climate 뗑 기후   waterwheel 뗑 물레방아   grind 통 빻다, 갈다   grain 뗑 곡식   coal 뗑 석탄   creation 뗑 탄생, 생성   steam engine 증기 기관   current 톙 현재의   solar energy 태양 에너지   slow down ~을 늦추다

13회 영어듣기 모의고사

1	④	2	⑤	3	①	4	③	5	②	6	③	7	②	8	④	9	⑤	10	①
11	②	12	④	13	③	14	⑤	15	②	16	③	17	①						

• 각 문제의 정답 근거는 굵은 글씨로, Dictation 정답은 밑줄로 표시되어 있습니다.

1 목적 파악

정답 ④

M Excuse me. I'd like to make an announcement. **I want to thank all of you** ¹⁾**for volunteering here at Buckington Cares.** Our charity organization could not exist without your time and hard work. You have helped the ²⁾homeless by serving free meals. **We want to show our appreciation in our own small way by holding a dinner party for you at Jerry's Restaurant.** The dinner will be held on December 3rd at 7 p.m. Feel free to ³⁾wear casual clothes, and don't forget to bring your invitation. I hope you'll all be able to attend. Once again, thank you so much for your dedication.

남 실례합니다. 안내 말씀드리겠습니다. 여기 Buckington Cares에서 자원봉사를 해주신 여러분 모두에게 감사드립니다. 여러분의 시간과 노고가 아니라면 저희 자선 단체는 존재할 수 없을 것입니다. 여러분은 무료 급식을 제공함으로써 노숙자들을 도왔습니다. 저희는 여러분을 위해 Jerry's Restaurant에서 저녁 만찬회를 열어 저희만의 소소한 방식으로 감사를 표하고 싶습니다. 만찬회는 12월 3일 오후 7시에 열릴 예정입니다. 자유롭게 평상복을 입고 오시되, 초대장 가져오는 것을 잊지 마십시오. 여러분 모두 참석할 수 있기를 바랍니다. 다시 한번 여러분의 헌신에 감사드립니다.

남자가 자원봉사자들에게 감사를 표하며 저녁 만찬회 계획을 공지하고 있다. 따라서, 남자가 하는 말의 목적으로 ④ '자원봉사자들을 위해 열리는 만찬회를 공지하려고'가 가장 적절하다.

[어휘] charity organization 자선 단체 exist 통 존재하다 homeless 형 노숙자의 appreciation 명 감사; 감상 feel free to 자유롭게 ~하다 casual 형 평상시의, 격식을 차리지 않는; 우연한 dedication 명 헌신, 전념

2 의견 파악

정답 ⑤

M Are you feeling okay, honey?
W I'm just tired. I had a long week.
M Why don't you ¹⁾go back to bed? It is Saturday morning after all.
W Well, I want to start keeping a more ²⁾regular sleep schedule. **I think there are a lot of health benefits to waking up at the same time every day.**
M Even if you're feeling tired?
W Yeah. I've read that it really helps your overall health.
M Interesting. What are some of the benefits?
W A steady sleep schedule ³⁾keeps your mood stable. It makes you less likely to get sad or upset.
M I can see that. I get a bit depressed when I oversleep.
W Me too. Most importantly, getting up at a regular time makes it easier to get a good night's sleep consistently.
M Well, then you'd better stay awake.

남 괜찮아, 여보?
여 그냥 피곤한 거야. 한 주가 참 길었어.
남 다시 잠자리에 드는 게 어때? 어쨌든 토요일 아침이잖아.
여 음, 나는 좀 더 규칙적인 수면 일정을 지켜 나가고 싶어. 매일 같은 시간에 일어나는 것에는 많은 건강상의 이점이 있다고 생각하거든.
남 피곤해도?
여 응. 그게 전반적인 건강에 정말 도움이 된다는 걸 읽은 적 있어.
남 흥미롭네. 이점 중엔 어떤 게 있는데?
여 규칙적인 수면 일정은 기분을 안정적으로 유지해 줘. 우울해지거나 심란해질 가능성을 줄여주지.
남 알 것 같아. 늦잠을 자면 좀 우울해지거든.
여 나도 그래. 가장 중요한 건, 규칙적인 시간에 일어나면 꾸준히 숙면을 취하기가 더 쉬워진 거야.
남 그래, 그러면 당신은 깨어 있는 게 좋겠어.

여자는 토요일 아침이니 다시 잠자리에 들라는 남자의 제안을 거절하면서, 매일 같은 시간에 일어나는 것에 건강상의 이점이 많다고 했다. 따라서, 여자의 의견으로 ⑤ '규칙적인 기상 시간을 유지하는 것이 건강에 좋다.'가 가장 적절하다.

[어휘] after all 어쨌든 regular 형 규칙적인 overall 형 전반적인 steady 형 규칙적인; 지속적인 mood 명 기분 stable 형 안정적인 likely to ~할 가능성이 있는, ~할 것 같은 depressed 형 우울한 consistently 부 꾸준히, 한결같이

3 관계 파악

정답 ①

M Thanks for meeting with me today, Ms. Lincoln.
W Of course. **I understand that you're interested in an internship here at our company.**
M That's right. I want to ¹⁾design great buildings myself one day, so I need as much work experience as possible.
W That's good to hear. **And you're majoring in architecture, right?**
M Correct. I'm ²⁾entering my senior year in the fall.
W Have you used computer programs to make architectural designs before?
M Sure. I use them regularly in my courses.
W Okay. **That's essential to the work you would do for us. You would** ³⁾assist me with checking construction drawings.

남 오늘 만나주셔서 감사합니다, Lincoln 씨.
여 당연한걸요. 우리 회사에서 인턴으로 근무하는 것에 관심이 있으신 걸로 알고 있는데요.
남 맞아요. 저는 언젠가는 직접 멋진 건물들을 설계하고 싶고, 그래서 가능한 한 많은 업무 경험이 필요합니다.
여 다행이네요. 그리고 건축학을 전공하고 있군요, 그렇죠?
남 정확합니다. 가을에 졸업 학기에 들어갑니다.
여 이전에 컴퓨터 프로그램을 사용해서 건축 디자인을 만들어 본 적이 있나요?
남 물론이죠. 수업에서 그걸 정기적으로 사용합니다.
여 알았어요. 그건 우리를 위해 해줄 업무에 필수적이에요. 제가 공사 도면을 확인하는 일을 보조할 거예요.

M I think I can do that.	남 그 일을 제가 할 수 있다고 생각합니다.
W All right. I hope you have a good experience here at our company.	여 좋아요. 여기 우리 회사에서 좋은 경험을 하길 바랄게요.
M Thank you. I'll do my best.	남 감사합니다. 최선을 다하겠습니다.

남자가 여자의 회사에서 인턴 면접을 보고 있다. 남자는 건축학 전공자이며 가을에 졸업 학기에 들어간다고 했으며, 여자는 인턴의 업무 내용으로 여자의 공사 도면 확인 작업을 보조한다고 설명하는 것으로 보아 두 사람의 관계로 ① '대학생 — 건축사무소 직원'이 가장 적절하다.

어휘 internship 명 인턴사원 근무 as ~ as possible 가능한 한 ~한/하게 major in ~을 전공하다 architecture 명 건축학 (architectural 형 건축의) senior year 졸업 학년, 최고 학년 essential 형 필수적인 assist 동 보조하다 construction 명 공사, 건설 drawing 명 도면; 그림 do one's best 최선을 다하다

---

4 그림 내용 불일치 파악 정답 ③

M Thanks for recommending this dentist's office, Lisa. The lobby is beautiful.	남 이 치과를 추천해 줘서 고마워, Lisa. 로비가 훌륭하다.
W Right? It makes 1)waiting for your appointment nicer.	여 그렇지? 진료 기다리는 걸 좀 더 기분 좋게 만들어 줘.
M Exactly. The three potted plants give it a pleasant atmosphere. I don't think I'll go back to my old dentist after coming here.	남 정확해. 세 개의 화분에 심긴 나무가 로비에 즐거운 분위기를 주고 있어. 여기 와 보니까 예전 치과에는 다시 안 갈 것 같아.
W That fish tank looks great, too. Do you want to sit in the two chairs in front of it?	여 저기 수조도 멋져 보여. 그 앞에 놓인 두 개의 의자에 앉을래?
M They look pretty uncomfortable. **How about that 2)checked couch by the window?**	남 의자가 꽤 불편해 보여. 창가에 있는 체크무늬 소파는 어때?
W Sure. Can you hand me one of those magazines?	여 물론이야. 저기 잡지들 중 하나를 내게 건네줄래?
M Oh, where are they?	남 아, 어디에 있는데?
W 3)On the square table.	여 네모난 탁자 위에 있어.
M Right. Here you go. [Pause] I still have some time before my appointment, right?	남 그래. 여기 있어. [잠시 멈춤] 내 진료 예약 시간 전까지 아직 시간이 좀 남았지, 맞지?
W It's in 15 minutes. Mine is right after.	여 15분 후야. 난 그 바로 뒤로.
M That's enough time for coffee. Can we use the coffee machine on the cabinet?	남 커피 마실 시간으로는 충분하네. 수납장 위에 있는 커피 머신기를 써도 되지?
W Of course. Would you mind getting some coffee for me?	여 당연하지. 나도 커피 좀 줄래?
M No problem. I'll make two cups.	남 문제없어. 두 잔 내릴게.

대화에서 남자가 창가에 있는 체크무늬 소파에 앉자고 제안했는데, ③에는 무늬가 없는 소파가 그려져 있다.

어휘 atmosphere 명 분위기; 대기 fish tank 수조 hand 동 건네주다 명 손 cabinet 명 수납장, 캐비닛

---

5 부탁한 일 파악 정답 ②

W Honey, it's 6 o'clock already. I don't think we'll ever be ready for the party.	여 여보, 벌써 6시야. 우리 파티할 준비가 안 될 것 같아.
M Relax. The house looks fine. It just needs a few more finishing touches.	남 진정해. 집은 괜찮아 보여. 몇 가지 마무리 작업만 더 필요할 뿐이야.
W Do we have enough snacks?	여 간식은 충분해?
M Yes. I'm 1)cutting fruit and making a cheese plate.	남 응. 내가 과일을 자르고 치즈 한 접시를 만들고 있어.
W Okay. What about the drinks?	여 알겠어. 음료는 어때?
M I have some iced tea chilling out back. There's also plenty of soda.	남 뒤쪽에 아이스티를 차게 식혀 두고 있어. 탄산음료도 많이 있어.
W How about the 2)plates and cutlery?	여 접시와 식기류는 어때?
M It's all taken care of. We just need to do some last-minute cleaning.	남 다 해결됐어. 우리는 그냥 막판 청소를 하기만 하면 돼.
W I already mopped and dusted in the dining room.	여 내가 이미 식당은 대걸레로 닦고 먼지를 털었어.
M Great. **Can you also take care of the living room floor? It needs 3)to be vacuumed.**	남 좋아. 거실 바닥도 맡아줄 수 있어? 진공청소기로 청소해야 해.
W **Okay. I'll do it while you keep working on the snacks.**	여 알겠어. 당신이 계속 간식을 준비하는 동안 그걸 할게.
M Sounds like a plan.	남 좋은 생각이야.

두 사람이 파티 준비를 하고 있다. 남자가 여자에게 거실 바닥을 진공청소기로 청소해 달라고 하자, 여자가 알겠다고 했으므로 남자가 여자에게 부탁한 일로 ② '청소기 돌리기'가 가장 적절하다.

어휘 be ready for ~할 준비가 되다 finishing touch 마무리 작업 plate 명 접시 chill out 차게 식히다 plenty of 많은 cutlery 명 식기류 last-minute 형 막판의, 마지막 순간의 mop 동 대걸레로 닦다 명 대걸레 dust 동 먼지를 털다 명 먼지 vacuum 동 진공청소기로 청소하다

6 금액 정보 파악
정답 ③

M	Welcome to the National Science Museum. How can I help you?
W	Hi. is it right that there's a special offer on tickets today?
M	I'm sorry. It's ¹⁾not available now. We only offer the 10% discount on tickets sold in the evening.
W	Okay. Well, I'm here with my grandparents. You have a ²⁾special rate for senior citizens, right?
M	Yes. **Tickets are $20 for adults and $15 for seniors.**
W	Okay. **I'll take two senior tickets and one adult.**
M	**Did you want to attend the special exhibition? It's** ³⁾**an extra $10 per person.**
W	Is there a senior price for that?
M	I'm afraid not.
W	That's fine. **I'll take three tickets for that as well.**
M	Got it. So I've got three general admissions tickets, two with the senior rate, and three special exhibit tickets. Is that correct?
W	That's everything. Thanks.

남 국립 과학박물관에 오신 것을 환영합니다. 무엇을 도와드릴까요?
여 안녕하세요. 오늘 입장권 특별 할인이 있는 게 맞나요?
남 죄송합니다. 지금은 가능하지 않습니다. 저녁에 판매되는 입장권에 대해서만 10% 할인을 제공합니다.
여 알겠습니다. 음, 저는 여기 조부모님과 함께 왔어요. 경로 우대 할인 요금이 있죠, 맞나요?
남 네. 입장권은 성인 20달러, 경로자 15달러입니다.
여 알겠어요. 경로자 2장과 성인 1장 주세요.
남 특별 전시에 참석하고 싶으셨나요? 추가로 1인당 10달러입니다.
여 그것도 경로 우대 가격이 있나요?
남 유감이지만 없습니다.
여 괜찮아요. 그것도 3장 주세요.
남 알았어요. 그럼 2장은 경로 우대 요금으로 해서 일반 입장권 3장, 그리고 특별 전시 입장권 3장 시키셨습니다. 맞을까요?
여 그게 다예요. 감사합니다.

여자가 특별 할인 없이 경로자 입장권 2장($15×2= $30)과, 성인 입장권 1장($20), 그리고 특별 전시 입장권 3장($10×3= $30)을 구매했으므로 정답은 ③ '$80'이다.

어휘 special offer 특별 할인, 특가품 exhibition 몡 전시 senior price 경로 우대 가격 general 혱 일반의

7 이유 파악
정답 ②

W	Hey, Nathan. How are your classes going?
M	I'm ¹⁾taking physics this semester, and it's tough!
W	You must be so busy. Didn't you start taking a cooking course on Saturdays?
M	Actually, I decided not to sign up for it.
W	Ah, you probably need more time to study, right?
M	Not really. I'm still free on the weekends usually.
W	Are you ²⁾not interested in cooking anymore?
M	Oh, no. I still cook whenever I can. **Actually, my uncle** ³⁾**is in the hospital. I've been visiting him on Saturdays.**
W	How is he doing?
M	He's feeling better. But his recovery will take a long time.
W	It sounds like he needs your help, then. Well, ⁴⁾let me know when you are free. We can go skateboarding while the weather is still nice.
M	That's a good idea. I will.

여 안녕, Nathan. 수업은 잘 되고 있니?
남 이번 학기에 물리학을 듣고 있는데, 어려워!
여 정말 바쁘겠다. 토요일마다 요리 수업을 듣기 시작하지 않았어?
남 사실, 그건 신청하지 않기로 했어.
여 아, 아마 넌 공부할 시간이 더 필요하겠구나, 맞니?
남 그렇지 않아. 나는 보통 주말에는 여전히 한가해.
여 더 이상 요리에 흥미가 없는 거야?
남 오, 아니. 난 여전히 할 수 있을 때마다 요리를 해. 실은, 우리 삼촌이 병원에 입원해 계셔. 난 토요일마다 삼촌 병문안을 가.
여 삼촌은 어떠셔?
남 좀 나아지셨어. 하지만 회복에는 오랜 시간이 걸릴 거야.
여 그러면 네 도움이 필요하겠다. 음, 한가할 때 알려줘. 날씨가 아직 좋을 때 스케이트보드를 타러 갈 수 있잖아.
남 좋은 생각이야. 그럴게.

남자는 토요일 요리 수업을 신청하지 않기로 했다면서 토요일마다 삼촌 병문안을 간다고 했으므로, 남자가 수업을 신청하지 않은 이유는 ② '삼촌 병문안을 매주 가야 해서'이다.

어휘 physics 몡 물리학 semester 몡 학기 sign up for ~을 신청하다 recovery 몡 회복 take time 시간이 걸리다

8 언급 유무 파악
정답 ④

	[Telephone rings.]
M	Watford Travel, this is William speaking.
W	Hi, William. This is Elizabeth Bowers. I left a message earlier about the Venice Tour Package.
M	I was just going to call you. We still have ¹⁾**five spaces** left for the trip.
W	Great. I'm interested in taking my family, but I wanted to confirm a few things first.
M	Sure. What did you want to ask?
W	The tour takes place from **September 14th to September 20th**, right?
M	That's correct.
W	²⁾What's the weather like in Venice at that time of year?
M	It's lovely, but it gets cool in the evening. You'll want to pack **a light jacket**.
W	I'll keep that in mind. And does the travel package on your website ³⁾include transportation?
M	It does. The total cost of **$900** includes airfare, accommodations, and boat tours of the city.
W	Fantastic. Let's book it.

남 Watford Travel의 William 전화 받았습니다.
여 안녕하세요, William. 저는 Elizabeth Bowers입니다. 아까 베네치아 여행 패키지에 관해 메시지를 남겼어요.
남 제가 마침 전화 드리려던 참이었어요. 아직 자리가 5석 남아 있습니다.
여 좋아요. 저희 가족을 데려갈 의향이 있는데, 먼저 몇 가지 확인하고 싶었어요.
남 물론이죠. 무엇을 묻고 싶으셨어요?
여 여행이 9월 14일부터 9월 20일까지 진행되는 거죠, 맞나요?
남 정확합니다.
여 그 시기 베네치아의 날씨는 어때요?
남 아주 훌륭하지만, 저녁에는 쌀쌀해져요. 가벼운 재킷을 챙기고 싶으실 수도 있어요.
여 명심할게요. 그리고 웹사이트에 나온 여행 패키지에 교통편이 포함되어 있나요?
남 포함되어 있습니다. 총 900달러의 비용에는 항공료, 숙박 시설, 그리고 도시 보트 투어가 포함되어 있습니다.
여 환상적이에요. 예약할게요.

잔여석 수(5석), 기간(9월 14일부터 9월 20일까지), 추천 복장(가벼운 재킷), 총비용(900달러)에 대해 언급했고, ④ '출발 장소'는 언급하지 않았다.

[어휘] confirm ⑧ 확인하다 take place 진행되다 pack ⑧ 챙기다 light ⑱ 가벼운 ⑲ 빛 keep in mind 명심하다 airfare ⑲ 항공료 accommodation ⑲ 숙박 시설; 수용

---

9 내용 불일치 파악   정답 ⑤

W Welcome to the city's second Annual Guitar-Playing Contest. This year we have 30 participants. As you know, our participants are amateur guitarists. I know all of them have been ¹⁾practicing hard for the contest. You won't want to miss any of their performances today. The participants have been ²⁾divided into three groups, which will be judged separately. These are junior, young adult, and adult. Each performer will play a single song on stage. Our judging panel consists of ³⁾professional musicians and will be selecting winners from each group. Awards will be given after all of the contestants have performed. **While the judges are deciding on the winners, we'll ⁴⁾have a special performance by the city choir.**	여 우리 시의 두 번째 Annual Guitar-Playing Contest에 오신 것을 환영합니다. 올해는 30명의 참가자가 있습니다. 여러분도 아시다시피, 저희 참가자들은 아마추어 기타리스트입니다. 제가 알기로 그들 모두가 대회를 위해 열심히 연습해 왔습니다. 여러분은 오늘 그들의 공연을 놓치고 싶지 않을 것입니다. 참가자들은 3개 그룹으로 나뉘어 따로 심사를 받을 것입니다. 청소년, 청년, 성인 그룹입니다. 각 연주자는 무대에서 한 곡을 연주할 것입니다. 심사위원단은 프로 연주자들로 구성되어 있으며 각 그룹에서 수상자를 선정할 예정입니다. 모든 참가자가 공연한 후에 시상할 것입니다. 심사위원들이 수상자를 결정하는 동안, 시립 합창단의 특별 공연이 있겠습니다.

기타 연주 대회에 대한 안내 방송이다. 여자가 심사위원들이 수상자를 결정하는 동안 시립 합창단의 특별 공연이 있겠다고 했으므로 ⑤ '수상자가 발표된 후 특별 공연이 이어질 것이다.'는 내용과 일치하지 않는다.

[어휘] divide ⑧ 나누다 separately ⑨ 따로 judging panel 심사위원단 consist of ~로 구성되다, 이루어지다 select ⑧ 선정하다 contestant ⑲ 참가자 choir ⑲ 합창단

---

10 도표 정보 파악   정답 ①

W Hi, I need to get a bat for my daughter. She's joining a softball league, but I'm ¹⁾not sure which one to get. M Of course. Let's start with material. **I wouldn't recommend a wooden bat.** W Why not? M Well, they're generally ²⁾not as durable. W Okay. **I'll get one made from some other material.** I want her to use this for a while. M Has your daughter played before? W Only a month. Why? M Well, **she may need one with a leather handle.** It's ³⁾easier to swing, especially for beginners. W Sure. I think that's right for her. That leaves only three good options. M How much were you thinking of spending? W **Not more than $150.** M Got it. Okay... length is another thing to consider. W Right. **I think ⁴⁾the shorter one will fit her better.** I'll take it. M Great choice.	여 안녕하세요, 제 딸이 쓸 배트를 사야 해요. 소프트볼 리그에 참가할 건데, 어떤 것을 사야 할지 모르겠어요. 남 당연합니다. 소재부터 시작해보죠. 나무 배트는 추천하지 않겠습니다. 여 왜요? 남 음, 일반적으로 내구성이 좋지 않아요. 여 알겠습니다. 다른 소재로 만들어진 걸 살게요. 제 딸이 얼마 동안은 사용하기를 바라거든요. 남 따님이 이전에 소프트볼을 해 본 적이 있나요? 여 한 달밖에 안 됐어요. 왜요? 남 음, 가죽 손잡이가 있는 게 필요할지도 몰라요. 특히 초보자의 경우, 그게 휘두르기가 더 쉬워요. 여 그럼요. 그게 알맞을 것 같아요. 그러면 세 가지 좋은 선택지가 남았네요. 남 얼마나 돈을 쓰실 생각이셨나요? 여 많이 써야 150달러요. 남 알겠습니다. 좋아요... 길이도 고려해야 할 사항입니다. 여 맞아요. 짧은 게 딸에게 더 잘 맞을 것 같아요. 그걸로 살게요. 남 훌륭한 선택이십니다.

여자는 나무가 아닌 다른 소재로 만들어진 것 중에서, 가죽 손잡이가 있고, 가격대는 많아야 150달러이며, 길이가 짧은 소프트볼 배트를 골랐다.

[어휘] wooden ⑱ 나무의 generally ⑨ 일반적으로 durable ⑱ 내구성이 좋은 leather ⑲ 가죽 swing ⑧ 휘두르다; 흔들다 not more than 많아야 ~인 length ⑲ 길이 fit ⑧ 맞다

---

11 짧은 대화의 응답 파악   정답 ②

W David, ¹⁾you're sweating a lot. What happened? M I ran all the way over here, and now I'm late anyway. I'm so sorry. W But you're 10 minutes early! **I think you ²⁾looked at the time wrong.** M No way! I thought I was hopelessly late.	여 David, 너 땀을 많이 흘리고 있는데. 무슨 일이야? 남 여기까지 줄곧 달려왔는데, 어쨌든 내가 늦었어. 정말 미안해. 여 하지만 넌 10분이나 일찍 왔는걸! 시간을 잘못 본 것 같아. 남 말도 안 돼! 난 내가 형편없이 늦었다고 생각했어.
	[선택지] ① 오, 이런! 너 지금 땀투성이야. ② 말도 안 돼! 난 내가 형편없이 늦었다고 생각했어. ③ 고마워. 날 기다려 주다니 정말 친절하구나. ④ 알았어. 하지만 다음번에는 좀 더 일찍 출발해야 해. ⑤ 미안해. 다른 시간에 다시 올게.

늦은 줄 알고 달려온 남자에게 여자가 시간을 잘못 본 것 같다고 했으므로, 이에 대한 응답으로는 착각했다고 말하는 ② 'No way! I thought I was hopelessly late.'가 가장 적절하다.

[어휘] sweat ⑧ 땀을 흘리다, 땀이 나다 (sweaty ⑱ 땀투성이의) all the way 줄곧, 처음부터 끝까지 No way! 말도 안 돼! hopelessly ⑨ 형편없이, 어찌할 도리 없이 My apologies. 미안해.

12 짧은 대화의 응답 파악

[Telephone rings.]	*[전화기가 울린다.]*
M Hello, this is Noah's Restaurant.	남 안녕하세요, Noah's Restaurant입니다.
W Hi. ¹⁾I'm calling to make a reservation for 6 p.m. this Saturday.	여 안녕하세요. 이번 주 토요일 오후 6시에 예약하려고 전화했어요.
M Let me see. *[Pause]* How many guests will there be? We only have ²⁾tables for two left on that day.	남 어디 볼게요. *[잠시 멈춤]* 몇 분이나 오실 건가요? 그날은 2인용 자리만 남아 있어요.
W That's okay. It'll be just me and my husband.	여 <u>괜찮아요. 저와 제 남편뿐이에요.</u>

선택지 ① 좋아요. 6인용 자리를 예약하고 싶어요.
② 유감스럽네요. 더 일찍 전화 주셨어야 했어요.
③ 아쉽네요. 그럼, 예약을 취소할 수 있나요?
④ 괜찮아요. 저와 제 남편뿐이에요.
⑤ 안 돼요. 이번 주 토요일은 예약이 꽉 찼어요.

레스토랑에 예약 전화를 하는 상황이다. 남자가 몇 명이 올 것인지 물으면서 그날은 2인용 자리만 남아 있다고 했으므로, 이에 대한 응답으로는 방문할 인원수를 대답하는 ④ 'That's okay. It'll be just me and my husband.'가 가장 적절하다.

어휘 make a reservation 예약하다 reserve 통 예약하다 cancel 통 취소하다

13 긴 대화의 응답 파악

W Welcome back, Thomas. How can I help you this morning?	여 또 오셨네요, Thomas. 오늘 아침엔 뭘 도와드릴까요?
M Hi, Taylor. I'd like a croissant. Oh, and are those new peanut butter cookies?	남 안녕하세요, Taylor. 크루아상 하나 주세요. 오, 저건 새로 나온 땅콩버터 쿠키인가요?
W Yeah! They're made with ¹⁾a special recipe I've been working on for a while. Would you like to try a sample?	여 그래요! 그건 제가 한동안 공을 들인 특별한 레시피로 만든 거예요. 샘플 하나 드셔보실래요?
M I'd love to. *[Pause]* It's really good. This is going to be a popular item at your bakery.	남 그러고 싶어요. *[잠시 멈춤]* 정말 좋은데요. 이건 당신의 빵집에서 인기 있는 품목이 될 거예요.
W I thought so too, but so far the ²⁾sales have been pretty slow.	여 저도 그렇게 생각했는데, 지금까지 매출은 꽤 부진했어요.
M Are you doing some kind of promotion?	남 홍보라든지 그런 걸 하고 있나요?
W Right now, if you buy two, you get a third one free.	여 지금 당장은, 두 개를 사면, 세 번째 쿠키는 공짜로 드려요.
M Perfect. I'm sure business will pick up soon, then.	남 완벽해요. 그러면 분명 장사가 곧 잘될 거예요.
W I hope so, but I'm getting a little worried.	여 그러면 좋겠는데, 걱정이 좀 되네요.
M It might help to ³⁾do some advertising online.	남 온라인으로 광고를 하는 게 도움이 될지도 몰라요.
W **Actually, would you mind spreading the word on social media?**	여 실은, 당신이 소셜 미디어에 말 좀 퍼뜨려 주실래요?
M **No problem. What do you ⁴⁾need me to do?**	남 문제없죠. 제가 어떻게 해드릴까요?
W How about posting a picture of the cookie and mentioning our bakery?	여 쿠키 사진을 올리고 우리 빵집을 언급하는 건 어때요?

선택지 ① 또 다른 홍보 행사를 진행하는 게 현명할 것 같아요.
② 당신의 웹사이트에 쿠키 레시피를 올려보는 건 어때요?
③ 쿠키 사진을 올리고 우리 빵집을 언급하는 건 어때요?
④ 땅콩버터 쿠키의 가격을 낮추는 건 어떨까요?
⑤ 가장 인기 있는 쿠키를 더 많이 만들기 시작해도 돼요.

빵집에서 신제품을 시식하는 상황이다. 여자가 새로 나온 쿠키를 소셜 미디어에 광고해달라고 부탁하자 남자가 승낙하며 어떻게 해주길 바라는지 물었으므로, 이에 대한 응답으로는 광고 방식을 제안하는 ③ 'How about posting a picture of the cookie and mentioning our bakery?'가 가장 적절하다.

어휘 work on ~에 공을 들이다 promotion 명 홍보 (행사) pick up (장사가) 잘되다 advertise 통 광고하다 spread 통 퍼뜨리다 lower 통 낮추다

14 긴 대화의 응답 파악

M Hey, Hannah. How was your weekend?	남 안녕, Hannah. 주말 어떻게 보냈니?
W Good. I went to see a comedy movie called *Noisy Neighbors*.	여 좋았어. <Noisy Neighbors>라는 코미디 영화를 보러 갔어.
M Oh, yeah? I've been meaning to watch that.	남 아, 그래? 나 그거 보러 갈 셈이었는데.
W ¹⁾It's hilarious. I really recommend it.	여 그건 진짜 웃겨. 정말 추천이야.
M Where did you see it? It wasn't playing at the theater near my house.	남 어디서 봤어? 우리 집 근처에 있는 극장에서는 상영하지 않던걸.
W I had to take the subway over to West End Village. It's only playing in a few places.	여 웨스트 엔드 빌리지로 가는 지하철을 타야 했어. 겨우 몇 곳에서만 상영 중이거든.
M Were there many people in the theater?	남 극장에 사람들은 많았어?
W Yes. It was almost full. But I don't think the movie will be in theaters ²⁾much longer.	여 응. 거의 꽉 찼어. 하지만 그 영화가 극장에 더 오래 걸려 있을 것 같지는 않아.
M Yeah... It came out a month ago. I'm worried that I ³⁾will miss it.	남 그러게... 한 달 전에 개봉했잖아. 그걸 놓칠까 봐 걱정이야.
W In any event, it should be on streaming services pretty soon.	여 어쨌든 꽤 금방 스트리밍 서비스로 나올 거야.
M I don't know... It's not the same when you watch a movie at home.	남 모르겠어... 집에서 영화를 볼 때랑 똑같지 않아.
W **You can still ⁴⁾catch it at the theater I went to, but you'd better hurry.**	여 내가 갔던 극장에서 아직 볼 수 있어, 그런데 서두르는 게 좋겠다.

M Okay, I'll check the movie times right now.

남 　알겠어, 지금 바로 영화 시간을 확인해 볼게.

선택지 ① 코미디 영화는 다른 사람들이 웃는 소리가 들려서 재미있어.

② 우리 집으로 그 영화를 보러 와도 돼.

③ 극장이 여기서 멀지 않으니까, 우리는 택시를 타면 돼.

④ 응, 영화 티켓은 금방 매진될 거야.

⑤ 알겠어, 지금 바로 영화 시간을 확인해 볼게.

여자가 주말에 관람한 영화에 대해 이야기하는 상황이다. 그 영화를 극장에서 보고 싶어 하는 남자에게 여자가 자신이 갔던 극장에서 서둘러 보기를 권했으므로, 이에 대한 응답으로는 그렇게 하겠다고 답하는 ⑤ 'Okay, I'll check the movie times right now.'가 가장 적절하다.

어휘 mean to ~할 셈이다　hilarious 형 진짜 웃긴, 유쾌한　come out 개봉하다　in any event 어쨌든, 아무튼　sold out 매진된, 다 팔린

15 　상황에 적절한 말 파악　　　　　정답 ②

M Mary is a member of her town's chess club. She is ¹⁾a talented player and beats most of the other members of the club. Last week, she played several games against a chess master online. Unfortunately, she lost every match they played. As a result, she is ²⁾feeling discouraged. One experienced member of the chess club, Russel, notices that she seems very disappointed. Russel thinks that Mary still has a lot to learn from the way that ³⁾stronger opponents play. If she wants to reach her full potential as a player, she needs to learn the strategies the master used against her. **Therefore, Russell wants to suggest that she ⁴⁾study the matches she lost last week.** In this situation, what would Russell most likely say to Mary?

남 　Mary는 동네 체스 동호회의 회원입니다. 그녀는 재능 있는 선수이고, 대부분의 다른 동호회 회원들을 능가합니다. 지난주, 그녀는 온라인에서 체스 고수를 상대로 여러 게임을 했습니다. 불행하게도, 그녀는 모든 경기에서 졌습니다. 결과적으로, 그녀는 낙담하고 있습니다. 체스 동호회의 경험 많은 회원인 Russel은 그녀가 매우 실망스러워 보인다는 것을 알아차립니다. Russel은 더 강한 상대가 경기하는 방식으로부터 Mary가 배울 것이 아직 많다고 생각합니다. 만약 그녀가 선수로서 그녀의 잠재력을 최대한 발휘하고 싶다면, 그녀는 체스 고수가 그녀를 상대로 사용한 전략을 배워야 합니다. 따라서, Russel은 그녀가 지난주에 졌던 경기들을 연구해야 한다고 제안하고 싶습니다. 이러한 상황에서, Russell이 Mary에게 가장 할 것 같은 말은 무엇입니까?

선택지 ① 다음번에는 네가 이길 거라고 난 확신해.

② 이전 게임들을 분석해 보는 게 어때?

③ 배우고 싶다면 전략을 가르쳐 줄 수 있어.

④ 이번에는 다른 전술로 다시 경기하자.

⑤ 도서관에서 체스 서적을 빌리는 건 어때?

Mary가 고수와의 경기에서 패배하여 매우 실망한 것을 보고, Russell은 더 강한 상대의 경기 방식으로부터 배울 점이 있으므로 그녀가 지난주에 졌던 경기들을 연구하는 것을 제안하려고 한다. 따라서, Russell이 할 말로 ② 'Why don't you analyze the previous games?'가 가장 적절하다.

어휘 talented 형 재능 있는　beat 통 능가하다; 이기다　as a result 결과적으로　discouraged 형 낙담한　experienced 형 경험 많은, 숙련된　disappointed 형 실망한　opponent 명 상대
reach one's full potential ~의 잠재력을 최대한 발휘하다　strategy 명 전략　confident 형 확신하는; 자신감 있는　analyze 통 분석하다　previous 형 이전의　tactic 명 전술
check out 빌리다, 대출하다

16-17 　세트 문항　　　　　정답 16 ③ 17 ①

W Good morning, everyone. In the previous unit, I gave some background information about different methods of plant pollination. **Today, I want to discuss how different seeds can ¹⁾move from one place to another.** First of all, let's consider **maple trees**. Maple tree seeds have wings that spin. These make them fly like a helicopter and ²⁾carry them far in the wind. The second example is the **coconut tree**. Its seeds are ³⁾waterproof and float quite easily in the ocean. Thus, they move through the water to new places. Next, there's the **blackberry tree**. Tiny blackberry seeds are spread by animals who eat them, travel elsewhere, and then leave the seeds in droppings. Finally, and most unusually, we have the **pine tree**. Certain pine seeds don't drop off the tree. These are covered in a thick material that only ⁴⁾melts off under high heat. In other words, these seeds can only be spread by forest fires. Let's look at some photos comparing the seeds I've mentioned.

여 　안녕하십니까, 여러분. 이전 단원에서는, 식물 수분의 다양한 방식에 관한 배경지식을 설명했습니다. 오늘은, 어떻게 여러 가지 씨앗들이 한 장소에서 다른 장소로 이동할 수 있는지 논의하고 싶습니다. 가장 먼저, 단풍나무를 생각해 봅시다. 단풍나무 씨앗에는 회전하는 날개가 있습니다. 이 날개는 씨앗이 헬리콥터처럼 날아가게 하고 바람을 타고 씨앗을 멀리 옮깁니다. 두 번째 예시는 코코넛 나무입니다. 그것의 씨앗은 방수가 되고 바다에서 꽤 쉽게 떠다닙니다. 따라서, 그것은 물을 통해 새로운 장소로 이동합니다. 다음은 블랙베리 나무입니다. 작은 블랙베리 씨앗은 그것을 먹고, 다른 곳으로 이동하고, 그리고 나서 그 씨앗을 배설물 안에 남기는 동물들에 의해 퍼집니다. 마지막으로, 그리고 가장 특이하게도, 소나무가 있습니다. 어떤 소나무 씨앗들은 나무에서 떨어지지 않습니다. 이것들은 고열에서만 녹는 두꺼운 물질로 덮여 있습니다. 다시 말해서, 이 씨앗들은 산불에 의해서만 퍼질 수 있습니다. 제가 언급한 씨앗의 비교 사진을 몇 장 보겠습니다.

선택지 16 ① 스스로 수분할 수 있는 다양한 나무

② 혹독한 환경에서 식물의 생존 전략

③ 씨앗이 새로운 장소로 이동하는 다양한 방법

④ 이토록 매우 다양한 씨앗 종류가 있는 이유

⑤ 기후가 어린 식물의 성장에 영향을 끼치는 방식

17 ① 떡갈나무　② 단풍나무　③ 코코넛 나무

④ 블랙베리 나무　⑤ 소나무

16 어떻게 여러 가지 씨앗들이 한 장소에서 다른 장소로 이동할 수 있는지에 대해 논의하고 있으므로 여자가 하는 말의 주제로 ③ 'various ways that seeds travel to new places'가 가장 적절하다.

17 단풍나무, 코코넛 나무, 블랙베리 나무, 소나무를 언급했지만, ① 'oak tree'는 언급하지 않았다.

어휘 pollination 명 수분　spin 통 회전하다　waterproof 형 방수의　float 통 떠다니다　droppings 명 배설물　be covered in ~으로 덮여 있다　melt 통 녹다　in other words 다시 말해서
survival 명 생존　harsh 형 혹독한　a wide variety of 매우 다양한　climate 명 기후　growth 명 성장

1	③	2	①	3	②	4	④	5	③	6	⑤	7	②	8	④	9	③	10	④
11	③	12	④	13	②	14	①	15	②	16	②	17	⑤						

• 각 문제의 정답 근거는 굵은 글씨로, Dictation 정답은 밑줄로 표시되어 있습니다.

1 목적 파악

정답 ③

| W | Attention, shoppers. We would like to remind you that the Waterford Mall will be closing at 8 p.m. **Therefore, I'd like to recommend that you** ¹⁾finish your shopping **within the next 15 minutes.** Please make your final selections soon. If you have chosen all the items you want to buy, please bring them to the checkout counter right now. We may not be able to assist you with ²⁾completing your purchases after 8. Keep in mind that our self-checkout kiosks are available, which will let you skip the line at the cash register. Thank you for ³⁾your cooperation, and enjoy the rest of your evening. | 여 | 주목해주세요, 쇼핑객 여러분. Waterford Mall이 오후 8시에 문을 닫을 예정임을 다시 한번 알려드립니다. 그러므로, 여러분에게 앞으로 15분 안에 쇼핑을 끝내시기를 권하고 싶습니다. 빠르게 최종 선택을 해주세요. 사고 싶은 물건을 다 고르셨다면, 지금 바로 계산대로 가져와 주세요. 8시 이후에는 구매 완료를 도와드리지 못할 수도 있습니다. 계산대에서 줄을 서지 않고, 저희 셀프 무인 계산대를 이용하실 수 있다는 점도 명심해 주세요. 협조에 감사드리며, 남은 저녁 시간도 즐겁게 보내세요. |

여자가 쇼핑객들에게 쇼핑몰 폐장 시간을 안내하면서, 앞으로 15분 안에 쇼핑을 끝내기를 권하고 있다. 따라서, 여자가 하는 말의 목적으로 ③ '쇼핑몰 폐장 전까지 쇼핑 마치기를 재촉하려고'가 가장 적절하다.

어휘 make a selection 선택하다 checkout counter 계산대 assist 통 돕다 complete 통 완료하다 keep in mind 명심하다 self-checkout kiosk 셀프 무인 계산대 skip a line 줄을 서지 않다 cash register 계산대, 금전 등록기 cooperation 명 협조

2 의견 파악

정답 ①

W	Hey, Terry. Your son wasn't at soccer practice this morning. Is he still on the team?	여	안녕, Terry. 네 아들 오늘 아침 축구 연습에 안 왔더라. 아직 축구팀에 있는 거지?
M	Actually, he's decided not to play, Michelle.	남	실은, 축구 그만하기로 했어, Michelle.
W	Is there anything wrong?	여	무슨 문제라도 있니?
M	He wasn't enjoying soccer anymore. **Besides, I don't think sports are** ¹⁾always healthy for children.	남	아들이 더 이상 축구를 즐겁게 여기지 않아. 게다가, 난 운동이 항상 아이들의 건강에 좋은 건 아니라고 생각해.
W	Really? Isn't it a great way to learn teamwork?	여	정말? 그건 협동심을 배우는 좋은 방법이지 않아?
M	I'm worried that he might get hurt. Head injuries in particular can ²⁾harm children's brain development.	남	나는 다칠까 봐 걱정되거든. 특히 머리 부상은 아이들의 두뇌 발달에 해로울 수 있어.
W	You have a point. There are a lot of fitness benefits, though.	여	일리가 있는 말이야. 그래도, 건강상 많은 이점이 있잖아.
M	Sure, but the competition has negative emotional effects. The pressure to win creates too much stress.	남	물론이야, 하지만 경쟁은 정서적으로 부정적인 영향을 끼쳐. 이겨야 한다는 압박감이 너무 많은 스트레스를 유발하거든.
W	Hmm... it seems like you've made up your mind.	여	흠... 결단을 내린 것 같네.
M	Yeah. I ³⁾support my son's decision.	남	응. 난 우리 아들의 결정을 지지해.
W	Well, I hope he finds an activity that he enjoys more.	여	음, 네 아들이 더 즐길 거리를 찾길 바랄게.
M	That would be great.	남	그러면 정말 좋겠어.

남자는 자신의 아들이 축구를 그만하기로 했다고 하면서 운동이 항상 아이들의 건강에 좋은 것은 아니라고 생각한다고 했다. 따라서, 남자의 의견으로 ① '운동이 아이들의 건강에 좋지 않을 수 있다.'가 가장 적절하다.

어휘 besides 부 게다가 teamwork 명 협동심, 협력 injury 명 부상 in particular 특히 You have a point. 일리가 있는 말이야. fitness 명 건강; 적절함 negative 형 부정적인 pressure 명 압박감; 압력 make up one's mind 결단을 내리다

3 관계 파악

정답 ②

W	My name is Sara Porter, and **I will be interviewing Brandon Harper today. Welcome to the show, Mr. Harper.**	여	저는 Sara Porter이고, 오늘 Brandon Harper를 인터뷰할 예정입니다. 쇼에 오신 것을 환영합니다, Harper 씨.
M	Thanks. I'm a little nervous. I've never been on TV before.	남	고마워요. 조금 긴장되네요. 저는 TV에 한 번도 나온 적이 없거든요.
W	¹⁾Being on camera isn't so scary, especially compared to the work you usually do.	여	카메라 앞에 서는 건, 특히 당신이 평소에 하시는 일에 비하면 그렇게 무섭지 않은걸요.
M	Well... I have training for that.	남	음... 그건 훈련을 받으니까요.
W	You're doing fine. Let's talk about what happened on May 15th. **You saved three people** ²⁾from a burning house, **right?**	여	지금 잘하고 계세요. 5월 15일에 있었던 일에 관해 이야기해 보죠. 불타는 집에서 세 사람을 구하셨죠, 맞나요?
M	Yes. I'm just glad that I rescued everyone.	남	네. 모두 구조해서 참 다행이죠.

W Was anyone injured?	여 다친 사람은 없었나요?
M One person had some scratches, but nothing serious.	남 한 사람이 찰과상을 입긴 했지만, 심각한 건 아니었어요.
W So how does it feel to be a hero?	여 그래서, 영웅이 되신 기분이 어떠세요?
M I don't think I'm a hero. I did what ³⁾<u>anyone with my job</u> would do. I'm just glad I was able to help.	남 전 영웅이라고 생각하지 않아요. 제 직업을 가진 사람이라면 누구나 할 일을 한 거예요. 제가 도움이 될 수 있었다니 기쁠 뿐이죠.
W You are so humble! I'm sure most of my viewers think what you did was amazing.	여 정말 겸손하시네요! 제 시청자들 대부분은 당신이 한 일이 대단하다고 생각할 거예요.
M Thanks. I really appreciate that.	남 고마워요. 정말 감사합니다.

두 사람이 최근에 일어난 화재 사고의 인명 구조에 대해 이야기하고 있다. 여자는 진행하는 TV쇼를 소개하며 인터뷰를 진행하고 있고, 남자는 화재 사고에서 세 사람을 구조했다고 답하고 있는 것으로 보아 두 사람의 관계로 ② 'TV쇼 진행자 — 소방관'이 가장 적절하다.

[어휘] nervous ⑧ 긴장한, 초조한 compared to ~에 비하면, ~에 비해 save ⑧ 구하다; 저장하다 rescue ⑧ 구조하다 scratch ⑲ 찰과상 humble ⑧ 겸손한

---

4 그림 내용 불일치 파악   정답 ④

M Hi, Emily!	남 안녕, Emily!
W Hey, Luke. What's all this outside the library?	여 안녕, Luke. 도서관 밖에 이게 다 뭐야?
M It's an event to ¹⁾<u>encourage children to read</u>.	남 아이들에게 독서를 장려하기 위한 행사장이야.
W Oh, I love the balloons over the entrance.	여 오, 난 입구에 걸린 풍선들이 마음에 든다.
M Yeah. It seems like a fun event.	남 응. 재미있는 행사 같아.
W Why is that table set up on the pathway?	여 저 탁자는 왜 보도 위에 설치되어 있지?
M That's where they have books recommended for kids.	남 아이들에게 추천할 만한 책들이 거기에 있어.
W I see. And they must have set up those ²⁾<u>chairs on the grass</u> so people could read outside, right?	여 그렇구나. 그럼, 잔디 위 의자들을 분명 사람들이 밖에서 독서할 수 있도록 설치했을 거야, 그렇지?
M Yeah! They're open to anyone. Why don't we go sit down?	남 응! 누구나 이용할 수 있어. 우리도 가서 앉는 게 어때?
W Absolutely! Just let me return my books first. **Do you want to meet up at the bench ³⁾<u>underneath the tree</u>?**	여 물론이야! 일단 나는 책 먼저 반납할게. 나무 아래에 있는 벤치에서 만날까?
M Sure. Oh, I'm going to get one of those drinks they're selling over at that booth with the ⁴⁾<u>striped roof</u>. Do you want anything?	남 그래. 아, 나는 줄무늬 지붕이 있는 부스에서 파는 음료수를 하나 살 거야. 넌 뭐 원하는 거 있어?
W Yeah. Could you get me a lemonade?	여 응. 레모네이드 한 잔 사 줄래?
M Of course! See you in a minute.	남 당연하지! 이따 봐.

대화에서 여자가 나무 아래에 있는 벤치에서 만나자고 제안했는데, ④에는 나무 아래에 돗자리가 그려져 있다.

[어휘] encourage ⑧ 장려하다 entrance ⑲ 입구 set up ~을 설치하다 pathway ⑲ 보도; 오솔길 underneath ⑳ ~ 아래에

---

5 할 일 파악   정답 ③

[Cell phone rings.]	[휴대폰이 울린다.]
W Honey, will you be home soon? We're supposed to be at the parent-teacher conference in an hour.	여 여보, 곧 집에 도착할 거야? 우리는 한 시간 후에 학부모 상담에 참석하기로 했잖아.
M I'll be leaving the office in a minute.	남 난 잠시 후에 퇴근할 거야.
W Don't forget to get the dry cleaning on the way home.	여 집에 오는 길에 드라이클리닝 맡긴 것 찾아오는 걸 잊지 마.
M Sorry, but I don't think I can. And honestly, I'm not sure if I have enough time to ¹⁾<u>pick you up</u>, either.	남 미안한데, 못할 것 같아. 그리고 솔직히, 당신 데리러 갈 시간도 충분할지 모르겠어.
W Okay, never mind. We can do that later. I'll head over to the school myself.	여 알겠어, 신경 쓰지 마. 그건 나중에 하면 돼. 학교도 내가 알아서 갈게.
M Are you taking your car there?	남 거기로 당신 차 타고 갈 거야?
W No. It'll be easier to just call a taxi.	여 아니. 그냥 택시를 부르는 게 더 쉬울 거야.
M Okay, that makes sense. We can go home in my car.	남 그래, 그럴 수 있겠네. 집에 갈 땐 내 차로 가면 돼.
W Great. Let's meet ²⁾<u>by the main entrance</u> of the school in 30 minutes.	여 좋아. 30분 후에 학교 정문 옆에서 만나.
M Sure. **I just need to turn in a report to my manager, and then I'll be out of here.**	남 그래. 부장님에게 보고서만 제출하면 되니까, 그러고 나서 나갈게.
W Got it. Call me if ³⁾<u>there's any delay</u>.	여 알겠어. 늦을 것 같으면 전화 줘.

부부가 학부모 상담에 가려 하고 있다. 여자가 남자에게 30분 후에 학교 정문 옆에서 만나자고 하자, 남자가 보고서만 제출하고 나서 나간다고 답했으므로 남자가 할 일로 ③ '보고서 제출하기'가 가장 적절하다.

[어휘] parent-teacher conference 학부모 상담 head over to ~로 가다, 향하다 turn in ~을 제출하다

6   금액 정보 파악

정답 ⑤

M	Welcome to the Delta Baseball Stadium. How can I help you?
W	Hi, I was wondering if you ¹⁾had any tickets left for tonight's game.
M	Sure. We have seats on the upper level for $30 and seats on the lower level for $50.
W	Okay, great. **I'll take five tickets in ²⁾the lower part of the stadium.**
M	We also have a special offer this afternoon. **You can buy a baseball player figure for only $5.**
W	Those are cute. Why not? **I'll take two of those.**
M	Great. You should see the total price on your screen.
W	Oh, just a moment. Is there ³⁾a group discount for the tickets?
M	I'm sorry. You need to buy more than 10 tickets to ⁴⁾qualify for the 20% group discount.
W	Ah, that's fine. Here's my credit card.
M	Great. Enjoy the game, tonight!
W	Thank you.

남	델타 야구 경기장에 오신 것을 환영합니다. 무엇을 도와드릴까요?
여	안녕하세요, 오늘 밤 경기 표가 남아 있는지 궁금해서요.
남	그럼요. 경기장 위층에 30달러짜리 좌석과 아래층에 50달러짜리 좌석이 있어요.
여	네, 좋아요. 경기장 아래쪽으로 다섯 장 주세요.
남	오늘 오후에는 특가 상품도 있어요. 단돈 5달러에 야구선수 피규어를 살 수 있답니다.
여	귀엽군요. 그거 좋죠. 그것들 두 개 주세요.
남	좋아요. 화면에서 총액을 확인해 주세요.
여	아, 잠깐만요. 단체 할인이 있나요?
남	죄송합니다. 20%의 단체 할인 혜택을 받으려면 열 장 이상 구매하셔야 합니다.
여	아, 괜찮습니다. 여기 제 신용카드요.
남	좋아요. 오늘 밤 경기 즐겁게 보세요!
여	감사합니다.

여자가 야구 경기장 아래층 좌석을 다섯 장($50×5=$250), 야구선수 피규어 두 개($5×2=$10)를 구매했으므로 정답은 ⑤ '$260'이다. 단체 할인 혜택은 열 장 이상 구매 시에만 적용되므로 할인은 받지 못했다.

[어휘] stadium 뗑 경기장   wonder 통 궁금하다   Why not? 그거 좋죠.

7   이유 파악

정답 ②

W	Welcome back to Toronto, Tom!
M	It's good to finally be back home, Liz.
W	How was your flight? Did you get any sleep?
M	No. I was ¹⁾awake the whole time.
W	Did you watch some movies?
M	No. I didn't really feel like doing that.
W	Were the other ²⁾passengers too noisy? That's the worst.
M	Actually, it was pretty quiet, and it wasn't a bumpy flight.
W	Did you drink too much coffee? That always keeps me awake.
M	No. **It was because I didn't have enough ³⁾room to get comfortable. I couldn't stretch my legs out at all.**
W	You'll need some rest, then. How about taking a nap this afternoon?
M	I'd better try to stay awake so I can avoid jet lag.
W	That's a good idea.

여	토론토로 돌아온 걸 환영해, Tom!
남	마침내 고향으로 돌아오게 돼서 좋다, Liz.
여	비행은 어땠어? 잠은 좀 잤니?
남	아니. 계속 깨어 있었어.
여	영화 좀 봤었어?
남	아니. 정말 그럴 기분이 아니었어.
여	다른 승객들이 너무 시끄러웠니? 그게 최악인데.
남	사실, 꽤 조용했고, 심하게 흔들리는 비행은 아니었어.
여	커피를 너무 많이 마셨니? 커피는 날 항상 잠 못 자게 해.
남	아냐. 편하게 있을 공간이 부족해서 그랬어. 다리를 전혀 쭉 뻗을 수가 없었거든.
여	그러면 좀 쉬어야겠다. 오늘 오후에 낮잠을 자는 건 어때?
남	시차 적응을 하도록 깨어 있으려고 노력하는 게 낫겠어.
여	좋은 생각이야.

남자가 고향으로 돌아오는 비행기에서 계속 깨어 있었다고 하면서 편하게 있을 공간이 부족해 다리를 뻗을 수 없었다고 말했으므로, 남자가 계속 깨어 있었던 이유는 ② '다리를 뻗을 공간이 부족해서'이다.

[어휘] feel like (doing) ~할 기분이다   passenger 뗑 승객   bumpy 뼹 심하게 흔들리는, 험난한; 울퉁불퉁한   stretch one's legs out 다리를 쭉 뻗다   take a nap 낮잠 자다

stay awake 깨어 있다   avoid jet lag 시차 적응을 하다

8   언급 유무 파악

정답 ④

W	Chris, are you going to Heather's birthday party?
M	I was planning to. What about you?
W	Of course. It's going to be ¹⁾on the 7th of January, right?
M	Yeah. And the party will be held at **Heather's house.**
W	She said that her house was going to be decorated for the party.
M	Right. It's going to have ²⁾a pirate theme.
W	Oh, that sounds fun. So, should I wear a costume or something?
M	I don't think so. We can just wear **casual clothes.**
W	Okay. One other thing, ³⁾what kind of present are you going to get her?
M	I'm thinking of buying her **a ticket to the musical *Captain Hook*. She is a huge fan of it.**
W	Oh, right! I'm sure she'll like your present.
M	Yeah. I hope so. This party will be a lot of fun, anyway.

여	Chris, 너 Heather의 생일 파티에 갈 거니?
남	그럴 계획이었어. 너는?
여	당연히 가지. 1월 7일에 하는 거지, 그렇지?
남	그래. 그리고 Heather의 집에서 열릴 거야.
여	집이 파티에 맞춰서 꾸며질 거랬어.
남	맞아. 해적 테마일 거야.
여	오, 재미있겠다. 그러면, 코스튬이나 뭐 그런 걸 입어야 할까?
남	그렇지 않을걸. 그냥 평상복을 입어도 돼.
여	알겠어. 하나만 더, 어떤 선물을 사줄 거야?
남	난 뮤지컬 <Captain Hook>의 티켓을 사줄까 생각 중이야. 그것의 엄청난 팬이잖아.
여	아, 맞다! 분명 네 선물을 마음에 들어 할 거야.
남	응. 그러면 좋겠다. 어쨌든 파티는 정말 재미있을 거야.

날짜(1월 7일), 장소(Heather의 집), 복장(평상복), 선물(뮤지컬 <Captain Hook>의 티켓)에 대해 언급했고, ④ '제공 간식'은 언급하지 않았다.

어휘 decorate 통 꾸미다, 장식하다 pirate 명 해적 casual 형 평상시의; 우연한 be a huge fan of ~의 엄청난 팬이다

9 내용 불일치 파악
정답 ③

W Welcome to the Parkwood Dance Program. My name is Marilyn Higgins, and I'll be one of the ¹⁾four instructors who will guide you for the next two weeks of intensive practice. The classes are held from 8 a.m. to 6 p.m. every day. Obviously, this will require a lot of energy. **But considering that ²⁾only experienced dancers are allowed to join our program**, all of you will be fine. Throughout the program, you'll have lots of time to practice, and you'll get feedback from the instructors. So you'll really improve if you work hard. At the end of the program, we'll ³⁾hold a performance for your friends and family. It'll be a perfect opportunity to show off what you've learned. Okay, let's get to it!	여 Parkwood Dance Program에 오신 걸 환영합니다. 저는 Marilyn Higgins라고 하며, 앞으로 2주간의 집중 훈련 동안 여러분을 지도할 네 명의 강사 중 한 명입니다. 수업은 매일 오전 8시부터 오후 6시까지 진행됩니다. 분명히, 많은 에너지가 필요할 것입니다. 하지만 오직 숙련된 댄서들만 저희 프로그램에 참여할 수 있다는 점을 고려하면, 여러분 모두는 괜찮을 겁니다. 프로그램 내내, 여러분은 연습할 시간을 많이 가질 것이고, 강사들로부터 피드백을 받을 겁니다. 그래서 열심히 연습한다면 정말 발전하게 될 것입니다. 프로그램의 말미에는, 여러분의 친구들과 가족들을 위해 공연을 열 것입니다. 그것은 여러분이 배운 것을 뽐낼 수 있는 완벽한 기회가 될 것입니다. 좋습니다, 시작해봅시다!

댄스 프로그램 수강자들을 대상으로 한 안내 방송이다. 여자가 오직 숙련된 댄서들만 프로그램에 참여할 수 있다고 했으므로 ③ '초보자들을 대상으로 열리는 수업이다.'는 내용과 일치하지 않는다.

어휘 intensive 형 집중적인 obviously 부 분명히 require 통 필요로 하다 experienced 형 숙련된, 경험이 풍부한 throughout 전 ~ 내내 show off ~을 뽐내다, 자랑하다
Let's get to it! 시작해봅시다!

10 도표 정보 파악
정답 ④

M Jennifer, can you help me choose a shirt?	남 Jennifer, 셔츠 고르는 것 좀 도와줄래?
W Sure, but there are a lot of options. Is there one you had your eye on in particular?	여 물론이야, 그런데 선택할 게 많네. 특별히 눈여겨본 게 있니?
M Not really. But I want a bigger one than what I got last time.	남 그렇지 않아. 하지만 지난번에 산 것보다 더 큰 걸 원해.
W You ¹⁾bought a medium-sized shirt, right? **We should look at large shirts, then.**	여 중간 치수의 셔츠를 샀었지, 그렇지? 그러면 큰 셔츠를 봐야겠어.
M Oh, and I shouldn't spend more than $25 on a shirt.	남 아, 그리고 셔츠 한 장에 25달러 이상은 쓰면 안 돼.
W That's helpful. What do you think of this one?	여 도움이 되는 얘기야. 이건 어때?
M Hmm... It ²⁾feels a little rough when I touch it. It wouldn't be comfortable.	남 흠... 만지니까 느낌이 좀 거칠어. 편하지 않겠어.
W In that case, I'd recommend getting something that's made of 100% cotton. It will be the softest choice.	여 그렇다면, 면 100%로 된 걸 사길 권할게. 그게 가장 부드러울 거야.
M I agree. That still leaves a couple of options.	남 동감이야. 여전히 2개의 선택지가 남아 있어.
W Do you want ³⁾long sleeves?	여 긴 소매를 원해?
M No. I'm planning to wear the shirt during the summer.	남 아니. 난 여름 동안 그 셔츠를 입을 거야.
W Okay, then this half-sleeve shirt should be perfect for you.	여 그래, 그러면 이 반소매 셔츠가 네게 딱이겠어.
M You're right. I'll take it.	남 네 말이 맞아. 그걸로 할게.

남자는 큰 사이즈이면서, 한 장에 25달러 이하인 것 중에서, 면 100%로 된, 반소매 셔츠를 골랐다.

어휘 have one's eye on 눈여겨보다 rough 형 거친 cotton 명 면, 솜 sleeve 명 소매

11 짧은 대화의 응답 파악
정답 ③

W Are you almost ¹⁾ready to leave for the bus station, Jamie?	여 버스 터미널에 갈 준비 거의 다 된 거니, Jamie?
M I just need to put a few things in my suitcase, Mom. Give me five more minutes.	남 여행 가방에 물건 몇 개만 넣으면 돼요, 엄마. 5분만 더 주세요.
W I'm a little worried. Our bus leaves in 40 minutes. **Do you think we'll ²⁾get to the station on time?**	여 난 조금 걱정되는구나. 우리 버스는 40분 후에 출발이야. 제시간에 터미널에 도착할 수 있을 것 같니?
M It won't take us long to get there by taxi.	남 택시로 가면 오래 안 걸릴 거예요.
	선택지 ① 버스에서 함께 앉을 수 있으면 좋겠어요.
	② 버스푯값은 이미 내셨나요?
	③ 택시로 가면 오래 안 걸릴 거예요.
	④ 여행 가방 옮기는 데 도움이 필요하세요?
	⑤ 저는 터미널에서 한 시간째 기다리고 있어요.

두 사람이 버스 터미널에 갈 준비를 하는 상황에서 여자가 늦을까 봐 걱정된다면서 제시간에 터미널에 도착할 수 있을 것 같은지 물었으므로, 이에 대한 응답으로는 택시로 가면 오래 안 걸릴 것이라고 말하는 ③ 'It won't take us long to get there by taxi.'가 가장 적절하다.

어휘 bus station 버스 터미널 suitcase 명 여행 가방 carry 통 옮기다, 나르다

12 짧은 대화의 응답 파악   정답 ④

[Cell phone rings.] **M** Hi, Beth. I was thinking of ¹⁾going to a movie this evening. Are you interested? **W** I'd love to, but I have a yoga class. It won't finish until 9. **M** **Oh, that's too bad. I haven't ²⁾seen you in a while, and I want to spend some time with you.** **W** I'm free tomorrow if you want to go then.	[휴대폰이 울린다.] 남 안녕, Beth. 나 오늘 저녁에 영화 보러 갈까 생각 중이었어. 관심 있니? 여 그러고 싶지만, 요가 수업이 있어. 9시는 되어야 끝날 거야. 남 오, 유감이다. 우리 못 본 지 꽤 돼서, 너랑 시간을 보내고 싶은데. 여 난 내일 한가해, 만약 네가 그때 가는 것도 괜찮다면 말이야. 선택지 ① 어젯밤 영화 티켓을 사줘서 고마워. ② 우리가 본 영화 어땠어? ③ 우리 이렇게 많이 어울려 놀아서 좋아. ④ 난 내일 한가해, 만약 네가 그때 가는 것도 괜찮다면 말이야. ⑤ 요가 수업에 새로운 회원들이 많아.

오늘 저녁에 영화를 보러 가자는 남자의 제안에 여자가 거절하자 남자가 유감을 표현했으므로, 이에 대한 응답으로는 내일은 한가하다고 말하는 ④ 'I'm free tomorrow if you want to go then.'이 가장 적절하다.

어휘   not A until B B는 되어야 A하다   That's too bad. 유감이다.   hang out 어울려 놀다

13 긴 대화의 응답 파악   정답 ②

W Thanks for making dinner, Grandpa. That was delicious. **M** I'm glad you liked it. It's a very old recipe that I ¹⁾got from my dad. **W** It was very tasty. Do you need some help cleaning up? **M** That would be great. Could you do the dishes? **W** Sure. I'll ²⁾take care of that right now. **M** Thanks. You can just put everything into the dishwasher. **W** That seems easy. Cleaning up won't take long at all. **M** Oh, hold on... **Those pans have a lot of oil on them. I don't think they can ³⁾go straight into the dishwasher.** **W** Should I rinse them out first? **M** That's right. And maybe wipe them with the cloth. **W** **Hmm... If I am going to do that, I might as well ⁴⁾just wash them by hand.** **M** **Then, make sure to use lots of dish soap.**	여 저녁 요리해 주셔서 감사합니다, 할아버지. 맛있었어요. 남 마음에 들었다니 다행이구나. 그건 내가 아버지께 물려받은 아주 오래된 요리법이야. 여 아주 맛있었어요. 치우는 걸 도와드릴까요? 남 그러면 좋겠구나. 설거지를 해줄래? 여 물론이죠. 지금 바로 할게요. 남 고맙구나. 그냥 전부 식기세척기에 넣으면 돼. 여 쉬워 보이네요. 치우는 데 전혀 오래 안 걸릴 거예요. 남 아, 잠시만... 저 프라이팬에는 기름이 많이 묻어 있구나. 식기세척기에 바로 넣으면 안 되겠어. 여 먼저 헹궈야 할까요? 남 그래. 그리고 어쩌면 천으로 닦아내는 게 좋겠구나. 여 흠... 그럴 거면, 그냥 직접 설거지하는 게 낫겠어요. 남 그렇다면, 주방 세제를 많이 사용하도록 하렴. 선택지 ① 식기세척기 켜는 걸 깜빡할 뻔했구나. ② 그렇다면, 주방 세제를 많이 사용하도록 하렴. ③ 내가 준비한 음식이 마음에 들었다니 다행이구나. ④ 내가 아직 설거지를 끝내지 못했단다. ⑤ 내게 요리법 복사본을 한 장 보내주렴.

저녁 식사 후 정리하는 상황에서 기름진 프라이팬을 식기세척기에 바로 넣으면 안 되겠다는 남자의 말에 여자가 그럼 직접 설거지하는 게 낫겠다고 했으므로, 이에 대한 응답으로는 설거지 방법을 충고하는 ② 'Then, make sure to use lots of dish soap.'이 가장 적절하다.

어휘   tasty 톙 맛있는   clean up 치우다   do the dishes 설거지하다   dishwasher 톙 식기세척기   rinse 툉 헹구다   wipe 툉 닦다   might as well ~하는 것이 낫다
      by hand 직접, (기계가 아닌) 사람 손으로   turn on ~을 켜다

14 긴 대화의 응답 파악   정답 ①

M Hi, Natalie. Did you go to the book signing last night? **W** I did! I also ¹⁾got a chance to speak with the author, Kate Snow. **M** You've been reading her books for years. That must have been exciting. **W** You can say that again! She gave me some advice about ²⁾writing science fiction stories, too. **M** Wow. That was very kind of her. **W** I know. She's great. Have you ever read any of her books? **M** No, I haven't. But I am planning to soon. **W** You should start with *The Golden Coral*. It's one of my favorite books. **M** Let me write down the title. I'll get a copy next time I'm at the library. **W** ³⁾**You can borrow mine if you like.** **M** **That would be great. I want to find out why you're such a big fan.** **W** Great. I'll go get the book for you.	남 안녕, Natalie. 어젯밤에 책 사인회에 갔었니? 여 갔었어! Kate Snow 작가님과 이야기할 기회도 얻었어. 남 넌 몇 년 동안 그분의 책을 읽어 왔잖아. 분명 아주 신나는 일이었겠어. 여 정말 그래! 작가님은 공상과학 소설을 쓰는 것에 관해서도 조언을 해주셨어. 남 와우. 정말 친절하신걸. 여 그래. 훌륭한 분이셔. 넌 그분의 책을 읽어본 적 있니? 남 아니, 안 읽어봤어. 하지만 곧 읽어보려고. 여 <The Golden Coral>부터 시작해 봐. 내가 가장 좋아하는 책 중 하나야. 남 제목을 적어 놓을게. 다음에 도서관에 가면 한 권 빌려야지. 여 괜찮다면 내 것을 빌려 가도 돼. 남 그러면 정말 좋지. 네가 왜 그렇게 팬인지 알고 싶어. 여 좋아. 네게 그 책을 갖다 줄게.

① 좋아. 네게 그 책을 갖다 줄게.

② 여기 봐. 그녀가 첫 장에 사인해줬어.

③ 동의해. 그 책에 흥미진진한 이야기가 있는 것 같아.

④ 알겠어. 사서 선생님에게 그게 반납됐는지 물어보자.

⑤ 고맙지만 괜찮아. 요즘 책 읽을 시간이 부족하거든.

좋아하는 작가에 대해 이야기하는 상황에서 책을 빌려주겠다는 여자의 제안을 남자가 승낙하면서 왜 그 작가의 팬인지 알고 싶다며 관심을 드러냈으므로, 이에 대한 응답으로는 관심을 반기며 책을 갖다 주겠다고 대답하는 ① 'Great. I'll go get the book for you.'가 가장 적절하다.

어휘 author 명 작가 You can say that again! 정말 그래! write down ~을 적어 두다 librarian 명 사서

---

15 상황에 적절한 말 파악

정답 ②

W Emma is a high school student who wants to [1]become a vet one day. She is eager to know as much as she can, so she has been thinking about volunteering at [2]a local animal shelter. Today, she finally visited the shelter in her neighborhood. Unfortunately, Emma learns that she cannot volunteer today. As Marcus, the receptionist, explains, the shelter [3]already has enough volunteers working at the moment. Furthermore, all volunteers are required to register online in advance, which she has not done. **Therefore, Marcus wants to suggest that Emma fill out [4]a registration form on the shelter's website so that she can volunteer later.** In this situation, what would Marcus most likely say to Emma?

여 Emma는 언젠가 수의사가 되고 싶은 고등학생입니다. 그녀는 가능한 한 많은 것을 알고 싶어 해서, 지역 동물 보호소에서 자원봉사 하는 것에 대해 생각해왔습니다. 오늘, 그녀는 마침내 동네에 있는 보호소를 방문했습니다. 유감스럽게도, Emma는 오늘 자원봉사 할 수 없다는 것을 알게 됩니다. 접수 담당자인 Marcus가 설명한 것처럼, 보호소에는 현재 자원봉사자들이 충분히 있습니다. 게다가, 모든 자원봉사자들은 미리 온라인에 등록하도록 되어 있는데, 그녀는 이를 하지 않았습니다. 따라서, Marcus는 Emma가 나중에 자원봉사 할 수 있도록 보호소 웹사이트에서 등록 양식을 작성하라고 제안하고 싶습니다. 이러한 상황에서, Marcus가 Emma에게 가장 할 것 같은 말은 무엇입니까?

선택지 ① 죄송하지만 접수 담당자 자리에는 공석이 없습니다.

② 여기서 자원봉사를 하려면 온라인 양식을 작성하셔야 합니다.

③ 동네에 있는 다른 보호소에 가서 도와주는 게 어때요?

④ 펜으로 개인정보를 적어주시길 바랍니다.

⑤ 자원봉사자에게 당신의 반려동물을 도와달라고 부탁할게요.

Emma가 동물 보호소에 미리 온라인 등록을 하지 않은 것을 보고, 접수 담당자인 Marcus는 나중에 자원봉사를 할 수 있도록 웹사이트에서 등록 양식을 작성할 것을 제안하려고 한다. 따라서, Marcus가 할 말로 ② 'You will need to complete an online form in order to volunteer here.'가 가장 적절하다.

어휘 vet 명 수의사 be eager to ~하고 싶어 하다 animal shelter 동물 보호소 neighborhood 명 동네; 이웃 receptionist 명 접수 담당자 furthermore 부 게다가
be required to ~하도록 되어 있다 in advance 미리 fill out ~을 작성하다 complete a form 양식을 작성하다 personal information 개인정보

16-17 세트 문항

정답 16 ② 17 ⑤

M Hello, everyone. Last Friday, we discussed the [1]origins of various music genres. **I want to discuss how music can have a major impact on an economy this time.** First, let's look at **Nashville**, the center of country music. Nashville is famous for hundreds of music venues. Live music here is a true industry. It contributes $5 billion annually to the small city's economy. Another notable example is **Seoul**. K-pop albums and concerts [2]generate huge revenue on their own. But the genre has also boosted the city's tourism. Next up is **New Orleans**, which is considered one of the jazz capitals of the world. [3]Millions of tourists visit the city every year to hear jazz music. The money they spend on concerts, hotels, and restaurants are an important part of the city's economy. Finally, I'll mention **Vienna**. During the time of Mozart and Beethoven, it was the center of the music world. Publishers in the city generated [4]major wealth selling copies of their sheet music. Now, let's have a quick look at a video.

남 안녕하십니까, 여러분. 지난 금요일, 우리는 다양한 음악 장르의 기원에 관해 논의했습니다. 이번에는 음악이 어떻게 경제에 큰 영향을 줄 수 있는지에 관해 논의하고 싶습니다. 먼저, 컨트리 음악의 중심지인 내슈빌을 살펴보겠습니다. 내슈빌은 수백 개의 음악 공연장으로 유명합니다. 이곳에서 라이브 음악은 진정한 산업입니다. 그것은 이 작은 도시의 경제에 매년 50억 달러를 기여합니다. 또 다른 주목할 사례는 서울입니다. K-pop 앨범과 콘서트는 그 자체로 엄청난 수익을 창출합니다. 하지만 이 장르는 또한 도시의 관광사업을 부흥시켰습니다. 다음은 뉴올리언스인데, 이곳은 세계에서 재즈의 중심지 중 하나로 여겨집니다. 매년 수백만 명의 관광객들이 재즈 음악을 듣기 위해 그 도시를 방문합니다. 그들이 콘서트, 호텔, 그리고 식당에 쓰는 돈은 그 도시 경제에서 중요한 부분입니다. 마지막으로, 빈을 언급하겠습니다. 모차르트와 베토벤의 시대 동안, 그곳은 음악계의 중심이었습니다. 도시의 출판업자들은 악보를 판매하여 큰 부를 창출했습니다. 자, 이제 동영상을 잠깐 보겠습니다.

선택지 16 ① 음악 장르의 기원

② 음악이 경제에 영향을 끼치는 방식

③ 여러 도시가 음악가들을 유치하는 방식

④ 서로 다른 음악적 스타일의 비교

⑤ 특정 지역에서 인기 있는 음악이 생겨나는 이유

17 ① 내슈빌 ② 서울 ③ 뉴올리언스 ④ 빈 ⑤ 시드니

16 음악이 어떻게 경제에 큰 영향을 줄 수 있는지에 관해 논의하고 있으므로 남자가 하는 말의 주제로 ② 'ways that music affects economies'가 가장 적절하다.
17 내슈빌, 서울, 뉴올리언스, 빈은 언급했지만 ⑤ 'Sydney'는 언급하지 않았다.

어휘 origin 명 기원 have an impact on ~에 영향을 주다 be famous for ~으로 유명하다 venue 명 공연장, 장소; 현장 industry 명 산업 contribute A to B A를 B에 기여하다
annually 부 매년 notable 형 주목할 generate 동 창출하다, 생성하다 revenue 명 수익, 수입 boost 동 부흥시키다, 신장시키다 tourism 명 관광사업; 관광 capital 명 중심지, 수도
publisher 명 출판업자, 출판사 sheet music 악보 attract 동 유치하다; 끌다 comparison 명 비교

1	①	2	④	3	②	4	③	5	②	6	③	7	④	8	④	9	③	10	③
11	①	12	②	13	⑤	14	①	15	⑤	16	④	17	④						

• 각 문제의 정답 근거는 굵은 글씨로, Dictation 정답은 밑줄로 표시되어 있습니다.

---

1 목적 파악

정답 ①

W May I have your attention, please? **The Emergency Care Club is asking for volunteers to help with the** ¹⁾victims of the wildfire. Our club needs volunteers to prepare and serve meals for those whose homes were burned. If you do not have ²⁾experience doing this, we can provide training. Please visit the club at the corner of Main and Fifth Streets. **Our club is also looking to receive donations of cash, old clothes, bottled water, and canned goods.** You may ³⁾bring your donations at any time. We ask that volunteers not donate fruit, vegetables, or other food items that can go bad quickly.

여 주목해 주시겠습니까? Emergency Care Club은 산불 피해를 본 이재민들을 돕기 위해 자원봉사자들을 찾고 있습니다. 저희 재단은 집이 불에 탄 사람들에게 식사를 준비하여 제공할 자원봉사자들이 필요합니다. 이런 일을 해본 경험이 없으시다면, 저희가 훈련을 제공할 수 있습니다. 메인가와 5번가 모퉁이에 있는 재단을 방문해주십시오. 저희 재단은 또한 현금, 헌 옷, 생수, 통조림 제품의 기부를 받길 기대하고 있습니다. 기부품은 언제든지 가지고 오셔도 됩니다. 자원봉사자들께 과일, 채소, 또는 다른 빨리 상할 수 있는 음식은 기부하지 말아 주시기를 부탁드립니다.

여자가 산불 피해를 본 이재민에게 식사를 제공할 자원봉사자 및 물품 기부가 필요하다고 호소하고 있다. 따라서, 여자가 하는 말의 목적으로 ① '봉사활동과 물품 기부 참여를 요청하려고'가 가장 적절하다.

[어휘] ask for ~를 찾다; 요청하다 victim 명 이재민, 피해자 wildfire 명 산불; 들불 look to ~하기를 기대하다 receive 동 받다 bottled water 생수 go bad 상하다, 썩다

---

2 의견 파악

정답 ④

M Shelly, our reservation is for 7 p.m. Let's head to the restaurant.
W Sure, but I want to stop by the convenience store here to get a candy bar.
M Right now? Won't that ¹⁾ruin your appetite for dinner?
W **Actually, eating a little dessert first is a good way to eat healthier.**
M You're going to have to explain this to me.
W Well, let me ask you this. What were you thinking of ordering for dinner?
M I wanted tacos with some nachos on the side.
W Right, nachos are a rather unhealthy side dish. **But if you have a** ²⁾small dessert first, you might want something healthier instead.
M Oh, I see. So it ³⁾satisfies the appetite for something unhealthy.
W Exactly. So you'll end up ordering a salad afterward.

남 Shelly, 우리 예약은 오후 7시야. 식당으로 가자.
여 물론이야, 그런데 초코바 하나 사러 여기 편의점을 들르고 싶어.
남 지금? 그러면 저녁 먹을 입맛을 해치지 않을까?
여 사실, 먼저 디저트를 살짝 먹는 게 더 건강하게 먹을 수 있는 좋은 방법이야.
남 내게 설명을 해줘야야겠는걸.
여 음, 하나 물어볼게. 저녁으로 뭘 주문할 생각이었어?
남 타코에 나초를 곁들이고 싶었지.
여 그래, 나초는 꽤 건강에 좋지 않은 사이드 요리야. 하지만 네가 디저트를 먼저 소량 먹으면, 대신 더 건강에 좋은 걸 먹고 싶어질 거야.
남 아, 그렇구나. 그러니까 그게 건강에 좋지 않은 걸 먹고 싶은 욕구를 충족시켜주는 거구나.
여 정확해. 그래서 결국 넌 이후에 샐러드를 주문하게 될 거야.

저녁 식사 전에 초코바를 먹으려는 여자를 남자가 말리자, 여자가 식사 전에 디저트를 살짝 먹는 게 더 건강하게 먹을 수 있는 좋은 방법이라고 했다. 따라서, 여자의 의견으로 ④ '식전 디저트가 건강한 식사를 위한 방법일 수 있다.'가 가장 적절하다.

[어휘] stop by 들르다 convenience store 편의점 candy bar 초코바 ruin 동 해치다; 파괴하다 appetite 명 입맛, 식욕; 욕구 satisfy 동 충족시키다, 만족시키다 end up 결국 ~하게 되다

---

3 관계 파악

정답 ②

W Hello. Can I ask you a favor?
M Sure. What is it?
W **I'm looking for a patient who was admitted to this hospital two days ago. I think he's on this floor.**
M **Can you tell me his name, please?**
W It's Kyle Bradley.
M Okay, just give me a moment. [Pause] I'm sorry, but I don't see that name on ¹⁾my list of patients. Are you sure you have the right floor?
W Well, I'm not absolutely sure. He injured his elbow playing tennis, and he is supposed to ²⁾have surgery tomorrow.
M **I see. I'll check the full list of the patients in our hospital. So please hold on a second.**
W All right.

여 안녕하세요. 부탁 좀 드려도 될까요?
남 물론이죠. 뭐가요?
여 이틀 전에 이 병원에 입원한 환자를 찾고 있어요. 이 층에 있는 것 같아요.
남 환자분 이름을 말씀해 주시겠어요?
여 Kyle Bradley예요.
남 네, 잠시만 기다려 주세요. [잠시 멈춤] 죄송하지만, 제 환자 명단에 그 이름이 없네요. 층수가 확실히 맞나요?
여 음, 확실히는 모르겠어요. 테니스를 치다가 팔꿈치를 다쳤고, 내일 수술을 받기로 되어 있어요.
남 그렇군요. 저희 병원의 전체 환자 명단을 확인해 보겠습니다. 그러니까 잠시만 기다려주세요.
여 알겠습니다.

M *[Typing sound]* Ma'am, he's on the sixth floor. That's Room 614. You can ³⁾take the elevator down the hall.	남 *[타자 치는 소리]* 선생님, 그분은 6층에 있습니다. 614호실입니다. 복도를 따라 내려가셔서 엘리베이터를 타세요.
W Thank you so much.	여 정말 감사합니다.

두 사람이 병원에서 이야기하고 있다. 여자는 병원에 입원한 환자를 찾고 있다고 말했고, 남자는 환자 명단에서 환자를 찾아주며 병실 가는 길을 알려주는 것으로 보아 두 사람의 관계로 ② '문병객 — 간호사'가 가장 적절하다.

어휘 be admitted to hospital 병원에 입원하다 elbow 명 팔꿈치 surgery 명 수술 hold on 기다리다

---

4 그림 내용 불일치 파악   정답 ③

M Hi, Louise. I heard you're going to have a garage sale. How are your preparations for it going?	남 안녕, Louise. 너희 차고에서 중고 물품 판매를 할 거라고 들었어. 준비 잘 돼가?
W Great. These two tables that I'm selling were the last things I ¹⁾needed to set up.	여 아주 좋아. 내가 판매하려 하는 이 두 개의 탁자가 내가 배치해야 했던 마지막 물건이었어.
M I see you have some children's toys in a bin to the right of the tables.	남 탁자들 오른편에 있는 통에 아이들 장난감이 몇 개 있네.
W Yes, since my kids are all grown up, we don't need them anymore.	여 응, 우리 애들이 다 커서, 그건 더 이상 필요 없어.
M Are you also selling that ²⁾round rug behind the bin?	남 통 뒤에 있는 둥근 러그도 팔 거야?
W I'm not selling it, but I want to clean it before any customers come.	여 팔 건 아니지만, 손님이 오기 전에 청소해두고 싶어서 말이야.
M What about the ³⁾fan by the door?	남 문가에 있는 선풍기는?
W It needs to be fixed, so I'm not charging a lot of money for it.	여 그건 수리가 필요해서, 가격을 높게 매기지는 않을 거야.
M You've ⁴⁾organized those hats on the shelf to the left really well.	남 왼편에 있는 선반에 저 모자들을 정말 잘 정리해놨구나.
W They're mostly out of fashion.	여 대부분 유행이 지난 것들이야.
M Well, they look great. I bet lots of people will want them.	남 글쎄, 좋아 보이는걸. 분명 많은 사람들이 탐낼 거야.
W Thanks! I hope you're right.	여 고마워! 네 말이 맞았으면 좋겠다.

대화에서 남자가 장난감 통 뒤에 있는 둥근 러그도 팔 것인지 물었는데, ③에는 네모난 러그가 그려져 있다.

어휘 preparation 명 준비 bin 명 통, 상자; 쓰레기통 fan 명 선풍기; 부채 charge 통 (돈을) 매기다, 청구하다 out of fashion 유행이 지난

---

5 할 일 파악   정답 ②

W Alex, I'm planning to ¹⁾form a band.	여 Alex, 난 밴드를 결성할 계획이야.
M Really? Are you going to record an album?	남 정말? 음반 녹음하는 거야?
W No, nothing like that. I'm looking for friends who are interested in playing music ²⁾as a hobby.	여 아니, 그런 건 전혀 아니야. 취미로 음악을 할 의향이 있는 친구들을 찾고 있어.
M You're a singer, right? So I suppose you're looking for people to play instruments.	남 네가 노래를 부르겠구나, 맞지? 그러면 악기를 연주할 사람들을 찾는 중이겠어.
W Yeah, I am. I'd love to recruit three or four other people.	여 맞아, 내가 노래할 거야. 다른 서너 명의 사람들을 모집하고 싶어.
M Have you found anyone yet?	남 누구 찾은 사람 있니?
W Not yet. But I know you have been taking guitar lessons. ³⁾Would you like to join?	여 아직 못 찾았어. 하지만 내가 알기로 넌 기타 수업을 계속 듣고 있잖아. 나랑 함께 할래?
M Well, I'm pretty busy these days. I would only be able to practice on Saturday afternoons.	남 글쎄, 내가 요즘에 꽤 바빠. 난 토요일 오후에만 연습할 수 있을 거야.
W That's fine. I can schedule our rehearsals for then.	여 괜찮아. 내가 그때로 우리 총연습 날을 잡을게.
M Okay, I'll be ⁴⁾in your band.	남 알겠어, 네 밴드에 들어갈게.
W Great! This is going to be fun!	여 좋아! 재미있을 거야!

여자의 밴드 결성 계획에 대해 이야기하고 있다. 여자가 남자에게 자신의 밴드에 함께 할 것을 제안하며 일정을 맞춰주겠다고 하자 남자가 승낙하였으므로 남자가 할 일로 ② '밴드 가입하기'가 가장 적절하다.

어휘 form 통 결성하다 명 유형 hobby 명 취미 instrument 명 악기 recruit 통 모집하다 schedule 통 일정을 잡다 명 일정

6 금액 정보 파악
정답 ③

M	Welcome to the Harborview Amusement Park. What can I do for you today?
W	Hi. How much is the entrance fee?
M	**It is $40 for adults and $20 for children.**
W	**Okay. I'd like to pay for two adults and one child, please.**
M	Of course. **Oh, I just realized it is after 4 p.m. That means you get 20% ¹⁾off the normal price.**
W	Oh, that's great. Thanks for letting me know.
M	No problem. Do you want to buy any ²⁾ride tickets in advance?
W	How much do they cost?
M	**A set of 10 tickets is $15.**
W	**I'll get ³⁾two sets, please.** Can I pay with credit card?
M	Of course. Let me confirm your purchases.
W	Sure, go ahead.
M	Entrance tickets for two adults and ⁴⁾one child with a 20% discount, and two sets of ride tickets. Is it correct?
W	Yes. Here is my card.

남	하버뷰 놀이공원에 오신 것을 환영합니다. 오늘 무엇을 도와드릴까요?
여	안녕하세요. 입장료가 얼마인가요?
남	어른은 40달러, 어린이는 20달러입니다.
여	알겠습니다. 어른 둘, 어린이 하나로 계산해 주세요.
남	물론이죠. 아, 지금 오후 4시가 넘었다는 걸 이제야 알았네요. 그렇다면 정상가에서 20% 할인받으실 수 있어요.
여	오, 잘됐네요. 알려주셔서 감사합니다.
남	천만에요. 미리 놀이기구 탑승권을 구매하시고 싶으신가요?
여	그건 가격이 얼마죠?
남	10개의 탑승권 세트에 15달러입니다.
여	두 세트 주세요. 신용카드로 계산할 수 있나요?
남	물론이죠. 구매 내역을 확인해 드릴게요.
여	그럼요, 해주세요.
남	어른 2명, 어린이 1명으로 20% 할인된 입장권과 놀이기구 탑승권 두 세트입니다. 맞나요?
여	네. 여기 제 카드 드릴게요.

여자가 어른 둘, 어린이 한 명의 놀이공원 입장권을 구매했고($40×2+$20=$100), 오후 4시 이후에 입장하여 20% 할인($100×0.8=$80)을 받았다. 또한, 탑승권 두 세트를 구매했으므로 ($15×2=$30) 정답은 ③ '$110'이다.

[어휘] entrance fee 입장료 normal 휑 정상적인, 일반적인 ride ticket 기구 탑승권 in advance 미리 confirm 통 확인하다

7 이유 파악
정답 ④

W	Jim, you must be excited about your trip to your hometown in December.
M	Actually, I may need to ¹⁾delay my trip by a month.
W	Oh, no. Was your leave request rejected by your manager?
M	No. He was very understanding and ²⁾approved it right away.
W	Are there no more train tickets available?
M	That doesn't seem to be an issue yet. There are many seats left.
W	Then, ³⁾what's the reason for the delay?
M	Well, my sister has to go on a business trip that month and won't be back until January.
W	**Oh, so you want to visit when all your family can be together, right?**
M	**That's it. We're trying to find the dates when ⁴⁾we'll all be around.**
W	I hope everything works out for you.

여	Jim, 12월에 고향으로 향하는 여행 기대되겠어.
남	사실, 여행을 한 달 정도 미뤄야 할지도 몰라.
여	오, 이런. 부장님이 네 휴가 신청을 거부하셨니?
남	아니야. 그분은 매우 이해심이 많으셔서 바로 승인해주셨어.
여	더 이상 구할 수 있는 기차표가 없는 거야?
남	그건 아직 문제가 되지 않는 것 같아. 자리가 많이 남아 있어.
여	그러면 미루려는 이유가 뭐야?
남	음, 내 여동생이 그달에 출장을 가야 해서 1월에나 돌아올 거야.
여	아, 그러니까 너희 가족 모두가 함께 할 수 있을 때 방문하고 싶은 거구나, 맞니?
남	바로 그거야. 우리는 모두가 함께할 날짜를 찾으려 하고 있어.
여	일이 잘 풀리길 바랄게.

남자는 여행을 한 달 정도 미뤄야 할지도 모른다고 하면서 가족 모두가 함께할 날짜를 찾으려 하고 있다고 말했으므로, 남자가 여행을 미루려는 이유는 ④ '가족 모두가 함께 모이기를 원해서'이다.

[어휘] hometown 휑 고향 leave request 휴가 신청 reject 통 거부하다, 거절하다 approve 통 승인하다 business trip 출장

8 언급 유무 파악
정답 ④

M	Hi, Jill. Are you going to the Artists Convention?
W	Oh, I hadn't heard about it. Please tell me more.
M	It's an event where people can show their work to ¹⁾professional artists and get feedback.
W	That would be really useful for me. Is it happening soon?
M	It's being held on **April 28th.**
W	Great. I think I can make it.
M	If you want to come, you would just need to ²⁾bring **some art pieces you've been working on.**
W	I can do that. Where is it being held?
M	It's going to be at **Parker Community College.**
W	Okay. Do I just show up, or do I need to register?
M	³⁾Registration is required. There's a **website** for it. I'll send a link to it in an email.
W	Thanks for letting me know about this event!

남	안녕, Jill. 너 Artists Convention에 갈 거니?
여	아, 난 그것에 관해 들은 바가 없어. 좀 더 말해줘.
남	사람들이 전문 예술가에게 그들의 작품을 보여주고 피드백을 받을 수 있는 행사야.
여	그건 내게 정말 유용할 거 같네. 조만간 열리는 거야?
남	4월 28일에 열려.
여	잘됐다. 갈 수 있을 것 같아.
남	가고 싶은 거라면 만들고 있는 작품들을 가져가기만 하면 될 거야.
여	그렇게 할 수 있어. 어디서 열려?
남	파커 전문대에서 열릴 거야.
여	알겠어. 내가 그냥 가면 되니? 아니면 신청해야 하니?
남	신청이 필요해. 그걸 위한 웹사이트가 있어. 그 링크를 이메일로 보내줄게.
여	이런 행사를 알려줘서 고마워!

날짜(4월 28일), 준비물(만들고 있는 작품), 장소(파커 전문대), 신청 방법(웹사이트)에 대해 언급했고, ④ '참가자 수'는 언급하지 않았다.

어휘 professional 휑 전문의 make it 가다, 참석하다 community college (2년제) 전문대 show up 가다, 나타나다

---

9 내용 불일치 파악　　　　　　　　　　정답 ③

M Good morning, students. I'm the head librarian at Monroe Public Library. We are holding a special event [1]from September 21st to 27th. It's called Teen Readers Week, and it's aimed at encouraging teenagers to read more. Teenagers usually associate reading with preparing for a class or studying for an exam. But reading can be enjoyable, too! **From Monday through Friday, teenagers who sign up for this event will** [2]**participate in informal discussions.** They can talk about their favorite books or books they have read recently. Participants can also share lists of books they've [3]read over the year. These lists will be posted on the Teen Readers' board on our website. Sign up, and read for fun!

남 안녕하십니까, 학생 여러분. 저는 먼로 공공 도서관의 도서관장입니다. 저희는 9월 21일부터 27일까지 특별한 행사를 열 예정입니다. 그 행사의 이름은 Teen Readers Week이며, 십 대들이 더 많이 독서하도록 장려하는 것을 목표로 하고 있습니다. 십 대들은 보통 독서를 수업 준비나 시험공부와 연관시킵니다. 하지만 독서가 재미있을 수도 있답니다! 월요일부터 금요일까지, 이 행사를 신청한 십 대들은 약식 토론에 참여할 것입니다. 그들이 가장 좋아하는 책이나 최근에 읽은 책에 관해 이야기할 수 있습니다. 참가자들은 또한 그들이 한 해 동안 읽은 책의 목록을 공유할 수 있습니다. 이 목록은 저희 웹사이트의 Teen Readers' 보드에 게시될 것입니다. 신청하시고, 재미있게 독서하십시오!

도서관 행사에 대한 안내 방송이다. 남자가 월요일부터 금요일까지 이 행사를 신청한 십 대들이 약식 토론에 참여할 것이라고 했으므로 ③ '금요일과 토요일에는 약식 토론이 열릴 것이다.'는 내용과 일치하지 않는다.

어휘 be aimed at ~을 목표로 하다 encourage 동 장려하다, 권장하다 associate A with B A를 B와 연관시키다 informal 휑 약식의, 격식을 차리지 않는

---

10 도표 정보 파악　　　　　　　　　　정답 ③

W What are you looking at, Josh?

M I'm getting some fish to keep as pets. But first I need to buy a fish tank for them.

W This one looks really nice. I like its unique shape.

M It caught my eye as well. **But it's** [1]**made from plastic, and I don't like that material.**

W How big of a tank do you need?

M **It has to hold at least** [2]**25 liters of water.** I'm planning to get three fish.

W Well, that leaves you with a few options.

M Yeah, but I think I can eliminate this one. **I don't want to spend more than $60 on the tank.**

W Oh, look! One of the remaining tanks comes with a stand.

M **I definitely want one with a stand.** That will make it [3]easier to set it up on my table.

W Then, I guess your choice is clear.

여 뭘 보고 있니, Josh?
남 반려동물로 기를 물고기를 좀 구하고 있어. 하지만 먼저 물고기를 놓을 어항을 사야 해.
여 이게 정말 멋져 보여. 독특한 모양이 마음에 들어.
남 그게 내 눈길을 끌긴 했어. 하지만 그건 플라스틱으로 만들어졌고, 난 그 소재를 좋아하지 않아.
여 어항 크기는 얼마나 큰 게 필요해?
남 최소한 25L의 물을 담을 수 있어야 해. 물고기 세 마리를 데려올 계획이거든.
여 음, 그럼 몇 가지 선택지가 남겠다.
남 맞아, 그런데 이건 제거할 수 있을 것 같아. 어항에 60달러 이상을 쓰고 싶지 않아.
여 오, 봐! 남은 어항 중 하나에는 받침대가 딸려 있어
남 난 꼭 받침대가 있는 걸 원해. 그러면 내 탁자 위에 설치하는 게 더 쉬워질 거야.
여 그렇다면, 네 선택이 확실해진 것 같아.

남자는 플라스틱 소재로 만들어지지 않았으며, 최소 25L의 물을 담을 수 있고, 60달러 이상이 아닌 것 중에서, 받침대가 있는 어항을 골랐다.

어휘 unique 휑 독특한 catch one's eye 눈길을 끌다 hold 동 담다, 수용하다; 잡다 at least 최소한 eliminate 동 제거하다 remaining 휑 남은, 남아 있는 come with ~이 딸려 있다

---

11 짧은 대화의 응답 파악　　　　　　　　　　정답 ①

M What's the matter, honey? **There's water** [1]**all over the floor here.**

W I'm not sure. [2]The faucet is turned off. I just checked it!

M Let me see. *[Pause]* Oh, the pipe under the kitchen sink is leaking.

W We should call someone to fix it.

남 이게 무슨 일이야, 여보? 여기 바닥에 물이 흥건해.
여 잘 모르겠어. 수도꼭지는 잠겨 있어. 내가 방금 확인했거든!
남 어디 볼게. *[잠시 멈춤]* 아, 부엌 싱크대 밑에 있는 파이프에서 물이 새고 있네.
여 <u>수리할 사람을 불러야겠어.</u>

선택지 ① 수리할 사람을 불러야겠어.
② 제발 접시는 싱크대에 놓아 줘.
③ 그냥 바닥을 수리하기만 하면 돼.
④ 다음에는 꼭 수도꼭지를 잠가.
⑤ 어제부터 싱크대 청소를 못 했어.

바닥에 물이 흥건한 상황에서 남자가 부엌 싱크대 밑에 있는 파이프에서 물이 새고 있다고 말했으므로, 이에 대한 응답으로는 해결책을 말하는 ① 'We should call someone to fix it.'이 가장 적절하다.

어휘 faucet 휑 수도꼭지 turn off ~을 잠그다 leak 동 물이 새다

12 짧은 대화의 응답 파악

정답 ②

W Hi. I'm $^{1)}$sorry to bother you, but is this your car?	여 안녕하세요. 귀찮게 해드려서 죄송하지만, 이게 당신 차인가요?
M It is. Oh, it seems I've parked too close to yours.	남 제 차예요. 아, 제가 당신 차에 너무 가까이 주차한 것 같군요.
W Would you $^{2)}$mind moving it over a bit so I can open my door?	여 제가 차 문을 열 수 있도록 당신 차를 좀 옮겨 주시겠어요?
M No problem. Just give me a moment.	남 문제 없어요. 그냥 잠시만 기다려 주세요.

선택지
① 그런 것 같네요. 전 새 차가 필요해요.
② 문제없어요. 그냥 잠시만 기다려 주세요.
③ 걱정 마세요. 이동하실 때까지 기다릴게요.
④ 괜찮아요. 원하시면 거기에 주차하셔도 돼요.
⑤ 물론이죠. 제가 문을 열어 드릴 수 있어요.

남자의 차가 너무 가까이 주차되어 있어 여자가 차를 좀 옮겨달라고 부탁했으므로, 이에 대한 응답으로는 부탁을 들어주는 ② 'No problem. Just give me a moment.'가 가장 적절하다.

어휘 bother 통 귀찮게 하다, 괴롭히다   Give me a moment. 잠시만 기다려 주세요.

13 긴 대화의 응답 파악

정답 ⑤

M It's raining again, Christine.	남 또 비가 오네, Christine.
W That's too bad. It's been raining so much these days.	여 정말 곤란해. 요즘 비가 너무 많이 내려.
M I know! I $^{1)}$had to cancel basketball with my friends. We were going to play in the park.	남 그러니까 말이야! 난 친구들과의 농구를 취소해야 했어. 공원에서 하려고 했는데 말이야.
W You can always play on an indoor court.	여 실내 경기장에서 언제든지 농구 할 수 있잖아.
M I wasn't $^{2)}$able to reserve the one at the gym. Some other group is using it.	남 체육관에 예약을 못 했어. 누군가 다른 사람들이 쓰고 있을 거야.
W You could do another $^{3)}$indoor sport like table tennis.	여 탁구 같은 또 다른 실내 운동을 할 수도 있어.
M My friends and I aren't into table tennis.	남 내 친구들과 난 탁구를 좋아하지 않아.
W You could also go bowling. A new place just opened on Pine Street.	여 볼링 치러 갈 수도 있어. 파인가에 새로운 곳이 막 개업했어.
M That sounds like a good idea. I think I'll do that.	남 그거 좋은 생각인 것 같아. 그렇게 해야겠어.
W Could I go with you?	여 내가 같이 가도 될까?
M Do you know how to bowl?	남 너 볼링 칠 줄 알아?
W I $^{4)}$went bowling regularly in my first year of college.	여 대학교 1학년 때 주기적으로 볼링 치러 다녔어.
M I didn't know that. Are you good at bowling?	남 그건 몰랐네. 볼링 잘 치니?
W Not really. But I enjoy playing.	여 그렇지는 않아. 그래도 치는 걸 좋아해.

선택지
① 진정해. 네가 생각하는 것보다 훨씬 쉬워.
② 모르겠어. 한 번도 안 해봤어.
③ 포기하지 마. 시도도 안 해봤잖아.
④ 나도 그래. 대학 시절은 정말 즐거웠지.
⑤ 그렇지는 않아. 그래도 치는 걸 좋아해.

비가 내려 농구를 못하게 된 상황에서 남자는 볼링을 치러 가는 것으로 계획을 변경하려고 한다. 남자가 여자에게 볼링을 잘 치는지 물었으므로, 이에 대한 응답으로는 볼링 실력을 말해주는 ⑤ 'Not really. But I enjoy playing.'이 가장 적절하다.

어휘 indoor 형 실내의   reserve 통 예약하다   table tennis 탁구   be into ~을 좋아하다   be good at ~을 잘하다   Take it easy. 진정해.   give up 포기하다

14 긴 대화의 응답 파악

정답 ①

[Phone rings.]	[전화기가 울린다.]
M Golden Travel Agency. May I help you?	남 Golden Travel Agency입니다. 도와드릴까요?
W Hi. Can you recommend a Southeast Asian country to visit at this time of year?	여 안녕하세요. 이 시기에 방문할 동남아시아 국가를 추천해 주시겠어요?
M Actually, it's now the $^{1)}$typhoon season in Southeast Asia.	남 사실, 지금 동남아시아는 태풍이 오는 계절이에요.
W Oh, I didn't know that. Hmm... Where can I go instead?	여 아, 그건 몰랐어요. 흠... 대신 어디로 가야 될까요?
M May I suggest Turkey? It has a nice Mediterranean climate.	남 튀르키예를 추천해도 될까요? 그곳은 멋진 지중해성 기후를 가지고 있어요.
W Is there anything to do there?	여 거기서 할 게 있나요?
M Absolutely! Aside from its many $^{2)}$historical sites, there are excellent seaside resorts.	남 물론이죠! 많은 유적지 외에도, 바닷가에 훌륭한 휴양지가 있어요.
W Well, other countries also have resorts on the beach.	여 글쎄요, 다른 나라에도 바닷가에 휴양지는 있는걸요.
M Turkey also has stunning natural scenery. There are many reasons why it's the sixth $^{3)}$most popular tourist destination in the world.	남 튀르키예에는 또한 굉장히 아름다운 자연경관이 있어요. 그곳이 세계에서 여섯 번째로 인기 있는 관광지인 데에는 여러 이유가 있죠.
W I didn't realize that. I'd like to know more about the country.	여 그건 몰랐어요. 그 나라에 관해 더 알아보고 싶네요.
M Well, I can send you an electronic brochure about Turkey if you want.	남 음, 원하시면 튀르키예에 관한 전자 책자를 보내드릴 수도 있어요.
W That would be great. Can you $^{4)}$send it to me today?	여 그거 정말 좋겠네요. 오늘 중으로 보내주실 수 있을까요?
M Of course. I just need your email address.	남 물론이죠. 단지 이메일 주소가 필요할 뿐입니다.

① 물론이죠. 단지 이메일 주소가 필요할 뿐입니다.

② 다행이네요. 너무 오래 걸릴 것 같았거든요.

③ 이것 참. 제게 튀르키예 여행을 갈 여유가 있을지 모르겠어요.

④ 좋아요! 그래서 언제 의견을 주실 수 있나요?

⑤ 고마워요. 제가 이메일로 티켓을 보내드릴게요.

여자가 여행 상품을 추천받고 있는 상황이다. 남자가 튀르키예에 대한 전자 책자를 보내준다고 하자 여자가 오늘 중으로 보내줄 수 있는지 물었으므로, 이에 대한 응답으로는 그렇게 하겠다며 이메일 주소가 필요하다고 하는 ① 'Of course. I just need your email address.'가 가장 적절하다.

어휘 typhoon 명 태풍 Southeast Asia 동남아시아 Mediterranean 형 지중해의 aside from ~외에도 historical site 유적지 seaside 형 바닷가의, 해변의 stunning 형 굉장히 아름다운 scenery 명 경관, 풍경 tourist destination 관광지 electronic 형 전자의 What a relief. 다행이네요.

15 상황에 적절한 말 파악

정답 ⑤

W Abigail and her brother are university students. They live together in an apartment during the school year and 1)split the chores. Abigail buys groceries and does the laundry. Her brother does the dishes and cleans the house. This week, Abigail has to travel out of town. She will not be able to buy groceries or clean their clothes. Her brother will have to do all the chores by himself. But he has been busy lately, and having more chores will 2)create more stress for him. Abigail doesn't want her brother to feel stressed. **So she wants to tell him that she will do all the grocery shopping, laundry, and cleaning 3)the following week instead.** In this situation, what would Abigail most likely say to her brother?

여 Abigail과 그녀의 오빠는 대학생입니다. 그들은 학기 중에는 아파트에서 함께 살면서 집안일을 나눠 합니다. Abigail은 식료품을 사고 빨래를 합니다. 그녀의 오빠는 설거지를 하고 집을 청소합니다. 이번 주에, Abigail은 마을 밖으로 여행을 가야 합니다. 그녀는 식료품을 사거나 빨래하는 일을 할 수 없을 것입니다. 그녀의 오빠가 모든 집안일을 혼자서 해야 할 것입니다. 하지만 그는 최근에 바빴고, 더 많은 집안일을 히는 것은 그에게 더 많은 스트레스를 줄 것입니다. Abigail은 오빠가 스트레스 받기를 원하지 않습니다. 그래서, 그녀는 대신 그다음 주에는 그녀가 식료품 구매, 빨래, 청소를 모두 다 할 것이라고 그에게 말하고 싶습니다. 이러한 상황에서, Abigail이 그녀의 오빠에게 가장 할 것 같은 말은 무엇입니까?

선택지 ① 괜찮아. 대신 다음 주에는 그냥 음식을 주문하면 돼.

② 이해해. 내가 아파트로 이사 올 다른 사람을 찾아보면 돼.

③ 미안해. 다음 주에 여행 갈 계획인지 몰랐어.

④ 잘됐다. 청소부에게 전화해서 다음 주에 가능한지 알아볼게.

⑤ 걱정하지 마. 다음 주에는 모든 집안일을 내가 처리할게.

Abigail이 여행 때문에 집을 비우게 되어 오빠가 모든 집안일을 혼자 해야 하는 상황이다. Abigail은 오빠가 스트레스를 받지 않았으면 해서 그다음 주에 그녀가 그의 몫까지 다 하겠다고 말하려 한다. 따라서, Abigail이 할 말로 ⑤ 'Don't worry. I'll take care of all the household chores next week.'가 가장 적절하다.

어휘 split 동 나누다 chore 명 집안일 grocery 명 식료품 do the laundry 빨래하다 do the dishes 설거지하다 by oneself 혼자서

16-17 세트 문항

정답 16 ④ 17 ④

M Good afternoon, class. Last time we discussed insects that live in large communities. **Today, we are going to discuss the 1)unique physical traits of ants.** First off, their **feet** have special sticky pads on them. These allow ants to 2)grip any surface, which is why it is easy for them to climb up walls and even walk while upside down. Second, ants have amazingly strong **necks**. These make it easy for ants to carry heavy loads and allow them to lift weights 3)10 to 50 times heavier than their bodies. Third, ants have two **stomachs**. One of these is used for digesting food as you would expect. The other is capable of carrying food so that it can be 4)transported back home and shared with other ants. Lastly, there is a pair of long, thin **antennae** on their heads. They use these antennae to smell scents. They help ants find food and their way back home. Now, let's take a quick look at a video on ants.

남 안녕하십니까, 학급 여러분. 지난 시간에 우리는 큰 규모의 집단을 이루고 살아가는 곤충에 관해 논의했습니다. 오늘은, 개미의 독특한 신체적 특징에 관해 이야기할 것입니다. 우선, 그것들의 발에는 끈적거리는 특별한 깔개가 붙어 있습니다. 이것은 개미가 어떤 표면이든 잡을 수 있게 해주는데, 이것이 개미가 쉽게 벽을 타고 올라가고 심지어 거꾸로 뒤집혀서도 걸을 수 있는 이유입니다. 두 번째로, 개미는 놀라울 정도로 튼튼한 목을 가지고 있습니다. 이는 개미가 무거운 짐을 운반하는 것을 쉽게 하고, 몸보다 10배에서 50배 무거운 무게를 들어 올리도록 해줍니다. 세 번째로, 개미는 두 개의 위를 가지고 있습니다. 이 중 하나는 여러분이 예상하는 대로 음식을 소화하는 데 사용됩니다. 나머지 다른 하나는 먹이를 개미집으로 운반하여 다른 개미와 나눠 먹을 수 있도록 먹이를 운반하는 기능이 있습니다. 마지막으로, 개미의 머리에는 한 쌍의 길고 가는 더듬이가 달려 있습니다. 개미는 이 더듬이를 냄새 맡는 데 사용합니다. 더듬이는 개미가 먹이와 집으로 돌아오는 길을 찾도록 도와줍니다. 이제, 개미에 관한 동영상을 간단히 살펴보겠습니다.

선택지 16 ① 개미들이 함께 일하는 방법

② 개미 종들 사이의 차이

③ 개미가 큰 집단을 이루고 살아가는 이유

④ 개미 신체의 특별한 특징

⑤ 개미가 가진 놀라운 근력의 이유

17 ① 발 ② 목 ③ 위 ④ 눈 ⑤ 더듬이

16 개미의 독특한 신체적 특징에 관해 이야기하고 있으므로 남자가 하는 말의 주제로 ④ 'special characteristics of ants' bodies'가 가장 적절하다.

17 발, 목, 위, 더듬이는 언급했지만 ④ 'eyes'는 언급하지 않았다.

어휘 sticky 형 끈적거리는 grip 동 잡다 upside down 거꾸로 뒤집혀 load 명 짐 weight 명 무게 stomach 명 위 digest 동 소화하다 be capable of ~하는 기능이 있다, 능력이 있다 transport 동 운반하다 antenna 명 더듬이, 안테나 (pl. antennae) scent 명 냄새, 향기 incredible 형 놀라운

1	③	2	①	3	④	4	③	5	②	6	⑤	7	③	8	⑤	9	④	10	①
11	③	12	③	13	④	14	①	15	⑤	16	②	17	④						

• 각 문제의 정답 근거는 굵은 글씨로, Dictation 정답은 밑줄로 표시되어 있습니다.

---

1 목적 파악

정답 ③

M	Attention, students. This is a message for anyone who is interested in a career in science. **Next Monday, our school will host a special** ¹⁾**information session organized by faculty from the science department of Chester University.** They will be setting up promotional booths, where you can find out about science-related jobs. Professors of ²⁾chemistry, biology, and geology will be at the booths to answer any questions you might have. There will also be a talk by Professor Tess Harrison about her work ³⁾collecting fossils. This event will be held in the school gym from 5 to 7 p.m. **If you're interested, just drop by after school.** Thank you.	남	주목해 주십시오, 학생 여러분. 과학 분야의 직업에 관심이 있는 모든 학생들에게 전달하는 내용입니다. 다음 주 월요일, 체스터 대학의 과학과 교수진이 준비한 특별 설명회를 열 것입니다. 그분들께서는 홍보 부스를 설치할 예정인데, 그곳에서 여러분은 과학과 관련된 직업들을 알게 될 수 있습니다. 화학, 생물학, 지질학 교수님들이 여러분의 질문에 답해주기 위해 부스에 계실 것입니다. 또한 Tess Harrison 교수님의 화석 수집에 관한 강연도 있을 예정입니다. 이 행사는 오후 5시부터 7시까지 학교 체육관에서 열립니다. 관심 있으시면, 방과 후에 들러주십시오. 감사합니다.

남자가 과학과 교수진이 준비한 특별 설명회에 대한 내용을 설명하면서, 관심 있는 학생들의 참석을 부탁했다. 따라서, 남자가 하는 말의 목적으로 ③ '학교에서 열릴 설명회를 홍보하려고'가 가장 적절하다.

어휘 information session 설명회 faculty 몡 교수진; 능력 department 몡 학과; 부서 find out ~을 알게 되다 chemistry 몡 화학 geology 몡 지질학 fossil 몡 화석 drop by 들르다

---

2 의견 파악

정답 ①

M	Susan, did you give money to that violinist performing on the street?	남	Susan, 너 길거리에서 공연하는 저 바이올린 연주자에게 돈을 준 거니?
W	Yes. Her playing was beautiful, so I gave her $5.	여	응. 그녀의 연주가 아름다워서, 5달러를 줬어.
M	That's a lot, isn't it?	남	그건 꽤 많은데, 그렇지 않아?
W	**I think people ought to** ¹⁾**donate money to artists who perform on the street.** It can help them launch their careers.	여	난 사람들이 거리 공연을 하는 예술가들에게 돈을 기부해야 한다고 생각해. 그건 예술가가 직업적 활동을 시작하는 데 도움이 될 수 있어.
M	Do you think she's talented enough to be a professional?	남	그녀가 프로가 될 만큼 충분히 재능이 있다고 생각해?
W	It's possible. And every artist needs support if they are going to succeed.	여	가능한 일이야. 그리고 모든 예술가는 성공하려면 지원이 필요해.
M	I guess earning money lets them practice more.	남	돈을 버는 게 그들이 더 많이 연습할 수 있게 해주겠구나.
W	Exactly. It encourages them to ²⁾keep trying hard.	여	정확해. 그건 그들이 계속 열심히 노력할 수 있도록 격려해주잖아.
M	I just don't feel comfortable giving away money.	남	난 단지 돈을 거저 준다는 게 불편하게 느껴져.
W	Well, she provided that music to us for free. Giving something back seemed fair.	여	음, 그녀는 그 음악을 우리에게 무료로 제공했어. 뭔가를 되돌려 주는 게 공평한 것 같아.
M	I see what you mean.	남	무슨 말인지 알겠어.
W	And if my money helps her start a professional career, it ³⁾will be worthwhile.	여	그리고 만약 내 돈이 그녀가 전문적인 경력을 시작하는 데 도움이 된다면, 그건 보람찬 일이 될 거야.

길거리 연주자에게 돈을 준 여자를 보고 남자가 탐탁지 않아 하자, 여자는 사람들이 거리 공연을 하는 예술가들에게 돈을 기부해야 한다고 했다. 따라서, 여자의 의견으로 ① '거리 공연을 하는 예술가에게 돈을 기부해야 한다.'가 가장 적절하다.

어휘 perform 몽 공연하다 launch 몽 시작하다 talented 휑 재능이 있는 encourage 몽 격려하다, 권장하다 give away ~을 거저 주다 give back ~을 되돌려주다 worthwhile 휑 보람찬, 가치 있는

---

3 관계 파악

정답 ④

W	Excuse me. I have a complaint.	여	실례합니다. 불편 사항이 있어요.
M	Sure. **Do you live here in the apartment complex?**	남	말씀하세요. 여기 아파트 단지에 살고 계시나요?
W	**Yes. I live in Unit 901.**	여	네. 901호에 살고 있어요.
M	What seems to be the problem?	남	뭐가 문제인 것 같으세요?
W	**A bird has** ¹⁾**built a nest outside of my bedroom window, and I'd like you to remove it.**	여	새 한 마리가 침실 창문 밖에 둥지를 틀었는데, 그걸 치워주시면 좋겠어요.
M	Is it causing you problems?	남	그게 문제를 일으키고 있나요?
W	Yes! I ²⁾hear it making sounds, and it disturbs my sleep. Why do you ask?	여	네! 새가 내는 소리가 들려서 제 수면을 방해받아요. 왜 물어보시는 거죠?
M	There are rules protecting wildlife, so we need to make sure it's necessary.	남	야생동물을 보호하는 규칙이 있기 때문에, 꼭 필요한 일인지 확실히 할 필요가 있어요.

W	I also can't open my window because of where the nest is located.	여	그리고 둥지가 있는 곳 때문에 창문을 열 수도 없어요.
M	Okay. I will get in touch with ³⁾animal control right away.	남	알겠습니다. 제가 바로 동물 관리소에 연락하겠습니다.
W	Thanks. **Also, someone will need to clean the window after it's removed.**	여	고마워요. 또한, 그걸 치운 뒤에는 창문을 청소해주셔야 할 거예요.
M	**Of course. I'll take care of that for you.** Thank you for reporting the problem, ma'am.	남	물론이죠. 제가 처리해 드릴게요. 문제를 알려 주셔서 감사합니다, 선생님.

두 사람이 불편 사항에 대해 이야기하고 있다. 아파트 단지에 살고 있는 여자가 새 둥지를 치워줄 것과 창문 청소를 남자에게 요청하고 있고, 남자는 여자의 요청을 처리해주겠다고 하는 것을 보아 두 사람의 관계로 ④ '아파트 주민 — 관리소 직원'이 가장 적절하다.

어휘 complaint 명 불편 사항, 불평 nest 명 둥지 remove 통 치우다 disturb 통 방해하다 wildlife 명 야생동물 get in touch with ~와 연락하다 report 통 알리다; 보도하다

---

4 그림 내용 불일치 파악   정답 ③

M	I see you remodeled the dance studio, Laura.	남	춤 연습실을 리모델링한 것 같네, Laura.
W	That's right. What do you think?	여	맞아. 어때?
M	The ¹⁾mirror on the left wall makes the room look much bigger.	남	왼쪽 벽에 있는 거울은 연습실이 훨씬 더 커 보이게 하네.
W	It does, but it's also important because students can watch themselves.	여	그렇기도 하고, 학생들이 자기 자신을 볼 수 있어서 중요하기도 해.
M	Are those two big speakers on the table?	남	탁자 위에 있는 건 2개의 큰 스피커니?
W	Yes. Now, I can play the music loudly.	여	응. 이제 음악을 크게 틀 수 있어.
M	**I notice you installed a flower-shaped light on the ceiling.**	남	천장에는 꽃 모양의 조명을 설치했네.
W	Yes, it's to change the mood of the studio.	여	응, 연습실 분위기를 바꿔보려고.
M	Why do you need the ²⁾striped gym mat on the floor?	남	바닥에 깔린 줄무늬 매트는 왜 필요한 거야?
W	When students learn difficult dances, they sometimes fall and hurt themselves. It is safer to practice on the mat.	여	학생들이 어려운 춤을 배울 때, 때때로 넘어져서 다치거든. 매트 위에서 연습하면 더 안전해.
M	And I see that you ³⁾replaced the shoe rack by the door, too.	남	그리고 문 옆에 있는 신발장도 교체했구나.
W	Yeah, I'd been meaning to do that for a while.	여	응, 전부터 그렇게 하려고 했어.
M	Well, everything looks great.	남	음, 모든 게 좋아 보여.
W	Thanks. I hope my students like the changes.	여	고마워. 우리 학생들도 이 변화를 마음에 들어 하면 좋겠어.

대화에서 남자가 천장에 꽃 모양의 조명을 설치했다고 말했는데, ③에는 둥근 미러볼 조명이 그려져 있다.

어휘 loudly 부 크게 install 통 설치하다 ceiling 명 천장 mood 명 분위기; 기분 replace 통 교체하다 shoe rack 신발장 mean to ~하려 하다

---

5 할 일 파악   정답 ②

	[Phone rings.]		[전화기가 울린다.]
W	Smile Broadband. How may I help you?	여	Smile Broadband입니다. 무엇을 도와드릴까요?
M	Hi. I had cable TV installed yesterday, but some channels don't work.	남	안녕하세요. 어제 케이블 TV를 설치했는데, 일부 채널이 작동하지 않아요.
W	Have you checked whether your television is ¹⁾set to cable mode?	여	텔레비전이 케이블 모드로 설정되어 있는지 확인해 보셨나요?
M	I'm not sure how to do that.	남	그건 어떻게 하는지 잘 모르겠어요.
W	That's okay. I can help you ²⁾change the setting now. Do you see the Mode button on your remote control?	여	괜찮습니다. 제가 지금 설정을 변경하시도록 도울 수 있어요. 리모컨에 있는 모드 버튼이 보이시나요?
M	Yes. I just pressed it. Now, there are three mode options on the screen.	남	네. 방금 눌렀어요. 이제, 화면에 세 가지 모드 옵션이 나오네요.
W	Then, select cable mode. It's the second option.	여	그러면, 케이블 모드를 고르세요. 두 번째 옵션입니다.
M	Okay. That worked. But it would be useful to have more information in case I have any other problems.	남	네. 됐어요. 그런데 제게 다른 문제가 있을 경우를 대비해서 더 많은 정보가 있으면 유용할 것 같아요.
W	Of course. **I'll ³⁾send you a link to the user's manual on our website.**	여	물론이죠. 저희 웹사이트의 사용 설명서 링크를 보내드릴게요.
M	Please do. But what if there is something I don't understand?	남	부디 그렇게 해주세요. 그런데 제가 이해하지 못하는 게 있으면 어떡하죠?
W	Just call us back at this number, and we can help.	여	그냥 이 번호로 다시 전화 주시면, 저희가 도와드리겠습니다.
M	All right. Thanks a lot.	남	알겠습니다. 정말 감사합니다.

남자의 케이블 TV에 문제가 있어 해결 방법에 대해 이야기하고 있다. 여자가 남자에게 사용 설명서 링크를 보내겠다고 하자, 이에 남자가 그렇게 해달라고 했으므로 여자가 할 일로 ② '사용 설명서 링크 전달하기'가 가장 적절하다.

어휘 press 통 누르다 select 통 고르다, 선택하다 user's manual 사용 설명서

6 금액 정보 파악 정답 ⑤

M Welcome to Wilson Jewelry. How may I help you?	남 Wilson Jewelry에 오신 것을 환영합니다. 무엇을 도와드릴까요?
W Hi. Can I see your 1)selection of friendship rings?	여 안녕하세요. 갖고 계신 우정 반지들을 볼 수 있을까요?
M Of course. I have some options in this display over here.	남 물론이죠. 여기 이 진열대에 선택하실 수 있는 것들이 몇 개 있어요.
W How much is this ring? It's beautiful.	여 이 반지는 얼마예요? 아름답네요.
M It's $45 in silver. If you'd like a gold one, it will be $60.	남 은으로 된 건 45달러예요. 금으로 하시려면, 60달러입니다.
W Okay, I'd like two of the 2)gold rings.	여 네, 금반지로 두 개 주세요.
M Perfect. We also offer an engraving service. It's $10 per ring.	남 아주 좋군요. 저희는 각인 서비스도 제공해 드립니다. 반지 하나당 10달러예요.
W Great! I want to put both my name and my friend's name on each ring.	여 좋아요. 저는 반지마다 저와 제 친구 이름을 둘 다 새기고 싶어요.
M Okay, so you'd like two gold engraved rings. Do you need anything else?	남 네, 그렇다면 금반지 두 개에 각인 서비스를 받으시는 거군요. 그 밖에 또 필요한 게 있으실까요?
W No, that will be all. Oh, isn't there a 10% off sale at the moment?	여 아뇨, 그게 다예요. 아, 지금 10% 할인이 되지 않나요?
M Actually, that 3)ended last week.	남 실은, 그건 지난주에 끝났어요.
W That's okay. Can I pay in cash?	여 괜찮아요. 현금으로 계산할 수 있나요?
M Certainly. Let me ring that up for you.	남 물론이죠. 제가 계산해 드릴게요.

여자가 금반지 두 개($60×2=$120)를 구매했고, 각 반지에 각인 서비스($10×2=$20)를 받았으므로, 정답은 ⑤ '$140'이다. 10% 할인은 지난주에 끝났으므로 할인은 받지 못했다.

[어휘] friendship 명 우정 engraving service 각인 서비스 (engrave 동 새기다) ring ~ up ~을 계산해주다

7 이유 파악 정답 ③

W Hey, Mark. When did you 1)dye your hair pink?	여 안녕, Mark. 너 언제 머리를 분홍색으로 염색했니?
M I got it done last weekend.	남 지난 주말에 했어.
W I love it. Were you tired of having black hair?	여 너무 좋다. 검은 머리엔 싫증 난 거야?
M Thanks. The bright color is nice, but I like my natural black hair color, too.	남 고마워. 밝은색이 좋지만, 내 타고난 검은 머리카락 색도 좋아하긴 해.
W It makes you look like a singer. Did you join a rock band?	여 그러니까 꼭 가수처럼 보여. 록 밴드에 들어간 거야?
M No. I'm not very musical.	남 아니. 난 음악엔 소질 없어.
W Well, were you trying to 2)look like a celebrity? It's a trendy style right now.	여 음, 연예인처럼 보이려고 했던 거야? 그건 지금 유행하는 스타일이야.
M Actually, I dyed it for 3)a play I'm acting in. My character has pink hair.	남 사실, 내가 연기할 연극 때문에 염색한 거야. 내 배역이 분홍 머리거든.
W That makes sense. When is the performance?	여 이해했어. 공연은 언제야?
M It's next weekend. You should come see it!	남 다음 주말이야. 꼭 보러 와!
W I'll be there. Do you think you'll keep your pink hair afterwards?	여 갈게. 그 후에도 분홍 머리를 유지할 생각이니?
M I think so. It's fun to have a new look.	남 그럴 것 같아. 새로운 스타일을 해보는 게 즐거워.

남자는 머리를 분홍색으로 염색한 이유를 답하면서 자신이 연기할 연극에서 분홍 머리 배역을 맡았기 때문이라고 말했으므로, 남자가 염색한 이유는 ③ '맡은 배역을 연기할 때 필요해서'이다.

[어휘] dye 동 염색하다 be tired of ~에 싫증 나다 musical 형 음악적 소질이 있는; 음악의 celebrity 명 연예인, 유명 인사 trendy 형 유행하는 afterwards 부 그 후에, 나중에 have a ~ look ~한 스타일을 해보다

8 언급 유무 파악 정답 ⑤

M I want to take my kids somewhere interesting this summer, Rosa.	남 이번 여름에 우리 애들을 어딘가 재미있는 곳으로 데려가고 싶어, Rosa.
W How about bringing them to the Central Science Museum?	여 중앙 과학박물관에 데려가는 건 어때?
M Oh, right. That just opened last year. Have you been there?	남 아, 맞네. 거기 작년에 막 문을 열었지. 넌 거기 가 봤어?
W Yes, and my kids really enjoyed it. It has many exhibits that teach kids about 1)different physical forces.	여 응, 그리고 내 애들이 정말 좋아했어. 그곳엔 아이들에게 다양한 물리적 힘에 관해 가르쳐주는 많은 전시가 있어.
M Are there any hands-on activities?	남 체험 활동은 있어?
W The museum has a chemistry room. The staff help kids 2)perform safe experiments, like making colorful bubbles.	여 박물관에 화학실이 있거든. 직원들이 알록달록한 비눗방울 만들기처럼 안전한 실험을 아이들이 할 수 있게 도와줘.
M That sounds great. Do they have any food options at the Museum?	남 그거 좋네. 박물관에서 먹을 수 있는 음식이 있을까?
W There's a cafeteria that sells some snacks.	여 간식을 몇 가지 파는 매점이 있어.
M That's perfect. If your kids are interested in going back there, maybe we could go together.	남 딱 좋다. 네 애들이 거길 다시 가 볼 의향이 있다면, 우리 함께 가는 게 좋을지도 몰라.
W That works. In fact, the museum also has 3)special tours for groups.	여 가능하겠네. 사실, 그 박물관에는 단체객들을 위한 특별 관람도 있거든.
M Even better.	남 훨씬 더 좋은걸.
W Let's pick a day to go soon.	여 조만간 갈 날을 정해보자.

개관 시기(작년), 전시 주제(다양한 물리적 힘 학습), 체험 활동(알록달록한 비눗방울 만들기), 취식 공간(매점)에 대해 언급했고, ⑤ '단체 할인'은 언급하지 않았다.

[어휘] physical 형 물리적인; 신체의 force 명 힘 hands-on 형 체험의, 직접 해 보는 experiment 명 실험

9　내용 불일치 파악　　　　　　　　　　　　정답 ④

W　Attention, please. I'd like to inform you about an upcoming Graphic Design Competition. It will be hosted by Super Tech Academy on September 12th. The contest is [1]open to anyone who has enrolled in one of the academy's courses. Participants must design a 3D logo for any type of product. The logo must be attractive and [2]match the product that it represents. There will be one grand prize winner and three consolation prizes. [3]**The judging panel will be composed of three professionals from the graphic design industry.** If you're interested, please sign up for the competition by the August 31st deadline. Details about the competition are available on posters at the academy and on its website.	여　주목해 주십시오. 다가오는 Graphic Design Competition에 관해 알려드립니다. 그것은 Super Tech Academy에서 주최하는 것으로, 9월 12일에 열릴 것입니다. 학원의 강좌 중 하나에 등록한 사람이라면 누구든지 이 대회에 참가할 수 있습니다. 참가자들은 어떤 종류의 제품에 쓰일 3D 로고를 디자인해야 합니다. 로고는 매력적이면서 그것이 나타내는 제품과 어울려야 합니다. 대상 수상자 1명과 장려상 수상자 3명이 있겠습니다. 심사위원단은 그래픽 디자인 업계의 전문가 3명으로 구성될 것입니다. 관심이 있으시다면, 마감일인 8월 31일까지 대회 신청을 해주십시오. 대회에 관한 자세한 내용은 학원에 걸려 있는 포스터와 웹사이트에서 확인하실 수 있습니다.

학원에서 주최하는 그래픽 디자인 대회에 대한 안내 방송이다. 여자가 심사위원단은 그래픽 디자인 업계의 전문가 3명으로 구성될 것이라고 했으므로, ④ '5명의 그래픽 디자인 업계 전문가들이 심사한다.'는 내용과 일치하지 않는다.

어휘　inform 통 알리다　upcoming 형 다가오는　enroll in ~에 등록하다　attractive 형 매력적인　match 통 어울리다 명 성냥　represent 통 나타내다　consolation prize 장려상, 위로상
be composed of ~로 구성되다　deadline 명 마감일　detail 명 자세한 내용, 세부 사항

10　도표 정보 파악　　　　　　　　　　　　정답 ①

W　Tony, why are you looking up suitcases? Are you going somewhere? M　Yeah. I have plans to take a trip to Rocky Island. However, my old suitcase has [1]a broken wheel, so I need to buy a new suitcase. Can you help me pick one? W　Oh, I like that one. The red color is nice. M　It's not bad, but **I don't want a red suitcase.** It's too bright. W　That's fair. Do you have a budget in mind? M　I'd like to [2]keep it under $150. W　What about size? Do you need something large? M　Not really. I'll only be there for a few days. W　Then, you can get a [3]small or medium one that you can bring on the plane. Do you need a lock? M　No, I [4]don't want one. I always worry I'll forget the combination to the lock. W　Then, I think the decision is made for you. M　Right. There's only one good option.	여　Tony, 왜 여행 가방을 찾아보고 있니? 어디 가게? 남　응. 난 로키섬으로 여행 갈 계획이야. 하지만 내 낡은 여행 가방은 바퀴가 고장 나서, 새 가방을 하나 사야 해. 내가 고르는 것 좀 도와줄래? 여　아, 난 저게 마음에 들어. 빨간색이 근사해. 남　나쁘지 않은데, 빨간색 여행 가방은 원하지 않아. 너무 밝거든. 여　일리 있는 말이야. 생각하고 있는 예산이 있니? 남　150달러 미만으로 하고 싶어. 여　크기는? 큰 게 필요해? 남　그렇지 않아. 며칠 동안만 거기 있을 거야. 여　그러면 비행기에 가지고 탈 수 있는 작은 거나 중간 것을 살 수 있어. 자물쇠는 필요하니? 남　아니, 자물쇠는 원하지 않아. 항상 자물쇠 비밀번호 조합을 잊어버릴까 봐 걱정하거든. 여　그렇다면, 결정이 내려진 것 같네. 남　맞아. 좋은 선택지가 하나뿐이네.

남자는 빨간색이 아니고, 가격대가 150달러 미만인 것 중에서, 중간이나 작은 사이즈의, 자물쇠가 없는 여행 가방을 골랐다.

어휘　look up ~을 찾아보다, 검색하다　suitcase 명 여행 가방　wheel 명 바퀴　lock 명 자물쇠 통 잠그다　combination 명 (자물쇠를 열 수 있는 번호) 조합

11　짧은 대화의 응답 파악　　　　　　　　　정답 ③

M　Mom, I think I'll be [1]a bit late for dinner this evening. W　Are you doing something after school? M　**My friends and I [2]formed a study group. We're going to get together at the library after class.** W　I will leave some food for you in the fridge, then.	남　엄마, 저 오늘 저녁 식사에 좀 늦을 것 같아요. 여　방과 후에 뭔가 할 거니? 남　친구들과 스터디 그룹을 만들었어요. 수업 끝나고 도서관에서 모일 거예요. 여　그럼, 네 몫의 음식을 냉장고에 남겨 놓도록 하마.
	선택지　① 난 오늘 밤에 집에 조금 늦게 도착할 것 같구나. ② 다음 주에 내 친구들을 저녁 식사에 초대할 거란다. ③ 그럼, 네 몫의 음식을 냉장고에 남겨 놓도록 하마. ④ 내 생각에 넌 공부에 좀 더 집중해야겠구나. ⑤ 분명 넌 방과 후 수업으로 많은 걸 배울 거란다.

남자가 오늘 저녁 식사에 늦을 것 같다면서 스터디 그룹을 결성한 친구들과 수업 끝나고 도서관에서 모일 거라고 말했으므로, 이에 대한 응답으로는 저녁 식사를 남겨놓겠다고 말하는 ③ 'I will leave some food for you in the fridge, then.'이 가장 적절하다.

어휘　a bit 조금　form 통 만들다, 형성하다　get together 모이다　fridge 명 냉장고　after-school program 방과 후 수업

12 짧은 대화의 응답 파악

정답 ③

W	Ted, who was it you were [1]talking to on the phone just now?
M	**It was a receptionist from my dentist's office.**
W	Oh? What was the [2]call about? **Are you finally getting that cavity filled?**
M	Yes. My appointment for tomorrow is confirmed.

여	Ted, 방금 누구랑 통화했어?
남	치과 접수 담당자였어.
여	어? 뭐에 관한 전화였어? 드디어 충치 때우는 거야?
남	응. 내일 진료 예약을 확인받았어.

선택지 ① 아니. 접수 담당자가 내게 다시 전화해 주지 않았어.
　　　② 물론이지. 내가 치과 선생님에게 어떤 치약을 써야 하는지 물어볼게.
　　　③ 응. 내일 진료 예약을 확인받았어.
　　　④ 맞아. 난 이제 충치 치료 다 했어.
　　　⑤ 안됐어. 넌 양치질을 더 꼼꼼히 해야 했어.

남자가 치과 접수 담당자와 통화했다고 하자 여자가 충치를 때우기로 한 것인지 물었으므로, 이에 대한 응답으로는 그렇다면서 예약했다고 말하는 ③ 'Yes. My appointment for tomorrow is confirmed.'가 가장 적절하다.

어휘 receptionist 몡 접수 담당자　fill a cavity 충치를 때우다　toothpaste 몡 치약　treat 통 치료하다; 대우하다　brush one's teeth 양치질하다

13 긴 대화의 응답 파악

정답 ④

W	Wow, this cookie tastes really good. Where did you get it, Neal?
M	I bought it at the bakery on Green Street.
W	There's always a long line in front of that place, right?
M	Yeah, exactly. Mr. and Mrs. Nelson, the owners of the bakery, have [1]an incredible recipe. Apparently, they spent two years developing it.
W	Well, their efforts really paid off. This cookie is delicious.
M	I was thinking of opening a bakery like theirs one day.
W	You are a really talented baker. I bet your business would be successful.
M	Maybe, but I'll need to create my own [2]signature item first.
W	Yeah, every good bakery has something they specialize in. What would you make?
M	**Well, cupcakes are my favorite. So I want to sell those.**
W	**Do you have [3]your own special way of making them?**
M	Not yet. I'm still developing my own cupcake recipe.

여	우와, 이 쿠키 정말 맛있다. 이거 어디서 났어, Neal?
남	그린가에 있는 빵집에서 샀어.
여	그곳 앞에는 항상 줄이 길게 있더라, 그렇지?
남	응, 맞아. 빵집 주인인 Nelson씨 부부에겐 놀라운 레시피가 있거든. 듣자 하니, 그들은 그걸 개발하는 데 2년을 썼대.
여	음, 그들의 노력이 정말 성과가 있었네. 쿠키 맛있어.
남	난 언젠가 그들의 것과 같은 그런 빵집을 개업할 생각이었어.
여	넌 정말 재능 있는 제빵사잖아. 분명 네 사업은 성공할 거야.
남	그럴지도 모르지만, 난 먼저 나만의 특징적인 아이템을 만들어야겠어.
여	그래, 좋은 빵집에는 모두 특화된 뭔가가 있지. 뭘 만들 거야?
남	음, 컵케이크는 내가 가장 자신 있는 거야. 그래서 그것들을 팔고 싶어.
여	컵케이크 만드는 너만의 특별한 방법이 있니?
남	아직 아냐. 계속 나만의 컵케이크 레시피를 개발 중이야.

선택지 ① 난 동의하지 않아. 차라리 다른 빵집에 가는 게 낫겠어.
　　　② 좋아. 가족들에게 쿠키를 좀 사다 주자.
　　　③ 그런 것 같지 않아. 컵케이크는 굽기 어려울 수 있어.
　　　④ 아직 아냐. 계속 나만의 컵케이크 레시피를 개발 중이야.
　　　⑤ 그건 진짜 맛있다. 넌 너만의 빵집을 열어도 될 것 같아.

두 사람이 한 빵집의 성공 사례에 대해 이야기하는 상황에서 남자가 자신도 컵케이크를 만들어 팔고 싶다고 했다. 여자가 컵케이크를 만드는 남자만의 특별한 방법이 있는지 물었으므로, 이에 대한 응답으로는 그의 레시피에 대해 말하는 ④ 'Not yet. I'm still developing my own cupcake recipe.'가 가장 적절하다.

어휘 Mr. and Mrs. ~ 부부　apparently 된 듣자 하니　effort 몡 노력　pay off 성과가 있다　I bet 분명 ~하다　signature 몡 특징; 서명　specialize in ~에 특화되다
favorite 혱 가장 자신 있는; 가장 좋아하는　would rather 차라리 ~하는 게 낫다

14 긴 대화의 응답 파악

정답 ①

M	Hey, Mandy. What are you up to?
W	I'm just looking through a Spanish dictionary.
M	Oh, it's so cool that you're [1]studying another language!
W	Yeah, but it's tough! I've been studying Spanish for years, but I feel like I'm still a beginner.
M	What makes you say that? Do you have [2]difficulty memorizing the vocabulary?
W	No. I can understand most of the words used in everyday conversation.
M	Then, it sounds like you're not a beginner.
W	I'm having trouble with speaking. Whenever I have to say something, my mind goes blank.
M	Have you tried studying with a tutor?
W	No, because I always [3]get more nervous in front of a teacher.
M	How about joining a club for Spanish learners?
W	I don't know. Would that be helpful?
M	**Other students may have the same problems you do, so you may feel [4]more comfortable speaking Spanish with them.**
W	I'd better look for a club to join, then.

남	안녕, Mandy. 뭐 하고 있어?
여	그냥 스페인어 사전을 훑어보고 있어.
남	아, 다른 언어를 공부하다니 정말 멋지다!
여	그래, 그런데 힘들어! 몇 년째 스페인어를 공부하고 있는데, 아직도 초보자 같은 걸.
남	왜 그런 말을 해? 어휘 암기가 힘드니?
여	아니. 일상적인 대화에서 쓰이는 단어 대부분은 이해할 수 있어.
남	그러면 초보자가 아닌 것 같은데.
여	말을 하는 게 문제야. 뭔가 말해야 할 때마다 머릿속이 새하얘져.
남	과외 선생님과 함께 공부해 봤니?
여	아니, 왜냐하면 선생님 앞에서는 항상 더 긴장하거든.
남	스페인어 배우는 사람들을 위한 동호회에 가입하는 건 어때?
여	잘 모르겠어. 그게 도움이 될까?
남	다른 학생들이 너와 같은 문제를 겪고 있을 수 있어서, 그들과 스페인어로 말하는 게 더 편하게 느껴질 수 있어.
여	그러면, 가입할 동호회를 찾아보는 게 좋겠어.

두 사람이 스페인어 공부에 대해 이야기하는 상황이다. 여자가 스페인어로 말을 잘하고 싶다고 하자 남자가 스페인어 동호회 가입을 추천했으므로, 이에 대한 응답으로는 추천을 받아들이는 ① 'I'd better look for a club to join, then.'이 가장 적절하다.

[어휘] look through ~을 훑어보다 memorize 통 암기하다, 외우다 conversation 명 대화 go blank 새하얗게 되다 worth 형 ~의 가치가 있는

15 상황에 적절한 말 파악

정답 ⑤

W Charles and Abby are classmates in a global history class. Today, their teacher explained the final exam for the course. The exam will ¹⁾cover material from the entire school year and test each student's knowledge of global history over the past 100 years. Charles and Abby are now studying hard for the test, but Abby is ²⁾losing confidence. She feels that there is too much to study for, so it will be almost impossible to be fully prepared. However, Charles ³⁾is not concerned because the test will only review topics they have already studied. **So he wants to tell Abby that she is familiar with the material on the exam and that she should not worry.** In this situation, what would Charles most likely say to Abby?

여 Charles와 Abby는 세계사 수업을 함께 듣는 급우입니다. 오늘, 그들의 선생님이 그 과목의 기말고사에 관해 설명했습니다. 시험은 한 학년도 전체에서 배운 자료를 다룰 것이고 지난 100년 동안의 세계사에 대하여 각 학생의 지식을 시험할 것입니다. Charles와 Abby는 현재 열심히 시험공부를 하고 있지만, Abby는 자신감을 잃고 있습니다. 그녀는 공부할 것이 너무 많아서, 완전히 준비하는 것은 거의 불가능할 것이라고 생각합니다. 하지만, Charles는 그 시험이 그들이 이미 공부한 주제들만 확인할 것이기 때문에 걱정하지 않습니다. 그래서, 그는 Abby에게 그녀가 이미 시험 자료를 잘 알고 있으니까 걱정하지 않아도 된다고 말하고 싶습니다. 이러한 상황에서, Charles가 Abby에게 가장 할 것 같은 말은 무엇입니까?

[선택지] ① 진정해. 우리 시험은 다음 달에나 있잖아.
② 괜찮아. 나도 시험을 잘 못 봤어.
③ 걱정 그만해! 새로 오신 선생님은 정말 친절하셔.
④ 나도. 세계사는 내가 가장 약한 과목이야.
⑤ 염려하지 마. 이거 전부 전에 공부한 거야.

Abby가 공부할 것이 너무 많아서 완전히 준비를 못 할까 봐 걱정하는 것을 보고, Charles는 그녀가 이미 시험 자료를 잘 알고 있으니까 걱정하지 않아도 된다고 말하려 한다. 따라서, Charles가 할 말로 ⑤ 'Take it easy. We've studied all of this before.'가 가장 적절하다.

[어휘] cover 통 다루다; 덮다 material 명 자료; 재료 knowledge 명 지식 confidence 명 자신감 concerned 형 걱정하는 be familiar with ~을 잘 알고 있다, 친숙하다

16-17 세트 문항

정답 16 ② 17 ④

M Good afternoon, everyone. Yesterday, we briefly talked about the importance of a balanced diet. **Today, I'd like to look at foods you should never eat when you ¹⁾have a stomachache because they will make it worse.** First, try not to drink any **coffee**. It is ²⁾highly acidic and will likely make your stomach hurt more. Another type of food you should avoid is **nuts**. These contain a lot of fiber, which can ³⁾stimulate a weakened stomach too much. This stimulation can lead to a number of digestive problems, including diarrhea. Next, you should not drink **milk** or eat any food that contains it. Milk is hard for the body to digest, and it can cause ⁴⁾painful gas to develop. Finally, greasy foods such as **French fries** should obviously not be eaten if you have a stomachache. In fact, they are often the cause of a stomachache. I hope this lesson has given information that will be helpful if you ever have an upset stomach.

남 안녕하십니까, 여러분. 어제, 우리는 균형 잡힌 식사의 중요성에 관해 간단히 이야기했습니다. 오늘은, 배탈을 악화시키기 때문에 배가 아플 때 절대로 먹으면 안 되는 음식들을 살펴보려고 합니다. 첫째, 커피를 마시지 않도록 하십시오. 그것은 매우 산성을 띠고 있고, 여러분의 위장을 더욱 아프게 할 가능성이 있습니다. 여러분이 피해야 할 또 다른 종류의 음식은 견과류입니다. 이것은 섬유질을 많이 함유하고 있는데, 이것은 약해진 위를 지나치게 많이 자극할 수 있습니다. 이러한 자극은 설사를 포함하여 많은 소화 문제로 이어질 것입니다. 다음으로, 여러분은 우유를 마시거나 우유가 함유된 음식을 먹으면 안 됩니다. 우유는 몸이 소화하기 어렵고, 고통스러운 가스가 생겨나게 만들 수 있습니다. 마지막으로, 감자튀김과 같은 기름진 음식은 배탈이 났다면 당연히 먹지 말아야 합니다. 사실, 그것들은 종종 배탈의 원인이기도 합니다. 이 수업이 여러분에게 배탈이 났을 때 도움이 될 정보를 주었기를 바랍니다.

[선택지] 16 ① 정크 푸드를 먹지 말아야 할 이유
② 아픈 위를 악화시키는 음식
③ 건강한 방법으로 음식을 요리하는 방법
④ 식단과 건강 사이의 관계
⑤ 균형 잡힌 식사를 하는 것이 중요한 이유
17 ① 커피 ② 견과류 ③ 우유 ④ 초콜릿 ⑤ 감자튀김

16 배탈을 악화시키기 때문에 배가 아플 때 절대로 먹으면 안 되는 음식들을 살펴보고 있으므로 남자가 하는 말의 주제로 ② 'foods that worsen a sore stomach'가 가장 적절하다.
17 커피, 견과류, 우유, 감자튀김은 언급했지만 ④ 'chocolate'은 언급하지 않았다.

[어휘] balanced 형 균형 잡힌 stomachache 명 배탈, 복통 acidic 형 산성을 띠는, 산성의 fiber 명 섬유질; 섬유 stimulate 통 자극하다 (stimulation 명 자극) weaken 통 약화시키다 diarrhea 명 설사 develop 통 (병이) 생기다; 개발하다 greasy 형 기름진 obviously 부 당연히; 분명히 have an upset stomach 배탈이 나다 worsen 통 악화시키다

1	①	2	②	3	②	4	③	5	⑤	6	②	7	①	8	③	9	④	10	②
11	④	12	①	13	③	14	①	15	④	16	⑤	17	②						

• 각 문제의 정답 근거는 굵은 글씨로, Dictation 정답은 밑줄로 표시되어 있습니다.

---

1 목적 파악

정답 ①

M Good morning, everyone. Thank you for coming. I'm the director of the Greenwich Hospital. **I'm happy to announce that the construction of our 1)<u>new cancer center</u> has just finished.** It is located next to the hospital's parking facilities. The center includes a number of new patient rooms and surgery areas. It also has 2)<u>examination rooms</u> equipped with state-of-the-art medical devices. We recently hired 20 new staff members who specialize in cancer treatment. We hope this will demonstrate the hospital's 3)<u>commitment to providing</u> our patients with excellent medical service. Now, I'll take a few minutes to answer any questions you might have.

남 안녕하십니까, 여러분. 와주셔서 감사합니다. 저는 그리니치 병원의 원장입니다. 저희의 새로운 암 센터 건설이 막 완료되었음을 알리게 되어 기쁩니다. 암 센터는 병원의 주차 시설 옆에 위치해 있습니다. 이 센터에는 다수의 신식 입원실과 수술 구역이 포함되어 있습니다. 또한 최첨단 의료기기를 갖춘 검사실도 있습니다. 최근에는 암 치료를 전문으로 하는 20명의 직원을 새로 고용했습니다. 이것이 환자들에게 훌륭한 의료 서비스를 제공하려는 저희 병원의 헌신을 잘 보여주길 바랍니다. 이제 몇 분간 여러분의 질문에 대답해 드리겠습니다.

남자가 병원에 암 센터 건설이 완료됐음을 알리며 위치 및 시설을 소개하고 있다. 따라서, 남자가 하는 말의 목적으로 ① '병원의 암 센터 완공을 발표하려고'가 가장 적절하다.

어휘 director 명 원장; 책임자 construction 명 건설 cancer 명 암 facility 명 시설 a number of 많은 surgery 명 수술 examination 명 검사 equipped with ~을 갖춘 state-of-the-art 형 최첨단의 specialize in ~을 전문으로 하다 demonstrate 동 잘 보여주다, 입증하다 commitment 명 헌신

---

2 의견 파악

정답 ②

W Greg, why are you lying on the couch?
M Hi, Mom. I 1)<u>sprained my ankle</u> on the stairs.
W Oh, no. How are you treating it?
M I heated up this towel and put it on my ankle.
W You shouldn't do that. **When you have a sprain, you need to apply an ice pack to the area immediately.** A hot pack doesn't help.
M Are you sure?
W Yes. After getting a sprain, the 2)<u>injured area swells up</u>. Ice reduces the blood flow there, which prevents swelling.
M But I thought heat was useful for healing.
W It isn't at the moment. Swelling is the main problem now. The ice will reduce your pain and 3)<u>prevent bruises</u>.
M I didn't realize that.
W Just take that off your ankle. I'll get you some ice.
M Thanks, Mom.

여 Greg, 왜 소파에 누워 있니?
남 안녕하세요, 엄마. 전 계단에서 발목을 삐었어요.
여 오, 이런. 어떻게 치료하고 있니?
남 이 수건을 데워서 발목 위에 올려뒀어요.
여 그러면 안 된단다. 염좌를 당했을 때는, 즉시 그 부위에 냉찜질을 해야 해. 온찜질은 도움이 안 되거든.
남 정말요?
여 그래. 염좌를 당한 후에는 다친 부위가 부어올라. 냉찜질은 그 부위의 혈류를 감소시켜서 붓는 걸 예방해줘.
남 하지만 저는 온찜질이 치료에 유용하다고 생각했어요.
여 지금은 아니야. 부기가 지금 가장 큰 문제란다. 냉찜질이 통증을 줄여주고 멍이 드는 걸 예방해 줄 거야.
남 그건 몰랐어요.
여 일단 그걸 발목에서 치우렴. 내가 얼음을 갖다 줄게.
남 고마워요, 엄마.

발목을 삐어서 온찜질을 하는 남자에게 여자가 염좌를 당했을 때는 즉시 그 부위에 냉찜질을 해야 한다고 했다. 따라서, 여자의 의견으로 ② '염좌를 당한 직후에는 냉찜질을 해야 한다.'가 가장 적절하다.

어휘 lie 동 눕다 sprain 동 삐다 명 염좌 heat up ~을 데우다 apply an ice pack 냉찜질을 하다 swell 동 붓다 at the moment 지금, 마침 bruise 명 멍 동 멍이 들다

---

3 관계 파악

정답 ②

M Sorry I'm late. There was 1)<u>heavy traffic</u> on the highway.
W That's fine. But we should get started right away. **Our art gallery has an exhibition opening next Tuesday.**
M No problem. **You need some work done on the garden, right?**
W Yes. And I'd like you to 2)<u>plant some cherry blossom trees</u> by the front gate, too.
M Sure. They will look nice there.
W Mainly I want you to focus on the garden, though. It needs to be more attractive for visitors.
M I've been 3)<u>designing outdoor spaces</u> for years, so I'm sure I can come up with some good ideas.

남 늦어서 죄송합니다. 고속도로가 꽉 막혔어요.
여 괜찮아요. 하지만 지금 당장 시작해야 해요. 우리 미술관에서 다음 주 화요일에 전시회가 열리거든요.
남 그럼요. 정원 작업을 끝내야 하는 거죠, 맞나요?
여 네. 그리고 정문 옆에 벚꽃 나무도 좀 심어주시면 좋겠어요.
남 물론이죠. 벚꽃 나무는 거기에서 멋지게 보일 거예요.
여 그래도 대게는 정원에 집중해주시면 좋겠어요. 그곳이 방문객들에게 더 매력적이어야 해요.
남 전 몇 년 동안 야외 공간을 디자인해 왔기 때문에, 좋은 아이디어를 분명 생각해 낼 수 있을 거예요.

W I'm glad to hear that.	여 그 말을 들으니 다행이네요.
M Is there anything in particular that I should be aware of?	남 특별히 제가 알고 있어야 할 점이 있을까요?
W Yes. There are a few 4)sculptures from our collection that I'd like to display in the garden.	여 네. 저희 소장품 중에서 정원에 전시하고 싶은 조각이 몇 점 있어요.
M Could I see them?	남 제가 좀 볼 수 있을까요?
W Of course. Let's go take a look at them.	여 물론이죠. 가서 그걸 살펴보도록 하죠.

두 사람이 미술관 정원 조경 작업에 관해 이야기하고 있다. 남자는 여자가 요구하는 정원 작업에 대해 확인하면서 야외 공간을 디자인한 경험이 있다고 했고, 여자는 남자에게 미술관의 조각 소장품을 보여주겠다고 하는 것으로 보아 두 사람의 관계로 ② '조경사 — 미술관 직원'이 가장 적절하다.

어휘 highway 명 고속도로 get started 시작하다 cherry blossom tree 벚꽃 나무 focus on ~에 집중하다 attractive 형 매력적인 outdoor 형 야외의 come up with ~을 생각해 내다 in particular 특별히 be aware of ~을 알고 있다 display 통 전시하다 take a look at ~을 살펴보다

4 그림 내용 불일치 파악

정답 ③

M Lisa, is everything ready for the 1)interschool baseball match?	남 Lisa, 학교 대항 야구 경기 준비는 다 됐니?
W Yes, I think so. What do you think of the field decorations?	여 응, 그런 것 같아. 야구장 꾸민 게 어떤 것 같아?
M They're perfect. I love the two logos painted on the grass.	남 완벽한걸. 잔디 위에 그려진 두 개의 로고가 마음에 들어.
W As the teams are called The Dragons and The Tigers, I put the letters D and T there.	여 팀 이름이 The Dragons와 The Tigers라서, 내가 D와 T 글자를 거기에 썼어.
M Is that person in front of the fence 2)wearing a tiger costume?	남 펜스 앞에 있는 사람이 호랑이 코스튬을 입고 있는 거지?
W That's right. It's our team's mascot.	여 맞아. 우리 팀의 마스코트야.
M And that banner on the fence looks good. The design with the bat and ball turned out well.	남 그리고 펜스에 걸린 저 현수막이 좋아 보여. 배트와 공으로 된 디자인이 잘 됐어.
W I'm glad you like it.	여 마음에 든다니 기쁘다.
M Oh, is there water available for the players?	남 아, 선수들이 마실 수 있는 물은 있니?
W Yes. It's in the cooler on the right side of the field.	여 응. 야구장 오른쪽에 있는 아이스박스 안에 있어.
M Ah, I see it. And the two players 3)in striped uniforms are already on the field.	남 아, 보인다. 그리고 줄무늬 유니폼을 입은 두 명의 선수가 이미 야구장에 나와 있네.
W I think they're stretching to get ready for the game.	여 경기 준비를 하려고 스트레칭 중인 것 같아.
M Yeah. I can't wait to get started!	남 그러게. 빨리 시작하면 좋겠다!

대화에서 남자가 펜스에 걸린 현수막의 배트와 공으로 되어 있는 디자인이 잘 됐다고 말했는데, ③에는 글러브가 그려져 있다.

어휘 interschool 형 학교 대항의, 학교 간의 field 명 야구장, 경기장; 벌판 turn out well 잘 되다 cooler 명 아이스박스; 냉장고 can't wait to 빨리 ~하면 좋겠다

5 할 일 파악

정답 ⑤

W Welcome to Pearson Mall's customer service desk. How can I help you?	여 Pearson Mall의 고객 서비스 데스크에 잘 오셨습니다. 무엇을 도와드릴까요?
M I tried to use this gift card to buy some books at the mall's bookstore, but it didn't work.	남 쇼핑몰의 서점에서 책을 사려고 이 기프트 카드를 사용하려 했는데, 작동이 안 됐어요.
W I'm sorry about that. Did you check if there was 1)enough money left on the card?	여 죄송합니다. 카드에 남은 돈이 충분한지 확인하셨나요?
M Yes. There is still $50 left.	남 네. 아직 50달러가 남아 있어요.
W Hmm... Maybe the store's 2)payment system isn't working properly. In that case, I'll contact the bookstore.	여 흠... 아마도 그 가게의 결제 시스템이 제대로 작동하지 않는 것 같습니다. 그렇다면, 제가 서점에 연락해 보겠습니다.
M You don't have to. I saw other customers using their cards there.	남 그러실 필요 없어요. 거기서 다른 손님들이 기프트 카드를 쓰는 걸 봤어요.
W That's strange. Could I take a look at it?	여 이상하네요. 제가 봐도 될까요?
M Here you go.	남 여기 있습니다.
W Well, the card doesn't 3)appear to be damaged.	여 음, 카드가 손상된 것 같지는 않네요.
M What can I do, then? Should I fill out a refund request form?	남 그러면 어떻게 하면 되죠? 환불 신청서를 작성해야 하나요?
W No. I'll just replace the card with one that has the same amount of money.	여 아니요. 그냥 같은 금액이 들어 있는 카드로 교체해드릴게요.
M Thanks. I really appreciate that.	남 고맙습니다. 정말로 감사드려요.

쇼핑몰 고객 서비스 데스크에서 불량 기프트 카드에 관해 이야기하고 있다. 남자가 환불 신청서를 작성해야 하는지 묻자 여자가 아니라고 하면서 카드를 교체해 주겠다고 했으므로 여자가 할 일로 ⑤ '카드 교체해주기'가 가장 적절하다.

어휘 payment 명 결제 properly 부 제대로, 적절히 appear 통 ~인 것 같다; 나타나다 fill out ~을 작성하다 refund 명 환불 request form 신청서 replace A with B A를 B로 교체하다

6 금액 정보 파악   정답 ②

M	Hi. I'm looking for a new printer.	남	안녕하세요. 새 프린터기를 찾고 있어요.
W	I'd recommend a laser printer. They ¹⁾print thousands of pages with a single cartridge of ink.	여	레이저 프린터기를 추천할게요. 그건 하나의 잉크 카트리지로 수천 장을 인쇄해요.
M	I heard that some brands can print 9,000 pages.	남	어떤 브랜드는 9천 장을 인쇄할 수 있었다고 들었어요.
W	Our models can print about 10,000 pages with just one cartridge.	여	저희 모델은 카트리지 하나로 약 만 장을 인쇄할 수 있어요.
M	That's impressive. How much does this one cost?	남	인상적이네요. 이건 얼마죠?
W	It's normally $250, but we're having a sale this week, so it's now 20% off.	여	보통 때는 250달러인데, 이번 주에 세일을 해서 지금은 20% 할인해요.
M	Do you have other models?	남	다른 모델은 없나요?
W	**We have another model which normally costs $200. You will ²⁾get 10% off at the moment, though.**	여	보통 때는 200달러 하는 다른 모델이 있어요. 하지만 지금은 10% 할인돼요.
M	**In that case, I'll go for the cheaper model.**	남	그렇다면, 더 싼 모델로 할게요.
W	That's a good choice, sir.	여	좋은 선택이십니다, 손님.
M	Oh, I also need to buy some A4 printer paper.	남	아, A4 프린터기 용지도 좀 사야 해요.
W	Sure. **A box of 500 sheets is $10.** How many do you need?	여	그럼요. 500장짜리 한 상자에 10달러입니다. 몇 상자 필요하세요?
M	**I'll take ³⁾three boxes of them.** Here's my credit card.	남	세 상자 주세요. 여기 제 신용카드요.

남자가 더 싼 모델의 레이저 프린터를 10% 할인($200×0.9=$180) 받아서 구매했고, 추가로 A4 프린터기 용지를 세 상자($10×3=$30) 구매했으므로 정답은 ② '$210'이다.

[어휘] impressive 혱 인상적인   normally 튄 보통 때는, 보통   sheet 몡 (종이) 한 장; 시트

7 이유 파악   정답 ①

W	Hi, Drake. What are you looking at?	여	안녕, Drake. 뭘 보고 있어?
M	I'm searching for a way to ¹⁾cancel my phone service online.	남	온라인으로 휴대폰을 해지할 방법을 찾고 있어.
W	Didn't you sign up for it a couple of weeks ago?	여	몇 주 전에 휴대폰 개통하지 않았어?
M	It was last month, actually.	남	사실은 지난달이었지.
W	What happened? Is there a problem with the call quality?	여	무슨 일이야? 통화 품질에 문제가 있니?
M	No. The calls sound great, and I never ²⁾get disconnected.	남	아니. 통화음도 좋고, 끊기는 일도 없어.
W	Ah, I guess you want a new phone. Some companies offer discounts if you sign a new contract.	여	아, 새 휴대폰을 원하나 보구나. 어떤 회사는 새로 계약하면 할인을 해주잖아.
M	I'm not planning to replace my current phone.	남	지금 휴대폰을 바꿀 계획은 없어.
W	Oh, does another phone company have ³⁾a cheaper plan?	여	아, 다른 통신사에 더 저렴한 요금제가 있니?
M	That's not it. This is the cheapest option available.	남	그게 아냐. 이게 가능한 가장 저렴한 요금제야.
W	Then, what's the problem?	여	그러면, 뭐가 문제야?
M	**Do you remember I applied for a ⁴⁾study abroad program? I got accepted, so I won't need my phone service anymore.**	남	내가 유학 프로그램에 지원했던 거 기억나? 거기 합격해서 더 이상 휴대폰을 개통해둘 필요가 없을 거야.
W	That's great. Good luck with your studies!	여	잘됐다. 공부 잘하길 바랄게!

남자는 온라인으로 휴대폰 해지 방법을 찾고 있다면서 이는 유학 프로그램에 합격해 더 이상 휴대폰을 개통해둘 필요가 없기 때문이라고 말했으므로, 남자가 휴대폰을 해지하려는 이유는 ① '유학을 가게 돼서'이다.

[어휘] search for ~을 찾다   quality 몡 품질   disconnect 동 연결을 끊다   contract 몡 계약   apply for ~에 지원하다   good luck with ~을 잘하길 바라다

8 언급 유무 파악   정답 ③

M	Julie, are you interested in learning how to play the piano?	남	Julie, 피아노 치는 법을 배우는 데 관심 있니?
W	Not really. I don't have much free time these days. Why do you ask?	여	그렇진 않아. 요즘 여유 시간이 별로 없거든. 왜 물어보는 거야?
M	My sister gives piano lessons ¹⁾on **Fridays and Saturdays**, and she's looking for more students.	남	내 여동생이 금요일과 토요일마다 피아노 수업을 하는데, 더 많은 학생을 찾고 있어.
W	Oh, I can see if my friends want to learn. Does she mainly teach ²⁾beginner or advanced students?	여	아, 내 친구들이 배우고 싶어 하는지 알아봐 줄 수 있어. 주로 초급 학생을 가르치니? 아니면 상급 학생을 가르치니?
M	She works with **students of all levels**.	남	모든 수준의 학생을 대상으로 일해.
W	Oh, that's good. Where does she teach? I know some piano teachers visit the students' houses.	여	오, 그거 좋네. 어디서 가르쳐? 몇몇 피아노 선생님들이 학생 집을 방문하는 걸로 알고 있는데.
M	Normally, she asks students to ³⁾come to **her studio**.	남	보통, 학생들에게 자기 스튜디오로 오라고 해.
W	What about the type of music?	여	음악의 종류는 어때?
M	She gives lessons in both **classical and jazz styles**.	남	클래식과 재즈 모두 가르쳐.
W	Okay. I'll make sure to share that information with my friends.	여	알겠어. 이 정보를 친구들과 꼭 공유할게.
M	Thanks. She will really appreciate your help.	남	고마워. 여동생이 네 도움에 정말 고마워할 거야.

수업 요일(금요일과 토요일), 수업 대상(모든 수준의 학생), 수업 장소(자기 스튜디오), 가르치는 음악(클래식과 재즈)에 대해 언급했고, ③ '수업료'는 언급하지 않았다.

어휘 look for ~을 찾다 mainly 🔒 주로 advanced 🔒 상급인, 고등인; 전진한 share 🔒 공유하다

---

9 내용 불일치 파악   정답 ④

M Attention, please. The Global Language Institute is holding an English Speaking Competition. If you're studying English ¹⁾<u>as a second language</u>, this contest will give you a chance to use your speaking skills! It will be held on April 5th, but the deadline for signing up is March 10th. If you're interested in participating, please ²⁾<u>submit a short video</u> of yourself speaking in English when you sign up. The video should be less than five minutes long. We will divide the competitors into three levels based on their English ability. **The winners of each level will be announced the day after the contest.** Prizes ³⁾<u>include free language classes</u> at our institute. For more details, visit our website or call 555-3333.	남 주목해 주십시오. 글로벌 어학원에서 English Speaking Competition을 개최할 것입니다. 만약 여러분이 제2외국어로 영어를 공부하고 있다면, 이 대회는 여러분의 말하기 기량을 발휘할 기회를 제공할 것입니다! 대회는 4월 5일에 열리지만, 참가 신청 마감일은 3월 10일입니다. 참가할 의향이 있으시다면, 신청하실 때 영어로 말하는 모습을 담은 짧은 동영상을 제출해주십시오. 동영상은 5분 이내여야 합니다. 영어 실력에 따라 참가자들을 세 단계로 나눌 것입니다. 단계별 우승자는 대회 다음날 발표됩니다. 상품에는 저희 학원의 무료 수강권이 포함되어 있습니다. 더 자세한 사항을 원하시면, 저희 웹사이트를 방문하시거나 555-3333으로 전화 주십시오.

글로벌 어학원에서 개최하는 영어 말하기 대회 안내 방송이다. 남자가 단계별 우승자는 대회 다음날 발표된다고 했으므로 ④ '우승자는 대회 당일에 발표된다.'는 내용과 일치하지 않는다.

어휘 deadline 🔒 마감일 submit 🔒 제출하다 divide 🔒 나누다 competitor 🔒 참가자; 경쟁자 based on ~에 따라

---

10 도표 정보 파악   정답 ②

W Peter, is that a furniture catalog you're reading?	여 Peter, 네가 읽고 있는 게 가구 카탈로그니?
M Yes. I'm thinking of buying a table. Since I enjoy cooking, I'd like to invite people over for dinner.	남 응. 식탁을 살까 생각 중이야. 내가 요리를 좋아해서, 사람들을 저녁 식사에 초대하고 싶거든.
W That's a great idea. How many ¹⁾<u>people should it fit</u>?	여 좋은 생각이야. 몇 인용이어야 해?
M **It should be big enough for at least six people.**	남 적어도 여섯 명이 쓸 정도로는 충분히 커야 해.
W Do you have any preference between wood and plastic?	여 목재와 플라스틱 중에 선호하는 게 있니?
M Oh, **I definitely want wood.** Wood is stronger than plastic.	남 아, 꼭 목재를 원해. 목재가 플라스틱보다 더 튼튼해.
W Okay. How much are you willing to spend?	여 알았어. 얼마를 쓸 의향이 있는데?
M I can ²⁾<u>spend up to</u> $250.	남 250달러까지 쓸 수 있어.
W Then, it looks like you have two choices left. **Do you prefer a table you can fold and put away?**	여 그러면 두 가지 선택지가 남는 것 같아. 접어서 넣어둘 수 있는 식탁이 더 좋니?
M **Yeah, that would be ideal.**	남 응, 그게 이상적일 거야.
W I think you've made your decision, then.	여 그럼, 결정을 내린 것 같아.
M Yes, I'd ³⁾<u>better get the foldable one</u>.	남 그래, 접을 수 있는 걸 사야겠어.

남자는 적어도 6명은 쓸 수 있을 정도로 크면서, 목재로 되어 있고, 250달러 이하인 것 중에서, 접을 수 있는 식탁을 골랐다.

어휘 furniture 🔒 가구 invite A over B A를 B에 초대하다 preference 🔒 선호 be willing to ~할 의향이 있다 fold 🔒 접다 (foldable 🔒 접을 수 있는) put away ~을 넣어두다 ideal 🔒 이상적인

---

11 짧은 대화의 응답 파악   정답 ④

M Honey, our upstairs neighbor's TV is ¹⁾<u>too loud</u>.	남 여보, 우리 윗집 TV 소리가 너무 시끄러워.
W I know. I'm trying to read a book, but the noise is ²⁾<u>really distracting</u>.	여 그러니까 말이야. 책을 읽으려고 하는데, 소음 때문에 정말 집중이 안 돼.
M **Maybe I should go up and ask her to turn down the volume.**	남 어쩌면 내가 올라가서 소리 좀 줄여 달라고 하는 게 좋겠어.
W We should complain to the building manager instead.	여 <u>그보다는 건물 관리인에게 항의해야 해.</u>
	선택지 ① 당신에게 방해된다면 TV를 끌게.
	② 그녀는 그 아파트에서 약 1년째 살고 있어.
	③ 오늘 밤 TV에는 볼 만한 재미있는 게 아무것도 없어.
	④ 그보다는 건물 관리인에게 항의해야 해.
	⑤ 이 책을 다 읽은 후에 빌려줄게.

남자가 윗집에 올라가서 TV 소리를 줄여달라 하는 것이 좋겠다고 했으므로, 이에 대한 응답으로는 다른 대안을 제시하는 ④ 'We should complain to the building manager instead.' 가 가장 적절하다.

어휘 upstairs 🔒 위층의 🔒 위층에 distracting 🔒 집중이 안 되게 하는, 방해하는 turn down ~을 줄이다 turn off ~을 끄다 complain 🔒 항의하다; 불평하다

12 짧은 대화의 응답 파악 정답 ①

W I'm really excited, Justin. A new amusement park just opened in our city. It is ¹⁾supposed to be amazing.	여 정말 신난다, Justin. 우리 도시에 새로운 놀이공원이 막 개장했어. 거긴 굉장할 거야.
M Yeah. I've seen several advertisements for it already.	남 그러게. 난 벌써 그곳에 대한 광고를 여러 개 봤어.
W I really want to check it out. **Do you want to ²⁾go with me on Saturday?**	여 정말 거기 가보고 싶어. 나랑 토요일에 같이 갈래?
M Of course. It sounds like it'll be fun.	남 <u>물론이지. 재밌을 것 같아.</u>

선택지 ① 물론이지. 재밌을 것 같아.
　　　② 정말? 넌 토요일 밤에 뭘 했는데?
　　　③ 나도 그래. 놀이기구 타는 건 관심 없어.
　　　④ 괜찮아. 놀이공원 티켓도 전부 매진이야.
　　　⑤ 맞아. 내가 광고를 다시 확인해 볼게.

여자가 새로 개장한 놀이공원에 토요일에 같이 가자고 제안했으므로, 이에 대한 응답으로는 제안을 수락하는 ① 'Of course. It sounds like it'll be fun.'이 가장 적절하다.

어휘 amusement part 놀이공원　several 형 여러 개의　advertisement 명 광고　check out ~에 가보다; ~을 확인하다　go on rides 놀이기구를 타다　sold out 매진인

13 긴 대화의 응답 파악 정답 ③

W Honey, I was thinking of adopting a pet. What do you think?	여 여보, 난 반려동물을 입양할까 생각 중이었어. 당신 생각은 어때?
M Really? I thought you ¹⁾had a fur allergy.	남 정말? 당신 털 알레르기가 있는 줄 알았는데.
W Cats and dogs make me sneeze. But what about getting a bird?	여 고양이와 개라면 재채기하게 돼. 그렇지만 새를 데려오는 건 어떨까?
M That's an interesting choice. What kind of bird?	남 흥미로운 선택이네. 어떤 종류의 새로?
W Actually, my friend is looking for someone to ²⁾adopt her parrots. I want to get one of them.	여 실은, 내 친구가 자기 앵무새들을 입양해 줄 사람을 찾고 있어. 내가 한 마리 데려 오고 싶은데.
M Well, I've never had a pet bird before. Is taking care of them difficult?	남 음, 난 반려동물로 새를 키워본 적이 없어. 새를 돌보는 게 어렵나?
W I think it's pretty easy. You just need to feed them, clean their cages, and let them have some exercise.	여 꽤 쉬운 것 같아. 먹이를 주고, 새장을 청소하고, 운동하도록 두기만 하면 돼.
M Exercise? What do you mean by that?	남 운동? 그게 무슨 말이야?
W You let them ³⁾out of their cage for a couple of hours every day.	여 매일 두어 시간씩 새를 새장 밖으로 내보내 주는 거야.
M You've really done your research.	남 당신 정말로 조사를 다 해뒀네.
W I have. I'm excited about getting a parrot.	여 그랬어. 앵무새를 데려오는 게 기대돼.
M **In that case, we should visit your friend to see her parrots soon.**	남 그렇다면, 조만간 앵무새 보러 당신 친구네를 방문하자.
W Do you want to head over there this weekend?	여 <u>이번 주말에 거기 갈래?</u>

선택지 ① 앵무새 먹이는 조금 비쌀 수 있어.
　　　② 대신 고양이를 원하지 않는다는 게 분명한 거야?
　　　③ 이번 주말에 거기 갈래?
　　　④ 새장에서 새를 꺼내놓는 걸 잊지 마.
　　　⑤ 난 새에 관한 책을 많이 읽었어.

부부가 반려동물 입양에 관해 이야기하는 상황이다. 여자가 친구에게서 앵무새 한 마리를 데려오고 싶다고 하자 남자가 조만간 친구를 방문하자고 했으므로, 이에 대한 응답으로는 구체적인 방문 날짜를 제안하는 ③ 'Do you want to head over there this weekend?'가 가장 적절하다.

어휘 adopt 동 입양하다　fur 명 털　allergy 명 알레르기　sneeze 동 재채기하다　parrot 명 앵무새　cage 명 새장, 우리　What do you mean by that? 그게 무슨 말이야?
head over ~로 가다

14 긴 대화의 응답 파악 정답 ①

W Hey, Andrew. What's wrong?	여 어머, Andrew. 무슨 일이야?
M I have a splitting headache, and ¹⁾nothing I do makes it go away.	남 머리가 깨질 듯이 아파, 그리고 뭘 해도 두통이 사라지지 않아.
W What have you tried so far?	여 지금까지 뭘 시도해 봤어?
M I've tried taking a nap, going for a walk, and drinking some water.	남 낮잠도 한번 자보고, 산책도 가보고, 물도 좀 마셔봤어.
W I think you ²⁾missed something important. How about taking medicine?	여 중요한 걸 놓친 것 같네. 약을 먹는 게 어때?
M Actually, I like to avoid taking medicine. I'm worried about ³⁾its side effects.	남 사실, 약 먹는 건 피하고 싶어. 부작용이 걱정돼.
W But it will ease your pain. And unless you take it too often, there is nothing to worry about.	여 하지만 통증을 완화해 줄 거야. 그리고 너무 자주 복용하지 않는다면, 걱정할 건 없어.
M You're right. But it will be better if I can recover through other means.	남 네 말이 맞아. 하지만 다른 방법으로 회복할 수 있다면 더 좋겠지.
W Well, you said you've tried other methods, and you still have that headache.	여 글쎄, 다른 방법을 시도해 봤다고 했는데 아직도 두통이 있는 거잖아.
M That's true. I'm not sure what else I can do about it.	남 맞아. 달리 더 뭘 할 수 있을지 모르겠어.
W **I have some aspirin right here. You should ⁴⁾give it a try.**	여 여기 아스피린이 좀 있어. 한번 먹어 봐.
M All right. I guess I don't have any other choice.	남 <u>알았어. 다른 선택의 여지가 없는 것 같네.</u>

선택지 ① 알았어. 다른 선택의 여지가 없는 것 같네.
　　　② 좋은 생각이야. 오늘 늦게 약국에 들를게.

③ 좋아. 지금 당장 약을 먹어야 하는 건 아니야.

④ 확실해? 넌 약을 좀 먹어봐야 해.

⑤ 모르겠어. 두통이 점점 심해지는 것 같아.

남자가 두통을 호소하는 상황에서 약 먹는 것을 꺼려하는 남자에게 여자가 아스피린을 먹어보라고 충고했으므로, 이에 대한 응답으로는 충고에 수긍하는 ① 'All right. I guess I don't have any other choice.'가 가장 적절하다.

[어휘] have a splitting headache 머리가 깨질 듯이 아프다 go away 사라지다 so far 지금까지 take a nap 낮잠 자다 go for a walk 산책 가다 side effect 부작용 ease 图 완화하다 recover 图 회복하다 means 图 방법, 수단 stop by ~에 들르다 pharmacy 图 약국

15 상황에 적절한 말 파악   정답 ④

W George and Teresa are looking for a good place to bring their children on a weekend evening. They think that the kids will enjoy looking at ¹⁾space through a telescope. They check the schedule of an observatory, which is open to the public on Fridays and Saturdays only. However, the schedule mentions that it is ²⁾closed on cloudy, rainy nights. George and Teresa make a reservation for the following Saturday evening. However, on Saturday morning, the sky is cloudy, so George checks the weather forecast. It says there is a 90% chance of rain that night. **So he wants to suggest to Teresa that they should ³⁾change the reservation date to a different week.** In this situation, what would George most likely say to Teresa?

여 George와 Teresa는 주말 저녁에 아이들을 데려갈 좋은 장소를 찾고 있습니다. 그들은 아이들이 망원경으로 우주 보는 것을 즐길 것이라고 생각합니다. 그들은 천문대의 일정표를 확인하는데, 그곳은 금요일과 토요일에만 대중에게 공개되는 곳입니다. 하지만, 일정표에 흐리고 비가 오는 밤에는 그곳이 문을 닫는다고 쓰여 있습니다. George와 Teresa는 다음 주 토요일 저녁으로 예약합니다. 하지만 토요일 아침, 하늘이 흐려서 George는 일기예보를 확인합니다. 일기예보에는 그날 밤 비가 올 확률이 90%라고 나와 있습니다. 그래서, 그는 Teresa에게 예약 날짜를 다른 주로 변경하자고 제안하고 싶습니다. 이러한 상황에서, George가 Teresa에게 가장 할 것 같은 말은 무엇입니까?

[선택지] ① 망원경은 밤에만 효과적으로 사용할 수 있어.

② 늦은 밤이 되면 날씨가 훨씬 더 좋아질 거야.

③ 예약하기 전에 일기예보를 확인해야 해.

④ 예약일을 다른 주로 옮기는 게 좋을 것 같아.

⑤ 천문대가 토요일마다 문을 여는지 알아봐야 해.

두 사람이 예약한 천문대는 비가 오는 밤에는 문을 닫는데, 예약 당일 밤에 비가 올 확률이 높은 것을 보고 George는 예약 날짜를 변경할 것을 제안하려고 한다. 따라서, George가 할 말로 ④ 'I think we'd better move our reservation to another week.'가 가장 적절하다.

[어휘] telescope 图 망원경 observatory 图 천문대, 전망대 following 图 그 다음의 weather forecast 일기예보 chance 图 확률, 가능성

16-17 세트 문항   정답 16 ⑤ 17 ②

M Good afternoon, everyone. As we discussed last week, communication was important for the survival of early humans. **But how did people do this without modern communication devices? Today, we'll discuss some of the** ¹⁾methods they used. First, storytelling was a common form of passing on information. Through stories, humans could share knowledge with each other and ²⁾younger generations. Then, communication became easier with the creation of early **writing systems**. The ancient Egyptians developed a type of writing that was made up of symbols. Ancient people also found ways of communicating ³⁾over long distances. **Drumming** was the first example of this. The sound could act as a warning signal or announce certain events. Similarly, **smoke signals** were used to send messages to people who were far away. For example, people made smoke to inform of ⁴⁾an approaching enemy. Now, let's watch a video about some of these early forms of communication.

남 안녕하세요, 여러분. 지난주에 논의했듯이, 초기 인류의 생존을 위해서는 의사소통이 중요했습니다. 하지만 현대적인 통신 장치 없이 사람들은 어떻게 이것을 할 수 있었을까요? 오늘은, 그들이 사용한 몇 가지 방법에 대해 알아보겠습니다. 첫째, 이야기하기는 정보를 전달하는 일반적인 형태였습니다. 이야기를 통해, 인간은 서로 간에, 그리고 젊은 세대와 지식을 공유할 수 있었습니다. 그 후, 초기 문자 체계가 만들어지면서 의사소통이 더 쉬워졌습니다. 고대 이집트인들은 기호로 구성된 일종의 문자를 개발했습니다. 고대 사람들은 또한 먼 거리에서 의사소통하는 방법을 발견했습니다. 북 치기가 첫 번째 예입니다. 이 소리는 경고 신호의 역할을 하거나 특정 사건을 알릴 수 있습니다. 비슷하게, 연기 신호는 멀리 있는 사람들에게 메시지를 보내기 위해 사용되었습니다. 예를 들어, 사람들은 다가오는 적을 알리기 위해 연기를 피웠습니다. 이제, 이러한 초기 형태의 의사소통에 대한 영상을 보시겠습니다.

[선택지] 16 ① 글쓰기의 발명이 역사를 변화시킨 방법

② 고대 문화에서 이야기하기의 중요성

③ 의사소통이 인류 문화에 영향을 끼친 방법

④ 통신 장치로 사용된 악기

⑤ 초기 인류가 소통했던 다양한 방법

17 ① 이야기하기 ② 동굴 벽화 ③ 문자 체계 ④ 북 치기 ⑤ 연기 신호

16 초기 인류가 현대적인 통신 장치 없이 의사소통을 하기 위해 사용한 몇 가지 방법에 대해 알아보고 있으므로 남자가 하는 말의 주제로 ⑤ 'different ways that early humans communicated'가 가장 적절하다.

17 이야기하기, 문자 체계, 북 치기, 연기 신호는 언급했지만 ② 'cave paintings'는 언급하지 않았다.

[어휘] survival 图 생존 modern 图 현대적인 device 图 장치 pass on ~을 전달하다 generation 图 세대 be made up of ~으로 구성되다 symbol 图 기호; 상징 distance 图 거리 act as ~의 역할을 하다 signal 图 신호 inform of ~을 알리다 approach 图 다가오다 enemy 图 적 invention 图 발명 musical instrument 악기

문제 pp.118~119 | Dictation pp.120~123

1	②	2	③	3	①	4	④	5	⑤	6	④	7	④	8	③	9	⑤	10	④
11	②	12	③	13	①	14	④	15	②	16	③	17	⑤						

• 각 문제의 정답 근거는 굵은 글씨로, Dictation 정답은 밑줄로 표시되어 있습니다.

---

1 목적 파악

정답 ②

M Hello, everyone. I have good news for those who are looking for some new books to read. A ¹⁾<u>book publishing exhibition</u> **will be held at the Gilman Center next month.** The participating publishers will display the books they published over the course of the year. They will also give ²⁾<u>attendees a preview</u> of their upcoming books. These will include e-books, which are popular among readers these days. The exhibition will also include ³⁾<u>lectures by critics</u> and talks by authors. **Make sure to be there, and start making a list of the books you want to read in the future.** Thank you.	남 안녕하십니까, 여러분. 새로운 읽을 책을 찾는 사람들에게 좋은 소식이 있습니다. 도서 출판 전시회가 길만 센터에서 다음 달에 열릴 예정입니다. 참여하는 출판사들은 그들이 한 해 동안 출판한 책들을 전시할 것입니다. 그들은 또한 참석자들에게 곧 나올 책에 대한 미리보기를 제공할 것입니다. 그 책에는 요즘 독자들 사이에서 인기 있는 전자책까지 포함됩니다. 전시회에는 또한 비평가들의 강연과 작가들의 대담도 있을 것입니다. 꼭 그곳에 가셔서 여러분이 앞으로 읽고 싶은 책의 목록을 만들기 시작하십시오. 감사합니다.

남자가 길만 센터에서 열릴 도서 출판 전시회에 대해 알려주면서, 꼭 그곳에 가보기를 권하고 있다. 따라서, 남자가 하는 말의 목적으로 ② '도서 출판 전시회를 홍보하려고'가 가장 적절하다.

어휘 publisher 명 출판사 over the course of ~ 동안 attendee 명 참석자 preview 명 미리보기, 시사회 upcoming 형 곧 나올, 다가오는 critic 명 비평가

---

2 의견 파악

정답 ③

M Honey, let's buy this coffee machine.	남 여보, 이 커피 머신을 사자.
W We do need to ¹⁾<u>replace our current one</u>, but let's wait a little.	여 지금 있는 걸 정말 교체해야 하긴 하지만, 조금만 기다리자.
M Why should we wait? Our current coffee machine hardly works!	남 왜 기다려야 해? 지금 커피 머신은 거의 잘 작동하지 않잖아!
W **I think it's always better to ²⁾<u>compare prices</u> before buying something.**	여 물건을 사기 전에는 항상 가격을 비교하는 게 좋다고 생각해.
M This coffee machine is pretty cheap, though. And it's on sale.	남 그래도 이 커피 머신은 꽤 저렴한걸. 그리고 할인 중이야.
W There are frequently better deals online. We need to look.	여 온라인에서는 종종 더 싼 게 있어. 살펴봐야 해.
M But isn't it worth a little more money to have it right away?	남 하지만 당장 그걸 가지기 위해 약간 더 돈을 지불할 만하지 않아?
W Sometimes. But it doesn't ³⁾<u>take long to check</u>, and shipping is fast these days.	여 가끔은. 하지만 확인하는 데 시간이 오래 걸리지 않고, 요즘은 배송이 빠르잖아.
M Maybe we could compare prices on my phone.	남 아마 내 휴대폰으로 가격을 비교해 볼 수 있을 거 같아.
W Great idea. Why don't we look up prices right now, then? If we don't see a better deal, we'll buy this one.	여 좋은 생각이야. 그럼, 지금 당장 가격을 찾아보는 게 어때? 더 싼 게 안 보이면, 이걸 사는 거야.
M Okay, let's check.	남 좋아, 확인해 보자.

커피 머신을 사려는 남자에게 여자가 물건을 사기 전에는 항상 가격을 비교하는 것이 좋다고 했다. 따라서, 여자의 의견으로 ③ '제품을 구매하기 전에 가격을 비교해야 한다.'가 가장 적절하다.

어휘 replace 통 교체하다 current 형 지금의, 현재의 compare 통 비교하다 frequently 문 종종 shipping 명 배송, 운송 look up ~을 찾아보다

---

3 관계 파악

정답 ①

W Hello, Mr. Harrison. Thanks for coming.	여 안녕하세요, Harrison 군. 와주셔서 감사합니다.
M I appreciate you meeting with me. **I've ¹⁾<u>collected some questions</u> to ask from my classmates.**	남 만나주셔서 감사합니다. 제가 반 친구들로부터 물어볼 질문 몇 가지를 모아왔어요.
W I'm glad to hear that. Go ahead.	여 그 말을 들으니 기쁘네요. 물어보세요.
M What made you dedicate your life to helping others?	남 무엇이 당신의 인생을 다른 사람들을 돕는 데 바치게 했나요?
W I was born in a poor family and received help from the community. So I always felt that I needed to give back.	여 저는 가난한 가정에서 태어났고 지역 사회의 도움을 받았습니다. 그래서 항상 돌려줘야 한다고 느꼈죠.
M I see. When did you start volunteering?	남 그렇군요. 언제부터 자원봉사를 시작하셨나요?
W **I helped out ²⁾<u>at local orphanages</u> when I was still a CEO. But it became my full-time job after I sold my investment company.**	여 제가 아직 CEO였을 때 지역 보육원에서 일을 도왔어요. 하지만 제가 투자 회사를 매각한 후 그건 제 전업이 되었죠.
M What is your focus nowadays?	남 최근 집중하시는 건 무엇인가요?
W These days, I run an organization that ³⁾<u>provides free medical care</u> and trains doctors.	여 요즘엔, 무료 의료 서비스를 제공하고 의사들을 훈련시키는 단체를 운영하고 있어요.
M I think many of our readers will want to volunteer after they see my article.	남 많은 독자가 제 기사를 보고 나서 자원봉사를 하고 싶어 할 것 같네요.
W I hope they do!	여 그러면 좋겠어요!
M Thank you for your time. **I'll send you a copy of the school newspaper later.**	남 시간 내주셔서 감사합니다. 나중에 학교 신문을 한 부 보내드릴게요.

두 사람이 여자의 삶에 관해 인터뷰하고 있다. 여자는 보육원 자원봉사를 시작한 뒤 다른 사람을 돕는 게 전업이 되었다고 했고, 남자는 반 친구들에게 받아온 질문을 던지며 나중에 학교 신문을 보내주겠다고 하는 것으로 보아 두 사람의 관계로 ① '자선 사업가 — 학생 기자'가 가장 적절하다.

어휘 | dedicate A to B A를 B에 바치다 be born in ~에서 태어나다 help out 일을 돕다 orphanage 명 보육원 investment 명 투자 run 동 운영하다; 달리다

---

4 그림 내용 불일치 파악   정답 ④

M	Mary, look at this photo of the living room in our old house.	

M Mary, look at this photo of the living room in our old house.
W Whoa... I haven't thought about that place in a while, Dad.
M I forgot that we had that 1)rug with the flower pattern on it.
W Mom threw it out when we moved. We still have that dolphin poster on the wall, though.
M Exactly. It's in storage now.
W Oh, right. Hmm... I like how our furniture was set up.
M Yeah, we had a 2)bookshelf next to the TV, so we spent some time reading books instead of watching TV.
W Right. **And it was nice to have that 3)square table between the couch and the chair.**
M That tall floor lamp in the back-left corner was useful, too.
W This brings back so many memories!
M Let's take a picture of this room so we can remember it.
W Good idea! I'll go get my camera.

남 Mary, 여기 우리 옛날 집 거실 사진 좀 보렴.
여 우와... 한동안 그곳 생각은 해본 적 없었어요, 아빠.
남 우리한테 꽃무늬 러그가 있었다는 걸 잊고 있었어.
여 우리가 이사할 때 엄마가 그걸 버리셨어요. 그래도 벽에 붙어 있던 돌고래 포스터는 아직 있지만요.
남 맞아. 지금은 창고에 있지.
여 아, 그래요. 흠... 저는 가구가 배치됐던 방식이 마음에 들어요.
남 응, TV 옆에 책장이 있어서, TV를 보는 대신 책을 읽으며 시간을 보냈지.
여 맞아요. 그리고 소파와 의자 사이에 사각 테이블이 있는 것도 좋았었죠.
남 왼쪽 뒤편 구석에 있는 저 키 큰 스탠드 조명도 유용했지.
여 이게 정말 많은 추억을 떠올리게 하네요!
남 우리가 기억할 수 있도록 이 방도 사진을 찍자.
여 좋은 생각이에요! 제가 카메라를 가져올게요.

대화에서 여자가 소파와 의자 사이에 사각 테이블이 있는 것이 좋았었다고 말했는데, ④에는 둥근 테이블이 그려져 있다.

어휘 | throw out ~을 버리다 storage 명 창고; 저장 bring back ~을 떠올리게 하다 memory 명 추억, 기억

---

5 할 일 파악   정답 ⑤

W Simon, why are you still awake? Your violin performance is tomorrow.
M I know, Mom. But I couldn't sleep. I'm feeling nervous.
W I'm sure it will go well. You've been practicing so much.
M Yes. I can play all the songs in my sleep.
W Then, maybe you just need to go over all the things you need. That always helps.
M Okay. I already put my violin and 1)two bows in the case.
W Great. Do you know what you're going to wear? Maybe you need to iron your clothes.
M Let me check. [Pause] Oh, no! **There's a 2)stain on my shirt.**
W **Hmm... You should wash it by hand with cold water.**
M **All right, I'll go do that now.**
W When you're done, 3)let it soak in baking soda. I'll put it in the dryer tomorrow morning.
M Thanks, Mom.

여 Simon, 왜 아직도 깨어 있니? 너 내일 바이올린 공연이잖아.
남 저도 알아요, 엄마. 하지만 잠을 잘 수가 없었어요. 긴장돼요.
여 분명히 잘될 거야. 연습을 아주 많이 해왔잖니.
남 네. 저는 자면서도 모든 곡을 연주할 수 있어요.
여 그러면 그냥 네게 필요한 전부를 점검해보면 되겠어. 그건 항상 도움이 되지.
남 알았어요. 저는 이미 바이올린과 활 두 개를 케이스에 넣어 뒀어요.
여 좋구나. 옷은 뭘 입을 건지 알고 있니? 어쩌면 네 옷을 다림질해야겠는걸.
남 확인해 볼게요. [잠시 멈춤] 오, 이런! 셔츠에 얼룩이 있어요.
여 흠... 찬물에 그걸 손빨래해야겠구나.
남 좋아요, 지금 가서 할게요.
여 다 끝나면, 베이킹 소다에 담가두렴. 내가 내일 아침에 건조기에 넣어 둘게.
남 고마워요, 엄마.

바이올린 공연을 앞두고 점검해야 하는 것들에 대해 이야기하고 있다. 여자가 얼룩진 셔츠를 찬물에 손빨래하라고 하자, 남자가 지금 가서 하겠다고 했으므로 남자가 할 일로 ⑤ '찬물에 손빨래하기'가 가장 적절하다.

어휘 | awake 형 깨어 있는 go over ~을 점검하다 bow 명 활 동 절하다 iron 동 다림질하다 명 철 stain 명 얼룩 soak 동 담그다; 잠기다 dryer 명 건조기

6 금액 정보 파악   정답 ④

M Hello. May I help you?	**남** 안녕하세요. 도와드릴까요?
W Yes. How much are these scarves in the display window?	**여** 네. 쇼윈도에 놓인 목도리들은 얼마인가요?
M **They're normally $20, but our store is selling them at 10% off right now.**	**남** 보통 20달러인데, 저희 가게에서 지금 10% 할인해서 팔고 있어요.
W Are they on sale because they are older designs?	**여** 오래된 디자인이라 할인하는 건가요?
M That's right. **But if you'd like the latest designs, we have some with very nice ¹⁾checkered patterns for $24.**	**남** 맞아요. 하지만 최신 디자인을 원하신다면, 24달러짜리 아주 멋진 체크무늬 목도리가 있습니다.
W **How about those long knitted scarves?**	**여** 저 긴 뜨개 목도리는 어떻죠?
M Those are really warm. **They go for $30.**	**남** 저건 정말 따뜻해요. 30달러에 팝니다.
W Hmm... I don't know which one I should choose for my brother.	**여** 흠... 제 남동생을 위해 어떤 걸 골라야 할지 모르겠어요.
M If he would like something simple, the knitted one would be a good choice.	**남** 만약 동생분이 단순한 걸 원하신다면, 뜨개 목도리가 좋은 선택이 될 거예요.
W **Yeah, that red ²⁾knitted one will suit him. And I'll take a checkered one for myself.**	**여** 네, 저 빨간 뜨개 목도리가 동생에게 어울릴 거예요. 그리고 제 거는 체크무늬로 할게요.
M So you want two full-priced scarves.	**남** 그러니까, 정가에 파는 목도리 두 개를 원하시는 거네요.
W Oh, wait. **I'll also get two more with the older design.**	**여** 아, 잠시만요. 오래된 디자인으로 두 개 더 살게요.
M No problem. ³⁾Will that be all?	**남** 문제없습니다. 그게 전부일까요?
W That's everything! Here's my credit card.	**여** 그게 다예요! 여기 제 신용카드요.

여자가 뜨개 목도리 하나($30)와 체크무늬 목도리 하나($24), 그리고 10% 할인 중인 오래된 디자인의 목도리 두 개($20×2×0.9=$36)를 구매했으므로 정답은 ④ '$90'이다.

어휘 latest 휑 최신의   knitted 휑 뜨개질된, 뜬   go for ~의 가격에 팔리다   suit 통 어울리다 명 정장   full-priced 휑 정가의, 할인하지 않은

7 이유 파악   정답 ④

M Hey, Charlotte. Did you find your lost wallet?	**남** 안녕, Charlotte. 잃어버린 지갑은 찾았니?
W Yes, I did. It had fallen behind my couch.	**여** 응, 찾았어. 소파 뒤에 떨어져 있었어.
M That's a relief. Do you want to ¹⁾join me for lunch at the Thai restaurant?	**남** 다행이다. 나랑 태국 음식점에서 점심 같이 먹을래?
W Actually, I can't do that today.	**여** 실은, 오늘은 안 되겠어.
M Why not? If you don't have enough money, I can treat.	**남** 왜 안 돼? 만약 돈이 부족한 거면, 내가 한턱낼게.
W I just got paid on Friday, so that's not an issue.	**여** 금요일에 막 월급을 받아서, 그건 문제가 아니야.
M Don't you like the food there? We could go somewhere else.	**남** 거기 음식이 마음에 안 드니? 다른 곳으로 갈 수도 있어.
W I like the Thai place. There are a lot of good ²⁾items on the menu.	**여** 난 태국 음식점 좋아해. 메뉴에 맛있는 음식이 많잖아.
M Do you have a test coming up you need to prepare for?	**남** 준비해야 하는 시험이 곧 있니?
W I took the last of my tests yesterday.	**여** 어제 마지막 시험을 봤어.
M Then, what's the issue?	**남** 그럼, 뭐가 문제야?
W I ³⁾already made lunch plans with someone else. I'm sorry!	**여** 이미 다른 사람과 점심 약속이 있어. 미안해!
M That's okay. Let's meet another day.	**남** 괜찮아. 다른 날 만나자.

여자가 오늘은 같이 점심을 먹을 수 없다고 하면서 이미 다른 사람과 점심 약속이 있다고 말했으므로, 여자가 점심을 함께 할 수 없는 이유는 ④ '점심 선약이 있어서'이다.

어휘 That's a relief. 다행이다.   treat 통 한턱내다; 치료하다   get paid 월급을 받다   have ~ coming up 곧 ~가 있다

8 언급 유무 파악   정답 ③

W Hey, Paul. What do you have in that large box?	**여** 안녕, Paul. 그 큰 상자 안에 뭐가 있니?
M It's full of vegetables. I ¹⁾subscribe to a vegetable delivery service.	**남** 채소로 가득 차 있어. 채소 배송 서비스를 구독하고 있거든.
W Oh, so they send them straight to your house?	**여** 아, 그러니까 너희 집으로 바로 채소를 보내준다는 거지?
M Yeah. I get a box of ²⁾fresh vegetables **every week**.	**남** 응. 매주 신선한 채소를 한 상자씩 받고 있어.
W That's convenient. What's the service called?	**여** 편리하네. 서비스 이름이 뭐야?
M It's called **Lilly's Veggies**. I really recommend it.	**남** Lilly's Veggies라고 해. 정말 추천이야.
W Where do the vegetables come from?	**여** 그 채소들은 어디서 생산된 거야?
M Everything is ³⁾grown in **the farms of Greenford County**.	**남** 전부 그린포드주의 농장에서 재배된 거야.
W Wow. The produce must be really fresh.	**여** 우와. 농산물이 틀림없이 아주 신선하겠어.
M It is. And it's a pretty good deal too. It's **$20 per week**.	**남** 그래. 그리고 꽤 싸기도 해. 일주일에 20달러야.
W I think I might be interested in subscribing. Can anyone sign up online?	**여** 구독하고 싶어질 것 같아. 누구나 온라인으로 신청할 수 있니?
M Yes, but they only ⁴⁾accept new registrations on Mondays.	**남** 응, 하지만 월요일에만 신규 등록을 받아줘.
W Oh, I guess I missed out this time.	**여** 아, 이번엔 놓친 것 같네.
M That's true, but you should try it next week!	**남** 맞아, 하지만 다음 주에는 꼭 시도해 봐!

배송 주기(매주), 서비스명(Lilly's Veggies), 채소 원산지(그린포드주의 농장), 서비스 가격(일주일에 20달러)에 대해 언급했고, ③ '채소 종류'는 언급하지 않았다.

어휘 be full of ~으로 가득 차 있다   subscribe 통 구독하다   convenient 휑 편리한   produce 명 농산물, 생산물 통 생산하다   miss out 놓치다

9 내용 불일치 파악

정답 ⑤

W May I have your attention, please? I'd like to invite you all to join the Milton Community Center Health Run. It will be held on Sunday, August 25th. This five-kilometer race is open to local residents. However, you must be ¹⁾16 or older to enter. If you'd like to participate, please sign up on our center's website by August 18th. On the morning of the race, you will need to register with event staff. So remember to ²⁾bring an identification card such as a school ID or a driver's license. There will be volunteers passing out bottles of water along the course of the race. The first three finishers will be given awards, and **all participants will get ³⁾a souvenir bag.**	여 주목해 주시겠습니까? Milton Community Center Health Run에 여러분 모두 함께하도록 초대하고 싶습니다. 이 행사는 8월 25일 일요일에 열릴 예정입니다. 이 5km 경기는 지역 주민분들에게 열려 있습니다. 그러나 참가하려면 16세 이상이어야 합니다. 참가하고 싶으시다면, 8월 18일까지 저희 센터 웹사이트에서 신청해주십시오. 경기 당일 오전에는 행사 직원에게 등록해야 합니다. 그러므로 학생증이나 운전면허증과 같은 신분증을 가져오는 것을 기억하십시오. 경기의 코스를 따라 생수를 나눠주는 자원봉사자들이 있을 것입니다. 최초 완주자 3명에게는 상이 주어지며, 참가자 전원은 기념 가방을 받을 것입니다.

주민센터의 달리기 경기에 대한 안내 방송이다. 여자가 참가자 전원이 기념 가방을 받을 것이라고 했으므로 ⑤ '최초 완주자 3명에게만 기념 가방이 주어진다.'는 내용과 일치하지 않는다.

[어휘] resident 명 주민 enter 동 (시합에) 참가하다, 출전하다; 입장하다 identification card 신분증 pass out ~을 나눠주다 souvenir 명 기념품

10 도표 정보 파악

정답 ④

M Welcome to Wallace Home Store. Can I help you?	남 Wallace Home Store에 오신 것을 환영합니다. 제가 도와드릴까요?
W Yes, thanks. I just got a new bed, and I'm looking for sheets.	여 네, 감사합니다. 방금 새 침대를 사서, 침대 시트를 찾고 있어요.
M What is your price range?	남 가격대가 어떻게 되세요?
W Hmm... I want something nice, **but I don't want to ¹⁾spend more than $150.**	여 흠... 좋은 것을 원하지만, 150달러보다 많이 쓰고 싶지 않아요.
M Okay, sure. Is there a color you prefer?	남 네, 물론이죠. 선호하시는 색상이 있으신가요?
W The walls of my bedroom are blue, **so I'd prefer to get a color, ²⁾other than blue.**	여 침실 벽이 파란색이라서, 파란 게 아닌 색깔로 하고 싶어요.
M Did you want only one set of bedsheets? Some of our sheets are sold in a pack of two.	남 침대 시트는 한 세트만 원하시나요? 저희 시트 중 일부는 두 세트씩 묶음으로 판매되고 있어요.
W **I think it would be better to get sheets that ³⁾come in a pack of two so I have an extra set.**	여 여분의 세트를 가지고 있을 수 있도록 두 세트씩 묶음으로 나오는 걸 사는 게 좋을 것 같아요.
M That makes sense. All that's left is the fabric.	남 일리 있는 말이에요. 남은 것은 원단뿐이에요.
W **Cotton is not warm enough in the winter. I prefer the other type.**	여 면은 겨울에 충분히 따뜻하지 않아요. 다른 종류가 좋겠어요.
M It looks like you've made your choice.	남 선택을 다 하신 것 같군요.

여자가 가격이 150달러 이하인 것 중에서, 파란색이 아니며, 두 세트씩 묶음으로 나오는 것 중, 면이 아닌 다른 종류의 침대 시트를 골랐다.

[어휘] price range 가격대 fabric 명 원단, 직물 cotton 명 면; 목화

11 짧은 대화의 응답 파악

정답 ②

W Hey, Walter. What is the bandage on your hand for?	여 어머, Walter. 너 손에 붕대 뭐야?
M I ¹⁾cut my finger chopping some onions last night. I should have been more careful.	남 어젯밤에 양파를 썰다가 손가락을 베었어. 좀 더 조심했어야 했는데.
W **Does it hurt when you write or ²⁾pick things up?**	여 필기하거나 물건을 집을 때 아프니?
M Luckily, there's no pain at all.	남 다행히 통증은 전혀 없어.

선택지
① 응, 네게 짧은 편지를 썼어.
② 다행히 통증은 전혀 없어.
③ 아니, 병원에 가 봐야겠어.
④ 붕대를 좀 더 사야겠어.
⑤ 네게 줄 양파 수프를 좀 준비했어.

손가락을 베인 남자에게 여자가 필기하거나 물건을 집을 때 아픈지 물었으므로, 이에 대한 응답으로는 아프지 않다고 말하는 ② 'Luckily, there's no pain at all.'이 가장 적절하다.

[어휘] bandage 명 붕대 cut one's finger 손가락을 베다 chop 동 썰다

12 짧은 대화의 응답 파악 · 정답 ③

M Emma, have you seen the leather jacket I ¹⁾was wearing earlier? I thought I left it in the living room. **W** Yeah. It was on the floor, Dad. **So I ²⁾hung it up. Why do you ask?** **M** I need to get my keys out of one of the pockets. **W** Don't worry. You can find it in the closet by the door.	남 Emma, 아까 내가 입고 있던 가죽 재킷 봤니? 내가 거실에 뒀던 것 같은데. 여 네. 바닥에 있었어요, 아빠. 그래서 걸어뒀어요. 왜 물어보시는 거예요? 남 주머니에서 열쇠를 꺼내야 하거든. 여 걱정하지 마세요. 문 옆의 옷장 안에서 찾으실 수 있어요. [선택지] ① 괜찮아요. 재킷은 곧 마를 거예요. ② 죄송해요. 추워서 그걸 입기로 했어요. ③ 걱정하지 마세요. 문 옆의 옷장 안에서 찾으실 수 있어요. ④ 맞아요. 전 앞주머니에 열쇠를 넣어뒀어요. ⑤ 잠깐만요. 그건 나머지 세탁물과 같이 있어요.

여자가 남자의 재킷을 걸어뒀다고 한 뒤 찾는 이유를 묻자 남자가 주머니에서 열쇠를 꺼내야 한다고 했으므로, 이에 대한 응답으로는 재킷이 걸려 있는 위치를 말하는 ③ 'Don't worry. You can find it in the closet by the door.'가 가장 적절하다.

[어휘] hung up 걸다; 전화를 끊다 dry off 마르다 closet 뎽 옷장 rest 뎽 나머지; 휴식

13 긴 대화의 응답 파악 · 정답 ①

M Hi, Ms. Fielder. Can I ask for your advice? **W** Sure, Nathan. I'm always happy to help a member of the film club. **M** Well, I was considering ¹⁾submitting a documentary to the Neo City Film Festival. **W** That's great. What is it about? **M** It's about a group of students who helped prevent a local forest from being cut down. **W** That sounds really interesting. Have you edited it yet? **M** Not yet. I wanted to ²⁾ask you about editing, actually. **W** I see. It can be one of the hardest parts of filmmaking. **M** Yeah, I don't know which parts to use in the film. **I have a few hours of good video.** **W** Hmm... That's too long. You should ³⁾keep it short. **M** Why do you think so? **W** The organizers of that festival don't often accept movies that are more than 30 minutes long. **M** That sounds tough. But I'll try to cut it down.	남 안녕하세요, Fielder 선생님. 조언을 부탁드려도 될까요? 여 물론이지, Nathan. 영화부원을 돕는 건 항상 반갑단다. 남 음, 저는 Neo City Film Festival에 다큐멘터리를 제출하는 걸 고려해보고 있어요. 여 잘됐구나. 뭐에 관한 거니? 남 지역 삼림이 벌목되는 걸 막도록 도운 학생들 무리에 관한 이야기예요. 여 그거 정말 흥미롭구나. 편집은 했니? 남 아직이요. 사실 편집에 관해 여쭙고 싶었어요. 여 그렇구나. 그게 영화 제작에서 가장 어려운 부분 중 하나일 수 있지. 남 네, 영화에 어떤 부분을 써야 할지 모르겠어요. 몇 시간짜리의 좋은 촬영본이 있거든요. 여 흠... 그건 너무 길구나. 짧게 해야겠어. 남 왜 그렇게 생각하세요? 여 그 영화제의 주최 측에서 30분이 넘는 영화는 종종 받아주지 않는단다. 남 힘든 일이 될 것 같네요. 하지만 줄이려고 노력할게요. [선택지] ① 힘든 일이 될 것 같네요. 하지만 줄이려고 노력할게요. ② 정말 감사해요. 그 세부 내용을 제 촬영분에 포함시킬게요. ③ 좋은 생각이에요. 제 영화를 다른 부원들과 함께 볼게요. ④ 그렇지 않은 것 같아요. 그 영화제는 다큐멘터리만 받아줘요. ⑤ 잘 모르겠어요. 저는 아직 그 숲에서 학생들을 촬영해야 해요.

영화제에 출품할 작품의 편집 방향을 상담하는 상황이다. 여자가 촬영한 분량을 짧게 줄여야 한다면서 영화제에서 30분이 넘는 영화는 종종 받아주지 않는다고 조언했으므로, 이에 대한 응답으로는 힘들겠지만 조언을 따르겠다는 ① 'That sounds tough. But I'll try to cut it down.'이 가장 적절하다.

[어휘] submit 뎡 제출하다 prevent A from B A가 B하는 것을 막다 cut down a forest 삼림을 벌목하다 edit 뎡 편집하다 accept 뎡 받아주다, 수락하다 detail 뎽 자세한 내용

14 긴 대화의 응답 파악 · 정답 ④

W Honey, can you take the kids to their ¹⁾dental appointment tomorrow afternoon? You get off work early on Fridays, right? **M** Sorry, but I can't do it. I have a meeting with a client at 5 tomorrow. **W** Hmm... I see. But I'm not quite sure what to do, then. **M** I don't understand the problem. Why can't you take them there? **W** I have a tennis lesson, and it's too late to cancel ²⁾without a penalty fee. **M** Isn't that normally on Sundays? **W** It used to be, but the schedule changed recently. **M** What is the fee for canceling? **W** If you cancel less than 24 hours beforehand, you should pay for the whole lesson. **M** Oh, that doesn't sound fair. **W** Yeah, that's why I don't think canceling is a good option. **M** **I think you should contact your tennis coach. Why don't you try ³⁾explaining the situation to him?** **W** I'll call and see what he says, then.	여 여보, 내일 오후에 아이들 치과 예약에 데려다줄 수 있어? 당신 금요일마다 일찍 퇴근하잖아, 맞지? 남 미안하지만, 못해. 내일 5시에 의뢰인과 회의가 있어. 여 흠... 그렇구나. 그런데 그러면 내가 어떻게 해야 할지 잘 모르겠네. 남 문제가 뭔지 모르겠어. 왜 당신이 못 데려다주는 거야? 여 테니스 수업이 있는데, 위약금 없이 취소하기에는 너무 늦었어. 남 그거 보통 일요일에 하지 않아? 여 예전에는 그랬는데, 최근에 일정이 바뀌었어. 남 취소 위약금이 얼마인데? 여 24시간 전에 미리 취소하면 수업료를 전부 내야 해. 남 아, 그건 불공평한 것 같아. 여 응, 그래서 취소가 좋지 않은 선택이라고 생각한 거야. 남 테니스 코치에게 연락해 봐야 할 것 같아. 상황을 한번 설명해 보는 게 어때? 여 그러면 내가 전화해서 그가 뭐라고 하는지 볼게.

① 우리는 퇴근 후에 치과로 운전해 갈 거야.

② 그런데 내가 아이들을 치과에 내려 줬어.

③ 당신은 그냥 위약금만 내면 돼.

④ 그러면 내가 전화해서 그가 뭐라고 하는지 볼게.

⑤ 우리는 테니스를 더 자주 쳐야 해.

테니스 수업을 취소할지 고민하는 상황이다. 여자가 취소 위약금 때문에 고민하자 남자가 테니스 코치에게 연락해서 상황을 설명해 볼 것을 제안했으므로, 이에 대한 응답으로는 제안을 수락하는 ④ 'I'll call and see what he says, then.'이 가장 적절하다.

[어휘] get off work 퇴근하다 client 명 의뢰인 penalty fee 위약금 cancel 동 취소하다 beforehand 부 ~ 전에 미리 drop off ~를 내려주다

15 상황에 적절한 말 파악

정답 ②

M Allison has recently gotten into cooking. She finds it ¹⁾fun to learn to make new dishes every week and is constantly searching for recipes. Today, Allison is at a bookstore looking for ²⁾an old cookbook she read good reviews about online. However, she can't find it in the cooking section. So she approaches Brad, one of the store employees, for help. Allison tells Brad what the title of the book is. Brad knows that the store does not have ³⁾a new copy of it, but he thinks it may have a used one. **Therefore, Brad wants to suggest to Allison that she should search in the ⁴⁾used books section of the bookstore.** In this situation, what would Brad most likely say to Allison?

남 Allison은 최근에 요리를 시작했습니다. 그녀는 매주 새로운 요리 만들기를 배우는 것이 재미있다고 생각하며 끊임없이 요리법을 찾고 있습니다. 오늘, Allison은 온라인에서 좋은 평을 읽어봤던 오래된 요리책을 찾기 위해 서점에 왔습니다. 하지만, 그녀는 그것을 요리 코너에서 찾지 못합니다. 그래서 그녀는 가게 직원 중 한 명인 Brad에게 도움을 요청하기 위해 다가갑니다. Allison은 Brad에게 책의 제목이 무엇인지 말해줍니다. Brad는 가게에 새 책이 없다는 것을 알지만, 중고 책은 있을 수도 있다고 생각합니다. 따라서 Brad는 Allison에게 서점의 중고 책 코너에서 찾아보라고 제안하고 싶습니다. 이러한 상황에서, Brad가 Allison에게 가장 할 것 같은 말은 무엇입니까?

① 어떤 요리법을 배우는 데 관심이 있으신가요?

② 저희 중고 책 코너에서 확인해 보시는 건 어떠신가요?

③ 원하시면 그 책 한 부를 주문해 드릴 수 있어요.

④ 저희 매장의 재고 시스템에서 찾아보시는 건 어떠신가요?

⑤ 제가 같은 작가님이 쓴 다른 요리책을 추천해드릴 수 있어요.

Allison이 찾고 있는 책이 서점의 중고 책 코너에 있을 수 있으므로, Brad는 중고 책 코너에서 찾아보라고 제안하려고 한다. 따라서, Brad가 할 말로 ② 'Why don't you check in our used books section?'이 가장 적절하다.

[어휘] get into ~을 시작하다 constantly 부 끊임없이 approach 동 다가가다 used book 중고 책 inventory 명 재고

16-17 세트 문항

정답 16 ③ 17 ⑤

W Welcome back, class. Earlier, we discussed how human settlements first formed. **Now, I'd like to talk about the ¹⁾various professions that began to appear in early human civilizations.** First off, **farmers** made up the largest group of people in this era. Farming ²⁾required a huge amount of work back then, so most people worked in the fields to produce grain. Next up, we have **bakers**. Their special skills were essential for turning grain into food that could ³⁾feed the growing towns and cities. **Soldiers** are the third distinct group that emerged at this time. They were able to fight and train for fighting full-time because, for the first time in history, there was a ⁴⁾surplus of food. And they became necessary to protect the city's resources from attack. Lastly, **merchants** were another class that began to appear at this time. They were needed to trade the extra resources of one town or city for those of another. Now, let's watch a video on early civilizations in the Middle East.

여 잘 왔습니다, 학급 여러분. 앞서, 우리는 인류의 정착지가 처음에 어떻게 형성되었는지에 대해 논의했습니다. 이제는, 초기 인류 문명에 나타나기 시작한 다양한 직업에 관해 이야기하고 싶습니다. 우선, 농부는 이 시대에 가장 큰 집단을 이루었습니다. 그 당시 농사는 엄청난 양의 일을 필요로 했기 때문에, 대부분의 사람이 곡식을 생산하기 위해 밭에서 일했습니다. 다음으로 제빵사입니다. 그들의 특별한 기술은 곡식을 성장하는 마을과 도시를 먹여 살릴 수 있는 식량으로 바꾸는 데 필수적이었습니다. 군인은 이 시기에 나타난 세 번째 독특한 집단입니다. 역사상 처음으로 잉여 식량이 있었기 때문에, 그들은 온종일 전투하고 훈련할 수 있었습니다. 그리고 그들은 공격으로부터 도시의 자원을 보호하기 위해 꼭 필요한 이들이 되었습니다. 마지막으로 상인은 이 시기에 등장하기 시작한 또 다른 계층이었습니다. 그들은 한 마을이나 도시의 여분의 자원을 다른 곳의 자원과 거래하는 데 필요했습니다. 이제 중동의 초기 문명에 대한 동영상을 보겠습니다.

16 ① 사람들이 상품을 거래하기 시작한 후 일어난 일

② 초기 인류 문명에서 농사가 변화한 방식

③ 초기 인류 문명에 나타난 여러 직업

④ 초기 인류 역사에서 직업상 요구된 특별한 기술

⑤ 인류가 더 큰 정착지에서 함께 살기 시작한 이유

17 ① 농부 ② 제빵사 ③ 군인 ④ 상인 ⑤ 사제

16 초기 인류 문명에 나타나기 시작한 다양한 직업에 관해 이야기하고 있으므로 여자가 하는 말의 주제로 ③ 'different jobs that emerged in early human civilization'이 가장 적절하다.
17 농부, 제빵사, 군인, 상인은 언급했지만 ⑤ 'priests'는 언급하지 않았다.

[어휘] settlement 명 정착지 form 동 형성하다 profession 명 직업 civilization 명 문명 make up ~을 이루다 era 명 시대 grain 명 곡식 turn A into B A를 B로 바꾸다 distinct 형 독특한, 뚜렷한 emerge 동 나타나다 surplus 명 잉여 merchant 명 상인 trade 동 거래하다 priest 명 사제

1	①	2	③	3	②	4	⑤	5	④	6	③	7	②	8	③	9	④	10	⑤
11	①	12	④	13	①	14	②	15	④	16	④	17	⑤						

• 각 문제의 정답 근거는 굵은 글씨로, Dictation 정답은 밑줄로 표시되어 있습니다.

---

1 목적 파악

정답 ①

M Hello, pet owners. Do you ever worry about your pet when you're out of the house? **Then, you should consider** 1)getting our new product, **Pet Viewer.** This is an Internet-connected camera that can be used to 2)monitor and interact with your pet. You can watch your pet through the camera at any time by connecting it to an app on your phone. It has 360-degree views and can detect both sound and motion. These features allow it to 3)send alerts if anything is wrong with your pet. The camera also includes a speaker. This will allow you to give your pet commands while you're away. So place an order for your pet today.

남 안녕하십니까, 반려동물 주인 여러분. 집 밖에 나와 있을 때 반려동물이 걱정된 적이 있으십니까? 그렇다면, 저희 신제품인 Pet Viewer를 사는 것을 고려해 보셔야 합니다. 이것은 인터넷에 연결되는 카메라로, 여러분의 반려동물을 지켜보고 상호작용하는 데 사용될 수 있습니다. 휴대폰의 앱에 연결해두면 언제든지 카메라를 통해 반려동물을 지켜볼 수 있습니다. 그것은 360도로 바라볼 수 있고 소리와 움직임을 모두 감지할 수 있습니다. 이러한 기능을 통해 반려동물에게 뭔가 이상이 있으면 경보를 보낼 수 있습니다. 카메라에는 또한 스피커도 포함되어 있습니다. 이것은 여러분이 없는 동안에도 반려동물에게 명령을 내릴 수 있게 해 줄 것입니다. 그러니 오늘 여러분의 반려동물을 위해 주문하십시오.

남자가 반려동물을 위해 신제품 Pet Viewer를 사는 것을 고려해 보라고 하면서, 제품 관련 정보를 주고 있다. 따라서, 남자가 하는 말의 목적으로 ① '반려동물 관찰 카메라를 광고하려고'가 가장 적절하다.

어휘 monitor 图 지켜보다; 감시하다 interact 图 상호작용하다 at any time 언제든지 connect A to B A를 B에 연결하다 detect 图 감지하다 motion 圆 움직임 feature 圆 기능 alert 圆 경보 command 圆 명령 place an order 주문하다

---

2 의견 파악

정답 ③

M Hey, Jasmine. You look tired. Did you stay up late last night?
W Yeah. I couldn't fall asleep.
M Let me guess. Were you using your phone before bedtime?
W Yes. I didn't feel sleepy, so I was playing a game and waiting until I got tired.
M That's probably why you couldn't sleep. **You shouldn't** 1)look at your phone before bedtime.
W But doesn't everyone do it?
M Maybe so. But the blue light from the screen 2)keeps you awake.
W My phone wasn't very bright, though. Why would it be a problem?
M Blue light is like the light from the sun. Seeing it makes your brain 3)think it's daytime.
W Really? What should I do instead of looking at my phone?
M You should try reading a book. Drinking milk could help, too.
W Okay. I'll try that.

남 안녕, Jasmine. 피곤해 보여. 어젯밤에 늦게까지 깨어 있었니?
여 응. 잠들지 못했어.
남 내가 맞춰볼게. 너 자기 전에 휴대폰 쓰고 있었니?
여 응. 잠이 안 와서, 피곤해질 때까지 게임을 하며 기다렸어.
남 아마 그래서 잠을 못 잤을 거야. 자기 전에는 휴대폰을 보면 안 돼.
여 하지만 모두 그렇게 하지 않나?
남 그럴지도 모르지. 하지만 화면에서 나오는 블루라이트가 계속 깨어있게 하거든.
여 그런데 내 휴대폰은 그렇게 밝지 않았어. 이게 왜 문제가 됐을까?
남 블루라이트는 태양에서 나오는 빛과 똑같아. 그걸 보는 것은 두뇌가 지금이 낮이라고 생각하게 만들어.
여 정말? 휴대폰을 보는 대신 뭘 해야 할까?
남 책을 한번 읽어 봐. 우유를 마시는 것도 도움이 될 수 있어.
여 알았어. 한번 해볼게.

자기 전에 휴대폰을 사용하다가 잠을 설친 여자에게 남자가 자기 전에 휴대폰을 보지 말고 대신 책을 한번 읽어보라고 했다. 따라서, 남자의 의견으로 ③ '자기 전에는 휴대폰을 보지 말아야 한다.'가 가장 적절하다.

어휘 stay up late 늦게까지 깨어 있다 fall asleep 잠들다 bright 图 밝은 instead of ~ 대신

---

3 관계 파악

정답 ②

M Good morning, Ms. Miller. Did you sleep well?
W Yes. The room was quite comfortable. **I'm really satisfied with your inn.**
M That's good to hear. I made some coffee. Would you like some?
W Yes. That would be lovely.
M Ms. Miller, you're in our town for a conference, aren't you? Are you doing a presentation?
W Well, it's something like that. I'm participating in a seminar on 1)global economic trends.
M Oh, are you studying economics?
W **Actually, I teach economics at Kensington University.**

남 좋은 아침입니다, Miller 씨. 안녕히 주무셨나요?
여 네. 방이 꽤 편안했어요. 저는 당신의 여관에 정말 만족해요.
남 다행이네요. 제가 커피를 내렸어요. 좀 드시겠어요?
여 네. 그러면 정말 좋겠군요.
남 Miller 씨, 학회 때문에 저희 동네에 오신 거죠, 그렇지 않나요? 발표를 하실 건가요?
여 음, 그런 셈이죠. 세계 경제 동향에 대한 세미나에 참석할 거라서요.
남 아, 경제학을 공부하고 계시나요?
여 사실, 저는 켄싱턴 대학에서 경제학을 가르치고 있어요.

M	Wow, that's impressive!
W	Thanks. Oh, I had a question for you. I was thinking of seeing some of the museums in the area after the conference. **Could I** 2)**extend** **my** **stay** **by one night?**
M	**Certainly!** There are plenty of great sights around here. I can give you 3)a list of tours if you like.
W	Yes, I'd really appreciate that.

남	와, 멋지시네요!
여	감사합니다. 아, 저 물어볼 게 있었어요. 학회가 끝난 후에 이곳의 박물관들을 몇 군데 볼 생각이었거든요. 숙박을 하루 더 연장할 수 있을까요?
남	물론이죠! 이 근처에는 멋진 관광지가 많이 있답니다. 원하시면 관광지 목록을 드릴 수도 있어요.
여	네, 그렇게 해주시면 정말 감사하겠습니다.

두 사람이 숙박 목적 및 관광 계획에 관해 이야기하고 있다. 남자는 여자의 숙박 연장 요청을 수락해 주었고, 여자는 대학에서 경제학을 가르치고 있다고 하는 것으로 보아 두 사람의 관계로 ② '숙박업소 사장 — 경제학 교수'가 가장 적절하다.

어휘 be satisfied with ~에 만족하다 inn 명 여관, 여인숙 trend 명 동향, 추세 economics 명 경제학 extend 통 연장하다 sights 명 관광지

---

4 그림 내용 불일치 파악　　　　　　　　　　정답 ⑤

W	Honey, is that the new playground you were talking about?
M	Yes. I think it's opening next week.
W	It looks so nice. That's a really big slide in the back of the playground.
M	Yes, but it's a bit high for small children. They can use the 1)smaller slide to the left of it.
W	The two swings next to the smaller slide look fun, too. Our kids are going to love those.
M	They look well-built, too. So even if the kids get a little wild, the 2)swings won't break.
W	Is that a sandbox over on the left?
M	Yes. Small children can bring buckets and shovels to play in the sand.
W	Where can parents sit while the children are playing?
M	**On** 3)**that curved bench** **in the front of the sandbox.**
W	Oh, it looks pretty comfortable.

여	여보, 저기가 당신이 말한 새로운 놀이터야?
남	응. 다음 주에 개장하는 것 같아.
여	정말 근사해 보여. 놀이터 뒤쪽에 정말 큰 미끄럼틀이 있어.
남	그러게. 하지만 어린애들이 쓰기엔 좀 높다. 왼쪽에 있는 더 작은 미끄럼틀을 쓸 수 있겠어.
여	작은 미끄럼틀 옆에 있는 두 개의 그네도 재미있어 보여. 우리 애들이 저걸 좋아할 거야.
남	튼튼해 보이기도 해. 그래서 애들이 약간 거칠게 놀아도, 그네가 망가지지 않을 거야.
여	저기 왼쪽 너머에 있는 게 모래밭이야?
남	응. 어린애들은 모래에서 놀 양동이와 삽을 가져올 수 있어.
여	아이들이 노는 동안 부모는 어디에 앉으면 돼?
남	모래밭 앞에 있는 곡선형 벤치 위에.
여	오, 꽤 편안해 보이네.

대화에서 남자가 모래밭 앞에 곡선형 벤치가 있다고 말했는데, ⑤에는 직선형 벤치가 그려져 있다.

어휘 slide 명 미끄럼틀 swing 명 그네 well-built 형 튼튼한; 체격이 좋은 wild 형 거친; 야생의 bucket 명 양동이 shovel 명 삽 curved 형 곡선형의

---

5 할 일 파악　　　　　　　　　　정답 ④

W	Are we ready for our family trip, Dad?
M	We should be. But let's check one last time to make sure.
W	Mom told me that she finished booking a room at a hotel near the beach.
M	And I 1)bought all the equipment including masks and wetsuits for our family to go snorkeling.
W	Perfect. Did you download a 2)tourist information map on your phone? We can look around if we have extra time.
M	Yes. I got it already. Do you want me to upload it on our group chat room?
W	No. I don't think it's necessary.
M	Okay. Is that everything? It sounds like we're ready.
W	Oh, one more thing. Did you decide where to eat dinner after snorkeling? Maybe we should 3)make a dinner reservation.
M	Good point. **Then, I'll search for some good restaurants first.**
W	Thanks. I'm really looking forward to our trip!

여	우리 가족 여행 준비는 다 됐나요, 아빠?
남	다 됐어야지. 하지만 확실히 해두기 위해 마지막으로 한번 더 확인해보자.
여	엄마가 해변 근처 호텔에 방 예약을 끝냈다고 말씀하셨어요.
남	그리고 난 우리 가족이 스노클링 하기 위한 마스크와 잠수복을 포함한 모든 장비를 사뒀지.
여	완벽해요. 아빠 휴대폰에 관광 안내 지도를 다운받아 놓으셨나요? 남는 시간이 있으면 주변을 둘러볼 수도 있잖아요.
남	응. 이미 받아뒀어. 내가 단체 채팅방에 올려줄까?
여	아니요. 그럴 필요는 없을 것 같아요.
남	알겠구나. 이게 다지? 준비가 된 것 같구나.
여	아, 한 가지 더요. 스노클링 후에 어디서 저녁을 먹을지 정하셨나요? 아마도 저녁 식사 예약을 해야 할 것 같아요.
남	좋은 지적이야. 그럼, 내가 우선 괜찮은 식당을 좀 찾아보마.
여	고마워요. 전 여행이 정말 기대돼요!

가족 여행 계획에 관해 이야기하고 있다. 여자가 저녁 먹을 곳을 예약해야겠다고 하자, 남자가 자신이 괜찮은 식당을 찾아보겠다고 했으므로 남자가 할 일로 ④ '식당 검색하기'가 가장 적절하다.

어휘 equipment 명 장비, 용품 wetsuit 명 잠수복 tourist information map 관광 안내 지도 Good point. 좋은 지적이야. search for ~을 찾다

6　금액 정보 파악

정답 ③

M Welcome to Dalton's Highway Snack Stand. How can I help you?	남 Dalton's Highway Snack Stand에 잘 오셨습니다. 무엇을 도와드릴까요?
W Hi. I'd like some ¹⁾grilled potatoes for my kids, please.	여 안녕하세요. 저희 애들이 먹게 통감자구이를 좀 사려고요.
M No problem. Would you like the regular or large size?	남 그럼요. 보통 사이즈로 드릴까요, 큰 사이즈로 드릴까요?
W How much are they?	여 얼마죠?
M **The regular one is $4, and the large is $6.**	남 보통 사이즈는 4달러이고, 큰 건 6달러입니다.
W **I'll take ²⁾two of the regular size, please.** I don't want the kids fighting over their food.	여 보통 사이즈로 두 개 주세요. 애들이 음식을 두고 싸우는 건 원치 않아요.
M Sure. Will there be anything else for you today?	남 물론이죠. 오늘 더 필요한 게 있으실까요?
W **I'll get ³⁾three hotdogs as well.** How much are those?	여 핫도그도 세 개 주세요. 그건 얼마죠?
M **They're $4 each.** So that'll be two regular-sized grilled potatoes and three hotdogs. Is it correct?	남 한 개에 4달러예요. 그럼, 보통 사이즈의 통감자구이 두 개와 핫도그 세 개입니다. 맞나요?
W That's right. **And can I use this coupon for a 10% discount?**	여 맞아요. 그리고 이 10% 할인 쿠폰을 쓸 수 있나요?
M Sure. But it's only valid if you pay ⁴⁾in cash.	남 물론이죠. 하지만 현금으로 결제하셔야 유효합니다.
W Let's see... *[Pause]* **Ah, yes, I've got some.** Here you go.	여 어디 볼게요... *[잠시 멈춤]* 아, 네, 있네요. 여기요.

여자가 보통 사이즈의 통감자구이 두 개($4×2=$8)와 핫도그 세 개($4×3=$12)를 구매했고, 현금 결제로 10% 할인($20×0.9=$18)을 받았으므로 정답은 ③ '$18'이다.

어휘 **regular** 형 보통의; 규칙적인　**valid** 형 유효한

7　이유 파악

정답 ②

M Danielle, you look exhausted.	남 Danielle, 진이 다 빠져 보여.
W Hi, Tyler. I just went jogging along the river. My ¹⁾legs are so stiff.	여 안녕, Tyler. 난 방금 강을 따라 조깅하러 갔다 왔어. 다리가 너무 뻐근해.
M Oh, I see. I'm planning to go camping this weekend. Do you want to come?	남 아, 그렇구나. 내가 이번 주말에 캠핑을 갈 계획이거든. 너도 갈래?
W I'd love to, but I can't make it.	여 그러고 싶지만, 못 가.
M That's too bad. Do you think you'll ²⁾still feel sore?	남 유감이야. 다리가 계속 아플 것 같니?
W No. I'll feel fine once I get some rest.	여 아니. 좀 쉬면 괜찮아질 거야.
M Are you behind on your science project, then?	남 그러면, 과학 수행평가가 밀렸니?
W No. I'm almost done with it. **Actually, my father ³⁾turns 60 on Saturday. So I'm going to his birthday party.**	여 아니. 거의 다 했어. 사실, 우리 아버지가 토요일에 예순이 되셔. 그래서 아버지 생신 잔치에 갈 거야.
M I didn't know! Send him my best wishes!	남 몰랐어! 아버님께 안부 전해드려!
W I will. Are you going to be back on Sunday afternoon for our study group?	여 그럴게. 너는 우리 스터디 모임 하러 일요일 오후에 돌아올 거니?
M No. I couldn't get a bus ticket ⁴⁾for an early time. I'll be back around 10 p.m.	남 아니. 이른 시간대의 버스표를 구하지 못했어. 밤 10시쯤에 돌아올 거야.
W Alright. Have fun!	여 알겠어. 재미있게 보내!

여자가 남자의 캠핑 하러 가자는 제안을 거절하면서 아버지의 예순 기념 생신 잔치에 가야 한다고 말했으므로, 여자가 캠핑을 갈 수 없는 이유는 ② '아버지 생신 잔치에 가야 해서'이다.

어휘 **exhausted** 형 진이 다 빠진　**stiff** 형 뻐근한, 결리는　**sore** 형 아픈　**be behind on** ~이 밀리다　**be done with** ~을 다 하다　**send ~ one's best wishes** ~에게 안부를 전하다

8　언급 유무 파악

정답 ③

W Zack, where did you go last night?	여 Zack, 어젯밤에 어디 갔었어?
M I was at the Public Speaking Club meeting. I joined it a couple weeks ago.	남 Public Speaking Club 모임이 있었어. 몇 주 전에 가입했지.
W That club meets at **the Lincoln library**, right?	여 그 동호회는 링컨 도서관에서 모이지, 맞니?
M Exactly. It's ¹⁾right across from our school.	남 정확해. 그곳은 우리 학교 바로 맞은편에 있어.
W What do you do during club meetings? Do you give speeches every time?	여 동호회 모임 때 뭐 해? 매번 발표하니?
M Yes. **Everyone ²⁾speaks in front of the other members for two minutes about a chosen topic.**	남 응. 모든 사람은 선정된 주제에 관해 다른 회원들 앞에서 2분 동안 이야기해.
W Is there usually a big audience?	여 보통 듣는 사람이 많아?
M Yeah. The club has **over 50 members.** So there are usually a lot of people.	남 그래. 동호회 회원이 50명이 넘거든. 그래서 보통 사람이 많아.
W I see. I was thinking of joining myself, but I'm not sure I can.	여 그렇구나. 나도 가입할까 했는데, 내가 할 수 있을지 모르겠어.
M What's the problem?	남 뭐가 문제야?
W Doesn't the club always meet on **Wednesdays**?	여 그 동호회는 항상 수요일마다 모이지 않니?
M That's right. Do you ³⁾have a scheduling conflict?	남 맞아. 겹치는 일정이 있는 거야?
W I'm busy with my part-time job on those nights.	여 수요일 밤에는 아르바이트 때문에 바빠.
M Well, if your schedule changes, you should sign up.	남 음, 일정이 바뀌게 되면 꼭 가입해.

모임 장소(링컨 도서관), 활동 내용(선정된 주제에 관해 다른 회원들 앞에서 2분간 이야기하기), 회원 수(50명이 넘음), 모임 요일(수요일)에 대해 언급했고, ③ '가입 방법'은 언급하지 않았다.

어휘 **speech** 명 발표; 연설　**audience** 명 듣는 사람, 청중　**scheduling conflict** 겹치는 일정, 일정 충돌

9 내용 불일치 파악

정답 ④

W Attention, residents. The city government has recently begun offering the Digital Drawing Course for seniors. Any resident of our city who is 65 or older is <u>1)encouraged to participate</u> in this course. Classes will be held at Parker Community Center. During the course, our instructors' goal is to teach seniors how to make drawings of people on a tablet computer. Students will practice <u>2)drawing and coloring</u> on this digital device. The entire six-week course will cost only $20. **But please make sure to <u>3)bring your own</u> tablet computer to the classes.** To make the program easier to attend, a shuttle bus will be available to take students to and from classes. If you're interested, you can register online or in person at the community center.	여 주목해 주십시오, 주민 여러분. 시 정부에서 최근 노년층을 위한 Digital Drawing Course를 제공하기 시작했습니다. 65세 이상의 우리 시 주민 누구에게든 이 수업에 참여할 것이 장려됩니다. 수업은 파커 주민센터에서 열릴 것입니다. 수업 동안, 저희 강사님들의 목표는 노년분들에게 태블릿 PC로 인물화를 그리는 방법을 가르치는 것입니다. 수강생들은 이 디지털 기기로 그림을 그리고 색칠하는 것을 연습할 것입니다. 전체 6주간의 수업 비용은 겨우 20달러일 뿐입니다. 하지만 수업 시간에 여러분의 태블릿 PC를 꼭 가지고 오십시오. 프로그램에 더 쉽게 참여하실 수 있도록, 수강생들을 수업에 등하교시켜주는 셔틀버스가 운행될 것입니다. 관심 있으시면, 온라인이나 주민센터에서 직접 등록하시면 됩니다.

노년층 주민 대상 디지털 그림 수업에 대한 안내 방송이다. 여자가 수업 시간에 각자의 태블릿 PC를 꼭 가지고 오라고 했으므로 ④ '수업에 개인 태블릿 PC를 따로 가져올 필요는 없다.'는 내용과 일치하지 않는다.

어휘 encourage 통 장려하다 instructor 명 강사 goal 명 목표 device 명 기기, 장치 register 통 등록하다 in person 직접

10 도표 정보 파악

정답 ⑤

W Good afternoon. Please let me know if you need help finding anything.	여 안녕하세요. 무엇이든 찾으시는 데 도움이 필요하시면 알려주세요.
M I'd like to buy some shampoo. Can you help me choose?	남 샴푸를 좀 사고 싶은데요. 제가 고르는 걸 도와주시겠어요?
W Sure. <u>1)What size would you like?</u> We have three different sizes.	여 물론이죠. 어떤 사이즈를 원하세요? 세 가지 다른 사이즈가 있어요.
M I think a 200-milliliter one will run out too quickly. **So 500 milliliters or more would be good.**	남 200ml짜리는 너무 빨리 다 떨어질 것 같아요. 그래서 500ml 이상이 좋을 것 같아요.
W Okay. Do you know what hair type you have?	여 알겠습니다. 손님의 모발이 어떤 타입인지 아시나요?
M **I would say it's normal.** It's not too <u>2)dry or oily.</u>	남 보통이라고 말할 수 있겠네요. 너무 건조하지도 않고 기름지지도 않아요.
W And do you have a price range in mind?	여 그럼 생각하고 계신 가격대가 있으신가요?
M **It should be no more than $20.**	남 20달러를 넘지 않아야 해요.
W Then, here are a couple of options. What kind of scent would you prefer?	여 그럼, 여기 두 개의 선택지가 있어요. 어떤 향을 선호하시나요?
M Hmm... I'm not picky. **But I don't want it to <u>3)smell too flowery.</u>**	남 흠... 제가 까다롭지는 않은데요. 하지만 너무 꽃향기가 나는 건 싫어요.
W All right. Then, this one would be perfect for you.	여 좋습니다. 그렇다면, 이게 손님에게 딱 맞을 거예요.
M Yeah, I'll take that. Thanks for your help.	남 네, 그걸로 할게요. 도와주셔서 고마워요.

남자는 500ml 이상이면서, 보통 모발을 위한 것이고, 20달러를 넘지 않는 것 중에서, 꽃향기가 나지 않는 샴푸를 골랐다.

어휘 run out 다 떨어지다 oily 형 기름진 scent 명 향 picky 형 까다로운 flowery 형 꽃향기가 나는; 꽃무늬의

11 짧은 대화의 응답 파악

정답 ①

W Andy, I can't believe the movie ended like that. I feel like the story isn't finished.	여 Andy, 나는 영화가 저렇게 끝났다는 게 믿기지 않아. 아직 이야기가 끝나지 않은 것 같은데.
M Yeah. The story isn't over. The next film in the series will <u>1)cover the lawyer</u> character's story in detail. **But the movie was pretty short, wasn't it?**	남 그래, 이야기는 아직 안 끝났어. 그 시리즈의 다음 영화에서 변호사 캐릭터의 이야기를 자세히 다룰 거야. 하지만 영화가 꽤 짧긴 했어, 그렇지 않니?
W **Actually, it was <u>2)over two hours long.</u>**	여 사실, 그건 두 시간도 더 넘었어.
M <u>Really? The time really flew by.</u>	남 <u>진짜? 시간이 정말 순식간에 지나갔네.</u>
	선택지 ① 진짜? 시간이 정말 순식간에 지나갔네.
	② 그렇겠지! 분명 너는 그 이야기를 좋아할 거야.
	③ 맞아. 그 영화는 한 시간짜리야.
	④ 물론이지. 다음 영화 같이 보자.
	⑤ 나도 그래. 그 변호사는 내가 가장 좋아하는 캐릭터였어.

남자가 영화의 길이가 짧았다고 하자 여자가 사실은 두 시간도 더 넘었다고 했으므로, 이에 대한 응답으로는 의외의 사실에 놀라워하는 ① 'Really? The time really flew by.'가 가장 적절하다.

어휘 cover 통 다루다; 덮다 lawyer 명 변호사 in detail 자세히, 상세하게 fly by (시간이) 순식간에 지나가다

12 짧은 대화의 응답 파악

정답 ④

M Honey, when is our daughter's first swimming lesson?	남 여보, 우리 딸 첫 수영 수업이 언제지?
W It's tomorrow morning. I ¹⁾can't wait to see how she reacts to the water.	여 내일 아침이야. 난 우리 딸이 물에 어떻게 반응하는지 빨리 보고 싶어.
M Me too. **She might need some help, though. Should we ²⁾go in the pool with her?**	남 나도 그래. 그런데 아이에게 도움이 필요할지도 모르겠어. 우리가 함께 수영장에 들어가야 할까?
W Yes. One of us has to hold her the entire time.	여 응. 우리 중 한 명이 그녀를 내내 잡고 있어야 해.

선택지 ① 완벽해. 그 수영복은 그녀에게 너무 귀여워.
② 물론이지. 6번 수업치고는 좋은 가격이야.
③ 문제없어. 난 내일 아침에는 바쁘지 않아.
④ 응. 우리 중 한 명이 그녀를 내내 잡고 있어야 해.
⑤ 그럴지도 몰라. 그녀는 두 달째 수업을 듣고 있잖아.

남자가 딸의 첫 수영 수업 때 아이에게 도움이 필요할지도 모른다면서 수영장에 함께 들어가야 할지 물었으므로, 이에 대한 응답으로는 그렇다고 대답하는 ④ 'Yes. One of us has to hold her the entire time.'이 가장 적절하다.

[어휘] react 图 반응하다 pool 图 수영장 the entire time 내내

13 긴 대화의 응답 파악

정답 ①

[Phone rings.]	*[전화기가 울린다.]*
M You've reached Jake Larsen.	남 Jake Larsen입니다.
W Hi. I'm calling to remind you about your appointment at Dr. Carter's office for 11 a.m. tomorrow.	여 안녕하세요. 내일 오전 11시에 Carter 선생님 병원에 예약하신 것을 다시 한번 알려드리려고 전화 드렸습니다.
M Thanks! Um... the doctor mentioned that I would need to ¹⁾get a blood test. Do I need to do anything special?	남 감사합니다! 음... 의사 선생님이 혈액검사를 받아야 할 거라고 말씀하셨어요. 제가 뭔가 특별히 해야 하나요?
W Yes. Please follow the guidelines that we sent you through text message.	여 네. 저희가 문자 메시지로 보내드린 안내 사항을 지켜주세요.
M I was ²⁾warned not to have breakfast. Is that right?	남 아침을 먹지 말라는 주의를 받았어요. 맞나요?
W Correct. You shouldn't eat anything for 12 hours beforehand.	여 정확해요. 검사 전 12시간 동안 아무것도 드시지 마셔야 합니다.
M Well, I don't like to skip breakfast.	남 음, 저는 아침을 거르는 걸 좋아하지 않아요.
W Is there a medical reason that requires you to eat?	여 아침을 먹어야만 하는 의학적 이유가 있으신가요?
M No, but that's a long time to go without eating.	남 아니요, 하지만 먹지 않고 보내기엔 너무 긴 시간이잖아요.
W I understand this requirement can cause difficulty. But we won't get accurate results from the blood test if you eat.	여 이 요구사항이 곤란을 일으킬 수 있다는 점은 이해합니다. 하지만 음식을 드시면 혈액 검사에서 정확한 결과를 얻지 못할 거예요.
M ³⁾What if I get thirsty?	남 목이 마르면 어떡해요?
W You are allowed to drink water. **The instructions we sent you ⁴⁾include these details.**	여 물은 마셔도 돼요. 저희가 보내드린 안내 사항에는 이러한 세부 내용들이 포함되어 있습니다.
M All right. I'll read through the text message.	남 알겠습니다. 제가 문자 메시지를 꼼꼼히 읽어 볼게요.

선택지 ① 알겠습니다. 제가 문자 메시지를 꼼꼼히 읽어 볼게요.
② 걱정하지 마세요. 저는 아침을 많이 먹을 계획이에요.
③ 그러셔야죠. 그렇지 않으면 검사를 다시 받으실 겁니다.
④ 맞아요. 전 이미 혈액 검사 결과를 확인했어요.
⑤ 사실이에요. 예약 시간을 변경해야 할 것 같습니다.

혈액검사 전 안내 사항을 확인하는 상황이다. 남자가 궁금해하는 내용은 이미 병원에서 문자 메시지로 보낸 안내 사항에 포함되어 있다고 여자가 말했으므로, 이에 대한 응답으로는 문자 메시지를 확인하겠다고 대답하는 ① 'All right. I'll read through the text message.'가 가장 적절하다.

[어휘] blood test 혈액검사 guideline 图 안내 사항, 지침 warn 图 주의를 주다, 경고하다 skip 图 거르다 accurate 휑 정확한 thirsty 휑 목이 마른 instruction 图 안내 사항, 설명
read through ~을 꼼꼼히 읽다 otherwise 閈 그렇지 않으면

14 긴 대화의 응답 파악

정답 ②

W Honey, do you want me to make pasta tonight?	여 여보, 오늘 밤에 파스타 만들어 줄까?
M You ¹⁾don't need to cook dinner again. You've cooked every night this week.	남 당신 또 저녁 요리하지 않아도 돼. 이번 주에 매일 밤 요리를 했잖아.
W I suppose it would be nice to have a night off. Maybe we could order some food?	여 하룻밤 쉬면 좋을 것 같긴 해. 음식을 좀 주문하는 게 좋을까?
M Sure. You can decide on the place.	남 물론이지, 장소는 당신이 정해도 돼.
W Hmm... I don't really like the delivery options.	여 흠... 배달하는 건 정말 안 내켜.
M We don't have to stay at home and get delivery.	남 집에만 머물면서 배달을 받을 필요는 없어.
W **Do you want to ²⁾go out to eat somewhere downtown?**	여 시내 어디 가서 식사할까?
M **Yes! It would be nice to get out of the house.**	남 그래! 집 밖으로 나가면 좋을 것 같아.
W Do you know if the Indian restaurant on Main Street is open?	여 메인가에 있는 인도 음식점이 영업 중인지 알아?
M It is, but the service is so slow there.	남 영업 중이긴 한데, 거긴 서비스가 너무 느려.

W Then, maybe we should try that new barbecue place ³⁾down the block from it.

M Perfect! We've been talking about going there for a while. **But do we have to** ⁴⁾make a reservation?

W I'll call now to check if we do.

여 그러면, 거기서 한 블록 밑에 있는 새로 생긴 바비큐 음식점에 가봐도 좋겠어.

남 완벽해! 우리 거기 가는 것에 대해 한동안 얘기했었잖아. 그런데 예약해야 할까?

여 내가 지금 전화해서 그래야 하는지 확인해볼게.

선택지 ① 내가 파스타 요리를 시작할게.
② 내가 지금 전화해서 그래야 하는지 확인해볼게.
③ 내가 5분 전에 주문을 넣었어.
④ 난 오늘 먹을 게 아무것도 없었어.
⑤ 어쨌든 난 인도 음식을 먹고 싶은 기분이 아니야.

두 사람이 저녁에 외식하기로 한 상황에서 남자가 음식점을 예약해야 할지 물었으므로, 이에 대한 응답으로는 확인해보겠다고 대답하는 ② 'I'll call now to check if we do.'가 가장 적절하다.

어휘 have a night off 하룻밤(일을) 쉬다 get out of ~에서 나가다 get started 시작하다 put in an order 주문을 넣다 feel like ~하고 싶은 기분이다

15 상황에 적절한 말 파악

정답 ④

M Thomas and Celine are artists who frequently work together. They recently heard about a local contest in which all of the art has to be made out of ¹⁾recycled materials. They thought it sounded fun, so they decided to make their own recycled art piece. Thomas and Celine made a sculpture together using old cans, plastic, and cardboard. Both of them feel certain they will ²⁾win the contest. However, the prize for winning is only $100. Celine thinks that they can make more money ³⁾selling the sculpture themselves, so they shouldn't just give it away. **Therefore, she wants to tell Thomas that they should find someone to** ⁴⁾purchase it instead. In this situation, what would Celine most likely say to Thomas?

남 Thomas와 Celine은 자주 협업하는 예술가입니다. 그들은 최근에 모든 예술품이 재활용 재료로 만들어져야 하는 지역 대회에 대해 들었습니다. 그들은 그것이 재미있을 것 같다고 생각했고, 그래서 그들은 그들만의 재활용 예술 작품을 만들기로 결정했습니다. Thomas와 Celine은 헌 깡통, 플라스틱, 그리고 판지를 사용하여 함께 조각품을 만들었습니다. 그들 둘 다 그 대회에서 우승할 것이라고 확신합니다. 하지만, 우승 상금은 겨우 100달러입니다. Celine은 그들이 그 조각품을 직접 팔아서 더 많은 돈을 벌 수 있으므로, 그것을 그냥 거저 주면 안 된다고 생각합니다. 따라서, 그녀는 Thomas에게 대신 그것을 구매할 사람을 찾아봐야 한다고 말하고 싶습니다. 이러한 상황에서, Celine이 Thomas에게 가장 할 것 같은 말은 무엇입니까?

선택지 ① 난 그 대회에 상금이 있는지 몰랐어.
② 내가 쓸 만한 더 많은 재활용 재료를 찾아볼게.
③ 그걸 비영리 단체에 기부하자.
④ 우리 조각품을 살 구매자를 찾아야 해.
⑤ 우리 예술 작품이 우승할 만큼 충분히 좋다고 생각하지 않니?

Thomas와 Celine은 대회에 출품하기 위해 함께 조각품을 만들었지만, 이후 Celine은 우승 상금보다 더 많은 돈을 벌기 위해 조각품을 구매할 사람을 찾아보자고 제안하려 한다. 따라서, Celine이 할 말로 ④ 'We ought to look for a buyer for our sculpture.'가 가장 적절하다.

어휘 frequently 뷔 자주 recycled 혱 재활용된 sculpture 몡 조각품 cardboard 몡 판지, 마분지 feel certain ~을 확신하다 give away ~을 거저 주다, 기부하다

16-17 세트 문항

정답 16 ④ 17 ⑤

W Good morning, class. Last time, I talked about the invention of ¹⁾virtual reality technology. **Today, I want to discuss how the metaverse may be used in the future.** First, the field of **medicine** could be transformed by the metaverse. Doctors will have access to 3D simulations of the inside of their patients' bodies. These accurate simulations will make surgeries ²⁾safer and more predictable. Next, **fashion** may work differently. Instead of making clothes by hand, designers can create them virtually and ³⁾try them on avatars, which would save time and money. Third, **education** has the potential to be very different in the metaverse. Students will have more chances for "hands-on" learning. Instead of reading about a famous historic site, they could walk around it. Lastly, ⁴⁾entertainment would likely change the most. In the metaverse, people will be able to attend live concerts remotely. Interactive movies could also become possible, where the viewer plays a part in the story. Now, let's watch a brief video on this topic.

여 안녕하십니까, 학급 여러분. 지난 시간, 저는 가상 현실 기술의 발명에 관해 이야기했습니다. 오늘은, 메타버스가 미래에 어떻게 사용될 수 있는지에 대해 논의하고 싶습니다. 첫째, 의학 분야가 메타버스에 의해 바뀔 수 있습니다. 의사들은 환자의 신체 내부를 3D로 모의실험할 수 있습니다. 이러한 정확한 모의실험은 수술을 더 안전하고 예측 가능하게 만들 것입니다. 다음으로, 패션계가 다르게 돌아갈지도 모릅니다. 손으로 옷을 만드는 대신, 디자이너들은 가상으로 옷을 만들고 아바타에게 입혀볼 수 있는데, 이는 시간과 돈을 절약해줄 것입니다. 셋째, 교육은 메타버스에서 매우 달라질 수 있는 잠재력을 가지고 있습니다. 학생들은 '체험' 학습의 기회를 더 많이 갖게 될 것입니다. 유명한 유적지에 관해 읽는 대신, 그들은 그 주변을 걸을 수 있습니다. 마지막으로, 연예계가 가장 많이 바뀔 가능성이 있습니다. 메타버스에서, 사람들은 원격으로 라이브 콘서트에 참석할 수 있을 것입니다. 또한 상호작용하는 영화가 가능해질 수 있는데, 여기서 관람자들은 이야기에 일조합니다. 이제 이 주제에 관한 짧은 동영상을 보겠습니다.

선택지 16 ① 처음에 가상현실이 어떻게 발명되었는지
② 성공적인 메타버스 상품 사례
③ 가상현실이 왜 미래에 채택될 것인지
④ 메타버스가 사용될 수 있는 미래의 방식
⑤ 시간이 지남에 따라 매체가 변화한 방식
17 ① 의학 ② 패션 ③ 교육 ④ 연예 ⑤ 관광

16 메타버스가 미래에 어떻게 사용될 수 있는지에 대해 논의하고 있으므로 여자가 하는 말의 주제로 ④ 'future ways that the metaverse may be used'가 가장 적절하다.

17 의학, 패션, 교육, 연예는 언급했지만 ⑤ 'tourism'은 언급하지 않았다.

어휘 virtual reality 가상 현실 transform 통 바꾸다, 변형하다 have access to ~할 수 있다, 접할 수 있다 simulation 몡 모의실험 predictable 혱 예측 가능한 by hand 손으로, 수동으로 potential 몡 잠재력 hands-on 혱 체험의, 직접 해보는 historic site 유적지 remotely 뷔 원격으로 interactive 혱 상호작용하는 play a part in ~에 일조하다 adopt 통 채택하다; 입양하다

| 1 | ② | 2 | ⑤ | 3 | ① | 4 | ④ | 5 | ③ | 6 | ② | 7 | ⑤ | 8 | ③ | 9 | ④ | 10 | ④ |
| 11 | ② | 12 | ① | 13 | ③ | 14 | ⑤ | 15 | ④ | 16 | ② | 17 | ④ | | | | | | |

• 각 문제의 정답 근거는 굵은 글씨로, Dictation 정답은 밑줄로 표시되어 있습니다.

---

1 목적 파악

정답 ②

W Good evening, and welcome to the Luna Kidswear fashion show. I'm designer Chloe Levine. **It's an honor for me to be here this evening to introduce my** [1)]**new children's clothing line.** I was inspired to create it after having my own kids. All the pieces are soft, light, and comfortable, making them perfect for active children. They come in neutral colors that can be easily [2)]mixed and matched. And everything is made of 100% organic cotton or other natural materials that are easy to care for. To [3)]purchase any of the items shown here today, please visit the Luna Kidswear pop-up store in London. You can also check out our online shop at www.lunakids.com. Thank you.

여 안녕하십니까, 그리고 Luna Kidswear 패션쇼에 오신 것을 환영합니다. 저는 디자이너 Chloe Levine입니다. 오늘 저녁 저의 새 아동복 라인을 소개하기 위해 이 자리에 서게 되어 영광입니다. 제 아이들을 낳고 나서 이 라인을 만들 마음이 생기게 되었습니다. 모든 옷이 부드럽고, 가볍고, 편안해서 활동적인 어린이들에게 딱 맞는 옷이 되었습니다. 옷은 쉽게 섞어서 매치할 수 있는 중간 색상으로 출시됩니다. 그리고 모든 것은 100% 유기농 면이나 관리하기 쉬운 다른 천연 소재로 만들어졌습니다. 오늘 이곳에서 선보이는 상품을 구매하시려면, 런던에 있는 Luna Kidswear 팝업 스토어를 방문해주십시오. www.lunakids.com에서 저희 온라인 매장을 확인해보실 수도 있습니다. 감사합니다.

여자가 Luna Kidswear 패션쇼장에서 자신의 새 아동복 라인을 소개하면서, 그 라인의 상품이 가진 장점들을 말해주고 있다. 따라서, 여자가 하는 말의 목적으로 ② '출시된 아동복 라인을 소개하려고'가 가장 적절하다.

어휘 **inspire** 통 (~할 마음이) 생기게 하다; 영감을 주다 **come in** ~으로 출시되다, 나오다 **neutral** 형 중간 색상의; 중립의 **organic** 형 유기농의 **care for** ~을 관리하다

---

2 의견 파악

정답 ⑤

M Caroline, are you still studying for your physics class?
W Yeah, Dad. I'm having trouble.
M Don't get worked up. Physics is a tough subject.
W But even when I review the chapter several times, I still don't [1)]get the main concepts.
M Have you been asking questions in class when you don't understand something?
W Not really. I'm too shy to speak up in front of everyone.
M In my opinion, you should [2)]never be afraid to ask questions. That's the best way to learn.
W Sometimes I don't know what to ask, though.
M You need to try. If nothing else, it will help you figure out what you don't know.
W That make sense, but I [3)]feel so embarrassed when I talk in class.
M Then, why don't you speak with your teacher after class?
W That's a good idea. Thanks, Dad.

남 Caroline, 아직 물리 수업 공부 중이니?
여 네, 아빠. 애먹고 있어요.
남 속상해하지 말렴. 물리학은 어려운 과목이야.
여 하지만 이 챕터를 몇 번이나 복습해도, 여전히 주요 개념을 이해하지 못하겠어요.
남 이해가 안 될 때는 수업 시간에 질문하고 있니?
여 그렇지는 않아요. 모두 앞에서 크게 말하기엔 전 너무 부끄럼이 많아요.
남 내 생각에, 넌 결코 질문하는 걸 두려워해선 안 돼. 그건 배우는 데 가장 좋은 방법이야.
여 하지만 가끔은 뭘 물어봐야 할지 모르겠어요.
남 노력해야지. 적어도, 네가 뭘 모르는 건지 알아내는 데는 도움이 될 거야.
여 일리 있는 말씀이세요. 그렇지만 수업 시간에 이야기할 때 너무 창피해요.
남 그러면 방과 후에 선생님과 이야기하는 건 어떠니?
여 좋은 생각이에요. 고마워요, 아빠.

수업 시간에 말하는 것을 부끄러워해서 이해가 안 될 때도 질문하지 않는다는 여자에게 남자가 결코 질문하는 것을 두려워해서는 안 된다고 했다. 따라서, 남자의 의견으로 ⑤ '모르는 것에 대해 질문하는 것을 두려워하면 안 된다.'가 가장 적절하다.

어휘 **physics** 명 물리학 **get worked up** 속상해하다 **subject** 명 과목; 주제 **concept** 명 개념 **speak up** 크게 말하다 **in one's opinion** ~의 생각에 **if nothing else** 적어도 **figure out** ~을 알아내다 **embarrassed** 형 창피한, 부끄러운

---

3 관계 파악

정답 ①

W Dr. Carson, it's great to have you back on *Morning Talk*.
M I'm happy to be on the show, Laura.
W I understand that you want to tell our viewers about food safety.
M Yes. Many people come to my clinic because their pets have [1)]eaten something poisonous.
W What are some foods that animals shouldn't eat?
M Not every animal is the same. But, for instance, chocolate is dangerous for dogs.

여 Carson 박사님, <Morning Talk>에 다시 모시게 되어 기쁩니다.
남 저도 쇼에 출연하게 돼서 기뻐요, Laura.
여 시청자분들께 식품 안전에 관해 알려주고 싶어 하신 것으로 알고 있는데요.
남 네. 많은 사람이 그들의 반려동물이 독성이 있는 것을 먹어서 제 병원에 옵니다.
여 동물이 먹으면 안 되는 음식에는 어떤 것들이 있나요?
남 모든 동물이 같지는 않아요. 하지만, 예를 들어, 초콜릿은 개에게 위험합니다.
여 그렇군요. 반려동물을 보호하기 위해 사람들이 어떻게 하기를 추천하시겠습니까?

W	I see. What would you recommend that people do to protect their pets?	남	권장되는 반려동물 사료만 먹이세요. 그리고 위험한 것은 냉장고나 진열장 안에 넣어 두세요.
M	2)Feed them only recommended pet foods. And put anything dangerous in the refrigerator or a cabinet.	여	그래도 반려동물이 위험한 걸 먹으면 어떻게 해야 할까요?
W	But what should they do if their pet eats something dangerous?	남	빠르게 행동해야 해요. 병원에 가거나 반려동물 도움 긴급 직통 전화로 바로 전화하세요.
M	You need to act fast. 3)Go to a clinic or call the pet help hotline right away.	여	지금 그 전화번호를 화면에 띄우겠습니다. 좋아요, 이 주제에 대해서는 잠시 광고를 보고 나서 좀 더 논의해 보겠습니다.
W	We'll display that phone number on the screen now. Okay, let's discuss this topic more after a quick commercial break.		

두 사람이 반려동물의 식품 안전에 관해 이야기하고 있다. 여자는 쇼를 진행하면서 시청자들에게 내용을 정리해주고 있고, 남자는 많은 경우 반려동물이 독성이 있는 음식을 먹어서 자신의 병원에 온다고 하는 것으로 보아 두 사람의 관계로 ① 'TV쇼 진행자 — 수의사'가 가장 적절하다.

어휘 clinic 명 병원 poisonous 형 독성이 있는 feed 통 먹이다 hotline 명 긴급 직통 전화, 핫라인

4 그림 내용 불일치 파악

정답 ④

M	Hi, Maria. It looks like you've changed the setup of your art supply shop.	남	안녕, Maria. 너희 미술용품점의 배치를 변경한 것 같네.
W	Yes. I think it'll be easier for customers to find what they need.	여	응. 고객들이 필요한 걸 찾는 게 더 쉬워질 것 같아.
M	What's inside those two big boxes on the left?	남	왼쪽에 있는 저 큰 상자 두 개 안에는 뭐가 들었니?
W	The paints are in those. I should organize them later on.	여	물감이 그 안에 있어 나중에 정리해야 해.
M	And all the 1)frames are hanging on the back wall now.	남	그리고 지금 모든 액자가 뒤쪽 벽에 걸려 있네.
W	Yeah. I displayed them to show all the different styles. The diamond-shaped one is the most popular.	여	그래. 난 여러 가지 스타일을 전부 보여주려고 전시해놨어. 다이아몬드 모양이 가장 인기 있는 거야.
M	What's the easel in the front for?	남	앞에 있는 이젤은 뭘 위한 거야?
W	Customers can try out the paint samples there.	여	고객들이 그곳에서 물감 샘플을 테스트해 볼 수 있어.
M	Oh, I see. **So that must be why you put the brushes and paint samples on the 2)square table next to it.**	남	아, 그렇구나. 그래서 이젤 옆 네모난 탁자 위에 붓과 물감 샘플을 올려뒀구나.
W	That's right. And what do you think of the poster of an 3)elephant by the door?	여	맞아. 그리고 문 옆에 있는 코끼리 포스터는 어떤 것 같아?
M	Oh, I like that. It reminds customers of your store's name, Elephant Paints.	남	아, 맘에 들어. 고객들에게 너희 가게 이름인 Elephant Paints를 떠올리게 하잖아.
W	Thank you.	여	고마워.

대화에서 남자가 이젤 옆 네모난 탁자 위에 붓과 물감 샘플을 올려뒀다고 말했는데, ④에는 동그란 탁자가 그려져 있다.

어휘 setup 명 배치 organize 통 정리하다; 조직하다 frame 명 액자, 틀 try out ~을 테스트해 보다 remind A of B A에게 B를 떠올리게 하다

5 할 일 파악

정답 ③

W	Steven, did you go shopping today? What's in that shopping bag?	여	Steven, 오늘 쇼핑하러 갔었니? 그 쇼핑백에는 뭐가 들었어?
M	These are my pants. I just picked them up 1)from the tailor.	남	이건 내 바지야. 방금 재단사에게서 찾아왔어.
W	What did you bring them in for? Was there a problem with them?	여	뭐 때문에 가져간 거야? 바지에 문제가 있었니?
M	They were too long, so I needed to 2)get them shortened.	남	너무 길어서, 짧게 줄여야 했어.
W	Did the tailor do a good job?	여	재단사가 잘 해줬니?
M	Let me check. [Pause] Oh, he didn't fix the hole in the back.	남	확인해 볼게. [잠시 멈춤] 아, 뒤에 난 구멍을 수선해 주지 않았네.
W	Huh? Why is there a hole in your pants?	여	어? 왜 바지에 구멍이 났어?
M	I accidentally cut them when I was removing the tags. I asked the tailor to fix the hole, but he 3)must have forgotten.	남	가격표를 제거하다가 잘못해서 바지를 잘랐어. 재단사에게 구멍을 수선해 달라고 부탁했는데, 분명 잊어버렸나 봐.
W	**You should take them back to the tailor.** The hole is small, so it shouldn't take him too long to fix.	여	재단사에게 다시 맡겨야 해. 구멍이 작아서, 수선하는 데 그리 오래 걸리지 않을 거야.
M	Yeah. I should 4)take them back there now.	남	응. 지금 거기에 다시 맡겨야겠어.

남자가 수선집에서 찾아온 바지에 관해 이야기하고 있다. 여자가 남자에게 바지 구멍을 수선하려면 재단사에게 다시 맡겨야 한다고 하자, 남자가 다시 맡기겠다고 했으므로 남자가 할 일로 ③ '바지 수선 맡기기'가 가장 적절하다.

어휘 pick up (맡긴 물건을) 찾아오다 tailor 명 재단사, 재봉사 shorten 통 짧게 줄이다 accidentally 부 잘못해서; 우연히 tag 명 가격표, 태그

6 금액 정보 파악

정답 ②

W	Welcome to Green Valley Campground. How can I help you?	여	Green Valley Campground에 오신 것을 환영합니다. 무엇을 도와드릴까요?
M	Hi. **I'd like to stay at this campground with my family tonight.**	남	안녕하세요. 오늘 밤 가족들과 이 야영장에서 묵고 싶습니다.
W	Okay. **All of our sites cost $40 ¹⁾per night.**	여	알겠습니다. 저희 부지는 모두 1박에 40달러입니다.
M	Oh, I have this coupon. Can I use it?	남	아, 이 쿠폰이 있는데요. 쓸 수 있을까요?
W	Let me see. [Pause] Yes. **You'll get 10% off the campsite itself, but not on additional purchases.**	여	어디 볼게요. [잠시 멈춤] 네. 야영장 자체에는 10% 할인받으시겠지만, 추가적인 구매에는 적용이 안 됩니다.
M	That's fine. **We will need to buy some ²⁾wood for a fire tonight.** How much are your packs of firewood?	남	괜찮아요. 오늘 밤에 모닥불을 피울 장작을 좀 사야 하는데요. 장작 묶음은 얼마죠?
W	**Those are $10 each.**	여	한 묶음에 10달러입니다.
M	**Okay, then I'll take two.** Please add that to my bill.	남	네, 그러면 두 묶음 할게요. 제 계산서에 추가해 주세요.
W	And would you also like to buy some marshmallows? We sell a ³⁾set with roasting sticks. It's great for kids.	여	그리고 마시멜로도 좀 사시겠어요? 구이용 막대와 함께 세트로 판매하고 있어요. 아이들에게 아주 좋죠.
M	How much is a set?	남	한 세트에 얼마예요?
W	It's $5.	여	5달러예요.
M	No. I think we'll be fine. We have plenty of food.	남	아뇨. 괜찮을 것 같아요. 음식이 많아요.
W	All right. Then, I'll take your card for the payment now.	여	좋아요. 그럼, 지금 카드로 결제해 드리겠습니다.

남자가 야영장에서 10% 할인을 받아 하룻밤을 묵기($40×0.9=$36)로 했고, 장작을 두 묶음($10×2=$20) 구매했으므로 정답은 ② '$56'이다.

[어휘] campground 몡 야영장, 캠프장 site 몡 부지, 장소 firewood 몡 장작 bill 몡 계산서 roast 동 굽다

---

7 이유 파악

정답 ⑤

W	Hi, Brent. Did you start your earth science report?	여	안녕, Brent. 지구과학 보고서 시작했니?
M	Yeah. I'm almost done. I'll be finished by Friday.	남	그래. 거의 다 했어. 금요일까지는 끝낼 거야.
W	Really? It's due next Monday. Why are you in such a hurry?	여	정말? 그거 다음 주 월요일이잖아. 너 왜 그렇게 서둘러?
M	I'm visiting my cousin this weekend. ¹⁾How far along is your report?	남	이번 주말에 사촌을 방문하거든. 네 보고서는 어느 정도 진행됐어?
W	Actually, I haven't started yet.	여	사실, 아직 시작 못 했어.
M	Are you having trouble coming up with a topic?	남	주제를 생각해내는 데 애를 먹고 있니?
W	No. I've already decided what I'll write about.	여	아니. 뭐에 관해 쓸지는 이미 정했어.
M	Then, you must be occupied with your other classes.	남	그럼, 다른 수업 때문에 바쁜 거구나.
W	Not really. My other classes haven't ²⁾assigned much homework.	여	그렇지 않아. 다른 수업에서는 숙제를 많이 내주지 않았어.
M	Is it because you are busy with practice for the school orchestra?	남	학교 오케스트라 연습 때문에 바빠서 그런 거야?
W	It's not that. **Actually, I ³⁾couldn't borrow the books for my report from the library.** They were checked out.	여	그게 아니야. 사실, 도서관에서 보고서에 쓸 책을 빌리지 못했어. 그것들은 대출 중이었거든.
M	Oh no. So, what are you going to do?	남	오 이런. 그래서, 어떻게 할 거야?
W	I'll go back tomorrow. They should be available by then.	여	내일 다시 갈 거야. 그때면 빌릴 수 있을 거야.

여자가 지구과학 보고서를 아직 시작하지 못했다고 하면서 도서관에서 보고서에 쓸 책을 빌리지 못했다고 말했으므로, 여자가 보고서 작성을 시작하지 못한 이유는 ⑤ '필요한 책을 빌리지 못해서'이다.

[어휘] earth science 지구과학 be in a hurry 서두르다 come up with ~을 생각해내다 be occupied with ~으로 바쁘다 assign 동 내주다; 부여하다 check out ~을 대출하다

---

8 언급 유무 파악

정답 ③

M	Honey, I don't want to waste our Sunday afternoon. We should do something fun!	남	여보, 난 우리 일요일 오후를 허비하고 싶지 않아. 뭔가 재미있는 걸 해야 해!
W	How about going to the Classic Cars Motor Show?	여	Classic Cars Motor Show에 가는 게 어때?
M	I'd love that! I didn't even know it was running right now.	남	정말 좋아! 난 그게 아직 진행 중인지도 몰랐네.
W	Yes. It **started on March 10th and will ¹⁾end on March 19th.**	여	응. 3월 10일에 시작했는데, 3월 19일에 끝날 거야.
M	Where is it being held?	남	어디서 열려?
W	At the Clifton Convention Center.	여	클리프턴 컨벤션 센터에서.
M	That's pretty close to us. We should buy tickets in advance, though. That way, we won't have to wait in the ticket line.	남	우리 집에서 꽤 가깝네. 그래도 우리는 미리 표를 사야 해. 그렇게 하면, 표를 사려고 줄 서서 기다릴 필요가 없을 거야.
W	I agree. Tickets are $20 ²⁾for adults.	여	동의해. 입장료는 어른은 20달러야.
M	Okay. What time should we go?	남	알았어. 몇 시에 가야 할까?
W	Well, it ³⁾runs until **6 p.m.** So I think we should be there by 4 p.m.	여	음, 그건 오후 6시까지 운영해. 그래서 오후 4시까지는 거기 도착해야 할 것 같아.
M	All right. And let's go out for dinner afterwards.	남	좋아. 그리고 끝나고 저녁 먹으러 가자.
W	Sounds good.	여	좋지.

기간(3월 10일부터 3월 19일까지), 장소(클리프턴 컨벤션 센터), 입장료(어른 20달러), 종료 시각(오후 6시)에 대해 언급했고, ③ '전시 차량'은 언급하지 않았다.

어휘 run 통 진행되다; 운영하다 in advance 미리 wait in line 줄 서서 기다리다

---

9 내용 불일치 파악

정답 ④

W Hello, everyone. The Oldfield Harbor Fishing Competition will take place again this year. It'll be held on May 28th. The fishing boats will ¹⁾depart from the Oldfield Harbor at 8 a.m., so everyone who wants to enter the competition will need to arrive at the harbor before 7 a.m. All boats must ²⁾return to the port by 5 p.m., which is when the competition officially ends. **This year, ³⁾the maximum number of boats will be 20, but five participants are allowed per boat, so there are 100 places available in total.** Prizes of $1,000 will be awarded to both the person who catches the most fish and the person who catches the biggest fish. Visit our website to register now for this exciting event.	여 안녕하십니까, 여러분. Oldfield Harbor Fishing Competition이 올해도 다시 열릴 예정입니다. 그것은 5월 28일에 열릴 것입니다. 낚싯배가 올드필드항에서 오전 8시에 출발할 예정이므로, 대회에 참가하기를 원하시는 모든 분들은 오전 7시 전에 항구에 도착해야 할 것입니다. 모든 낚싯배는 대회가 공식적으로 끝나는 오후 5시까지 항구로 돌아와야 합니다. 올해는 낚싯배의 수가 최대 20척이지만, 한 척당 5명이 탑승할 수 있으므로, 총 100자리가 가능합니다. 가장 많은 물고기를 잡은 사람과 가장 큰 물고기를 잡은 사람 둘에게 1,000달러의 상금이 수여될 것입니다. 이 흥미로운 이벤트에 지금 등록하시려면 저희 웹사이트를 방문하십시오.

올드필드항에서 열리는 낚시 대회에 대한 안내 방송이다. 여자가 20척의 배에 한 척당 5명이 탑승하여 총 100자리가 가능하다고 했으므로 ④ '참가 가능 인원은 총 20명이다.'는 내용과 일치하지 않는다.

어휘 depart 통 출발하다 port 명 항구 officially 부 공식적으로 maximum 명 최대

---

10 도표 정보 파악

정답 ④

W Hey, Ron, what are you shopping for?	여 이봐, Ron, 뭘 사려고 하니?
M I want to buy a bag of rice. I recently bought a rice cooker, so I want to use it.	남 쌀 한 포대를 사고 싶어. 최근에 밥솥을 사서, 그걸 사용하고 싶거든.
W That sounds good. How much are you looking to buy?	여 그거 좋네. 얼마나 사려고 하는데?
M Well, I don't want to buy too ¹⁾much at one time, **so I don't want more than 10 kilograms.**	남 음, 한 번에 너무 많이 사고 싶지 않으니까, 10kg 이상은 원하지 않아.
W That makes sense. Do you prefer white rice or brown rice?	여 일리 있는 말이야. 백미가 좋아, 아니면 현미가 좋아?
M **They say that ²⁾brown rice is healthier, so I'll get that.**	남 현미가 더 건강에 좋다고 하니까, 그걸로 사려고.
W What about grain size? That's an important factor.	여 곡물 크기는? 그건 중요한 요인이야.
M I'm going to make Indian curry. **So I better go with the long-grain rice.**	남 난 인도식 카레를 만들 거야. 그래서 길쭉한 쌀을 선택하는 게 좋겠어.
W That leaves you with two good options.	여 그러면 두 가지 좋은 선택지가 남게 돼.
M Hmm... The $25 one is cheaper, but I'd ³⁾**get better value with** the $30 bag **considering its size.**	남 흠... 25달러짜리가 더 저렴하지만, 사이즈를 고려하면 30달러짜리가 더 가성비가 좋을 것 같아.
W So do you want the more expensive one?	여 그래서, 더 비싼 걸 원하는 거야?
M Yes, I think so. I'll order it now.	남 응, 그런 것 같아. 지금 주문할게.

남자가 10kg 이상이 아니며, 현미 중에서, 길쭉한 크기의, 30달러짜리인 쌀을 골랐다.

어휘 rice cooker 밥솥 brown rice 현미 grain 명 곡물, 낱알 factor 명 요인 considering 전 ~을 고려하면

---

11 짧은 대화의 응답 파악

정답 ②

W Excuse me, sir. Is the traffic here usually this slow? I'm worried our bus won't ¹⁾arrive in time.	여 실례합니다, 기사님. 여기는 원래 이렇게 차가 많이 막히나요? 버스가 제시간에 도착하지 못할까 봐 걱정이에요.
M I've been driving buses in this area for 10 years, and I've never seen it this bad.	남 제가 이 지역에서 10년 동안 버스를 운전해 왔는데, 이렇게 심한 건 본 적이 없어요.
W Really? **Do you know what is ²⁾causing the heavy traffic?**	여 정말요? 교통 체증의 원인이 뭔지 아시나요?
M There is a lot of road construction at the moment.	남 현재 도로 공사하는 곳이 많아요.
	선택지 ① 그래서 이 조용한 길로 지름길을 택한 거예요. ② 현재 도로 공사하는 곳이 많아요. ③ 저는 버스 대신 지하철을 탈 거예요. ④ 우리는 제시간에 목적지로 도착할 거예요. ⑤ 차가 막히지 않으면 좋겠어요.

여자가 교통 체증의 원인을 알고 있는지 물었으므로, 이에 대한 응답으로는 그 원인을 말하는 ② 'There is a lot of road construction at the moment.'가 가장 적절하다.

어휘 heavy traffic 교통 체증 shortcut 명 지름길 destination 명 목적지 run into traffic 차가 막히다

12 짧은 대화의 응답 파악   정답 ①

M Ms. Brown, I ¹⁾found this wallet left in the school restroom. **W** Oh, how kind of you! Is there a student ID card in it? **M** Luckily, there is. But I don't know him. I ²⁾was wondering if you might return this to him. **W** Certainly. I'll find the owner.	남 Brown 선생님, 제가 학교 화장실에 남겨진 지갑을 발견했어요. 여 오, 정말 친절하구나! 안에 학생증이 들어 있니? 남 다행히도, 있어요. 하지만 저는 그 학생을 몰라요. 선생님이 이걸 돌려주실 수 있을지 궁금해요. 여 물론이지. 내가 주인을 찾아볼게. 선택지 ① 물론이지. 내가 주인을 찾아볼게. ② 좋아. 신분증을 새로 발급해 줄게. ③ 미안하구나. 화장실은 수리 중이야. ④ 당연하지. 반드시 제시간에 반납하렴. ⑤ 고맙구나. 내 지갑을 찾고 있었어!

남자가 발견한 지갑을 주인에게 돌려줄 수 있는지 물었으므로, 이에 대한 응답으로는 그렇게 하겠다고 대답하는 ① 'Certainly. I'll find the owner.'가 가장 적절하다.

어휘 wonder 통 궁금하다 issue 통 발급하다 under repair 수리 중인

13 긴 대화의 응답 파악   정답 ③

W Harold! It's so good to see you! How was ¹⁾your research project in Antarctica? **M** Incredible, but I'm happy to be back. **W** I'll bet. By the way, you've become my daughter's hero. She really looks up to her Uncle Harold. **M** Does she still want to major in science when she ²⁾goes to college? **W** Yes! And now she wants to explore Antarctica. **M** I'm sure she can do it! Is she at home now? **W** No. She's out with some friends. **M** That's too bad. I have a lot of great photos I think she would be interested in. **W** Oh, I'm sure she would. Are you going to be in town for long? **M** I'll be staying at Mom and Dad's house for a couple of weeks. **W** My daughter would love it if you ³⁾invited her over there to tell her about your experience. **M** I'll ask her to come listen to my stories about Antarctica.	여 Harold! 널 보니 정말 반갑구나! 남극에서의 연구 프로젝트는 어땠니? 남 놀랍도록 좋았지만, 돌아와서 기뻐. 여 틀림없이 그렇겠어. 그런데, 넌 우리 딸의 영웅이 되었어. 딸이 Harold 삼촌을 정말 존경하고 있어. 남 그녀는 여전히 대학에 가면 과학을 전공하고 싶어 하는 거야? 여 응! 그리고 이제는 남극을 탐험하고 싶어 해. 남 분명히 할 수 있을 거야! 지금 집에 있어? 여 아니. 친구들과 외출 중이야. 남 유감이야. 그녀가 관심을 가질 만한 멋진 사진들이 많이 있는데. 여 오, 분명 그럴 거야. 너 동네에 오래 있을 거니? 남 부모님 집에서 몇 주 동안 있을 거야. 여 네가 우리 딸을 초대해서 네 경험담을 말해주면 그 애가 정말 좋아할 텐데. 남 그녀에게 남극에 관한 이야기를 들으러 오라고 할게. 선택지 ① TV 화면에 내 사진들을 띄워도 될까? ② 안타깝게도 며칠 후에 동네를 떠나야 해. ③ 그녀에게 남극에 관한 이야기를 들으러 오라고 할게. ④ 내가 기꺼이 대학 추천서를 써 줄게. ⑤ 극소수의 과학자만이 남극을 방문할 기회를 얻어.

남극에서 돌아온 남자와 이야기하는 상황이다. 여자가 남자에게 남극을 탐험하고 싶어 하는 자기 딸을 초대해서 경험담을 말해주면 좋겠다고 제안했으므로, 이에 대한 응답으로는 제안을 수락하는 ③ 'I'll ask her to come listen to my stories about Antarctica.'가 가장 적절하다.

어휘 Antarctica 명 남극 I'll bet. 틀림없이 그렇겠어. by the way 그런데 look up to ~를 존경하다 major in ~을 전공하다 recommendation letter 추천장

14 긴 대화의 응답 파악   정답 ⑤

M Mom, can I ask you something? **W** Sure, Paul. What is it? **M** How did you learn to cook so well? **W** Well, I followed a lot of recipes at first. Once I knew the basics, I started experimenting more. **M** I see. I've been watching some cooking videos online. But I've failed each time I ¹⁾tried to copy them. **W** What's the hardest part about cooking for you? **M** Well, I don't know how long to cook things. The dishes I make are usually overcooked. **W** I think that's something you have to learn from experience. ²⁾Practice makes perfect. **M** But I don't get a chance to cook very often. **W** Then, why don't you start helping me when I make dinner? You can make a dish tonight. **M** Great! But can you let me know when to ³⁾turn off the gas? **W** Definitely. I'll help you avoid cooking it for too long.	남 엄마, 뭐 좀 여쭤봐도 돼요? 여 물론이지, Paul. 뭔데? 남 엄마는 어떻게 그렇게 요리를 잘 배우셨어요? 여 음, 처음에는 많은 요리법을 따라 했어. 일단 기본적인 것을 알게 되자, 더 많은 시도를 해보기 시작했지. 남 그렇군요. 저는 온라인으로 요리 동영상을 좀 보고 있어요. 그런데 그걸 따라 하려고 할 때마다 실패했어요. 여 요리할 때 가장 어려운 부분이 뭐니? 남 글쎄요. 얼마나 오래 요리해야 할지 모르겠어요. 제가 만드는 요리들은 보통 너무 익었어요. 여 그건 경험에서 배워야 할 것 같구나. 연습이 완벽을 만든단다. 남 하지만 요리할 기회가 자주 없어요. 여 그러면 내가 저녁을 만들 때 도와주는 게 어떠니? 오늘 밤에도 요리를 할 수 있어. 남 좋아요! 하지만 언제 가스 불을 꺼야 하는지 알려주실 수 있나요? 여 물론이지. 너무 오래 요리하지 않도록 도와줄게.

① 좋아. 요리 실력이 정말 많이 늘었구나.

② 꼭 그렇지는 않아. 요리법을 따를 필요는 없어.

③ 맞아. 넌 매일 밤 요리를 만들어야 해.

④ 확실해. 그건 내가 먹어본 음식 중에 가장 맛이 없었어.

⑤ 물론이지. 너무 오래 요리하지 않도록 도와줄게.

요리를 잘하는 방법에 관해 이야기하는 상황에서 적당한 조리 시간을 잘 모르는 남자가 언제 가스 불을 꺼야 하는지 알려달라고 부탁했으므로, 이에 대한 응답으로는 그러겠다고 대답하는 ⑤ 'Definitely. I'll help you avoid cooking it for too long.'이 가장 적절하다.

어휘 once 접 일단 ~하자 experiment 통 시도하다; 실험하다 copy 통 따라 하다; 복사하다 overcooked 형 너무 익힌 get a chance to ~할 기회를 얻다

15 상황에 적절한 말 파악

정답 ④

W Brandon is a park ranger at a national park. Recently, many visitors have been [1]leaving the designated trails and walking through off-limits parts of the forest. This is harming the forest environment. So Brandon has decided to post signs that warn visitors not to leave the trails. Last week, he went to a sign maker, Alice, and asked her to make a design. However, when Alice showed him the design today, Brandon was not pleased. He requested that the word *trail* be [2]written in red letters on the sign, but instead it is written in black. **Therefore, he wants to ask that she redesign the sign [3]using his guidelines.** In this situation, what would Brandon most likely say to Alice?

여 Brandon은 국립공원의 삼림 경비원입니다. 최근, 많은 방문객이 지정된 등산로를 벗어나 삼림의 출입 금지 구역을 걷고 있습니다. 이것은 삼림 환경을 해치고 있습니다. 그래서, Brandon은 방문객들에게 등산로를 벗어나지 말라고 경고하는 표지판을 세우기로 정했습니다. 지난주에, 그는 표지판 제작자인 Alice에게 가서 디자인을 만들어 달라고 부탁했습니다. 하지만, 오늘 Alice가 그에게 디자인을 보여주었을 때, Brandon은 만족스럽지 않았습니다. 그는 표지판에 '등산로'라는 단어를 빨간색 글씨로 써달라고 요청했는데, 그것은 대신 검은색으로 쓰여 있습니다. 따라서, 그는 그녀에게 그의 지시 사항을 가지고 표지판을 다시 디자인해달라고 요청하고 싶습니다. 이러한 상황에서, Brandon이 Alice에게 가장 할 것 같은 말은 무엇입니까?

선택지 ① 이번 달 말까지 디자인이 끝났으면 좋겠습니다.

② 이 표지판은 친환경 재료로 만들어져야 합니다.

③ 등산로의 다른 구역에 둘 다른 디자인이 필요합니다.

④ 제 지시에 따라 표지판을 다시 만들어 주셨으면 좋겠습니다.

⑤ 빨간색은 규칙 위반의 위험성을 강조해 줍니다.

Alice가 Brandon이 원한 대로 표지판 디자인을 해주지 않았기에, Brandon은 자기 지시 사항대로 표지판을 다시 디자인해달라고 요청하려 한다. 따라서, Brandon이 할 말로 ④ 'I'd like you remake this sign according to my directions.'가 가장 적절하다.

어휘 ranger 명 삼림 경비원 designated 형 지정된 trail 명 등산로 off-limits 형 출입 금지 구역의 harm 통 해치다 post a sign 표지판을 세우다 pleased 형 만족스러운; 기쁜 eco-friendly 형 친환경의 emphasize 통 강조하다 break a rule 규칙을 위반하다

16-17 세트 문항

정답 16 ② 17 ④

M Good afternoon, class. In the last lecture, we looked at plants that appear in Korean paintings throughout history. **Today, we will examine the [1]symbolic meanings of animals in traditional Korean art.** First, there's the **pig**, which most people associate with wealth. This idea is so common that there is a saying that when you see a [2]pig in your dream, you'll have good luck. Similarly, the **bat** is a traditional symbol of good fortune. Therefore, the pattern of bats' wings was carved on furniture and buildings in the past to [3]bring good luck. Next, there is the long-lived **turtle**. Many of them can live for centuries. Not surprisingly, this animal symbolizes longevity in Korean artwork. Lastly, the **tiger** is a familiar symbol. These animals [4]represent bravery and protection, so paintings of them were often hung on gates to keep away evil. Now, please turn your attention to the screen. I'll show you some examples of these creatures in traditional paintings.

남 안녕하십니까, 학급 여러분. 지난 강의에서, 우리는 역사를 통틀어 한국화에 등장하는 식물들을 살펴봤습니다. 오늘은, 한국 전통 예술에서 동물이 갖는 상징적인 의미에 대해 살펴보겠습니다. 첫째, 돼지가 있는데, 대부분의 사람이 그걸 부유함과 연결 지어 생각합니다. 이런 생각은 아주 흔해서 꿈에서 돼지를 보면, 행운이 생긴다는 말이 있습니다. 비슷하게, 박쥐는 전통적으로 행운의 상징입니다. 그러므로, 박쥐의 날개 문양은 행운을 불러들이려고 과거 가구와 건물들에 조각되었습니다. 다음으로, 장수하는 거북이가 있습니다. 많은 거북이가 수 세기 동안 살 수 있습니다. 놀랄 것도 없이, 이 동물은 한국 예술 작품에서 장수를 상징합니다. 마지막으로, 호랑이는 친숙한 상징입니다. 이 동물은 용맹과 보호를 나타내므로, 호랑이 그림은 종종 악귀를 물리치기 위해 대문에 걸렸습니다. 이제, 화면으로 주의를 돌려주십시오. 전통적인 그림에서 이 동물들의 몇 가지 예시를 보여드리겠습니다.

선택지 16 ① 동물과 관련된 한국의 옛날 속담

② 한국의 전통 예술에서 동물이 상징하는 것

③ 한국 문학에서 동물 캐릭터의 묘사

④ 한국에서 행운을 가져온다고 알려진 흔한 동물

⑤ 고대 한국 그림에 나오는 신화적인 동물

17 ① 돼지 ② 박쥐 ③ 거북이 ④ 닭 ⑤ 호랑이

16 한국 전통 예술에서 동물이 갖는 상징적인 의미에 관해 살펴보고 있으므로 남자가 하는 말의 주제로 ② 'what animals stand for in traditional Korean art'가 가장 적절하다.

17 돼지, 박쥐, 거북이, 호랑이는 언급했지만 ④ 'chicken'은 언급하지 않았다.

어휘 throughout 전 ~을 통틀어; ~ 내내 examine 통 살펴보다 symbolic 형 상징적인 (symbolize 통 상징하다) associate A with B A를 B와 연결 지어 생각하다 wealth 명 부유함, 부 fortune 명 운 carve 통 조각하다 longevity 명 장수 represent 통 나타내다 keep away ~을 물리치다 turn one's attention to ~으로 주의를 돌리다 stand for ~을 상징하다 depiction 명 묘사 mythical 형 신화적인

1	③	2	④	3	①	4	④	5	②	6	④	7	④	8	②	9	⑤	10	③
11	①	12	③	13	⑤	14	③	15	②	16	④	17	②						

• 각 문제의 정답 근거는 굵은 글씨로, Dictation 정답은 밑줄로 표시되어 있습니다.

---

1 목적 파악

정답 ③

W Attention, listeners. This is Melinda Kim with a news update. **Air quality in the Central City area is expected to be very poor for the next few days, with** 1)high levels of fine dust. **So please remain indoors as much as you can for the time being.** As physical activities in these conditions can be dangerous, **it is** 2)advisable to wear **a mask if you need to do work outside.** To improve air quality, the city council has decided to limit the number of cars on the road and make public transportation 3)temporarily free during rush hour. These policies are expected to remain in place until at least Friday. Stay tuned for more updates.

여 청취자 여러분, 주목해주세요. 최신 소식을 가지고 온 Melinda Kim입니다. 앞으로 며칠간 미세먼지 농도가 높아지면서, 센트럴 시티 지역의 대기질이 매우 나쁠 것으로 예상됩니다. 그러니 당분간은 가급적 실내에 머무르시기를 바랍니다. 이런 환경에서 신체활동을 하면 위험할 수 있기 때문에, 야외활동을 해야 한다면 마스크를 착용하시기를 권합니다. 대기질을 개선하기 위해, 시의회는 도로의 차량 수를 제한하고 출퇴근 시간 동안 대중교통을 일시적으로 무료화 하기로 결정했습니다. 이러한 정책은 적어도 금요일까지는 유지될 것으로 예상됩니다. 더 많은 최신 정보를 위해 채널을 고정해주세요.

여자가 며칠간 미세먼지 농도가 높아질 것으로 예상되니 실내에 머무르고 야외활동 시 마스크를 착용하는 등 주의 사항을 설명하고 있다. 따라서, 여자가 하는 말의 목적으로 ③ '고농도 미세먼지 대응 요령을 설명하려고'가 가장 적절하다.

어휘 fine dust 미세먼지 for the time being 당분간 advisable 휑 권할 만한, 바람직한 council 몡 의회; 위원회 temporarily 闬 일시적으로 policy 몡 정책 remain in place 계속 유지되다 stay tuned 채널을 고정하다

---

2 의견 파악

정답 ④

W What are you watching, Charles?

M I'm watching a short video about the Industrial Revolution. It's for my history report.

W Well, it doesn't seem like it 1)includes enough information for a report.

M I'll watch a few more videos, though. I find them more interesting than other ways of researching.

W I understand, **but you should refer to academic books or journals** 2)when doing research.

M But that sounds more difficult and boring.

W It is, but you'll find they have much more information.

M I guess that's true.

W You'll get a better grade if you don't cut corners. Plus, those materials are 3)accurate and reliable.

M Yeah, I would hate for anything in my report to be incorrect.

W You can even find many books and journals online nowadays.

M You're right. I'll start doing some research now.

여 뭘 보고 있니, Charles?

남 산업혁명에 관한 짧은 동영상을 보고 있어. 내 역사 보고서를 위해서야.

여 글쎄, 거기에 보고서에 쓸 충분한 정보가 담겨 있을 것 같지 않아.

남 그래도 동영상 몇 개를 더 볼래. 그게 다른 조사 방법보다 더 흥미롭다고 생각하거든.

여 이해는 하지만, 조사할 때는 학술서나 학술지를 참고해야 해.

남 하지만 그건 더 어렵고 지루할 것 같아.

여 그렇긴 하지만, 너는 그것들에 훨씬 더 많은 정보가 있다는 것을 알게 될 거야.

남 그건 사실인 것 같아.

여 쉽게 하려고 원칙을 무시하지 않는다면, 넌 더 좋은 점수를 받을 수 있을 거야. 게다가, 그런 자료들은 정확하고 신뢰할 수 있잖아.

남 응, 내 보고서에 실린 어떤 것도 부정확한 건 싫어.

여 요즘에는 심지어 온라인으로 많은 도서와 학술지를 찾을 수 있어.

남 네 말이 맞아. 지금부터 조사를 시작할게.

동영상을 보고 역사 보고서를 쓰려는 남자에게 여자가 보고서를 쓰기 위해 조사할 때는 학술서나 학술지를 참고해야 한다고 했다. 따라서, 여자의 의견으로 ④ '자료 조사 시 학술서나 학술지를 참고해야 한다.'가 가장 적절하다.

어휘 Industrial Revolution 산업혁명 refer to ~을 참고하다 journal 몡 학술지; 일지, 일기 cut corners (쉽게 하려고) 원칙을 무시하다 accurate 휑 정확한 reliable 휑 신뢰할 수 있는

---

3 관계 파악

정답 ①

W Hi, Mr. Davis. How are you feeling today?

M I'm okay. But my 1)back is quite sore.

W I see. **You suffered your injury during a recent golf tournament, right?**

M That's correct. It was 2)the most painful injury **I've experienced playing sports.**

W My husband was watching the golf tournament, actually. He was cheering for you.

여 안녕하세요, Davis 씨. 오늘 몸은 좀 어떠세요?

남 괜찮아요. 하지만 허리가 꽤 아파요.

여 그러시군요. 최근 골프 대회에서 부상을 당하셨죠?

남 맞아요. 그건 제가 운동을 하면서 겪었던 것 중 가장 고통스러운 부상이었어요.

여 제 남편이 실제로 그 골프 대회를 보고 있었어요. 그는 당신을 응원하고 있었어요.

M That's good to hear, but is there anything you recommend eating that would speed up my recovery? **I know you've helped other** [3])athletes with their diets **in the past.**	남 듣기 좋은 말이네요. 그런데 제 회복 속도를 높일 수 있는 추천할 만한 음식이 있나요? 제가 알기로 당신은 과거에 다른 운동선수들의 식단을 도왔잖아요.
W The most important thing is to increase your protein intake.	여 가장 중요한 것은 단백질 섭취를 늘리는 거예요.
M Does that mean eating more meat?	남 고기를 더 많이 먹으라는 뜻인가요?
W Not exactly. You'll need to avoid food that is high in fat. Fish is a better choice.	여 꼭 그렇지는 않아요. 지방이 많은 음식은 피해야 하거든요. 생선이 더 나은 선택이에요.
M I can do that. Is there anything else you'd recommend?	남 그건 할 수 있어요. 더 추천할 만한 것이 있나요?
W **I'll make a** [4])comprehensive meal plan **for you, with all the vitamins and minerals you need.**	여 필요한 모든 비타민과 미네랄이 포함된 종합적인 식단 계획을 세워 드릴게요.
M I see. That sounds helpful.	남 그렇군요. 도움이 될 것 같네요.

두 사람이 남자의 식단 계획에 관해 이야기하고 있다. 여자는 과거에 다른 운동선수들의 식단을 도운 적이 있으며 지금도 남자의 식단 계획을 세워주겠다고 하고 있고, 남자는 골프 대회에 출전했다가 부상을 당했다고 하는 것으로 보아 두 사람의 관계로 ① '영양사 ─ 골프 선수'가 가장 적절하다.

어휘 sore 형 아픈 suffer 동 (부상 등을) 당하다, 겪다 cheer for ~를 응원하다 protein 명 단백질 intake 명 섭취 comprehensive 형 종합적인

---

4 그림 내용 불일치 파악   정답 ④

W Hey, Ian. What are you looking at on your phone?	여 안녕, Ian. 휴대폰으로 뭘 보고 있니?
M Hi, Morgan. It's a picture my dad took by the lake last weekend.	남 안녕, Morgan. 이건 지난 주말 호숫가에서 우리 아버지가 찍어주신 사진이야.
W Can I see? [Pause] Oh, it looks beautiful. That tree next to you is huge.	여 봐도 될까? [잠시 멈춤] 오, 아름다워 보인다. 네 옆에 있는 저 나무는 진짜 커.
M Yeah, it provided a lot of shade.	남 그래, 나무가 큰 그늘을 드리웠어.
W Is that why you [1])put your round mat there?	여 그래서 거기에 둥근 매트를 둔 거야?
M Right. We sat on it and looked out at the lake.	남 맞아. 우리는 그 위에 앉아서 호수를 내다봤어.
W I like [2])that striped T-shirt you're wearing. How was the weather there?	여 네가 입고 있는 줄무늬 티셔츠가 마음에 들어. 거기 날씨는 어땠어?
M It was perfect. But the path was in the sun, so I sweated a bit while walking.	남 완벽했어. 하지만 산책길에는 햇빛이 잘 들어서 걷는 동안 땀을 좀 흘렸어.
W **Those three flowers** [3])by the path **are also lovely.**	여 산책길 옆에 있는 세 송이의 꽃도 사랑스러워.
M Yeah. And did you notice the duck floating on the water?	남 응. 그리고 물 위에 떠 있는 오리를 알아차렸니?
W That's so cute. It seems like you had a great time.	여 너무 귀여워. 즐거운 시간을 보냈던 것 같네.
M We did. You should try to go there soon, too.	남 그랬지. 너도 조만간 거기 가 보도록 해.

대화에서 여자가 산책길 옆에 세 송이의 꽃이 있다고 말했는데, ④에는 두 송이의 꽃만 그려져 있다.

어휘 shade 명 그늘 path 명 산책길, 길 sweat 동 땀을 흘리다 float 동 떠 있다, 뜨다

---

5 할 일 파악   정답 ②

W Honey, are you ready for our trip tomorrow?	여 여보, 우리 내일 여행 갈 준비는 다 됐어?
M I just [1])finished packing my suitcase. But I need to check a few things. Do we have any sunscreen?	남 방금 여행 가방을 다 쌌어. 하지만 몇 가지 확인해야 해. 자외선 차단제는 있어?
W Yeah! I bought some this afternoon. It's in my bag.	여 응! 오늘 오후에 좀 샀어. 내 가방 안에 있어.
M Okay. And you arranged for a cat sitter, right?	남 알았어. 그리고 당신이 고양이를 돌봐줄 사람을 준비한 거 맞지?
W Yes. My cousin is [2])coming to feed our cat.	여 응. 내 사촌이 우리 고양이에게 먹이를 주러 올 거야.
M And what about transportation to the airport? Did you arrange for a taxi?	남 그리고 공항까지 가는 교통편은? 택시 예약했어?
W Oh, I canceled that. Instead, I booked express train tickets.	여 아, 그건 취소했어. 대신에, 급행 기차표를 예매했어.
M Yeah, that will be much faster. **When does it leave?**	남 그래, 그게 훨씬 빠르겠다. 언제 출발이야?
W I can't remember off the top of my head. **I will check** [3])the departure time **on the website right away.**	여 당장 생각이 안 나네. 지금 바로 웹사이트에서 출발 시간을 확인해 볼게.
M Thanks. Why don't I take out the trash in the meantime?	남 고마워. 그동안 내가 쓰레기를 밖에 내놓을까?
W Good idea. That's something we don't want to forget!	여 좋은 생각이야. 그건 우리가 잊고 싶지 않은 것이니까!

다음 날 갈 여행을 위한 준비 사항을 점검하고 있다. 남자가 급행 기차가 언제 출발하는지 묻자, 여자가 지금 바로 웹사이트에서 확인해 보겠다고 했으므로 여자가 할 일로 ② '기차 출발 시간 확인하기'가 가장 적절하다.

어휘 sunscreen 명 자외선 차단제 arrange for ~을 준비하다, 마련하다 off the top of one's head 당장 생각나는 대로, 즉석에서 departure 명 출발 in the meantime 그동안에

6 금액 정보 파악

정답 ④

W I see you've found ¹⁾our new fountain pens.	여 저희의 새로 나온 만년필을 발견하셨군요.
M Yes. This one looks nice. **I was thinking of buying it with ²⁾a bottle of blue ink.**	남 네. 이거 괜찮아 보여요. 저는 파란색 잉크 한 병과 함께 그걸 살 생각이었어요.
W Great! I should mention that there's a discount. **It's 10% off the original price of both.**	여 좋아요! 할인이 있다는 것을 말씀드려야겠군요. 둘 다 원래 가격에서 10% 할인 돼요.
M Okay, and how much is that?	남 좋아요, 그러면 얼마죠?
W **Normally, the pen would be $80, and the ink would be another $10.**	여 보통은 펜이 80달러이고, 잉크는 별도로 10달러예요.
M That works for me. My son is going to love this.	남 괜찮네요. 저희 아들이 이걸 좋아할 거예요.
W Oh, is it a present for your son?	여 아, 아드님에게 줄 선물인가요?
M Yes. He's graduating this weekend, so I need it to be wrapped.	남 네. 이번 주말에 졸업하거든요, 그러니 포장해주세요.
W **There is an additional fee for wrapping.**	여 포장에는 추가 금액이 있습니다.
M How much ³⁾is the charge?	남 요금이 얼마인데요?
W **It's $5 on top of the discounted total.**	여 할인된 총액 외에 5달러입니다.
M **That sounds reasonable.** It wouldn't look good if I tried to ⁴⁾wrap it myself.	남 적당한 것 같네요. 제가 직접 포장을 하려 하면 보기 좋지 않을 테니까요.
W I'll have it ready for you in a couple of minutes.	여 금방 준비해 드릴게요.

남자가 사려는 펜과 잉크는 각각 원래 가격에서 10% 할인($80×0.9+$10×0.9=$81)이 되었고, 포장비($5)가 추가로 발생하였으므로 정답은 ④ '$86'이다.

어휘 fountain pen 만년필 original 휑 원래의 That works for me. 괜찮네요. wrap 동 포장하다 charge 명 요금 동 청구하다 on top of ~ 외에 reasonable 휑 (가격이) 적당한; 합리적인

7 이유 파악

정답 ④

W Hey, Steven. Did you sign up for those tennis lessons I told you about?	여 안녕, Steven. 내가 말한 테니스 수업 신청했니?
M I did. I was surprised the class ¹⁾was almost full when I signed up.	남 했어. 신청할 때 수업이 거의 꽉 차 있어서 놀랐어.
W Yeah. I actually ended up not registering for them.	여 그렇구나. 사실 난 결국 등록 안 하게 됐어.
M Why? Is your back still bothering you?	남 왜? 아직도 허리가 아파?
W No. I've had some physical therapy, and it's much better now.	여 아니. 물리치료를 좀 받았더니, 지금은 훨씬 나아졌어.
M Then, ²⁾is it because of a scheduling conflict? I know you also have piano classes.	남 그러면 일정이 겹쳐서 그래? 내가 알기로 넌 피아노 수업도 있잖아.
W Those usually take place on different days.	여 그건 대개 다른 날이야.
M Then, why didn't you sign up?	남 그러면 왜 신청하지 않은 거야?
W **Well, we're moving to another area near my mother's new office. The problem is that it's ³⁾too far away from where the lessons are held.**	여 음, 우리는 어머니의 새 사무실이 근처에 있는 다른 지역으로 이사 갈 거야. 문제는 그곳이 수업이 열리는 곳에서 너무 멀다는 거지.
M Oh, I see. I'm sorry you'll miss the lessons, but I'm sure you're looking forward to moving.	남 아, 그렇구나. 수업을 못 듣게 된 건 유감이지만, 넌 분명 이사 가는 걸 기대하고 있겠네.
W Definitely. I hope you enjoy them, though.	여 물론이지. 그래도 넌 수업을 즐기길 바랄게.
M Thanks. I'm sure I will.	남 고마워. 분명 그럴 거야.

여자가 테니스 수업을 신청하지 않았다고 하면서 이사 갈 곳이 수업이 열리는 곳에서 너무 멀다고 말했으므로, 여자가 수업을 신청하지 않은 이유는 ④ '수업 장소가 너무 멀어서'이다.

어휘 sign up for ~을 신청하다 end up 결국 ~하게 되다 bother 동 아프게 하다; 괴롭히다 physical therapy 물리치료 scheduling conflict 겹치는 일정, 일정 충돌
look forward to ~을 기대하다

8 언급 유무 파악

정답 ②

M Lily, do you still want to get together on Sunday?	남 Lily, 여전히 일요일에 만나고 싶은 거지?
W Yes, Mark. I'd love to.	여 응, Mark. 그러고 싶어.
M Well, the Wiltshire Vintage Market ¹⁾is being held downtown in front of city hall if you want to go.	남 음, 네가 가고 싶다면 말이야, Wiltshire Vintage Market이 시내의 시청 앞에서 열리고 있어.
W Oh, that sounds great. Is it a big market?	여 오, 그거 좋아서. 큰 시장이야?
M Yes. Apparently there will be **around ²⁾150 different vendors** there selling secondhand clothes.	남 응. 듣자 하니 그곳에는 중고 의류를 파는 150여 개의 다른 노점상이 있을 거야.
W Wow. I bet they'll have some high-quality items, then. What time should we go?	여 와. 그렇다면 분명 질 좋은 물건들이 있겠네. 몇 시에 갈까?
M The market **opens at 9 a.m. and closes at 3 p.m.**, so maybe we could go in the morning?	남 시장은 오전 9시에 열고 오후 3시에 닫는데, 아침에 가도 될까?
W Yeah. I don't want to miss out on anything.	여 응. 아무것도 놓치고 싶지 않아.
M Oh, and the website says we should bring ³⁾our own fabric shopping bags. It's a sustainable market.	남 아, 그리고 웹사이트에 천으로 된 장바구니를 직접 가져와야 한다고 쓰여 있어. 지속 가능한 시장이거든.
W All right. I've never heard of this market, though. Does it happen every week?	여 알겠어. 그런데 난 한 번도 이 시장에 대해 들어본 적이 없어. 그게 매주 열려?
M No. It's just a one-time event. It'll end next month.	남 아냐. 그냥 일회성 행사야. 다음 달에 끝나.

장소(시내의 시청 앞), 노점상 수(150여 개), 운영 시간(오전 9시부터 오후 3시), 준비물(천으로 된 장바구니)에 대해 언급했고, ② '날짜'는 언급하지 않았다.

어휘 get together 만나다 apparently 및 듣자 하니; 분명히 vendor 명 노점상, 행상인 secondhand 형 중고의 I bet 분명 ~이다 high-quality 형 질 좋은, 고급의 miss out on ~을 놓치다 sustainable 형 지속 가능한

9 내용 불일치 파악   정답 ⑤

M Good evening, everyone. I'm honored to be here at ¹⁾the opening ceremony of the Edwards City Film Festival. From today, the city's theaters will ²⁾be filled with great new films for one week. If you have purchased a festival pass, you will be able to attend these movies. However, some events and lectures may have an extra charge. For more information on these events, check the festival's website. As always, we are committed to showing the work of exciting up-and-coming filmmakers. This year, we'll show more than 50 debut movies by ³⁾promising young directors. In addition, we have more international films than ever, including this opening film, *The Clockwork Canary*. **To introduce the film, here is** ⁴⁾its lead actor, **Carlos Forman.** Everyone, please give him a warm welcome!	남 여러분 안녕하십니까. Edwards City Film Festival의 개막식에 서게 되어 영광입니다. 오늘부터 일주일 동안, 도시의 극장들은 멋진 신작 영화들로 가득 찰 것입니다. 축제 입장권을 구매하셨다면, 이 영화들을 관람하실 수 있습니다. 하지만, 일부 행사와 강연에는 추가 요금이 있을 수 있습니다. 이러한 행사들에 대한 더 많은 정보를 원하시면, 축제의 웹사이트를 확인하십시오. 항상 그랬듯이, 저희는 멋지고 전도유망한 영화 제작자들의 작품을 선보이려 최선을 다하고 있습니다. 올해는 유망한 젊은 감독들의 데뷔작을 50편 이상 선보일 예정입니다. 게다가, 이번 개막작인 <The Clockwork Canary>를 포함하여, 그 어느 때보다 더 많은 국제적인 영화들이 있습니다. 개막작을 소개하러 온, 여기 주연 배우인 Carlos Forman입니다. 여러분, 그를 따뜻하게 맞아주십시오!

에드워즈시의 영화제의 개막식 방송이다. 남자가 개막작을 소개하기 위해 주연 배우가 자리에 와 있다고 했으므로 ⑤ '감독이 개막작 영화를 소개할 예정이다.'는 내용과 일치하지 않는다.

어휘 be committed to ~하는 데 최선을 다하다, 전념하다 up-and-coming 형 전도유망한 promising 형 유망한 lead actor 주연 배우 give ~ a warm welcome ~를 따뜻하게 맞이하다

10 도표 정보 파악   정답 ③

M Hi, Sarah. Could I ¹⁾ask for your opinion on coffee makers? I've found some recommendations online.	남 안녕, Sarah. 커피 메이커에 대해 의견을 물어도 될까? 온라인에서 몇 가지 추천 제품을 찾았어.
W These all look good, but how much coffee do you usually brew?	여 전부 괜찮아 보이긴 한데, 보통 얼마나 많이 커피를 내리니?
M I usually make about four cups at once for me and my family.	남 보통 나와 우리 가족이 마시려고 한 번에 네 잔 정도 내려.
W I don't think you want anything smaller than that, then.	여 그러면 그보다 더 작은 것은 원하지 않겠어.
M Very true! That rules out one of the coffee makers.	남 정말 그러네! 커피 메이커 중 하나는 제외됐어.
W What kind of budget are you working with?	여 예산은 어떻게 돼?
M I want to ²⁾keep it under $200.	남 200달러 이하로 하고 싶어.
W That sounds reasonable. **Do you have a coffee grinder?**	여 적당한 것 같네. 커피 분쇄기는 있어?
M No, I don't. Is that important?	남 아니, 없어. 그게 중요해?
W ³⁾Freshly ground coffee always tastes better.	여 갓 간 커피가 항상 더 맛있잖아.
M All right. **I'd better get one with that built-in, then.**	남 좋아. 그러면 그게 내장된 걸로 사는 게 낫겠어.
W That still leaves two options.	여 아직 두 가지 선택지가 남아 있어.
M Hmm... **I think I'll go with the one that offers a free tumbler in that case.**	남 흠... 그렇다면 텀블러를 무료로 제공하는 걸로 할래.
W I think that's a good choice.	여 그게 좋은 선택인 것 같아.

남자는 한 번에 4잔 이상을 내릴 수 있으며, 200달러 이하인 것 중에서, 커피 분쇄기가 내장되어 있고, 텀블러를 무료로 제공하는 커피 메이커를 골랐다.

어휘 brew 통 (커피, 차 등을) 내리다, 끓이다; (술을) 양조하다 at once 한 번에 rule out 제외시키다 grinder 명 분쇄기, 가는 기구 (grind 통 갈다, 빻다) built-in 형 내장된, 붙박이의

11 짧은 대화의 응답 파악   정답 ①

W Professor Mathews, can I ask you a question about ¹⁾the essay assignment for your politics course?	여 Mathews 교수님, 정치학 강의의 에세이 과제에 대해 질문을 드려도 될까요?
M I'm busy right now, Matilda. I ²⁾have several lectures this morning. **Can you come back later today?**	남 내가 지금은 바쁘구나, Matilda. 오늘 오전에 강의가 여러 개 있거든. 오늘 늦게 다시 올 수 있겠니?
W Sure. **Will you be around this afternoon?**	여 물론이죠. 오늘 오후쯤에 계실 건가요?
M I will be back in my office after lunch.	남 점심 이후에 내 연구실로 돌아올 거란다.

선택지 ① 점심 이후에 내 연구실로 돌아올 거란다.
        ② 정치학 강의는 오후 2시쯤에 끝났단다.
        ③ 에세이에 관해 물어보러 내가 나중에 다시 올 수도 있겠구나.
        ④ 나는 오늘 오전에 과제를 제출해야 한단다.
        ⑤ 오늘 오후에 에세이 파일을 보내주마.

과제 문의를 하러 온 여자에게 남자가 오늘 늦게 다시 와 달라고 부탁하자 여자가 오늘 오후에는 자리에 있을지 물었으므로, 이에 대한 응답으로는 돌아올 시점을 말하는 ① 'I will be back in my office after lunch.'가 가장 적절하다.

어휘 assignment 명 과제 politics 명 정치학, 정치 be around (부근에) 있다, 체재하다 turn in 제출하다

21회 고난도 영어듣기 모의고사 **125**

고난도 영어듣기 모의고사 해커스 수능영어듣기 모의고사 20+4회 실전

12 짧은 대화의 응답 파악

정답 ③

M Did you want to ¹⁾<u>see</u> <u>anything</u> <u>else</u> in the gallery, Tanya?	남 미술관에서 다른 보고 싶은 게 있었니, Tanya?
W **Let's check out the East Wing.** I heard they have some great impressionist paintings there.	여 동관을 살펴보자. 거기에 인상파 화가들의 멋진 그림들이 있다고 들었어.
M That's fine with me, **but the gallery closes** ²⁾<u>in</u> <u>just</u> <u>under an hour.</u>	남 난 괜찮은데, 미술관이 한 시간도 안 돼서 폐장할 거야.
W <u>In that case, we'd better get a move on!</u>	여 <u>그렇다면, 우리 서둘러야겠어!</u>
	[선택지] ① 인상파 화가들의 화풍은 내 취향이 아니야.
	② 미술관에서 그 그림들을 판매하는지 확인해 보자.
	③ 그렇다면, 우리 서둘러야겠어!
	④ 미술관의 영업시간은 온라인에 게시되어 있어.
	⑤ 내 그림 수업은 한 시간 후에 시작해.

여자가 동관을 보고 싶다고 하자 남자가 미술관이 한 시간 이내에 폐장할 것이라고 주의를 줬으므로, 이에 대한 응답으로는 서두르자고 대답하는 ③ 'In that case, we'd better get a move on!'이 가장 적절하다.

[어휘] check out 살펴보다 impressionist 몡 인상파 화가 taste 몡 취향 통 맛보다 get a move on 서두르다, 빨리 하다

13 긴 대화의 응답 파악

정답 ⑤

M Thanks for looking after the kids, Mom. They really ¹⁾<u>appreciate</u> <u>spending</u> <u>time</u> with you.	남 아이들을 돌봐줘서 고마워요, 엄마. 애들도 함께 시간을 보낸 걸 정말 고마워하고 있어요.
W No problem. It's always nice to see my grandchildren.	여 천만에. 손자들을 보는 건 항상 좋단다.
M What did you do with them today?	남 오늘은 애들과 뭘 하셨나요?
W We went to the zoo in the morning, and then we came home and had lunch.	여 아침에 동물원에 갔다가, 집에 와서 점심을 먹었단다.
M Were they well-behaved?	남 아이들이 얌전했나요?
W Mostly. Benji got ²⁾<u>a little irritable</u> at the zoo, but I think he was just hungry. Both of the kids loved seeing the monkeys, though.	여 대부분은. Benji는 동물원에서 조금 짜증을 냈지만, 그냥 배가 고팠던 것 같아. 그래도 두 아이 모두 원숭이 보는 걸 무척 좋아했어.
M That's so cute. I hope you got some photos!	남 너무 귀엽네요. 사진을 좀 찍었길 바랄게요!
W I took a few. I'll send them to you.	여 몇 장 찍었단다. 보내줄게.
M Thanks. What did you do for lunch?	남 고마워요. 점심으로는 뭘 하셨어요?
W I just heated up the leftover chicken and broccoli.	여 그냥 먹다 남은 닭고기와 브로콜리를 데웠어.
M Oh, wait... **Did Laura** ³⁾<u>eat</u> <u>her</u> <u>vegetables</u>? She's been refusing to eat them lately.	남 아, 잠깐만요... Laura가 채소를 먹었어요? 최근에 채소 먹기를 거부하고 있었는데요.
W That's right. **I tricked her into eating everything.**	여 맞아. 난 그 애가 전부 먹도록 꾀어냈다.
M **How did you do that?**	남 어떻게 하신 거예요?
W <u>I chopped up the broccoli and mixed it with the chicken.</u>	여 <u>브로콜리를 잘게 썰어서 닭고기와 섞었지.</u>
	[선택지] ① 그녀에게 동물원에 가려면 그것을 먹어야 한다고 말했지.
	② 동물원 직원에게 사진을 찍어달라고 부탁했지.
	③ 점심을 다 먹고 나면 원숭이를 볼 거란다.
	④ 만약 여전히 배가 고프다면, 아직 남은 음식이 있단다.
	⑤ 브로콜리를 잘게 썰어서 닭고기와 섞었지.

남자가 여자에게 아이들을 맡긴 뒤 하루가 어땠는지 이야기하는 상황이다. 남자가 채소 먹기를 거부하는 자녀를 어떻게 전부 먹도록 꾀어냈는지 물었으므로 정답은 그 비결을 알려주는 ⑤ 'I chopped up the broccoli and mixed it with the chicken.'이 가장 적절하다.

[어휘] look after ~를 돌보다 appreciate 통 고마워하다 well-behaved 웽 얌전한, 행실이 바른 irritable 웽 짜증을 내는, 화를 곧잘 내는 leftover 웽 먹다 남은 몡 남은 음식
trick A into B A가 B하도록 꾀어내다 chop 잘게 썰다, 다지다 mix A with B A와 B를 섞다

14 긴 대화의 응답 파악

정답 ③

[Cell phone rings.]	[휴대폰이 울린다.]
W You've reached the Easton Police Department. This is Officer Philips speaking.	여 이스턴 경찰서입니다. 전 Philips 경관입니다.
M Hi. I'm Neal Sanchez. I'm calling to follow up on a ¹⁾<u>report</u> I <u>made</u> last week.	남 안녕하세요. 전 Neal Sanchez입니다. 지난주에 한 신고에 대해 더 알아보고 싶어서 전화했어요.
W Ah, yes. I remember your case. **Some items were stolen from your jewelry store, correct?**	여 아, 네. 그 사건 기억납니다. 선생님의 보석상에서 일부 물건들이 도난당했었죠, 맞나요?
M That's right. A thief took ²⁾<u>several</u> <u>valuable</u> <u>necklaces.</u>	남 맞아요. 도둑이 값비싼 목걸이 여러 점을 가져갔습니다.
W Let me check our files. *[Typing sound]* **So it looks like our officers arrested the man who did it this morning.**	여 사건 기록을 확인해 볼게요. [타자 치는 소리] 그러니까 오늘 아침에 저희 경찰관들이 그 일을 저지른 남자를 체포한 것 같군요.
M How do you know it's the right person?	남 그 사람이 맞는지 어떻게 아세요?
W Actually, we identified him from your CCTV video.	여 사실, 선생님의 CCTV 동영상에서 그의 신원을 확인했어요.
M Great! I'm glad that helped.	남 잘됐네요! 그게 도움이 되었다니 다행입니다.
W **He also had stolen items from several local stores, including the necklaces you mentioned.**	여 그 남자는 또한 선생님이 언급하신 목걸이를 포함해서 몇몇 지역 상점에서 훔친 물건들을 소지하고 있었어요.
M I see. Will we be able to ³⁾<u>get</u> <u>them</u> <u>back</u>?	남 그렇군요. 그것들을 돌려받을 수 있을까요?

| W | We have to hold the stolen items for now, but yes. **We will return them to you ⁴⁾as soon as we can.** |

| W | We have to hold the stolen items for now, but yes. **We will return them to you** **<u>as soon as we can.</u>** |
| M | What a relief. I was worried I wouldn't get them back. |

여 지금은 저희가 도난품들을 보관하고 있어야 하지만, 그래요. 가능한 한 빨리 돌려드리겠습니다.

남 다행이네요. 돌려받지 못할까 봐 걱정했어요.

선택지 ① 그럴 것 같았어요. 동영상에서 도둑의 얼굴을 볼 수 있어요.
② 유감스럽게도 아닙니다. 목걸이 중 일부는 심하게 파손됐어요.
③ 다행이네요. 돌려받지 못할까 봐 걱정했어요.
④ 맞아요. 그 남자는 아마 다른 몇 가지 물건을 훔쳤을 거예요.
⑤ 괜찮아요. 저희 보석상은 보험을 잘 들어놨어요.

도난 사고에 관해 이야기하는 상황이다. 물건을 도난당한 남자에게 여자가 범인을 체포했으며 되찾은 도난품을 가능한 한 빨리 돌려주겠다고 했으므로, 이에 대한 응답으로는 돌려받게 되어 다행이라고 말하는 ③ 'What a relief. I was worried I wouldn't get them back.'이 가장 적절하다.

어휘 follow up on ~에 대해 더 알아보다 valuable 혱 값비싼; 귀중한 arrest 통 체포하다 identify 통 신원을 확인하다 What a relief. 다행이네요. insurance 몡 보험

15 상황에 적절한 말 파악   정답 ②

| W | Mary is a very talented student who loves to ¹⁾<u>write plays</u>. Recently, her school drama club decided to put on a musical that she wrote. However, her play has 15 different characters and the drama club only has 10 actors. So the club needs to ²⁾<u>hold open auditions</u> to fill the extra parts. Mary knows that her friend Jared has a ³⁾<u>great singing voice</u>. He hasn't acted before, but she thinks that he would be ⁴⁾<u>able to play</u> one of the parts in the play. **So Mary wants to suggest to Jared that he should try out for the drama club's musical.** In this situation, what would Mary most likely say to Jared? |

여 Mary는 극본을 쓰는 것을 좋아하는 매우 재능 있는 학생입니다. 최근에, 그녀의 학교 연극 동아리는 그녀가 쓴 뮤지컬을 상연하기로 결정했습니다. 하지만, 그녀의 연극에는 15명의 서로 다른 등장인물들이 나오는데 연극 동아리에는 10명의 배우뿐입니다. 그래서 동아리에서는 나머지 배역을 채우기 위해 공개 오디션을 열어야 합니다. Mary는 그녀의 친구 Jared의 노래하는 목소리가 훌륭하다는 것을 알고 있습니다. 그가 이전에 연기를 해본 적은 없지만, 그녀는 그가 연극에서 한 배역을 잘 연기할 수 있을 것이라고 생각합니다. 그래서 Mary는 Jared에게 연극 동아리의 뮤지컬에 도전해 보라고 제안하고 싶습니다. 이러한 상황에서, Mary가 Jared에게 가장 할 것 같은 말은 무엇입니까?

선택지 ① 널 위해서라면 기꺼이 이 부분을 다시 써줄게.
② 넌 뮤지컬 오디션을 보러 와야 해.
③ 그 노래를 부를 때 너의 목소리는 분명 아주 멋졌어.
④ 내가 동아리 회원들에게 너의 연기력에 대해 말해줄게.
⑤ 뮤지컬의 주인공이 된 걸 축하해!

Jared의 노래하는 목소리가 훌륭하다는 것을 알고, Mary는 그에게 연극 동아리의 뮤지컬에 도전해 보라고 제안하려 한다. 따라서, Mary가 할 말로 ② 'You ought to come audition for the musical.'이 가장 적절하다.

어휘 drama club 연극 동아리 put on 상연하다 try out for (오디션 등에) 도전하다

16-17 세트 문항   정답 16 ④ 17 ②

| M | Hello, class. Last week we discussed threats to biodiversity. **This afternoon, I'd like to show how predators help other ¹⁾**<u>species within an ecosystem.</u> First off, they prevent harmful insect populations from becoming too large. **Bats**, for instance, play a big role in ²⁾<u>reducing the number</u> of insects that spread deadly diseases. Second, predators can actually increase a prey species' population. For **buffaloes** and other herd species, this is especially true. Since predators generally hunt ³⁾<u>weak or injured prey</u>, healthier animals have access to more food and are more likely to reproduce. Third, larger predators are vital to the existence of scavengers. **Eagles** and other scavengers rely on the meat large predators ⁴⁾<u>leave behind</u>. Lastly, predators can protect plant life by influencing the behavior of their prey. **Wolves** are a perfect example of this. They scare away animals that eat young trees. With these grazing animals gone, the trees are free to grow again. Now, let's open our books to page 232. |

남 안녕하세요, 학생 여러분. 지난주에 우리는 생물 다양성에 대한 위협에 대해 논의했습니다. 오늘 오후에는, 포식자들이 생태계 내에서 다른 종들을 어떻게 돕는지 보여드리고 싶습니다. 우선, 그들은 해로운 곤충의 개체수가 너무 많아지는 것을 막아줍니다. 예를 들어, 박쥐는 치명적인 질병을 퍼뜨리는 곤충의 수를 줄이는 데 큰 역할을 합니다. 둘째로, 포식자들은 실제로 먹잇감의 개체수를 증가시킬 수 있습니다. 버펄로와 다른 떼를 짓는 종들에게, 이것은 특히 사실입니다. 포식자들이 일반적으로 약하거나 다친 먹잇감을 사냥하기 때문에, 더 건강한 동물들은 더 많은 먹이에 접근할 수 있고 번식할 가능성이 더 높습니다. 셋째, 몸집이 큰 포식자는 썩은 고기를 먹는 동물들의 생존에 필수적입니다. 독수리와 다른 썩은 고기를 먹는 동물들은 몸집이 큰 포식자들이 남기고 간 고기에 의존합니다. 마지막으로, 포식자들은 먹잇감의 행동에 영향을 줌으로써 식물의 생명을 보호할 수 있습니다. 늑대는 이것의 완벽한 예입니다. 그것들은 어린나무를 먹는 동물들을 겁주어 쫓아냅니다. 이 풀을 뜯어 먹는 동물들이 사라지면서, 나무는 다시 자유롭게 자랄 수 있습니다. 이제 책의 232페이지를 펴보도록 합시다.

선택지 16 ① 생물 다양성에 대한 위협이 환경을 해치는 이유
② 자연에서 포식자 개체수를 늘리는 방법
③ 동물에 의해 옮겨지는 치명적인 질병의 원인
④ 포식자들이 다른 종을 돕는 방법
⑤ 종의 개체수 과잉을 막는 방법
17 ① 박쥐 ② 곰 ③ 버펄로 ④ 독수리 ⑤ 늑대

16 포식자들이 생태계 내에서 다른 종을 어떻게 돕는지 보여주고 있으므로 남자가 하는 말의 주제로 ④ 'ways that predators aid other species'가 가장 적절하다.
17 박쥐, 버펄로, 독수리, 늑대는 언급했지만 ② 'bears'는 언급하지 않았다.

어휘 biodiversity 몡 생물 다양성 predator 몡 포식자 species 몡 종 ecosystem 몡 생태계 population 몡 개체수; 인구 play a role in ~에 역할을 하다 spread 통 퍼뜨리다 deadly 혱 치명적인 prey 몡 먹잇감 herd 몡 떼, 무리 have access to ~에 접근할 수 있다 reproduce 통 번식하다; 복제하다 vital 혱 필수적인, 중요한 existence 몡 생존; 존재 scavenger 몡 썩은 고기를 먹는 동물 rely on ~에 의존하다 scare away 겁주어 쫓아내다 graze 통 풀을 뜯다 animal-borne 혱 동물에 의해 옮겨지는 aid 통 돕다

1	①	2	③	3	②	4	④	5	⑤	6	②	7	④	8	③	9	⑤	10	④
11	②	12	④	13	①	14	⑤	15	①	16	③	17	③						

• 각 문제의 정답 근거는 굵은 글씨로, Dictation 정답은 밑줄로 표시되어 있습니다.

---

1 목적 파악

정답 ①

M Good morning, Trafford High School students. This is your principal, Mr. Burns, speaking. As most of you know, our school's Spring Festival will take place in a matter of weeks. **Therefore, any last-minute booth proposals from school clubs 1)must be submitted by noon this Friday at the latest.** After that, any new applications will not be accepted. Before submitting an idea, check the 2)list of booths that have already been confirmed for the festival on our school's website. We currently have clubs running booths that will serve food, host games, and 3)provide arts and crafts activities. I hope to see many more new ideas in the coming days, and I look forward to celebrating at the Spring Festival with you all.

남 안녕하십니까, 트래포드 고등학교 학생 여러분. 교장 Burns 선생님입니다. 여러분 대부분이 알고 있듯이, 우리 학교의 Spring Festival이 약 몇 주 후에 열릴 것입니다. 따라서 학교 동아리들의 마지막 부스 제안서는 늦어도 이번 주 금요일 정오까지 제출돼야 합니다. 그 이후에는, 어떤 새로운 신청서도 받아주지 않을 것입니다. 아이디어를 제출하기 전에, 우리 학교 웹사이트에서 이미 확정된 축제 부스 목록을 확인하십시오. 현재 음식을 제공하고, 게임을 열고, 미술 공예 활동을 제공하는 부스들을 운영하는 동아리들이 있습니다. 저는 앞으로 더 많은 새로운 아이디어들을 볼 수 있기를 바라며, 여러분 모두와 함께 Spring Festival에서 즐겁게 놀기를 기대합니다.

남자가 몇 주 후 열릴 학교 축제의 부스 제안서를 늦어도 이번 주 금요일 정오까지는 제출해야 한다고 말하고 있다. 따라서, 남자가 하는 말의 목적으로 ① '축제 부스 제안서 제출을 재촉하려고'가 가장 적절하다.

어휘 a matter of 약, 대충; ~의 문제 last-minute 휑 마지막의, 막바지의 proposal 휑 제안서; 제안 at the latest 늦어도 application 휑 신청서; 적용 arts and crafts 미술 공예 celebrate 통 즐겁게 놀다; 기념하다

---

2 의견 파악

정답 ③

M Are you already leaving the gym, Carla?
W Yeah. I'm all done with my 30-minute group class.
M Is that enough time for a good workout?
W It is! The class is 1)brief but intense. **Such workouts are the most efficient way to get in shape.**
M Why do you say that?
W Your body keeps burning calories for several hours after a high-intensity session.
M Are you saying that you 2)get the benefits of exercising while you're recovering?
W Yes. The after-burn effect can last up to 16 hours. And when you exercise like that, you quickly build muscles.
M I can see why that would be. You can't take it easy in an intense class.
W Also, the short period helps you 3)stay focused on your workout.
M I want to try that. When is your next group class?
W It's at 7 p.m. on Tuesday. You should come!

남 벌써 체육관을 떠나려는 거야, Carla?
여 응. 30분짜리 단체 수업을 다 끝냈거든.
남 그게 좋은 운동이 되기에 충분한 시간이니?
여 충분해! 수업이 짧지만 격해. 이런 운동은 좋은 몸 상태를 유지하는 데 가장 효율적인 방법이야.
남 왜 그렇게 생각해?
여 우리 몸은 고강도 활동 후 몇 시간 동안 계속해서 열량을 소모해.
남 쉬는 동안에도 운동의 이점을 얻을 수 있다는 말이야?
여 응. 운동 후에도 열량이 소모되는 효과는 16시간까지 지속될 수 있어. 그리고 그렇게 운동을 하면, 근육이 금방 생겨.
남 왜 그런지 알 것 같아. 격한 수업에서는 쉬엄쉬엄하지 못하잖아.
여 또한, 짧은 시간이라는 점이 운동에 집중한 채로 있을 수 있게 도와줘.
남 나도 그거 시도해볼래. 다음 단체 수업이 언제야?
여 화요일 저녁 7시에 있어. 꼭 와야 해!

남자가 30분짜리 단체 운동 수업이 효과적인지 궁금해하자 여자가 짧지만 격한 운동은 좋은 몸 상태를 유지하는 데 가장 효율적인 방법이라고 했다. 따라서, 여자의 의견으로 ③ '짧지만 격한 운동은 효율적인 신체 관리법이다.'가 가장 적절하다.

어휘 be done with ~을 끝내다, 마치다 intense 휑 격한, 강렬한 get in shape 좋은 몸 상태를 유지하다 burn calories 열량을 소모하다 last 통 지속되다 휜 마지막에 high-intensity 휑 고강도 take it easy (일을) 쉬엄쉬엄하다

---

3 관계 파악

정답 ②

M Hi, Dr. Williams! It's a pleasure to meet you.
W Likewise. I hope I 1)haven't kept you waiting.
M No problem. The cappuccino at this café is very good. Do you want to try one?
W No, thanks. Let's get straight into the interview.
M Sure. 2)Do you mind if I take notes?
W Go ahead. I imagine you'll need them when you're writing.

남 안녕하세요, Williams 박사님! 만나서 반가워요.
여 마찬가지예요. 오래 기다리시게 한 게 아니었으면 좋겠네요.
남 괜찮아요. 이 카페의 카푸치노가 매우 맛있는데요. 한 잔 드셔 보실래요?
여 아뇨, 됐습니다. 바로 인터뷰로 들어가죠.
남 물론이죠. 제가 메모해도 될까요?
여 그렇게 하세요. 글을 쓰실 때 그게 필요할 것 같네요.

M That's right. **I want to be as accurate as possible** ³⁾<u>with</u> <u>my</u> <u>novels</u> **when it comes to science.**	남 맞아요. 저는 과학에 관해서라면 제 소설을 가능한 한 정확하게 쓰고 싶어요.
W I admire that in your books. I just read your last one.	여 당신의 저서에서 그 점에 감탄했어요. 제가 방금 당신의 마지막 저서를 읽었거든요.
M Wow, thank you! Now, I want to ask you about black holes first.	남 우와, 고마워요! 그러면 이제, 블랙홀에 관해 먼저 묻고 싶은데요.
W Sure. **I've been studying them** ⁴⁾<u>with</u> <u>space</u> <u>telescopes.</u>	여 그래요. 저는 우주 망원경으로 그것들을 연구해 왔어요.
M I'm wondering how you do that.	남 그걸 어떻게 하시는지 궁금해요.
W Just a moment. Let me draw you a picture. I think it will illustrate this point well.	여 잠깐만요. 제가 그림을 그려 드릴게요. 그게 요점을 분명하게 잘 보여줄 것 같아요.

두 사람이 여자의 블랙홀 연구 방법에 관해 이야기하고 있다. 남자는 과학에 관해서는 본인의 소설을 정확하게 쓰고 싶다고 했고, 여자는 우주 망원경으로 블랙홀을 연구해 왔다고 하는 것으로 보아 두 사람의 관계로 ② '소설가 — 천문학자'가 가장 적절하다.

어휘 likewise ⑤ 마찬가지로, 똑같이 get straight into 바로 ~으로 들어가다 take notes 메모하다, 필기하다 when it comes to ~에 관해서라면 admire ⑧ 감탄하다; 존경하다 telescope ⑲ 망원경 illustrate ⑧ 분명하게 보여주다; 삽화를 넣다

4 그림 내용 불일치 파악   정답 ④

M Hey, April. Would you help me get ready to paint your sister's room?	남 얘, April. 네 여동생 방을 페인트칠할 준비를 하는 걸 도와줄래?
W Sure, Dad. What do you need me to do?	여 그럼요, 아빠. 제가 뭘 하면 될까요?
M Let's move a few things into the hallway. Can you ¹⁾<u>grab</u> <u>the</u> <u>chair</u> in front of the window?	남 몇 가지 물건을 복도로 옮기자. 창문 앞에 있는 의자를 가져가 줄래?
W Got it. What about the round mirror between the bookcase and the window?	여 알겠어요. 책장과 창문 사이에 있는 둥근 거울은 어쩌죠?
M I'll take care of that.	남 그건 내가 처리하마.
W And we'd better leave the bookcase where it is. It's too big and heavy.	여 그리고 책장은 지금 있는 곳에 두는 게 좋겠어요. 너무 크고 무거워요.
M You're right. Then, just move the two plant pots ²⁾<u>on</u> <u>top</u> <u>of</u> <u>it.</u>	남 맞아. 그러면 그 위에 있는 화분 두 개만 옮겨줘.
W Okay. **What about this rainbow-shaped rug?**	여 알았어요. 이 무지개 모양의 러그는요?
M Can you take that downstairs? We'd better replace it.	남 그건 아래층으로 가져가 줄래? 그건 교체하는 게 낫겠어.
W No problem. Is there anything else?	여 문제없어요. 다른 건 없어요?
M We need to remove the ³⁾<u>wall</u> <u>sticker</u> <u>of</u> <u>the</u> <u>giraffe.</u>	남 벽에 붙인 기린 스티커를 제거해야 해.
W It will be easier to peel off if we heat it up a little bit first.	여 먼저 열을 조금 가하면 벗기기 쉬울 거예요.
M Good thinking. I'll try using a hair dryer. Let's get started!	남 좋은 생각이야. 드라이기를 한번 써볼게. 시작하자!

대화에서 여자가 무지개 모양의 러그를 어떻게 할지 물었는데, ④에는 물방울 모양의 러그가 그려져 있다.

어휘 hallway ⑲ 복도 bookcase ⑲ 책장 take care of ~을 처리하다 downstairs ⑤ 아래층으로 replace ⑧ 교체하다 peel off 벗기다 heat up 열을 가하다, 데우다

5 할 일 파악   정답 ⑤

M Annie, I'm looking forward to our club trip to Mount Helens National Park this weekend.	남 Annie, 난 이번 주말에 헬렌스산 국립공원으로 동호회 여행을 가는 게 기대돼.
W Me too. Everyone in the hiking club ¹⁾<u>has</u> <u>signed</u> <u>up</u> <u>for</u> it, so I hope it goes well.	여 나도 그래. 등산 동호회 사람들이 다 신청했으니, 잘 됐으면 좋겠어.
M Should we check our preparations, then?	남 그러면 준비 사항들을 확인해 볼까?
W Sure. I booked a van yesterday.	여 물론이지. 내가 어제 승합차를 예약했어.
M Perfect. And what about snacks for the hike?	남 아주 좋아. 등산용 간식은 어때?
W I've got some protein bars and fruit already.	여 단백질 바와 과일을 이미 좀 구비해뒀어.
M Okay. I also ²⁾<u>polled</u> <u>our</u> <u>members</u> about which trails they want to do.	남 알았어. 나도 회원들에게 어떤 등산로를 가고 싶은지 설문 조사했어.
W What was the result?	여 결과는 어땠어?
M Most of them want to go up the north peak of the mountain.	남 그들 대부분은 산의 북쪽 봉우리를 오르고 싶어 해.
W Okay. We'll need to leave around 6:30 a.m., then. Let's send everyone a text message ³⁾<u>about</u> <u>the</u> <u>schedule.</u>	여 알겠어. 그러면 오전 6시 30분쯤에 출발해야겠어. 모두에게 일정에 관한 문자 메시지를 보내자.
M Can you take care of that? I don't have everyone's number.	남 그건 네가 처리해 줄래? 내겐 모든 사람의 번호가 없어.
W Sure. **And I'd better call the hotel and make sure that our booking is all set.**	여 물론이지. 그리고 호텔에 전화해서 예약이 다 준비되었는지 확인해야겠어.
M **Don't worry about it. I'll do that later today.**	남 걱정하지 마. 이따가 오늘 중에 내가 할게.

등산 동호회 여행을 앞두고 준비 사항을 확인하고 있다. 여자가 호텔에 전화해서 예약이 다 준비되었는지 확인해야겠다고 하자, 남자가 오늘 중으로 자신이 하겠다고 했으므로 남자가 할 일로 ⑤ '호텔 예약 확인하기'가 가장 적절하다.

어휘 preparation ⑲ 준비 사항; 준비 van ⑲ 승합차, 밴 poll ⑧ 설문 조사하다 ⑲ 선거, 투표 trail ⑲ 등산로; 자국, 흔적 peak ⑲ 봉우리, 정상; 정점 be all set 준비가 되어 있다

6 금액 정보 파악   정답 ②

M Welcome to Office Supply World. May I help you?	남 Office Supply World에 오신 것을 환영합니다. 무엇을 도와드릴까요?
W Hello. I need a new planner for work.	여 안녕하세요. 업무용 플래너가 새로 필요해요.
M Our planners are over here. Do you have ¹⁾any specific requirements?	남 플래너는 이쪽에 있어요. 구체적인 요구 사항이 있으실까요?
W I'd like a small one.	여 전 작은 게 좋아요.
M Then, I would consider these two. **This blue one here is $20, and the pink one is $30.**	남 그렇다면, 여기 두 가지를 고려해 보겠습니다. 이 파란색 플래너는 20달러이고 분홍색 플래너는 30달러예요.
W Oh, I like the ²⁾blue one. I'll take it.	여 아, 파란색이 좋아요. 그걸로 살게요.
M Great. And do you need anything else?	남 좋아요. 더 필요한 게 있으실까요?
W Yes. I'd also like some good pens.	여 네. 좋은 펜도 좀 갖고 싶어요.
M Well, this three-piece set here is our bestseller. It's $20.	남 음, 여기 있는 이 세 개짜리 세트가 가장 잘 팔리는 거예요. 20달러입니다.
W I'll ³⁾take two of those, then. I think my husband also needs a set.	여 그러면 그걸로 두 세트 주세요. 제 남편도 한 세트가 필요한 것 같아요.
M Okay, great. So you're getting the blue planner and two sets of pens. Is that right?	남 네, 좋습니다. 그러니까 파란색 플래너와 펜 두 세트를 사시는 거군요. 맞죠?
W Yes. **Also, I have this 10% discount coupon. Does that apply to these items?**	여 네. 그리고 이 10% 할인 쿠폰도 있어요. 그게 이 물건들에 적용되나요?
M It applies to the pen sets, but ⁴⁾not the planner.	남 펜 세트에는 적용되지만, 플래너에는 안 됩니다.
W That's fine. Here's my card.	여 괜찮아요. 여기 제 카드요.

여자가 파란색 플래너 하나($20), 펜 두 세트($20×2=$40)를 구매했고, 펜 세트에만 10% 할인을 받았으므로($20+$40×0.9=$56) 정답은 ② '$56'이다.

[어휘] specific ® 구체적인 requirement ® 요구 사항 consider ⑧ 고려하다 apply to ~에 적용되다

7 이유 파악   정답 ④

M Hi, Rachel. How was your weekend?	남 안녕, Rachel. 주말은 어떻게 보냈니?
W It was good, but ¹⁾I missed you at the five-kilometer race on Saturday.	여 좋았는데, 토요일에 있었던 5km 달리기 대회에서 널 보고 싶었어.
M I know. I'm sad I missed it. I wanted to set a new personal record.	남 그러게. 나도 놓쳐서 아쉬워. 개인 신기록을 세우고 싶었는데.
W Yeah, you cut a few seconds off your record at the last practice. But why couldn't you come? Was it that injury you had last month?	여 응, 넌 지난 연습 때 네 기록을 몇 초 줄였었잖아. 그런데 왜 못 온 거야? 지난달에 다친 부상 때문이었어?
M No. My ²⁾knee is fully recovered.	남 아니. 무릎은 완전히 회복됐어.
W Then, did you not wake up on time? I know it was early in the morning.	여 그러면 제때 못 일어났니? 이른 아침이었다는 건 알아.
M I was up early. **I actually couldn't go because I had to take my grandmother to the hospital.**	남 난 일찍 일어났어. 실은 할머니를 병원에 모셔다드려야 해서 못 갔어.
W Oh, I'm sorry. I hope she's feeling better now.	여 아, 유감이야. 할머니께서 지금은 좀 나아지신 거면 좋겠다.
M Thanks. Luckily, she just had ³⁾a mild cold, and she's fine.	남 고마워. 다행히도, 가벼운 감기였고 괜찮으셔.
W Glad to hear that.	여 다행이야.
M I'll be sure to run in the next race. See you at the next practice!	남 난 꼭 다음 달리기 대회 때는 달릴 거야. 다음 연습 때 보자!

남자가 5km 달리기 대회에 못 가서 아쉽다고 하면서 할머니를 병원에 모셔다드려야 했다고 말했으므로, 남자가 대회에 참가하지 못한 이유는 ④ '할머니를 병원에 모셔다드려야 해서'이다.

[어휘] miss ⑧ 보고 싶어 하다; 놓치다 set a record 기록을 세우다 cut off ~을 줄이다 injury ® 부상 mild ® 가벼운; 유순한 be sure to 꼭 ~하다

8 언급 유무 파악   정답 ③

W Hi, Joseph. Did your son enjoy Junior Robotics Class last weekend?	여 안녕, Joseph. 네 아들은 지난 주말의 Junior Robotics Class를 재미있게 들었니?
M He loved it. Were you ¹⁾thinking of signing up your son Ryan for the next one?	남 엄청나게 좋아했어. 다음 수업에 네 아들 Ryan을 등록시킬 생각 중인 거야?
W Oh, I didn't realize there was another class scheduled.	여 아, 또 한 번의 수업이 예정되어 있는지는 몰랐어.
M Yeah, the robotics class is held on the ²⁾first Saturday of every month.	남 응, 로봇 공학 수업은 매달 첫째 주 토요일에 열려.
W Oh, interesting. Is it always held in the **Bluemont Community Center**?	여 오, 흥미로운걸. 수업이 항상 블루몬트 주민센터에서 열리는 거야?
M That's right. So it's just a quick walk from our apartment complex.	남 맞아. 그래서 우리 아파트 단지에서 금방 걸어갈 수 있어.
W I heard the class is ³⁾four hours long. Is that correct?	여 수업 시간이 4시간이라고 들었는데. 그게 맞아?
M It is. The class lasts from 11 a.m. to 3 p.m.	남 그래. 수업은 오전 11시부터 오후 3시까지 진행돼.
W Are you sure Ryan can sign up? He's a sixth-grader now.	여 Ryan이 들을 수 있는 게 확실해? 이제 초등학교 6학년이야.
M Sure! It's open to kids who are ⁴⁾between the ages of 8 and 14.	남 물론이지! 그 수업엔 8세에서 14세 사이의 아이들이 참여할 수 있어.
W I'll see if he's interested. It sounds like a good opportunity.	여 Ryan이 관심이 있는지 알아봐야겠다. 좋은 기회인 것 같아.
M I think he'd like it!	남 내 생각엔 좋아할 것 같아!

수업 요일(매달 첫째 주 토요일), 수업 장소(블루몬트 주민센터), 소요 시간(4시간), 대상 연령(8세에서 14세)에 대해 언급했고, ③ '수업료'는 언급하지 않았다.

[어휘] apartment complex 아파트 단지 last ⑧ 진행되다, 계속되다 ⑨ 마지막에 opportunity ® 기회

9 내용 불일치 파악   정답 ⑤

W Hello, listeners. This is Mayor Janet Harrison. I'm glad to announce that our city government has decided to ¹⁾<u>organize the first ever</u> Winslow Christmas Food Donation Event. The event will run for a month beginning on December 1st. We will set up the event booths by city hall and have ²⁾<u>staff members on-site</u> to collect any donations that you bring. We will accept food donations and monetary contributions. If you want to donate food, only canned or dry food is acceptable. **The collected food and funds will be given to five local institutions, including ³⁾<u>both orphanages and senior centers</u>.** We thank you so much for your time and any help you can offer. I hope all of you enjoy the holiday season!	여 안녕하십니까, 청취자 여러분. 저는 시장 Janet Harrison입니다. 우리 시 정부가 사상 최초로 Winslow Christmas Food Donation Event를 개최하기로 했다는 것을 알리게 되어 기쁩니다. 이 행사는 12월 1일부터 한 달간 진행됩니다. 시청 옆에 행사 부스를 설치하고, 여러분이 가져오실 기부 물품을 모을 직원들을 현장에 배치하겠습니다. 저희는 식품 기부와 현금 기부를 받을 것입니다. 만약 식품을 기부하고 싶으시면, 통조림이나 건조식품만 가능합니다. 모인 식품과 기금은 보육원과 경로당을 모두 포함하여 5개의 지역 기관에 전달될 것입니다. 시간을 내주시고 도와주셔서 정말 감사합니다. 여러분 모두 연휴 기간을 즐기시기를 바랍니다!

크리스마스 기념 식품 기부 행사에 대한 안내 방송이다. 여자가 이렇게 모인 식품은 보육원과 경로당을 모두 포함하여 총 5개의 지역 기관에 전달될 것이라고 했으므로 ⑤ '기부된 식품은 다섯 곳의 보육원에 전달될 것이다.'는 내용과 일치하지 않는다.

어휘   on-site 형 현장의, 건물 내의   monetary 형 현금의, 금전의   contribution 명 기부, 기여   institution 명 기관   orphanage 명 보육원

10 도표 정보 파악   정답 ④

W Hey, Jasper. Have you picked out a bike yet? **M** No, but I went to the used bike shop yesterday, and I've narrowed it down to a few options. Do you want to ¹⁾<u>help me select</u> one? **W** Sure. What is the most you want to spend on it? **M** **I want to pay $300 ²⁾or less.** That seems reasonable for a used bike. **W** Okay, so not this one. And what about the material of the bike? **M** Steel and titanium are fine, but **I don't want to deal with aluminum.** It's ³⁾<u>too hard to repair</u>. **W** Okay, then **does the bike have to be foldable?** **M** I think that would be more convenient for storing it, **so yeah.** **W** Then, all you have to do is pick a color. These are the ones left. **M** **The ⁴⁾green one looks nicer**, so I'll go for that.	여 안녕, Jasper. 이제 자전거는 골랐니? 남 아니, 하지만 어제 중고 자전거 가게에 갔었는데, 몇 가지 선택지로 좁혔어. 내가 고르는 걸 도와줄래? 여 물론이지. 자전거에 돈을 최대 얼마큼까지 쓰고 싶어? 남 300달러 이하로 내고 싶어. 그게 중고 자전거엔 적당한 것 같아. 여 알겠어, 그러면 이건 아니겠다. 그리고 자전거의 소재는 어때? 남 스틸과 티타늄은 괜찮은데, 알루미늄은 취급하고 싶지 않아. 그건 수리하기가 너무 어려워. 여 그래, 그리고 자전거가 접을 수 있어야 해? 남 그게 보관하는 데 더 편리할 것 같으니까, 응. 여 그러면 색깔만 고르면 되겠어. 이것들이 남은 거야. 남 초록색이 더 좋아 보이니까 그걸로 할게.

남자가 300달러 이하인 것 중에서, 알루미늄이 아니고, 접을 수 있으며, 초록색인 중고 자전거를 골랐다.

어휘   pick out 고르다, 선택하다   narrow down to ~으로 좁히다   deal with ~을 취급하다, 다루다   foldable 형 접을 수 있는, 접히는   store 동 보관하다 명 가게

11 짧은 대화의 응답 파악   정답 ②

W Honey, I'm so excited that it's ¹⁾<u>our wedding anniversary</u> this Friday. **M** Me too. It was really hard to pick out your gift, but I think you're going to love it. **W** I'm sure I will. **I also can't wait to go to a nice dinner after a long day of work. Did you ²⁾<u>make the reservation</u> yesterday?** **M** Yes. We're booked for dinner at 7 p.m.	여 여보, 이번 주 금요일이 우리 결혼기념일이라서 너무 설레. 남 나도 그래. 당신 선물 고르느라 정말 힘들었지만, 당신이 좋아할 것 같아. 여 분명 그럴 거야. 긴 일과 끝에 근사한 저녁을 먹으러 가는 것도 너무 기대돼. 당신 어제 예약은 해뒀어? 남 응. 저녁 7시로 예약했어.
	선택지 ① 아니. 아직 선물 못 샀어. ② 응. 저녁 7시로 예약했어. ③ 알았어. 그러면 스테이크와 샐러드를 만들어줄게. ④ 괜찮아. 선물이 마음에 들지 않으면 반품해도 돼. ⑤ 했어. 내일 업무하려면 발표를 끝내둬야 해.

여자가 결혼기념일에 근사한 저녁을 먹으러 갈 것이 기대된다고 하면서 예약했는지 물었으므로, 이에 대한 응답으로는 예약을 해뒀다고 대답하는 ② 'Yes. We're booked for dinner at 7 p.m.'이 가장 적절하다.

어휘   wedding anniversary 결혼기념일   can't wait to ~이 너무 기대되다, 빨리 ~하고 싶다   return 동 반품하다; 돌아오다

12 짧은 대화의 응답 파악

정답 ④

M	Hello, I'd like a ticket to see the new action movie starring Harry Golding.
W	Well, the movie ¹⁾<u>includes</u> <u>some</u> <u>violent</u> <u>scenes</u>, so **those under 18 years are not allowed to watch it. May I ask how** ²⁾**<u>old you are</u>?**
M	Oh, I didn't know that. **I'm only 17.**
W	<u>I'm sorry. Then, you can't buy a ticket for this movie.</u>

남 안녕하세요, Harry Golding 주연의 새 액션 영화표를 사고 싶습니다.
여 음, 그 영화에는 폭력적인 장면들이 포함되어 있어서, 18세 미만은 관람할 수 없어요. 나이가 어떻게 되시죠?
남 아, 몰랐어요. 저는 겨우 17살이에요.
여 죄송합니다. 그러면 손님은 이 영화표를 사실 수 없어요.

선택지 ① 알아요. 그는 많은 액션 영화에서 주연을 맡았어요.
② 그것참 곤란하네요. 저는 18살이 되려면 몇 달 더 있어야 해요.
③ 그러면 다 되셨습니다. 손님의 영화는 3관입니다.
④ 죄송합니다. 그러면 손님은 이 영화표를 사실 수 없어요.
⑤ 괜찮아요. 다음 상영 시간의 표는 아직 남아 있습니다.

남자가 보려는 영화는 18세 미만 관람 불가인데 남자가 17살이라고 했으므로, 이에 대한 응답으로는 영화표를 구매할 수 없다고 말하는 ④ 'I'm sorry. Then, you can't buy a ticket for this movie.'가 가장 적절하다.

어휘 star 통 주연을 맡기다; 주연을 맡다 형 별 violent 형 폭력적인 scene 명 장면

13 긴 대화의 응답 파악

정답 ①

W	Honey, are you done packing for the trip to my parents' house tomorrow?
M	Not yet. I can start right now.
W	My parents said it's been really hot, so be sure to ¹⁾<u>grab</u> <u>some</u> <u>T-shirts and</u> <u>shorts</u>.
M	Got it. And we'd better take our sunglasses, too.
W	Okay. I also looked up the ²⁾<u>expected</u> <u>traffic</u> <u>conditions</u> for tomorrow. Apparently, the roads will be very busy since everyone's going out of town.
M	I guess that's not a surprise.
W	Yeah, so we should leave early tomorrow to beat traffic.
M	Well, **we can't leave until after 11:30 a.m. because of** ³⁾**<u>my doctor's</u>** **<u>appointment</u>.**
W	Oh, I totally forgot about that.
M	Yeah, it's just a checkup, but it's the only time I could get an appointment in the next few weeks.
W	That's okay. **So** ⁴⁾**<u>what</u> <u>time</u> <u>do</u> <u>you</u> <u>think</u>** **we can leave for my parents' house, then?**
M	<u>Let's aim to head out at 12 p.m.</u>

여 여보, 내일 우리 부모님 댁에 가기 위한 짐은 다 챙겼어?
남 아니 아직. 지금 시작하면 돼.
여 우리 부모님이 날씨가 진짜 덥다고 하셨으니까, 티셔츠와 반바지 좀 꼭 챙겨.
남 알았어. 그리고 선글라스도 가져가는 게 좋겠어.
여 그래. 내가 내일 예상 교통 상황도 찾아봤어. 분명, 사람들이 모두 도시를 떠나려 해서 도로가 무척 혼잡할 거야.
남 놀랄 일은 아닌 것 같네.
여 응, 그러니 교통 체증을 피하려면 내일 일찍 출발해야 해.
남 음, 내 진료 예약 때문에 우리는 오전 11시 반은 되어야 출발할 수 있어.
여 아, 그걸 완전히 잊고 있었어.
남 응, 그냥 검진일 뿐이지만, 앞으로 몇 주 안으로는 예약을 잡을 수 있는 유일한 시간이야.
여 괜찮아. 그럼, 몇 시에 우리 부모님 댁으로 출발할 수 있을 것 같아?
남 오후 12시에 출발하는 걸 목표로 하자.

선택지 ① 오후 12시에 출발하는 걸 목표로 하자.
② 그러면 내가 티셔츠와 반바지 몇 벌을 챙길게.
③ 10분 후에 부모님을 뵈러 갈게.
④ 예약을 더 이른 시간으로 바꿀 수 있어.
⑤ 교통 체증을 고려하면 기차가 더 빠를 거야.

여자의 부모님 댁으로 출발할 시간을 정하려는 상황이다. 남자가 검진 예약 때문에 11시 반 이후에야 출발할 수 있다고 하자 여자가 그러면 몇 시에 출발할 수 있을지 물었으므로, 이에 대한 응답으로는 출발 가능 시간을 언급한 ① 'Let's aim to head out at 12 p.m.'이 가장 적절하다.

어휘 shorts 명 반바지 look up (정보를) 찾아보다 beat traffic 교통 체증을 피하다 not A until B B가 되어서야 A하다 totally 부 완전히 checkup 명 검진, 건강 진단 aim 통 목표로 하다 head out 출발하다

14 긴 대화의 응답 파악

정답 ⑤

	[Cell phone rings.]
W	Hi, Justin. Are we still meeting this afternoon?
M	Of course. I was ¹⁾<u>calling</u> <u>to</u> <u>ask</u> if I could bring my dog. It would be nice to get him out of the house.
W	Sure! There's actually a great dog park inside the park we're going to.
M	Oh, perfect. What else is in that area?
W	There's a really nice café nearby. We can walk there from the park for a coffee.
M	Is it ²⁾<u>pet friendly</u>?
W	It is. I see dogs there all the time.
M	Then, I'd love to check it out. **But I have to think about parking.**
W	**Oh, right. You'll need to drive if you're bringing your dog.**
M	Would I be able to leave my car in your building's garage?
W	I don't think that would be helpful. It's a long walk from my place.
M	Well, is there ³⁾<u>a parking lot</u> at the park?
W	Yes. But parking costs $2 per hour.

[휴대폰이 울리다.]
여 안녕, Justin. 우리 여전히 오늘 오후에 만나는 거지?
남 당연하지. 내 개를 데려가도 될지 물어보려고 전화한 거야. 그 녀석을 외출시키면 좋을 것 같거든.
여 물론이지! 사실 우리가 갈 공원 안에 괜찮은 강아지 놀이터가 있어.
남 오, 딱 좋다. 그 구역에 또 뭐가 있니?
여 근처에 정말 근사한 카페가 있어. 커피 마시러 공원에서 거기까지 걸어가면 돼.
남 반려동물에 친화적인 곳이야?
여 그래. 난 거기에 항상 개가 있는 걸 봤어.
남 그러면 한번 가보고 싶어. 하지만 주차를 생각해 봐야겠지.
여 아, 맞다. 개를 데리고 오려면 운전을 해야겠구나.
남 내 차를 네 집의 차고에 두고 갈 수 있을까?
여 그건 도움이 안 될 것 같아. 우리 집에서 걸어가기엔 멀거든.
남 음, 공원에 주차장이 있니?
여 응. 하지만 주차료가 시간당 2달러야.

① 좋아. 내 주차 공간을 이용하면 돼.

② 아니. 카페에서 왼쪽 말고 오른쪽으로 돌면 돼.

③ 물론이지. 하지만 개를 데려온 사람들은 밖에 앉아야 해.

④ 걱정하지 마. 대신 걸어갈게.

⑤ 응. 하지만 주차료가 시간당 2달러야.

약속 장소에 개를 데려가도 되는지 양해를 구하는 상황이다. 개를 데려가기 위해 운전을 해야 하는 남자가 공원에 주차장이 있는지 물었으므로, 이에 대한 응답으로는 주차장이 있지만 주차료가 든다고 대답하는 ⑤ 'Yes. But parking costs $2 per hour.'가 가장 적절하다.

어휘 pet friendly 반려동물 친화적인 garage 몡 차고 parking spot 주차 공간

15 상황에 적절한 말 파악   정답 ①

W Jessica is a singer, and Albert is a songwriter. She asked him to write a new song that she will perform at her next concert. She wants the song to ¹⁾<u>express her gratitude</u> to her fans. Albert has finished creating the music for the song. It has a very ²⁾<u>bright and calm melody</u>. But he is having difficulties writing the lyrics. He is finding it hard to express ³⁾<u>such a personal message</u>. He also thinks that Jessica's fans would appreciate it if she was involved in the songwriting process. **So he wants to suggest to Jessica that she ⁴⁾<u>write her own lyrics</u>.** In this situation, what would Albert most likely say to Jessica?

여 Jessica는 가수이고, Albert는 작사가 겸 작곡가입니다. 그녀는 그에게 다음 콘서트에서 공연할 새로운 노래를 써 달라고 부탁했습니다. 그녀는 그 노래가 그녀의 팬들에 대한 고마움을 표현하기를 원합니다. Albert는 그 노래를 위한 음악을 다 만들었습니다. 그것은 매우 밝고 차분한 멜로디로 되어 있습니다. 하지만 그는 가사를 쓰는 데 어려움을 겪고 있습니다. 그는 그런 개인적인 메시지를 표현하는 것을 어려워합니다. 그는 또한 Jessica의 팬들이 그녀가 곡을 쓰는 과정에 참여한다면, 이를 고맙게 여길 것이라고 생각합니다. 그래서 그는 Jessica에게 그녀 자신만의 가사를 쓰라고 제안하고 싶습니다. 이러한 상황에서, Albert가 Jessica에게 가장 할 것 같은 말은 무엇입니까?

선택지 ① 당신이 직접 노랫말을 생각해내는 건 어떨까요?

② 저는 저번에 당신의 공연을 보고 정말 감명받았습니다.

③ 저는 당신의 콘서트가 큰 성공을 거둘 것이라고 확신합니다.

④ 이 가사가 당신의 생각을 표현하고 있는지 알려주실래요?

⑤ 팬들이 당신의 최신곡을 굉장히 좋아할 것 같군요.

Jessica가 의뢰한 새 노래를 작곡하는 중에, Albert는 Jessica가 직접 가사를 쓰는 것을 제안하려 한다. 따라서, Albert가 할 말로 ① 'Why don't you come up with the words for the song yourself?'가 가장 적절하다.

어휘 songwriter 몡 작사가 겸 작곡가 gratitude 몡 고마움 lyrics 몡 가사 be involved in ~에 참여하다, 관련되다 come up with ~을 생각해내다 positive 혱 확신하는; 긍정적인

16-17 세트 문항   정답 16 ③ 17 ③

M Good morning, everyone. Last time, we discussed reasons why city planning became necessary in ancient civilizations. **Today, I want to give you a brief overview of ¹⁾<u>ancient construction methods</u>.** At first, builders could only create simple structures ²⁾<u>out of wood</u>. These homes did not protect people from rain and wind well because of the gaps between the sticks or logs. Eventually, builders found ways to make ³⁾<u>structures with fewer gaps</u>. They started to use **bricks** that fit together tightly. This method is at least 9,000 years old. Later, ancient builders began to make beautiful and durable structures from **stone**. However, the material was difficult to work with, so it was only used for special structures like temples or monuments. The last example I want to look at is the surprising use of **concrete** in Roman times. Concrete's strength and cost-effectiveness allowed builders to create structures ⁴⁾<u>on a huge scale</u>, so it became the go-to material for public buildings. Now, let's take a look at some pictures of ancient buildings.

남 안녕하십니까, 여러분. 지난 시간에, 우리는 고대 문명에서 도시 계획이 필수가 된 이유를 논의했습니다. 오늘은, 여러분에게 고대 건축 방법에 대한 간략한 개요를 설명해드리려 합니다. 처음에, 건축자들은 목재로 간단한 구조물만 만들 수 있었습니다. 이런 집은 나무막대기나 통나무 사이의 틈 때문에 비와 바람으로부터 사람들을 잘 보호하지 못했습니다. 결국, 건축자들은 틈이 더 작은 구조물을 만드는 방법을 찾았습니다. 그들은 서로 꼭 들어맞는 벽돌을 사용하기 시작했습니다. 이 방법은 적어도 9,000년은 된 것입니다. 이후 고대의 건축자들은 석재로 아름답고 튼튼한 구조물을 만들기 시작했습니다. 하지만, 이 재료는 작업하기가 어려워서, 사원이나 기념비와 같은 특별한 구조물에만 사용되었습니다. 마지막으로 제가 살펴보고자 하는 사례는 놀랍게도 로마 시대의 콘크리트의 사용입니다. 콘크리트의 강도와 비용적 효율성은 건축자들이 거대한 규모로 구조물을 만들 수 있게 해주었고, 그래서 그것은 공공 건축물을 지을 때 믿고 쓸 수 있는 재료가 되었습니다. 이제, 고대 건축물의 사진들을 살펴보겠습니다.

선택지 16 ① 고대 도시들의 크기가 확장된 방식

② 문명에 있어 튼튼한 구조물의 중요성

③ 고대에 건축물이 만들어진 다양한 방법

④ 로마 시대 건축에 대한 오해

⑤ 고대에 도시가 계획된 방식

17 ① 목재 ② 벽돌 ③ 유리 ④ 석재 ⑤ 콘크리트

16 고대 건축 방법에 대한 간략한 개요를 설명하고 있으므로 남자가 하는 말의 주제로 ③ 'various ways buildings were made in ancient times'가 가장 적절하다.

17 목재, 벽돌, 석재, 콘크리트는 언급했지만 ③ 'glass'는 언급하지 않았다.

어휘 civilization 몡 문명 give an overview of ~의 개요를 설명하다 gap 몡 틈, 간격 fit together 꼭 들어맞다 durable 혱 튼튼한, 내구성이 있는 temple 몡 사원, 절 monument 몡 기념비, 기념물 scale 몡 규모 go-to 혱 믿음직한, 기댈 수 있는 misconception 몡 오해 expand 동 확장하다

1	②	2	③	3	⑤	4	④	5	⑤	6	②	7	②	8	③	9	⑤	10	③
11	②	12	①	13	②	14	④	15	⑤	16	②	17	④						

• 각 문제의 정답 근거는 굵은 글씨로, Dictation 정답은 밑줄로 표시되어 있습니다.

---

1   목적 파악

정답 ②

W Good morning, everyone. This is Drama Club President, Sally Howard. As you know, the Drama Club's first meeting of the year will be held today at 5 p.m. We will start by ¹⁾introducing the new club members, and then we will begin planning this year's performances. Since we accepted so many students into our club this semester, our group will have ²⁾twice as many members as before. **That's why we've decided to change the location of our meeting to ³⁾accommodate the larger group. Instead of taking place in the student council room, it will now be held in the auditorium so that we'll have plenty of space.** I look forward to seeing all of you there and hope you have a great rest of the day!

여 안녕하십니까, 여러분. 저는 연극부 회장 Sally Howard입니다. 여러분도 알듯이, 연극부의 올해 첫 회의가 오늘 오후 5시에 열립니다. 새로운 부원을 소개하는 것으로 시작해서, 올해 공연을 계획하도록 하겠습니다. 이번 학기에는 많은 학생을 우리 동아리에서 받아줬기 때문에, 이전보다 부원수가 두 배 더 많아졌습니다. 그래서 더 많은 인원을 수용하기 위해 회의 장소를 변경하기로 했습니다. 학생회실에서 여는 대신, 공간을 충분히 확보할 수 있도록 강당에서 열리겠습니다. 그곳에서 여러분 모두를 볼 수 있기를 기대하고 남은 하루도 즐겁게 보내길 바랍니다!

여자가 연극부의 올해 첫 회의를 안내하면서, 회의 장소를 강당으로 변경하겠다는 사실과 그 이유를 말하고 있다. 따라서, 여자가 하는 말의 목적으로 ② '동아리 회의 장소 변경을 공지하려고'가 가장 적절하다.

어휘 semester 몡 학기 location 몡 장소 accommodate 통 수용하다 student council 학생회

---

2   의견 파악

정답 ③

M Sarah, it's such a nice day. Isn't this beach beautiful?
W Yes. The water is so blue, and there aren't any clouds in the sky.
M Oh, look! There's a pretty seashell. I want to take it home with me.
W Hmm... **You shouldn't ¹⁾carelessly take natural objects like seashells and stones from the beach.**
M I disagree. It's not a living creature.
W Sure, but removing those things from a habitat can ²⁾break its natural balance.
M Really? I had no idea that they were so important.
W Many animals and plants need these objects for specific purposes. For example, a crab could use that shell for shelter.
M Well, I definitely don't want to ³⁾harm the wildlife here.
W You can take a picture of it instead or just enjoy looking at it now.
M You're right. Thanks for letting me know.

남 Sarah, 날이 너무 좋다. 여기 해변 아름답지 않니?
여 응. 물이 아주 파랗고 하늘에는 구름 한 점 없어.
남 오, 봐! 예쁜 조개껍데기가 있어. 이걸 집에 가지고 갈래.
여 흠... 해변에서 조개껍데기나 돌 같은 자연물을 함부로 가져가면 안 돼.
남 난 동의하지 않아. 그건 살아있는 생명체도 아닌걸.
여 그건 그렇지만, 서식지에서 그런 것들을 가져오면 자연의 균형을 깨뜨릴 수 있어.
남 정말? 그게 그렇게 중요한지 전혀 몰랐어.
여 많은 동물과 식물엔 특정한 목적을 위해 이런 것들이 필요해. 예를 들어, 게는 그 조개껍데기를 은신처로 사용할 수 있지.
남 음, 난 절대 이곳의 야생동물들에 피해를 주고 싶지 않아.
여 넌 대신 사진을 찍어도 되고, 아니면 그냥 지금 즐겁게 보면 돼.
남 네 말이 맞아. 알려줘서 고마워.

해변에서 발견한 조개껍데기를 집에 가져가려는 남자에게 여자가 그러한 자연물을 함부로 가져가면 안 된다고 했다. 따라서, 여자의 의견으로 ③ '해변에서 조개껍데기 같은 것을 함부로 가져가면 안 된다.'가 가장 적절하다.

어휘 carelessly 凰 함부로, 부주의하게 creature 몡 생명체, 생물 habitat 몡 서식지 balance 몡 균형 shelter 몡 은신처; 대피소 definitely 凰 절대로; 분명히 wildlife 몡 야생동물

---

3   관계 파악

정답 ⑤

W Mr. Dillon, thank you for your time today.
M You're welcome, Ms. Charles. I'm happy to talk to you and your viewers.
W I want to first congratulate you ¹⁾on your recent election.
M Thank you. I'm honored to represent our city's residents.
W Many claim they voted for you due to your crime prevention policies. Can you give us more details?
M Sure. I want to increase the budget of local police departments.
W Why is that necessary?
M Well, with more money, we'll ²⁾replace the old equipment being used by our police.

여 Dillon 씨, 오늘 시간 내주셔서 감사합니다.
남 천만에요, Charles 씨. 당신과 시청자분들에게 이야기할 수 있어 기쁘네요.
여 먼저 당신의 최근 당선을 축하드리고 싶어요.
남 감사합니다. 제가 우리 도시의 주민들을 대표하게 되다니 영광입니다.
여 많은 사람이 당신의 범죄 예방 정책 때문에 당신에게 투표했다고 주장하는데요. 좀 더 자세히 말씀해 주시겠어요?
남 물론이죠. 저는 지방 경찰청의 예산을 늘리고 싶습니다.
여 그게 왜 필요한가요?
남 음, 돈이 더 생기면, 우리 경찰이 쓰는 낮은 장비를 교체할 거예요.

W	Do you have any other future plans for the city?	여	도시를 위한 다른 미래 계획이 있나요?
M	Yes. I also hope to provide more public transportation options. This is necessary to ³⁾reduce air pollution and traffic jams.	남	네. 저는 또한 더 많은 대중교통 선택지를 제공하고 싶습니다. 이건 대기 오염과 교통 체증을 줄이기 위해 필요해요.
W	And do you have any final messages for our viewers today?	여	그리고 오늘 시청자들에게 전할 마지막 메시지가 있을까요?
M	I do. I appreciate your votes, and I won't let you down.	남	있습니다. 시민 여러분의 투표에 감사드리며, 실망시키지 않겠습니다.
W	Great. **Now, it's time for the weekly weather report.**	여	좋습니다. 이제, 주간 일기예보 시간입니다.

두 사람이 남자의 당선에 관해 인터뷰하고 있다. 여자는 남자의 정책에 대해 물어봤으며 인터뷰 후에 일기예보가 이어질 것이라고 했고, 남자는 최근에 당선되어 도시의 주민들을 대표하게 되었다고 하는 것으로 보아 두 사람의 관계로 ⑤ '뉴스 앵커 — 정치인'이 가장 적절하다.

어휘 represent 동 대표하다 claim 동 주장하다 due to ~ 때문에 equipment 명 장비 public transportation 대중교통 traffic jam 교통 체증 let ~ down ~를 실망시키다

---

4 그림 내용 불일치 파악
정답 ④

M	Wow, honey. I love how you decorated the backyard for our son's birthday party.	남	우와, 여보. 당신이 우리 아들 생일 파티하려고 뒤뜰을 꾸며놓은 방식이 정말 마음에 쏙 들어.
W	Thank you. But do you think he will like it?	여	고마워. 그런데 아들이 좋아할 것 같아?
M	Definitely. That soccer goal ¹⁾between the two trees is perfect. I'm sure the kids will enjoy that.	남	물론이지. 두 그루의 나무 사이에 있는 축구 골대는 완벽해. 아이들이 분명 좋아할 거야.
W	That's what I thought. Our dog is already playing with the ball on the grass.	여	나도 그렇게 생각했어. 우리 강아지가 이미 잔디 위에서 공을 가지고 놀고 있네.
M	I saw that. But what's that table ²⁾with three chairs for?	남	봤어. 그런데 의자가 세 개가 놓인 저 탁자는 뭘 위한 거야?
W	That's for face painting.	여	그건 페이스페인팅을 위한 거야.
M	I see. It's nice that there will be so many activities.	남	그렇구나. 많은 활동이 있을 것 같아서 좋네.
W	Yes. **And I've also put some heart-shaped balloons next to the table.**	여	응. 그리고 탁자 옆에 하트 모양의 풍선도 몇 개 뒀어.
M	They look good. ³⁾Those circular containers you have his gifts in are unique.	남	보기 좋아. 선물이 들어 있는 원형 용기도 독특한걸.
W	Do you think they're okay next to the balloons there?	여	그게 풍선 옆에 있는 게 괜찮은 것 같아?
M	Yes. Everything is perfect just as it is.	남	응. 모든 게 있는 그대로 완벽해.
W	Thanks. I really hope our son has a wonderful time.	여	고마워. 우리 아들이 아주 멋진 시간을 보내면 좋겠어.

대화에서 여자가 탁자 옆에 하트 모양의 풍선을 몇 개 두었다고 말했는데, ④에는 별 모양의 풍선들이 그려져 있다.

어휘 backyard 명 뒤뜰 grass 명 잔디 balloon 명 풍선 circular 형 원형의 container 명 용기, 그릇 just as it is 있는 그대로

---

5 할 일 파악
정답 ⑤

W	Hey, Eric. Is everything ready for our bookstore's signing event next week?	여	안녕하세요, Eric. 다음 주에 있을 우리 서점 사인회 준비는 다 되었나요?
M	Almost. I actually just emailed all our customers about it.	남	거의요. 사실 방금 모든 고객들에게 사인회 관련 이메일을 보냈어요.
W	And did you pick up that banner we're hanging in the store?	여	그리고 우리 매장에 걸어둘 현수막은 찾아왔나요?
M	I did. It looks great.	남	찾아왔어요. 현수막이 근사해 보이던걸요.
W	Excellent. I ¹⁾called the author this morning to confirm all of the event details.	여	훌륭하네요. 전 오늘 아침에 작가님에게 전화를 걸어서 행사의 세부 사항들을 확인했어요.
M	Does he have any requests?	남	작가님이 뭔가 요청하신 게 있었나요?
W	He said he'd appreciate it if we put his other books on display.	여	우리가 작가님의 다른 책들도 진열해두면 고맙겠다고 하셨어요.
M	Do we have ²⁾enough copies of them in the store?	남	매장에 책이 충분한 부수가 있나요?
W	I think so, but I ordered a few more just in case.	여	그런 것 같지만, 만약을 위해서 몇 권 더 주문했어요.
M	I guess the only thing we have to worry about is ³⁾moving the bookshelves around for the event.	남	우리가 걱정해야 할 단 한 가지는 행사를 위해 책장을 여기저기로 옮기는 것뿐인 것 같아요.
W	Yeah, we'll need more open space. **I'll get here early that day to handle it.**	여	네, 더 넓은 공간이 필요할 거예요. 제가 그날 일찍 와서 처리할게요.
M	**No, I'll take care of that now.** You've done enough.	남	아뇨, 그건 지금 제가 할게요. 당신은 할 만큼 했어요.
W	Thanks. That's very kind of you.	여	고마워요. 정말 친절하시군요.

서점의 사인회 준비 상황에 대해 이야기하고 있다. 책꽂이를 옮기는 일을 걱정하는 남자에게 여자가 자신이 그 일을 하겠다고 했으나, 결국 남자가 본인이 지금 하겠다고 했으므로 남자가 할 일로 ⑤ '책꽂이 옮기기'가 가장 적절하다.

어휘 pick up ~을 찾아오다, 찾다 author 명 작가 confirm 동 확인하다 detail 명 세부 사항 put ~ on display ~을 진열하다, 전시하다 copy 명 책 한 부; 복사 just in case 만약을 위해서 space 명 공간; 우주 handle 동 처리하다 명 손잡이

6 금액 정보 파악 · 정답 ②

M	Welcome to Carter Movie Theater. How can I help you?
W	Do you have ¹⁾any tickets left for *Future Seems Good*?
M	**We have tickets for both 11 a.m. and 1 p.m. The 11 a.m. showing has an early-bird price.**
W	Oh, what's ²⁾the price difference?
M	**It's $10 for a ticket instead of $12.**
W	**In that case, I'd like three tickets for 11 o'clock.**
M	Great. And would you be interested in buying a mini movie poster? **They're $5 each.**
W	Oh, I like those. **Um, I'll take ³⁾two of them.** And can I use my VIP membership card?
M	Yes. **You're actually entitled to a 20% discount. However, that will ⁴⁾only apply to the tickets.**
W	Sure. That's fine.
M	Okay. Your total is on the screen, ma'am.
W	Here you go.
M	Enjoy the movie!

남	Carter Movie Theater에 오신 것을 환영합니다. 무엇을 도와드릴까요?
여	<Future Seems Good> 티켓 남은 것 있어요?
남	오전 11시와 오후 1시 모두 자리가 있어요. 오전 11시 영화는 조조할인이 있습니다.
여	아, 가격 차이가 얼마나 나요?
남	티켓 한 장에 12달러가 아니라 10달러예요.
여	그렇다면, 11시로 세 장 주세요.
남	좋아요. 그리고 미니 영화 포스터를 살 의향이 있으신가요? 한 장에 5달러입니다.
여	오, 마음에 드네요. 음, 그중 두 장을 살게요. 그리고 제 VIP 회원 카드를 사용할 수 있나요?
남	네. 실제로 20% 할인받을 자격이 있으시네요. 하지만, 그건 티켓에만 적용됩니다.
여	그럼요. 괜찮아요.
남	알겠습니다. 총액이 화면에 표시되었습니다, 손님.
여	여기요.
남	영화 재미있게 보세요!

여자가 오전 11시 영화 티켓 세 장($10×3=$30)과, 미니 영화 포스터 두 장($5×2=$10)을 구매했고, 영화 티켓에 대해서만 20% 할인($30×0.8=$24)을 받았으므로 정답은 ② '$34'이다.

어휘 early-bird price 조조할인 be entitled to ~을 받을 자격이 있다, ~이 주어지다

7 이유 파악 · 정답 ②

W	Hi, Adam. Come in.
M	Is there something wrong, Ms. Barnes?
W	I just graded your English test from last week. Your score was ¹⁾much lower than usual.
M	I see.
W	Did you forget about the test?
M	Not at all. I had a math test last week, too. So I ²⁾reminded myself about both test dates every day.
W	Then, did you run out of time to study?
M	No. It wasn't that, either. **It was actually because I ³⁾had a stomachache on the exam day.** I couldn't focus on the exam.
W	Oh, I'm very sorry that happened. Are you feeling better now?
M	Yes. I'm okay now. I'll work hard on ⁴⁾my upcoming report to make up for it.

여	안녕, Adam. 들어오렴.
남	무슨 문제라도 있나요, Barnes 선생님?
여	지난주에 본 영어 시험을 막 채점했단다. 네 점수가 평소보다 훨씬 낮았어.
남	그렇군요.
여	시험에 대해 잊어버렸니?
남	전혀요. 지난주에 수학 시험도 있었어요. 그래서 매일 스스로 두 시험 날짜를 되새겼어요.
여	그렇다면 공부할 시간이 부족했니?
남	아니요. 그것도 아니었어요. 실은 시험 당일에 배탈이 나서 그랬어요. 시험에 집중할 수가 없었어요.
여	이런. 그런 일이 일어났다니 안됐구나. 이젠 좀 괜찮아졌니?
남	네, 지금은 괜찮아요. 전 그걸 만회하기 위해 곧 있을 보고서를 열심히 쓸 거예요.

남자의 시험 점수가 평소보다 훨씬 낮았다고 하는 여자에게 남자는 시험 당일에 배탈이 나서 집중을 할 수 없었다고 말했으므로, 남자가 시험에서 좋은 성적을 받지 못한 이유는 ② '배탈 때문에 집중을 못 해서'이다.

어휘 grade 통 채점하다, 성적을 매기다 명 등급 run out of ~이 부족하다, ~을 다 써버리다 make up for ~을 만회하다, 보충하다

8 언급 유무 파악 · 정답 ③

W	Rick, what are you looking at on your phone?
M	Hi, Angela. I'm reading about this year's Junior Bowling Tournament.
W	Oh, I heard it was fun last year. When is it?
M	It starts at **5 p.m. on November 23rd**.
W	Wow, that's soon. Are you ¹⁾going to compete?
M	Yes, but it requires participants to register as part of a **four-person team**. So do you want to ²⁾enter with me? I'll also ask some other friends to join.
W	Hmm... Is there any entry fee?
M	Yeah. It costs **$20** to enter. Is that too much?
W	No. It's fine. Count me in. ³⁾Where is it happening?
M	It will be at the **Astro Bowling Center** downtown.
W	Perfect. I hope we have a great time together.

여	Rick, 휴대폰으로 뭘 보고 있는 거야?
남	안녕, Angela. 난 올해 Junior Bowling Tournament에 대해 읽고 있어.
여	아, 작년에 재미있었다고 들었어. 그게 언젠데?
남	11월 23일 오후 5시에 시작해.
여	우와, 그거 곧이네. 너도 참가할 거니?
남	응, 그런데 참가자들에게 4인 팀의 일원으로 등록하도록 요구하고 있어. 그러니 나랑 함께 참가할래? 다른 친구들에게도 함께하자고 부탁할 거야.
여	흠... 참가비가 있니?
남	응. 참가하는 데 20달러가 들어. 너무 과하니?
여	아니. 괜찮아. 나도 끼워줘. 어디에서 열려?
남	시내에 있는 아스트로 볼링 센터에서 열릴 거야.
여	딱 좋다. 우리가 함께 즐거운 시간을 보내면 좋겠어.

일시(11월 23일 오후 5시), 참가팀 인원(4인), 참가비(20달러), 장소(아스트로 볼링 센터)에 대해 언급했고, ③ '신청 방법'은 언급하지 않았다.

어휘 compete 통 (시합에) 참가하다; 경쟁하다 enter 통 참가하다; 들어가다 entry fee 참가비 count ~ in ~를 끼워주다

9 내용 불일치 파악

정답 ⑤

W Hello, parents. As you know, technology is becoming ¹⁾more and more important to our world. So why don't you give your kids a head start at mastering it? Sign them up for Winter Computer Camp to provide them with the skills they need for their future. Our instructors are ²⁾computer science professors who will help your children learn about different computer programs and features. This course is open to children who are 12 or older. Classes will be held from 9 a.m. to 4 p.m. ³⁾daily for two weeks on the campus of Andersen College. And only 20 students can register. **Registration is open online ⁴⁾until this Friday at 5 p.m.** Don't let this opportunity pass you by, and register today. We hope to see you soon!

여 안녕하십니까, 학부모 여러분. 아시다시피, 기술은 세상에서 점점 더 중요해지고 있습니다. 그렇다면, 여러분의 자녀가 기술을 통달하기에 유리한 출발점에 서도록 하는 것이 어떻겠습니까? 자녀의 미래에 필요한 기술을 제공하려면 그들을 Winter Computer Camp에 등록시키십시오. 저희 강사진은 컴퓨터 공학 교수들로, 여러분의 자녀가 다양한 컴퓨터 프로그램과 기능에 대해 배울 수 있도록 도와줄 것입니다. 이 과정에는 12세 이상의 아이들이 참여할 수 있습니다. 수업은 안데르센 대학의 캠퍼스에서 2주 동안 매일 오전 9시부터 오후 4시까지 열릴 예정입니다. 그리고 오직 20명의 학생만 등록할 수 있습니다. 온라인 등록은 이번 주 금요일 오후 5시까지입니다. 이 기회를 놓치지 말고 오늘 등록하십시오. 곧 뵙기를 바랍니다!

학부모를 대상으로 한 겨울 컴퓨터 캠프 홍보 방송이다. 여자가 온라인 등록은 이번 주 금요일 오후 5시까지라고 했으므로 ⑤ '금요일 오후 5시부터 등록 신청을 받는다.'는 내용과 일치하지 않는다.

[어휘] a head start 유리한 출발 provide A with B A에게 B를 제공하다 instructor 명 강사 feature 명 기능; 모습 register 동 등록하다 (registration 명 등록)

10 도표 정보 파악

정답 ③

W Robert, did you ¹⁾reserve a booth to sell our photographs at the art market next Saturday yet?

M I'm looking at the website to book a booth now.

W Oh, let's see. *[Pause]* Well, this one is too small. **I think it should be over five square meters.**

M Okay, and ²⁾what about the cost?

W **Let's try to keep it under $200.**

M Good idea. That still leaves us with a few options.

W Right. What about the rental time?

M I don't think the afternoon will be as busy, **so let's book a booth ³⁾for the morning.**

W Then, this one won't work.

M And I don't think we need a premium spot at the market.

W I disagree. **By ⁴⁾choosing a premium spot, we will have a booth right by the entrance. People will see us easily.**

M **Okay. Let's go for it, then.**

W That sounds good.

여 Robert, 다음 주 토요일에 우리 사진을 판매할 아트 마켓 부스를 예약했니?
남 지금 예약하려고 웹사이트를 보고 있는 중이야.
여 아, 어디 봐. [잠시 멈춤] 음, 이건 너무 작아. 5m²는 넘어야 할 것 같아.
남 알겠어, 그리고 비용은 어쩌지?
여 200달러 미만으로 유지해 보자.
남 좋은 생각이야. 여전히 우리에게는 몇 가지 선택지가 남아있어.
여 맞아. 대여 시간은 어떻게 하지?
남 오후에는 바쁘지 않을 것 같으니, 오전으로 부스를 예약하자.
여 그럼, 이건 안 되겠네.
남 그리고 마켓에서 프리미엄 자리는 필요 없을 것 같아.
여 난 동의하지 않아. 프리미엄 자리를 선택하면, 우리 부스가 입구 바로 옆이 될 거야. 사람들이 우리를 쉽게 보러 오겠지.
남 알았어. 그러면 그걸로 할게.
여 좋았어.

두 사람은 면적이 5m²가 넘는 것 중에서, 가격은 200달러 미만이며, 대여 시간은 오전이고, 프리미엄 자리에 있는 부스를 골랐다.

[어휘] square meter 제곱미터 disagree 동 동의하지 않다 entrance 명 입구

11 짧은 대화의 응답 파악

정답 ②

W Honey, there's ¹⁾something wrong with the bathroom sink. When I brush my teeth, the water doesn't drain.

M Oh, no. The pipe must be blocked. **I guess we have to ²⁾call the plumber.**

W I can do it. **When should I ask him to come?**

M **Let's try to get it fixed as soon as possible.**

여 여보, 화장실 세면대에 뭔가 문제가 있어. 양치질할 때, 물이 안 빠져.
남 오, 이런. 파이프가 막힌 게 틀림없어. 배관공을 불러야 할 것 같아.
여 내가 부를 수 있어. 언제 와달라고 할까?
남 가능한 한 빨리 그걸 고치려고 하자.

[선택지] ① 메모장에 배관공의 번호가 있어.
② 가능한 한 빨리 그걸 고치려고 하자.
③ 나는 방금 몇 분 전에 양치질을 했어.
④ 일단 세면대에서 손만 씻을게.
⑤ 사실 오늘 아침에 화장실 청소를 했어.

화장실 세면대에 물이 빠지지 않아 수리가 필요한 상황에서 여자가 배관공을 언제 불러야 좋을지 남자에게 물었으므로, 이에 대한 응답으로는 가능한 빨리 수리하자고 하는 ② 'Let's try to get it fixed as soon as possible.'이 가장 적절하다.

[어휘] brush one's teeth 양치질하다 drain 동 물이 빠지다 block 동 막다, 차단하다 plumber 명 배관공 as soon as possible 가능한 한 빨리

12 짧은 대화의 응답 파악

정답 ①

[Cell phone rings.] **M** Hey, Julie. Are you on your way to the café? Did you forget we are supposed to meet here today? **W** Hi, Mark. **I'm stuck in traffic, so I'm running a little late.** I'm sorry ¹⁾<u>about the</u> inconvenience. **M** No, it's okay. **If you want, I can go ahead and** ²⁾<u>order</u> **you** <u>something</u>. **W** Sure. I'll take an iced latte, please.	[휴대폰이 울린다.] 남 안녕, Julie. 카페로 오는 중이야? 오늘 여기서 만나기로 한 거 안 잊었지? 여 안녕, Mark. 차가 막혀서 조금 늦어지고 있어. 불편하게 해서 미안해. 남 아냐, 괜찮아. 원한다면, 내가 먼저 가서 널 위해 뭔가 주문해 놓을게. 여 그래. 아이스 라테로 부탁할게. 선택지 ① 그래. 아이스 라테로 부탁할게. ② 알겠어. 카페 주소를 보내줄게. ③ 맞아. 사고 때문에 차가 막히는 거야. ④ 서둘러 줘. 네 커피가 식을 거야. ⑤ 걱정하지 마. 대신 내 차를 끌고 갈게.

여자와 남자가 카페에서 만나기로 약속한 상황에서 남자가 카페에 먼저 가서 주문해 놓겠다고 했으므로, 이에 대한 응답으로는 음료 주문을 부탁하는 ① 'Sure. I'll take an iced latte, please.' 가 가장 적절하다.

어휘 be one's way to ~로 오는[가는] 중이다 be supposed to ~하기로 하다 stuck in traffic 차가 막히는, 교통이 정체된 be running late 늦어지다

13 긴 대화의 응답 파악

정답 ②

M Hey, Tina. ¹⁾<u>Great</u> <u>job on</u> your history essay. **W** Thank you, Mr. Roberts. **M** It was very well written. It seems like your writing has improved a lot this year. **W** Yes, I joined the student newspaper a couple months ago and ²⁾<u>wrote some</u> <u>articles</u>. It's taught me a lot about how to be an effective writer. **M** I bet. Are you interested in journalism as a career? **W** I think so. I really love telling stories and interviewing people. **M** So what article are you working on right now? **W** I'm writing an ³⁾<u>article</u> <u>on a</u> <u>lecture</u> that's going to take place at the local museum next week. **M** Do you mean the one about the founding of our city? **W** That's right! **M** Well, I know the lecturer. If you want, I can put you in touch with him. **W** Thank you! That would help. **Do you think he would** ⁴⁾<u>mind being interviewed?</u> **M** I'm sure he would love to talk with you.	남 안녕, Tina. 역사 에세이 잘 썼더구나. 여 감사합니다, Roberts 선생님. 남 그건 아주 잘 써졌어. 올해는 네 글쓰기가 많이 좋아진 것 같구나. 여 네, 몇 달 전에 학교 신문반에 들어가서 기사를 좀 썼어요. 어떻게 하면 유능한 기자가 될 수 있는지 많이 배웠어요. 남 그렇겠구나. 직업으로 언론 일 쪽에 관심이 있니? 여 그런 것 같아요. 저는 이야기를 들려주고 사람들과 인터뷰하는 걸 정말 좋아하거든요. 남 그래서 지금은 무슨 기사를 쓰고 있니? 여 다음 주에 지역 박물관에서 열릴 강의에 관한 기사를 쓰고 있어요. 남 우리 도시의 설립에 관한 강연을 말하는 거니? 여 맞아요! 남 음, 내가 그 강연자를 알고 있단다. 네가 원한다면, 그와 연락이 닿도록 해 줄 수 있어. 여 감사합니다! 그러면 도움이 될 거예요. 그분이 인터뷰 받는 것을 꺼리실 것 같으세요? 남 그는 분명 너와 이야기하고 싶어 할 거란다. 선택지 ① 역사 에세이는 다음 주까지만 제출할 수 있단다. ② 그는 분명 너와 이야기하고 싶어 할 거란다. ③ 내 기사를 다시 확인해야 할 것 같구나. ④ 내일 인터뷰에서 보자꾸나. ⑤ 그건 매우 흥미로운 강의가 될 거야.

여자의 기사에 관해 이야기하는 상황이다. 지역 박물관에서 열릴 강의에 관한 기사를 쓰고 있다는 여자에게 남자가 그 강연자와 연결해주겠다고 제안하자 여자가 그가 인터뷰 받는 것을 꺼릴 것 같은지 물었으므로, 이에 대한 응답으로는 강연자의 반응을 예상하는 ② 'I'm sure he would love to talk with you.'가 가장 적절하다.

어휘 journalism 뗑 언론 career 뗑 일, 직업; 경력 founding 뗑 설립, 창립 lecturer 뗑 강연자 put A in touch with B A를 B와 연락이 닿게 하다

14 긴 대화의 응답 파악

정답 ④

M Where do you want to go for a vacation this year, honey? **W** We went to the beach last year, so let's visit a place ¹⁾<u>with different scenery</u> this time. **M** We could rent a cabin by a lake. There are many good places nearby. **W** I'd rather go abroad. **M** Okay. Then, maybe we should visit a city in Europe. **W** I really want to be close to nature, too. I don't want to just be in a city the whole time. **M** Hmm... How about going to Finland? Then, we can stay in a place close to ²⁾<u>both</u> <u>mountains</u> <u>and</u> <u>a city</u>. **W** That sounds perfect. **M** Great. So we should decide when we want to go.	남 올해 휴가는 어디로 가고 싶어, 여보? 여 작년에 해변으로 갔으니까, 이번에는 경치가 다른 곳을 방문하자. 남 호숫가에서 오두막집을 빌릴 수도 있어. 근처에 좋은 장소들도 많아. 여 차라리 해외로 가고 싶어. 남 알았어. 그럼, 유럽의 도시를 방문하는 게 좋을 수도 있겠어. 여 자연에도 가까운 곳에 정말로 있고 싶어. 내내 도시에만 있고 싶지 않아. 남 흠... 핀란드에 가는 건 어때? 그러면 산과 도시 모두 가까운 곳에 머물 수 있어. 여 완벽한 것 같아. 남 좋아. 자, 우리 언제 가고 싶은지 정해야 해.

W I think summer would be best. It's too cold there at other times of the year. M That makes sense. **But summer is peak season, so we better hurry to get all of** ³⁾our reservations **sorted.** W That's true. I'll start looking at flights and hotels now.	여 여름이 가장 좋을 것 같아. 거긴 다른 때는 너무 춥잖아. 남 이해가 되네. 하지만 여름은 성수기니까 서둘러서 모든 예약을 정리하는 게 좋겠어. 여 맞아. 내가 지금부터 항공편과 호텔을 알아보기 시작할게.

선택지 ① 정확해. 거기서는 여름에 자외선 차단제를 발라야 할 거야.
② 맞아. 성수기에는 가격이 더 비싸.
③ 물론이지. 작년에 우리 유럽에서 멋진 휴가를 보냈잖아.
④ 맞아. 내가 지금부터 항공편과 호텔을 알아보기 시작할게.
⑤ 괜찮아. 그냥 다음번에 해변으로 가면 돼.

두 사람이 휴가 계획을 세우고 있는 상황이다. 남자가 여름은 성수기이므로 모든 예약을 서둘러 하자고 했으므로, 이에 대한 응답으로는 그렇게 하겠다고 말하는 ④ 'That's true. I'll start looking at flights and hotels now.'가 가장 적절하다.

어휘 scenery 명 경치, 풍경 cabin 명 오두막집; 객실 would rather 차라리 ~하고 싶다 abroad 부 해외로 the whole time 내내 peak season 성수기
sort 동 잘 정리하다, 해결하다 명 종류

15 상황에 적절한 말 파악   정답 ⑤

M Steve and Diana are ¹⁾interested in space. They both spend their free time reading books about it. So both of them were excited when their science class started studying the solar system this week. Today, they were given a group project. The students were ²⁾told to pick a space-related topic for a class presentation. Each student submitted a piece of paper with their choice of topic written on it. Since both Steve and Diana have been reading about asteroids in their spare time, they both wrote "asteroids." **After Steve finds out that he and Diana have the same idea, he wants to suggest to her that they** ³⁾work together on the project. **In this** situation, what would Steve most likely say to Diana?	남 Steve와 Diana는 우주에 관심이 있습니다. 그들은 둘 다 우주에 관한 책을 읽으며 여가 시간을 보냅니다. 그래서 그들 모두 이번 주 과학 시간에 태양계를 공부하기 시작하자 신이 났습니다. 오늘, 그들은 조별 과제를 받았습니다. 학생들은 수업 발표를 위해 우주와 관련된 주제를 고르라는 말을 들었습니다. 각 학생은 자신이 선택한 주제가 적힌 종이를 제출했습니다. Steve와 Diana 둘 다 여가 시간에 소행성에 관해 읽고 있었기 때문에, 그들은 둘 다 '소행성'이라고 썼습니다. Steve는 자신과 Diana가 같은 생각을 하고 있다는 것을 알게 된 후, 그녀에게 이 과제를 함께 하자고 제안하고 싶습니다. 이러한 상황에서, Steve가 Diana에게 가장 할 것 같은 말은 무엇입니까?

선택지 ① 우주에 관한 좋은 주제를 하나 더 찾을 수 있을 것 같아.
② 우리 둘 다 소행성에 관해 써도 된나고 생각하니?
③ 태양계에 관한 네 과제를 내게 공유해줄래?
④ 우와, 난 소행성이 그렇게 흥미로운지 몰랐어.
⑤ 우리 팀을 짜서 수업 발표를 하는 게 어때?

Diana가 자신과 같은 발표 주제를 고른 것을 보고 Steve는 수업 발표 과제를 함께 하자고 제안하려 한다. 따라서, Steve가 할 말로 ⑤ 'Why don't we team up to work on the class presentation?'이 가장 적절하다.

어휘 solar system 태양계 submit 동 제출하다 asteroid 명 소행성 spare time 여가 시간 team up 팀을 짜다

16-17 세트 문항   정답 16 ② 17 ④

W Hello, class. In today's lecture, I'm going to talk about elections. **Specifically, I'd like to look at some successful methods** ¹⁾to encourage voting. The first one is mandatory voting. For example, people in **Switzerland** have to ²⁾pay a fine if they don't vote. According to one study, this increased voting by around 10%. Next, in **Argentina**, there is a ³⁾political penalty for not voting. If people do not go to the polls, they are prohibited from holding government positions for three years. Another effective approach is to make election day a national holiday. **Belgium** is one such country. Thanks to its holiday, the country has a voting rate of nearly 75%. ⁴⁾The final tactic is to make voting a fun and welcoming experience. We can see one example of this in **Australia**. Its people often host barbecues outside of its polling places and cook so-called "democracy sausages." Nine out of ten people there vote. Now, let's take a look at a quick video clip on this subject.	여 안녕하십니까, 학급 여러분. 오늘 강의에서, 저는 선거에 관해 말하려고 합니다. 구체적으로, 투표를 장려하기 위한 몇 가지 성공적인 방법들을 살펴보고 싶습니다. 첫 번째는 의무 투표입니다. 예를 들어, 스위스 사람들은 투표하지 않으면 벌금을 내야 합니다. 한 연구에 따르면, 이것이 투표율을 약 10% 증가시켰습니다. 다음으로, 아르헨티나에서는 투표하지 않으면 정치적 불이익이 있습니다. 만약 사람들이 투표소에 가지 않는다면, 그들은 3년 동안 정부 직책을 맡는 것이 금지됩니다. 또 다른 효과적인 접근법은 선거일을 국경일로 만드는 것입니다. 벨기에가 그런 나라 중 하나입니다. 휴일 덕분에, 그 나라는 거의 75%의 투표율을 보입니다. 마지막 전략은 투표를 재미있고 환대받는 경험으로 만드는 것입니다. 우리는 이것의 한 예를 호주에서 볼 수 있습니다. 그곳 사람들은 종종 투표소 밖에서 바비큐 파티를 열고 이른바 '민주주의 소시지'를 요리합니다. 그곳 사람들은 10명 중 9명이 투표합니다. 이제, 이 주제에 관한 짧은 동영상을 살펴보겠습니다.

선택지 16 ① 사람들이 투표하지 않는 이유
② 사람들이 투표하도록 동기부여 하는 방법
③ 누구에게 투표할지 고르는 방법
④ 낮은 투표율의 결과
⑤ 국제적 선거의 결과
17 ① 스위스 ② 아르헨티나 ③ 벨기에 ④ 프랑스 ⑤ 호주

16 투표를 장려하기 위한 몇 가지 성공적인 방법들에 대해 살펴보고 있으므로 여자가 하는 말의 주제로 ② 'ways of motivating people to vote'가 가장 적절하다.
17 스위스, 아르헨티나, 벨기에, 호주는 언급했지만 ④ 'France'는 언급하지 않았다.

어휘 mandatory 형 의무적인 fine 명 벌금 형 좋은 penalty 명 불이익; 형벌 go to the poll 투표소에 가다 be prohibited from ~하는 것이 금지되다 approach 명 접근법 동 접근하다
thanks to ~ 덕분에 tactic 명 전략, 전술 so-called 형 이른바, 소위 democracy 명 민주주의 motivate 동 동기부여 하다 vote for ~에게 투표하다 consequence 명 결과

1	②	2	①	3	④	4	⑤	5	④	6	④	7	①	8	⑤	9	③	10	②
11	④	12	①	13	⑤	14	②	15	③	16	③	17	⑤						

- 각 문제의 정답 근거는 굵은 글씨로, Dictation 정답은 밑줄로 표시되어 있습니다.

---

1 목적 파악
정답 ②

M Hello, listeners. **Do you want to create art from the comfort of your home? Then,** ¹⁾sign up for an Easy Art online course and make beautiful pieces where you live! With Easy Art courses, you don't need to go out and ²⁾buy art supplies. Instead, we send kits including paintbrushes, paints, and canvases right to your door. Make your own work and learn about art with the help of our professional instructors online in either live streaming classes or recorded sessions. To register, just visit our website at www.easyart.com. We can't wait to ³⁾help you get started!

남 안녕하십니까, 청취자 여러분. 집에서 편안하게 미술 작품을 만들고 싶으신가요? 그렇다면 Easy Art 온라인 강의를 신청하고 지내시는 곳에서 아름다운 작품을 창작하세요! Easy Art 강의를 들으면, 미술용품을 사러 외출할 필요가 없습니다. 대신, 저희가 페인트 붓, 물감, 캔버스를 포함한 키트를 바로 현관 앞까지 보내드립니다. 온라인으로 실시간 강의나 녹화 강의를 듣고 전문 강사의 도움을 받아, 여러분만의 작품을 만들고 미술에 대해 배우십시오. 등록하시려면 그냥 저희 웹사이트 www.easyart.com을 방문하시면 됩니다. 여러분의 시작을 너무나 돕고 싶습니다!

남자가 Easy Art 온라인 강의의 장점에 대해 설명하며, 강의를 신청하여 집에서 편하게 미술 작품을 창작하라고 홍보하고 있다. 따라서, 남자가 하는 말의 목적으로 ② '온라인 미술 강의를 홍보하려고'가 가장 적절하다.

[어휘] from the comfort of ~에서 편안하게 art supplies 미술용품 right to one's door (~의) 바로 현관 앞까지 live streaming 실시간 방송, 생중계 방송

---

2 의견 파악
정답 ①

W Ron, what is that medicine you're taking?
M I have a slight cold, so I'm ¹⁾taking some antibiotics.
W I don't think that's a good idea. You shouldn't use them to treat a cold.
M Why not?
W Every time you use antibiotics, it can ²⁾make germs stronger.
M But I need to get better fast. Aren't antibiotics helpful for that?
W Actually, no. They can't cure a cold.
M Really? I thought antibiotics would kill the cold virus.
W That's a common misunderstanding. Antibiotics are only effective at getting rid of bacteria. They have no effect on viruses.
M Oh, I didn't realize that. So antibiotics won't help me at all.
W Exactly! You'll ³⁾get no benefit, and the drug may be less effective when you actually need it.
M Okay. I'll stop taking it. Thanks for the advice.

여 Ron, 네가 먹으려는 약 뭐야?
남 감기 기운이 있어서 항생제를 먹으려고 해.
여 그건 좋은 생각이 아닌 것 같아. 감기를 치료하려고 그걸 쓰면 안 돼.
남 왜 안 돼?
여 항생제를 사용할 때마다, 그건 세균을 더 강하게 만들 수 있어.
남 하지만 난 빨리 나아야 해. 그러려면 항생제가 도움이 되지 않니?
여 사실, 아니야. 그건 감기를 고칠 수 없어.
남 정말? 항생제가 감기 바이러스를 죽일 거라고 생각했는데.
여 그건 흔한 오해야. 항생제는 박테리아를 없애는 데만 효과가 있어. 바이러스에는 영향을 주지 않아.
남 아, 그건 몰랐어. 그러면 항생제는 전혀 도움이 안 되겠네.
여 정확해! 아무런 이득도 얻지 못할 테고, 실제로 그 약이 필요할 때는 덜 효과적일 수도 있어.
남 알았어. 복용하지 않을게. 조언해 줘서 고마워.

감기 기운이 있어서 항생제를 먹으려고 하는 남자에게 여자가 감기를 치료하려고 항생제를 쓰면 안 된다고 했다. 따라서, 여자의 의견으로 ① '감기 치료제로 항생제를 쓰면 안 된다.'가 가장 적절하다.

[어휘] have a slight cold 감기 기운이 있다 antibiotic 圀 항생제 germ 圀 세균 get rid of ~을 없애다 have an effect on ~에 영향을 주다 not ~ at all 전혀 ~ 아니다

---

3 관계 파악
정답 ④

M Thank you for meeting with me, Ms. Michaels.
W Of course. I'm ¹⁾a huge fan of your magazine articles, so I'm excited to be featured in one.
M I'm happy to hear it. **So you've recently been** ²⁾recognized for your groundbreaking research on sea turtles. Can you tell me more about that?
W Yes. I've been tracking different species of sea turtles to get a better idea of their movements.
M Why is this data helpful?
W Well, ³⁾the more we know about their movements, the easier they are to protect.
M Why is their protection so important?

남 저를 만나주셔서 감사합니다, Michaels 씨.
여 당연한 걸요. 저는 당신이 쓴 잡지 기사의 열렬한 팬이에요, 그래서 거기 실리게 되어 설레요.
남 그 말을 들으니 기쁘네요. 자, 당신은 최근에 바다거북에 관한 획기적인 연구로 인정을 받으셨죠. 그것에 대해 좀 더 말씀해 주시겠어요?
여 네. 저는 바다거북의 이동을 더 잘 알기 위해 여러 종의 바다거북을 추적해 왔어요.
남 이 데이터가 왜 도움이 될까요?
여 음, 우리가 그것들의 이동에 대해 더 많이 알면 알수록, 더 쉽게 보호할 수 있거든요.
남 그것들을 보호하는 게 왜 그렇게 중요한가요?

W	Sea turtles are critical to the health of our oceans. They keep our reefs [4]in good shape and transport nutrients from the water to land.	여	바다거북은 바다의 건강성에 매우 중요해요. 암초를 좋은 상태로 유지하게 하고 바다에서 육지로 영양분을 옮기거든요.
M	That's amazing. What's your next goal, then?	남	정말 놀랍군요. 그러면 다음 목표는 어떻게 되시나요?
W	**I'm going to examine fish that live in and around reefs.**	여	전 암초 속과 그 주변에 사는 물고기들을 조사할 거예요.
M	I see. I hope your studies go well. And thank you so much for your time.	남	그러시군요. 연구가 순조롭게 진행되기를 바랍니다. 그리고 시간 내주셔서 감사합니다.

여자의 연구에 관해 인터뷰하는 상황이다. 남자는 잡지 기사를 쓴 적이 있으며 인터뷰를 주도하고 있고, 여자는 바다거북을 연구했고 이후 암초 속과 그 주변에 사는 물고기를 조사할 예정이라고 하는 것으로 보아 두 사람의 관계로 ④ '잡지 기자 — 해양 생물학자'가 가장 적절하다.

어휘 be featured in (신문, 잡지 등에) 실리다 groundbreaking 형 획기적인 track 통 추적하다 get a better idea of ~을 더 잘 알다 critical 형 중요한 reef 명 암초 transport 통 옮기다 nutrient 명 영양분 go well 순조롭게 진행되다

---

4 그림 내용 불일치 파악

정답 ⑤

W	Well, it looks as if everything is ready for the school's band auditions, Kevin.	여	음, 학교 밴드부 오디션을 위한 모든 것이 준비된 것 같아, Kevin.
M	I think so. What catches your eye the most?	남	내 생각에도 그래. 가장 네 눈길을 끄는 건 뭐야?
W	I really love the banner with "Good Luck" on it above the stage.	여	무대 위쪽에 걸린 'Good Luck'이라고 적힌 배너가 정말 마음에 들어.
M	Thanks. I thought it might help the students feel more comfortable.	남	고마워. 그게 학생들이 좀 더 편안함을 느끼도록 도와줄 거라고 생각했어.
W	Why did you set up a chair [1]in the middle of the stage?	여	왜 무대 중앙에 의자를 설치했어?
M	Each participant will sit there and play.	남	각 참가자들은 거기 앉아서 연주할 거야.
W	I see the microphone is already set up [2]in front of that. Did you test the sound system?	여	그 앞에 마이크가 이미 설치되어 있구나. 음향 시스템은 시험해봤어?
M	I did that this morning. We're all good to go.	남	오늘 아침에 했어. 우리는 모두 시작할 준비됐어.
W	Great! What is the rectangular table facing the stage for?	여	좋아! 무대 쪽을 향해 있는 직사각형 탁자는 뭘 위한 거야?
M	That's where the senior band members will sit.	남	거기에 선배 밴드부원들이 앉을 거야.
W	I see. **And did you put the [3]laptops on the table?**	여	그렇구나. 그리고 네가 탁자 위에 노트북을 올려둔 거니?
M	**Yeah, but I brought only two. I should find out who brought the other one.**	남	응, 그런데 난 두 대만 가져왔어. 나머지 한 대는 누가 가져왔는지 알아봐야겠어.
W	Maybe it's one of the senior members.	여	아마 선배 부원들 중 한 명일 거야.

대화에서 남자가 탁자 위에 올려둔 노트북 중 두 대만 본인이 가져왔고 나머지 한 대는 누가 가져왔는지 알아봐야겠다고 말했는데, ⑤에는 두 대의 노트북만 그려져 있다.

어휘 catch one's eye 눈길을 끌다 set up 설치하다 good to go 시작할 준비가 된 rectangular 형 직사각형의 face 통 ~쪽을 향하다 명 얼굴 senior 형 선배의; 연상인

---

5 할 일 파악

정답 ④

W	Honey, you seem really stressed. Is everything okay?	여	여보, 정말 스트레스를 많이 받는 것 같아. 괜찮아?
M	Well, our clothing shop's [1]sales have dropped this month. I'm so worried about it.	남	음, 우리 옷 가게의 이번 달 매출이 떨어졌어. 그게 너무 걱정돼.
W	I think it's because of the cold weather. It'll be all right soon.	여	그건 추운 날씨 때문이라고 생각해. 곧 괜찮아질 거야.
M	I still think we should find a way to bring in more customers.	남	그래도 더 많은 고객을 끌어들일 방법을 찾아야 할 것 같아.
W	Do you have any ideas?	여	무슨 아이디어 있어?
M	Why don't we have a sale? If we [2]offer a discount on new arrivals, more shoppers might stop by.	남	세일을 하는 게 어때? 만약 우리가 신상품에 할인을 제공하면, 더 많은 쇼핑객들이 들를지도 몰라.
W	I think we would lose money from that. How about handing out flyers instead?	여	그렇게 하면 손해를 볼 것 같아. 대신 광고지를 나눠주는 건 어떨까?
M	Good idea. **I can make a design on the computer today.**	남	좋은 생각이야. 내가 오늘 컴퓨터로 디자인하면 돼.
W	**No, let me [3]contact my friend.** She's a great designer, so she can create an impressive flyer.	여	아냐, 내 친구에게 연락해 볼게. 그녀는 훌륭한 디자이너라서, 인상적인 광고지를 만들 수 있어.
M	That sounds great. Then, I'll buy some ink for the printer so we can just print them out here.	남	그거 좋다. 그러면 여기에서 출력할 수 있도록 프린터기 잉크를 사 올게.
W	All right. I hope it helps with business!	여	그래. 이게 우리 일에 도움이 되면 좋겠다!

옷 가게의 매출 하락을 걱정하며 모객 방법을 고민하고 있다. 여자가 광고지를 나눠주자고 제안했고 남자가 자신이 디자인하겠다고 했으나, 여자가 디자이너 친구에게 연락해 보겠다고 했으므로 여자가 할 일로 ④ '친구에게 연락하기'가 가장 적절하다.

어휘 bring in ~를 끌어들이다, 유치하다 new arrival 신상품 stop by 들르다 lose money 손해를 보다 hand out ~을 나눠주다, 배포하다 flyer 명 광고지; 비행사 impressive 형 인상적인

6 금액 정보 파악

정답 ④

W	Good afternoon. Is there anything in particular you're looking for?
M	Yes. I need to ¹⁾buy 12 lightbulbs, please.
W	Okay. Well, we have yellow bulbs and white bulbs.
M	How much are they?
W	**The yellow bulbs are $3 each, and the white ones are $5 each.**
M	I see. Do they ²⁾last the same amount of time?
W	Yes. Now that you mention it, **we also have an LED bulb that's $8.**
M	That's expensive compared to the others.
W	It is, but it's very long-lasting. It also uses ³⁾less electricity, so it's cheaper in the long run.
M	Got it. **Then, I'll take six LED bulbs and six yellow bulbs.**
W	All right. [Pause] Oh, I'm sorry. **It looks like the yellow bulbs are out of stock.**
M	In that case, **I'll get ⁴⁾six of the white bulbs instead.**
W	No problem. Here you go.

여	안녕하세요. 특별히 찾으시는 게 있으신가요?
남	네. 저는 전구 12개를 사야 해요.
여	알겠습니다. 음, 노란색 전구와 흰색 전구가 있어요.
남	얼마인가요?
여	노란색 전구는 개당 3달러이고, 흰색 전구는 개당 5달러입니다.
남	그렇군요. 그것들의 지속 시간은 같나요?
여	네. 그 말을 듣고 보니, 저희에겐 8달러짜리 LED 전구도 있어요.
남	다른 것들에 비해 비싸네요.
여	그렇긴 한데, 아주 오래 지속된답니다. 또한 전기를 덜 쓰기 때문에, 장기적으로는 더 저렴한 거예요.
남	알겠습니다. 그러면, LED 전구 6개랑 노란색 전구 6개로 주세요.
여	좋습니다. [잠시 멈춤] 아, 죄송합니다. 노란색 전구 재고가 떨어진 것 같아요.
남	그럼, 대신 흰색 전구를 6개 살게요.
여	문제없어요. 여기 있습니다.

남자가 LED 전구 6개($8×6=$48)를 구매했고, 노란색 전구 대신에 흰색 전구를 6개($5×6=$30) 구매했으므로 정답은 ④ '$78'이다.

어휘 lightbulb 명 전구 last 통 지속되다 Now that you mention it 그 말을 듣고 보니 compared to ~에 비해 electricity 명 전기 in the long run 장기적으로
out of stock 재고가 떨어진

7 이유 파악

정답 ①

M	Hi, Angela. How was your performance at the festival last Friday?
W	Hey, Mark. Do you mean my dance group performance?
M	Yeah! I was looking forward to seeing you, but I had to help out at my family's shop that evening.
W	We actually didn't end up ¹⁾going on stage.
M	Was someone in your group sick? The flu is going around.
W	That's true. But everyone was feeling good that day.
M	Oh, wasn't there a problem with the lighting? I heard that ²⁾a stage light broke during the magic show.
W	You are right about the lighting problem, **but we couldn't perform because of the weather. There were ³⁾severe winds, so the whole event ended early.**
M	That's bad luck! Is it going to be rescheduled?
W	No. It's canceled, but we'll have another show next week.
M	Break a leg! I'll definitely be there!

남	안녕, Angela. 지난 금요일 축제에서 공연은 잘했어?
여	안녕, Mark. 내 댄스부 공연을 말하는 거니?
남	응! 무척 보고 싶었는데, 그날 저녁에 가족의 가게 일을 거들어야 했어.
여	사실 우리는 끝내 무대에 서지 못했어.
남	부원 중에 누군가 아팠니? 독감이 유행 중이야.
여	그건 맞아. 그런데 그날은 모두 컨디션이 좋았어.
남	아, 조명에 문제가 있지 않았니? 마술쇼 도중에 무대 조명이 깨졌다고 들었어.
여	조명 문제가 있었던 건 맞는데, 우리가 공연을 못 한 건 날씨 때문이었어. 바람이 심하게 불어서, 전체 행사가 일찍 끝났거든.
남	운이 없었네! 일정이 다시 잡혔니?
여	아니. 그건 취소됐어, 그런데 우리는 다음 주에 또 공연이 있을 거야.
남	행운을 빌어! 내가 꼭 갈게!

여자는 축제에서 공연하지 못 한 이유는 바람이 심하게 불어서 전체 행사가 일찍 끝났기 때문이고 결국 공연은 취소되었다고 했으므로, 여자가 축제 무대에 서지 못한 이유는 ① '강풍으로 무대가 취소돼서'이다.

어휘 help out 거들다, 돕다 end up 끝내 ~하게 되다 flu 명 독감 go around 유행하다, 퍼지다 lighting 명 조명 reschedule 통 일정을 다시 잡다 Break a leg! 행운을 빌어!

8 언급 유무 파악

정답 ⑤

	[Telephone rings.]
W	Hi. This is Cheryl Williams. I wanted to talk to you about The Poetry Night.
M	Oh, do you mean the poetry-reading event I'm hosting?
W	Yeah. We've had to make a few changes.
M	Go on.
W	Well, there has been ¹⁾a change in the venue. We're moving the event to the **Hampton Center.**
M	Will it still be on the same night?
W	Yeah. It will ²⁾take place as scheduled on **September 12th.**
M	Okay, good. And will I be introducing the same poets?
W	Yes. All ³⁾three of the poets will be participating.
M	Is there anything else I need to know?
W	Oh, make sure to be there by **6.** That's when we will begin rehearsing.
M	No problem. I'll be there then.
W	That's perfect. Thanks.

	[전화기가 울린다.]
여	안녕하세요. Cheryl Williams입니다. The Poetry Night에 관해 말씀드리려고요.
남	아, 제가 사회를 볼 시 낭송 행사를 말씀하시는 건가요?
여	네. 몇 가지 변경 사항이 있었거든요.
남	계속 말씀하세요.
여	음, 장소가 바뀌었어요. 우리는 행사를 햄프턴 센터로 옮길 거예요.
남	여전히 같은 날 밤에 진행되는 건가요?
여	네. 예정대로 9월 12일에 진행될 거예요.
남	네, 좋습니다. 그리고 제가 동일한 시인들을 소개하나요?
여	네. 세 명의 시인 모두 참석할 거예요.
남	제가 더 알아야 할 것이 있나요?
여	아, 6시까지 거기로 꼭 와 주세요. 그때부터 리허설을 시작할 거예요.
남	문제없어요. 그때 갈게요.
여	완벽해요. 감사합니다.

변경 장소(햄프턴 센터), 행사 날짜(9월 12일), 참여 시인 수(3명), 리허설 시작 시간(6시)에 대해 언급했고, ⑤ '기념품'은 언급하지 않았다.

어휘 poetry-reading 명 시 낭송 venue 명 장소 as scheduled 예정대로 make sure to 꼭 ~하다

9 내용 불일치 파악

정답 ③

| W | Good evening. I'm here to discuss an event that I organize every year. Last week, we held the most recent Earth All Together concert in Griffith Park. As always, the purpose of the concert was to ¹⁾emphasize the importance of protecting the environment. **We were inspired by John Graham, ²⁾the former vice president of Green Planet Network, who was dedicated to protecting our planet.** We have carried on his mission with Earth All Together ever since our first concert in 1969. Thanks to our close collaboration with musicians and activists, we've been ³⁾able to raise $12 million and spread awareness about key issues. I really appreciate your support and interest in our concert. We'll be back with even better performances next year. | 여 | 안녕하십니까. 제가 매년 주관하는 행사에 대해 말씀드리려 이 자리에 섰습니다. 지난주, 저희는 그리피스 공원에서 가장 최근의 Earth All Together 콘서트를 열었습니다. 언제나 그랬듯이, 콘서트의 취지는 환경 보호의 중요성을 강조하는 것이었습니다. 저희는 지구를 보호하는 데 전념한 Green Planet Network의 전임 부회장인 John Graham에게서 영감을 받았습니다. 1969년 첫 콘서트 이후로 저희는 Earth All Together 콘서트로 그의 사명을 계속해왔습니다. 음악가들 및 운동가들과의 긴밀한 협력 덕분에, 저희는 1,200만 달러를 모을 수 있었고 주요 이슈에 대한 인식을 확산시킬 수 있었습니다. 저희 콘서트에 보내주신 성원과 관심에 정말로 감사드립니다. 내년에는 더 좋은 공연으로 다시 찾아뵙겠습니다. |

환경 보호의 취지로 열린 콘서트에 대한 안내 방송이다. 여자가 Green Planet Network의 전임 부회장에게서 영감을 받았다고 했으므로 ③ 'Green Planet Network의 전임 회장에게 영감을 받았다.'는 내용과 일치하지 않는다.

어휘 organize 동 주관하다; 조직하다 emphasize 동 강조하다 inspire 동 영감을 주다 former 형 이전의 vice president 부회장, 부통령 be dedicated to ~에 전념하다
carry on 계속하다 mission 명 사명, 임무 collaboration 명 협력 activist 명 운동가 raise 동 모으다; 올리다 awareness 명 인식

10 도표 정보 파악

정답 ②

M	After visiting Paris, we're planning to get to Marseille by train, right?	남	우리 파리를 방문한 후에, 열차를 타고 마르세유에 갈 계획이지, 그렇지?
W	I was thinking of heading down on the 26th.	여	난 26일에 내려갈까 생각 중이었어.
M	Have you booked train tickets, yet? It looks like there are quite a few options on the schedule.	남	기차표 예매했어? 일정표에 선택할 수 있는 것들이 꽤 있는 것 같은데.
W	Oh! Let me see that. *[Pause]* **Leaving before 4 p.m. seems too early.**	여	오! 어디 볼게. *[잠시 멈춤]* 오후 4시 전에 떠나는 건 너무 이른 것 같아.
M	Okay. What about taking the high-speed train? That could ¹⁾save us some time.	남	알았어. 고속열차를 타는 건 어때? 그러면 시간을 좀 절약할 수 있을 거야.
W	It's not really important one way or the other. **So let's take a standard one.** It should be quick enough.	여	어느 쪽이든 정말 중요한 건 아니야. 그러니 일반 열차를 타자. 그것도 충분히 빠를 거야.
M	Yeah, maybe it's ²⁾more relevant to look at the number of times we would have to change trains.	남	그래, 어쩌면 열차를 갈아타야 하는 횟수를 살펴보는 게 더 적절할지도 모르겠어.
W	Good point. **We don't want to stop twice if we can avoid it.**	여	좋은 지적이야. 피할 수 있다면 두 번은 멈추고 싶지 않아.
M	It looks like there are still a couple of good choices, then.	남	그러면 아직 두 가지 좋은 선택지가 남아 있는 것 같아.
W	**Let's just go with ³⁾the cheaper one.**	여	그냥 더 싼 걸로 하자.

두 사람은 오후 4시 이후에 떠나는 것 중에서, 일반 열차이고, 두 번은 멈추지 않으며, 더 싼 열차 편을 골랐다.

어휘 head 동 가다, 향하다 명 머리 standard 형 일반적인; 표준의 명 표준 relevant 형 적절한; 관련 있는 change trains 열차를 갈아타다

11 짧은 대화의 응답 파악

정답 ④

[Telephone rings.]	*[전화기가 울린다.]*
M Hi, this is Jack's Car Wash Service. How can I help you?	남 안녕하세요, Jack's Car Wash Service입니다. 무엇을 도와드릴까요?
W Hello. I'm just calling to see ¹⁾what time you close today. I want to visit later this afternoon.	여 안녕하세요. 그냥 오늘 몇 시에 문을 닫는지 알아보려고 전화했어요. 오늘 오후 늦게 방문하고 싶거든요.
M **We close at 8 p.m., but you should ²⁾come before 7 if you want your car to be washed today.**	남 오후 8시에 문을 닫기는 하는데, 오늘 중으로 세차 받으시려면 7시 전에 오셔야 해요.
W Great. I'll come by around 6 o'clock then.	여 좋아요. 그러면 6시쯤에 들를게요.
	선택지 ① 말도 안 돼요. 서비스가 너무 비싸네요.
	② 걱정하지 마세요. 필요하신 만큼 천천히 하세요.
	③ 오, 잠깐만요. 그러면 오늘은 밤늦게서야 문을 닫을게요.
	④ 좋아요. 그러면 6시쯤에 들를게요.
	⑤ 감사합니다. 제 차가 정말 멋져 보여요.

폐점 시간을 문의하는 여자에게 남자가 오늘 세차 받으려면 7시 전에 와야 한다고 했으므로, 이에 대한 응답으로는 방문 예정 시간을 말하는 ④ 'Great. I'll come by around 6 o'clock then.' 이 가장 적절하다.

어휘 take time 천천히 하다 No way. 말도 안 돼요. come by 들르다

12 짧은 대화의 응답 파악

정답 ①

W	Hey, Chris. I heard you ¹⁾moved into a new apartment recently. How do you like it?
M	It could be better. It is closer to my dad's work, **but I can't walk to school anymore.**
W	²⁾**How far away is it now?**
M	It's a 45-minute bus ride both ways.

여　안녕, Chris. 최근에 새 아파트로 이사했다고 들었어. 어때?
남　그저 그래. 아버지 직장에는 더 가까워졌는데, 난 더 이상 걸어서 학교에 갈 수 없어.
여　지금 거리가 얼마나 되는데?
남　버스로 편도 45분 거리야.

[선택지]　① 버스로 편도 45분 거리야.
　　　② 지금 저쪽으로 걸어갈래?
　　　③ 다음 주에 이사하면 알게 될 거야.
　　　④ 아버지에게 부탁하면 우리를 거기까지 태워다 주실 수도 있어.
　　　⑤ 사실 거긴 내 직장에서 꽤 멀어.

남자가 최근 이사 간 아파트에서 학교까지 걸어서 갈 수 없다고 하자 여자가 거리가 얼마나 되는지 물었으므로, 이에 대한 응답으로는 구체적인 거리를 말하는 ① 'It's a 45-minute bus ride both ways.'가 가장 적절하다.

[어휘]　It could be better. 그저 그래.

13 긴 대화의 응답 파악

정답 ⑤

M	What's wrong with your phone, Daisy?
W	What do you mean?
M	I called you, but ¹⁾your phone was off again.
W	Oh, sometimes it just turns off randomly. It's a really old phone.
M	How long have you had it?
W	About five years. It's probably time for me to get a new one, but I ²⁾can't afford it at the moment.
M	I see. Well, maybe you could buy a secondhand phone instead of a new one. It wouldn't be so expensive that way.
W	But I'm worried a ³⁾secondhand phone would break easily.
M	Don't worry. Some of them are in perfect condition. You just need to check them carefully. Plus, many sellers offer money-back guarantees.
W	I'll go online and look then.
M	I know some really good websites where you can find them.
W	Really? Do you ⁴⁾mind sending the links to me?
M	Not at all. I'll text them to you now.

남　휴대폰에 무슨 문제 있니, Daisy?
여　무슨 말이야?
남　너한테 전화했는데, 휴대폰이 또 꺼져 있었어.
여　아, 휴대폰이 가끔 그냥 무작위로 꺼지기도 해요. 정말 오래됐거든.
남　얼마나 오래 썼어?
여　5년 정도. 아마 내가 새것을 살 때가 된 것 같은데, 지금 당장은 그럴 여유가 없어.
남　그렇구나. 음, 어쩌면 새것 대신 중고폰을 살 수도 있을 거야. 그렇게 하면 별로 안 비쌀걸.
여　하지만 중고폰은 쉽게 고장 날까 봐 걱정돼.
남　걱정하지 마. 그중 일부는 상태가 완벽해. 그저 그것들을 주의 깊게 확인하기만 하면 돼. 게다가, 많은 판매자가 환불 보증을 제공하고 있어.
여　그러면 인터넷으로 찾아볼게.
남　내가 중고폰 찾아보기에 정말 좋은 웹사이트들을 알고 있어.
여　정말? 링크를 내게 보내주는 건 별로야?
남　전혀 아니야. 지금 문자 메시지 줄게.

[선택지]　① 기다리지 마. 지금 바로 휴대폰 수리기사에게 보내.
　　　② 물론 아니지. 난 이미 돈을 많이 모았어.
　　　③ 아니, 그렇지 않아. 난 웹사이트에서 그걸 찾을 수 없었어.
　　　④ 미안해. 어젯밤에 휴대폰이 고장 났어.
　　　⑤ 전혀 아니야. 지금 문자 메시지 줄게.

휴대폰이 오래됐지만 새것을 살 여유가 없다는 여자에게 남자가 중고폰을 사는 것을 권유하는 상황이다. 남자가 중고폰 찾아보기에 좋은 웹사이트들을 알고 있다고 하자 여자가 링크를 보내달라고 요청했으므로, 이에 대한 응답으로는 요청을 수락하는 ⑤ 'Not at all. I'll text them to you now.'가 가장 적절하다.

[어휘]　turn off 꺼지다　randomly [부] 무작위로　afford [동] ~할 여유가 있다　break [동] 고장 나다; 깨다　money-back [형] 환불이 가능한　guarantee [명] 보증

14 긴 대화의 응답 파악

정답 ②

M	What are you looking at, Jane?
W	Dad, I found some old photographs in a box. ¹⁾They were taken when my brother and I were kids.
M	Wow, I forgot about these. I remember this day, though. We were at your grandparents' house.
W	I don't remember it at all.
M	That's natural. You were only four at the time.
W	I wish we went to see grandmother and grandfather more often like we used to.
M	I know. But your schedules became busier on the weekends ²⁾the older you both got.
W	I guess that's true. It makes these pictures very special to me.
M	**Then, why don't you put them in a nice album?**
W	Like a photo album? ³⁾Do we have any?
M	We don't, but we can go buy one. **Then, you could take it to your grandparents' house the next time we go.**

남　뭘 보고 있니, Jane?
여　아빠, 제가 상자에서 오래된 사진들을 발견했어요. 오빠와 제가 어릴 때 찍은 거예요.
남　우와, 이걸 내가 잊고 있었구나. 그래도 이날은 기억이 난단다. 우리는 너희 조부모님 댁에 있었어.
여　저는 전혀 기억이 안 나요.
남　그건 당연한 거야. 넌 그때 겨우 4살이었거든.
여　우리가 예전에 그랬던 것처럼 할머니 할아버지를 더 자주 뵈러 가면 좋겠어요.
남　그러게 말이야. 하지만 너희 둘 다 나이를 먹을수록 주말마다 일정이 바빠졌잖니.
여　그건 사실인 것 같아요. 그래서 이 사진들이 제게 매우 특별해졌어요.
남　그럼, 근사한 앨범에 넣는 게 어떻니?
여　사진첩 같은 거요? 저희가 갖고 있는 게 있나요?
남　없지만, 하나 사러 가면 되지. 그러고 나서 다음에 조부모님 댁에 갈 때 그걸 가져가면 되겠어.

| W | That's a great idea. I bet they'd both love that. |

여 좋은 생각이에요. 분명 두 분 다 좋아하실 거예요.

선택지 ① 이 앨범이 좋아 보여요. 그리고 겨우 20달러예요.
② 좋은 생각이에요. 분명 두 분 다 좋아하실 거예요.
③ 전혀요. 원하시면 사진을 가지고 계셔도 돼요.
④ 맞아요. 우리는 오후 3시쯤에 그들의 집으로 출발할 거예요.
⑤ 다들 모이세요. 사진을 빨리 찍고 싶어요.

조부모님 댁에서 찍은 어릴 적 사진에 관해 이야기하는 상황이다. 남자가 사진을 앨범에 잘 보관해서 다음에 조부모님 댁을 방문할 때 가져가자고 제안했으므로, 이에 대한 응답으로는 제안에 동의하는 ② 'That's a great idea. I bet they'd both love that.'이 가장 적절하다.

어휘 natural 형 당연한, 자연스러운 get together 모이다

15 상황에 적절한 말 파악 정답 ③

| M | Katie is an aspiring author who is writing her first book. Recently, she was invited to join a weekly writer's workshop in which people critique one another's work. Katie is worried that she will 1)receive severe criticism. She discusses the issue with her friend Max, who also writes stories, and asks for his advice about joining the workshop. Max believes that Katie should 2)welcome feedback from other writers as it can highlight what parts of her story to work on. He thinks that this can benefit the overall quality of her work. **So Max wants to tell Katie that she should consider joining the group in order to 3)improve her book.** In this situation, what would Max most likely say to Katie? |

남 Katie는 그녀의 첫 번째 책을 집필 중인 작가 지망생입니다. 최근, 그녀는 사람들이 서로의 작품을 비평하는 주간 작가 워크숍에 초대받았습니다. Katie는 혹평을 받을까 봐 걱정입니다. 그녀는 마찬가지로 글을 쓰는 친구 Max와 이 문제에 대해 논의하고, 워크숍에 참여하는 것에 대해 조언을 구합니다. Max는 Katie가 다른 작가들의 피드백을 기꺼이 받아들여야 한다고 생각하는데, 그게 그녀의 이야기에서 공을 들여야 하는 부분을 강조하도록 할 수 있기 때문입니다. 그는 이것이 그녀의 작품의 전반적인 질에 도움이 될 수 있다고 생각합니다. 그래서, Max는 Katie에게 그녀의 책을 개선하기 위해 그 그룹에 들어가는 것을 고려해야 한다고 말하고 싶습니다. 이러한 상황에서, Max가 Katie에게 가장 할 것 같은 말은 무엇입니까?

선택지 ① 잊지 말고 다음 글쓰기 워크숍을 준비해.
② 지금 당장은 네가 집필 목표에 집중해야 한다고 생각해.
③ 네 책을 더 좋게 만들려면 워크숍에 참여해야 해.
④ 우리 서로의 책을 읽고 피드백을 주는 건 어때?
⑤ 책을 끝내려면 집필하는 데 더 많은 시간을 쓰는 게 좋겠어.

Katie가 작가 워크숍에 참여해야 할지 고민하는 것을 보고, Max는 그녀의 책을 개선하기 위해 워크숍 그룹에 들어가는 것을 고려해야 한다고 말하려 한다. 따라서, Max가 할 말로 ③ 'You should join the workshop to make your book better.'가 가장 적절하다.

어휘 aspiring author 작가 지망생 critique 통 비평하다 severe criticism 혹평 highlight 통 강조하다, 두드러지게 하다 work on ~에 공을 들이다, 애쓰다 overall 형 전반적인 focus on ~에 집중하다 in order to ~하려면

16-17 세트 문항 정답 16 ③ 17 ⑤

| W | Good morning, students. Last class, we talked about why Pluto is no longer considered a planet. **Today, we'll learn about the 1)different characteristics of planets in our solar system.** First, we have **Mercury**. Not only is this the smallest planet, but it is also closest to the sun. This planet has a rocky surface that 2)closely resembles that of our own moon. Next, there is **Venus**. Venus is the hottest planet in our solar system with a surface temperature of around 475 degrees Celsius. It's 3)also covered in volcanoes, which might be still active. Thirdly, **Mars** is a unique planet with seasons, canyons, and even polar ice caps. It's also been explored extensively because scientists believe that 4)life once existed there. Lastly, **Jupiter** is the largest planet in our solar system. The Great Red Spot of Jupiter is visible from space. This is actually a vast storm that's larger than some planets, and it's been brewing for hundreds of years. Now, let's watch a video about these planets. |

여 안녕하십니까, 학생 여러분. 지난 수업에서, 우리는 왜 명왕성이 더 이상 행성으로 여겨지지 않는지에 대해 이야기했습니다. 오늘은, 태양계에 있는 행성들의 다양한 특징들에 대해 배울 것입니다. 먼저 수성이 있습니다. 이것은 가장 작은 행성일 뿐만 아니라, 태양에 가장 가깝기도 합니다. 이 행성은 우리의 달과 매우 흡사하게 바위가 많은 표면적을 가지고 있습니다. 다음으로 금성입니다. 금성은 표면적 온도가 섭씨 475도 정도로 태양계에서 가장 뜨거운 행성입니다. 그것은 또한 화산으로 덮여 있는데, 아직 활화산일지도 모릅니다. 세 번째로, 화성은 계절, 협곡, 그리고 심지어 극지방의 만년설이 있는 독특한 행성입니다. 그것은 또한 과학자들이 한때 생명체가 그곳에 존재했다고 믿었기 때문에 광범위하게 탐사되었습니다. 마지막으로, 목성은 태양계에서 가장 큰 행성입니다. 목성의 대적점은 우주에서 보입니다. 이것은 사실 몇몇 행성보다도 더 큰 광대한 폭풍이고, 이것은 수백 년 동안 계속해서 진행 중에 있습니다. 이제, 이 행성들에 대한 동영상을 봅니다.

선택지 16 ① 명왕성이 행성으로 분류되지 않는 이유
② 생명체가 존재할 수 없는 행성
③ 태양계의 행성들이 가진 다양한 특징
④ 일부 행성이 다른 것보다 큰 이유
⑤ 태양계의 행성들이 형성된 방식
17 ① 수성 ② 금성 ③ 화성 ④ 목성 ⑤ 토성

16 태양계에 있는 행성들의 다양한 특징들에 대해 배우고 있으므로 여자가 하는 말의 주제로 ③ 'various features of our solar system's planets'가 가장 적절하다.
17 여자가 수성, 금성, 화성, 목성은 언급했지만 ⑤ 'Saturn'은 언급하지 않았다.

어휘 no longer 더 이상 ~이 아닌 characteristic 명 특징 not only A but also B A뿐만 아니라 B도 rocky 형 바위가 많은 surface 명 표면적 resemble 통 ~과 흡사하다, 닮다 canyon 명 협곡 polar ice caps 극지방의 만년설 extensively 부 광범위하게 vast 형 광대한, 방대한 brew 통 (폭풍우가) 진행 중이다; 양조하다 be classified as ~으로 분류되다

MEMO

MEMO

수능 1등급을 위한 **완벽한 실전 대비서**

해커스
수능영어듣기
모의고사 20+4회
실전

수능·내신 한 번에 잡는
해커스 불변의 패턴 시리즈

해커스 수능 어법 불변의 패턴

[기본서]

필수편 [고1]

· 역대 수능·모의고사 기출에서 뽑아낸
55개의 불변의 패턴

· 출제포인트와 함정까지 빈틈없이 대비하는
기출 예문 및 기출 문제

[훈련서]

실력편 [고2]

· 역대 수능·모의고사 기출 분석으로
실전에 바로 적용하는 **37개의 불패 전략**

· **핵심 문법 설명**부터 **실전 어법**까지
제대로 실력을 쌓는 **단계별 학습 구성**

해커스 수능 독해 불변의 패턴

[기본서]

유형편 [예비고~고1]

· 역대 수능·모평·학평에서 뽑아낸
32개의 불변의 패턴

· 끊어 읽기와 구문 풀이로
독해 기본기 강화

[실전서]

실전편 [고2~고3]

· 최신 수능·모평·학평 출제경향과 패턴을
그대로 반영한 **실전모의고사 15회**

· 고난도 실전모의고사 3회분으로
어려운 수능에 철저히 대비

HackersBook.com 해커스북 중·고등

해커스 중고등 교재 MAP | 나에게 맞는 교재 선택!

	예비중	중1	중2	중3
문법	Hackers Grammar Smart Starter	Hackers Grammar Smart Level 1	Hackers Grammar Smart Level 2	Hackers Grammar Smart Level 3
		기출로 적중 해커스 중학영문법 1학년	기출로 적중 해커스 중학영문법 2학년	기출로 적중 해커스 중학영문법 3학년
서술형		해커스 쓰기 자신감 Level 1	해커스 쓰기 자신감 Level 2	해커스 쓰기 자신감 Level 3
구문				
독해	Hackers Reading Smart Level 1	Hackers Reading Smart Level 2	Hackers Reading Smart Level 3	Hackers Reading Smart Level 4
		Hackers Reading Path Level 1	Hackers Reading Path Level 2	Hackers Reading Path Level 3
			해커스 첫수능 영어 기초독해	해커스 첫수능 영어 유형독해
듣기		해커스 중학영어듣기 모의고사 24회 Level 1	해커스 중학영어듣기 모의고사 24회 Level 2	해커스 중학영어듣기 모의고사 24회 Level 3
어휘		해커스 3연타 중학영단어		
		해커스 보카 중학 기초	해커스 보카 중학 필수	해커스 보카 중학 고난도
		해커스 보카 중학 숙어		

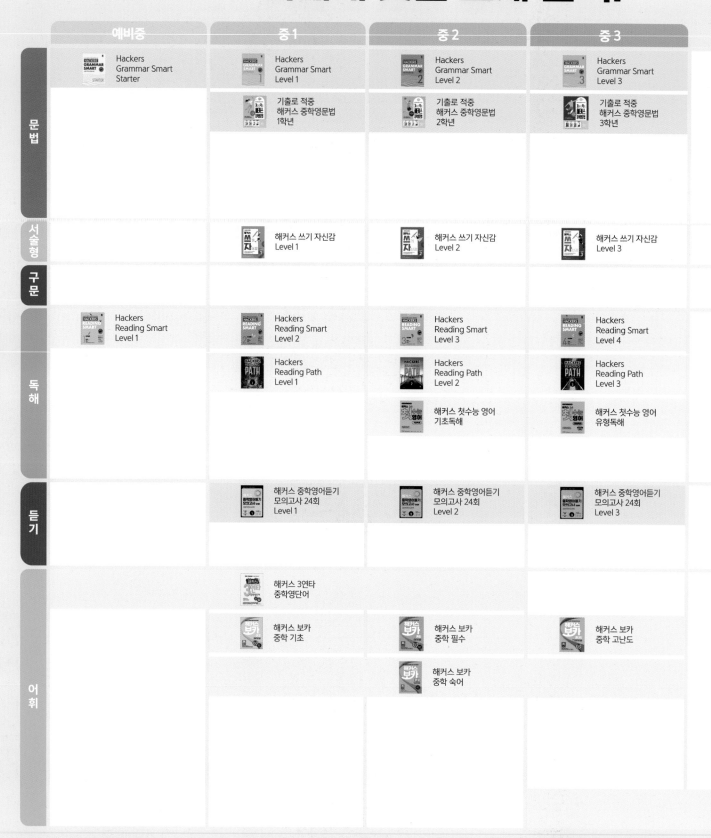

	READING	LISTENING	VOCA
토플	HACKERS APEX READING for the TOEFL iBT Basic/Intermediate/Advanced/Expert	HACKERS APEX LISTENING for the TOEFL iBT Basic/Intermediate/Advanced/Expert	HACKERS APEX VOCA for the TOEFL iBT HACKERS VOCABULARY